Western Australia

the Bradt Guide

Scott Dareff

edition

www.bradtguides.com

Bradt Guides Ltd, UK
The Globe Pequot Press Inc, USA

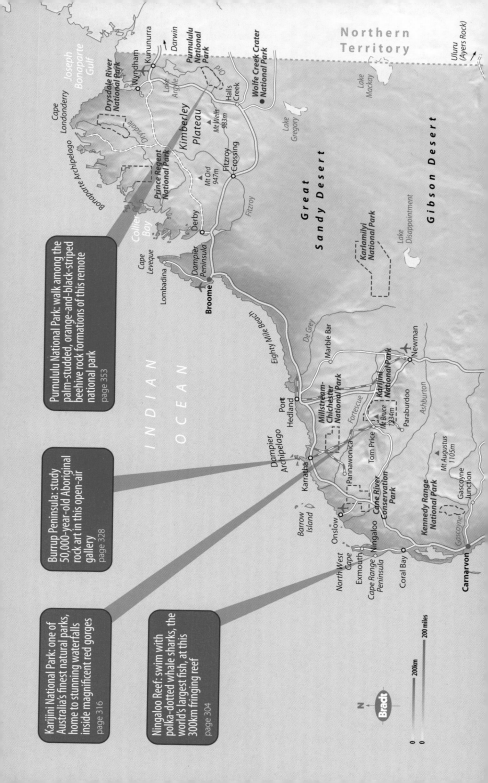

Northern Territory

Uluru (Ayers Rock)

Purnululu National Park: walk among the palm-studded, orange-and-black-striped beehive rock formations of this remote national park
page 353

Burrup Peninsula: study 50,000-year-old Aboriginal rock art in this open-air gallery
page 328

Karijini National Park: one of Australia's finest natural parks, home to stunning waterfalls inside magnificent red gorges
page 316

Ningaloo Reef: swim with polka-dotted whale sharks, the world's largest fish, at this 300km fringing reef
page 304

INDIAN OCEAN

Great Sandy Desert

Gibson Desert

Joseph Bonaparte Gulf

Darwin

Kununurra

Wyndham

Drysdale River National Park

Cape Londonderry

Bonaparte Archipelago

Prince Regent National Park

Collier Bay

Cape Leveque

Lombadina

Dampier Peninsula

Broome

Derby

Fitzroy Crossing

Mt Ord 947m

Halls Creek

Mt Wells 983m

Kimberley Plateau

Lake Argyle

Lake Gregory

Lake Mackay

Wolfe Creek Crater National Park

Ord

Fitzroy

De Grey

Eighty Mile Beach

Port Hedland

Marble Bar

Karlamilyi National Park

Lake Disappointment

Dampier Archipelago

Karratha

Barrow Island

Onslow

Ningaloo

Coral Bay

North West Cape

Exmouth

Cape Range Peninsula

Pannawonica

Millstream-Chichester National Park

Fortescue

Karijini National Park

Mt Bruce 1234m

Tom Price

Paraburdoo

Newman

Ashburton

Cane River Conservation Park

Kennedy Range National Park

Gascoyne Junction

Mt Augustus 1105m

Gascoyne

Carnarvon

N

Bradt

0   200km
0   200 miles

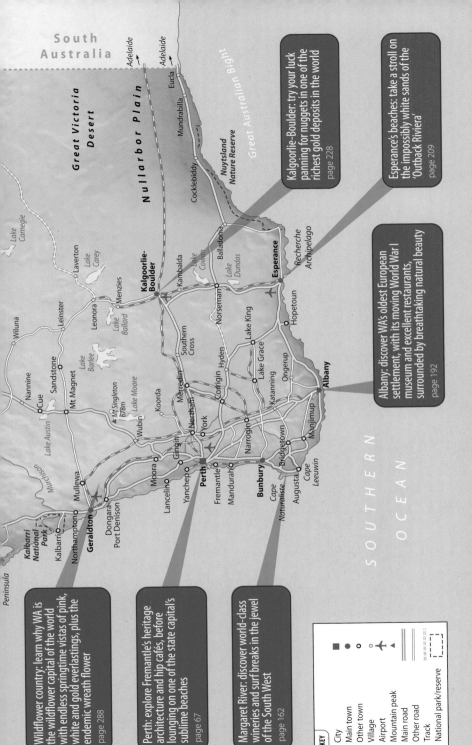

South Australia

Great Victoria Desert

Nullarbor Plain

Great Australian Bight

Adelaide

Adelaide

Eucla

Mundrabilla

Cocklebiddy

Nuytsland Nature Reserve

Kalgoorlie-Boulder: try your luck panning for nuggets in one of the richest gold deposits in the world
page 228

Esperance's beaches: take a stroll on the impossibly white sands of the 'Outback Riviera'
page 209

Albany: discover WA's oldest European settlement, with its moving World War I museum and excellent restaurants, surrounded by breathtaking natural beauty
page 192

Wildflower country: learn why WA is the wildflower capital of the world with endless springtime vistas of pink, white and gold everlastings, plus the endemic wreath flower
page 288

Perth: explore Fremantle's heritage architecture and hip cafés, before lounging on one of the state capital's sublime beaches
page 67

Margaret River: discover world-class wineries and surf breaks in the jewel of the South West
page 162

Lake Carnegie

Wiluna

Nannine

Cue

Mt Magnet

Sandstone

Leinster

Leonora

Laverton

Lake Carey

Menzies

Lake Ballard

Kalgoorlie-Boulder

Kambalda

Southern Cross

Lake Cowan

Lake Dundas

Balladonia

Norseman

Esperance

Recherche Archipelago

Lake Barlee

Koorda

Hyden

Lake King

Hopetoun

Lake Moore

Mt Singleton 678m

Wubin

Merredin

Corrigin

Lake Grace

Ongerup

Albany

Moora

Gingin

Northam

York

Narrogin

Katanning

Manjimup

Lancelin

Yanchep

Perth

Fremantle

Mandurah

Bunbury

Bridgetown

Cape Naturaliste

Augusta

Cape Leeuwin

Mullewa

Geraldton

Dongara Port Denison

Kalbarri National Park

Kalbarri

Northampton

Peninsula

Murchison

SOUTHERN OCEAN

KEY

■ City
● Main town
○ Other town
○ Village
✈ Airport
▲ Mountain peak
Main road
Other road
Track
National park/reserve

Western Australia Don't miss...

Rottnest Island's quokkas
These smiley creatures have been dubbed the 'world's happiest animal' (TA) page 96

Karijini National Park
With its dramatic gorges, world-class plunge pools and colourful terrain, this is one of Australia's finest national parks; pictured here, Hamersley Gorge
(AH/S) page 316

Sensational beaches

WA's coastline stretches for some 12,800km, so it's no surprise its sands are some of the world's best — such as Little Beach, pictured here

(TA) page 198

Aboriginal art

The Kimberley is an excellent place to learn about the state's Aboriginal art; pictured here, Waringarri Aboriginal Arts

(TWA) page 359

Margaret River

No trip to the state would be complete without a visit to its surf and wine capital

(ADH/S) page 162

Western Australia in colour

Above   Anchored by vast Kings Park, the city's signature attraction, central Perth feels more laidback than other capitals (b/S) page 67

Left   Meaning 'many stories' in Noongar, WA Museum Boola Bardip showcases the diverse tales, characters and events that have shaped Western Australia (A/S) page 86

Below   Fremantle's Heritage-listed covered market has stood at the heart of this lively suburb since 1897 (EQR/S) page 95

Above   Cottesloe is the focal point of Perth's beach scene, home to the iconic Beach Pavilion (DHP/S) page 90

Below left   The showcase of central Perth's pointy Bell Tower are the 18 Swan Bells, of which a dozen were donated by Buckingham Palace's parish church in London (BM/S) page 84

. Bottom left   The Subiaco neighbourhood is known for its wealth of magnificent 19th-century architecture, with grand verandas and stained-glass 'leadlights' (BM/S) page 88

Below right   The spectacular 40m cascade of Lesmurdie Falls, situated in the Perth Hills, is one of WA's best-known waterfalls (PIP/S) page 107

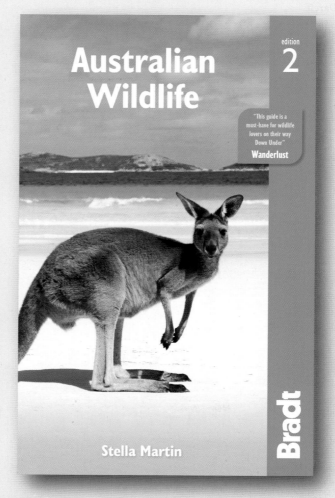

AUTHOR

Scott Dareff has been in education for 20 years as a teacher, advisor and researcher in a number of international settings. Having worked for several years in the Middle East and former Soviet Union, he and his wife migrated to Australia in 2015 and settled in rural Western Australia, after doing a grand tour of the country in search of the perfect country spot.

AUTHOR'S STORY

I have used Bradt guidebooks extensively in my own overseas travel and became motivated to write this book when using Nigel Roberts's excellent *Belarus* guide in 2018. From Minsk, I went to visit my in-laws in southern Europe and, one morning, I turned to my wife and told her I wanted to write a guidebook about my adopted home state. A few weeks after we got back home, I sent in the proposal to Bradt – and was fortunate enough that it was the right time for them.

Having driven some 500,000km across Western Australia (WA) over the past seven years, I felt that I knew this fantastic state pretty well, but during the research for this book I have found that it still surprises, amazes and confounds at every turn. The landscapes, stories, history and people here are one of a kind and reward the kind of off-the-beaten-path exploration that Bradt readers love so much. One of the motivations for writing this book is that I live in a rural part of the state. Existing travel guides to the state tend to be Perth-centric and while Perth is great, the West Australian countryside is, from my perspective, one of the best places on the planet and deserved a guidebook championing its wonders. Trying to capture the state's beauty and spirit in just a few hundred pages has been an amazing experience and I hope that I can do Western Australia justice.

First edition published September 2022
Bradt Guides Ltd
31a High Street, Chesham, Buckinghamshire, HP5 1BW, England
www.bradtguides.com
Print edition published in the USA by The Globe Pequot Press Inc,
PO Box 480, Guilford, Connecticut 06437-0480

Text copyright © 2022 Scott Dareff
Maps copyright © 2022 Bradt Guides Ltd; includes map data © OpenStreetMap contributors
Photographs copyright © 2022 Individual photographers (see below)
Project Manager: Laura Pidgley
Cover research: Ian Spick, Bradt Guides

ISBN: 9781784777531

British Library Cataloguing in Publication Data
A catalogue record for this book is available from the British Library

Photographs Alamy.com: Ian Beattie IB/A); Anna Pretorius Photography (APP); AWL Images: Marco Bottigelli (MB/AWL), Danita Delimont (DD/AWL); Christmas Island Tourism Association (CITA); iStock.com: Overviews (O/IS); Naturaliste Charters (NC); Ngurrangga Tours (NT); Nick Thake (NTH); Sarah Duguid Photography (SDP); Shutterstock: Adwo (A/S), alybaba (AY/S), Adeline Helg (AH/S), Adriena Halasi (ADH/S), anne-tipodees (at/S), beeboys (b/S), Benny Marty (BM/S), Carl Nelson (CN/S), Darkydoors (D/S), David Henry Photography (DHP/S), Dianne Wickenden (DW/S), Emily Hamley (EH/S), EQRoy (EQR/S), Frank McClintock (FM/S), Happy Auer (HA/S), Heather Ruth Rose (HRR/S), imagevixen (i/S), iSKYDANCER (iSD/S), Ian Geraint Jones (IGJ/S), John Crux (JC/S), Jordan Tan (JT/S), Ken Griffiths (KG/S), Kirsty Hulme (KH/S), Kathryn Willmott (KW/S), Jukka Jantunen (JJ/S), lepir (l/S), Lewis Burnett (LB/S), LIBIN THOMAS OLAPRATH (LTO/S), mcography (m/S), Marion Carniel (MC/S), Martin Helgemeir (MH/S), Michelle Marks (MM/S), Marc Witte (MW/S), PomInPerth (PIP/S), Ric Jacyno (RJ/S), trabantos (t/S), Taras Vyshnya (TV/S), Wright Out There (WOT/S); Tourism Australia (TA); Tourism Western Australia (TWA); Voyager Estate (VE); Valley of the Giants Tree Top Walk (VG); WA Museum: Bellette Photography (BP/WAM); Walking Into Luxury (WIL)

Front cover Nature's Window, Kalbarri National Park (MB/AWL)
Back cover Kangaroo, Lucky Bay (TA); Tree Top Walk, Valley of the Giants (VG)
Title page York Town Hall (RJ/S); Kangaroo paw (KW/S); Ningaloo Coast (TA)
Part openers Page 65: Swan Bell Tower, Perth (t/S); Page 223: Lake Ballard (TA); Page 259: The Pinnacles (BM/S); Page 311: Horizontal Falls (HRR/S)

Maps David McCutcheon FBCart.S

Typeset by Ian Spick, Bradt Guides
Production managed by Jellyfish Print Solutions; printed in India
Digital conversion by www.dataworks.co.in

Acknowledgements

Where do I start… too many to fit in. First, to my wife Flavia, for putting up with endless nights of me tapping away on the laptop on the kitchen counter, promising just *one more page tonight*, and my in-laws Claudio and Loredana for helping to inspire and encourage me to do this. Thanks to my colleagues, who had to deal with 18 months of staff-room chatter about every shire in this state. Thanks to all the people at Bradt – Laura, Sue, Anna, Claire and everyone behind the scenes – for making this project go and sticking with it when the pandemic hit, and for the invaluable and insightful feedback. Thanks to my mechanics, Paul and Jamie, for keeping my car rolling past half a million kilometres. Thank you as well to every tourism operator in WA, of all stripes, for showing what you were made of during unprecedented times for us all these past few years and continuing your vital work of connecting visitors to our great state.

Contents

Introduction

Western Australia is full of oddities and superlatives. If the state were its own country, it would be the tenth largest in the world – yet outside the Perth Metropolitan area, there are no towns with over 100,000 people. There have been times here where I have driven for 8 hours and not passed another town – and if you drive the nearly 700km stretch between Collie in the South West and Kalgoorlie in the Goldfields, you won't pass a single traffic light.

Many people equate WA with the vast, empty landscapes of the Outback – and it is true that much of the state is taken up by desert. But it would be wrong to equate the sparsely populated landscape with a sense of nothingness. Indeed, some of Australia's most spectacular attractions are found in the west. Ningaloo Reef, the world's largest fringing reef at 300km long, is every bit as astounding as the more famous Great Barrier Reef – and far more accessible, as you can just walk off the beach into the water and among the reefs and marine life. Up north in the remote Kimberley, Karijini's magnificent gorges have earned it a well-deserved place in the Australian psyche as one of the nation's finest national parks. You can also head east and prospect for gold and precious metals in some of the world's most productive goldfields – and keep what you find.

And there are plenty of other landscapes to explore besides endless red dirt. The fertile southwest is known for its magnificent jarrah and karri forests, home to some of the tallest trees on earth, while one of the world's biggest and most dazzling displays of wildflowers appears every spring throughout the state – with some 12,000 species, 60% of which are found nowhere else. In the Mid West, the Great Western Woodlands – spanning some 16 million hectares – are Australia's lungs, the largest (and healthiest) remaining temperate woodland on the planet. The state is also known for its remarkable rocks – the massive striped granite outcrops in the Wheatbelt look like giant waves, while the eerie limestone pinnacles at Cervantes are reminiscent of a moonscape.

Perth itself has a reputation for being a relaxed and tranquil city – the sort of place where one of the biggest attractions is sitting back with a coffee at one of the many promenades strung along the city's dozens of sparkling beaches. It's also Western Australia's eating and drinking hub, and the Cappuccino Strip in Fremantle, where innovative eateries and trendy bars line the historic main drag, is the best place to do so. The city's signature highlight, however, is Kings Park, one of the nation's best botanical gardens – a good place to acquaint yourself with banksias, kangaroo paws and many others of the state's native flora.

The state is an excellent place to learn more about Australia's Aboriginal heritage, as this this was one of the first places Aboriginal people settled in when they arrived in Western Australia 50,000 years ago. Aboriginal art here is some of the best in the state, but the premier site is undoubtedly the Burrup Peninsula, home to rock art that is thousands of years old. Gazing at some of these ancient drawings, you can't help but wonder if some of the animals you can't quite recognise are actually extinct.

One of the myths of Western Australia is that it is inaccessible – that to do a trip here justice, you need a massive 4x4, a month off work, and a whole lot of money. But this is all completely untrue. One of the things I hope this guidebook does is help connect the reader to the most wonderful sites in this state in an accessible, practical way – so that a trip to WA is not the 'trip of a lifetime', but just the first of many trips you take to this great state.

HOW TO USE THIS GUIDE

AUTHOR'S FAVOURITES Finding genuinely characterful accommodation or that unmissable off-the-beaten-track café can be difficult, so the author has chosen a few of his favourite places throughout the country to point you in the right direction. These 'author's favourites' are marked with a ✳.

PRICE CODES Throughout this guide we have used price codes to indicate the cost of those places to stay and eat listed in the guide. For a key to these price codes, see the boxes on page 58 for accommodation and page 60 for restaurants.

MAPS
Keys and symbols Maps include alphabetical keys covering the locations of those places to stay, eat or drink that are featured in the book. Note that regional maps may not show all hotels and restaurants in the area: other establishments may be located in towns shown on the map.

Grids and grid references Several maps use gridlines to allow easy location of sites. Map grid references are listed in square brackets after the name of the place or site of interest in the text, with page number followed by grid number, eg: [79 C3].

FEEDBACK REQUEST

At Bradt Guides we're aware that guidebooks start to go out of date on the day they're published – and that you, our readers, are out there in the field doing research of your own. You'll find out before us when a fine new family-run hotel opens or a favourite restaurant changes hands and goes downhill. So why not write and tell us about your experiences? Contact us on ☏ 01753 893444 or e info@bradtguides.com. We will forward emails to the author who may post updates on the Bradt website at w bradtguides.com/updates. Alternatively, you can add a review of the book to w bradtguides.com or Amazon.

Part One

GENERAL INFORMATION

WESTERN AUSTRALIA AT A GLANCE

Location The entire western third of the Australian continent (32.9%). It is a massive landmass bordered by the Indian Ocean to the west, the Timor Sea to the north, the Southern Ocean to the south, and the Northern Territory and South Australia to the east.

Size 2,646,000km²

Climate Owing to the state's huge size, the climate is varied and contrasting, from tropical to arid to Mediterranean

Population 2,667,130 (2020)

State capital Perth (population two million; 2020)

Other main towns Bunbury, Geraldton, Albany, Kalgoorlie-Boulder

Administrative divisions Nine regions and the Perth Metropolitan Area, plus external territories of Christmas Island and Cocos (Keeling) Islands, which do not fall under state jurisdiction but generally apply West Australian law and use West Australian public services

Western Australia Premier Mark McGowan (Labor)

Main airport Perth Airport

Main language Australian English

Religion Multiple, with Anglican and Catholic having a plurality of adherents

Currency Australian dollar (A$)

Exchange rate (June 2022) £1 = A$1.75, US$1 = A$1.45, €1 = A$1.51

International telephone code +61; state telephone code 8; mobile telephone code 4 (don't dial the 8 if dialing a West Australian mobile)

Time Australian Western Standard Time (AWST) GMT +8. WA is 3 hours behind Sydney, Melbourne and Canberra; 2 hours behind Brisbane; 2½hrs behind Adelaide; and 1½hrs behind Darwin. WA does not observe Daylight Saving Time.

Electrical voltage 230V/50Hz, three-prong UK-style plug

Flag Similar to the Australian flag with a Union Jack in the top left, but also with a yellow circle bearing a black swan replacing the Southern Cross

1

Background Information

GEOGRAPHY AND GEOLOGY

The state of Western Australia is truly immense. At 2,646,000km², it is the largest of Australia's six states and, if it were its own nation, it would be the tenth-largest in the world, behind Kazakhstan and ahead of Algeria. If you were to drive from south to north, it would take you four days to get from Augusta, in the far southwest, to Kununurra, in the far northeast, while driving west to east would take you two days to get from Perth in the southwest to Eucla on the eastern border with South Australia. Some 12,800km of coastline binds the state on three sides, with land borders with Northern Territory and South Australia to the east.

GEOGRAPHY As you would expect for a region this size, the landscape and topography vary extensively. Vast **deserts** make up the eastern part of the state; five of Australia's six largest deserts lie in WA, at least in part. The Great Victoria Desert tops the list at 422,466km² and covers large swathes of both WA (in the Goldfields-Esperance Region) and South Australia. The Great Sandy Desert, Australia's second largest at 285,000km², sprawls across the Pilbara and Mid West and into the southwestern fringes of Northern Territory. There is also the Tanami (260,000km²; Kimberley), Gibson (156,000km²; Mid West) and Little Sandy (112,000km²; Mid West).

In the West Australian psyche, these deserts often blend together into a vague 'Big Empty' that's out in the 'Great Beyond'. But in actual fact they vary considerably in terrain, from sandy with large dune systems to mulga and other scrub, or red hills and salt lakes. If you are imagining them as boring and brown, don't – flying over them allows you to witness one of the planet's most beautiful natural portraits, with an array of reds, oranges, purples, whites and yellows alongside dazzling white and pink salt lakes. A flight from Perth to Darwin covers some of this scenery, but going east from Perth to Sydney or Melbourne usually doesn't. But take note: these are some of the world's most isolated and remote locations, so you don't just drive out here.

The extreme southeast of WA is covered by the treeless, 200,000km² **Nullarbor Plain** (Nullarbor is Latin for 'no trees'), bordered to the north by the Great Victoria Desert and stretching over the border with South Australia. It is the world's largest exposure of limestone bedrock – an ancient seabed dating from when this part of the state was underwater 14 million years ago. 'The Nullarbor' is often used colloquially, and incorrectly, to refer to the entire area between Adelaide and Norseman, while 'crossing the Nullarbor' is an Australian colloquialism meaning to go to WA from the Eastern States. The drive from Adelaide to Perth (or vice versa) is also seen as one of Australia's great road journeys.

In the far northeast, the **Kimberley** has a tropical and subtropical landscape, with monsoonal rainforest and tropical and subtropical savannah and grasslands.

The northern part of the region is plateau while the central part is hilly and mountainous, and red sandy plains exist around Broome. Just to the south is the **Pilbara**, where you find the classic 'Outback' red earth, as well as huge mineral and iron-ore deposits, massive gorges and WA's highest mountains – though the state, like most of Australia, is relatively flat with occasional ranges little more than 1,000m high, as well as gentle hills and scarp.

To the west, the Gascoyne's peninsula has **Ningaloo Reef**, Australia's largest fringing reef, which stretches for around 300km from the tip of the North West Cape near Exmouth south to Red Bluff north of Carnarvon. The reef forms part of the **Ningaloo Coast World Heritage Area**, one of WA's crown jewels, which was inscribed on the UNESCO list in 2011 owing to its natural beauty, biological diversity and important natural habitats. The rugged browns and oranges of the canyons of the Cape Range adjacent to the sugar-white beaches form one of the most visual and scenic contrasts in the state. Nearly 500 species of fish can be found here, as well as whale sharks, and the area is also a vital marine turtle habitat.

The **Mid West and Wheatbelt** form the heart of Australia's pastoral and grazing industry, dominated by sheep and cereal crops. These areas are heavily reliant on rainfall – about 350mm annually, but rainfall can be fickle – for agriculture and as a water source, and the area is pocked by ancient granite outcrops, rolling pastures and dry salt lakes. Heading further south into the **Peel, South West and Great Southern** areas, rainfall becomes more regular and this is reflected into yet another landscape change – cool climates, hilly terrain, huge karri and jarrah forests (page 7) and a thunderous coastline. The Darling Scarp gently rolls through here at an elevation of roughly 600m.

What West Australians refer to as '**mountains**' would be thought of by North Americans and Europeans as anthills; the state's highest point is Mt Meharry in the Pilbara at 1,249m, though Bluff Knoll in the Great Southern (1,099m) is better known and more accessible. Ranges tend to cover small pockets across the state: the Stirling Range is about 65km wide in the Great Southern (and about half that north–south), the Hamersley Range stretches for about 260km, and the Kennedy Range in the Gascoyne has a land area size similar to, if somewhat larger, than the Stirling Range.

Many of WA's **rivers and lakes** are dry and only fill in flooding or downpour conditions. Do not assume that just because you see something labelled as a 'river' or a 'lake' on a map that it has water in it. Flash flooding is a fact of life here, and driving around the regions you are likely to see long, white measuring sticks rising up several metres next to dry river beds. Standing up next to tracks of dirt, they may look foolish and humorous when it's bone dry out, but they are there for a reason – to indicate to drivers how deep the water is during flood conditions. Never drive your vehicle through water of unknown depth – cars can washout even in knee-deep water, and the currents are deceptively strong – people have died from that. Pay close attention to weather forecasts and warnings during inclement weather.

The longest river is the Gascoyne (865km), which passes east–west through Gascoyne Junction, just south of the Kennedy Range, and out to Carnarvon. Here, however, it is a dry river except during floods, when water levels can rise as high as 15m quickly and precipitously. Closely following in length is the Murchison (820km), which flows out to Kalbarri. The Blackwood River is the longest in the South West (300km), while Perth's Swan River, the state's best known, is only 72km.

GEOLOGY Australia separated from the Gondwana super-continent 160 million years ago, from what is now India and Africa. Dinosaurs lived in WA 130 million years ago; the world's biggest known dinosaur footprints, 1.7m wide, were found here north of Broome (page 344). Theories differ as to why megafauna went extinct in WA, with some attributing it to climate change and increases in arid conditions, and others theorising that it was the arrival of Aboriginal Australians at least 50,000 years ago, and their use of fire in environmental management. Others believe that Aboriginal people co-existed with megafauna, at least for a while, before overhunting wiped them out.

There are no **tectonic plate** boundaries in WA, and so the state is very stable geologically. There are no active volcanoes, and felt earthquakes are rare but do happen, with the 1968 Meckering earthquake (magnitude 6.5; Wheatbelt Region) being the most prominent example (see box, page 246). Such earthquakes are thought to be partly the result of compressive stress from the Australian Plate colliding into the Eurasian and Pacific Plates offshore. As the stress builds up, rock deep underground can break and release the stress.

Geologically, WA has some of the world's richest **mineral deposits** and the largest stores of iron ore and gold. Diamonds, including the famously rare pink diamonds (page 358), are found in the East Kimberley, near Kununurra, while emeralds have been found at Poona, near Cue in the Murchison – the so-called 'Emerald Desert' – and Menzies in the Goldfields. Aquamarine is found in the Gascoyne and near Coolgardie, opal around Cue and Kalgoorlie, and sapphires and rubies have been found in the Wheatbelt, near Southern Cross and Beverley, but not in commercial quantities.

WA is one of the best places in the world to observe 'living' **stromatolites** – microbial reefs created by cyanobacteria (algae). With a 3.5-billion-year ancestry, these resemble the earliest life forms on earth – life forms that contributed to the rise of the oxygen levels in the atmosphere and thus played a vital role in the development of life on earth. Hamelin Pool at Shark Bay (page 296) is the best place to see them, though less impressive stromatolites live in Lake Thetis (page 269) near Cervantes, while similar **thrombolites** – which differ from stromatolites as non-layered, as opposed to layered, sedimentary formations – thrive in Yalgorup National Park (page 140).

CLIMATE

In a state this big you get all sorts of weather, from monsoonal rains to scorching hot summers, and – yes – even snow and ice.

Much of the north Kimberley is tropical savannah, with very hot, humid and rainy summers, and mild, dry winters, and that extends down the coastal Pilbara as well. The south Kimberley and inland Pilbara feature very hot and dry summers, with mild winters; the inland Mid West, Goldfields-Esperance and Wheatbelt see hot summers and cold, dreary and wet winters. The South West, Great Southern, Peel and Perth have temperate climates with warm summers, cool winters and a winter rainy season.

Australia's famed 'wet' and 'dry' seasons are present in the north. The 'wet' lasts from November to April and can see torrential rains, especially relatively short, powerful bursts in the afternoon with copious helpings of lightning. Many roads, particularly in the north Kimberley, can become impassable for months and attractions close seasonally. The 'dry' is from May to October when tourist numbers bulge, as Perth residents and those in the southern part of the state take advantage of the north's mild winters compared with the much colder, wetter and greyer ones down south. Daytime temperatures will be between 20°C and 30°C; although inland, it can get near freezing here too at times.

AVERAGE TEMPERATURES IN WESTERN AUSTRALIA

The average daily maximum and minimum temperatures for key places are:

	January	July
Perth	30/19°C	18/10°C
Albany	23/16°C	17/9°C
Broome	33/26°C	29/14°C
Bunbury	28/16°C	17/9°C
Denham/Shark Bay	31/22°C	22/13°C
Esperance	26/16°C	17/8°C
Exmouth	38/23°C	24/11°C
Geraldton	32/18°C	20/9°C
Kalgoorlie	34/19°C	17/5°C
Karratha	36/27°C	26/14°C
Kununurra	36/25°C	31/15°C

Though Perth winters can be cold and rainy, the city still has some of the most days of sunshine of any Australian city. In the southern part of the state, summers can be mild, and winter temperatures will hover in the teens before dropping to near-freezing levels at night – even in summer. Wheatbelt residents sometimes have to scrape ice off their windshields in the morning and drive to work or the farm in sub-zero temperatures. Snow doesn't happen often, but the top of Bluff Knoll can see some every few years or so; when it's forecast, people flock to the national park to hike and catch a rare glimpse of the white stuff, to the point that numbers sometimes have to be restricted and visitors can camp out before dawn to make sure they can get a chance to go up. Getting naked at the summit in the snow – 'buff on the Bluff' – is something of a dubious tradition. It has snowed in places like Norseman, Wheatbelt and South West, but these are once-in-a-generation events.

EXTREME WEATHER Hot, dry conditions are very dangerous in WA due to the threat of **bushfire**, and no part of the state is immune – neighbourhoods in metropolitan Perth have even gone up. The state has a comprehensive bushfire warning system – when weather conditions are conductive to bushfires, you are likely to hear of shires declaring 'total fire bans' where it's illegal to drive on unsealed roads or hold outdoor barbecues, for instance. The three levels of warning are: 'Advice' – there is a bushfire, but no threat; 'Watch and Act' – there is a possible threat, consider leaving; and 'Emergency Warning' – you need to take immediate action to survive. When planning bush activities, check the bushfire situation beforehand and have an emergency plan in case one pops up in your area. Bushfires can move with lightning speed; I recall once seeing one start from a workplace window just before leaving, and within two hours, a town 50km away was under threat.

WA is also prone to **cyclones**, usually with at least one, but often more, hitting each year. This is especially true in (but not limited to) the Pilbara and the Kimberley during the wet, and flooding and damage can be severe. WA's cyclone alert system is colour-coded; a Blue Alert means an area can see cyclone conditions within 48 hours (similar to a 'Hurricane Watch' in the US); a Yellow Alert warns of cyclone conditions within 12 hours (similar to a 'Hurricane Warning'), and a Red Alert means the cyclone will arrive imminently. That being said, cyclones can strike much further south, and one, Alby, even hit Busselton in the late 1970s, severely damaging the jetty and also impacting Perth. During any cyclone alerts, pay careful attention to local authorities and evacuation orders. When the cyclone hits, the emergency services baton down their own hatches and have to seek shelter themselves; they won't be able to help you if you blow off evacuation orders and find yourself in trouble.

NATURAL HISTORY AND CONSERVATION *With Stella Martin*

FLORA With more than 10,000 vascular plants recorded, the state is a botanical treasure house. Largely isolated from the rest of the continent by deserts, a fairly large proportion of its flora and fauna is endemic (ie: found nowhere else). Thanks to good rainfall, the southwest corner supports some of Australia's most magnificent tall forests of endemic karri (*Eucalyptus diversicolor*), tingle (*E. jacksonii*) and jarrah (*E. marginata*) eucalypts. Precipitation decreases with distance from the coast and vegetation progresses through woodland, mallee shrubland and mulga (where rainfall is inadequate for eucalypts) to arid spinifex, saltbush and bluebush plains. Summer monsoonal rainfall in the north supports savannah woodlands.

WA is famous for its spring **wildflowers**, almost two-thirds of which are unique to the state. Good rain in preceding winter months results in vast, multi-coloured carpets of blooms, at their most prolific between the months of July and November, with August–October the peak season. Naturally, the flowers attract large numbers of nectar-feeding birds, insects and possums. Wildflower enthusiasts should start in the north of the state early in the season and gradually head towards the South West, where the kwongan heathlands are considered a biodiversity hotspot of global significance. Infertile, sandy soils here have led to the evolution of numerous species, including many carnivorous plants and over 300 types of terrestrial orchid, including intriguing spider orchids with elongated petals.

Fat, conical-shaped **banksias** (Proteaceae) are a much-loved icon of the state. Some 60 different species occur in southwestern Australia, coming in many colours – red and yellow being the most common. If you are bushwalking in autumn or winter, you are likely to come across them. Closer to ground level, the many endemics include the state floral emblem, the **red-and-green kangaroo paw** (*Anigozanthos manglesii*), which derives its name from the appearance of the cluster of hairy, unopened flowers. Vast, colourful displays of **everlasting daisies** (*Helipterum roseum*) carpet the mulga woodlands, while a narrow area around Morawa and Mullewa is famous for its **wreath flowers** (*Lechenaultia macrantha*), which grow as circular, flat pads, up to 50cm across, ringed with pink, red or yellow flowers. They thrive in disturbed soils, sometimes stopping traffic where they line the road. Other prominent wildflowers include bottlebrushes, acacias and eucalypts.

The South West is seeing a significant decline in rainfall, which has collapsed by some estimates by as much as 20% since the 1970s, and this is having a visible effect on the area's flora. Possible theories for this range from human-induced climate change to a shift in fronts out over the Southern Ocean to the possibility that the higher rainfall totals themselves were the outlier, and that the South West is returning to a historically more normal level of precipitation. Future issues are expected to include overdrawing of water from underground aquifers; increasing salinity in soil and its impact on agriculture and food production; and managing the continued growth of Perth and its impact on the surrounding environment.

1

MAMMALS

Marsupials Synonymous with Australia, marsupials are mammals with pouches. The infant is born while still a tiny embryo, the size of a jellybean, and hauls itself into the mother's pouch where it attaches to a teat and continues to develop. When older, it emerges from the pouch but returns frequently. Australia has 159 species ranging from tiny 4g planigales to 90kg male red kangaroos, which can stretch to over 2m in height. Most species tend to be nocturnal and crepuscular.

Red kangaroos (*Macropus rufus*) are found in arid and semi-arid parts of WA while smaller **western grey kangaroos** (*M. fuliginosus*) tend to be south of Shark Bay. Both species are gregarious unlike the more solitary **euro** (*Osphranter robustus*), found in more hilly terrain throughout WA except for the South West.

Wallabies are small kangaroos, frequenting less open terrain. **Agile wallabies** (*Notamacropus agilis*) form large mobs in northern coastal plains and open forests. About five species of **rock wallabies** (*Petrogale* spp) live in large colonies restricted to small ranges in rocky areas. They emerge at night from caves bounding effortlessly up and down steep inclines. **Quokkas** (*Setonix brachyurus*) are small wallabies that thrive in large numbers on fox-free islands – most notably Rottnest Island (page 96), off the coast of Perth, so-called because early Dutch explorers thought they were rats.

Possums are climbing marsupials, not unlike nocturnal squirrels, and WA is home to both one of the largest species and the smallest. The 4kg, leaf-eating **common brushtail possum** (*Trichosurus vulpecula*), about the size of a domestic cat, is found in the South West and north of the state and can be quite tame in urban areas. The 5–10g **honey possum** (*Tarsipes rostratus*) is endemic to WA, feeding on nectar and pollen in the heathlands of the South West. Its foraging behaviour has been described as a cross between that of a monkey and a honeybee. Females produce the world's smallest mammal baby, weighing just 0.0005g. **Sugar gliders** (*Petaurus breviceps*), found in the north of the state, extend flaps of skin on their sides to glide between trees harvesting tree sap.

Dasyurids are nocturnal, carnivorous marsupials which are ferocious, but mostly small. Living fast, most die young, with many males lasting just one year and females two or three. Brown, with attractive white spots, **western quolls** (*Dasyurus geoffroii*) are confined to the South West while the **northern quoll** (*D. hallucatus*) is restricted to small areas of the north and west. The faunal emblem of WA is the diurnal **numbat** (*Myrmecobius fasciatus*). Once widespread, it is now found only in small patches of wandoo and jarrah forest in the South West where it eats only termites.

WA is home to a number of smaller marsupials such as bandicoots, bettongs and potoroos, some of which are endemic and many endangered owing to feral animal predation, habitat destruction and bushfires in sometimes limited ranges. Chocolate versions of the **bilby** (*Macrotis lagotis*), with its oversized ears, are sold as an alternative to the Easter bunny to raise awareness of its plight. Once widespread, it is now largely restricted to small pockets in the state's northwest. Barnia Mia

---

LOCAL LINGO

In WA, local names are often used for mammals and can cause confusion. Those most commonly encountered include **woylie** for brush-tailed bettong (*Bettongia penicillata*); **chuditch** for western quoll (*D. geoffroii*); **quenda** for southern brown bandicoot (*Isoodon obesulus*); **boodie** for burrowing bettong (*B. lesueur*); and **marl** for western barred bandicoot (*Perameles bougainville*).

(page 256), a captive breeding site, is an excellent place to view bilbies and other rare local marsupials while nearby Dryandra Woodland (page 256) is one of the best places to find numbats and rare nocturnal mammals.

Monotremes These are found only in Australia and New Guinea. They combine features of reptiles and mammals, with females laying eggs but feeding their young on milk. The **short-beaked echidna** (*Tachyglossus aculeatus*) roams widely in WA. About the size of a rabbit, it is covered with sharp spines which grow through a coat of fur. It uses a long snout, equipped with electro-sensors, to detect ants and termites, lapping them up with a sticky tongue. Echidnas are active both by day and night, wandering along with a slow, rolling gait, rather like a monitor lizard, but rolling into a tight, spikey ball if disturbed.

Placental mammals Most placental mammals, which nurture the young in the womb, arrived after Australia collided with the Asian plate, about 15 million years ago. Nonetheless, rodents comprise about 25% of Australia's native mammal species. They include the delightful **spinifex hopping mouse** (*Notomys alexis*), which can appear in large numbers after rain in arid zones. The large native **water rat** (*Hydromys chrysogaster*) is found around water in the South West. Less welcome are recently introduced **black rats** (*Rattus rattus*) and **house mice** (*Mus musculus*), which can reach serious plague proportions but are a boon for predators.

The **dingo** (*Canis lupus dingo*) hitched a lift from Asia with seafaring humans about 4,000 years ago. It is a primitive dog that howls but does not bark, although many have crossbred with domestic dogs. They hunt alone or in packs, and are generally found in the central and northern parts of the state.

Many species of insectivorous bats are found in WA, including the largest, the **ghost bat** (*Macroderma gigas*), and the only Australian bat to prey on large vertebrates such as birds and reptiles. Larger fruit bats are represented in the tropics by **black flying-foxes** (*Pteropus alecto*) and the partially nomadic **little red flying-foxes** (*P. scapulatus*), which can gather in very large camps in spring. Remote Tunnel Creek National Park (page 350) is a good place for bat spotting.

BIRDS Of approximately 550 bird species recorded in WA, 18 are endemic and a number are unique subspecies.

Water birds In Europe, the term **black swan** (*Cygnus atratus*) signified the impossible – until 1697, when a Dutch navigator spotted some in Perth's Swan Estuary. Although found throughout Australia, the black swan is particularly associated with WA where it is the state emblem. This lovely bird, whose white wing feathers are generally hidden until it takes flight, can be seen in fresh and salt water. It is one of many waterbirds, including pelicans, cormorants, spoonbills, egrets, herons, ibises, bitterns, cranes, storks, ducks and geese, which frequent the 12 Ramsar sites in WA, listed for the values as wetlands.

In addition to residents, vast numbers of **migratory waders** leave their breeding grounds in the Arctic and head down under during the northern winter (September–March). WA hosts significant numbers of these; the Broome Bird Observatory has listed over 50 species (nearly a quarter of the world's total) while more than 472,000 have been counted on Eighty Mile Beach. The Broome Bird Observatory, run by Birdlife Australia, offers accommodation, tours, courses and educational facilities. Also check out the Broome Wastewater Treatment Plant and Derby Sewage Ponds for birds.

Another significant Ramsar site is Lake Argyle (page 359), the largest freshwater body in northern Australia, which has recorded up to 74 waterbird species. There are other important Ramsar sites near Perth, Busselton (with the state's largest breeding colony of black swans), Manjimup, Narrogin and Esperance, which shelter about one-third of the world's vulnerable **hooded plovers** (*Thinornis rubricollis*).

Albatrosses, shearwaters, petrels, gannets and prions frequent the Southern Ocean and may be seen on pelagic bird-spotting trips or from shore in winter. Boobies, tropicbirds and frigatebirds prefer tropical seas; the last, lacking waterproof feathers, feed by hassling other seabirds and forcing them to drop their catch. Terns and gulls frequent the coast, but many are found inland wherever there is water. The **little penguin** (*Eudyptula minor*), the world's smallest penguin, breeds in burrows in colonies on rocky cliff-bases and sand dunes on islands, including Penguin Island (page 100).

Parrots Many of Australia's lovely parrots are found in WA including several endemic species. The **red-capped parrot** (*Purpureicephalus spurius*) of southwestern woodlands is a beauty with crimson crown, yellow cheeks, green back and purple-blue underparts. The largely nocturnal, ground-dwelling **western ground parrot** (*Pezoporus flaviventris*), from the same zone, is one of the world's rarest birds; perhaps only 150 individuals remain. By contrast, **budgerigars** (*Melopsittacus undulatus*), in their natural green and yellow plumage, occur in drier areas in dense, wheeling flocks. Huge flocks of pink and grey **galahs** (*Eolophus roseicapilla*) are common in drier areas.

Black-cockatoos are large, gregarious birds, up to 65cm, with slow, lazy wingbeats. **Red-tailed black-cockatoos** (*Calyptorhynchus banksii*) are a fairly common sight but the **Carnaby's black-cockatoo** (*Zanda latirostris*) and very similar **Baudin's black-cockatoo** (*Z. baudinii*), with white cheek patches and tail panels, are endangered. The Great Cocky Count, held annually since 2009, surveys black-cockatoos, with a focus on Carnaby's black-cockatoo which has declined 35% in the last decade, thanks largely to severe habitat loss, owing to clearing as well as bushfires. Exotic pine plantations, which have displaced much native vegetation, provide an alternative food source, but when they are logged the birds go hungry. Supporters have replanted the areas with thousands of native eucalypts and banksias and have also installed Cockatubes – artificial nesting hollows.

Ground birds Standing almost 2m tall, the **emu** (*Dromaius novaehollandiae*) is a flightless nomad found throughout arid plains and woodlands. In 1932, when about 20,000 of the birds were raiding WA wheat fields, soldiers were employed to machine gun them during the 'emu wars'. The birds proved elusive and fences more effective, though thousands continue to perish on these barriers.

Also known as the plains turkey, the **Australian bustard** (*Ardeotis australis*) is one of the world's heaviest flying birds (males reach 1.5m in height) but prefers to stride through grasslands. The vulnerable **malleefowl** (*Leipoa ocellata*), from dry inland scrub in the South West, builds an enormous nesting mound of vegetation and soil. The decomposing material generates heat to incubate the eggs; chicks are independent immediately after hatching. The Yongergnow Australian Malleefowl Centre (see box, page 186) is dedicated to conserving these birds.

Passerines Male bowerbirds build elaborate structures to seduce females. The **great bowerbird** (*Chlamydera nuchalis*), from the state's north, and the **western bowerbird** (*C. guttata*) further south, both build avenue bowers comprising two parallel walls of upright twigs, decorated with hundreds of white and green objects, both natural and humanmade.

At least 34 of Australia's ubiquitous **honeyeater** species are found in WA, including some endemics. Along with lorikeets, they play an important role as plant pollinators for over 1,000 Australian plants species.

Little fairywrens, with their bright colours, cocked tails and twittering gregarious family groups, are among Australian's favourite birds. The **red-winged fairywren** (*Malurus elegans*) is endemic to the South West.

Twelve of Australia's 18 finch species occur in WA. Most, including the spectacular **Gouldian finch** (*Erythrura gouldiae*), can be found in the state's north while the endemic **red-eared firetail** (*Stagonopleura oculata*) inhabits the southwest corner.

Some other sought-after species include the **thick-billed grasswren** (*Amytornis purnelli*), which are quite confiding in the car park of Monkey Mia conservation park (page 297). Easier heard than seen, the endemic **noisy scrub bird** (*Atrichornis clamosus*), one of Australia's rarest birds, was thought to be extinct until rediscovered in Two Peoples Bay in 1961. Some have been relocated, notably to Waychinicup National Park near Albany. The endemic **western bristlebird** (*Dasyornis longirostris*) also frequents these sites as well as Fitzgerald River National Park (page 207) on the south coast.

REPTILES Warm habitats, particularly the hot, dry conditions of the arid zone, favour reptiles. These energy-efficient creatures use solar power to generate body heat and therefore need only about 10% as much food as mammals. If conditions are too cold or too hot, they can shut down and become inactive (aestivate). They are also very water-efficient thanks to their waterproof skins and their ability to excrete urine as crystals rather than as a liquid. Male lizards and snakes have two penises, used alternately, and kept within the body when not in use.

Crocodiles Two crocodile species inhabit northern Australia. They are more often seen in winter when they spend periods of time basking in the sun to increase their body temperatures; slide marks on river banks are a sure sign of their presence.

The **estuarine crocodile** (*Crocodylus porosus*) is the largest reptile in the world, some growing over 6m long. It is found in the tropical coastal regions of WA, mainly between Kununurra and Broome. This species is often referred to as the saltwater (or 'saltie') croc, but this term is misleading because many live in fresh water – billabongs, swamps, lakes and rivers – as well as estuaries, offshore islands and even the open sea. The jaw of an estuarine croc is irregular and teeth are visible when its mouth is shut. Eggs are laid in mounds of vegetation; incubation temperatures around 32°C produce males while higher and lower temperatures produce more females.

The **freshwater crocodile** (*C. johnstoni*) is found only in Australia and only in fresh water. Rarely reaching 3m in length, 'freshies' are slimmer and have narrow snouts with an even jawline. They catch fish, their main prey, along with frogs and other aquatic animals. Freshies do not eat people but have been known to bite, probably in self-defence. In the dry season, along with fish and waterbirds, they congregate in pools of the shrinking Lennard River in Kimberley's Windjana Gorge National Park (page 350). They may also be seen on boat tours in Danggu Geikie Gorge National Park, along with sawfish (*Pristis microdon*) and stingrays.

Deaths from crocodile attacks are minimal compared with road deaths, but they do happen. You must assume that all natural waterways in the tropical north contain crocodiles. Do not swim or stand in water and keep several metres away from the water's edge. See the box on page 350 for more on croc safety.

Snakes Pythons are non-venomous snakes, which may have evolved in Australia. A python seizes prey in its sharp, backward facing teeth and very swiftly coils its body around it. Each time the captive breathes out, the snake tightens its coils, quickly suffocating its victim. Growing to 2.5m, the **carpet** or **diamond python** (*Morelia spilota*) is found in WA's north and South West; it is richly patterned and varies greatly in colour. The **black-headed python** (*Aspidites melanocephalus*), with its distinctive glossy, dark head, inhabits savannah woodlands north of Exmouth. It is related to the **woma** (*A. ramsayi*) of the arid interior and west. Both these pythons prey mainly on other reptiles and are apparently immune to snake venom. The shiny, brown **water python** (*Liasis fuscus*) frequents waterways north of Broome.

Colubrid snakes produce venom, but it is relatively weak and delivered through fangs at the back of the mouth, allowing a deep bite into small prey; Australian species are not considered dangerous to adult humans. The diurnal **common tree snake** (*Dendrelaphis punctulata*) and nocturnal **brown tree snake** (*Boiga irregularis*) from the Kimberley area are slim, swift and agile climbers. In WA, the latter tend to be strongly banded and are known as night tigers. The **keelback** or **freshwater snake** (*Tropidonophis mairii*) frequents northern waterways, readily swimming to hunt frogs, tadpoles and fish.

Elapid snakes have fixed, front fangs, with deep grooves, connected to venom glands. Not all are highly dangerous, but it is best to give all snakes a wide berth. They tend to be nocturnal, secretive, rarely seen, most retreating from confrontations with humans. The **coastal taipan** (*Oxyuranus scutellatus*), one of Australia's most dangerous snakes, is found in the northern Kimberley. Fairly plain, and growing to over 3m, it has very long fangs which inject large amounts of powerful venom, designed to immobilise mammals. When cornered, it attacks aggressively and bites repeatedly. **Brown snakes** (*Pseudonaja* spp) are not always brown – individuals of the same species can vary enormously from bright orange to dull brown, with or without bands. They tend to act aggressively and are blamed for most snake-bite fatalities. The **western brown** or **gwardar** (*P. nuchalis*), growing to about 1.5m, inhabits most of the state except the southern coastal fringe where the endemic **dugite** (*P. affinis*) exists. **Black snakes** (*Pseudechis* spp) are not always black; the most widespread, the **mulga snake** (*P. australis*), is also known, confusingly, as the king brown. Growing to over 2.5m, it is found in most of the state except the southern coastal fringe. It feeds mainly on other snakes and is apparently immune to their venom. Different species of **death adders** (*Acanthophis* spp) are found in most parts of the state. They vary in colour but usually have irregular pale bands. Rarely reaching 1m, they have fat bodies which taper abruptly to a slender tail, terminating in a thin spine which they waggle to attract prey. They are very dangerous because, as ambush predators, they are well-camouflaged and, unlike most Australian snakes, do not retreat when disturbed.

Lizards Lizards are an Australian speciality and, next to birds, the most commonly seen vertebrates.

Skinks (Scincidae) are Australia's most diverse and most numerous vertebrates, with many of the 370-plus species inhabiting relatively small ranges. The majority are small (5–10cm), smooth and fast-moving. Most are diurnal and live on the ground, feeding mainly on invertebrates. Blue-tongues are unusually large, slow-moving skinks. When threatened they open pink mouths and stick out their large, contrasting, blue tongues while hissing and inflating their bodies. A very distinctive blue-tongue, the **shingleback** (*Tiliqua rugosa*), is found in the South West and on the Mid-West coast. Also known as the bobtail, stumpy tail, pinecone or sleepy lizard, it grows to 30cm and 1kg, with a short, blunt tail and very large, thick scales.

Geckos (Gekkonidae) are mostly small, soft-skinned, nocturnal lizards. When threatened, like some skinks, geckos readily drop their tails, which continue to wriggle, distracting predators while the owner escapes. The tails later regrow. Many are able to walk upside down and on vertical panes of glass. Their toes are coated with tiny hairs with flattened ends which exploit the weak attractive force between molecules, enabling the geckos' feet to stick. Most tropical dwellings have a resident population of geckos stationed around lights at night, pouncing on confused moths and other invertebrates. The **Asian house gecko** (*Hemidactylus frenatus*), a common, introduced species, has a distinctive, loud, scolding call. WA's most widespread native species, **Bynoe's gecko** (*Heteronotia binoei*) lives in dry, open areas. It is about 10cm long, with irregular bands and spots of brown, black and white. Females, some of which reproduce without males, often lay in communal nests containing up to 150 eggs. A number of **knob-tailed geckos** (*Nephrurus* spp), with strangely shrunken tails ending in a round ball, are found in dry to arid areas. Many species in the *Diplodactylus* genus have plump tails, which function as fat storage organs and can be used to plug the entrance to underground burrows.

Dragon lizards (Agamidae) have rough textured skins, often ornamented with spines and crests. Males in particular are quite brightly coloured at times. Diurnal, with an upright stance, they often perch on rocks, tree trunks or other vantage points. They pounce on prey but, if in danger, can sprint off on their hind legs; some reaching speeds over 20km/h, are called 'bicycle lizards'. The charismatic **frilled lizard** (*Chlamydosaurus kingii*) can grow to a metre in length. It has a frill around its neck which it can erect, rather like opening an umbrella, by gaping its mouth. Although common throughout northern savannah woodlands, it is rarely seen in the dry season when it is high in the trees. It can remain in a state of energy-saving torpor for three months. In the wet season it is active on, or close to, the ground feeding on ants, termites and other invertebrates.

The **thorny devil** (*Moloch horridus*), from arid sandy regions, feeds on ants. Its stuttering walk and thorny red, yellow and brown body are thought to camouflage it, persuading predators that it is just a windblown leaf. To drink, it stands on damp sand. Moisture is drawn, by capillary action, along grooves between its scales and up into its mouth. **Bearded dragons** (*Pogona* spp) have strong spines around the throat forming a 'beard'. The **western** or **dwarf bearded dragon** (*Pogona minor*) is widespread and may be spotted basking on fence posts. A number of medium-sized dragons, often with prominent white dorsal stripes or lines and long tails, are common in arid and savannah regions. Some *Amphibolurus* species are commonly called ta-ta lizards for their comical habit of waving their front legs. The extraordinary **pebble dragon** (*Tympanocryptis cephalus*) superbly mimics the stones of its arid habitat with an attached stick-like tail.

Monitor lizards (Varanidae), also known as goannas, have tough, loose skin often patterned with spots which may be arranged in bands. Large ones tend to lumber slowly and confidently but if threatened can run quickly and climb trees. The **perentie** (*Varanus giganteus*), sometimes exceeding 2.5m in length, is one of the world's largest lizards. It is strikingly patterned with rows of large, pale, dark-edged spots but hides well in rocky areas of arid regions. The widespread **sand monitor** (*V. gouldii*), also known as Gould's goanna, can grow to 1.5m long. A fast runner, it is also called the racehorse goanna. **Mertens' water monitor** (*V. mertensi*) frequents tropical watercourses, basking on rocks or using its laterally flattened tail to propel itself in the water and to herd fish.

THE MARINE ENVIRONMENT With over 10,000km of coastline, WA's diverse marine habitats range from temperate to tropical. Ningaloo Marine Park protects Australia's largest and most accessible fringing coral reef system; it is possible to snorkel from the shore at Coral Bay and Cape Range National Park.

Marine mammals Of the several whale species recorded in WA waters, two are seen regularly from about May to November when they move north from sub-Antarctic waters to give birth and mate. The **southern right whale** (*Eubalaena australis*) favours shallow, southern bays for calving and mating between late July and September; Point Ann in Fitzgerald River National Park (page 207) and Albany's southern bays are good places to observe this close to land.

The **humpback whale** (*Megaptera novaeangliae*) travels further up the west coast to breed in tropical waters in June/July, notably off the Kimberley's Camden Sound. Coastal vantage points include Cape Leveque, points near Exmouth, Shark Bay and Kalbarri. A swim-with-humpbacks programme operates in Ningaloo Marine Park.

The best vantage points on land for both species are between Cape Naturaliste and Cape Leeuwin, Conspicuous Cliffs in Walpole-Nornalup National Park, King George Sound near Albany and Point Ann. Whale-watching cruises operate around the coast between Esperance and Broome. It is also possible on these trips to see some of the many species of dolphins that inhabit WA's coastline and it is possible to swim with **bottlenose dolphins** (*Tursiops truncates*) on trips run from Rockingham, Mandurah and Bunbury.

Shark Bay (page 294) is home to 10% of the world's **dugongs** (*Dugong dugon*) – large marine mammals, related to elephants, that feed on seagrasses. They can be seen from boat trips here, along with turtles, rays, sharks and sea snakes, while bottlenose dolphins come to shore at nearby Monkey Mia (page 297) to be fed, under supervision.

The **New Zealand fur seal** (*Arctocephalus forsteri*) breeds on islands off the south coast, with colonies hauling out on rocky areas. **Australian sea lions** (*Neophoca cinerea*), only found in Australia, range south from Shark Bay. One of the rarest pinniped in the world, it is listed as endangered owing to declining numbers.

Sea turtles Five species of sea turtle frequent WA waters, roughly north from Shark Bay. Most cover great distances across the world's oceans as they move between feeding and breeding areas. From about October to January, females return to the beaches where they hatched, hauling themselves ashore at night to dig nesting pits in the sand and depositing about 100 ping-pong-ball-sized eggs, before covering them up. Cooler temperatures produce male hatchlings, and warmer ones females. Surviving hatchlings emerge about seven to 11 weeks later, usually at night, to run the gauntlet of crabs, birds and other predators as they aim for the sea. The Jurabi Turtle Centre (page 307) in Cape Range National Park runs tours.

Three species, with adult carapace lengths of 1–1.5m, are often seen by divers and snorkellers. Most common is the **green turtle** (*Chelonia mydas*), named after the green fat around its internal organs; it is a popular food for Aboriginal people. Adults are vegetarians, browsing on algae and seagrasses. Likely to be seen in sandy areas, the **loggerhead turtle** (*Caretta caretta*) has a relatively large head with powerful jaws used to crush molluscs and crustaceans, although it also eats jellyfish. The **hawksbill turtle** (*Eretmochelys imbricata*) has a distinctive beak-like mouth used to tear sponges and soft corals from the reefs.

Freshwater turtles Where sea turtles have flippers, freshwater turtles have clawed feet. The endemic **southwestern snake-necked turtle** (*Chelodina colliei*) and the **northern snake-necked turtle** (*C. rugosa*) have extremely long necks, which they fold sideways under their carapace. Both can, during dry times, bury into still-damp soil and remain in a state of torpor (aestivation) until the next rain. The former is found around the South West and is common in lakes of suburban Perth; the latter is from the Kimberley. Uniquely among turtles, it lays its eggs under water which would normally destroy them. However, they do not begin to develop until the water level drops during the dry season and hatch when the wet season brings more rain.

Whale sharks (*Rhincodon typus*) These fish can grow to over 12m in length, and come close to shore between March and July. Swimming with these harmless giants is big business at Coral Bay and Exmouth.

Corals Australia is world famous for its Great Barrier Reef, but WA is home to its very own showstopper – Ningaloo Reef, the world's largest fringing reef. Colonies grow as individual coral polyps divide but, once a year, they reproduce in orgies of mass spawning – around March and April. A few nights after the full moon, on a neap tide, the corals release massive numbers of eggs and sperm almost simultaneously, the spectacle having been compared to an upside-down snowstorm or underwater firework show.

Crustaceans The marron, or freshwater crayfish (*Cherax cainii*), is endemic to WA, inhabiting freshwater bodies between Hutt River in the northwest and Esperance. Considered a state specialty food, it is farmed in aquaculture.

INVERTEBRATES Australia is famous for its venomous **spiders**. Commonly making webs in dry sheltered spots, including urban areas, female redback spiders (*Latrodectus hasselti*), with a distinctive red stripe on the abdomen, can give a nasty bite, but no deaths have been recorded in Australia since antivenom was developed in 1956. Recent discoveries indicate that WA is a hotspot for endearing peacock spiders (*Maratus* spp); these jumping spiders (they do not make webs) are only the size of a grain of rice but the males put on a dazzling mating display in spring, hoisting their back legs and brilliantly coloured abdomens and dancing back and forward in an attempt to woo females. See page 49 for details on how to treat a spider bite.

Tiny, but with a gigantic impact, are **termites** (Isoptera). Across the savannah plains of the tropical north, these soft-bodied, blind builders band together in vast colonies to construct, grain by grain, massive earthen mounds, some over 6m high. Not all termites build mounds; many live underground or inhabit rotting timber or hollow out tree trunks and branches. They are excellent recyclers, breaking down cellulose and lignin, the main components of wood, and releasing nutrients back into the environment.

Beetles account for about 25% of all animal species on earth and WA has no shortage. The state's abundant flowers support an impressive variety of aptly named jewel beetles (Buprestidae), which feed on the nectar.

In terms of **butterflies**, standouts include the small but beautiful western jewel butterfly (*Hypochrysops halyaetus*), a favourite of Perth residents with its solidly violet wings framed by a golden border, and the red-spotted jezebel (*Delias aganippe*), with its red, yellow and white round splotches.

1

CONSERVATION EFFORTS Australia has a woeful record of wildlife extinctions. Since 1788 more than 115 plants and animals – including about 28 mammal, 23 bird and four frog species – have died out, owing largely to habitat destruction and invasive species, notably cats and foxes.

Work is being done to prevent any more extinctions. The Parks and Wildlife Service manages 1,224 protected areas, covering 6.3% of the state, including national and marine parks and various reserves. Non-governmental not-for-profit agencies, such as Bush Heritage, Australian Wildlife Conservancy (ACF) and Greening Australia, buy, protect and restore significant areas, often in partnership with local Traditional Owners (Aboriginal peoples who have traditionally been custodians of the land).

A number of endangered species are being raised in various captive breeding centres with the aim of reintroducing them into the wild, ideally in fenced, feral-predator-free areas. One of these is Project Eden, in the Shark Bay World Heritage Area, where a 3km fence across the neck of the Peron Peninsula provides a sanctuary for reintroduced malleefowl, bilbies, woylies and others. At least 18 reptile species also thrive on the peninsula.

Some fenced sanctuaries are also run by ACF, including Mt Gibson, 350km northeast of Perth, where at least ten regionally extinct mammal species have been reintroduced into a 7,800ha area behind a 43km-long fence. Closer to Perth, Karakamia is a 258ha fenced sanctuary with reintroduced quendas, woylies and tammar wallabies (*Notamacropus eugenii*) among others. Resident wildlife also thrives in these predator-free sanctuaries.

Revegetation projects are working to restore native habitat in many parts of the state. The ambitious Gondwana Link (w gondwanalink.org) aims to reconnect countryside across southwestern Australia, from the wet forests in the southwest corner to the dry woodlands and mallee bordering the Nullarbor Plain.

Getting involved There are plenty of opportunities for volunteers to become involved in conservation activities in WA. A good resource is SEEK Volunteer (w volunteer.com.au), a database of current listings in the state. More specifically, Birdlife Australia runs various programmes (w birdlife.org.au), including one to help the recovery of the southwest back-cockatoo, while Gondwana Link (see above) welcomes help with restoring the ecological integrity of land in the south of the state.

HISTORY

THE FIRST INHABITANTS Aboriginal peoples first arrived in Western Australia over 50,000 years ago, although some claim there is evidence of Aboriginal settlement on Rottnest Island dating back 70,000 years (sea levels were such that Rottnest Island was connected to the mainland then). The discovery of the Mungo Lady remains (1969) and Mungo Man remains (1974) at Lake Mungo in southwestern New South Wales were landmark discoveries that, when dated back to their origins 42,000 years ago, provided conclusive proof that Aboriginal peoples had lived in Australia for tens of thousands of years prior to European settlement. This makes Aboriginal Australian culture the world's oldest surviving culture. Some experts believe the first Aboriginal peoples in Australia were part of a larger African migration, and that they arrived in northern Australia from southeast Asia (including to the Kimberley, which at one point in the evolution of the land was only about 100km away from southeast Asia and Northern Territory). It is believed this happened either by boat, making Aboriginal Australians the first oceanic seafarers, and/or when Australia was still connected to New Guinea by a land bridge, allowing the first inhabitants to potentially arrive on foot through what is now Cape York in Queensland. Rising sea levels submerged the land bridge into what is now the Torres Strait approximately 8,000 years ago, and the Torres Strait Islands are remnants of this.

Aboriginal people arriving into northern Australia found a land rich in fresh water, plants, animals and environmental resources, and one highly conducive to settlement, though within a few thousand years Aboriginal people were living in all parts of the country. Disparate tribes, cultures and languages developed and helped Aboriginal culture evolve into a rich tapestry of diversity (see page 29 for more on this).

They encountered giant animals like Diprotodon, a huge marsupial wombat weighing two tons that became extinct around 12,000 years ago; there is some belief that in Aboriginal folklore the bunyip – a monster that drags unsuspecting people underwater – may in fact be a reference to Diprotodons trapped in muddy salt lakes. Also present were *Procoptodon goliah*, the largest known kangaroo, which was 2m tall – and could not hop! – and became extinct between 18,000 and 45,000 years ago. Ancient Aboriginal culture was a hunter-gatherer society, and there is evidence that Aboriginal peoples hunted these and other megafauna, as bones have been found at sites the animals could not have accessed, and images at rock art galleries such as that in Murujuga National Park depict them being hunted.

After the megafauna became extinct, Aboriginal people began using tools to better harvest and process plants. Multiple oscillations of global warming and cooling, and rising and falling sea levels, likely significantly impacted settlement patterns from the time of arrival to the end of the Ice Age 12,000 years ago. The Australian landmass used to be about one-third larger in the thousands of years before Europeans arrived, and recent archaeological finds of stone tools and grinders off the Pilbara coast raise the possibility that significant Aboriginal settlements laid on lands that have now been lost to the sea.

With the land forming such an important part of Aboriginal survival, a deep and significant knowledge of it was vital to thrive. Stone tools were used extensively, and stone was also used to carve and help produce wooden tools. Aboriginal people worked with the environment around them and also used shells, fibres and resins from trees to make glues, bags, containers, shields and baskets. Controlled fires

ABORIGINAL AUSTRALIANS AND TORRES STRAIT ISLANDERS

There is a distinction between Aboriginal Australians and Torres Strait Islanders – the latter being of Melanesian origin and hailing from the islands in the Torres Strait, though living across Australia. The term 'Indigenous Australian' refers to both, but you will often hear Aboriginal people referred to as 'Aboriginal and Torres Strait Islanders'. If you are unsure which to address a group by, don't assume – just ask. Do not use the term 'Aborigine', which is anachronistic and harkens back to segregationist days.

Boomerangs are estimated to have been invented around 10,000 years ago. A common myth of Aboriginal culture is that all Aboriginal people used boomerangs, but this is not true. While they were used in many parts of Australia, they were not used, for instance, in the Kimberley or in rainforest areas, where trees could limit their effectiveness. Another misconception is that all boomerangs 'return' to where they were thrown – in actuality, most only travelled in the direction they were launched, and killed their prey by hitting them with blunt force. In that sense, they were more useful than spears as the boomerang could cover a greater range and did not need to be as accurate as a spear to kill prey. Boomerangs had different shapes and were used for different purposes, such as weaponry in warfare, and different types of boomerangs were used for different types of prey.

were used as a fuel-management technique to prevent larger fires later on, and also as a hunting method to attract animals or cause them to flee, sometimes out into open areas where they could be captured more easily. Aboriginal culture continued to evolve, develop and grow – but changed forever when the Europeans arrived.

THE ARRIVAL OF THE EUROPEANS The Dutch were the first Europeans to sight the coast of WA, with explorer Dirk Hartog arriving on the island that now bears his name off Shark Bay in 1616. Hartog did not intend to arrive there – his destination was Batavia, now called Jakarta, the Indonesian capital, but strong winds blew him off course. The most common route for Dutch ships heading to what is now Indonesia was to round the southern tip of Africa, catch the westerly winds at the 'Roaring Forties' (westerly winds between 40°S and 50°S) and then turn north when they had reached Indonesia's longitude. However, without an exact way to calculate longitude, it was fairly easy to miss the 'turn-off' and end up on the Australian West Coast. Hartog's discovery was named Eendrachtsland after his ship, the *Eendracht*.

Other Dutch exploration and surveying missions occurred in the years following – Rottnest Island got its name because the Dutch who originally sighted it mistook the quokkas for giant rats (Rottnest is Dutch for 'rat's nest'). Ships belonging to the British East India Company also sailed by – and wrecked – off the coast in the early 1600s, and many of the first Europeans to put their feet on WA's shores were shipwreck survivors waiting for rescue. There were also voyages of exploration; William Dampier landed in the northwest part of the state in the late 1600s, recording the first significant European accounts of flora and fauna in what is now the Pilbara. Mostly, however, the Europeans did not find the land valuable enough to attempt settlement and were happy to just pass by on their way to Batavia. For a while, the land was called New Holland or Southland; but as an indication of how poorly the land was thought of, no European nation staked a claim to it.

This indifference changed in the late 1700s, however, as the world's geopolitical scene altered significantly. The Netherlands, Spain and Portugal had faded as colonial powers, leaving the British and French positions dominant. Britain, facing massive crime problems, had relied on its American colonies for convict transportation – but this was cut off when America gained its independence in 1776 (aided by France). Needing a new place to transport their convicts, the British turned to Australia. James Cook explored the east coast of Australia in the early 1770s aboard the HMS *Endeavour*, sailing into Botany Bay at what is now Sydney.

The British chose to establish new penal colonies in Australia over West Africa in part because of climate, agriculture potential and a miscalculation of the possibility of conflict with Aboriginal peoples. Arthur Phillip's First Fleet arrived in Port Jackson (now Sydney Harbour) on 26 January 1788 and established the colony of New South Wales. For many years, in the national psyche of European-descended Australians, the story of Australia was seen to have begun with Cook and the First Fleet, but more and more that is being seen as inaccurate and insensitive, with Cook's arrival being the start of a later, recent chapter of the Australian story rather than the beginning. Australians are becoming gradually more aware of the impact European arrival had on Aboriginal peoples, and the different perspectives that different groups may have regarding its effects.

The British claimed the whole eastern half of Australia – Dampier's poor and sobering account of the conditions in the northwest throwing a wet blanket on British interest there – and set up another penal colony in Van Diemen's Land – now Tasmania – in 1803. The colonies of Victoria, Queensland, South Australia and Tasmania would all be cut out of New South Wales by 1860.

Meanwhile, French exploration efforts picked up steam – a French ship, commanded by Jean-Francois de la Perouse, arrived on the coast of New South Wales just days after the First Fleet, and French scientists began to explore the west coast. Napoleon Bonaparte funded Nicolas Baudin's ships, the *Geographe* and the *Naturaliste*, which arrived in WA in 1801 – you will notice many things named after the ships and the captain, especially in the South West. Bruni d'Entrecasteaux arrived with his ships, the *Esperance* and the *Recherche*, a little before, officially searching for Perouse, who had gone missing after leaving the Australian East Coast and was never heard from again.

The British became anxious about French activity in the west, as well as American whaling activity, and decided to act – sending Edmund Lockyer and a party of soldiers and convicts there from New South Wales. In late 1826, what is now Albany was chosen as the first site for permanent English settlement, to forestall any French territorial claims – and the Brig *Amity* arrived from the east with over 50 men and formed a military installation. Albany, however, was formed as part of New South Wales and the British claim on the western half of the Australian continent was only settled in 1827 amid rumours of French interest in establishing their own penal presence in what is now Shark Bay in the Gascoyne.

ESTABLISHING WESTERN AUSTRALIA What we now think of as Western Australia began in 1829, as the free (not convict) Swan River Colony, with settlers and corporations being allocated land grants based on the size of their investments. Led by Captains James Stirling (who would become the colony's first governor) and Charles Fremantle, settlements were established at Fremantle (for shipping and trade), Guildford (for agriculture) and Perth (chosen as capital because it was halfway between the two). Part of the rationale for choosing Perth against the advice of previous explorers unimpressed with the potential of the land for agriculture, and the lack of transport access – as the Swan River mouth was blocked – was that Stirling felt Mt Eliza, in what is now Kings Park, would make the new colony easier to defend. Calamity struck immediately, though, with multiple ships carrying settlers running aground and striking rocks off the coast near Garden Island and Cockburn Sound – a poor omen for the colony.

Swan River Colony got off to a terrible start. Preparations for arriving settlers were non-existent, fresh water scarce, the soil poor for agriculture, and relationships between the Noongar and the settlers were violent. The colony struggled, and many settlers fled to New South Wales. Despite this, back in England Thomas Peel (see box, page 123) jumped on the Swan River bandwagon and formed a syndicate in which the British government promised him, after some negotiation, one million acres of land if he delivered 400 settlers to Swan River prior to 1 November 1829. The transport ran into trouble, however, and Peel's first settlers were six weeks late – the government denied Peel his land as a result and redistributed it to others, though eventually they came to a settlement of 250,000 acres of land south of Perth in what is now the Peel region. Peel's settlement floundered almost immediately owing to poor agricultural conditions, lack of labour and Peel's own unsuitable leadership temperament – and eventually Peel was the only one left as settlers drifted off to Fremantle and elsewhere.

Relations with Aboriginal peoples in early Swan River were poor and marked by violence. An Aboriginal man named Yagan (see box, page 89) led resistance to the early settlers, conducting raids on the colony; he was briefly captured and interred on Carnac Island before escaping, and a bounty was put on his head. Yagan conducted more raids, before getting shot by two young settlers in 1833. A year later, another Aboriginal man named Calyute, of the Noongar tribe, led further resistance, with more raids, resulting in tit-for-tat from Stirling and the settlers. After a raid on Thomas Peel's property that killed one and injured another, Stirling led a band of settlers to retaliate against Calyute in what is now the Peel Region – the battle between firearms and spears at Pinjarra was particularly noted for its brutality on the part of the settlers and though the number of Aboriginal dead is not known for certain, the Pinjarra Massacre likely resulted in around 80 dead (see box, page 133). Calyute survived, and reportedly moved south to the Lake Clifton area, but there are no records of what happened to him after. The Pinjarra Massacre itself backfired on Stirling; instead of calming the security fears of settlers, and thus encouraging additional settlement for the floundering colony, many panicked and tensions soared as the colony feared that the local Aboriginal groups would unite and retaliate to drive the settlers out. These fears persisted for decades, dampening further British settlement efforts.

The name Western Australia was formalised in the early 1830s, but Swan River continued to be used colloquially for most of the 19th century. Albany was incorporated into Swan River from New South Wales in 1831 and its convicts sent back to the east.

From Swan River, the thin population of only about 1,500 began spreading out in search of farmland. York was established in 1831, as the colony's first inland town; Northam quickly followed in 1833. Kojonup was established in 1837 (there was a freshwater spring there) as a halfway stopping point between Perth and Albany.

Swan River, however, continued to flounder and seemed to be on an eternal quest for more settlers. Stories of the less-than-desirable conditions and tensions with the Aboriginal population made their way back to the UK and other parts of Australia, and population growth (and with it, the colony's economy) stagnated. The population slowly drifted southwards and eastwards; Bunbury was established in 1843, and settlers fanned further southwards to Augusta from there. However, the population of the entire colony was still only 4,622 by the time of WA's first census in 1848.

CONVICT LABOUR As a result of the poor economic conditions and severe skills and labour shortages in essential fields, WA decided to seek convict settlement – known as 'transportation' – in 1850, and the results were immediate; the second census in 1854 recorded a population of 11,743 – not counting Aboriginal Australians, who were excluded (it would be over a century until they were counted in the census).

Transportation at the time was a controversial move; convicts had a social stigma and, in WA, a perception had taken hold that convict labour was linked to crime rates. Despite this, the labour shortage, especially in agriculture, and Britain's continuing need to find a solution to overcrowded prisons, led to the policy change over a two-decade period before transportation was halted in 1868. Convict labour proved instrumental in the development of WA's critical infrastructure, particularly roads, and many were sent to remote areas of the colony. When the British government wound up transportation, the colony protested and sought compensation owing to the loss of the labour pool.

Though the infusion of convict labour stabilised the economy, WA was far from flourishing. The colony continued to expand northwards, with pastoral lands being opened up for grazing in what is now the areas around Geraldton and the Pilbara. John Forrest (who would go on to become the first Premier of Western Australia) led an expedition across the Nullarbor to Adelaide to stake out the route for a telegraph line, which was completed in 1877 and dramatically improved communications, and exploration began in the interior and in the Kimberley. The traditional agricultural activities of wool and wheat production became firmly ingrained in the state's economy, where they remain today.

THE GOLD RUSH The colony's future did not become cemented, however, until 1885 with the discovery of some of the world's richest gold deposits, really taking off with the finds at Cue (1891), Coolgardie (1892) and Kalgoorlie-Boulder (1893). The timing was fortuitous; these finds came as the Victorian goldfields were exhausting, and so news of the new gold in WA set off a massive gold rush and population shift from the east. Prospectors and miners arrived by the thousands by boat into Albany, and from there would travel up to Broomehill and take the Holland Track to Coolgardie – a route you can still travel today (see box, page 185). Cue's population swelled to 10,000 residents – about the same size of Perth, though Perth would also balloon to three times that during the decade.

The population boom from the gold rush finally made the state large enough by the end of the 1880s to draft its own constitution, which was accepted by the British government in 1890, and WA became self-governing. The Legislative Assembly and Legislative Council were established, and WA finally had self-government and all-elected representatives, with John Forrest as its first premier. The funds from the influx of population and discovery of gold allowed the colony to boom. The water pipeline from Mundaring allowed permanent settlement in the Eastern Goldfields; the huge size of the find in Kalgoorlie-Boulder, along with reliable water supplies, allowed Kalgoorlie to become a permanent settlement while Cue and Coolgardie busted after their booms. Fremantle Harbour, which had never met its potential, was enlarged and became a premier facility, railways were developed and progressive legislation on things like women's rights and workers' compensation – but not Aboriginal rights – were passed.

A UNITED AUSTRALIA The Australian colonies were, effectively, like separate countries; but as Australia's population grew and its economy developed, this became to be seen as inefficient, particularly in business where colonies had their own tariffs and different railway gauges. The colonies had a common culture and language and a sense of a national 'Australian' identity had also developed. Interest in federating the colonies into one country – Australia – grew as people began to believe a national entity was needed to govern things like trade and defence, and federation conventions were held in the 1890s.

However, federation was a divisive issue in WA. The Gold Rush had sharply cleaved the population over the issue; long-standing settlers and farmers wanted to remain independent, while the influx of prospectors and miners from the eastern colonies wanted to join the federation. WA's distance from the other colonies, and fears that much more populous New South Wales and Victoria would dominate WA in parliament, also undermined support for federation. At one point, the Goldfields threatened to secede from WA and join the federation on its own, a notion which Albany joined as they were unhappy with the loss of business that resulted from the expanded and upgraded port at Fremantle. Such a threat helped swing the tide towards joining the proposed Australia, and in 1900 WA voted to join the federation as the second-smallest state by population, ahead of only Tasmania. An Australia that stretched from the Indian Ocean to the Pacific Ocean was born.

CONTEMPORARY ABORIGINAL CIVIL RIGHTS

Western Australia's Aboriginal history is littered with tragedy post-European settlement. When Federation occurred, the states had Aboriginal Protection Boards designed to control the population, with each state having a Chief Protector. One of the main purposes of the boards was to remove Aboriginal children from their families – a policy that led to what is now referred to as the Stolen Generations. In 1905, the West Australian Government passed an act declaring the Chief Protector to be the legal guardian of all Aboriginal children up to the age of 16. Carrolup, also called Marribank, near Katanning was one large reserve established for the purpose of relocating Aboriginal children, along with Moore River Settlement near New Norcia. Housing provided on native reserves were often made of tin – completely unsuitable for the state's hot climate and the interior would be rendered into ovens during the day.

Aboriginals were excluded from schools, were paid far lower wages than white people for the same jobs, could not marry non-indigenous people without permission, and suffered from a whole raft of other segregationist policy including forced labour, medical internment in lock hospitals on spurious grounds and more. Much of White Australia at that time believed in Social Darwinism and that 'inferior' races such as the Aboriginals would die out without White intervention to 'civilise' them. By 1937 this had evolved into the 'Assimilation Policy', in which Aboriginal Australians were expected to give up their culture and way of life and behave like White Australians. However, Aboriginals still did not have equal citizenship rights and were treated (at best) as second-class citizens.

The birth of the modern Civil Rights Movement can perhaps be traced to the 1938 Day of Mourning – on the Australia Day sesquicentenary (150 years) – when a march was held on the streets of Sydney that, for the first time, presented an alternative view of history to White Australians. In 1939, the Cummeragunja Walk-Off occurred in New South Wales, the first ever mass strike by Aboriginals, to protest poor and abusive working conditions – the strikers crossed the state border into Victoria, which was against the law for them. By the 1960s, television had brought the US Civil Rights Movement into Australian homes and was very influential in encouraging action. Aboriginal people gained citizenship in 1961 and the right to vote in 1962.

The Australian 'Freedom Rides' took place in 1965, when nearly three-dozen students went on a two-week bus ride around rural New South Wales – exposing segregation at a swimming pool and an RSL Club – and attracting huge publicity

THE EARLY 20TH CENTURY World War I drew many West Australian men from the state – an act that provided the death knell for many struggling Gold Rush communities. Once again the economy became dependent on wheat and wool, but this in turn lead to a dramatic fall in prices – and by the early 1930s, the state's economy was on the verge of collapse.

Despite the federation, secessionist sentiment continued to garner pace in the early 20th century and a referendum was held in 1933 on whether to remain part of Australia or become a separate nation called Westralia. The referendum to leave was successful by an almost 2:1 margin, but the British government refused to act on the petition and WA remained part of the federation. The secessionists lost steam fairly quickly after that, but secession as a political issue has never gone away completely – most recently indirectly implied by then-Premier Colin

and further public support for change. A year later, the Wave Hill Walk-Off occurred in response to the British Vestey Company's refusal to pay Gurundji farm and station workers a just wage; Vincent Lingiari, one of the most important activists in the movement, was able to talk Wave Hill into discussion and action about traditional land rights. By 1975, prime minister Gough Whitlam returned over 3,000km^2 of land to the Gurundji people.

Additionally, in 1967, a constitutional referendum was held asking Australians if Aboriginal people should be counted in the national census, and whether the federal government should have power to make laws impacting Aboriginal people, which had previously been the domain of the states. An overwhelming 91% of Australians voted yes, although WA had the lowest approval, at 81%. Though Aboriginals gained no new rights, the referendum is considered a historic landmark in the movement for equality.

One of the biggest issues for Aboriginal people in WA today is that of native title – the right of Aboriginal people to use land and water according to traditional customs. It seems unfathomable today, but as late as 1992, land management in Australia still operated under the idea of *terra nullius* – that the land here belonged to nobody until the arrival of Europeans. The historic *Mabo v Queensland* decision by the High Court of Australia in 1992 rejected this, and the Australian government responded with the Native Title Act of 1993, recognising Aboriginal links to the land.

The Federal Court is responsible for determining native title rights and interested groups must submit an application. Native title relating to exclusive use can only be acquired in limited cases (ie, unallocated Crown lands, etc); non-exclusive native title gives rights to use land in a traditional way (ie, hunting, fishing, etc) but not control access to, or the use of, allowing native title to co-exist with operations like stations, but there are other restrictions on where native title can be claimed. Determining and awarding native title, however, is an exhaustive process with many moving pieces.

Another landmark occurred in 2008, when prime minister Kevin Rudd issued a formal apology to Aboriginal people, particularly the Stolen Generations. However, with major gaps still between White Australians and Aboriginal Australians in health, housing, income, education and employment, the road to equality is still just at the beginning and people across racial lines are waiting for words to be translated into more tangible outcomes.

Barnett in 2015 over an argument with the federal government over the state's share of national tax revenue, and a 'WAxit Party' formed and (unsuccessfully) ran candidates at the 2021 state election.

World War II brought direct conflict to WA. A naval battle took place off the coast of Carnarvon in November 1941 between the German vessel *Kormoran* and the HMAS *Sydney*, resulting in the sinking of both vessels – 318 of the *Kormoran*'s 399-hand crew survived, while all 645 hands on the *Sydney* were lost, which is still today Australia's greatest naval tragedy. The *Sydney* was considered to be a far superior ship to the *Kormoran* and its sinking at the hands of the lesser vessel, off the coast of WA no less, shook the entire country. In March 1942 the Japanese bombed Broome, killing 88, and also launched raids against what is now Exmouth, Port Hedland, Wyndham and other northern parts of the state. As the Japanese continued moving south, there were significant fears that Perth would be invaded; extensive preparations were made to defend the city, and an allied submarine base was established at Fremantle, with American and Dutch submarines. The Australian Broadcasting Corporation (ABC) opened a tiny office in the Wheatbelt town of Wagin as a back-up to be able to continue broadcasting to West Australians if Perth fell. By 1944, however, the threat had subsided as the Japanese retreated and Perth was never seriously threatened.

POST-WAR ERA Iron ore had been discovered in the Pilbara in the late 1880s, and mining operations soon started, with exports aimed particularly at Japan. By the 1930s, with war drums beating in the Pacific, and concerns over how much iron ore stock was actually in the ground, the government put in place an export ban in 1938. However, by 1960, an increasing trade deficit, rising commodity prices and the reindustrialisation of a peaceful Japan led to a rethink and in November 1960 the export ban was reversed. The fate of WA was forever changed, and iron-ore mines blossomed over the Pilbara and nickel mines in the Goldfields, becoming the engine room for WA's economy and closely tethering the state's fortunes to minerals. Rio Tinto and BHP, among others, set up shop in the Pilbara; the BHP's Mount Whaleback mine opened in 1968 as the biggest open-pit iron-ore mine in the world, and the town of Newman was developed to service it; Rio Tinto opened the Mount Tom Price Mine in 1966. As of 2020, WA accounted for 39% of the world's iron-ore supply, more than double that of Brazil, the world's second-largest supplier. WA also realised its energy resources in the 1960s; today, Australia is the world's second-largest supplier of liquified natural gas after Qatar, with more than half of the Australian supply coming from WA.

But the 1960s also saw substantial natural disaster in the state. The 1961 Dwellingup bushfires, in the Peel Region, were the most intense in state history and were part of a shock fire season that also saw huge blazes at Pemberton, Margaret River and the Perth Hills. The Dwellingup fires were started by lightning and miraculously nobody died, but over 120 homes were lost and the town was destroyed. The fire changed the way the state viewed firefighting and the concept of fuel reduction became embedded in the state's consciousness. In 1968, the Meckering earthquake, with was a magnitude of 6.5 in the Wheatbelt, caused over A\$2 million in damage.

Viticulture was established in Margaret River and the South West in the early 1970s, fundamentally altering the region's economic prospects and super-charging the tourism industry. The closure of the Perth-to-Fremantle passenger train line in 1979 by the Liberal Party's Court government, owing to low passenger volume and the government's interest in building a highway on the tracks, proved to be a politically costly one; the railway had come to be seen as something akin to a community icon, of substantial sentimental value, and the closure attracted some of the biggest protests in West Australian history – with petitions attracting over 100,000 signatures.

Labor was elected in 1983 on a promise to restore service (which did occur the same year). The following years were watershed moments politically for WA. The Labor government, led by Brian Burke, abolished capital punishment but became enmeshed in a series of scandals dubbed 'WA Inc', a string of poor business deals that resulted in the loss of hundreds of millions of taxpayer dollars and corporate insolvencies, closely tied to a collection of businessmen, most notably Alan Bond and Laurie Connell. The estimated financial loss to the government neared A$1 billion; Burke resigned in 1988 and was sentenced to prison over corruption.

The late 20th and early 21st centuries saw commuter train services in Perth begin to expand; new trains were introduced on the Armadale line in 1991, the Joondalup line opened in 1992 and Mandurah in 2007. Another boom in the mining sector saw the face of Perth changed in the 2010s, with the government using royalty monies to redevelop Elizabeth Quay and build Optus Stadium; as a result, WA's economy entered a boom period, with the highest per-capita GDP in the nation, which stands to this day.

GOVERNMENT AND POLITICS

STATE GOVERNMENT The Government of Western Australia is a parliamentary constitutional monarchy. The government was established in 1890 and, upon joining the Federation in 1901, became one of Australia's six states. State government is based on the Westminster system, a form of parliamentary government based on the UK's model. The Parliament of Western Australia consists of the Queen of Australia (at the time of writing, Elizabeth II), represented by the Governor of Western Australia (at the time of writing, Kim Beazley); the Legislative Council (36 seats – the Upper House); and the Legislative Assembly (59 seats – the Lower House). Parliament sits at Parliament House in Perth.

The Premier of Western Australia is the executive leader of the state and by custom is a member of the Legislative Assembly. In practice, the leader of the party or coalition of parties with the most seats in the Legislative Assembly becomes premier.

The major political parties are the Liberal Party of Australia (centre-right), the Australian Labor Party (centre-left) and the National Part of Australia (centre-right). Unlike at the federal level, in WA there is no automatic coalition between the Liberals and Nationals, and the two parties have distinct identities and compete vigorously against one another for the right-of-centre vote in the state's rural areas.

The state's political instincts tend to be towards the right-of-centre, though at the state government level, voters can swing either way. The Liberals and Labor have tended to alternate power in seven-to-ten-year blocks in modern history.

The 2021 state election saw the incumbent Australian Labor Party returned to power in the largest landslide in state history, currently holding 53 seats in the Legislative Assembly, against four for the Nationals and two for the Liberals. Premier Mark McGowan, who represents Rockingham for the Labor Party in the Legislative Assembly, has enormous popularity and the result was seen as the state's voters rewarding him for his handling of the Covid-19 pandemic. Labor also won control of the Legislative Council with 23 seats, against six for the Liberals, four

The state is divided into nine regions plus the Perth Metropolitan Area, and that largely mimics the structure of this guidebook. There are also the remote external territories of Christmas Island and the Cocos (Keeling) Islands that, while not technically part of Western Australia, use West Australian governmental and administrative services.

However, the nine regions of WA are not political entities, do not have capitals, and do not have a government. Each one does have a 'Regional Development Commission' who seeks to promote economic, business and infrastructure growth and development – but these are not law-making bodies and its representatives are not elected by the population. Instead, governing in regional WA, below the state level, is done at the shire or city level.

The regions were established by the Regional Development Commissions Act of 1993. While their boundaries do generally follow informally recognised historical patterns, this was not an exact science. You may hear of some Wheatbelt towns being described as being part of the Great Southern, some Great Southern towns being described as part of the South West, and so on, because that's how they were thought of prior to 1993 act (and are still thought that way by some today). The nine regions were thought of by locals rather nebulously for most of their existence, but took on a much firmer place in the state consciousness during the Covid lockdowns, which in WA was done by region – and so everyone began googling to see exactly where their region started and ended, and where they could and couldn't go.

Perth Metropolitan Area A collection of independent cities with their own governments. The actual City of Perth itself is quite tiny – 12km^2, & with a population

for the Nationals and the rest split among minor parties. The 2017 election was also a landslide victory for Labor and McGowan, albeit on a smaller scale, and saw and end to nine years of Liberal government under Premier Colin Barnett, who represented the Perth suburb of Cottesloe.

At the federal level, WA sends 15 members to the Australian House of Representatives (out of 151 nationally). The state was the surprise epicentre of Labor's 2022 federal election win and saw a major swing of almost 11% to the ALP, resulting in Labor capturing nine of those 15 seats, with five remaining for the Liberals and one independent. The federal division of O'Connor, represented by Liberal MP Rick Wilson, has an area of almost 900,000km^2 and stretches from Nannup in the South West all the way to the South Australian Border, a distance of almost 1,500km; while the federal division of Durack, represented by Liberal MP Melissa Price, is even larger, covering 1.6 million km^2, covering parts of the Wheatbelt and the Mid West alongside the entirety of the Gascoyne, Pilbara and Kimberley.

WA utilises compulsory voting for those 18 and older, and this is enforced through fines of A\$20, increasing to A\$50 for repeat offenders.

LOCAL GOVERNMENT Below the state level, there are three types of Local Government Areas (LGAs) – city, town and shire. They have their own councils who are elected by the public in their areas. Perth is not one big urban government area, but rather a collection of over two-dozen LGAs that each have their own comparable to that of Albany or Geraldton. Perth City Council is responsible for just the area generally bounded by the Central Business District (CBD) & Kings Park. For the purposes of the visitor, however, all these councils & LGAs blur into one, & while each neighbourhood does have its own local identity & character, residents consider themselves to live in 'Perth.'

Peel Region 5,516km^2; population: 137,000; largest city: Mandurah (pop 86,000); famous for: seafood, dolphins, inlets & waterways. Mandurah & the part of the Peel region just north of it are considered to be part of the Perth Metropolitan Area.

South West Region 23,970km^2; population: 170,000; largest city: Bunbury (pop 70,000); famous for: wine, dairy, surfing, forests & beaches

Great Southern Region 39,000km^2; population: 60,000; largest city: Albany (pop 25,000); famous for: mountains & hills, wine, beaches, coastal national parks & long-distance hiking trails

Wheatbelt Region 155,000km^2; population: 74,000; largest town: Northam (pop 11,000); famous for: grain & sheep farming, granite rock outcrops, wildflowers, country pubs & turn-of-the-century architecture

Goldfields-Esperance Region 771,276km^2; population: 60,000; largest town: Kalgoorlie-Boulder (pop 25,000); famous for: gold, mining, gemstones, fossicking, woodlands, beaches, frontier atmosphere & Gold Rush-era architecture

Mid West Region 478,000km^2; population: 52,000; largest town: Geraldton (pop 30,000); famous for: beaches, grain & sheep farming, spectacular wildflowers & Kalbarri National Park

Gascoyne Region 135,000km^2; population: 9,000; largest town: Carnarvon (pop 6,000); famous for: coral reefs, marine life, dazzling beaches, the Kennedy Ranges & Mt Augustus

Pilbara Region 500,000km^2; population: 62,000; largest town: Karratha (pop 22,700); famous for: gorges, Karijini National Park, rock art, mining & classic Outback scenery

Kimberley Region 423,517km^2; population: 36,230; largest town: Broome (pop 15,000); famous for: Cable Beach, Aboriginal art, crocodiles, Purnululu National Park, boab trees, gorges & waterfalls

council and no other governing body above them until the state level. However, residents in these areas still unreservedly view themselves as living in Perth, and the area has a collective Perth identity.

If you are driving through country towns, you are likely to come across stately but small old buildings, still with their original 'Roads Board' branding. These were the initial government institutions in many country areas – the Roads Boards were responsible for, well, local roads, and were vitally important (and powerful) as they connected farmers with the railroads. The Roads Boards were the predecessors to the shire system – the Roads Boards and Roads Districts were converted into the shires in 1961.

ECONOMY

Mining powers the West Australian economy and as go prices, so goes the state. Almost half of Australia's exports leave from WA.

The state economy produces goods and services worth over A$300 billion each year, and accounts for about 16% of Australia's GDP. Mining is by far the largest sector, contributing about A$135 billion to the state economy – construction is second, accounting for about A$17 billion. Trade with China accounts for 50% of all West Australian trade, with Japan a distant second at 9.3%, and the UK third at 6%. With the current ebb in Australia–China relations, little prospect for recovery in the near- or medium-term, and punitive financial sanctions applied to Australia by the Chinese side, diversifying the economy away from a dependence on China has become a political issue and a priority for the federal and state governments. Of that 50% of total trade with China, 56% are exports from WA to China and only about 18% are Chinese imports to WA.

As of January 2022 the unemployment rate was 3.4% – the lowest in Australia (which has a 4.2% unemployment rate), and the lowest in WA since 2008. The state workforce is prone to significant swings between skills shortages and gluts of workers, depending on the health of the mining sector. When times are good – often defined in WA by mining booms – workers flock here from all parts of Australia; when times are bad, there is a net outflow of migration. The general strong state of the economy historically, coupled with high salaries available in the mining and minerals sectors, has meant that younger West Australians typically have not felt a need to migrate to New South Wales or Victoria to strike their fortunes or careers.

Fly-in, fly-out (FIFO) workers form a significant part of the West Australian workforce and in the employment psyche of the state. Typically found in mining, petroleum, energy and minerals, workers do weeks-long shifts at a remote site and then get weeks-long breaks. It is common for FIFO workers to live far away from their work site and then take charter flights with other miners and colleagues to the mine site at the start of their shifts. Looking at the domestic departures board at Perth Airport, when you see flights to places you don't recognise – like Cloudbreak – that is probably a charter flight to a mine site. That being said, however, mining does not employ the most workers in WA – the health-care sector does, followed by retail and construction.

Although eclipsed in recent decades by mining, agriculture, particularly wheat, barley, wool, cattle and canola (in that order), has historically been a major driver of the WA economy. Agricultural land takes up about 40% of the state; over half of WA's 7,300 farms are dedicated to grain-growing, or mixed grain-sheep or grain-beef farming. Grape and dairy farming, while having a prominent image owing to wine and cheese production in the state's South West and Great Southern holiday areas, actually only make up a small percentage of the state's farming profile.

Technological advances in agriculture and farming have significantly changed West Australian rural society in the past 50 years. The ability of technology to do the work of multiple farmhands, and at a faster rate, has significantly reduced the need for farm labour, which in turn has had significant negative effects on the population and economies of inland towns, especially in and around the Wheatbelt Region, which has seen significant population loss. A farm that 40 years ago may have needed three or four families on it to work the land may now only need two or three people. This then has knock-off effects on the ability of these communities to provide adequate essential services like education, shopping and health care. Many communities will share a doctor between them and some schools may only have a dozen or so students and be in danger of closing, while shops find it difficult to stock an adequate variety of goods for a small and decreasing customer base. This makes the town less appealing to people wanting to move, in turn reinforcing the negative cycle. It can be quite eerie to drive through some of the affected towns and see a main street full of boarded-up windows, wondering if anything can happen to bring back the vibrancy of yesteryear. Many of these communities, however, are increasingly attempting to turn to tourism and other industries to provide a shot of adrenaline to their economies, with some success.

Western Australia is the fourth-most-populous state in the country, with roughly 2.6 million residents – about 10% of the national population. About 80% of the state population lives in Perth, which is Australia's fourth-biggest city. The second-largest city in the state outside of the Perth Metropolitan Area is Bunbury, but it has a population of only 70,000. No other city in the state outside the metro area has more than 50,000 residents living in it.

Inside Australia, West Australians are known colloquially as 'sandgropers' (referring to a type of insect that lives underground). The State Library of Western Australia indicates the term may have originated as a derogatory one (though it is not considered so today) from the eastern colonies during the federation debate, but could also reference how sandy the land in WA is.

The state population is divided almost evenly between men and women. In the 2016 census, about two-thirds of the state population registered their ancestry as British, Irish or Australian and 3.1% identify as Aboriginal Australians, which is about the national average. However, only 60% of the population reported being Australian-born, while 40% reported that both of their parents were born overseas. England and New Zealand were the countries most identified as countries of birth, either for residents or their parents. Perth has one of the highest populations of UK-born residents in Australia and this voting bloc has often been accounted for as influential in state elections.

ABORIGINAL PEOPLES IN WA About 75,000 West Australians are Aboriginal. Those identifying as Aboriginal generally have to satisfy three criteria for governmental purposes: that they are of Aboriginal descent; that they identify as Aboriginal; and that they are accepted by the Aboriginal community where they live.

WELCOME TO COUNTRY

Aboriginal people have a special relationship with the land and view their role as custodians or managers rather than owners. Land has personal significance, particularly if it is ancestral; and Aboriginal spirituality comes from the land as well. Aboriginal people feel a deep responsibility to maintain and care for land and the environment. The relationship is also one or reciprocity; Aboriginal people live off of the land and its bounty, and so therefore have a need and responsibility to manage and tend to it.

Stemming from this is the 'Welcome to Country' protocol, which you are very likely to come across at the start of large events, business meetings or university lectures. This is a practice where 'Traditional Owners' – descendants of the original custodians – welcome people on to their traditional land. Though this has existed in Aboriginal culture for thousands of years, it has only recently become common statewide. There is no standard format; it often involves some short remarks acknowledging Traditional Owners and the history of the land. When this is done by an Aboriginal person who is a descendant of the original custodians on their own land, it is called a 'Welcome to Country'. Otherwise, the protocol is called an 'Acknowledgement of Country' and generally takes the form of a few sentences acknowledging the Traditional Owners of the land, and pledging respect.

Aboriginal Australians in WA are very culturally diverse – they have their own culture, laws, traditions and languages. The Australian Institute of Aboriginal and Torres Strait Islander Studies (AIATSIS) publishes what is considered to be the benchmark map of Aboriginal societies in Australia, including the dozens in WA; their map can be found at w aiatsis.gov.au/explore/map-indigenous-australia. Some of the larger Aboriginal groups in WA include:

- The **Noongar**, based mainly in the southwestern part of the state, along a diagonal line from Geraldton to Esperance, including parts of the Mid West, Wheatbelt, South West, Great Southern, Peel and Perth Metropolitan areas. It is estimated the Noongar have lived in their boodja (county) for at least 45,000 years.
- The **Yamatji** in the Mid West, Gascoyne and Murchison regions, covering an area from Jurien Bay and Geraldton up to Carnarvon and inland to Meekatharra.
- The Wongatha, or **Wongi**, based in the Goldfields and extending to the Nullarbor, with eight main groupings in society.
- The **Ngaanyatjarra** in the Central Deserts, crossing over into Northern Territory and South Australia. There are about 2,000 people living in 11 communities here.
- The **Karajarri** encompass parts of northern Pilbara and the Kimberley, stretching from the coast inland (including Broome) to the Great Sandy Desert. Bidyadanga Community, also known as La Grange, is thought to be the biggest Aboriginal community in WA, with nearly 1,000 residents (a permit is required to enter).
- The **Yindjibarndi** in the Pilbara is centred around the Karratha and Roebourne areas.

But this is just a small sampling of some of the larger and more well-known Aboriginal societies in WA; there are many, many others, and it is very important to understand that Aboriginal societies are very distinct from one another and have their own cultures, languages, laws, traditions and protocols. Some of these are not allowed to be shared outside the society or with non-Aboriginals, and some can only be shared by certain members of the society. There is no single 'Aboriginal' society or culture – there are hundreds. If you are unsure about where you can go, what can be shared with you, or other cultural protocols – ask. Visitor centres may have that information or can direct you to an Aboriginal council or corporation that can help. Many often offer cultural training.

You may notice the use of different spellings across WA – ie: Noongar, Nyoongar, etc. Different consultative bodies have come to different agreements on correct spellings and terms. If you are in doubt about which is correct for your context or situation – just ask someone.

THE SIX SEASONS

For the Noongar, much of the way of life was based around the 'six seasons' of the year, which were closely tied to the weather and dictated hunting and gathering activities. The six seasons are Birak, the 'first summer' (December and January); Bunuru, the 'second summer' (February and March); Djeran, 'autumn' (April and May); Makuru, 'the first rains' (June and July); Djilba, 'the second rains' (August and September); and Kambarang, 'wildflower season' (October and November).

THE DREAMING

Also known as the Dreamtime, the Dreaming are stories relating to the creation of the world. It is of major and central importance to Aboriginal culture, spirituality and beliefs. However, the creatures involved in creating the world and its living inhabitants are not part of the past – they continue to exist to this day and will help shape the future. It is important to remember that because Aboriginal cultures are very distinct, stories will be different.

Oral storytelling plays a major role in Aboriginal culture; as there was no written language, Dreaming stories were passed down orally. Stories could relate to history, location of food or water, detail warnings or talk about societal boundaries or other Aboriginal groups. Strict protocols surround storytelling – some stories are restricted to certain people or groups, and sometimes only select individuals are allowed to tell a particular story. One such group are Elders, respected custodians of an Aboriginal society's culture, traditions and knowledge who hold a place of deep respect. Simply being of a certain age does not qualify one to be an Elder. Though Aboriginal culture has defined gender roles – men's business and women's business – females can be Elders and can have more power than men.

There is also no one 'Aboriginal' language – Australia-wide there are over 200 separate indigenous language groups and WA is no exception to that diversity; 66 existed in WA alone at time of European settlement. The Pilbara alone has 31 Aboriginal languages, most with multiple dialects, and language group is often used as a marker to distinguish different societies within a larger Aboriginal group. Almost all languages, however, are in danger of dying out and there are very few fluent speakers outside the Elders. Restoration, preservation and education projects to ensure the survival of these languages are gaining more prominence in modern Australia. Virtually all Aboriginal people you meet will speak English. Noongar is perhaps the most recognised Aboriginal language in the state, as there is a large population of Noongar people in Perth and the South West. As you head outside these areas, language groups change. Yamatji is spoken in the Mid West, while Yindjibarndi is the largest remaining language of the Pilbara groups. Multiple languages survive in the Kimberley and the deserts. Main language groupings also have multiple dialects with varying degrees of mutual intelligibility to each other. For more information about Noongar and Aboriginal languages, see page 30.

'Aboriginal Communities' is a term generally used to denote Aboriginal settlements mainly in Outback or remote areas, particularly in the north and the deserts. Many are closed to non-residents and you may require a permit to enter or transit through these lands. The Department of Planning, Lands and Heritage (w dplh.wa.gov.au) can advise further if your itinerary is going to take you through one of these areas. However, there is very little interaction between tourists and Aboriginal communities, and that is by design. The communities are very small with limited facilities and travellers often don't have the ability as a permit condition to wander and interact.

RELIGION West Australians are not particularly religious – almost one-third identify as having no religion, and of those that do, 21% are Catholic and 14% are Anglican. Though churches have visibility, they don't have the same prominent role in society as they do in the United States or Europe. There is a small but vibrant

Jewish population in Perth, and also Muslims from southeast Asia, with the town of Katanning in the Great Southern becoming famous as an example of successful multi-cultural integration following migration programs in the 1970s (page 185).

LANGUAGE Three-quarters of West Australians report that they speak only English at home; the second-most spoken language in the state is Mandarin Chinese closely followed by Italian, but figures for both are less than 2%. Italian migration to the state was particularly strong in the post-war period and you will notice many Italian surnames in some Perth neighbourhoods, as well as in the South West regions, where family businesses were established and continue today. The dialect of English spoken in WA is Standard Australian English and is virtually indistinguishable from that spoken in the Eastern States. See page 374 for a glossary of terms.

EDUCATION Compulsory schooling in WA starts with pre-primary (generally 4½ to five years old) and continues to Year 12 (18 years old – though there are some circumstances where someone can leave school at 17 or a little earlier). Generally schools in the state are divided into primary schools, which go from kindergarden/ pre-primary up to Year 6, and then senior high schools, which go from Year 7 to Year 12 (graduation year). In the regions, smaller towns may have a district high school instead, which goes from kindergarden/pre-primary up to Year 10, and then students transport to a neighbouring community or board at a senior high school elsewhere for Years 11 and 12 – or a town may just have a primary school and then students bus elsewhere for senior high school. The school year runs from February to December and school sizes can vary wildly – from 2,000 students or more at a big senior high school in Perth, down to fewer than 10 students with combined-year classes at small primary schools in the Outback.

Some government schools also have boarding facilities. Depending on where one lives in the regions, sending the kids to a private school in Perth for boarding is a time-honoured, though expensive, tradition, with some tuition and board packages running as much as A$50,000 per year. Many families are loyal to the same private school and enrollment can be generational; the 'old school tie' – informal professional and social networks based on what school you went to – still has its place in state society. Australia's famed 'School of the Air' – correspondence schools for isolated and Outback families, that were legendarily taught by radio back in the day – is alive and well in WA, with five still operating with support from the state's School of Isolated and Distance Education. The radios have been replaced by the internet.

The state's universities are clustered in Perth though some have branch campuses in regional cities. The University of Western Australia is the state's flagship, though Murdoch, Curtin, Edith Cowan and Notre Dame all have robust enrollments, generally for three years. TAFEs – Technical and Further Education schools – offer a variety of vocational certificates, diplomas and advanced diplomas, often through single- or multi-year programmes undertaken after senior high school. TAFE Certificates – which come in four levels – and TAFE Diplomas are below university degrees in the Australian Qualifications Framework.

CULTURE

ABORIGINAL ART Though Perth is not the centre for Western-style art that Sydney and Melbourne are, WA is one of the best places in the world to find, browse, admire and buy Aboriginal art. Visiting Aboriginal art galleries and collectives is a highlight of any trip to the state. Numerous galleries exist, especially in Aboriginal communities in the Goldfields, Pilbara and Kimberley.

Traditionally Aboriginal art was often used for communication, as indigenous peoples did not have a written language. Art could tell stories, give warnings, describe locations of food and water and myriad other information. Much Aboriginal art has, at its heart, inspiration from the Dreaming – a series of creation stories and laws that spell out how Aboriginal people believe the land, humans, plants and animals were created (see box, page 31).

Dot paintings are perhaps the most well-known type of West Australian Aboriginal art and have become vogue in the past decade – often hailing from the state's Western Deserts. But, like all art, Aboriginal forms are distinctive and unique, and have intense regional variation. Some common forms of indigenous art are listed here, while wood carvings, sculpture and art on large boab nuts are also important forms of West Australian Aboriginal art. Well-known artists include Jack Britten, Shirley Purdie, Sandra Hill, Graham Taylor, Cynthia Burke, Daniel Walbidi and Rover Thomas – but there are many others.

Dot paintings These are often seen in art from West Australian desert communities, though owing to the extreme isolation of the Western Deserts, they only started to become well-known across the country in the late 20th century. Historically artists often used dots to disguise their sacred designs, so that Westerners could not determine the true meaning. Some of Australia's most famous indigenous artists use this style; if you are looking for a unique West Australian piece of Aboriginal art to take home, you should probably start here.

Bark paintings These come from large sheets cut from stringybark trees and are often produced in the Kimberley. They frequently feature the Wandjina, mythical cloud and rain spirits that are prominently displayed on rock art in the north and very important to many Aboriginal groups in the Kimberley.

Ochre paintings Made from rocks, soils and materials that come from the ground, which are then crushed and mixed with water, bright, vivid and vibrant colours are a hallmark of many ochre paintings. Predominant hues are earth tones – the reds, oranges, yellows, browns and purples that are synonymous with the Outback.

ARCHITECTURE West Australian architecture is full of character. Having been a British colony, many historic buildings reflect the trends of 19th-century England as well as showcasing Georgian, Gothic Revival, Queen Anne, Italianate, Edwardian and Victorian styles. As you explore the country's Heritage towns, you'll become familiar with a distinctive style of Australian architecture known as the Federation style – it is similar to Edwardian but evolved to embrace the country's outdoor lifestyle and distinctive climate, often featuring elaborate verandas. There are 12 main styles within this period including Federation Free, which is typically punctuated with Art Nouveau, unconventional use of classic architectural elements, lack of adherence to artistic rules and often asymmetrical designs.

Outside Perth, the best places for West Australian architecture are the Goldfields, specifically Kalgoorlie-Boulder and Coolgardie, and the Wheatbelt town of York, although a country drive through any Wheatbelt town will provide many examples. Town halls and hotels often stand out: York Town Hall (page 249) and Boulder Town

WA has several categories of heritage listing. The **State Register of Heritage Places** is managed by the Heritage Council of Western Australia and represents places that tell the story of Western Australia and its history – anything from buildings to gardens to cemeteries can qualify as long as they have state cultural heritage significance. Buildings on the State Register are legally protected and changes can only be made with approval and as long as they protect the heritage significance of the listing. The **National Heritage List** is managed by the Australian Heritage Council, and lists places (natural and manmade) that are of exceptional significance to Australia – in Western Australia, examples include the *Batavia* shipwreck site and the Burrup Peninsula (with its rock art) in the Pilbara. Local governments also have their own heritage lists, municipal inventories or surveys. The website inHerit (w inherit.stateheritage.wa.gov.au/Public) allows you to search for heritage information on West Australian sites across national, state and local databases. The **National Trust of Australia** is another key conservation organisation with autonomous branches in each state and territory – they granted Bridgetown 'Historic Town Status' in 2000.

Hall (page 237) are prominent examples, but strolls along the main streets of the Gold Rush towns of Coolgardie and Cue are delights for the eyes as well.

FILM WA's rich, dramatic Outback scenery, stunning beaches, rolling farmland and Perth's relaxed vibe make for great film backdrops, and several notable movies have been shot here in recent years. The best-known of these is probably Baz Luhrmann's 2008 epic drama, *Australia*, starring Nicole Kidman and Hugh Jackman, set in World War II during the Japanese bombing raids on northern Australia and partially shot in Kununurra.

Other Australian films shot in the state include the 2009 comedy-drama *Bran Nue Dae*, an adaptation of the 1990 musical set in Broome about an Aboriginal Australian's coming-of-age in the 1960s, and the 2012 surfer's classic *Drift*, which was shot in Nannup, though the setting in the film is Margaret River, 70km away; the film is about two brothers trying to make a name for themselves during the beginnings of the South West's surf culture. *Japanese Story*, winner of multiple awards in 2003, is a romance set in Perth and the Pilbara; the latter is also the setting for the 2011 comedy *Red Dog*, based on a true story of a canine who was adopted by the entire region (see box, page 327). Based on the highly successful 2009 novel of the same name (and widely read in West Australian high school English classes), the 2017 film adaptation of *Jasper Jones* (see opposite) takes place in Corrigin in the Wheatbelt.

Despite its popularity location-wise, the state's film infrastructure is only in its infancy, but the state government and Screenwest, the screen funding and development agency, are considering building the state's first film studio.

The late Heath Ledger was born in Perth and is the most famous actor to come out of the state. Actress Katherine Langford, the former a Teen Choice Awards winner and star of Netflix drama *13 Reasons Why*, is from the Perth suburb of Applecross, along with her younger sister Josephine, who is also an actress.

MUSIC WA is not particularly known for its music scene, but it has produced some artists of national and international acclaim. Contemporary rock band Birds of

Tokyo are from Perth, as are YouTube star Troye Sivan and Kevin Parker, known for his psychedelic project Tame Impala. Folk rockers The Waifs are also from Albany. Perth's isolation has been a major factor in the development of West Australian music, allowing for a thriving amateur and local scene; though this has been a negative as well, with many musicians leaving for larger markets on the east coast to try and find fame and fortune there.

The West Australian Opera (w waopera.asn.au) is based in Perth but does innovative outdoors performances annually, including at Kings Park and in the regions – their performance in Walpole's giant tingle forests has amazing acoustics and draws hundreds each year, and is well worth trying to attend if you are in the South West in late November or early December even if opera is not really your thing. Two of the state's biggest music festivals are also in the South West; the Boyup Brook Country Music Festival, in February, and the Nannup Music Festival, held during the March Labour Day weekend.

LITERATURE

LITERATURE WA's colourful history and vibrant landscapes make for some great plotlines and settings, and a rich body of literature has cropped up from around the state. Tim Winton, one of Australia's most celebrated writers, has written multiple award-winning books and grew up in the Perth suburb of Subiaco. His novel *Cloudstreet*, about two families sharing a house in Perth over 20 years, is an exemplar of Australiana for its exploration of the nation's cultural themes, and his thriller *Dirt Music* is set in the Kimberley and has been adapted for film. *Lockie Leonard* is popular with teenagers, about a schoolboy's adventures in the South West.

Albert Facey's *A Fortunate Life*, set in Geraldton, is about World War II's impact on West Australian families; Facey himself led a very interesting life and fought at Gallipoli. Louis de Bernier's book *Red Dog* encapsulates the spirit of the region, inspired by a real roving kelpie that was adopted by an entire Pilbara community in the 1970s (see box, page 327). It has since been adapted for film, as has Craig Silvey's *Jasper Jones*, set in Corrigin, which chronicles teenagers on a whodunit quest. A similar coming-of-age tale is *Boy on a Wire*, by Bridgetown's Jon Doust, about a teenage boy who has been sent to Perth for boarding school.

WA also has a robust Aboriginal literature scene. Indigenous publisher Magabala Books, based in Broome (page 342), is a major publishing house. From Perth, Sally Morgan's *My Place*, about her discovery of her past, is considered a landmark in the genre. Kim Scott's *Kayang and Me*, co-written alongside his aunt who is a Noongar Elder, is another landmark that is an oral history of Scott's family and people, while his novel, *That Deadman Dance*, set in Albany, explores early interactions between white settlers and indigenous peoples on the South Coast.

SPORT

SPORT WA falls squarely on the **Australian Football League (AFL)** side of the 'Barassi Line' – the invisible, southeasterly line from the northwest Queensland coast down to the southeastern edge of the New South Wales–Victoria border that divides Australia's sporting passions between AFL to the west and rugby to the east. The state's two main loves are the AFL's West Coast Eagles and Fremantle Dockers – unfortunately, for Freo supporters like me, in that order – and the teams share the sparkling-new Optus Stadium in the Perth neighbourhood of Burswood. AFL is the undisputed king of West Australian sport; almost every small town has some kind of team participating in the lower leagues.

The Eagles were founded in 1987 as Perth's first entry into what was then the Victorian Football League, precursor to today's AFL, and they chose to brand themselves in a way that represented the entire state. They have won four premierships, most recently in 2018, and were the first team from outside Victoria to win an AFL Grand Final. Following the early success of the Eagles, the AFL dipped into WA again, with the Fremantle Dockers playing their first game in 1995. While they have a strong following of passionate supporters, the Dockers have not been nearly as successful as the Eagles and have never won a Grand Final. It is something of a dubious tradition for Eagles supporters to point out that the Moon has more 'flags' than Freo does.

At the state level, the WAFL – West Australian Football League – was king before the arrival of the Eagles and Dockers. Featuring ten teams all from the Metro Perth Area plus one from Mandurah, who play from March to September, the league dates from 1885 and has multiple teams that were founded in 19th century. The WAFL is considered to be a lower level than the national AFL competition – Americans might equate it to Triple-A baseball.

Outside Perth, there are a huge number of regional leagues, and seemingly every community big enough to have a pub will also have a footy team. Leagues extend from the East Kimberley all the way out to Esperance, with some leagues carrying on with as few as three teams.

Basketball is also popular, with Denmark's Luc Longley being the state's most recognisable export to the NBA. The Perth Wildcats, who play in the National Basketball League (NBL), Australia's top domestic competition, have their games at RAC Arena. They have been one of the NBL's most successful and stable franchises, winning ten championships in their 39 seasons. While basketball doesn't have the same popularity or infrastructure as footy, it is growing substantially in appeal – most communities have recreational leagues, and it is extremely popular among younger West Australians. Almost every school in the state will have kids playing during breaktime.

Cricket is another favoured sport. The Western Australian Cricket Association was founded the same year (1885) as the WAFL, and their grounds – known as the WACA – are storied, with the stadium dating from 1890. The Big Bash League is Australia's main domestic competition, and the Perth Scorchers are WA's entry, playing their games at the WACA. The Scorchers have been wildly successful, winning the championship four times since 2013 and being the runners-up on three other occasions. Like footy and basketball, recreational leagues at the grass-roots level flourish across the state. There have been numerous West Australian cricketers who have made a splash including Dennis Lillee, Rod Marsh and Michael Hussey.

WA's experience with **rugby** has been less charmed, and the state's flagship rugby union team, the Western Force, participate in Super Rugby but have often been more interesting off the pitch than on it. The franchise was granted an expansion licence and began to play in 2006, in what was then the Super 12, a rugby league featuring teams from Australia, New Zealand and South Africa; the Force were Australia's fourth franchise. Though attendance was strong, the team floundered and never finished in the top half of the table before being wound-up in a stunning boardroom power play in 2017. The team then played in other lower-profile international competitions, thanks to the unqualified backing of state mining magnate Andrew Forrest, before experiencing a breathtaking twist of fate and being invited back into Super Rugby during the Covid-19 pandemic. There are no signs the Force will be kicked out again. However, WA is not a natural, fertile rugby area like New South Wales and Queensland, and the game has struggled to gain traction here on a grass-roots level against the AFL.

Having 12,000km of coastline, **watersports** are a natural fit in the state and WA has a rich sailing history that includes the Royal Perth Yacht Club's win in the 1983 America's Cup regatta, and subsequent hosting of the event in Fremantle in 1987, both of which were defining cultural moments in West Australian sport. The regatta, generally held every four years, had been successfully defended for 132 years – the longest winning streak in sport history – by the New York Yacht Club until its yacht, the *Liberty*, helmed by the legendary Dennis Conner, was defeated in stunning fashion by the Royal Perth Yacht Club's *Australia II* in 1983, skippered by John Bertrand. *Liberty* went ahead in the best-of-seven series three races to one, but *Australia II* scored three victories in a row to win the series in a shock upset. The win also meant that the 1987 defence was hosted by the Royal Perth Yacht Club, which chose Fremantle as the venue. The US's *Stars & Stripes 87*, led again by Dennis Conner, defeated Iain Murray's *Kookaburra III* in a sweep of four races to none and took the cup back to the US. The 1992 film *Wind* is about the 1983 and 1987 races. Aside from racing, sailing for sport and pleasure is a major pastime in the state. There are nearly two-dozen sailing clubs in the Perth area alone, and about that many in the regions as well.

Surfing, particularly in the South West, is a major draw and each year Margaret River hosts the Pro, an annual event of the World Surfing League. Surfing did not not become an icon of the South West until around the 1970s; Margaret River at the time was a relatively poor beef and dairy farming town (viticulture had not yet taken off there either, and was only beginning to stir) and the surfers were largely imported to the region. Their personalities and lifestyle clashed with what was then a buttoned-down farming town and they were not embraced (as highlighted by the 2012 film, *Drift*). The tandem rise of surfing and wine forever changed the South West and turned it into one of Australia's premier tourism destinations. From its Margaret River roots, surfing has spread throughout the state and you can find surf shops in any community with decent ocean swells and no crocs. More recently, shark attacks have plagued the Margaret River Pro and there has been talk of moving the event to Kalbarri, but that seems to have quieted of late.

2

Practical Information

WHEN TO VISIT

Western Australia is so vast, and the climate so varied, that the best time to visit depends on where you are going. The warmer, summer months are from October to April and the cooler, winter months are from May to September.

Wherever you go, however, summer gets *hot*. Heat stroke and heat exhaustion are real threats, and fresh water can be in short supply (this isn't the driest continent in the world for nothing). Even in the 'cool' South West, daytime temperatures can reach 40°C. It isn't a balmy yet bearable dry heat either – it's oppressive, and bushfires can pop up suddenly and threaten entire towns (and suburbs of Perth) within an hour (see page 51 for more on bushfires).

That being said, the hot, clear weather makes for ideal conditions to explore some of the world's best beaches in the South West, Great Southern and Esperance areas, and Perth has plenty of trendy cafés and restaurants to cool off in after a morning at Cottesloe or City Beach. Temperatures can also dip markedly by nightfall – into the single digits. It isn't uncommon in southern summers for it to be 35°C in the afternoon and as low as 8°C at night.

In the north, summer brings the 'wet' – tropical, monsoonal afternoon downpours – which can wash out roads. Many national parks and tourist sites in the north will close in the summer due to the weather. Further inland, like at Purnululu, tour operators actually close for the season as early as the end of September because it's already 50°C in the gorges and chasms. To give you the mindset: the slang term 'going troppo' (meaning crazy) refers to people in the north losing their minds from not being able to cope with the weather. Summer in the north also brings cyclones, box jellyfish and Irukandji – tiny jellyfish that pack an unfortunate wallop (see box, page 344) – so you can't even head to a place like Cable Beach to beat the heat.

The middle part of the state, around Geraldton, can also get dangerously hot in summer. I recall once being in Kalbarri in December when the temperature peaked in the high 40s and it was assessed as the hottest place in the world that particular day.

Winter is the ideal time to go to the Pilbara and Kimberley, where temperatures are in the high 20s and low 30s, the 'dry' presents clear days, Cable Beach is perfect and national parks and tour operators are in full swing. Spring sees some of the summer oppressiveness start to kick in as well as a return to the rains – it will be hot, but still doable. The tail end of autumn sees a refreshing cooling start to kick in and an increasingly bright mood spread across the region.

In the rest of the state, winter brings cold and rain, even as far north as Geraldton. Some places in the Wheatbelt and the Goldfields can see the mercury drop below zero overnight and in the early morning hours – although snow is rare. The rain does not come in downpour form like the north, but instead hours of drizzle or a steady fall. The cold and rain, however, does rule out swimming and a lot of hiking (though I have never minded throwing on the boots and hiking through the karri forests in winter). Autumn and spring, however, bring temperate weather – pleasant days, cool nights and more cooperative skies. The water can still be too cold for swimming but it is excellent weather for hiking, boating, wine-tasting and lots of other activities. Easter weekend traditionally sees holidaymakers jam the South West, taking advantage of the last bits of warm beach weather before the rains set in.

HIGHLIGHTS

If you love nature, beaches and vast, open space, there is no better place on the planet than WA. My top highlights are as follows, but I have also listed some regional highlights at the beginning of each part in this book.

KARIJINI NATIONAL PARK (Pilbara; page 316) One of Australia's finest parks, with dramatic gorges, plunge pools, lavender wildflowers and a deep-red Outback colour palette. Walking along the plateaux, it looks like the earth has simply been ripped open into huge canyons, and the bright lime-green spinifex contrasting with the red earthen walls of the gorges is a vivid and enduring image. Swimming in the many plunge pools, with this as your backdrop, is unforgettable.

NINGALOO REEF (Gascoyne; page 304) WA's answer to the Great Barrier Reef is so accessible for snorkellers that you can just walk right in off the beaches around Exmouth. The coral gardens are just as bright and colourful, the fish just as varied, and the whale sharks friendly and amenable to being swum with.

BEACHES OF ESPERANCE AND THE OUTBACK RIVIERA Put 'Western Australia' into Google and very quickly you will come across an adorable image of a kangaroo standing on the sand in front of some impossibly blue sea. You'll think it was staged by a marketing company – but it's the real deal in Lucky Bay (page 216), 65km east of Esperance, in Cape Le Grand National Park. The park has a resident mob of feral roos that wander the shoreline, presenting numerous opportunities for photographs – the water itself is some of the clearest you will find, and the ever-darker blue striping as it heads out into deeper depths, with the granite hills as a frame, is awesome. Another 100km east takes you to the splendid of Cape Arid (page 217), with its blue-and-purple hues contrasting against the white sands in another superb and isolated Outback beach.

FREMANTLE'S CAPPUCCINO STRIP (Perth; page 90) A stroll through the main drag of historic Fremantle is a journey through the 1800s spruced up with trendy cafés, gourmet eateries and UNESCO-listed convict sites. Instantly charming, this is the birthplace of modern Perth and oozes West Australian history. The boutique accommodation here also makes it a great place to base yourself in the capital.

MID WEST WILDFLOWERS (Page 288) If you are here in August or September, a trip to Mingenew, Morawa and Mullewa is a must-do for one of the planet's most spectacular displays of wildflowers. Many – such as the iconic wreath flower – exist only in WA. Massive carpets of paddock-covering pink, gold and white everlastings melt the hearts of even the most cynical travellers. Coalseam Conservation Park and the areas around Mullewa are the state's wildflower epicentre, but virtually every region of the state has their own displays.

BURRUP PENINSULA ROCK ART (Pilbara; page 328) One of the most important rock art galleries in the world, this site near Karratha has drawings, paintings and etchings dating back some 50,000 years. As you wander the pathways between these massive piles of red stone and earth, you are transported back thousands of years to a time before the animals in the art became extinct.

MARGARET RIVER (South West; page 162) Though older West Australians will claim that Margaret River has 'changed' and is no longer the surfer and hipster mainstay it once was, it is still pretty special and remains one of the world's premier surf spots. Aside from world-class swells, there are also superb wineries, fantastic hiking routes (the Cape to Cape is one of Australia's best multi-day hikes), brilliant swimming and snorkelling opportunities, and exciting caving and forest activities. The vibe may have changed, but the things that made Margaret River a gem in the state's jewellery box are still here.

SUGGESTED ITINERARIES

It's 2,700km from Kununurra to Esperance and 1,300km from Perth to Eucla, so unless you are a backpacker with your own wheels and have six months in your pocket, you can't see all of Western Australia in one trip. It's foolish to try, unless you want the lasting memory to be the inside of a car. Instead, it's better to pick a few adjoining regions to focus on.

The following itineraries are based along those lines. All start and end in Perth, since that will be the start and end point for the vast majority of travellers.

LONG WEEKENDS
South Western Explorer Base yourself in Dunsborough, & explore Busselton Jetty & Busselton Beach, Cape Naturaliste, Yallingup Reef & the Margaret River wineries.

South Coast Weekender Drive down to Albany & spend your time exploring the wineries of Denmark & William Bay National Park (Greens Pool & Elephant Rocks). On the next day see the Porongurups & do the Stirling Range scenic drive. On your last day, relax at Torndirrup National Park & Middleton Beach, or take a historical stroll through the Albany CBD.

Indian Ocean Drive Use Jurien Bay as a base, 2 hours north of Perth. On your drive up, visit the koalas & lagoon at Yanchep, the dunes at Lancelin, & have a wander through the shack settlement at Wedge Island. Explore the Pinnacles & the Jurien Bay foreshore, & do the Three Bays Walk at Green Head. Book a trip to swim with the sea lions, tour the facility at the Lobster Shack & drive through Lesueur National Park before heading back to the capital.

Geraldton and the Mid West A bit further north than Indian Ocean Drive, Geraldton makes a good base, boasting maritime history, a beach vibe & quality restaurants. Spend a day at Kalbarri National Park, taking in Horrocks Beach, Port Gregory's pink lake & the historic main street of Northampton on the way, & the yin-yang of Dongara-Port Denison's history & lovely oceanfront scenery before returning to Perth.

Perth
Long weekend On a 3-day stay in the state capital, base yourself in the CBD & on your first day, explore Kings Park, do a walking tour of the CBD, take in the Swan River waterfront & head to Cottesloe Beach. Devote your second day to Fremantle & the Cappuccino Strip, soaking up the history, visiting Fremantle Prison & stopping in at the area's quality cafés & restaurants. Spend day 3 in Guildford & the Swan Valley, with more history & wineries.

A week Do as above, but on day 4 head to the Perth Hills, its lookouts & Lesmurdie Falls. Day 5 should see you head to Penguin Island near Rockingham, while spend days 6 & 7 exploring Yanchep (koalas), Lancelin (dunes & beaches) or Scarborough (one of WA's best-known beach suburbs).

Ten days Do as above, but spend days 8 & 9 exploring Mandurah's waterways, & on day 10 head to York in the Wheatbelt, the oldest inland town in the state & famed for its colonial architecture.

LONGER STAYS

Wildflowers (Mid West; 5 days) Base yourself in either Moora or Geraldton (1-day drive from Perth). On day 2, visit Coalseam Reserve, & head to Canna. On day 3, do the Mullewa walks, & drive out to see the wreath flowers. On day 4, consult with the Shire Offices & meander along several of the wildflower drives, hunting down carpets of everlastings. End with a scenic drive through the Chapman Valley & head back to Perth on day 5.

Rock 'n Roll (Wheatbelt; 7 days) On a crisp autumn or winter day, take the hire car out into the Wheatbelt for some scenic yet gentle rock climbing – no special equipment needed. Base yourself in Merredin & explore the rocks around there (day 1) before heading to Elachbutting Rock & Mukinbudin on day 2, Mount Walker & Wave Rock on day 3, & Gorge Rock & Kokerbin Rock on day 4 before exploring the old inland towns of York, Northam & Toodyay on days 5–6 & then heading back to Perth on day 7.

Great National Parks (Mid West, Gascoyne & Pilbara; 13 days) Focus on Karijini & Cape Range (Ningaloo). On day 1, drive from Perth to Geraldton, stopping at the Pinnacles en route, & then on day 2, drive from Geraldton to Carnarvon, stopping at Kalbarri National Park to take in Nature's Window & the skywalks, & Hamelin Pool at the Shark Bay turn-off to see the stromatolites. On day 3, visit Kennedy Range National Park & hit Carnarvon's tropical fruit farm gates in the late afternoon. On day 4, drive to Exmouth, stopping on the way in Coral Bay – try to leave late enough in the morning to give yourself time to visit Carnarvon's Space & Technology Museum before setting off. Give yourself 3 full days based in Exmouth, exploring Turquoise Bay & the many other snorkelling spots, before heading to Tom Price on day 8. Give yourself another 3 full days at Karijini National Park, before returning to Perth along the inland highway through Newman & Cue (overnight at this historic gold rush town).

Surf 'n' Turf (Great Southern & Goldfields-Esperance; 13 days) Drive down to Albany (day 1), stopping at Kojonup's Kodja Place en route, & spend 3 days in the state's oldest European settlement. On day 2, visit Torndirrup National Park

& its crashing surf, William Bay National Park & its glorious swimming spots, & Denmark's wineries & gourmet farm gates on Scotsdale Road. Spend day 3 in historic Albany itself, taking in the scenic ocean vistas & Middleton Beach, as well as the ANZAC Museum, & day 4 in the Porongurups & Stirlings before driving out to Esperance on day 5. Spend 3 full days in Esperance (days 6–8), taking in its amazing coastal strip from Cape Le Grand to Cape Arid east of town, the beaches & the Great Ocean Road. Take a scenic flight to Lake Hillier, the breathtaking bubble-gum pink lake in the Recherche Archipelago. On day 9, drive to Kalgoorlie & spend 3 days (days 10–12) exploring the gold rush history & mining operations of the Super Pit, Coolgardie, Lake Ballard, Menzies & Leonora before doubling back to Norseman & taking the Great Western Woodlands drive (day 13) to Wave Rock. Overnight there, or continue on to Perth.

South West Spin – Bunbury to Albany (South West & Great Southern; 15 days) Make the 2-hour drive down to Bunbury (day 1) & spend a full day (day 2) exploring the beaches & CBD galleries, & then head into the Ferguson Valley to see Gnomesville & sample the art & craft galleries (day 3). On day 4, go to Collie & explore the dams, waterways & Honeymoon Pool, & then head to Busselton for three full days (days 5–7) exploring the jetty & sheltered bays & beaches along Cape Naturaliste. Book another 2 days (days 8–9) for the Margaret River area, Augusta & its wineries, caves & surfing, & then cut through the Blackwood Valley (day 10) to get to the karri forests in Pemberton. Spend two days (days 11-12) doing the scenic drives & hikes in Pemberton, Walpole & the Valley of the Giants before heading to Albany for three days (days 13–15) exploring Denmark, the Porongurups, Stirlings & south coast beaches before returning to Perth.

Far North Explorer (Pilbara & Kimberley; 17 days) Start in Karratha – either drive up from Perth (days 1–2) or save time by flying in & hiring a vehicle. Spend a full day exploring the rock art at Burrup Peninsula, the beautiful beaches at Hearson's Cove & the islands of the Dampier Archipelago, & then another full day at Millstream-Chichester National Park & Python Pool, with their rich Aboriginal history. On day 5, drive to Broome – with, if time permits, a diversion through the Coongan Hills to the jasper at Marble Bar – &

spend 3 full days in Broome, which in wintertime has a special vibrancy to it, & the superlative Cable Beach. Either take the Gibb River Road to Kununurra or, if you don't have a vehicle, take an organised tour to Derby, Windjana Gorge & Tunnel Creek (day 9), drive to Halls Creek & tour Purnululu (days 10–11), & then head up to Kununurra, taking in El Questro, Mirima & Lake Argyle (days 12–14). Then hit the long road back to Perth.

TOUR OPERATORS

Many tour operators in WA are independently owned and local in focus – see the regional chapters for more information on these.

AAT Kings w aatkings.com/wa. Pricey but highly reputable operator offering package tours from 4 to 19 days up & down the West Australian coast, including Kimberley, South West & the Mid West.

Abercrombie & Kent w abercrombiekent. com.au. Specialists in luxury travel, some of the multi-day options offered are air safaris & cruises through the Kimberley, gourmet South West tours, & Ningaloo experiences.

Audley Travel w audleytravel.com. Another luxury operator, arranging 2-week & longer packages highlighting the South West, Mid West coast, Ningaloo & Shark Bay, as well as hiking tours along the Cape to Cape, plus Kimberley cruises & wildlife-oriented journeys.

Australian Pacific Touring (APT) w aptouring. com.au. APT offers a large number of upmarket itineraries including the Kimberley, Karijini & wildflower tours. Their 15-day Perth to Broome tour is a comprehensive highlight of some of the state's gems. Again, a pricey option but a longstanding & respected operator.

Butterfield & Robinson w butterfield.com. Offers Outback journeys & the opportunity to craft one-on-one personalised tours with an expert.

Freedom Destinations w freedomdestinations. co.uk; see ad, inside back cover. Australia specialists Freedom Destinations can arrange everything from flights & stopovers to car & motorhome hire, rail journeys, tours & accommodation.

Intrepid w intrepidtravel.com. Specialising in small-group & adventure tours, with Cape-to-Cape hiking & northern overland trips.

RED TAPE

VISAS All visitors to Australia require a visa, which needs to be issued before arrival (managed by the Department of Home Affairs). If you are a citizen of the UK or the EU, as well as Andorra, Iceland, Liechtenstein, Monaco, Norway, San Marino, Switzerland or Vatican City, you can apply for the free 'e-visitor' visa (subclass 651), a multiple-entry visa valid for 12 months, with stays up to three months allowed at any one time. You are free to enter Australia as often as you wish, for up to three months, during the validity period of the visa. You can apply for this online at the department's website (w immi.homeaffairs.gov.au) – the visa must be applied for outside Australia and you also must be outside Australia when the government decides on your application.

You do not get a visa stamp in your passport when the visa is granted. Instead, your passport is digitally linked to the department's system. You will get a grant notice, however, and you should print that and take it with you just in case. Airlines check your Australian visa status at check-in and you will be denied boarding if they cannot find evidence that you have permission to enter Australia.

If you are a citizen of the US, Canada, Japan, South Korea, Singapore, Brunei, Malaysia or Hong Kong, you need to apply for an Electronic Travel Authority (ETA) visa (subclass 601). This is a multiple-entry visa that allows you to visit Australia in three-month increments over a 12-month period. The cost is A$20 and like the e-visitor, this visa is electronic (though do print the grant and take it with you in case).

ETAs and e-visitor visas cannot be extended, and it is illegal to work on these visas. Both are often granted almost instantaneously – when my in-laws, who are EU nationals, applied, they received the grant notice just after they closed their online application tab. But don't bank on that, and leave yourself plenty of processing time. If you are going to make multiple three-month entries into Australia – whether on an ETA or an e-visitor visa – be prepared to prove to immigration that you are a genuine visitor with sufficient funds to support yourself for an extended period.

If you are a citizen of New Zealand, you may receive the Special Category Visa (subclass 444) on arrival and do not need to apply for anything in advance. This is an indefinite-length visa that also allows you work rights.

If you are a citizen of a country not listed, then you will generally need to apply for a visitor visa (subclass 600; tourism stream) at a cost of A$145 per applicant. Check the Australian embassy's website in the country of your citizenship, or the Home Affairs website, for more details.

It is your responsibility to understand and comply fully with your entry requirements and visa conditions, and to make sure that you are eligible for visa grants, and do not have outstanding circumstances that may lead to a visa denial or entry refusal – ie: a criminal record, having the wrong visa for your intended purpose in the country, etc. Australian immigration authorities are switched-on, know all the tricks and are very adept at identifying overstayers, those working illegally and those entering on false pretences. Save yourself a multi-year visa ban and deportation and comply fully with your visa conditions. Be sure to check both the Home Affairs website and the Australian mission in your home country to ensure you understand which visa you need to apply for, entry requirements and conditions of the visa well in advance of any travel – particularly as requirements and conditions can change quickly. In January 2022, when world No 1 tennis player Novak Djokovic arrived at Melbourne Airport to defend his 2021 Australian Open championship, he was blocked from entering the country at immigration and subsequently deported for failing to meet entry requirements. If they will deport him for not meeting requirements, they will deport you too.

CUSTOMS AND QUARANTINE
There is a national-level customs and quarantine system, and WA also maintains its own state-level one in addition. The Australian Border Force (w abf.gov.au) manages customs and takes import requirements and bans very seriously. Agriculture is a multi-billion-dollar industry and invasive pests from overseas have a long history of decimating the local industry.

Generally speaking, fresh fruit, vegetables, animal products (meat, fish, honey, etc), untreated and unprocessed plant products (timber, etc) and homemade foods will be banned. If it's commercially packaged and unopened, it will probably be OK. You need to check the Border Force's website, which is clear and comprehensive, to see if your prescription medicine is OK or what conditions need to be met.

If you are unsure if something you have brought meets requirements – declare it. We never take a risk when we return to Australia, and the Border Force officers are very helpful. In all cases, however, it is your responsibility as the traveller to ensure you are cognisant of requirements and that you are aware of laws and regulations about what you can bring into the country or state and what you can't, and in what quantities.

Live animals will normally have a quarantine requirement, and sometimes will only be accepted from certain countries. Again, the Border Force's website has comprehensive explanations and directives.

Duty-free limits apply. You have a A$900 limit for general goods, 2.25 litres for alcohol and 25 cigarettes or 25g of tobacco. If you exceed those limits, you are liable for duty on the whole lot – not just the excess amounts.

Australia operates a Tourist Refund Scheme (TRS), in which your GST (goods and services tax) can be refunded from participating suppliers. You need to get a paper invoice, have spent at least A$300 with the same supplier, and be able to take the item in your hand luggage. The Border Force has precise qualification criteria and directions on its website.

The Department of Agriculture and Food – Western Australia (DAFWA) operates a state-level quarantine system to prevent diseases and pests from other parts of Australia entering the state. There are no problems bringing cats and dogs into WA from other parts of the country, but you may need a permit for birds, fish, reptiles or other animals. Fresh fruit and vegetables, as well as honey, from other parts of Australia are likely to be seized at the state border, but cheese and eggs are OK, as are fresh and frozen meat and fish. Visit the Department of Primary Industries and Regional Development's website (w agric.wa.gov.au/biosecurity-quarantine) for rules and regulations.

EMBASSIES AND CONSULATES For a list of offices in Perth, visit w embassypages.com/city/perth.

GETTING THERE AND AWAY

BY AIR With water on three sides, and an impenetrable desert system on the fourth, the vast majority of travellers arriving in WA do so by flying into Perth Airport. Wherever you're coming from, though, WA is a long way away. Jakarta (3,010km) is closer to Perth than Canberra (3,088km), and New York to London (5,570km) is roughly the same distance as Perth to Auckland (5,537km).

That being said, advances in aircraft technology in the past decade have greatly increased WA's connections to the world, and Perth Airport is growing. Qantas made world headlines in 2018 with the introduction of its non-stop Perth to London flight – taking 17 hours, 15 minutes – thus connecting Australia and the UK directly for the first time and ending the fabled 'Kangaroo Route' that, at its inception, used to take four days and make seven stops, and cost, in today's money, around A$44,000.

The main Australian operators are Qantas, Virgin Australia and Jetstar, with others such as Airnorth and Skippers and numerous international airlines filling out the airport's portfolio.

International flights From Asia, there are non-stop flights to/from Hong Kong (7hrs 35mins), Singapore (5hrs 20mins), Bangkok (6hrs 55mins), Jakarta (4hrs 50mins) and Kuala Lumpur (5hrs 45mins), with onward connections to the rest of the continent. Tokyo (12hrs 30mins) was added by ANA just before the pandemic. Qatar Airways and Emirates fly to Perth from Doha (11hrs) and Dubai (10hrs 30mins) and offer timely transfers to many parts of Europe and Africa.

To get to Perth from North America, the traditional way was to first fly to California, and then connect a second time in Sydney/Melbourne, but there are now a much greater range of options. If you are on the US or Canadian east coasts, you can fly to Perth on one of the Middle Eastern carriers with just one stop in Doha or Dubai; it takes the same amount of time as coming over the Pacific. Qantas introduced a flight from Dallas to Sydney in 2011 that has proven hugely popular and bypasses the traditional California connection. There are also Asian options available – my last flight to the US connected in Singapore and Tokyo – and depending on where your departure point is in North America, you might be able to get a one-stop option through Hong Kong.

Air New Zealand flies non-stop to Auckland (7hrs) and seasonally in summer to Christchurch. There are tons of one-stop connection options available via the Australian east coast.

Perth has a large expatriate South African population, and SAA offers non-stop flights between Perth and Johannesburg (9hrs 30mins).

Flights from elsewhere in Australia There are multiple daily flights to/from Sydney, Melbourne and Brisbane. The introduction of non-stop services to Canberra and Hobart in the late 2010s means that Perth now has direct flights to every state and territory capital in Australia. Roughly, flight times are as follows:

Sydney 5hrs	**Darwin** 3hrs 55mins
Melbourne 4hrs 10mins	**Canberra** 4hrs 30mins
Brisbane 5hrs 35mins	**Hobart** 4hrs 35mins
Adelaide 3hrs 25mins	

Owing to prevailing winds, it takes longer to fly east to west than west to east, so add 30 minutes to an hour to those times for flights in the other direction to Perth. The winds can cause those times to change wildly; I've been on flights that got to Melbourne in less than 3 hours, and a flight to Perth from Brisbane that took 6 hours.

Domestic fares fluctuate in breathtaking fashion depending on time of day or year, whether it's the school holidays or not, how far in advance you buy the tickets, whether or not Mars is in retrograde and a zillion other factors. These fluctuations are to such a degree that publishing any sample fares here would be like throwing a dart.

Perth Airport Perth Airport itself is fairly user-friendly and is located in between Perth CBD and the Perth Hills. The airport is busy enough to have a good range of services and amenities, but not so busy to feel constantly crushed by traffic volume or have exhaustive lines. Do check which terminal your flight arrives in and departs from. Terminals 1 and 2 are located near each other, and Terminals 3 and 4 are located near each other, but Terminals 1 and 2 and Terminals 3 and 4 are not near each other and there is no longer a bus that connects them. You will need to take a taxi, and you don't want to park your car in the car park for one set of terminals and then find that your flight actually leaves from the other set. The airport has a range of car-hire facilities and long-term parking is competitively priced.

BY TRAIN The *Indian Pacific* runs from Sydney and Adelaide across the Nullarbor to Perth, and is a holiday experience in itself. The trip from Sydney to Perth takes four days, three nights and starts from A$2,065 per person. Gourmet food and local wines are served, and off-train excursions en route include Adelaide, the Barossa Valley and Rawlinna (on the Nullarbor), among others. Varying service levels and cabin types are also on offer; see w journeybeyondrail.com.au for details. You can connect to the *Indian Pacific* in Adelaide from the *Great Southern* (Brisbane–Adelaide), the *Overland* (Melbourne–Adelaide) or the *Ghan* (Darwin/Alice Springs–Adelaide).

BY BUS There are no viable bus options to get from other states to Perth. Greyhound (w greyhound.com.au), however, offers services from the Northern Territory to the Kimberley, and from Broome you can connect to other bus options run by operators like Integrity. One-way from Darwin to Broome takes 26 hours and starts from upwards of A$300. If you are going to Perth, it is quicker and cheaper to fly.

BY CAR There are two roads into WA from other states and territories. The Eyre Highway crosses the Nullarbor from South Australia at the border village of Eucla. It's a long journey that will take you a minimum of three days – the drive from Adelaide to Perth is 2,700km. The 1,200km section from Ceduna in South Australia to Norseman in WA has no real towns along the way, just a string of roadhouses with motels attached. However, 'crossing the Nullarbor' has an iconic place in the Australian psyche and the trip will be just as memorable as your stay in WA (see page 219 for more details on this). The other road into the state is the Victoria Highway in the far north, connecting Kununurra to Katherine in the Northern Territory, a distance of 515km. It's a well-maintained scenic road, passing through rolling red hills and bluffs, and there are services at Timber Creek en route.

Note that both highways are part of Highway 1 – a circular highway or national ring road that circumnavigates Australia. So whether you are driving into WA from the north or the south, technically speaking, you are on the same road.

It's worth a safety reminder here that 'highway culture' in Australia is different than in North America, Europe or other parts of the world. If entering WA by car, make sure to take plenty of rest breaks over the vast distance, don't drive at night, watch for animals, fill your car at regular intervals, and make sure you can do simple repairs like change a flat tyre. See page 50 for more on road safety in WA.

There is a third option if you are an experienced 4x4 driver, and that is the 1,100km Great Central Road (see box, page 240), a track (though often used by truckies) connecting Yulara in the Northern Territory (from which you can drive onwards to Alice Springs) to Laverton in the Goldfields (from which you can drive on to Kalgoorlie). A series of roadhouses provide motel, restaurant and petrol services en route, but the track does pass through Aboriginal lands so you need to get a permit beforehand. Call each roadhouse individually beforehand to check road conditions. Though generally fine as a 4x4 road, it is not suitable for 2WD and the series of abandoned cars on the roadside along the journey is testament to that. There are other tracks into the state but they are only for seasoned, veteran and completely self-sufficient 4x4 drivers who can also make their own repairs.

BY BOAT There are no scheduled boat services into WA, though cruise ships do call in. If you will be arriving in the state by yacht or pleasure craft, check the Australian Border Force's website for entry requirements and directives.

HEALTH   *With Dr Felicity Nicholson*

WA is fully developed and has a comprehensive health-care system. Your main health risks are likely to come from sunburn, heat exhaustion, exposure to the elements, and in some areas, mosquito-borne viruses such as Ross River virus.

SAFETY IN THE SUN The sun in the southern hemisphere is like a microwave, and if you are coming from the northern hemisphere, you will not be accustomed to just how quickly and severely you can get sunburned here (especially in summer). A period of time that you can spend outdoors in Europe or America with no problem will turn you into a lobster here. Australia has one of the world's highest rates of skin cancers from UV exposure. 'Slip, slap, slop', a slogan referring to wearing suncream, became a national tagline in the 1980s, and make this a personal mantra. Cloudy days do not reduce the risk of UV or sunburn – the rays just penetrate right through them. I know people who have gotten melanomas on the right side of their faces or arms because of constant sun exposure over the years through the drivers' side window. Carry suncream, sunglasses and a wide-brimmed hat with you at all times, and reapply the cream at regular intervals. Ideally use at least a factor 25 (preferably higher) to protect against the UVB rays and ensure that it has a five-star UVA rating too.

Nationally, heatwaves cause more deaths than bushfires and storms combined. Heat-related illnesses occur when sweat alone is not enough to keep your body cool, whether that's because you can't sweat enough or because the conditions are too extreme for your body.

Symptoms of heat stress include headaches, dizziness, fatigue and tiredness, cramps, feeling less thirsty and urinating less. Rest in a cool area, drink water, remove excess clothing and apply a wet cloth to your skin, particularly the armpits and groin. If you are starting to feel the effects of heat stress or aren't sure, always assume heat stroke, which can cause permanent organ damage. Heat stroke comes with elevated body temperature, and signs include abnormal walking, confusion, strange speech patterns and seizures. Call 000 (Australia's emergency number) immediately as heat stroke is a life-threatening emergency. While waiting for assistance, strip as much clothing off the victim as possible, soak with water and fan vigourously.

To prevent heat-related illnesses, ensure you have adequate water, schedule rest breaks ahead of time (don't wait until you are tired or trust your body to tell you when to stop), and don't do strenuous activities in the heat of the day. Schedule bushwalks, particularly in summer, for early morning. Temperatures inside gorges can be up to 10 degrees hotter than at the surface.

MOSQUITO-BORNE DISEASES Ross River virus and Barmah Forest virus are the two most common mosquito-transmitted viruses in WA; both are nasty and have similar symptoms and effects on humans. In each case, you are infected by a mosquito carrying the relevant virus, and neither is transmissible person-to-person or animal-to-person. Though not fatal, crippling fatigue, joint pain and sore muscles, often lasting for months (and sometimes over a year), are common symptoms (though many people experience no symptoms at all). The viruses are at their most prevalent in warmer temperatures; the north can be exposed to them all year round, and they do occur in the south as well, particularly on the coast between Mandurah and Busselton, where you will sometimes see public awareness billboards and 'Fight the Bite' logos. Once you've been infected, however, you're unlikely to get it again.

SNAKES, SHARKS, SPIDERS AND STINGERS Though Australia's famously deadly and toxic animals have a robust presence in WA, you don't need to be paranoid and are likely to go your entire trip without even seeing one. In the event of a snake bite, the Australian Red Cross recommends getting the victim away from the snake quickly, putting the person at rest (no movement) and ringing 000 for an ambulance. Pressure bandages should then be applied to the bite site, and immobilise the limb with a splint or sling – do not wash. See page 12 for more on WA's snakes.

The pandemic was still ongoing in many parts of the world when this guide went to print. UK travellers should check the Foreign Commonwealth and Development Office travel advice (w gov.uk/government/organisations/foreign-commonwealth-development-office), including the country-specific pages, to get the latest information on travel restrictions, testing and quarantine requirements. Do this on a regular basis as changes can occur where there are rapid increases in case numbers. US travellers should do the same from the US State Department's site at w travel.state.gov. Visitors from other countries should consult relevant advice from your home country government before travelling.

For a jellyfish sting, the Red Cross advises that if the victim is showing signs of distress or the sting is from a venomous jellyfish, ring 000. Pour vinegar on the sting if it is from a tropical jellyfish; otherwise, for other jellyfish, hot water – but not so hot the victim can't bear it – should be run over the sting for 20 minutes. If there isn't hot water, use a cold press or an ice pack. Pick off tentacles (don't use your fingers) and monitor the victim, following up with medical attention.

For shark bites, ring 000 immediately, even if it is a minor bite. See box, page 214, for more on shark safety.

For spider bites, with highly venomous species like the funnel web or redback, the Red Cross recommends treating it the same way as you would do a snake bite and calling 000. For other types of spiders, treat with a cold compress and get immediate medical advice/assistance.

HEALTH CARE Australia has reciprocal health agreements with 11 countries – Belgium, Finland, Italy, Malta, the Netherlands, New Zealand, Norway, Ireland, Slovenia, Sweden and the UK. These agreements cover medically necessary care, but your definition of what is medically necessary may differ from the government's, and do not cover all medications – and in any case these agreements do not replace the need for private insurance. The Services Australia website (w servicesaustralia. gov.au) has more information, but ensure you have adequate insurance coverage to repatriate yourself to your home country if needed.

The medical system in WA is a private–public partnership; some hospitals are publicly run, and some are private. GPs are usually the first point of call for health services, though in emergencies go straight to the emergency department. In small towns and country areas, you may have no choice if the GP is shut and you need urgent advice.

Ambulance services are run by trained volunteers (St John) in country areas. Journeys can be quite expensive for visitors and even for Australians who are not covered by Medicare in WA; ensure your insurance covers this.

TRAVEL CLINICS AND HEALTH INFORMATION A full list of current travel clinic websites worldwide is available on w istm.org. For other journey preparation information, consult w travelhealthpro.org.uk (UK) or w wwwnc.cdc.gov/travel (USA). Information about various medications may be found on w netdoctor. co.uk/travel. All advice found online should be used in conjunction with expert advice received prior to or during travel.

LONG-HAUL FLIGHTS, CLOTS AND DVT   *Dr Felicity Nicholson*

Any prolonged immobility, including travel by land or air, can result in deep-vein thrombosis (DVT) with the risk of embolus to the lungs. Certain factors can increase the risk and these include:

- History of DVT or pulmonary embolism
- Recent surgery to pelvic region or legs
- Cancer
- Stroke
- Heart disease
- Inherited tendency to clot (thrombophilia)
- Obesity
- Pregnancy
- Hormone therapy
- Older age
- Being over 1.83m (6ft) or under 1.52m (5ft)

A DVT causes painful swelling and redness of the calf or sometimes the thigh. It is only dangerous if a clot travels to the lungs (pulmonary embolus). Symptoms of a pulmonary embolus – which commonly start three to ten days after a long flight – include chest pain, shortness of breath, and sometimes coughing up small amounts of blood. Anyone who thinks that they might have a DVT needs to see a doctor immediately.

PREVENTION OF DVT
- Wear loose comfortable clothing
- Do anti-DVT exercises and move around when possible
- Drink plenty of fluids during the flight
- Avoid taking sleeping pills unless you are able to lie flat
- Avoid excessive tea, coffee and alcohol
- Consider wearing flight socks or support stockings, widely available from pharmacies

If you think you are at increased risk of a clot, ask your doctor if it is safe to travel.

SAFETY

ROAD SAFETY Your biggest safety risk in WA is the roads. Traffic fatalities and accidents are alarmingly high. WA drives on the left, and country roads and highways are not multi-lane affairs as is the case in the US and Europe. Even between major towns, highways are usually only two lanes, can be windy and bendy, have lots of heavy vehicles from road trains to big pieces of farming machinery, and there are limited overtaking opportunities. Fatigue, drink-driving and speeding are major contributors to accidents. Schedule frequent rest breaks; the rolling pastureland of the Wheatbelt has some of the highest per-capita rates of accidents in the state – it is easy to zone out unintentionally during a monotonous, multi-hour drive.

Unsealed roads are a major fact of life in regional areas. Check your car-hire contract carefully, as some don't allow you to drive on them and others don't but allow exceptions for access roads to car parks in national parks – always worth asking the question to make sure. On an unsealed road, you need to drop your speed significantly and drive to the conditions. Slow down well in advance of any curves. Sudden stops or turns of the wheel could easily cause you to lose control and roll over, and that is true even of veteran country drivers. Never drive your vehicle through water of unknown depth – cars can washout even in knee-deep water, and the currents are deceptively strong – and people have died from that. Pay close attention to weather forecasts and warnings during inclement weather. Remember that speed kills; 'Drop 5, Save lives' – meaning drop 5kph from your driving speed – is a road safety slogan here.

One of the other major traffic risks in rural WA are animals. Kangaroos are most active at dawn, dusk and night, and can hop in front of your car without warning. While hitting one may total your car, it is unlikely to kill you unless you are particularly unlucky (though it can) – however, what may well kill you is swerving into oncoming traffic or a tree on the side of the road when one jumps out in front of your car. Keep your wits and situational awareness about you at all times. Kangaroos are everywhere outside of Perth; you need to pay attention in every part of the state.

Emus are another hazard, and they are also active during the day. Emus have a higher centre of gravity and hitting one may cause it to roll up on to your bonnet and through your windshield, with an unfortunate result for you. Again, this is an issue in every region outside Perth; pay attention, particularly in forested areas where you might not be able to see what is lurking even just a metre or two off the road.

In the northern half of the state, stations are often unfenced and cattle can and do wander right out into the road, including the major highways. They are easy to spot in the day, but not at night – when you'll also need to pay attention to difficult-to-spot carcasses in the road, as hitting one will probably cause your car to flip.

For all these reasons, many car-hire companies often have a 'sunset to sunrise' clause in their contracts forbidding you from driving at night. This is sound advice even if your car-hire contract doesn't contain that clause. Locals try to avoid driving at night in country areas and you should too. If doing long-distance driving, aim to be at your destination by about 18.00.

Services can be limited en route; many maps will note where petrol is available so be sure to make use of that information. Try not to let your car dip below half-full on an extended country or Outback drive. If you have a breakdown or get lost, stay with your car. It is very easy to get lost in the bush, and it is much easier for the authorities to find a car than a person. People die wandering off to look for assistance. Ensure you have a stock of emergency supplies, blankets and a first-aid kit. In an emergency – ring 000.

For more on driving in WA, see page 55.

NATURAL DISASTERS Bushfires, cyclones and floods all occur in Western Australia. The Emergency WA website (w emergency.wa.gov.au) has real-time information on natural disasters, warnings and advice, and is a vital service bookmarked by locals, particularly useful in bushfire season (Jun–Oct in the Kimberley, Sep–Apr elsewhere). Cyclone season runs from November to April, but is generally an issue only for the northern third of the state (though Cyclone Alby did hit Busselton in the 1970s). Floods following torrential rains or cyclones can also be disastrous, and the state's dry rivers, creeks and lakes can fill up quickly. Never drive through water of unknown depth.

DANGEROUS ANIMALS Australia is well-known for its venomous animals, many of which live in WA. A variety of highly toxic **snakes** including death adders, tiger snakes, dugites, taipans and brown snakes inhabit the state. Snake bites are very uncommon – the Royal Flying Doctor Service puts it at two deaths per year, with most coming from brown snakes, though bites occur in both city and rural areas. Don't stick your hand into any tree hollows or unknown spaces, try to avoid walking through tall grasses and, if you see a snake, give it a wide berth – though it is likely as scared of you as you are of it. Stomping the ground when you walk can also help as the snake will sense the vibrations and move away. If you see one, call the shire and tell them. See page 48 for advice on what to do in the event of a snake bite.

Saltwater **crocodiles** are human-eating, and live in the northern part of the state, especially the Kimberley. They need muddy water to help camouflage themselves, and they do so with amazing efficiency – you won't see a croc until it's got you. 'Saltwater' is a bit of a misnomer as they live in freshwater too, so it's safest to assume any waterway or waterhole is croc-infested unless definitively told otherwise by informed locals. Always keep a safe distance from the water's edge – the Department of Parks and Wildlife advises 50m – and that includes climbing up on branches as crocs can jump out of the water to grab animals from overhead. Crocs can also climb rocks, lounge at clearwater beaches and have been seen as much as a kilometre away from the water. See box, page 350, for more on croc safety.

Marine stingers (**jellyfish**) are common in WA waters. The deadly box jellyfish (Irukandji) inhabits the waters around the northern third of the state and is present year-round, though is at its most dangerous from November to April (the wet season) and puts places like Cable Beach and Exmouth off-limits during that period (see box, page 344). Box jellyfish can kill within minutes and quick medical help is essential. Irukandji jellyfish, about the size of a fingernail, pack an insane wallop and can also kill. The best advice is simply to stay out of the water in the north during the wet season. Stingers are present in southern waters as well but are far more likely to be painful than fatal. Stonefish can be present in northern waters and look like rocks until you step on one – the sting is enormously painful – and their spines will go right through any aquatic shoes. I always wear sandals in the water, as much to protect my feet against rocks as animals, but they won't protect against something like a stonefish. See page 49 for advice on how to treat a jellyfish sting.

Redback **spiders** (better known as black widows) also live in WA, but there is an effective antidote and nobody has died from a bite since 1955. I have seen them in the toilet in my house numerous times and they will try to avoid you, but don't do silly things like stick your hands or feet in dark places or hollows. See page 49 for more on spider safety.

Sharks are an increasing problem in southern waters, and there have been numerous attacks in Perth, the South West, Great Southern and Esperance. Often surfers are the victims, but sharks can come right up to the shore in knee- or hip-deep water and attack people there. You can download the Sharksmart WA App, which has updated information, and closely monitor any warnings that are given. If you do come across a carcass on the beach, stay out of the water – sharks will probably be attracted to the decomposition, and beaches are often closed pre-emptively in such cases. See box, page 214, for more on shark safety.

Blue-ringed **octopus** are common in shallow waters, and are routinely seen in Perth and the South West, among others. They will often hide in shells so be careful about picking up any rocks, shells or similar items. In 2018, at Coogee Beach south of Perth, a girl was collecting seashells, took them home, and only when her aunty was preparing to clean out the seashells at the house did the blue-ring crawl out (thankfully, there was no bite). The bite can paralyse within seconds and kill quickly; when it is provoked, the rings will turn a bright neon blue.

OTHER DANGERS WA doesn't present too much of a crime problem, but petty crime does exist and some areas of Perth (like Northbridge) are less-than-desirable at night. Standard precautions like locking your car and not leaving valuables inside, not walking alone at night and so on will more than do the trick. Take precautions even in rural regions; some Outback and country towns have monstrous crime rates, and car crime especially can be common.

Lastly, pay attention to rip currents at the beach. If you get caught, stay calm and don't try to swim against the rip; swim to the side and then when clear, swim back to shore. To spot a rip, look for calmer water with fewer breaking waves – that may be where a rip is – and for areas of significant water movement.

WOMEN TRAVELLERS WA is very safe and welcoming for solo female travellers, and that includes all forms of transportation and accommodation. Take the same safety precautions that anyone would normally take and there should be no issues.

LGBTQ+ TRAVELLERS Same-sex marriage is legal in Australia, and West Australians are generally very tolerant. However, this is not to say you won't come across homophobic attitudes here and there, more noticeable outside Perth, but this is the exception rather than the rule. Visitors should feel just as welcome in WA as they would elsewhere in Australia, if not more so, though legislation is a bit inconsistent – the state does not allow same-sex surrogacy, for instance, but it was the first state in the nation to grant full adoption rights to same-sex couples in 2002, and a West Australian same-sex couple were the first in the nation to adopt in 2007. The 2017 national postal survey on same-sex marriage – which provided the foundation for parliament to legalise same-sex marriage in the immediate aftermath (the bill was introduced by a West Australian MP, Senator Dean Smith) – passed in WA by the second-biggest margin of any of the states, behind only Victoria.

For more information on the LGBTQ+ community in WA, check out **Living Proud** (w livingproud.org.au) or **Pride WA** (w pridewa.com.au). The latter grew out of a protest movement against discriminatory laws and practices in the 1980s, and now provides a platform to celebrate and promote cultural diversity. They have a calendar of events on their website.

TRAVELLING WITH KIDS The fabulous nature scapes, beaches, national parks and cute animals make WA a delight for kids. Many attractions have child-specific features and exhibits, restaurants have kids' menus and changing facilities, and even the smallest town will usually have a playground. One of the biggest challenges you will face is keeping the kids occupied on long car trips, or the long flight out here, but otherwise it's a well-equipped family destination.

WHAT TO TAKE

Almost everything you need can be bought in WA when you get here. Be sure to bring an electricity converter or adapter from home; Australia is on 230V, 50Hz and electrical sockets feature three flat prongs, with two on top slanted opposite directions, and a third vertical prong under them.

You'll undoubtedly need protection from the sun, so bring suncream, a wide-brimmed hat and a good pair of sunglasses – and a fly net to put over your hat (which you will be exceptionally grateful for). A decent-quality raincoat is also a good idea; if you are planning on doing some hiking and outdoor activities, bring the appropriate footwear, though you will probably find that the latter can be bought here and will be more suited to Australian conditions than yours from back home. If you are coming in winter, bring a coat and a few jumpers – it can get chilly both inside and out. Be prepared to dress in layers at any time of year.

If you are planning to go camping but don't want to lug your own equipment out here, the BCF store chain (w bcf.com.au) – Boating, Camping, and Fishing – will have plenty of everything that you require, from tents to sleeping bags to cooking equipment. BCF has branches in most major cities in the state.

It makes sense to pick up a small first-aid kit if you are going to be doing bushwalking and outdoor activities – something with bandages, gauze, tweezers and scissors, disinfectant and the like. If you are going to be in rural areas, note that mobile phone reception can be patchy. If you're going camping, a satellite phone is a good investment and they can be hired – Rent a Satellite Phone (w rentasatphone.com.au) has an office in Subiaco.

MONEY AND BUDGETING

Western Australia uses the Australian dollar, which comes in A$1 and A$2 coins (often called 'gold coins'), and notes of A$5, A$10, A$20, A$50 and A$100. Coins come in 5c, 10c, 20c and 50c pieces – prices will be rounded up or down to the nearest five cents. Visa and Mastercard bankcards are accepted virtually everywhere – this is often called 'EFTPOS' (an acronym meaning 'electronic funds transfer at point of sale') – though it pays to have some small change as a few shops have a minimum spend (often A$10) to use a card. However, other cards – such as American Express, Discover, etc – are unlikely to be accepted or attract enormous fees, so don't rely on these.

ATMs can usually be found in even the smallest towns. You should be able to use your foreign Visa/Mastercard debit cards to withdraw Australian dollars at these machines (at a surcharge), but verify this with your bank ahead of time. It is advisable if you are travelling outside Perth and Peel to have enough cash to pay for a tank of petrol, in case the only petrol station in town's EFTPOS machine is down or there is a problem with your card. Physical bank branches in rural areas are slowly becoming a thing of the past, and many have restricted hours even during the work week – sometimes just from 09.30 to 13.00 or even less – and this can be true at some branches in Perth as well. Call ahead and verify opening hours if you are going to need to actually go inside a bank branch.

To change money, **Travelex** has 11 branches in Perth, including inside HSBC on St Georges Terrace in Perth and in the Murray Street Mall. Travelex also has a branch at the South Bunbury branch of Australia Post (123 Spencer St), but realistically you may have difficulty changing money outside the Perth metro area, or have trouble doing so in a quick and easy fashion – and so if you are unable to use your cards to withdraw funds, consider doing all of your money-changing in Perth before you leave.

There is a goods-and-services tax (GST) of 10% on purchases, and that is included in quoted prices. Bargaining and haggling over prices is not customary. Service charges are not added to bills and tipping is not common or expected.

1.5L of bottled water: A$1.15
Bottle/pint/24-case of beer: A$6/
  A$13/A$49
Loaf of bread: A$3.40

Take-away coffee: A$4
Fast-food sandwich: A$6
T-shirt: A$5
Litre of petrol: A$1.90

BUDGETING There are no two ways around it – WA is expensive. And as a general rule, the further you get from Perth, the more expensive things become. If you want to stay in mid-range accommodation and have a nightly meal in a family restaurant, budget about A$200–250 per day per person. If you are going upmarket for your accommodation and dining, plan on A$300–$400 per day not including alcohol, car-hire charges or petrol. For those on a budget, it is possible to stay in self-catering hostels and take public transport for around A$100 per day.

Petrol generally costs more than in North America, but less than in Europe. Expect to pay around A$1.90/litre in the Perth Metro, more in the regions, and more again in the Outback – though this can vary wildly. For a standard, mid-size vehicle, expect to pay around A$70 to fill the tank. Check w fuelwatch.wa.gov.au for up-to-date prices.

If you are visiting national parks, a tourist pass is a good idea. Standard entry fees are A$12 per vehicle, and so if you are planning to visit multiple parks that adds up quickly. However, DPaW (Department of Parks and Wildlife) sells five-day passes for A$25, two-week passes for A$40, four-week passes for A$60 and annual passes for A$120 – much more cost-effective. You can buy online at w parks.dpaw.wa.gov. au/know/parks-passes and print them at home.

GETTING AROUND

BY CAR The best way to get around is by car, especially if you are going to be travelling outside Perth. Many of the best spots in the regions simply are not viable on public transport.

Car-hire facilities exist at virtually all airports and in many towns, and all the major international companies are represented. Hiring a car at Perth Airport will usually give you unlimited kilometres (double-check when you book) and you can use this to travel the state – when travelling north we will often do this and leave our own car in long-term parking (which has attractive rates – figure on about A$150 for two weeks). If you hire away from the airport (ie, in Perth city or at a regional airport), you will often be slapped with an onerous restriction of 100km or 200km per day – that sounds like a lot if you are in Perth, but it is not in the regions where the kilometre counter can spin wildly from day to day, attracting significant extra charge to you.

You do not need a kitted-out 4x4 to leave Perth, visit the regions or go up north, unless you are planning on travelling to an area that is expressly noted as requiring a 4x4. That being said, there are plenty of 4x4 options available (though often pricey) from hire companies.

Perth-based **Britz** (471 Great Eastern Hwy; w britz.com; ⊕ 09.00–15.30 Mon–Sat) offer campervan hires, as do **Apollo** (65 Worrell Av; w apollocamper.com; ⊕ 08.00–16.00 daily). Apollo can also rent out motorhomes and 4x4s.

The South West's hills and the open skies of the Wheatbelt make for some great motorcycling. Two reliable hire outfits are **West Coast Motorcycle** (w westcoastmotorcyclehire.com.au) and **CR Motorcycle Training & Rental** (w crmotorcycletrainingandrental.com.au).

As a tourist, you are generally able to drive using your overseas licence, as long as you have an English translation of it by a NAATI translator. Consult the WA Department of Transport (w transport.wa.gov.au) for more information. Keep in mind that your 'International Drivers Licence' is not actually a licence, it is just a translation of your home country licence, and it isn't valid unless you have your original home country licence with you.

Speed limits in WA are generally 110km/hr on highways, 50km/hr in built-up areas and 40km/hr in school zones. Red lights mean stop – it is illegal to turn on a red light in WA unless expressly and directly stated, but there are often slip lanes with give way/yield markers and you can turn on those. Seatbelts are mandatory in the state, and it is an offence to drive on a blood alcohol limit (BAC) of 0.05 or above. Refusing to comply with police instructions to submit for testing is an offence. Huge penalties apply for using mobile phones while driving – if you are caught texting while driving, it's a A$1,000 fine. The state government's website (w wa.gov.au) can advise about laws regarding phones and so on while driving.

West Australian road planners love a roundabout, and you will see them everywhere on the roads. Traffic gives way to the right, and you must signal/ indicate – get into the left lane if you are taking the first exit and indicate left, and get into the right lane and indicate right if you are going straight or exiting at a later turn-off (then indicate left when you are going to exit). At uncontrolled intersections, traffic gives way to the right. West Australian drivers are generally courteous. Horn-honking, following too close and other aggressive driving tactics will be frowned upon.

Read and download the 'Drive Safe' handbook from the Department of Transport, which can be downloaded online, for more road rules.

For more on road safety, see page 50.

Maps Hema Maps (w hemamaps.com) produce definitive and detailed maps and atlases to just about every place in Australia, including remote areas, 4x4 desert tracks and unsealed highways. I keep their Australia-wide road atlas in my car at all times. As well as their online shop, many bookshops and newsagents, both inside and outside Australia, carry their products – my original Hema Australia atlas was actually purchased in Brussels, Belgium – and they also produce folding maps of localised areas like Perth, the South West, the Kimberley and the Nullarbor.

BY AIR Within WA, there is a robust roster of flights from Qantas and Virgin Australia, as well as regional operators Rex, Airnorth and Skippers. Perth is connected to/from Albany, Esperance, Kalgoorlie, Geraldton, Meekatharra, Mt Magnet, Leonora, Laverton, Wiluna, Denham/Monkey Mia, Carnarvon, Exmouth/ Learmonth, Onslow, Paraburdoo, Newman, Karratha, Port Hedland, Broome, Fitzroy Crossing, Halls Creek and Kununurra, as well as Christmas Island and the Cocos (Keeling) Islands.

However, intra-WA flights are, notoriously, often exorbitantly priced – to the point that it has become a political issue. International fares are sometimes cheaper than those within WA (which the local media often points out), and a parliamentary inquiry was held in 2017, which did play a role in Qantas's decision to cap airfares on some regional WA routes – but only for residents of those regional communities, not tourists. The state government is also working on a cap plan that has yet to be finalised or implemented – but this will also not apply to visitors. If you are looking to travel within the state, though distances are vast, you will need to consider carefully if flying really is your best option; a multi-day drive from, say, Perth to Broome can be significantly cheaper than air tickets.

BY TRAIN Railways within the state do exist, in limited form, but they are not particularly useful to tourists – you will still need to hire a car at your regional destination (Wheatbelt, Goldfields or Bunbury) to visit the worthwhile sights, and probably at a higher price than if you had just hired the car in Perth and drove out yourself. State operator Transwa (w transwa.wa.gov.au) runs the state's rail network, but the number of services is low. The most useful services for travellers are likely to be the *Australind* (Perth–Bunbury; 2hrs 30mins; from A$68.30 return), the *Prospector* (East Perth–Kalgoorlie; 6hrs 50mins; from A$187.30 return), the *AvonLink* (Midland (Perth)–Northam; 1hr 20mins; from A$43.10 return) and the *MerredinLink* (East Perth–Merredin; 3hrs 20mins; from $99.20 return).

BY BUS The vast distances involved in travelling WA make taking the bus a slow option. If you don't have your own vehicle and need to get to mid-range-distance destinations from Perth, such as Busselton, Albany or Geraldton, the bus can be a viable option but consider the travel times and costs carefully for longer distances – you may actually find it cheaper and more viable in some cases to hire a car. Major operators are listed here, each of which specialise in different parts of the state. Sample fares and travel times are given in the relevant regional sections of this guidebook.

Transwa w transwa.wa.gov.au. Their main hub is East Perth Terminal, & from there services run to Esperance, Albany, Augusta, Pemberton, Boyup Brook, Geraldton & Kalgoorlie. There are also some region-to-region services such as Kalgoorlie to Esperance, Albany to Hopetoun & Geraldton to Meekatharra.
South West Coach Lines w southwest coachlines.com.au. Focusing on the southwest, these services connect Bunbury, Busselton, Collie, Dunsborough, Margaret River & Manjimup with Perth's Elizabeth Quay & Perth Airport.

Integrity Coach Lines w integritycoachlines. com.au. Focuses on the coastal Mid West & northern part of the state, with its main Perth departure points being the Wellington Street tourist bus stop, Midland Station & Joondalup. They can take you from Perth all the way up to Broome, including Jurien Bay, Dongara, Geraldton, Carnarvon, Coral Bay, Exmouth, Karratha, Port Hedland, Newman & points in-between.
Greyhound w greyhound.com.au. Services the Kimberley & links Broome, Derby, Fitzroy Crossing, Halls Creek & Kununurra with points in-between, with onward services into the Northern Territory.

INTERCITY TRANSPORT Perth has an excellent public transport system, but once you leave the Perth Metropolitan Area and head into the country, public bus services become fewer and further between. If you want to travel outside Perth, getting to the main tourist sites will usually require your own vehicle.

ACCOMMODATION

You can find virtually every type of accommodation imaginable in Perth, from swanky five-star luxury resorts down to boutique bed and breakfasts, youth hostels, houseboats and even unique historical accommodation, like at Fremantle Prison.

Most have provisions for breakfast, even if it is just continental. But outside Perth, accommodation can be a real mixed bag. Some of the more tourist-oriented centres like Broome will have glitzy resorts, and some station accommodation – rooms on vast rural farming or ranching properties – can be breathtaking in beauty (with prices to match). Generally, however, regional WA towns are too small to support more than a couple of accommodation options, and sometimes not even that many. Lack of competition has lead some establishments to rest on their laurels and you can quite easily find yourself paying four-star prices for a tired three- or even two-star room. If you find a place you like – bookmark it, and keep coming back.

Beautiful character **hotel** accommodation in small Outback or inland towns look wonderful from the outside, but the original old structures did not have things like en suites and those rooms have often been converted to staff quarters. While the main building itself may have been restored, you may find yourself actually staying in dongas (often-creaky modular rooms, sometimes intended as temporary accommodation of highly variable quality), behind the building or across the street. It's always best to call or email and check before you book. If you don't like it, it may be a 100km drive to the next hotel in difficult conditions. Additionally, with B&Bs it's always a good idea to verify before booking that they actually serve breakfast.

The **hostel and homestay** scene tends to be proportional to the size of the town; you won't have any problems in Perth, Peel or most parts of the South West, and hostels are in all the major centres – Airbnb has also become a major competitor to hotels in some locations. But once you get to smaller towns you may struggle significantly.

Caravan parks are part of WA's travelling DNA, and many have motel- and cabin-style accommodation in addition to powered and unpowered sites. These can be really good-value options and highly competitive with hotels and motels, especially in small country areas. Major chains include BIG4 and Discovery Parks, but there are a variety of dependable local operators as well.

In Outback areas, **roadhouses** typically offer motel accommodation and spaces for caravans, with a restaurant on site.

Camping is possible at many caravan parks, and the Department of Parks and Wildlife (DPaW) manages a vast number of campsites at national parks and conservation areas with variable policies and amenities. Some require advance booking, while others don't accept advance bookings at all; some allow generators, some don't; some have powered sites, some don't; some have water and allow campfires, others don't. DPaW's website (w dpaw.wa.gov.au) is comprehensive in describing the amenities, prices and policies and the best thing to do is to check there for a campsite in your specific area.

Because of the small population and limited options of many towns, rooms can fill up very fast with FIFO workers or because of someone's wedding. Always book a room in advance, especially if doing so to break up a long road journey.

ACCOMMODATION PRICE CODES

Prices are the average per night for a double room.

$$$$	A$250–400	**$$**	A$100–150
$$$	A$150–250	**$**	Less than A$100

EATING AND DRINKING

Some of the world's finest produce comes from WA. The state's 12,000km of coastline produce outstanding seafood bounties – barramundi is a favourite in the Kimberley, Mandurah is known for its crabs and the area along Indian Ocean Drive is a haven for rock lobster. The South West's and Great Southern's cattle farms produce outstanding beef, and their dairy produce lends itself to exquisite cheeses. Apple and stonefruit orchards dot the Donnybrook and Blackwood Valley regions, and the inland South West, Peel, Swan and Chittering Valleys are known for citrus. Manjimup has an annual cherry festival and also produces award-winning truffles. Carnarvon has delectable bananas and tropical fruits. The state's wheat, canola and barley crops are exported all over the world, as is lamb from WA abattoirs – the Middle East being a particularly voracious market. West Australian honey, produced seemingly all over, is also top-notch. Many areas of the state have farm gates open to the public and going from orchard to orchard or farm gate to farm gate is a relaxing and delicious past time.

When I am in the mood for some WA 'comfort food', my go-tos are South West marron linguini, fish and chips with something locally caught (impossible to say what – if it's fresh, it will be whatever's just been caught!), or a good old-fashioned scotch fillet steak from a South West cattle farm. A pavlova – an Australian meringue dessert topped with fruit (usually berries) and whipped cream – is an excellent finish with a South West or Great Southern port.

The state is also famous for the high quality of its premium **wines**. Margaret River is the most well-known wine region, but most of the South West, Great Southern, Peel and Perth regions produce vintages. Margaret River is well-known for its Cabernet Sauvignon and Shiraz, while the Great Southern has outstanding Rieslings – I never fail to come back with a few bottles whenever I'm in Albany or the Porongurups. The Swan Valley, on Perth's northeastern fringe, is the state's oldest wine region – try the Chenin Blanc here – and the Perth Hills produce a number of good varieties (I aim for the Tempranillo when I'm there). There are also wine regions around Busselton, the Blackwood Valley and Pemberton/Southern Forests – I particularly like the fortifieds and ports that come out of the Blackwood. Many places have cellar doors open to the public and offer tastings – so much so that we virtually never actually buy wine from a bottle shop, only from cellar doors.

Numerous craft breweries cover the state, there are some good rum distilleries in the Mid West and Kimberley, while craft gin is also becoming big business. If you aren't into alcohol – Australians are proud of their coffee and tea palettes – you will have no problem finding a caffeine fix anywhere in the state. A 'long black' is a double espresso in hot water – the espresso is poured over the hot water instead of the other way around, as in an americano. American-style filter coffee can be hard to find, however, and you may need to explain to the barista what you want and see if they can do it (or if there is a close substitute). Bottled water is abundant and for sale everywhere, though the tap water is safe to drink.

EATING OUT Like any large Western, developed city, Perth has a range of dining options from high-end, five-star restaurants to fast-food outlets. The state's Italian and Asian heritage is reflected in its vast number of quality restaurants, although many others tout their use of West Australian products. Vegetarians and vegans will have no problem in the Perth Metropolitan Area, but outside the capital area and some parts of the South West you may struggle to find a wide variety of options and should plan ahead – many places have menus or Facebook pages with some of their

2

dishes online, and ringing ahead and asking will be helpful. Be sure to tell staff of any dietary requirements when you arrive.

The **pub** is still the lifeblood and hive of activity in country towns, sometimes branded as a tavern. In some places it might be the *only* place to get a meal. Most pubs and taverns will have a bar and then a separate dine-in family section; some also offer simple accommodation. Pubs serve hearty meals and should be tried at least once – though quality can range from excellent to inedible, and menus often vary little from one town to the next. Finding a good one can be a trial-and-error process. I've noted my own favourites with a ✳ symbol throughout this guide.

West Australian 'pub classics' generally include scotch fillets (what a ribeye steak is often called), burgers, chicken parmigiana, fish and chips, garlic prawns, salt and pepper squid, steak sandwiches, surf and turf, lamb shanks and sometimes a pizza option. Sticky date pudding – sponge cake with dates, toffee sauce and usually vanilla ice cream on the side – will be offered for dessert with a few other options.

On the highways, **roadhouses and petrol stations** will often offer dine-in and take-away coffees, cakes and filling fare like burgers and all-day breakfasts; some are tasty, but others are so greasy the bag it is in looks like it will dissolve.

Opening hours can be variable and just because business hours are posted and published doesn't mean they will be stuck to, especially if it's a slow day with few customers – this tends to happen a lot more in the regions but can also occur in Perth. Call ahead to make sure where you want to eat will be open; you don't want to arrive looking forward to a burger at that lunch spot you read about, only to find a sign on the door saying it closed early because the chef had a dentist's appointment, or the owner is on holiday for the week, or – as I once saw on the door of a café when I went looking for breakfast – 'closed today for a little R&R'. Also keep in mind that kitchen hours and opening hours can be different – you may find that a place has published that it is open until 20.00, but then walk in at 19.30 and find that the kitchen has already shut down and closed for the night.

For **self-caterers**, the main supermarket chains are Woolworth's and Coles, though Aldi has been making inroads in key markets of the state – the bigger regional towns like Busselton, Esperance, Broome, Manjimup and Kalgoorlie will all have the big chains. Small country towns will often instead have an IGA or IGA Express – ranging in size from a mini-supermarket to convenience store. Many towns host farmers' markets at least monthly showcasing local produce.

Vegetarians may be inconvenienced in smaller towns – limited to a few puny options on pub menus. It may be worth it to plan ahead and locate IGAs where you can buy vegetables and protein to make your own meals, or peruse menus online first and plan ahead.

Dishes highlighting **bush foods** that Aboriginal people have used for thousands of years, like wattle, native lime and other plants or meats like kangaroo, have made exceptionally limited headway into Australian menus – you are not going to find an 'Aboriginal restaurant' and will struggle to find restaurants or cafés that use any bush foods at all. You may very occasionally find a place serving kangaroo steaks, usually made from the meat in the tail – this is a very high-quality meat with low fat content, usually served medium-rare and well worth trying.

PUBLIC HOLIDAYS AND FESTIVALS

1 January	New Year's Day
26 January	Australia Day
First Monday in March	Labour Day
March/April	Good Friday
March/April	Easter Monday
25 April	Anzac Day
First Monday in June	Western Australia Day
Last Monday in September/first Monday in October	Queen's Birthday
25 December	Christmas Day
26 December	Boxing Day

FESTIVALS Throughout spring, many shires will host **agricultural shows**, which bring together a variety of events, games, food and displays. Some of the most famous are the Royal Perth Show, held at the end of September; Wagin's (Wheatbelt) Wool-o-Rama, usually held in early March; and the Dowerin Field Days (Wheatbelt), towards the end of August.

The Blackwood Valley hosts three major **music festivals** each year. The Boyup Brook Country Music Festival is one of the state's largest and is usually held the third weekend of February. The Blues at Bridgetown in November is hugely popular, and the Nannup Music Festival is over the Labour Day weekend. The Ord Valley Muster, usually in May, brings 10,000 people to Kununurra for dozens of acts. These festivals often feature local and national artists, and the occasional international artist.

Many towns in the regions, especially the Wheatbelt, Great Southern, Mid West and South West, host a wildflower show in August and/or September – these can be as small as a display of local wildflower specimens in the one-room town hall, or a grander affair held over a few weeks like Nannup's Flower and Garden Festival in August, which showcases open gardens in town with tours, as well as workshops, informative how-to talks, and celebrity presenters.

The Perth Festival is a month-long multi-arts festival showcasing film and visual art, dating back to the 1950s. Taking place in late summer (February–March), it was founded by the University of Western Australia and events are held across the city. Encompassing theatre, dance, literature, film and art, among others, participants come from around the state, country and the world.

SHOPPING

Western Australia is one of the best places in the world to buy Aboriginal art, and galleries that ship internationally can be found in Perth and throughout many Aboriginal Outback communities such as near Halls Creek; see box, page 352.

Aside from Aboriginal art and crafts like boomerangs, popular souvenirs include homewares like bowls and chopping boards, made from timber from WA's massive forests; clothing like jumpers and scarves from the state's vast flocks of wool-producing sheep; and 'Outback' items like Akubra hats – the iconic wide-brimmed fur felt hats – and jewellery from the state's historic pearling and pink diamond industries (page 358). Leather products like wallets are also popular.

Farmers' markets are popular state-wide, though they tend to be on the small side in the regions – hours and schedules vary (from a few hours once a month to weekly), but visitor centres in the relevant towns will be able to advise.

ARTS AND ENTERTAINMENT

Although not quite on the same level as that of Sydney and Melbourne, Perth and Western Australia's arts and entertainment scene is vibrant and growing.

Perth is the undisputed centre of it all, and many high-profile national and international performances call in to the various venues. You can expect to find the same options here that you would any major city of Perth's size, and it is a regular stop for touring artists, singers and bands of all genres. There is a vibrant theatre scene, with multiple venues in town. Prices for tickets are variable depending on your seats; expect to pay around A$40 and up for general entry.

In the regions, some of the bigger centres like Bunbury, Albany and Geraldton will show tours of lesser-known artists from time to time but rarely, if ever, major international artists. However, many regional towns have historic theatres (like Cummins Theatre in Merredin, page 252) and there are still performances there – it is well worth giving one of these a try and taking in the historic digs.

The West Australian Opera (w waopera.asn.au), the state opera company, has only been around since the 1960s but is highly regarded, performing traditional and modern work. They perform at multiple venues in Perth and occasionally head out to the regions – they have performed at the Pinnacles in Cervantes and the Valley of the Giants in Walpole. The forest provides amazing acoustics for opera.

Things like museum opening times can vary wildly and there are no particular rules-of-thumb; some may be open daily, some may be open on alternating days, some may only open in the mornings. In the regions they may be staffed by volunteers and opening hours reflect that. If you see a sign saying that entry is by a 'gold coin donation', you are expected – though technically not required – to drop an A$1 or A$2 coin in the box as you go in – those coins being gold in colour in Australia.

MEDIA AND COMMUNICATIONS

PRINT The *West Australian* is Perth's daily tabloid newspaper (w thewest.com.au), founded in 1833. It has a huge market share and is distributed across the state. The state's regions have their own newspapers, but only the *Kalgoorlie Miner* is a daily; most others are weekly or twice-weekly. They tend to be hyper-local in focus.

TV AND RADIO There are three commercial TV stations (Channels 7, 9 and 10), part of national networks, and two government TV stations (ABC and SBS). Many hotels and accommodation providers supplement this with Foxtel packages.

Perth has the same choice of radio offerings you would expect in any big city – but this will dwindle down considerably once you leave the capital, to maybe just one or two options. You can usually get ABC Radio in your car in the Outback but may have to play around with the dial to find it.

TELEPHONE The international dialling code for Australia is 61, and the state code for Western Australia is 8. For all mobiles, however, the code is 04 – if calling a mobile, you dial both the 0 and the 4 (and not 8).

West Australian phone numbers typically have eight digits. A phone number with a 1300 prefix is charged the same as a local call; an 1800 number is free to the caller (and is sometimes referred to as a 'freecall').

The emergency number in WA is 000 – referred to universally as triple zero.

Australia uses the GSM network – so you need to make sure your mobile phone is compatible before arriving. There is no shortage of prepaid products in WA, so you may find it easier to use that option than roaming. Prepaid SIMs can come for as little as A$10 per recharge, while companies like Boost Mobile offer 28-day SIMs for A$30, with 45GB of data. If you are planning on travelling to the regions, Telstra is the most common network as it has the most coverage, but you do pay a premium for using them. Optus and Vodafone are the two other networks in WA.

Wi-Fi and 4G signals in regional areas are improving all the time – you may struggle for a signal on a country or Outback road in between towns, or on some farms, but populated areas do not present any issues. Note that not all hotels in regional areas will offer in-room Wi-Fi.

CULTURAL ETIQUETTE

West Australians are generally a confident, outgoing people who welcome visitors with open arms. Society here is relaxed and informal, and being overdressed for an occasion can often be a bigger faux pas than being under-dressed. If unsure – ask someone. You'll be given honest guidance.

Egalitarianism is an important part of Australian culture, as is the concept of the 'fair go' (everyone gets an opportunity). What you make of that opportunity is your responsibility. 'Tall Poppy Syndrome' is when self-promoters get cut down to size – though at its darkest, it can mean that those who excel are ganged up on by those left behind.

Highly opinionated or loud people tend to make Australians uncomfortable, as can public criticism of others. Like people everywhere, Australians are proud of their country and talking about the country's or the state's shortcomings will not win you many friends.

It's rude to ask overly personal questions about politics, religion, salary and personal beliefs to people you don't know very well. If invited to someone's house, it is courteous to ask if you should bring something. If that is declined, a small gift (ie, a box of chocolates) is considered polite. The informal barbecue – ie: 'the barbie' – is a great tradition. Try to avoid the 'pop-in' and call beforehand if you want to stop by someone's house. It's not considered rude to decline food or drink if you aren't hungry or thirsty.

Australian culture can often have 'shouts' (buying a meal or round of drinks for someone). It is customary to take turns 'shouting' over time.

When shopping, saying please and thank you are vital, and gently getting a waiter's attention as they walk by is more appropriate than calling out. Haggling is not done, tipping is not customary, and queuing patiently rather than crowding a desk is an expectation. It is illegal to smoke in enclosed public areas, outdoor eating areas (unless in a designated area at an establishment with a licence), in taxis or on public transport, or in vehicles with children aged 17 and under. The Department of Health website (w ww2.health.wa.gov.au) has all the regulations.

Punctuality is important. If you have a dinner reservation for 17.30, it is expected that you will be there at 17.30. Don't be 'fashionably late'.

If you are interested in volunteering while in WA, you need to check with Home Affairs to make sure your visa allows this activity and, if so, how much of it is allowed – the immigration and legal definition of 'work' versus 'volunteering' can sometimes be cloudy and cause visitors problems.

If you are on an extended visa whose conditions allow volunteering, and will be in one place for an extended period of time, many West Australian rural fire services and ambulance services are staffed by volunteers. Signing up to either St John of God (w stjohnwa.com.au) or the DFES Volunteer Fire and Rescue Service (w dfes.wa.gov.au) can be a great way to contribute to a community, meet locals and gain new skills. You may one night find yourself driving the ambulance or the fire engine out to a call out, or spraying the fire hose or giving CPR. It is very serious work, however, and quite literally the lifeline of many small communities. Many who join stay involved for years.

The Parks and Wildlife Service can offer opportunities like animal monitoring and environment conservation; visit their website for more information (w dbca. wa.gov.au).

For broader opportunities, SEEK Volunteer (w volunteer.com.au) is an aggregation site where local agencies and organisations post adverts looking for volunteers.

Part Two

PERTH & THE SOUTH WEST

KINGS PARK Page 86. Perth's signature site, this botanical garden dates back to the foundation of the Swan River Colony. This is Perth's favourite place to relax, and the array of native plants showcase some of state's signature flora, like banksias and kangaroo paws. The views of Perth alone are reason enough to come.

FREMANTLE'S CAPPUCCINO STRIP Page 90. The quirky architecture, UNESCO heritage sites, spirited café and dining scene, and funky ambience of the Cappuccino Strip give Perth's most recognisable neighbourhood its instantly loveable flavour. The plethora of diverse restaurants, bars and character accommodation also make it a favourite base for visitors.

GUILDFORD AND THE SWAN VALLEY Page 113. Usually overshadowed by Fremantle, Guildford, in Perth's northeast, is just as historic, character-laden and charming, and has in its back yard the terrific wines and cellar doors of the Swan Valley. It's also Perth's best spot for antiquing – I come here often for reasonably priced vintage items like 1940s hat racks.

BUSSELTON JETTY AND CAPE NATURALISTE The Jetty – one of the world's longest at 1.8km – has become something of a cliché at Busselton (page 153), which at high school graduation time in December becomes Western Australia's answer to Florida during Spring Break (this is called 'Schoolies' here). Nevertheless, Busselton Beach's calm waters are simply beautiful, and I never get tired of seeing the majestic, white-trimmed jetty stretch out over the impeccably clear waters of the sheltered Geographe Bay, framed by the pines along the foreshore. A short hop west are the holiday home haven of Dunsborough and the splendid coastline of Cape Naturaliste (page 158), with its marvellous north-facing and sheltered beaches at Eagle Bay and Meelup, and whale-watching opportunities at the lighthouse.

MARGARET RIVER Page 162. WA's capital for both surfing and wine, 'Margs' has long been the South West's showpiece. The charms don't end with waves and grapes, though – it's also a base for one of Australia's most scenic multi-day hikes, the Cape to Cape, and there's plenty of caving in the area too.

STIRLINGS AND PORONGURUPS While lacking the height of the Rockies or the Alps, the Stirling Range (page 187) and Porongurup Hills (page 189) – about 40km from each other, near Mount Barker – are wonderfully scenic, with their purple hues brightening up the rolling landscape. There are good scenic drives and hikes here, and both are close enough to Albany to use the Great Southern's historic port city as a base.

ESPERANCE AND THE OUTBACK RIVIERA Page 203. Arguably the world's best beaches line this isolated stretch of Outback coast, where impossibly white sand meets impossibly blue water under impossibly clear skies. Even when it's 'busy' you'll find a stretch of sand to yourself.

3

Perth & the Metropolitan Area

Sandwiched between the Indian Ocean and the Perth Hills, 'Perth is pure relaxation' one long-time local, who spent many years overseas, tells me. It's hard not to notice it during your final descent into the airport – you'll see the sun sparkling over the water below (Perth is the country's sunniest state capital, with an annual average of 3,000 hours of sunshine), giving way to an almost continuously unbroken narrow line of sand, stretching seemingly forever in both directions. Your flight path is likely to then take you slightly inland past the gleaming cluster of skyscrapers serenely perched on Swan River, before a few turns over suburbia leads your plane to its final approach over the numerous vineyards chequerboarding the outskirts of the city to touchdown on the runway at the foot of the gently rolling Perth Hills.

Compared with the hectic urban bric-a-brac of the major southeast Asian cities to the north, and the hustle and bustle of Sydney and Melbourne to the east, the West Australian capital *is* pure relaxation. Scenic, tranquil rivers, hill estate wineries, endless kilometres of golden sand beaches, glorious parks and an easy-to-navigate town layout just beg you to grab a bicycle or a kayak for a day's leisurely exploration, and stop for a glass of wine on your way home. The city's neighbourhoods, while each distinct in their identity, share a common commitment to a chilled vibe and you will find excellent restaurants, cafés and shops catering to the stress-free, or those aspiring to that.

Despite being hemmed in by the ocean and the hills, Perth does not have the dense, packed-in and overbuilt feel to it that Sydney and Melbourne can sometimes have, and even the stop-and-go traffic on the highways here feels more chill. Although the metropolitan area stretches for 108km from Two Rocks in the north to Rockingham in the south, being in that corridor means nobody is ever very far from the beach or the hills. It's easy to forget that this is Australia's fourth-biggest city, and that over two million people – more than 80% of WA's population – live here. The city dominates the state in every conceivable way, and every person you meet in Western Australia's regions and Outback will know the fastest way to get here.

This is a young, wealthy and prosperous city. West Australians *love* Perth, and many would never dream of leaving here. Despite the oft-cited label of it being 'the world's most isolated city', the state's economic success and bounty of jobs make living here long term both feasible and desirable – those skyscrapers in the CBD aren't gleaming for nothing – and the climate and geographic setting simply add to the appeal. Young West Australians don't need to cross the Nullarbor to find their fortunes, and most don't try. This is an urbane and cultured big city, well-connected into the planet's global village, and it does not resemble an isolated frontier outpost in any way whatsoever.

Perth is the gateway to WA for almost all visitors, and even if it isn't you're likely to end up here or pass through at some point during your trip. Appropriately for

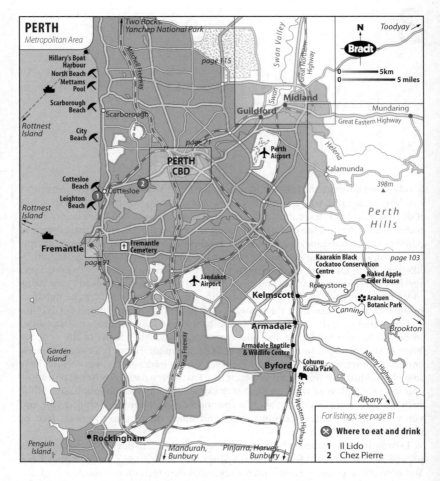

page 115

page 71

page 91

page 103

PERTH
Metropolitan Area

N

0 ——— 5km
0 ——— 5 miles

Toodyay

Swan Valley

Two Rocks,
Yanchep National Park

Mitchell Freeway

Great Northern Highway

Hillary's Boat
Harbour
North Beach
Mettams
Pool
Scarborough
Beach

Scarborough

Swan

Midland

Guildford

Mundaring

Great Eastern Highway

Rottnest
Island

City
Beach

PERTH
CBD

Perth
Airport

Helena

Kalamunda

398m

Cottesloe
Beach
Leighton
Beach

Cottesloe

Rottnest
Island

Fremantle

Fremantle
Cemetery

Perth
Hills

Kaarakin Black
Cockatoo Conservation
Centre
Roleystone

Naked Apple
Cider House

Araluen
Botanic Park

Canning

Jandakot
Airport

Kelmscott

Brookton

Garden
Island

Kwinana Freeway

Armadale

Armadale Reptile
& Wildlife Centre

Byford

Cohunu
Koala Park

Albany Highway

South Western Highway

Albany

Penguin
Island

Rockingham

Mandurah,
Bunbury

Pinjarra, Harvey,
Bunbury

For listings, see page 81

Where to eat and drink

1   Il Lido
2   Chez Pierre

a city whose DNA is geared this way, the sites are all low-key and understated – Perth's most famous attraction, after all, is a botanical garden. At times, this has left it open to criticism and accusations of being dull – Bill Bryson once memorably described its architectural profile as 'Minneapolis Down Under' – but the key to understanding and appreciating Perth is to home in on that relaxing vibe, and set your itinerary accordingly.

HISTORY

The Traditional Owners of the land where Perth now sits are the Whadjuk Noongar, and they have been present for at least 45,000 years – though there is evidence that it is perhaps as long as 70,000 years. They believe a serpent from the Dreamtime, Wagyl, dug the Swan River and still lives in it today. The area was well-equipped for habitation: the river ensured that the land around today's Perth was relatively rich with wildlife, honey could be found in banksias in what is now South Perth and the Indian Ocean provided a bounty as well. Unsurprisingly, the Noongar name for the Canning River – Djarlgarra – means 'place of abundance'; however, there is oral evidence that the Swan River was not known by just one name, and instead different parts of the river took on different names.

The Dutch arrived at Rottnest in 1658 but didn't stay. European settlement began in 1829, when the British government established the free Swan River Colony. Captain James Stirling was the first governor, and Perth got its name because the then-British Colonial Secretary, Sir George Murray, was from Perth, Scotland. Many things around the Perth and Peel Region – such as the Murray River – are named after him.

Fremantle, about 20km from Perth, was established at about the same time. Charles Fremantle was captain of the first ship that arrived for settlement, the HMS *Challenger*, but Stirling decided Perth would be the capital of the new colony. The site of Perth worked as the capital because it was at the halfway point between Fremantle and the farming districts further up the river, in what is known now as the Swan Valley. So Fremantle developed as the port, Guildford as the agricultural hub, and Perth, in between, governed.

When the British arrived, it's believed there were around 10,000 Noongar living in the Perth and the South West. Land for settlers was expropriated immediately and, with it, severe disruption to Aboriginal food sources occurred (both through land damage and denial of access to land). Introduced diseases like measles ravaged the population. Aboriginal resistance leaders were pursued, jailed and killed. Early battles took the form of ambushes and tit-for-tat strikes. Midgegooroo and Yagan – a father-and-son team that became famous as major Noongar resistance fighters against European settlement (see box, page 89) – were both killed; Midgegooroo in 1832 after he was executed without trial for the murder of two white settlers, and Yagan a year later in 1833 through an ambush (a bounty had been placed on his head). With early resistance leaders out of the way, expropriation continued unabated, with Europeans also forming and leading expeditions to subdue Aboriginals. In 1841, an Aboriginal jail opened on Rottnest Island – several thousand Aboriginals would be imprisoned here over the next century (see page 97 for more).

As a start-up, however, Perth was a disappointment. Much of the land around the river is quite sandy and did not live up to its agricultural potential. Population growth was not forthcoming and the colony floundered economically. In 1850, the decision was made to bring in convict labour to help jolt the situation; the influx of thousands of convicts forever changed the city's fortunes, effectively tripling the population (from around 5,000 to 15,000). Perth began to develop rapidly, including aesthetically, with the convict labour force professionalising the fledgling construction industry. Many grand buildings were constructed during this time, including Perth Town Hall and Fremantle Prison. The city also expanded its boundaries, with industry beginning to stake out East Perth and residences sprouting up in West Perth. However, growth was limited and the city's problems became so well-known that Swan River Colony was even cited by Karl Marx in *Das Kapital* in his critique of capitalist modes of production.

But the Kalgoorlie and Murchison gold rushes changed all that, and Perth became a boom town in the late 1800s. The city's population swelled, and newfound riches and receipts fundamentally changed the city and secured its long-term viability. Infrastructure, services and the economy all improved rapidly. In 1897 Fremantle Harbour opened, allowing greater ship access. Perth was supportive of Federation, and the 1900 referendum carried both Perth and Fremantle easily. Higher education came to the city, and the University of Western Australia was established and opened in 1911.

3

The 1905 Aborigines Act – anchored in a belief in Social Darwinism and that Aboriginals would 'die out' without European protection – established a 'Chief Protector' in Western Australia for Aboriginal society, provided for external control of Noongar society by white politicians, and was the legal basis for establishing Aboriginal exclusion areas in Perth in 1927 – the Noongar could not enter and stay in Perth unfettered. Most of today's CBD and Northbridge were thought to

PERTH Overview
For listings, see from page 76

◔ **Where to stay**

1   Tribe Kings Park

⊗ **Where to eat and drink**

2   Architects & Heroes
3   George's Meze
4   Lapa Brazilian BBQ
5   Nobu

Off map
Elie's Tent Lebanese
Victoria Park Hotel

be 'prohibited areas' for Aboriginal; however, the edict was actually quite vague and could (and was) applied to any suburb in the metro area. Aboriginal people required a specific purpose and a 'Native Pass' to be in a prohibited area, and a 18.00 curfew applied – being in Perth without a Native Pass could result in quick arrest. A 1947 review concluded that the prohibited area was too large to enforce and was scaled back in size dramatically, and abolished entirely in 1954.

On 25 February 2021, after years of battle in the courts, the South West Native Title Settlement took effect granting the Whadjuk Noongar people native title (see box, page 23 for more on native title) over what is now the Perth Metropolitan Area. This is the largest in Australian history, covering 200,000km². Though an important step in the reconciliation process, it is widely understood and acknowledged that there is still a long way to go.

The Americans arrived in World War II, with a Catalina Flying Boat base being established in the Swan River at Matilda Bay, along the waterfront in front of the University of Western Australia, and submarines came to Fremantle. Many ships arrived after Singapore fell, looking for refuge; the submarine base became one of the biggest in the war. After the war large-scale European migration arrived, particularly Italians. Another mining boom in the 1960s saw the city's fortunes continue to improve. Today, the city – and by extension, the state – remain tightly coupled to the mining and resources sector and growth continues to be among the highest in Australia. Perth routinely ranks highly in quality of life.

GETTING THERE AND AWAY

BY AIR Perth is very well connected to the rest of Australia and other countries – it's just really far away. (For details of routes and airlines, see page 45.)

Flights depart and arrive at Perth Airport (w perthairport.com.au), a major international and domestic gateway. It's 12km east of the CBD; there are two terminal areas – T1/T2 and T3/T4 – and they are not within walking distance of each other (about a 15-min drive apart), so note which terminal your flights arrives at/departs from. A free transfer bus connects the two.

To get downtown, TransPerth bus route 380 connects Elizabeth Quay and T1/T2, while route 40 connects Elizabeth Quay and T3/T4. By car, it is best accessed from the Tonkin Highway. There are competitively priced short- and long-term car parks at both terminals; parking can be booked online (see page 72 for more on car hire). A one-way taxi fare from the airport to the CBD is about A$45 and the ride takes about 20 minutes; to Fremantle it is about 30 minutes (A$65–70).

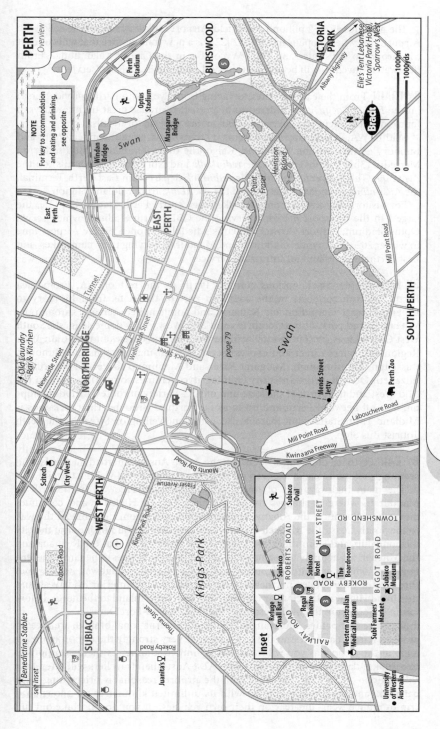

NOTE
For key to accommodation
and eating and drinking,
see opposite

Old Laundry
Bar & Kitchen

Scitech

City West

WEST PERTH

NORTHBRIDGE

Newcastle Street

Wellington Street

Barrack Street

Tunnel

East
Perth

EAST PERTH

Kings Park Road

Mounts Bay Road

Fraser Avenue

Kings Park

Roberts Road

Benedictine Stables

see inset

SUBIACO

Thomas Street

Rokeby Road

Juanita's

Point
Fraser

page 79

Swan

Mends Street
Jetty

Perth Zoo

Labouchere Road

Mill Point Road

Kwinaana Freeway

SOUTH PERTH

Mill Point Road

Heirisson
Island

Swan

Windan
Bridge

Matagarup
Bridge

Perth Stadium

Optus Stadium

BURSWOOD

5

VICTORIA
PARK

Albany Highway

Elie's Tent Lebanese
Victoria Park Hotel,
Sparrow's Nest

Bradt

N

0   1000m
0   1000yds

Inset

Subiaco Oval

Subiaco
Hotel

ROBERTS ROAD

HAY STREET

TOWNSHEND RD

The
Boardroom

4

BAGOT ROAD

Subiaco
Museum

ROKEBY ROAD

Western Australian
Medical Museum

Subi Farmers'
Market

3

Regal
Theatre

2

Refuge
Small Bar

RAILWAY ROAD

University
of Western
Australia

The new, nearly A\$2 billion Forrestfield-Airport Link – which will be called the Airport Line when it opens in winter 2022 – is a new train service that will connect the airport to Bayswater and High Wycombe, in the City of Kalamunda. From Bayswater, travellers will be able to access other useful TransPerth services.

BY TRAIN From the eastern states, voyaging from Sydney to Perth (or vice-versa) on the *Indian Pacific* is considered to be one of Australia's great train journeys: a four-day, three-night trip covering 4,300km. See page 46 for details.

Within WA, Transwa-operated trains (w transwa.wa.gov.au) connect Perth and Bunbury (2½hrs) on the *Australind*; Kalgoorlie (6hrs 50mins) by the *Prospector*; Merredin (3hrs 20mins) on the *MerredinLink*; and Northam (1hr 20mins) on the *AvonLink*. The *Prospector* and the *MerredinLink* depart from East Perth Terminal, the *Australind*, from Perth Station and the *AvonLink*, from Midland Station.

For visitors, the key stations will likely be central Perth Station [79 C2], the largest in the transport network, serving the CBD; Perth Stadium, which serves Optus Stadium; Airport Central, which is scheduled to open on the Airport Line in winter 2022; Fremantle, Guildford and Mandurah, serving their namesakes; and East Perth and Midland for intra-state services.

BY BUS Ample coach options connect Perth to the rest of WA. From East Perth, **Transwa** connects to the southern part of the state, from Bunbury to Esperance up to Geraldton and Kalbarri, and points in between and through the Wheatbelt and parts of the Goldfields and Mid West. As its name suggests, **South West Coach Lines** (w southwestcoachlines.com.au) specialises in the South West Region and offers direct and express services from major towns like Bunbury, Busselton, Dunsborough, Margaret River and Manjimup to Perth Airport and Elizabeth Quay Busport. **Integrity** (w integritycoachlines.com.au) focuses on the Mid West and the north of the state and offers a variety of routes, including hop-on, hop-off between Perth and up to as far north as Broome. Their terminus is Midland Train Station, but there is also a stop on Wellington Street, at the Perth Tourist Bus Stop.

BY CAR Perth is the central locus of the West Australian road network, and seemingly all roads lead here, even if you have no intention of visiting the city.

The main highways out of town are: the Kwinana Freeway, from Perth to Mandurah, where it changes its name to the Forrest Highway and continues onwards to Bunbury; the Albany Highway, which goes from the CBD all the way to the South Coast; the Mitchell Freeway, which will take you north out of the city to Joondalup, and from there, to Indian Ocean Drive (note that the Kwinana and the Mitchell are actually the same road, the name just changes); the Great Eastern Highway, which goes to Kalgoorlie; the Great Northern Highway, which goes through the Swan Valley northeast to the Murchison and Interior Mid West; and the Brand Highway, the circular Highway 1, which tacks inland to the north, before joining the coast in the Mid West just south of Dongara-Port Denison.

Car-hire companies, including all the major international brands, are located at Perth Airport and around the city. Consider very strongly the option of hiring a car at the airport as you will often get unlimited kilometres there, as opposed to a 100km daily limit in the city. Savvy West Australian travellers will often take this option – leave their personal car in the airport's reasonably priced long-term car park, and then take a hire car with its unlimited kilometres on a long road trip to reduce wear-and-tear on their own vehicles. If you do this, take out full insurance coverage and make sure you understand the conditions on the hire, including if there is a sunset-to-sunrise clause (see page 51 for more details).

GETTING AROUND

PUBLIC TRANSPORT Perth has a comprehensive public transport system, TransPerth (w transperth.wa.gov.au; ⊕ 05.00–00.30 Mon–Fri, 05.00–02.00 Fri–Sat, 05.00–midnight Sun), that consists of bus, ferry and train. Their online Journey Planner is useful to find the best route/method for reaching your destination. You can pay for tickets in cash, but more convenient are the reusable, reloadable SmartRider cards, which, after a A\$20 initial spend (A\$10 for the non-refundable A\$10 purchase of the card, and A\$10 for the initial minimum value), give you a 10% discount on fares (see website for a list of outlets where you can buy one). Tap the card on the kiosk as you enter and again when you leave and the fare is automatically deducted from your account; you can top-up at stations.

Fares are calculated on a zone system, and you are charged depending on the number of zones you cross. A fare through one zone will cost A\$3.20 (A\$2.88 using SmartRider); the maximum fare for a nine-zone trip is A\$13.10 (A\$11.79 on SmartRider). Your fare entitles you to travel anywhere within those set zones within a 2-hour limit, unless you are travelling through more than four zones at which point your time limit is 3 hours. The TransPerth app is free to download and offers maps and information on schedules.

DayRider (A\$13.10) passes allow unlimited travel on the day of purchase, but can only be used after 09.00 on weekdays. FamilyRider passes (A\$13.10) allow a group of seven unlimited travel on the day of purchase, but there are significant time restrictions involved.

By train Visitors will probably get most acquainted with the six TransPerth train lines, characterised by their silver-and-green carriages. The lines spoke out from Perth Station in the CBD to Joondalup (45mins), Armadale (40mins), Fremantle (30mins), Mandurah (50mins), Thornlie (25mins) and Midland (25mins) – each line named after the suburb that is its ultimate destination. The system is designed to carry people to Perth and back out again, so there's no circular line – to take the train from Mandurah (south of Perth) to Armadale (also south of Perth), you have to go into Perth, transfer there, and go back out on a different line. There is some overlap of stops on the Thornlie and Armadale lines.

The 'FTZ' is a Free Transit Zone where you are not charged a fare on buses and trains if you travel within that boundary. In Perth, this covers the area roughly west–east from Kings Park to the Swan River, and then north to Newcastle Street. For trains, the area is bounded by City West, Elizabeth Quay and Claisebrook stations.

By bus TransPerth offers a comprehensive public bus network, with fares payable through SmartRider. Additionally, TransPerth's CAT (Central Area Transit) buses are free and operate in loops. Red and Yellow CATs connect different parts of West Perth and East Perth, while Blue CATs link Northbridge to the Barrack Street Jetty and Green CATs go from Leederville to Elizabeth Quay. Services are frequent, about every 10 minutes or so. There are also CATs within Fremantle and Joondalup.

By boat The ferry crosses the Swan River to connect Elizabeth Quay, at the foot of the CBD, with the Mends Street Jetty in South Perth, near Perth Zoo. The ride takes 8 minutes and, while good fun, visitors are unlikely to get a lot of mileage out of it.

BY CAR Driving in Perth poses no particular hazards, though parking can be at a premium and traffic difficult. If you're heading into the CBD, it can pay off to plan your parking before you set out. **City of Perth Parking** (w cityofperthparking.com. au) facilities are denoted with orange and blue 'CPP' logos, while **Wilson Parking** (w wilsonparking.com.au) has a stylised white 'w' inside a red square – both websites show their car park locations. Metered parking exists elsewhere, with signs showing what hours meters operate and what hours are free. You collect a printed ticket from a machine (card payments accepted) and display it on your dashboard.

BY TAXI All taxis in WA are required to have a meter, and fares are governed by the Western Australia Department of Transport. In the metro area, flagfall is generally A\$4.50 during daylight hours and A\$6.50 from 18.00 to 06.00; the distance rate is A\$1.83/km and A\$52/hour of wait time. Along with those recommended outfits listed here, Uber also has a presence in the capital, and rides can be booked up to 30 days in advance, though pricing is variable.

Maxi Taxi ✆0406 553 313; w maxitaxiperth. com.au
Perth Taxi Services ✆0422 130 540; w perthtaxiservices.com

Swan Taxis ✆131 330; w swantaxis.com.au
Taxi Wizard ✆0476 519 665; w taxiwizard. com.au

BY BICYCLE Perth is by-and-large bike friendly – many major roads have bicycle lanes and there are dedicated bike shelters and lockers at TransPerth stations. That being said, Perth is not Amsterdam and most locals associate bikes with recreation rather than transportation. Helmets are required by law in WA, as are lights and reflectors on the bicycle. Bikes may share paths with pedestrians unless otherwise noted. For bike hire, try **Cycle Centre Perth** (23/326 Hay St; ✆9325 1176; w cyclecentre.com.au; from A\$25/day).

ON FOOT The Perth CBD, and some parts of the metro area like Fremantle, Guildford and Subiaco, are pedestrian-friendly and walking is a viable option. However, elsewhere distances can be great, the weather very hot and the sun intense – walking is a perfectly viable way to explore Perth in short bursts inside a concentrated area, but for longer journeys consider public transport, taxis or your own vehicle.

ORIENTATION

The Perth Metropolitan Area is quite big, but the City of Perth itself is quite small – as the metro area expanded, more and more suburbs decided to incorporate, and so the metro area is really a collection of small cities like Armadale, Canning, Stirling and Joondalup. As you travel through the metro area, where one of these cities ends and another begins is indistinguishable.

The metro area is shaped like a rectangle; roughly 110km from north to south, and 35km or so from the Indian Ocean to the west and the Perth Hills to the east. The Swan River divides the city between northern and southern halves; you'll often hear locals talk about a place being 'north' or 'south' of the river (which are metaphoric divisions since the river actually runs southwest to northeast). It is not a straight river, nor does it maintain roughly uniform size – it is fairly narrow near the ocean at Fremantle, then bulges out considerably almost into a lake near the CBD, before contracting again fairly dramatically on the other side of the city and petering out after about 70km – twisting and turning the whole way. The Canning River is a tributary and passes just south of the CBD.

The CBD sits on the northern bank of the Swan, with Kings Park and Subiaco to the immediate west, the Swan Valley to the north, the airport to the east and Rockingham to the south. The Swan River also divides Fremantle into North Fremantle, Fremantle and East Fremantle to the southwest of the CBD. It's about 25km from the CBD to Fremantle – they were separate towns in the colony's early days – 15km from the CBD north to Guildford, at the base of the Swan Valley, 27km east to Kalamunda in the Perth Hills, 48km south to Rockingham and 12km east to the airport. It's 34km to offshore Rottnest Island in the Indian Ocean, home of the quokka, but as there is no bridge, access is by ferry or air only. It might be easier to think of your orientation in terms of animal attractions – north to the koalas (Yanchep), south to the penguins (Rockingham/Penguin Island), west to the quokkas (Rottnest) and east to horses (equestrian in the Perth Hills).

Many visitors choose to stay in the CBD or near the Cappuccino Strip in Fremantle, but there are quality options across the whole metro area, and restaurants and amenities are spread fairly evenly through most neighbourhoods. Logistically it's probably easiest to stay in the CBD because the city's extensive transport system is mostly designed to take people to and from the CBD, rather than to connect suburb to suburb. But if you're spending more than a few days in the city, it is worth staying in a couple of neighbourhoods to soak up their individual character.

In terms of the CBD itself, the Mitchell Freeway, which changes its name to the Kwinana south of the river, is the main north–south artery in town and is the effective western boundary of the CBD, separating it from Kings Park. The Kwinana connects the Perth CBD with Mandurah; the road then changes its name again at Mandurah to the Forrest Highway and continues down to Bunbury. The main heart of the CBD roughly corresponds to an area bounded by the Mitchell Freeway and Plain Street running north–south, and Wellington Street and the Swan River running east–west. St Georges Terrace, Hay Street and Murray Street – running parallel to one another – are other key roads in the CBD.

Directly north of the CBD is the suburb of Northbridge – vibrant restaurants and cafés by day, rough-and-tumble by night – and Optus Stadium is to the east of the CBD – the Swan River makes one of its twists and turns directly north, and so in some sense is both the southern and eastern boundaries of the CBD (it is just beyond Plain Street). The pedestrian-only Matagarup Bridge, just east of the CBD, can be used to cross the Swan River and access the stadium from East Perth. Otherwise, take the Graham Farmer Freeway out of the CBD and East Perth across the river and exit on to Victoria Park Drive (you can't miss it).

TOURIST INFORMATION AND TOUR OPERATORS

There's no shortage of guided tours in Perth. The following operators are particularly recommended, but plenty of walking tours (both guided and self-guided) can be found and downloaded from the Visit Perth website (w visitperth.com/en/getting-around/walking-tours). One of the most popular is the 'Convicts and Colonials' tour, which takes in many government buildings such as the Town Hall and the Supreme Court, while the 'Icons of Influence' tour also takes in St Georges Terrace and explores Perth's history and rapid growth in the 19th century. For tourist information centres, see individual neighbourhoods in this chapter.

3

Aussie Perth Tours w aussieperthtours.com.
au. Offers intense full-day tours covering the CBD,
Fremantle, the Swan Valley & Kings Park. They also
organise Swan Valley wine & gourmet tasting tours
& trips to Yanchep National Park to see the koalas.
Best of Perth Tours w bestofperthtours.com.
au. Organises tours to the Swan Valley & the
Bickley-Carmel Wine Region in the Perth Hills, as
well as a city highlights tour.
Djurandi Dreaming w djurandi.com.au.
Tours showcasing Aboriginal culture, heritage &
Dreamtime stories, including in the CBD, Point
Peron in Rockingham & Kings Park. They also offer
Aboriginal art workshops.
Food Loose w foodloosetours.com.au. Branding
themselves as 'foodie experts' & 'ambassadors'
for Perth instead of tour guides, this company is
dedicated to helping visitors uncover the city's
authentic dining & drinking experiences. Featuring
different walking tours through the inner-city &
Chinatown, local culture & history is touched on
too. Private & group tours available from A$39 —
but this does not include food costs.

EMV Charter Vehicles and Kandu Tours
w emvchartervehicles.com.au. Led by Vicki, the
self-proclaimed friendliest tour operator in Perth,
this outfit offers Perth & Fremantle day tours with
a Swan River cruise, as well as a Swan Valley day
tour. A Yanchep tour to see koalas, going all the
way up to the Pinnacles in Cervantes, can also
be organised, as well as airport transfers.
Oh Hey WA w ohheywa.com.au. Offering
specialist focus on themes like architecture,
nightlife & history, this award-winning outfit has
a number of high-quality street art tours but also
bar & gin tours as well. Tours typically range about
2hrs & start from A$40.
Nyungar Tours w nyungartours.com.au. Offers
walks with Traditional Owners in Kings Park & the
rest of Perth, as well as trips to other cultural sites.
Owner Kerry-Ann Winmar is Whadjuk Noongar &
has been operating cultural tours for years.
Perth Explorer w perthexplorer.com.au. Hop-
on, hop-off bus tours across the CBD & Kings Park
with commentary.

CENTRAL PERTH

Perth's central area does not feel as rushed or as hurried as CBDs or downtowns
elsewhere, and why should it? The city's signature attraction, the massive Kings
Park botanical garden, is located here, as are the gentle flows of the Swan River, the
eclectic café and dining culture of the Subiaco and Northbridge neighbourhoods,
and the state's iconic beach at Cottesloe. The whole central region of the capital just
begs you to slow down, take a stroll, do some window shopping, find a gourmet bite
somewhere and then finish it off with a drink at a funky bar. The area sets the tone
for the relaxed vibe that defines the metro area. Even the traffic flows comparatively
gently here, providing an unintimidating atmosphere for pedestrians and cyclists,
unusual for the heart of such a major city.

A visit to WA should start with two or three days here, acclimatising to the
atmosphere, before branching out into Fremantle, the Swan Valley or the Perth Hills.

TOURIST INFORMATION
ℹ️ Western Australia Visitor Centre [79 C3]
55 William St; ☏ 9483 1111; w wavisitorcentre.

com.au; 🕐 09.00–16.00 Mon–Fri, 09.30–14.30
Sat–Sun

🏠 **WHERE TO STAY** Many of Perth's CBD hotels are oriented to business travellers,
but staying here ensures you a central location and access to the heart of the city's
transport network.

Luxury
✳️ 🏠 **COMO The Treasury** [79 D3] (48 rooms)
1 Cathedral Av; ☏ 6168 7888; w comohotels.
com/en/thetreasury. Luxury accommodation in

historic government buildings from the 1800s;
the restaurants, wellness facilities & colonial
atmosphere make this a unique experience in
the city. Though in historic digs, rooms aim for

contemporary luxury with hand-crafted furniture & posture-specialised beds. The oversized windows add extra light. Well worth it if your budget suits. **$$$$**

🏠 **QT** [79 D3] (184 rooms) 133 Murray St; 📞 9225 8000; **w** qthotels.com. Marble bathrooms with rain showers feature in this boutique hotel with standout purple, gold & black colour themes that give a sleek chic feel. The on-site Santini Grill features modern Italian fare, & there's a stylish rooftop bar. **$$$$**

🏠 **Ritz-Carlton** [79 C4] (205 rooms) 1 Barrack St; 📞 6559 6888; **w** ritzcarlton.com. One of hospitality's definitive luxury brands delivers nothing less in Perth, with a heated infinity pool overlooking the city, rooftop bars & superb river views from rooms, which boast seated areas & huge windows. The dining, spa treatments & sauna facilities are top notch. Recommended if you have the budget. **$$$$**

✱ 🏠 **Melbourne Hotel** [79 A2] (73 rooms) 33 Milligan St; 📞 9320 3333; **w** melbournehotel. com.au. Paying homage to the hotels of yore, this 1897 hotel has been completely refurbished in an attempt to restore it to its original glory. Heritage rooms are each unique with some opening on to an old-style veranda. A worthwhile stay in the CBD. **$$$**

Mid-range

🏠 **DoubleTree by Hilton Waterfront** [79 C4] (229 rooms) 1 Barrack Sq; 📞 6372 1000; **w** hilton. com. At 29m², rooms are spacious & arranged to capitalise on the bigger-than-normal feel. Some have panoramic views of the CBD skyline & it is worth booking one of these. The rooftop bar, 18 Knots, has great skyline views & a comprehensive wine list. **$$$**

🏠 **Duxton Hotel** [79 D4] (306 rooms) 1 St Georges Tce; 📞 9261 8000; **w** perth.duxtonhotels. com. In a hulking, imposing building, the Duxton looks like it is from a different era but the upscale, refurbished rooms inside are contemporary & comfortable, as are the en suites. Good deals are often on offer. The on-site Firewater Grille does an excellent beef tenderloin & the cocktail bar, with its retro motif, is great for an aperitif or digestif. **$$$**

✱ 🏠 **European Hotel** [79 D3] (52 rooms) 97 Murray St; 📞 9325 3900; **w** europeanhotel. au. What makes this CBD hotel a winner is the

competitive pricing & all-you-can-eat buffet b/fast which is known across Perth. Rooms are small but brightly decorated & surprisingly comfortable, with sparkling clean en suites. There is no on-site parking; you can pay to leave your car at a nearby garage. Very close to Perth Station. **$$$**

🏠 **Four Points by Sheraton** [79 A2] (278 rooms) 707 Wellington St; 📞 9327 7000; **w** marriott.com. Across from RAC Arena, functional but modern rooms have all the conveniences you would expect from this reliable global chain. The on-site restaurant does b/fast & there is a bar too; a good choice if you have business in this neighbourhood or need to be at the arena. **$$$**

🏠 **Intercontinental Perth City Centre** [79 B3] (240 rooms) 815 Hay St; 📞 9486 5700 **w** perth.intercontinental.com. Wide range of rooms here; the ones with city views, such as executive studios with 180-degree views, are worth booking. Décor is stylish & makes the rooms feel bigger. Penthouses are large (80m²) & have walk-in wardrobes. 24hr concierge, multiple restaurants using West Australian ingredients, drinks & canapes round out the features. **$$$**

🏠 **Mercure Perth** [79 D3] (239 rooms) 10 Irwin St; 📞 9326 7000; **w** mercureperth.com. au. With décor inspired by the city, rooms have flat-screen TVs, minibars & access to a laundry valet. Consider upgrading to a Privilege Room that has coffee machines & armchairs. The on-site restaurant & bar are good spots to wind down at the end of the day. **$$$**

🏠 **Pensione Perth** [79 D3] (98 rooms) 70 Pier St; 📞 9325 2133; **w** pensione.com.au/perth. A 1960s' theme permeates throughout with period furniture in the restored lobby; rooms here are functional but stylish. The free CAT stops across the street. **$$$**

🏠 **Tribe Kings Park** [map, page 71] (123 rooms) 4 Walker Av; 📞 6247 3333; **w** mytribehotel. com. Large, innovative hotel featuring intentionally designed 'living spaces' to promote relaxation & socialising. Rooms have park & city views, rain showers, floor-to-ceiling windows & smart TVs. **$$$**

Budget

🏠 **Bailey's Motel** [79 G3] (44 rooms) 150 Bennett St; 📞 9220 9555; **w** baileysmotel.com. au. Rooms are functional but what stands out here is the Bistro Bellavista pizzeria (5-time Gold Plate award winner) & the location – 10mins' walk from the stadium. **$$**

🏠 **Kangaroo Inn** [79 D3] (30 rooms) 123 Murray St; 📞 9325 3508; **w** kangarooinn.com.au. Private & shared rooms (2-, 4-, & 6-bunk) available at this high-quality backpackers' with communal facilities. Rooms have AC & there is a laundry, games room, reading room, theatre & kitchen facilities. **$**

✖ **WHERE TO EAT AND DRINK** The CBD has some good restaurants, particularly Asian, but large stretches of the area can become awfully quiet at night. Consider going into Northbridge (which has a vibrant restaurant and bar scene, but watch your valuables after dark) or Victoria Park – the Albany Highway here is chock-a-block with moderately priced eateries, again with an Asian focus. It pays to wander up and down the highway menu-gazing in the windows until you find something that interests you.

CBD

✖ **Amano Restaurant** [79 C4] Pier, Barrack St; 📞 9325 4575; **w** amanorestaurant.com. au; 🕐 noon–14.30 & 18.00–21.30 Wed–Thu, noon–14.30 & 17.30–21.30 Fri–Sun. With excellent views of the city from some tables, this Italian-Australian restaurant mixes good lasagne & tortellini with things like pumpkin ravioli, beetroot salad & kangaroo loin. Have the panna cotta for dessert. **$$$**

✳ ✖ **Angel Falls Grill** [79 B2] Shop 16 Shafto Ln; 📞 9468 7177; **w** angelfallsgrill.com. au; 🕐 11.00–14.30 & 17.00–20.00 Mon–Thu, 11.00–14.30 & 17.00–21.00 Fri, noon–21.00 Sat, noon–20.00 Sun. Venezuelan steakhouse offering arepas, empanadas, parrilla, pabellón & black beans & avocado. A great find in the CBD. **$$$**

✖ **Arirang Korean BBQ** [79 C3] 91–93 Barrack St; 📞 9225 4855; **w** arirang.com.au; 🕐 11.30–14.00 & 17.00–20.30 Mon–Thu, 11.30–15.00 & 17.00–21.30 Fri–Sat, 11.30–15.00 & 17.00–20.30 Sun. Popular Korean restaurant – a pioneer when they opened 20 years ago – with a grill in your table. Succulent bulgogi alongside bibimbap, ramen & fried chicken. **$$$**

PERTH CBD
For listings, see from page 76

🛏 **Where to stay**

1	Bailey's Motel	G3
2	COMO The Treasury	D3
3	DoubleTree by Hilton Waterfront	C4
4	Duxton	D4
5	European	D3
6	Four Points by Sheraton	A2
7	Intercontinental Perth City Centre	B3
8	Kangaroo Inn	D3
9	Melbourne	A2
10	Mercure Perth	D3
11	Pensione Perth	D3
12	QT	D3
13	Ritz-Carlton	C4

❌ **Where to eat and drink**

14	Amano	C4
15	Angel Falls Grill	B2
16	Arirang Korean BBQ	C3
17	Canton Bay	C1
18	La Veen Coffee	B2
19	Le Vietnam	D3
20	Louder Louder	C1
21	My Bayon	C1
22	New Sahara Middle Eastern Cuisine	D3
23	Outback Jack's	C1
24	Red Opium	E3
25	Sauma	C1
26	Twilight Hawkers Market	C2
27	Uma	E4

✖ **Uma** [79 E4] 207 Adelaide Tce; 📞 6211 7221; **w** umaperth.com.au; 🕐 17.30–21.30 Thu–Sat. Peruvian restaurant with an award-winning chef, adding a unique flavour to the Perth dining scene. An array of ceviches with local ingredients like Fremantle octopus are on offer, as well as tasty beef & seafood grills like Margaret River beef & rainbow trout. **$$$**

✖ **La Veen Coffee** [79 B2] 90 King St; 📞 9321 1188; **w** laveencoffee.com.au; 🕐 06.15–14.00 Mon–Fri, 07.15–14.00 Sat–Sun. Get your morning caffeine fix in this Heritage-listed, red-brick building in the CBD. Traditional cooked b/fasts plus items like smashed avo, hummus & espresso tiramisu make this a winner for b/fast or brunch. **$$**

✖ **Le Vietnam** [79 D3] 80 Barrack St; 📞 6114 8038; 🕐 10.00–15.00 Mon–Fri. Great bánh mì & lots of vegan options. Wide selection of beers. The word is out & it gets very busy. **$$**

✖ **New Sahara Middle Eastern Cuisine** [79 D3] 48 Pier St; 📞 6114 6143; **w** newsahararestaurants.com.au; 🕐 11.00–21.00 Sat–Thu, 11.00–22.00 Fri. Jordanian-

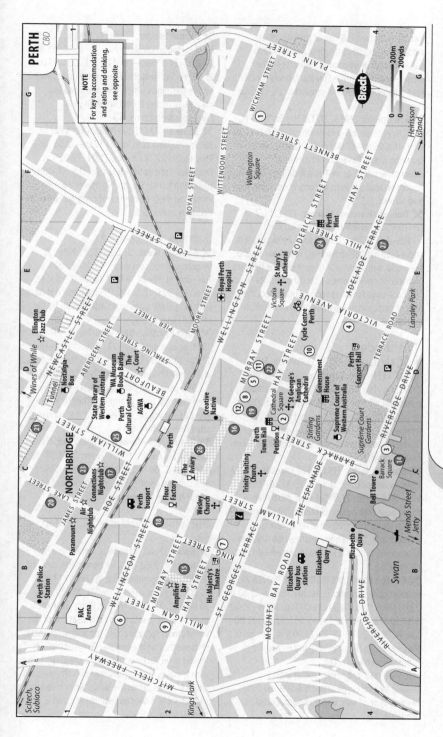

PERTH CBD

NOTE
For key to accommodation and eating and drinking, see opposite

Scitech, Subiaco

Kings Park

MITCHELL FREEWAY

RAC Arena

Perth Police Station

NORTHBRIDGE

Paramount Nightclub

Air Nightclub

Connections Nightclub

Wines of While

Ellington Jazz Club

Nostalgia Box

WA Museum Boola Bardip

The Court

State Library of Western Australia

Perth Cultural Centre

AGWA

Perth busport

Flour Factory

The Aviary

Creative Native

Trinity Uniting Church

Wesley Church

Amplifier Bar

His Majesty's Theatre

Perth Town Hall

Petition

St George's Anglican Cathedral

Cathedral Square

Stirling Gardens

Government House

Supreme Court of Western Australia

Supreme Court Gardens

Perth Concert Hall

St Mary's Cathedral

Victoria Square

Clyde Centre Perth

Royal Perth Hospital

Perth Mint

Elizabeth Quay

Elizabeth Quay bus station

Bell Tower

Barrack Square

Mends Street Jetty

Swan

Heirisson Island

Langley Park

WILLIAM STREET
LAKE STREET
JAMES STREET
ABERDEEN STREET
NEWCASTLE STREET
BEAUFORT STREET
ST GEORGES TERRACE
HAY STREET
MURRAY STREET
WELLINGTON STREET
MILLIGAN STREET
KING STREET
BARRACK STREET
PIER STREET
VICTORIA AVENUE
WELLINGTON STREET
MURRAY STREET
HAY STREET
ROE STREET
STIRLING STREET
LORD STREET
MOORE STREET
ROYAL STREET
WITTENOOM STREET
WICKHAM STREET
PLAIN STREET
GODERICH STREET
HILL STREET
BENNETT STREET
ADELAIDE TERRACE
TERRACE ROAD
RIVERSIDE DRIVE
THE ESPLANADE
MOUNTS BAY ROAD

Wellington Square

Tunnel

0 200m
0 200yds

N

1
2
3
4
5
6
7
8
9
10
11
12
13
14
15
16
17
18
19
20
21
22
23
24
25
26

owned restaurant – & one of the only places outside the Middle East where I've ever seen *mansaf* (lamb in fermented yoghurt) on the menu – featuring grilled meats, falafels & other Arab staples. The décor is simple but the cooking is good. $$

✖ **Red Opium** [79 E3] 21/326 Hay St; ✆ 9221 8780; w red-opium.business.site; ⊕ 18.00–21.30 Wed–Thu, 06.00–22.00 Fri–Sat. Thai restaurant featuring highly flavourful set menus at competitive prices, as well as stand-alone courses. Noodle-wrapped prawns are very good. Bring your own alcohol. $$

✖ **Twilight Hawkers Market** [79 C2] 1/7 Forrest Pl; w twilighthawkersmarket.com; ⊕ Nov–Feb 16.30–21.30 Fri only. Perth's biggest street-food market, showcasing food from around the world, with live music to ease into the summer nights & warm weekends. Check the website & Facebook page for who's serving, but expect the likes of empanadas, Japanese noodles & Turkish gözleme. $

Northbridge

☀ ✖ **My Bayon** [79 C1] 313 William St; ✆ 9227 1331; w mybayon.com.au; ⊕ 16.00–21.00 Sun–Thu, 16.00–21.30 Fri–Sat. Cambodian restaurant with beef lok lak & oyster sauce to go with strong stir-fries. The char kroeung & lemongrass chilli chicken are also good. An interesting addition to the CBD's southeast Asian dining scene. $$$

✖ **Outback Jack's** [79 C1] 124 James St; ✆ 9227 7346; w outbackjacks.com.au; ⊕ 11.30–21.00 Mon–Fri & 11.30–22.00 Sat–Sun. Australian steakhouse with flavourful burgers, ribs & steaks – & an intriguing selection of bush meats like crocodile ribs. Try the game platter with croc, emu, boar, camel, buffalo & kangaroo, served with bush chutney. $$$

✖ **Canton Bay** [79 C1] 20 Roe St; ✆ 9228 2198; w cantonbay.com.au; ⊕ 10.30–15.00 & 17.30–22.00 Mon–Wed, 10.30–15.00 Thu, 10.30–15.00 & 17.30–23.00 Fri, 10.00–15.00 & 17.30–23.00 Sat, 10.00–15.00 & 17.30–22.00 Sun. Our go-to for dim sum in the city – the prawn & chive is especially good, as is the soft-shell crab. Exhaustive menu with seemingly every type of meat & seafood done in every type of way. Banquet options also available. $$

✖ **Louder Louder** [79 C1] 47 Lake St; ✆ 9228 9358; w louderlouder.com.au; ⊕ 11.00–15.00 & 17.00–21.00 Sun–Thu, 11.00–15.00 & 17.00–22.00 Fri–Sat. Beautiful Thai food complemented by fine Australian wines. The prawn pad Thai, massaman curries & beef ribs with potato & pineapple are winners. $$

✖ **Sauma** [79 C1] 200 William St; ✆ 9227 8682; w sauma.com.au; ⊕ 17.00–22.00 Tue–Thu, 11.00–22.30 Fri–Sat, 11.00–22.00 Sun. Beautifully presented Indian street food. Paneer tikka with honey & pistachio makes a great entrée, while the banana leaf curry & the dal are delicious mains. $$

Subiaco *Map, page 71*

✖ **George's Meze** 26 Denis St; ✆ 9388 1585; w georgesmeze.com.au; ⊕ 17.30–20.00 Tue–Thu, 11.30–14.30 & 17.30–21.00 Fri–Sat, 11.30–14.30 & 17.30–20.00 Sun. Greek restaurant with tasty lamb souvlaki, tzatziki & dips. Try the seafood claypot. $$$

✖ **Lapa Brazilian BBQ** 375 Hay St; ✆ 9381 1323; w lapa.net.au; ⊕ 18.00–9.45 Wed–Thu, 17.30–20.00 Fri–Sat, 17.30–19.45 Sun. Named after a neighbourhood in Rio, the *churrasco* here – a BBQ feast of 16 different meats – will satisfy even the most finicky carnivore. There is also an all-you-can-eat veggie 'Endless Feast' featuring pasta, salad & vegetables. $$$

✖ **Architects & Heroes** 25 Rokeby Rd; ✆ 0450 308 224; ⨏ ArchitectsAndHeroes; ⊕ 06.30–13.30 Mon–Sat, 07.00–13.30 Sun. Some of Subiaco's best coffee is on offer here, plus good beef noodle salads & bagel burgers. $$

Burswood & Victoria Park *Map, page 71*

✖ **Nobu** Crown Metropol, Great Eastern Hwy, Burswood; ✆ 9362 7551; w crownperth.com.au/restaurants/premium/nobu; ⊕ noon–14.00 & 17.30–21.30 Sun–Thu, noon–14.00 & 17.30–20.00 & 20.30–22.30 Fri–Sat. If you are in the mood & want to splurge, do it here at one of the world's most recognisable & innovative Japanese restaurants. Truffle edamame, Wagyu striploins, lobster sushi, tartar with caviar & champagne to go with it makes for a decidedly memorable evening. Lunch features things like bento boxes with lobster spinach salad & beef tenderloin with truffle teriyaki sauce. $$$$

✖ **Victoria Park Hotel** 605 Albany Hwy, Victoria Park; ✆ 9460 9938; w victoriaparkhotel. com.au; ⏱ 11.00–22.00 Sun–Tue, 11.00–23.00 Wed–Fri, 11.00–midnight Sat. Popular pub with some twists on traditional classics like chilli maple chicken & coconut-battered snapper. Steaks, chicken parmis, loaded fries & vegetarian/vegan options available too. **$$$**

✳ ✖ **Elie's Tent Lebanese Restaurant** 610 Albany Hwy, Victoria Park; ✆ 6111 4145; w eliestent.com.au; ⏱ 11.00–21.00 Mon–Thu, 11.00–23.00 Fri–Sat, 17.30–21.00 Sun. Owned by a Lebanese couple who do all the cooking themselves & with *majlis* seating (cushions on the floor) to go with tables, every menu item here is done to perfection – it is hard to narrow down what to choose from on the long list of mezze. We try to eat here at least once every time we're in town; I usually go with the BBQ platter & never, ever regret it. Baklava & Lebanese coffee is a

great way to round off the meal. The owners are incredibly friendly & hospitable. **$$**

West towards Cottesloe *Map, page 68*

✖ **Chez Pierre** 131 Stirling Hwy, Nedlands; ✆ 9386 5886; w chezpierre.com.au; ⏱ noon–15.00 & 18.00–midnight Wed–Fri, 18.00–midnight Tue & Sat. French restaurant near Cottesloe with upscale cuisine. Regional menus highlighting a different part of France star & there are à la carte & degustation menus. Classics like French onion soup & cheese soufflé are done well, as is the beef. **$$$**

✖ **Il Lido** 88 Marine Pde, Cottesloe; ✆ 9286 1111; w illido.com.au; ⏱ 07.00–midnight daily. In a near-century-old Art Deco building, this Italian restaurant specialises in pastas though also has an 'Oyster Sunday' & extensive drinks list. There is also an espresso bar & pastries. **$$$**

ENTERTAINMENT AND NIGHTLIFE Perth may not be Ibiza or Miami, but it still offers a decent spread of nightlife options, mostly concentrated in and around the CBD. The epicentre of Perth's club scene is Northbridge, while Subiaco has a more upscale vibe and is better for boutique and trendy bars. The Esplanade in Scarborough also has a few noteworthy venues if you're staying up that way.

Bars and clubs

♀ **The Aviary** [79 C2] 140 William St; w theaviaryperth.com.au; ⏱ 11.00–21.00 Sun–Tue, 11.00–22.00 Wed–Thu, 11.00–01.00 Fri–Sat. Rooftop bar with skyline views. Menu of burgers, pizzas & crumbed halloumi to get you through to another cocktail.

♀ **The Boardroom** [map, page 71] 94 Rokeby Rd, Subiaco; w theboardroomsubi.com.au; ⏱ Mon–Sat 11.00–late; Sun 11.00–22.00. Neat cocktail bar serving espresso martinis alongside premium beers & pizzas, pasta & oysters.

♀ **Flour Factory** [79 C2] 16 Queen St; w theflourfactory.com; ⏱ 16.00–22.00 Wed–Thu, 16.00–midnight Fri–Sat. Rooftop bar on top of – you guessed it – a renovated flour factory. Gin specialists with Perth's largest collection, both from Australia & worldwide. If you can't decide they will spin a wheel to determine your fate.

♀ **Juanita's** [map, page 71] 341 Rokeby Rd, Subiaco; w juanitasbar.com.au; ⏱ 14.00–22.00 Tue–Wed, 14.00–23.00 Thu–Sat, Sun 15.00–21.00 Sun. Trendy wine bar with expansive array of

Australian & international wines, complemented with terrines & parfaits.

♀ **Old Laundry Bar & Kitchen** [map, page 71] 22 Angrove St; w theoldlaundry.net; ⏱ 07.00–22.00 daily. Cocktails & digestifs, along with an extensive wine menu & 3 meals a day. The interior pays tribute to old laundries that used to operate in Perth in the early 1900s.

♀ **Petition** [79 C3] Cnr St Georges Tce & Barrack St; w petitionperth.com; ⏱ call for hours. Multi-purpose venue situated within the State Buildings. Large wine list with plates to accompany them; the 'Beer Corner' has numerous European & North American offerings, the staff will guide you through West Australian options, & what's on tap is on constant rotation.

♀ **Refuge Small Bar** [map, page 71] 5/50 Subiaco Square Rd; w refugesmallbar.com.au; ⏱ noon–late Mon–Sat. Craft beer bar with a range of pub food like chicken wings, parmis & burgers.

♀ **Wines of While** [79 D1] 458 William St, Northbridge; ✆ 9328 3332; w winesofwhile.com; ⏱ 16.00–midnight Tue–Thu, noon–midnight

Perth is LGBTQ+-friendly, and many of the establishments listed cater to LGBTQ+ customers, but here are a few other recommendations.

✖ Sparrow's Nest   [map, page 71] 1/912 Albany Hwy; ■ TheSparrowsNestCafe; ⏰ 08.00–15.00 Sun–Mon, 07.00–15.00 Tue–Sat. Chilled hangout in Victoria Park, with games like Uno & Connect Four & eclectic décor – you're given a playing card for your table number. Well-priced & classic items like French toast or more unique creations like fried chicken benedict.

☆ Connections Nightclub   [79 C1] 81 James St, Northbridge; w connections

nightclub.com; ⏰ see website. The longest-running LGBTQ+ nightclub in the southern hemisphere, serving Northbridge since the 1970s, there is no dress code & they are known for wild & diverse themes – everything from lesbian mud wrestling to bingo. Also plenty of drinks & dancing.

☆ The Court   [79 D2] 50 Beaufort St; w thecourt.com.au; ⏰ see website. One of Perth's leading & best-known LGBTQ+ venues – 4 bars across 2 floors plus a pizza bar.

Fri–Sat, noon–22.00 Sun. Wine store & bar dedicated to sourcing handmade wines grown without chemicals. They serve seasonal plates too, changing daily.

☆ Air Nightclub   [79 C1] 139 James St, Northbridge; w airclub.com.au; ⏰ from 21.00 Fri–Sat. With an airplane theme, DJs, dancing & bottle service abound at this party hub.

☆ Amplifier Bar   [79 B2] 393 Murray St; w amplifierbar.com; ⏰ 20.00–04.00 Fri, 20.00–05.00 Sat. Combining live music (including house bands, & original & visiting acts) with bowling, this place jumps until sunrise.

☆ Ellington Jazz Club   [79 D1] 191 Beaufort St; ☎ 9228 1088; w ellingtonjazz.com.au; ⏰ contact for hours. Jazz club featuring acts from right across Australia – book by the seat or by the table.

☆ Paramount   [79 B1] 163 James St, Northbridge; w paramountnightclub.com.au; ⏰ 21.00–05.00 Fri–Sat. Massive club with 6 bars over 2 floors; live bands, house DJs & an attractive setting with disco balls & multi-coloured lights.

THEATRE AND THE ARTS   Theatre goers should try and catch a show at **His Majesty's Theatre** [79 B2] (827–905 Hay St; w ptt.wa.gov.au). When it opened on Christmas Eve 1904, it was the largest theatre of its kind in Australia. Today, shows range from black comedies like *Hell Hath No Fury* to Neil Diamond tribute acts. Guided tours of the facility are also on offer; check the website for times and prices. There are numerous theatre companies in Perth, one of the most notable being the **Black Swan State Theatre Company** (w bsstc.com.au) who put on many original performances at a range of venues.

Perth Concert Hall [79 D4] (5 St Georges Tce; w perthconcerthall.com.au) is the main venue of the West Australian Symphony Orchestra (w waso.com.au) and also hosts musicals and other performances such as the West Australian Opera (w waopera.asn.au).

The **Perth Cultural Centre** [79 C1] (Francis St & William St, Northbridge; w perthculturalcentre.com.au) is the hub of the state's arts scene. Alongside AGWA (page 85) and WA Museum Boola Bardip (page 86), it also houses the Perth Institute of Contemporary Arts (w pica.org.au) – one of the state's top exhibition spaces, including dance, theatre and interdisciplinary works – two independent theatres and the State Library of Western Australia (w slwa.wa.gov.au), which offers heaps of information about WA's heritage, including a film room, in addition to its books.

SPORT Opened in 2018 for the AFL's West Coast Eagles and Fremantle Dockers, the 60,000-seat **Optus Stadium** has been an immediate smash hit and, in addition to its signature footy contests, also hosts an array of rugby, cricket, concerts and other entertainment events. One of the highlights is actually getting there – the 600m-long **Matagarup Footbridge**, resembling two swans, with arches reaching 72m high, connects the stadium's surrounding parkland to East Perth over the Swan River.

SHOPPING Shopping in the CBD is concentrated around pedestrian malls and a few big centres; most of the more interesting boutique shopping is found in Fremantle and Guildford.

Creative Native [79 D2] 158 Murray St; w creativenative.com.au; ⊕ 10.00–17.00 Mon–Sat, 11.00–16.00 Sun. Showcases emerging Aboriginal artists & has an extensive collection of digeridoos & boomerangs – they also highlight rare works & host workshops & exhibitions.
Subi Farmers' Market [map, page 71] 271 Bagot Rd; w subifarmersmarket.com.au; ⊕ 08.00–noon Sat. On the grounds of Subiaco Primary School, this offers a range of seasonal produce from around the capital area as well as stalls with plants, pastries, honey & other goodies. Check the website, updated regularly, to see what stalls will be on when you're planning to visit.
Tunbridge Gallery Shop 6 Napoleon Close, Cottesloe; w tunbridgegallery.com.au; ⊕ 10.00–15.00 Thu–Sat. A good introduction to Aboriginal art, stocking work from the Kimberley, Pilbara, Western Deserts & top end of Northern Territory. It aims to educate customers about the art & artists too.

OTHER PRACTICALITIES
Perth Police Station [79 B1] 2 Fitzgerald St, Northbridge; ☎ 9422 7111
Royal Perth Hospital [79 E3] Victoria Sq; ☎ 9224 2244

WHAT TO SEE AND DO
The CBD As you drive in on the Mitchell or the Kwinana, Perth's CBD seems to rise up out of nowhere; a small cluster of gleaming skyscrapers that would not be out of place in Dubai or Tokyo. But Perth is not a dense urban jungle of high-rises; they are concentrated in the fairly compact (3km by 1km) and highly walkable CBD, providing a stark visible contrast to the rest of the city. The CBD forms a rectangle, with the Swan River forming its southern and eastern boundaries, Kings Park its western boundary and Wellington Street its northern boundary. Inside, ample one-way streets, pedestrian malls and a plethora of cafés and restaurants invite leisurely exploration – a big city without all the big city hassle. Even parking isn't a problem (well, not *that* big a problem anyway) – large ticketed garages are easy to find across the CBD.

Cathedral Square (w cathedralsquare.com.au) Perth was founded here in 1829, and this spot remains one of the CBD's focal points with its cathedral, town hall and old government buildings. Old and new contrast sharply here – with the hulking, modernist City of Perth's administration building now across the street.

Its most striking figure is the imposing **St George's Anglican Cathedral** [79 D3] (38 St Georges Tce; w perthcathedral.org; ⊕ 07.00–17.00 daily), a Gothic Revival church built in 1888 with handmade bricks. The showpiece of the Anglican Church in WA, it remains one of the most important religious institutions in the state – its brick interior arches and walls, chandeliers and deeply sloped roof give it an understated elegance. The grounds have memorials to important West Australians and soldiers, and a Soldiers' Chapel that honours Anglican soldiers who fought for Australia in World War I. The cathedral's choir is nationally acclaimed and there are often lunchtime concerts; see website for dates.

Opposite the cathedral are the **State Buildings** (St Georges Tce & Barrack St; w statebuildings.com). Western Australia's government centre since the 1870s, the site has seemingly hosted every government agency at one time or another, from immigration to treasury to the police court to the premier's office. Its final tenant was the Department of Land Administration, which left in 1993. Redevelopment some years later saw it begin to regain its former glory as an entertainment centre and today it is steeped in historical elegance with dozens of boutiques, dining options and a luxurious hotel (page 76).

In the northwest corner of the square – behind the skyscraper housing the David Malcolm Justice Centre – is **Perth Town Hall** [79 C3] (601 Hay St; ⊕ 10.00–16.00 Mon–Sat), built in 1870, Australia's only Gothic-style town hall and the only one built by convict labour (see box, above). Restored to its original glory between 1995 to 2005, it is one of Perth's most distinctive buildings with a medieval, castle-like appearance. It is still used as a hall and frequently hosts banquets and other civic events – though the interior is a much more simple and functional space. Its 38m-tall clock tower for many years hosted a series of shops on its ground level.

Barrack Square and Elizabeth Quay On the banks of the Swan, 400m south of Cathedral Square, Elizabeth Quay is the brainchild of former premier Colin Barnett – who said he decided the need for riverfront redevelopment after walking Brisbane's South Bank with his wife in 2009, making him realise Perth's vibrancy had fallen significantly behind not just Asian cities but Australian ones too. And so in 2016, the 10ha, A$440 million mixed-retail and housing centre with promenades, restaurants and shops was opened.

The area is dominated by the pointy, 82.5m-tall **Bell Tower** [79 C4] (Riverside Dr; w thebelltower.com.au; ⊕ 10.00–16.00 Thu–Sun), home to the 18 Swan Bells, a dozen of which came from St-Martin-in-the-Fields Church, Buckingham Palace's parish church in London. The bells rang in Trafalgar Square for centuries before being donated to WA for the nation's bicentenary celebrations in 1988. The bells ring Monday, Thursday and Sunday for an hour from noon, and there are interactive exhibits inside on how to ring the bells. If you think that bell ringing is just about standing around pulling ropes, a visit here will change your perception.

On the other side of Riverside Drive from the square are the well-manicured **Supreme Court Gardens** [79 C4] and **Stirling Gardens** [79 C3], Perth's oldest gardens, a landscape classified by the National Trust and originally used in the 1830s to help cultivate plants from seeds. Both gardens surround Perth's oldest building – the **Supreme Court of Western Australia** [79 C4], dating from 1836. Today this houses the **Old Court House Law Museum** (28 Barrack St; w lawsocietywa.asn.au; ◷ 10.00–16.00 Tue–Fri; free), one of the world's only law museums, home to over 2,000 artefacts that document the legal history of WA dating back to colonial times.

Nearby is the striking façade of **Government House** [79 D4] (13 St Georges Tce; w govhouse.wa.gov.au), the official residence of the Governor of Western Australia. The 1863 orange-pink Gothic Revival-style building was mostly built by convict labour and features chequerboard slate and stone floors, Victorian-era stained glass and a Bechstein boudoir grand piano. Visitor tours are not offered, but the gardens are open (◷ noon–14.00 Tue–Thu), and open days to see inside the house are periodically offered – check the website.

Perth Mint [79 E3] (310 Hay St; w perthmint.com; ◷ 09.00–17.00 Mon–Sat) Established as a branch of the UK Royal Mint in 1899 – and the only one in Australia still operating – this is where diggers would take their finds from the Goldfields for conversion into coins. Today it has branched out and, in addition to work with gold, also services other precious metals. Coins and bars made here are shipped out the world over. The world's largest coin, the Australian Kangaroo One Tonne Gold Coin, was made here in 2011 – a 1-tonne, 80cm x 12cm, 99.99%-pure gold coin with a kangaroo on it, still displayed here today. Tours include seeing a live gold pour.

Notable churches Dating from 1865, **St Mary's Cathedral** [79 E3] (Victoria Sq; w stmaryscathedralperth.com.au) is Perth's signature Catholic worship house, which was built in multiple stages over nearly 150 years. It is one of the oldest buildings in the state, and guided tours are offered (◷ Tue 10.30; A$10) that include the crypt. Heritage-listed **Wesley Church** [79 C2] (75 William St; w perthunitingchurch.org. au/wesley-church) is Perth's central Methodist church, built in the Victorian Gothic style in 1867; the organ inside is over 100 years old. With its twin towers, **Trinity Uniting Church** [79 C3] (72 St Georges Tce; w perthunitingchurch.org.au) is also Heritage-listed; it was built in 1893, in the American-Romanesque style, which distinguishes it from the British-influenced designs of the time.

Northbridge Northbridge is Perth's party and nightclub centre, and has a bit of an edge to it – one West Australian newspaper labelled James Street, Northbridge's main road, 'Perth's filthiest strip' due to the prevalence of 'grime and gum' from party animals. That being said, I have never felt particularly unsafe here and have no hesitation exploring on my own. Northbridge is also where you'll find **Chinatown**, a fairly new addition to the city's streetscape – dating from the 1980s – though there has been a Chinese population in WA since the 1840s. The entrance gate is along Roe Street, and every year tens of thousands gather here for the Lunar New Year celebrations.

Art Gallery of Western Australia (AGWA) [79 D2] (Francis St & William St; w artgallery.wa.gov.au; ◷ 10.00–17.00 Wed–Mon; donation welcomed, free guided tours available) Housed in the Perth Cultural Centre (page 82), the 18,000+ works here – the first one purchased in 1895, including paintings, sculptures and indigenous works – are the state's premier collection. The gallery is diverse, with art from Aboriginal and Torres Strait Islander peoples, 20th-century Australian and

British artists as well as those from the state. In late 2021, it launched 'The View From Here', the gallery's largest-ever showcase of West Australian art, involving 230 artists and 361 works. The rooftop has also been converted as a part of this, framed by the Perth skyline, with an open-air sculpture walk.

WA Museum Boola Bardip [79 D2] (Francis St & William St; w visit.museum. wa.gov.au; ⏱ 09.00–17.00 daily; free) Originally established in 1891 at the old Perth gaol, the name of this museum means 'many stories' in the Noongar language – appropriate for an institution that views itself as a centre for the exchange and communication of WA's stories. The connection between people and place is a special emphasis of this museum, and this permeates through all its exhibits, transforming the space from a dull display of objects into a vibrant showcase of Western Australia, its people, stories and land, in all entirety.

The museum is organised around three themes: 'Being West Australian', geared towards showcasing the state's diversity; 'Discovering Western Australia', offering visitors a gateway to the wonders of the state; and 'Exploring the World (Western Australia's place in it)', which aims to define the state and its contrasts and niche in the global community. Permanent exhibitions include 'Reflections', which explores perspectives of different West Australians that make the state what it is – from those descendent from millennia-old Aboriginal cultures to new migrants – while 'Changes' looks at how humans have changed the environment to suit their needs – from Aboriginal land management to contemporary financial uses like mining.

Nostalgia Box [79 D1] (1/16 Aberdeen St; w thenostalgiabox.com.au; ⏱ 11.00–16.00 Fri–Sun; A$18.70/13.20 adult/child) Gamers will love this museum dedicated to video game consoles, with over 100 on display including old-school Atari and Nintendo sets. There's also an area to play vintage games like old favourites, Pac-Man and Space Invaders.

Scitech (Cnr Railway St & Sutherland St; w scitech.org.au; ⏱ 09.30–16.00 Mon–Fri, 10.00–16.00 Sat–Sun; A$19/12 adult/child) Interactive planetarium and science museum aimed at children and school students, with some 160 hands-on exhibits covering everything from trees to the search for alien life, plus light shows and other science-themed programmes.

Kings Park ☀ (Fraser Av; w bgpa.wa.gov.au; ⏱ 24hrs, free guided tours at 10.00, noon & 14.00 daily) This huge 400ha botanical garden and nature reserve on the CBD's western border is undoubtedly Perth's signature attraction. Its beauty and importance was recognised almost immediately by the British upon settlement – John Septimus Roe, the first Surveyor-General of Western Australia, attempted to have the area protected as early as the 1830s but was unsuccessful and the area was logged, until his successor Malcolm Fraser persuaded then-Governor of Western Australia Frederick Weld to protect it in 1871; further governments periodically enlarged the area to its present size over the years. Aside from being one of the world's premier botanical gardens, it serves as a focal point for the entire Perth Metropolitan Area (and even the state) and is an integral part of the city's identity.

Enter the park through the red-flowering gum-lined **Fraser Avenue**, which leads to the entrance of two of the park's most-visited attractions – the Western Australian Botanic Garden and the State War Memorial. This is also where you'll find the visitor centre (from where you can pick up a map), Aspects of Kings Park (the gift shop, from where guided tours leave), Frasers Restaurant and the Floral

Clock, an operating timepiece on a huge bed of flora, originally designed in 1962. Strolling down Fraser Avenue is one of Perth's great pastimes, with its lemon-scented eucalypts lining both sides; a memorial plaque sits at the foot of each tree, commemorating a prominent West Australian. Just opposite the restaurant is the **Kaarta Gar-up Lookout,** from where the views over the Swan River and the city, as well as out to the Darling Scarp, are some of the best in WA – note two of Perth's tallest skyscrapers, 234m-high Brookfield Place (with the BHP Billiton name on it) and 249m Central Park (emblazoned with Rio Tinto) just to the left. At sunrise or sunset, it's a living postcard and a must-see on a Perth visit.

Fraser Avenue ends at the **State War Memorial precinct,** site of one of WA's largest ANZAC Dawn Services (40,000 people annually), which frames another spectacular view over the water and to the city skyline. An 18m obelisk honours all West Australians who have lost their lives in the service of Australia; the Flame of Remembrance in the Pool of Reflection in the same precinct is always burning, and represents the promise of West Australians. There are various other war memorials dotted around the park, and the **Memorials Walk** has 12 points of interest, including the South African War Memorial for West Australians who died serving in the Boer War and the Aboriginal and Torres Strait Islander War Memorial near the Roe car park. There are also monuments to those lost at Kokoda, Gallipoli, Crimea, Waterloo, Jews who died in both world wars, and those killed in the Bali terrorist attack in 2002.

Encompassing some 17ha, the **Western Australian Botanic Garden,** opened in 1965, features a staggering 25% of all flora found in WA. Much of it is grouped by region, and there are Wheatbelt and Great Southern plantings, as well as areas for Rottnest, Mulga and other WA locations. The wildflower display here in late winter is spectacular and showcases the state in miniature. The Conservation Garden is a highlight, featuring over 400 specimens of the state's endangered flora like the endemic Cranbrook bell, with a red-and-white flowering bell that droops upside-down, the Kalbarri yellow bell, whose bright-yellow flower resembles two five-pointed stars on top of each other, and the multi-fingered, yellow-with-red-fringe golden catspaw. The Banksia Garden is also a joy to explore; the plant is a point of pride and a symbol of WA identity, with 62 of the 76 species in Australia native to the state, and all are represented here. Above all of this, snaking through the treetops, is the 620m Lotterywest Federation Walkway, a highlight of which is the 22m-long steel, arched bridge up in the tops of the eucalypts.

Aboriginal culture features prominently within the garden. The 3.2km **Boodja Gnarning Walk** explores bush tucker (food), traditional medicines, Noongar language and indigenous use of plants, while on the Lotterywest Federation Walkway is a giant boab tree, the **Gija Jumulu,** which is estimated to be 750 years old and was a gift from the Gija people in the Kimberley region.

Roughly two-thirds of Kings Park is native bush, and the **Bushland Nature Trail** departs from the botanic garden car park, featuring banksias, wild violets, kangaroo paws and other flora in season. If you're with kids, the 6ha **Rio Tinto Naturescape** is a must. With the idea of reconnecting with nature at its core, the area aims to give city kids an interactive bush experience. Children can explore and play in a waterhole, and there are tunnels, bridges and ropes to scramble on and climb.

University of Western Australia (35 Stirling Hwy; w uwa.edu.au) Occupying an enviable position bordering Kings Park and the Swan River, the state's premier institution of higher learning welcomed its first students in 1913 and today hosts some 20,000. The signature building here, Winthrop Hall, invokes Spain and

Italy in its Mediterranean-style and with its clock tower; it was built in 1932 and designed by Rodney Alsop and Conrad Sayce, two Melbourne architects. American servicemen stayed here during World War II, and post-war the university continued to grow and expand to become one of Australia's most prestigious. You can tour the grounds – the university provides an audio tour that hits 15 highlights including Winthrop Hall, the Earth Science Museum and the New Fortune Theatre, which is said to be a reconstruction of its London namesake.

Perth Zoo (20 Labouchere Rd; w perthzoo.wa.gov.au; ⊕ 09.00–17.00 daily; A\$34/17 adult/child) Just across the river from Kings Park and the CBD in South Perth, this 125-year-old zoo houses both local favourites like bilbies, black cockatoos, potoroos, tree kangaroos and gliders and far-away exotics like lions, lemurs and penguins. You can get to the zoo by ferry from the CBD – the entrance is 500m from the Mends St Jetty.

Subiaco Known as 'Subi', this Perth suburb 5km west of the CBD is known for its upscale, hip bars and cafés, preserved architecture and stately homes. Originally settled by Benedictine Monks in 1851 – and named after the city of the same name in Lazio, Italy – the first building constructed in the area was a monastery. Restored in 2019, the **Benedictine Stables** (18 Barrett St; ☏ 9442 3444; ⊕ visits by appt only) remains the only structure left from the monks' time here – and technically the stables are actually in Wembley, just north of Subiaco. The monks planted olive trees when they arrived, and the city continues to plant them as an ode to its history.

When the Perth to Fremantle railway was constructed in the 1880s, a station was built in Subiaco that ignited an economic boom and an influx of settlers, business and industry. Many of the houses built during that period survived and are still in use today – 791 buildings in Subiaco are Heritage-listed. In particular, Subiaco houses are known for their **leadlights** – coloured, decorative and elaborate windows with glass separated by lead and metal bars. They are similar to stained glass, though leadlights are more associated with commercial enterprises and housing, and have a more simplistic design than the stained glass found in churches. Subiaco's **Leadlight Night** – usually in December – has free walking tours where residents are encouraged to leave their hallway lights on, making their door and window leadlights highly visible to the public. Ask the visitor centre for details. The city also offers a self-guided Leadlight Tour on its website (w subiaco.wa.gov.au) that starts and ends at the **Subiaco Museum** (239 Rokeby Rd; ☏ 9237 9227; ⊕ 13.00–16.00 Tue–Fri, 10.00–14.00 Sat; free).

One of Subi's most intriguing architectural examples is **Harvey House**, dating from 1896, with its twin domed spires, which was originally a school for orphans, before being converted into a maternity hospital in 1916. Today it houses the **Western Australian Medical Museum** (Railway Rd & Barker Rd; w wamedicalmuseum.org. au; ⏲ 10.30–16.00 Wed; A$5/2 adult/child), which has an interesting iron lung and polio display. Other noteworthy architectural treasures include the **Subiaco Oval** (304 Roberts Rd), with its limestone ticket office and Marseilles tile roof, built in 1935 to commemorate the Jubilee of King George V; the grey, Federation-Romanesque **Subiaco Hotel** (cnr Hay St & Rokeby Rd), with its decorative exterior walls and three-storey tower; and the 1938 **Regal Theatre** (474 Hay St; w regaltheatre.com.au), considered one of the state's most striking Art Deco constructions.

The Swan River At 72km long and 21m at its deepest point at Mosman Bay, WA's best-known river forms an integral part of the state's identity and was the lifeblood of the colony's original European settlements. It's also a focal point of Perth's outdoor activities, with miles of footpaths for walking, jogging and biking, and the waters teem with boaters, kayakers and swimmers. Some 130 species of fish can be found in its waters; there are also bottlenose dolphins and of course the ubiquitous black swan, the state bird, after whom the river was named. **Swans on the Swan** (w swansontheswan.com.au; ⏲ 10.00–17.00 Sat–Sun) hires out everything from pedal boats and SUPs (A$55/hr) to kayaks (A$35/hr), but if you need some guidance then **Water Wanderers** (w waterwanderers.com.au) offer kayak tours (from A$75pp) led by Leonie, who was long-term president of the Ascot Kayak Club and a veteran of kayaking expeditions in North America.

Located in the river between East Perth and Victoria Park and connected by a causeway is **Heirisson Island**, a nature reserve with a 2km walking trail, great birdwatching (look out for great egrets, ospreys and Australian ibis) and a kangaroo

A NOONGAR HERO

A Whadjuk Noongar warrior, Yagan was a key figure in Aboriginal resistance to European settlement in the Perth area in the early 19th century. His main country was Beeliar, south of the rivers. Feared and respected by both Aboriginals and Europeans, Yagan was seen as an accomplished warrior with a high level of status; he was an imposing figure of a great height who habitually carried a spear, and he had killed and wounded other Noongar from other groups in battle. He also reportedly had a ferocious temper, which added to his reputation.

Resistance to the early British settlers took the form of ambushes, tit-for-tat attacks and revenge killings. When Yagan's father, Midgegooroo, was executed without trial in 1832, accused of murdering two settlers, Yagan vowed to kill three white settlers in revenge. He was consequently outlawed, and a bounty of 80 pounds put on his head; in 1833, a young shepherd boy, William Keats, found him and shot him. Yagan was decapitated and his head taken to the Liverpool Museum in England.

Yagan's death was significant; the loss of someone of his stature had a serious negative impact on the resistance, and he is considered a hero to the Noongar today. His head (*kaat*) was repatriated by Noongar Elders in 1997 and was reburied at the Yagan Memorial Park in the Swan Valley (W Swan Rd). There is also a statue of him on Heirisson Island.

sanctuary. There is also a statue to Yagan, the Noongar leader during the Swan River Colony days (see box, page 89).

Beaches Some 15km from the city centre is the epicentre of Perth's beach culture, **Cottesloe Beach** ✻, which has been a see-and-be-seen place for over a century. With both reefs and waves, it's a great spot for surfers, snorkellers and beach cricketers, and the blue and green waters backed by the dense Norfolk pines behind make for a truly wonderful setting – though the beach was the site of one of WA's most notorious shark attacks, when in 2000 local resident Ken Crew was killed by a Great White. The star of the show here is the Cottesloe Beach Pavilion, sometimes called the Indiana after the Indiana Teahouse – originally constructed in the 1920s, it was demolished and replaced by another pavilion in 1983. This was deemed too small, however, and another new building (though designed to look traditional) was erected on the original foundations. Public interest in the teahouse remained muted until Taylor Swift visited in 2012 and shared on social media how much she loved the building. Now – partly due to publicity, and partly because it really is a lovely building in a popular spot – it is arguably Perth's most recognisable building with its wide arches, semicircular windows recalling an image of the sun and green dome roof.

Elsewhere, **City Beach**, 8km north of Cottesloe, is a beautiful all-purpose beach with groynes for fishing and good surfing – there is also a café/restaurant. South of Cottesloe is **Leighton Beach**; the waves are much gentler here, and the water remains shallow further out, making it a good option for families.

TransPerth's bus 102 and the Fremantle Line both pass near Cottesloe Beach; the latter also passes Leighton Beach. Buses 81 and 82 pass City Beach.

FREMANTLE

With its colourful and character-laden turn-of-the-century architecture, excellent museums and terrific café culture – the main street through here is nicknamed the 'Cappuccino Strip' – historic and colourful Fremantle (known as 'Freo' to locals) is a must-visit on any trip to Perth.

Aboriginal peoples call Fremantle Walyalup – 'place of the woylie', a type of small marsupial – and for thousands of years this was a meeting place and ceremonial ground. Fremantle was the first part of the Perth area to be settled by Europeans in 1829 – named after Charles Fremantle, captain of the HMS *Challenger*, who claimed the area for Britain (though he was not the first European here – the Dutch got here in the 1600s, but didn't stay). The settlement, like the colony, struggled until convict transportation was instituted, and in 1897 Fremantle Harbour was enlarged and deepened, and had the limestone bar and sand blockages to the Swan River removed, allowing Fremantle to become the primary commercial shipping centre for WA (instead of Albany) and igniting a round of prosperity. Fremantle was an important World War II base for the Allies and hosted the biggest submarine facility in the southern hemisphere. Large waves of Italian migration in the post-war period added a more diverse European cultural and culinary texture to the suburb. The hosting of the America's Cup boat race in 1987 is widely seen as the modern turning point in Fremantle's history; the influx of visitors and money from that event helping to turn it from a port town into a tourism destination, with the Cappuccino Strip emerging at the same time.

Fremantle today is now one of the cultural hearts of Perth, but it does have a bit of an edge to it – while you don't need to be paranoid, take the same precautions

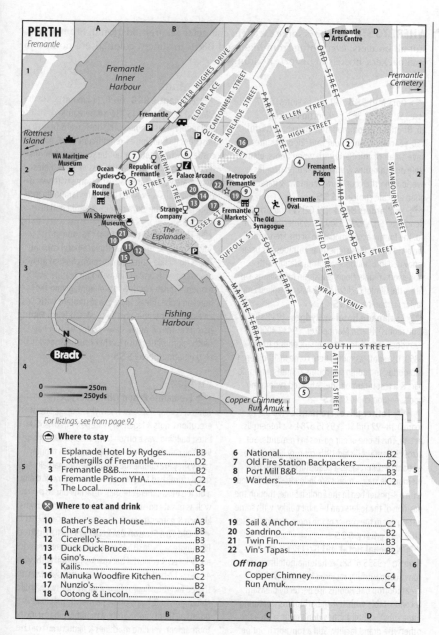

Fremantle
Inner
Harbour

Rottnest
Island

WA Maritime
Museum
Ocean
Cycles
Round
House
WA Shipwrecks
Museum

The
Esplanade

Fishing
Harbour

N

Bradt

0 ——— 250m
0 ——— 250yds

Republic of
Fremantle
Palace Arcade
Strange
Company

Fremantle

Metropolis
Fremantle
Fremantle
Markets
The Old
Synagogue

Fremantle
Arts Centre

Fremantle
Cemetery

Fremantle
Prison

Fremantle
Oval

Copper Chimney,
Run Amuk

For listings, see from page 92

Where to stay

1	Esplanade Hotel by Rydges	B3
2	Fothergills of Fremantle	D2
3	Fremantle B&B	B2
4	Fremantle Prison YHA	C2
5	The Local	C4
6	National	B2
7	Old Fire Station Backpackers	B2
8	Port Mill B&B	B3
9	Warders	C2

Where to eat and drink

10	Bather's Beach House	A3
11	Char Char	B3
12	Cicerello's	B3
13	Duck Duck Bruce	B2
14	Gino's	B2
15	Kailis	B3
16	Manuka Woodfire Kitchen	C2
17	Nunzio's	B2
18	Ootong & Lincoln	C4
19	Sail & Anchor	C2
20	Sandrino	B2
21	Twin Fin	B3
22	Vin's Tapas	B2

Off map

| Copper Chimney | C4 |
| Run Amuk | C4 |

you would take in any big city, and there isn't much reason for you to stray much
beyond the historical quarter and the Cappuccino Strip.

TOURIST INFORMATION

Fremantle Visitor Centre [91 B2] 155 High
St; 9431 7878; w visitfremantle.com.au;
09.00–17.00 Mon–Fri, 09.00–16.00 Sat,
10.00–16.00 Sun

WHERE TO STAY There is some excellent character accommodation in Fremantle to suit all budgets: everything from high-end B&Bs in stately, colonial-era homes, to backpackers' hostels in historic buildings.

Luxury

Port Mill B&B [91 B3] (4 suites) 3/17 Essex St; 9433 3832; w portmillbb.com. au. Boutique accommodation in a characterful 150-year-old former flour mill. Elegant suites have an air of chic Paris with wood floors, bistro-style dining tables & wrought-iron balconies overlooking the courtyard, fountain & garden. A good upscale choice. $$$$

Warders Hotel [91 C2] (11 rooms) 19–29 Henderson St; 9239 3300; w wardershotel.com. au. The former accommodation of the Fremantle Prison warders, these limestone cottages has been renovated into boutique accommodation with stonework, timber floors & tasteful furnishings. On site is the Gimlet cocktail bar & Asian-inspired Emily Taylor restaurant. $$$$

Esplanade Hotel by Rydges [91 B3] (300 rooms) 46–54 Marine Tce; 9432 4000; w rydges.com. A town landmark dating from 1850, the spotless rooms here come in 10 different categories, including spa rooms & suites. Multiple bars & a restaurant on site; 2 heated swimming pools. A good choice. $$$

✳ **Fothergills of Fremantle** [91 D2] (6 rooms) 18–22 Ord St; 9335 6784; w fothergills. net.au. This is one of our go-tos in Fremantle. Set across 3 Heritage-listed 19th-century houses, the elegant décor provides a beautiful backdrop to a memorable stay – rooms are individually furnished, with a 4-poster bed in the English Suite, though the position of the toilets can be a bit quirky, with some jutting out in the corner of the room, though walled-off & with privacy. $$$

National Hotel [91 B2] (12 rooms) 98 High St; 9335 6688; w nationalhotelfremantle. com.au. Beautifully restored building with a great rooftop bar. Rooms are perfectly pleasant & comfortable with stylish bathrooms (featuring huge tubs), although they don't quite match the otherwise grand facility. Still a top-notch option. $$$

Mid-range

Fremantle B&B [91 B2] (4 rooms) 5 Mouat St; 0403 945 284; w fremantle bedandbreakfast.com.au. The hotel website describes its building as 'reminiscent of a Bavarian castle', & while that may not be your first thought, it is striking, handsome & impressive nonetheless. Rooms are very homely & rustic, some with wood-panelled walls & exposed brick. The Tarantella attic suite is worth the extra money. Continental b/ fast. $$$

The Local Hotel [91 C4] (16 rooms) 282 South Tce; 6219 5510; w thelocalhotel.com.au. This is no cookie-cutter place; rooms are uniquely decorated with timber floors, bright feature walls, modern 4-poster beds & lots of light, giving the hotel an upbeat feel. There is a restaurant with an extensive menu – try the steak sandwich with bacon chutney & apple slaw – & the whisky bar (with appropriate plush leather couches) sets an elegant atmosphere. $$$

Budget

Fremantle Prison YHA [91 C2] 6A The Terrace; 9433 4305; w www.yha.com.au. Site of executions, riots & legendary escapes, this UNESCO-listed building was a prison from 1855 to 1991 (page 94). You can sleep in an actual prison cell – though today they are double the size of the original cells – simply furnished & with bars on the window. If that's a bit too much, there are shared-facility dorms as well as private en-suite rooms. Communal laundry, kitchen & games room. $

Old Fire Station Backpackers [91 B2] 18 Phillimore St; 9430 5454; w oldfirestation.com. au. Relaxed & colourful backpackers' hostel with 4-, 8-, & 12-bed dorms as well as private dbls with shared facilities. Rooms have a funky vibe, with bold statement art & hippy prints painted by previous guests, & there's free Netflix, a monthly ping-pong tournament, vending machines & laundry on site, as well as, interestingly, a tax-return service. $

WHERE TO EAT AND DRINK You will eat and drink well in Fremantle. One of Perth's culinary hubs, it is chock-a-block with great restaurants and cafés, and the buzzing atmosphere, Heritage-listed buildings and Italian influence have earned South Terrace the moniker of the Cappuccino Strip. Wandering up and down the street is an attraction itself, with plenty of alfresco options to choose from. There are a number of excellent seafood restaurants around the harbour too that have been popular with locals for years.

Cappuccino Strip

✗ Copper Chimney [91 C4] 1/330 South Tce; 9336 4414; w copperchimneyperth.com; ⏱ 17.30–21.30 Mon, 11.30–14.30 & 17.30–21.30 Tue–Fri, 09.00–11.00, 11.30–14.30 & 17.30–21.30 Sat–Sun. High-quality Indian restaurant that serves b/fasts on the weekend for your dosa fix. Solid dinner menu includes honey-&-ginger prawns as well as classics like butter chicken. **$$**

✗ Gino's [91 B2] 1/5 South Tce; 9336 1464; w ginoscafe.com.au; ⏱ 05.30–midnight daily. One of the pioneers of South Terrace's transformation, & the café is one of Freo's elder statesmen. They produce their own custom blend of coffees, & their longevity over the decades testifies to the quality. The huge selection of pastas, antipasti, risottos & fish & meat dishes won't leave you hungry. **$$**

✗ Ootong & Lincoln [91 C4] 258 South Tce; 9335 6109; f OotongAndLincoln; ⏱ 06.00–15.30 Mon–Fri, 06.30–15.30 Sat–Sun. Great little café serving hearty brunches, vegetarian options & a wide array of teas to go with their coffees. Plates are colourful in presentation & flavour, with chai pancakes, potato cakes & b/fast burgers just a few of the dishes on offer. **$$**

✗ Run Amuk [91 C4] 386A South Tce; 9335 1216; w runamuk.com.au; ⏱ 11.30–20.30 Thu–Sun. Hot dogs galore. The Ratbag is a real winner, with its kransky (Slovenian sausage), chives & sweet chili mayo, but the bratwurst options are good too. **$$**

✗ Sail & Anchor [91 C2] 64 South Tce; 9431 1666; w sailandanchor.com.au; ⏱ 10.00–23.00 Mon–Tue, 10.00–midnight Wed–Thu & Sun, 10.00–01.00 Fri–Sat. Landmark cocktail bar with a fantastic vintage lounge setting in the Freemasons Room that opens out on to a balcony. The food is good too – try the potato skins & the cheeseburger. **$$**

✗ Vin's Tapas [91 B2] 1/36 South Tce; 0402 523 592; w vinstapas.com; ⏱ 17.00–03.00 Wed–Thu, 17.00–04.00 Fri, noon–04.00 Sat, noon–03.00 Sun. Open until the wee hours, this Asian-inspired tapas bar has a distinct Freo vibe with dishes like cheeseburger spring rolls, ponzu pork belly & banana blossom bao. **$$**

Fishing Harbour

✗ Char Char Restaurant & Bar [91 B3] 44B Mews Rd; 9335 7666; w charcharrb.com.au; ⏱ 11.30–15.00 & 17.00–late daily. If you're tired of seafood, this sophisticated eatery has excellent steaks to complement their seafood selection. The kangaroo loin with lemon myrtle is especially good. **$$$**

✳ ✗ Cicerello's [91 B3] 44 Mews Rd; 9335 1911; w cicerellos.com.au; ⏱ 09.00–20.30 Mon–Thu & Sun, 09.00–21.00 Fri–Sat. A true WA landmark for over a century, home to the largest private aquarium in the state (but your dinner does not come from there!), from which you can safely view blue ring octopus. The menu has a variety of local fish & mussels, with a bit of pizza & pasta thrown in. **$$$**

✗ Bather's Beach House [91 A3] 47 Mews Rd; 9335 2911; w bathersbeachhouse.com.au; ⏱ 11.00–22.00 Sun–Thu, 11.00–midnight Fri–Sat. Beachfront restaurant with Italian-inspired mains & fresh catches. The seafood sharing plate comes loaded with oysters, squid, mussels & Tasmanian cold smoked salmon. **$$**

✗ Kailis [91 B3] 46 Mews Rd; 9335 7755; w kailis.com; ⏱ 11.00–late daily. Stylish harbourside restaurant with BBQ, fried & raw seafood highlighting local catches like Rottnest herring & Fremantle sardines. BBQ local snapper is a winner. **$$$**

✗ Twin Fin [91 B3] 8/47 Mews Rd; 6424 9503; w twinfin.com.au; ⏱ 11.00–20.00 Mon–Thu, 10.30–20.00 Fri, Sat 10.00–20.30 Sat, 10.00–20.00 Sun. The fish-&-chips specialists, serving up fried & grilled local catches including shark, snapper, mackerel & barramundi. **$$**

Elsewhere in Fremantle

✗ Duck Duck Bruce [91 B2] 18 Collie St; 6219 5216; w duckduckbruce.com.au; ⏱ 07.00–15.00 Sat–Tue. Great café with innovative, filling Indian-fused b/fasts & lunches. The chilli scrambled eggs with garam masala & vanilla pancake stacks are sure to fill you up, & the mango lassi muesli is genius. **$$**

✗ ✳ Manuka Woodfire Kitchen [91 C2] 134 High St; 9335 3527; w manukawoodfire.com.au;

17.30–22.30 Tue–Thu, noon–15.00 & 17.30–22.30 Fri–Sat. Stylish eatery with exposed-stone walls & black dining tables. Sharing plates include Abrolhos scallops, dorper lamb & wood-roasted octopus – good food well done. $$
✗ **Nunzio's** [91 B2] 20 Essex St; ☏6219 5441; w nunzios.net.au; ⏱ 17.00–21.00 Tue–Thu & Sat, noon–14.30 & 17.00–21.00 Fri. Family-run Italian with a rustic Mediterranean feel.

Homemade pasta & local seafood headline; the red emperor is tasty. $$
✗ **Sandrino** [91 B2] 95 Market St; ☏9335 4487; w sandrino.com.au; ⏱ 11.30–21.00 Mon–Thu, 11.00–22.00 Fri–Sat, Sun 11.00–21.00 Sun. Another Fremantle icon, serving up wood-fired pizzas & other Italian favourites but using local ingredients. The calzone is hearty, as are the pastas & risottos. $$

ENTERTAINMENT AND NIGHTLIFE

✴ ♀**The Old Synagogue** [91 C2] 92 South Tce; w theoldsynagogue.com.au; ⏱ see website. WA's first synagogue, built in 1902, now houses 4 bars & restaurants. At L'Chaim – meaning 'toast to life' – the coconut pandan negroni is a personal favourite.
♀**Palace Arcade** [91 B2] 96 High St; w thepalacearcade.com.au; ⏱ 16.00–midnight Wed–Thu, noon–01.00 Fri–Sat. 1980s & 90s nostalgia reign supreme at this cocktail bar & retro video game joint serving New York-style pizza. Also has branches in Northbridge & Victoria Park.
♀**Republic of Fremantle** [91 B2] 3 Packenham St; w republicoffremantle.com; ⏱ noon–midnight Wed–Sat. Gin & vodka distillery with a

gin school where you can put together your own bottle. Walk-ins only.
♀**Strange Company** [91 B2] 5 Naim St; w strangecompany.com.au; ⏱ 16.00–midnight Mon–Thu, noon–midnight Fri–Sun. Popular local favourite with small plates like garlic sardines mixed in with a huge wine list & hip, bamboo interior.
☆ **Metropolis Fremantle** [91 C2] 58 South Tce; w metropolisfremantle.com.au; ⏱ 21.00–late Fri–Sat. Popular among locals, visitors & backpackers alike, the club is divided into earth, air, fire & water chambers. Known for its good DJ line-up; free entry to the Fri 'House Party'.

WHAT TO SEE AND DO Fremantle is easily explored on foot, and one way to anchor together all its sights is on the 5.8km **Fremantle Discovery Trail** (downloadable as a PDF from w visitfremantle.com.au). The route starts at the 1907 Fremantle Railway Station [91 B1] and winds its way past the markets, prison, Round House, museums and a variety of other places before ending at the Fremantle Arts Centre. If you prefer to explore on two wheels, the 10km **Indian Ocean Explorer** (also downloadable from w visitfremantle.com.au) starts from the Round House and follows the coast across the Swan River, taking in North Fremantle's trendy beaches and finishing at Cottesloe. **Ocean Cycles** [91 A2] (2 Phillimore St; w oceancycles.com.au; ⏱ 10.00–16.00 Fri–Sun) has a huge range of bikes and e-bikes for hire and sale. They also do guided tours (min 5 people).

Fremantle Prison ✴ [91 C2] (1 The Terrace; w fremantleprison.com.au; ⏱ 09.00–17.00 daily; A$22/12 adult/child) Though not the first prison in Fremantle – the 1831 Round House (page 96) is older – this is one of 11 sites that form the group of Australian Convict Sites on UNESCO's World Heritage List. Built in 1859 by convict labour from limestone to hold 1,000 inmates, the prison was a maximum-security institution and life and punishments inside reflected that – such as the use of irons and beatings. All sorts were imprisoned here, including POWs from both world wars. The gallows arrived in 1888, and a women's division was started in 1889; the prison was also the site of executions before capital punishment was banned in WA in 1984. It finally closed its doors to inmates only on 8 November 1991.

THE TRAGIC TALE OF C Y O'CONNOR

Charles Yelverton O'Connor (1843–1902) is one of the most important figures in West Australian history. His work in creating Fremantle Harbour and the Goldfields Water Supply Scheme were landmarks in the development of the state and have stood the test of time in cementing Fremantle's importance and in making permanent settlement in the Goldfields possible.

Despite these achievements, O'Connor found himself the subject of brutal criticism, especially from the media, who accused him of incompetence and corruption. Government inquiries found no evidence or basis for corruption accusations; but the constant barrage was too much for O'Connor to bear. He got on his horse, rode out into the water from the beach in Fremantle that now bears his name, and shot himself.

A bronze statue of O'Connor on his horse was commissioned and placed 30m out in the water, roughly where he died. The forever-drowning bronze monument marks a horrible and tragic end to a man whose work is appreciated much more a century after his death than during his lifetime.

Significant restoration has since occurred and today it is considered to be one of the best-preserved convict buildings in Australia. The centrepiece once inside the gatehouse – which has twin towers on either side – is the enormous, four-storey main cell block with parade area, surrounded by a 4.6m wall; several of the cells have been restored to give visitors an idea of conditions during various times in the prison's operation. Guided tours are available; recommended are the Behind Bars tour, which takes you through the main cell block and exercise yard and shows the daily routines of life inside, and the night-time Torchlight Tour, which regales visitors with stories of the macabre such as executions, punishments and wrongful imprisonments.

Fremantle Markets ✳ [91 C2] (South Tce & Henderson St; w fremantlemarkets. com.au; ⏱ 09.00–18.00 Fri–Sun) Part farmers' market, part-bazaar, and one of the very few market halls left in Australia still used for its intended purpose, this soft yellow-and-red, Victorian-style Heritage building has housed a hall-style market since 1897. Today, some 150 stalls offer fresh produce, food, jewellery, Aboriginal crafts, sunglasses and more – this is where I had my first-ever taste of crocodile meat in a hot dog! Numerous vendors also sell snacks and drinks like pretzels and coffee, as well as bush teas.

WA Shipwrecks Museum [91 B3] (47 Cliff St; w museum.wa.gov.au/museums/shipwrecks; ⏱ 09.30–17.00 daily; donations welcomed) The rocks, reefs, tides, currents and storms off the coast of WA make for treacherous waters, and this museum, housed in a restored 1850s Commissariat building, is dedicated to documenting their stories. Widely billed as one of the best maritime museums in the southern hemisphere, the highlight here is the reconstructed *Batavia* stern built from relics of the Dutch ship that sank in 1629 (see box, page 279), after painstaking research. The Dutch Wrecks Gallery also has artefacts and relics from a series of ships that sank in the 17th century.

WA Maritime Museum [91 A2] (Victoria Quay; w museum.wa.gov.au/museums/maritime; ⏱ 09.30–17.00 daily; A$15/7.50/free adult/concession/child) Focusing on the relationship between WA and the Indian Ocean, highlights here include the *America II* – the yacht that won the America's Cup in 1983 – and you can take a guided tour of the Cold War-era submarine, HMAS *Ovens*. The museum also hosts special exhibits like Brick Wrecks – shipwrecks constructed in excruciating detail out of Lego. A good place to bring kids.

Round House [91 A2] (15 Captains Ln; ☎9336 6897; w fremantleroundhouse. com.au; ⊕ 10.30–15.30 daily; A$2) One of the oldest buildings in the state, dating from 1831, this dodecagonal stone prison was originally a holding facility until being converted into a storage house. At 13.00, the time-signal ceremony is re-enacted in which a cannon fires a blank – you can book in to be the one doing the firing (once a day on a first-come, first-served basis). Kids can get their photo taken in the stocks.

Fremantle Arts Centre [91 D1] (1 Finnerty St; w fac.org.au; ⊕ 10.00–17.00 daily) The building itself is the highlight here – a convict-built, limestone Victorian Gothic structure, though its simple gables, dormer windows and steep roof have sometimes been referred to as 'romantic' Gothic – and it has been put to use by the government in wildly diverse ways over the years. It began life in 1864 as an insane asylum, eventually drifting into use as a women's house in the mid-1900s, then a technical high school before finally becoming an arts centre in 1973. There are various exhibitions inside by local and international artists, as well as a shop and a café.

Fremantle Cemetery [91 D1] The grave of AC/DC lead singer Bon Scott, reportedly the most-visited grave in Australia, is among the 40,000 burials at this 1898 cemetery where most of the buildings were constructed out of limestone. Heath Ledger was also cremated here, though his ashes were then taken elsewhere. The modest (1½hrs) but somewhat macabre **Heritage Walk Trail** (available as a PDF from w mcb.wa.gov.au) explores 35 graves scattered across the area of notable Fremantle residents and others who made their mark in WA. You are struck by the egalitarian nature of those buried here – immigrant miners who never struck it rich and died penniless, like Russian Jack, are interred alongside the likes of Sir Henry Briggs, who was President of the Legislative Council in the Parliament of Western Australia. Scan the QR code for in-depth biographies as you go.

ROTTNEST ISLAND ✷

WA's offshore jewel, Rottnest ('Rotto' to locals) is famous for two things: its quokkas, dubbed the happiest animal on earth because of their ever-present smile, and its spectacular beaches, often rated among the best in the state. The limestone island got its name because when Dutch explorers first arrived here in the 1600s, they mistook the quokkas for giant rats – 'Rottnest' means 'Rat's Nest'.

Rottnest is believed to have separated from the mainland 7,000 years ago through rising sea levels, and is stunningly diverse, with six habitats packed into 19km². It was uninhabited at the time the Europeans arrived, though it is thought that people lived on Rottnest as far back as 70,000 years ago. The Whadjuk Noongar are the Traditional Owners, who call the island Wadjemup, meaning 'place across the water where the spirits are' – they believe the island is where spirits go as they transition from life as we know it to the afterlife, and as such the island holds major cultural importance to them.

Europeans settled Rottnest at the same time as they did the rest of the Perth area, with the idea being the land could be used for salt mining and agriculture. By 1838, an Aboriginal prison had been set up, and imprisonment and/or forced labour of Aboriginal peoples continued all the way to the 1930s. When forced labour and incarceration ended, Rottnest opened up to recreational possibilities, and its birth as a tourism and leisure centre for the capital began to emerge, despite a five-year closure between 1940 and 1945 when the island became a defence fortification.

Surfing has become hugely popular, and the island is known for its fantastic beaches and hiking trails – and of course its quokkas, which are arguably the main reason to come here and a highlight of any holiday to Perth.

There is some accommodation on the island, but most people day trip from Perth – usually from Fremantle, a 30-minute ferry ride away, though boats and ferries also leave from the Perth CBD and Hillary's Boat Harbour. The island is car free and, while there are a few shuttle buses, the most common method of getting around is by bicycle, which can be hired – indeed, one of the largest bike-hire facilities in the world is on Rotto.

GETTING THERE AND AWAY Rottnest Express (w rottnestexpress.com.au), **Rottnest Fast Ferries** (w rottnestfastferries.com.au) and **SeaLink Rottnest Island** (w sealinkrottnest.com.au) all offer ferry services to/from the island from various points in Perth: generally Fremantle (from A$45 return) is the closest and quickest option, but some services depart from Perth CBD or further north at Hillary's Boat Harbour (from A$88 same-day return). Note that on the island, 'the Settlement' is not a town per se, but rather the location of the visitor centre, the ferry dock and a few shops/cafés.

Flying to Rottnest is also possible (around 15–20mins from Perth). **Rottnest Air Taxi** (w rottnestairtaxi.com.au) offers private flights from Jandakot Airport in Perth's south, starting at A$165pp for three people and A$248pp for two. **Swan River Seaplanes** (w swanriverseaplanes.com.au) also offer departures from Jandkot as well as the Swan River on the Perth Foreshore, for similar prices. **Air Charters West** (w aircharterswest.com.au) flies to/from Bunbury Airport from A$295 return (30mins).

TOURIST INFORMATION AND ISLAND TOURS The cliché 'outdoor playground' is so overused these days it has lost much of its meaning – but not on Rottnest. The activities here are so varied that planning a trip can be a bit bewildering. Use the island's website (w rottnestisland.com) to orient yourself before you arrive, otherwise your first ports of call on arrival should be the **Rottnest Island Visitor Centre** (1 Henderson Av; 9372 9730; ⊕ 08.15–16.00 daily) and **Pedal and Flipper** (Bedford Av; 9292 5105; ⊕ 08.30–16.00 daily), which offers all sorts of equipment hire – including nearly 2,000 bicycles – as well as snorkel sets, wetsuits and more. They also do a call-out repair service if you have an issue with your bike while pedalling around.

Guided tours Bus tours are available on the island – the hop-on-hop-off **Island Explorer** runs at 30-minute intervals between 08.30 and 16.00 (18.00 on weekends), covering most of the island highlights. See the island website for more options.

Go Cultural Aboriginal Tours w gocultural.com.au. Runs a 60min walking tour of the island, exploring its Aboriginal culture & history.

The Hike Collective w hikecollective.com.au. Offers a number of guided hikes across the island, including a 12km route that takes in its wonderful bays & lakes.

Rottnest Voluntary Guides Association
w rvga.asn.au. Runs a number of free guided walks on various themes, with a focus on the island's history & culture.
Rottnest Cruises w rottnestcruises.com. Does a 'sea to plate' experience tour where you can catch & cook your own lobster, as well as sundowner cruises.
Sea Kayak Rottnest w rottnestkayak.com. au. Located on Pinky Beach, these run 1hr glass-bottom kayak tours around the island.

 WHERE TO STAY AND EAT Accommodation on Rotto is limited and can be expensive, sometimes exorbitantly so for what you get compared with the mainland. If you want to stay overnight, book ahead. For those on a budget, the Rottnest Island website (w rottnestisland.com/accommodation/accommodation-types) lists numerous shoestring options, from former military barracks with bunks (Governor's Circle and the Kingstown Dormitories) to a 50-bed hostel (Rottnest Island Hostel) and an unpowered campsite near The Basin.

Karma Rottnest (61 rooms) Kitson St; ☏ 9292 5161; w karmagroup.com/find-destination/karma-resorts/karma-rottnest. Housed in a Heritage-listed building, rooms somewhat lack the flash of the Rottnest Island setting but nonetheless are comfortable & get the job done – at less cost than the Samphire. Lakeside rooms are larger & suitable for families. **$$$$**

Samphire Rottnest (80 rooms) 1 Bedford Av; ☏ 9292 5011; e hello@samphirerottnest.com. au; w samphirerottnest.com.au. The ultimate in beachfront luxury. Large rooms have soft tones that capture the hues of the coast, & almost all have water views, though best to confirm you've got one that does. Expect to pay dearly to stay here, & book well in advance, but it is worth it if your budget suits. West Australian produce highlights at its 2 restaurants – the southeast Asian-inspired Lontara, & the Italian-based Isola Bar e Chibo. **$$$$**

Thomsons Colebatch Av; ☏ 9292 5171; w thomsonsrottnest.com.au; ⏱ 11.30–17.00 Sun–Thu, 11.30–20.30 Fri–Sat. Sleek seafood restaurant with good pastas – try the prawn spaghetti. The fish burger & local mussels are also good. **$$$**

Frankie's on Rotto 342 Somerville Dr; ☏ 0431 735 090; w frankiesonrotto.com.au; ⏱ 11.00–20.00 Tue, Thu & Fri, 08.00–20.00 Sat–Mon. Family-owned Italian specialising in pizzas, though they also have salad options & a decent b/fast menu. Good wine list. A relaxing place to wind up at in the evening. Also offers a delivery service. **$$**

Rottnest Bakery Maley St; ☏ 9292 5023; f RottnestBakery; ⏱ 08.00–16.00 daily. The famous island bakery bakes bread in-house & recently opened an on-site chicken restaurant, the Chook Shack. Great snack & coffee spot. The donuts are well-known. **$**

WHAT TO SEE AND DO The main attraction on Rotto is undoubtedly its **quokkas** (see box, opposite). Approximately 12,000 of these contented marsupials live here and, though they are nocturnal, they are quite opportunistic and you are likely to see them out and about trying to scavenge during daylight. The best way to find them is on a free 45-minute guided walk, which leaves from the Salt Store at 13.00. Note that it is illegal to touch or feed the quokkas. Elsewhere, the West End Boardwalk –

ROTTNEST CHANNEL SWIM

Held in February each year, the Rottnest Channel Swim (w rottnestchannel swim.com.au) is a 19.7km, open-water swim from Cottesloe Beach to the island. Over 2,000 swimmers usually participate in a variety of categories (team, tandem and solo); the 2022 winner was Kyle Lee, who completed the swim in 4 hours, 5 minutes and 19 seconds.

THE WORLD'S HAPPIEST ANIMAL

About the size of a housecat, quokkas are Rottnest Island's most recognisable face. Some 12,000 live on the island, although they are very rare on the mainland – only a few isolated pockets remain in the southern forests and in the Blackwood Valley around Nannup.

Mostly feeding on grasses, quokkas store fat in their tail and don't need much water – they can supposedly go up to a month without drinking. The animal is incredibly cute and photogenic – its facial muscles give it a perpetual smile, leading it to be dubbed the happiest animal on the planet – and 'quokka selfies' became hugely popular among tourists after several celebrities, including tennis legend Roger Federer, had theirs taken and posted on social media.

However, quokkas are classed as Vulnerable by the IUCN – the importation of European animals like foxes and cats has decimated Western Australia's native animals, and the quokka is no exception – and it is illegal to touch them. A local outrage occurred in 2007 when two players for Super Rugby's Western Force were convicted and fined for mistreating the animals – initial reports spoke of 'hammer throwing' the quokkas and attempting to catch them in milk crates, though that was walked back to inappropriate handling.

So, take your selfie, but hands-off. Don't feed them – human food is very unhealthy for them. And don't always trust a pretty face – they can bite when threatened, and also have the ability to climb.

constructed in 2012 from recycled plastic – is a great place to look for muttonbirds, ospreys and whales – some 35,000 pass by here each year on their migration routes, and the calm waters off some parts of the island make good nurseries for the calves. New Zealand fur seals can also be observed at New Cathedral Rocks, bats and frogs come out at night, currents bring green turtles, bottlenose dolphins are sighted regularly and the Leeuwin Current's influence results in over 100 different types of tropical fish in the water – over ten times more than found off the Perth coastline – such as moonlighters, butterflyfish and sweeps.

Rotto's other major draw is its **beaches** – all 63 of them. **The Basin**, 10 minutes from the ferry dock, is routinely judged as one of WA's best beaches. A natural pool inside a reef, the colours, soft sand, sheltered swimming and snorkelling are out of this world. **Little Salmon Bay** in the south, also sheltered, is a fantastic snorkelling spot, with its aqua waters forming a Y-shape against reef and rock. One of the island's bigger beaches is at semi-circular **Geordie Bay**, home to a jetty, good swimming and plenty of quokkas. Those three would be enough for a day trip; however, if you are staying longer, one of the pleasures of being on Rottnest is just taking your map, your bike or hopping on the Island Explorer and finding your own secluded patch of sand.

Rottnest is home to some terrific **surf** breaks, and attracts world-famous competitions such as the HIF Pro-AM, held at Strickland Bay. Stark Bay, Salmon Bay and the Rotto Box are other popular surf spots.

For those with more time on their hands, the 45km **Wadjemup Bidi Walking Trail** (w rottnestisland.com/wadjemupbidi) is broken into five sections and covers most of the island's sights, exploring its rich history as well as its natural wonders. 'Bidi' means 'trail' in Noongar, and highlights along the track include WWII defence installations, salt lakes and Wadjemup Lighthouse, WA's first stone lighthouse built in 1849 and the highest point on the island, with good views of Perth. Also on the trail is **Oliver Hill Battery**, with its restored 9.2-inch guns and underground tunnels, which defended the mainland ports during World War II and could fire shells 28km away. Guided tours are available (A$13/4 adult/child); you can also take the tourist train there from the settlement (A$20/13 adult/child).

One of the darker chapters of the island's history was that it was used as an Aboriginal prison between 1838 and 1903, and then with the prison's closure in 1904, forced Aboriginal labour was conducted here until 1931. Access to the island was restricted, with information about its use as a prison and labour camp largely concealed from the public until the 1980s. The 373 men who were imprisoned here are buried in unmarked graves at the **Wadjemup Aboriginal Burial Ground**. The conservation and acknowledgement of the burial ground is of significant importance to Aboriginal people, and to the reconciliation process.

ROCKINGHAM AND PENGUIN ISLAND

South from Fremantle, the landscape changes to dreary suburbs, commercial strips and unappealing industrial infrastructure before arriving at Rockingham at Perth's southern boundary, 50km from the CBD.

Rockingham got its name from one of the three ships hired by Thomas Peel to bring settlers to Swan River – they arrived off the coast in 1830, and then inauspiciously struck rocks and sunk, with survivors scrambling ashore and naming their campsite after their vessel. The town developed as a timber port and eventually urban sprawl morphed it into an unremarkable bedroom community of Perth, and as a support centre for the Royal Australian Navy base on Garden Island. In modern times, West Australians know it more as the home electorate of Premier Mark McGowan.

The main reason to come here is for the Rockingham Foreshore, and the beaches and activities nearby in Cape Peron, Shoalwater Islands Marine Park and Penguin Island.

GETTING THERE AND AROUND As a coastal suburb of Perth, Rockingham is well connected to the metro area's road and public transport network. From Perth or Bunbury, the Kwinana Freeway bypasses Rockingham, but take the Mundijong Road/Kulija Road exit and it's 11km west to the town centre. Alternatively, you can take Stock Road down from Fremantle, which turns into Rockingham Road – but it will likely take longer due to more traffic (and the scenery along the way – past a landfill and a refinery – is hardly endearing).

Rockingham is on the TransPerth's Mandurah Line – but the station is there to service locals, not tourists, and so it's a 9km walk from there to Point Peron and a 7km walk to Shoalwater Islands Marine Park. Bus 551 runs from the station to Point Peron in about 30 minutes, though you will still have to walk over 1km, and bus 552 runs from the station to the Shoalwater Foreshore in about 35 minutes. It's about a 5km walk from Point Peron to Shoalwater Islands Marine Park.

TOURIST INFORMATION
🄸 Rockingham Visitor Centre 19 Kent St; ☎ 9592 3464; w visitrockingham.com.au;   ⊕ 09.00–17.00 Mon–Fri, 09.00–16.00 Sat–Sun

 WHERE TO STAY AND EAT Rockingham is halfway between Perth and Mandurah, but you are probably better off staying in either one and driving here or taking public transport. However, there are a couple of decent options if you need to spend the night.

✳ 🏠 **Anchorage Guest House** (5 rooms) 2 Smythe St; ☎ 9527 4214; w anchorageguesthouse.com.au. Located a few minutes' walk from Rockingham Beach & very close to restaurants, elegant units are stylishly appointed & exceedingly comfortable. Continental b/fast inc. **$$$**

✳ 🏠 **Manuel Towers** (3 rooms) 32A Arcadia Dr; ☎ 9592 2698; w manueltowers.com.au. In a stone building on the foreshore, rooms are tastefully furnished to give an old-world feel. Choose from a huge b/fast menu in the morning. Can't beat the location or atmosphere. **$$$**

✖ **Ostro Eatery** 11A Rockingham Beach Rd; ☎ 0437 013 764; w ostroeatery.com.au; ⏱ 07.00–15.00 daily. Filling b/fasts – some with a kick, like chilli-infused scrambled eggs – headline at this arty foreshore café along with great coffee, organic teas & pressed juices. Good gnocchi too, with tomato sugo. **$$**

✖ **Steel Tree Sunset** 1 Railway Tce; ☎ 9528 1910; w steeltreesunset.com.au; ⏱ 08.30–21.00 Mon–Fri, 08.00–21.00 Sat–Sun. Varied but reliable menu here makes this a good dinner bet. The beef noodles & chilli prawn pasta are both done well & the wine list showcases West Australian makers. **$$**

WHAT TO SEE AND DO Rockingham is all about adventure activities. Its magnificent coastal geography makes it a good spot for jetpacking, and a 30-minute session with **Jetpack Flyboard Perth** (61 Rockingham Beach Rd; w jetpackperth.com.au) starts from A$189. They also offer 60- and 90-minute jet-ski tours (from A$240), as well as jet-ski hire (from A$60). For those seeking something even more adrenalin-charged, **SkyDive Australia** (w skydive.com.au/perth; from A$319) offers skydiving from 15,000ft (4,500m), travelling at an estimated 200km/h during a 7-minute freefall, floating down over Shoalwater Islands Marine Park and the Rockingham coastline.

If all that sounds too hectic, Rockingham has some beautiful beaches on which to chill out. Winner of the 2010 WA Clean Beaches Award, sweeping **Rockingham Beach** is great for swimming, while to the west towards Point Peron, **Palm Beach** has a photogenic jetty and similar swimming conditions. **Point Peron** itself and the **Shoalwater Foreshore** stretch west from Rockingham like a long, narrow finger. The calm waters here make for excellent snorkelling and kayaking, and you can kayak out to nearby Seal Island from the foreshore. **Rockingham Kayak and SUP Hire** (11 Cypress Mews; w rockinghamkayakhire.com.au) rents out equipment and also has a drop-off and pick-up service for gear.

Shoalwater Islands Marine Park and Penguin Island Just 2km south of Rockingham Beach by way of the Esplanade, this 6,540ha protected marine park consists of a series of limestone islands just off Point Peron. The islands are a hub of marine life, with plenty of penguins, seals, sea lions, dolphins and all sorts of fish in between. The most popular is **Penguin Island** (w penguinisland.com.au; ⏱ Sep–Jun); hourly ferries operate from Mersey Point (5 mins; A$32/25 adult/child), but as they only run during the day, sightings of the island's little penguins (see box, page 102) are unlikely as they usually hunt at that time (though it's not unheard of to find one sleeping under the steps or the boardwalks). The population has been in steep decline since 2017, by as much as 80%, down to about 300 birds. This has prompted significant concern in the community about the future of the colony and what sustainable measures can be taken, if any, to support the birds.

The **Penguin Island Discovery Centre** hosts penguin feedings at 10.30, 12.30 and 14.30 for birds not able to live in the wild, and hourly dolphin-spotting cruises

3

and sea kayaking tours can be booked through the island website. The island also operates a 'Swim with the Dolphins' tour (3–6hrs; from A\$200) from Rockingham, and though sightings and swimming is not guaranteed, they have a very high success rate. Although Penguin Island is closed during the breeding season, park rangers offer the **Penguin Island Wildlife Cruise** (A\$50/35 adult/child) during this time to a limited number of visitors – which encompasses a guided walk, plus a 1-hour glass-bottom boat cruise. See website to book.

Elsewhere on the island, there are plenty of opportunities for swimming, fishing and picnicking, not to mention birdwatching (pelicans, oystercatchers and pied cormorants are common sightings). Bring everything you think you might need, including your lunch.

THE PERTH HILLS

Gently rising out of the earth 25km east of the city, the Perth Hills – actually part of the Darling Scarp – are a forested refuge with a true 'escape to the country' feel. The region is best known for its wine, spectacular lookouts over the city, waterfalls, fine botanical gardens, and as a terminus for the Bibbulmun Track – billed as one of the world's greatest long-distance walking trails. This is long-weekend country for Perth residents and, with an elevation a few hundred metres higher than that of the city, can often be a cooler retreat in the summertime.

The hills don't have a defined centre, sprawling for 54km from Armadale to Gidgegannup. Kalamunda is the best-known population centre, home to the Bibbulmun Track's northern terminus, and makes a good place to base yourself if you're looking to explore for a few days. B&Bs are dotted across the hills, however, particularly in Lesmurdie, Araluen and the Bickley-Carmel Valley.

Though Aboriginal peoples had been here for millennia, European-style settlement did not begin until 1899, with the idea that the Perth Hills would be an agricultural reserve for Aboriginals. Within a few years, many Aboriginals from what is now the Perth CBD and the Wheatbelt had been forcibly relocated here.

European settlement came slowly; the area was not very accessible from Perth, and so growth was mostly related to small-scale fruit farming and the timber industry. As Perth sprawled out, it eventually came to encompass the Perth Hills and today they are effectively a suburb of the city and form the metro area's eastern boundary.

GETTING THERE AND AROUND From Perth, the Great Eastern Highway goes to Mundaring, 15km east of Midland. Armadale, in Perth's far southeast, sits at the junction of the Albany Highway and the South Western Highway, 35km from the CBD. Kalamunda is 27km from the CBD, on the aptly named

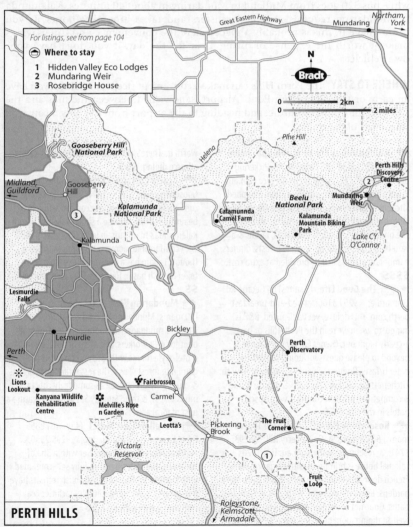

For listings, see from page 104

Where to stay

1 Hidden Valley Eco Lodges
2 Mundaring Weir
3 Rosebridge House

Kalamunda Road. Because the roads are so windy, and towns are not necessarily connected in a linear way (and sometimes not connected at all), you might want to get a map from the visitor centres in either **Kalamunda** (50 Railway Rd; ✆ 9257 9998; w experienceperthhills.com.au; ☼ 09.00–16.00 Mon–Fri, 10.00–16.00 Sat–Sun) or **Armadale** (40 Jull St; ✆ 9394 5410; w perthhillsarmadale.com. au; ☼ 09.00–16.00 Mon–Fri; 09.00–14.00 Sat–Sun) and orient yourself before setting off.

Armadale is served by TransPerth trains as the terminus of the Armadale Line. Getting to Kalamunda from the CBD on public transport is a bit complicated though, and typically requires a train ride to Welshpool station followed by a bus from there to Kalamunda – all in all, taking about an hour.

Buses 282 and 283 connect Kalamunda and Lesmurdie in about 30 minutes, while bus 320 goes from Midland to Mundaring in about 40 minutes. Kalamunda to Mundaring requires multiple transfers and takes around 2 hours. If you can manage it, this is probably a place where the convenience and time savings make it worth the expense of hiring a car for the day, if you don't have your own vehicle.

WHERE TO STAY The Perth Hills can make a convenient sleepover point if you have an early or late flight from Perth Airport, sandwiched between the hills and the CBD, 15km from Lesmurdie, and heading to the airport from the hills means you miss most of the traffic.

Hidden Valley Eco Lodges & Spa [map, page 103] (6 lodges) 85 Carinyah Rd, Pickering Brook; ✆ 9293 7337; w hiddenvalleyeco.com.au. Private heated jacuzzis, gas BBQs, fully equipped kitchens & spacious hammocks make these stylish lodges a great escape from Perth's urban bustle. The on-site Day Spa offers massages, facials & a variety of other treatments, while b/fasts, dinners, hampers & platters can be provided at extra cost. **$$$$**

✴ **The Good Life** (3 suites) 64 George Rd, Lesmurdie; ✆ 9291 3106; w bed-and-breakfast-perth.com. This deluxe, yet well-priced, B&B is our go-to when we're in the Perth Hills or have an early flight out. Owner Cherry goes above & beyond to please guests including cooked-to-order b/fasts. Rooms are very well appointed with kitchenette, reclining armchairs & private terrace, & competitive prices & comforts with upscale hotels in the city. **$$$**

Rosebridge House [map, page 103] (6 rooms) 86 Williams St, Gooseberry Hill; ✆ 9293 1741; w rosebridgehouse.com.au. This 1920s' colonial house is brimming with elegance, with French doors opening on to verandas & lush, leafy gardens. Some rooms come with spas or claw-foot baths. Gourmet cooked b/fasts enjoyed in the well-lit dining room or on the terrace. Pricey but

worth it. There's also a pool & BBQ for self-catered alfresco dining. **$$$**

Acacia Cottage (3 rooms) 15 The Ln, Gooseberry Hill; ✆ 6293 1441; w acaciacottage. com.au. Tranquil boutique accommodation in a beautiful red-brick house a short walk north from Kalamunda's main strip in leafy Gooseberry Hill. Very comfortable rooms, but shared facilities – though 1 room has a mini-ensuite with its own toilet & wash basin. Rates are very competitive. **$$**

Mundaring Weir Hotel [map, page 103] (10 rooms) Mundaring Weir Rd & Hall Rd; ✆ 9295 1106; w mundaringweirhotel.com.au. Originally built for weir workers, this elegant hotel offers motel-style rooms with kitchenette & either garden or forest views. The restaurant does b/fasts & counter meals (as well as some truly choctastic mudshakes), & their 'Sunday Session' gigs feature a host of local acts. **$$**

Travellers Rest Motel (4 rooms) 8855 Great Eastern Hwy, Mundaring; ✆ 9295 2950; w travellersrestwa.com.au. Set within 3ha of bushland, the suites here are fully self-contained with kitchen, while more rustic bush retreats have microwaves & en suites. Laundry facilities & a communal area with BBQ. **$$**

✕ WHERE TO EAT AND DRINK

✳ **✕ Embers Woodfired** 169 Railway Rd, Gooseberry Hill; 📞 9293 3663; **w** emberswoodfired.com.au; 🕐 11.00–21.00 Wed–Fri, 08.00–21.00 Sat–Sun. Italian restaurant specialising in pizzas, but with a whole lot of other items too, including filling pastas & hefty burgers. The spinach & ricotta cannelloni is my go-to here; the desserts are good too. **$$$**

✕ The Vault 21 Haynes St, Kalamunda; 📞 9293 3323; **w** thevaultrestaurant.com.au; 🕐 16.00–21.00 Wed–Thu & 11.00–21.00 Fri–Sun. Pasta primis at this community-driven Italian go well with the variety of secondis, & the tiramisu is a winner. There is also a good pizza list. **$$$**

✕ Vineyard Kitchen 5 Loaring Rd, Bickley; 📞 9227 7715; **w** thevineyardkitchen.net.au; 🕐 noon–15.00 Fri–Sun. Using free-range meats & local produce, this classy & innovative restaurant offers a seasonal menu of colourful mains from vodka-cured trout to twice-cooked duck leg & Manchego cheeseballs. **$$$**

✕ Kishi 3 Haynes St, Kalamunda; 📞 9293 0001; 🕐 17.30–20.30 Tue–Sat. Sushi bar with teriyakis, bento boxes & noodles. Food is well-presented & tasty – the menu is very authentic & caters to customers with a deep familiarity with Japanese cuisine. **$$**

✕ La Fattoria 211 Merrivale Rd, Pickering Brook; 📞 9293 7888; **w** lafattoria.com.au; 🕐 11.00–16.30 Thu–Sun. Offering set menus & platter options, this trattoria prides itself on bringing its version of the 'Italian experience' to diners. The Sicilian meatballs are excellent, as are the poached pears. They also have a cellar door, representing wines from different parts of Italy; the trattoria is also the start of the Bickley Valley Wine Trail (page 108). **$$**

✕ Mason & Bird 7 Williams St, Kalamunda; 📞 9293 1581; **w** masonandbird.com.au; 🕐 08.00–15.00 daily. Rustic café with Italian-inspired brunches, topped toasts & toasties, as well as good coffee. The speck & egg burger is a winner. **$$**

✕ Orchard Bistro at Core Cider House 35 Merrivale Rd, Pickering Brook; 📞 9293 7583; **w** corecider.com.au; 🕐 11.00–16.00 Wed–Mon. Operating within a 16ha orchard in an idyllic valley in Pickering Brook, this relaxing bistro offers set 2- & 3-course lunch menus featuring the likes of WA slow-cooked beef & Margaret River tempeh, washed down with ciders from 9 varieties of apple. When weather permits, you can also pick stonefruits & produce from their orchard, which has over 7,000 trees – this has to be done by booking; call for details. **$$**

FARM GATE PRODUCE

The Perth Hills have been an agricultural haven for over a century, and the fruit here is first-rate – stonefruits, apples, pears and grapes are particular highlights. Numerous orchards open their doors to the public in season for farm gate sales. Summer is the best time for plums and stonefruit, while the autumn brings apples and pears; winter is the time for citrus. Some of our favourites include:

The Fruit Corner 1 Bracken Rd, Pickering Brook; 📞 9293 8024; 📘 thefruitcornerpickeringbrook; 🕐 09.00–15.00 Thu–Sun. Passed down the generations since 1953, this family-run business specialises in apples but also makes artisan preserves.

Fruit Loop 211 Merrivale Rd, Pickering Brook; 📞 0411 271 714; 📘 fruitlooppickeringbrook; 🕐 call for hours. Small, family-run orchard selling stonefruits, apples, pears & figs from their shed, among others.

Irymple Orchard 140 Irymple Rd, Roleystone; 📞 0430 783 471; 📘 irympleorchardroleystone; 🕐 13.00–17.00 Wed–Fri, 10.00–17.00 Sat–Sun – call for season dates. Run by the Bettenay family since 1901, these guys are specialists in cherries.

Leotta's 741 Canning Rd, Carmel; 📞 9293 5226; 📘 Leottas; 🕐 Dec–Mar 08.00–16.00. Small, longstanding orchard with a reputation for stonefruits.

WHAT TO SEE AND DO

Kalamunda and around In many respects, this is the closest thing the Perth Hills have to an anchor point, and the town is easily explorable on foot. A good starting point for learning about the area is **Kalamunda History Village** (56 Railway Rd; w kalamundahistoricalsociety.com; ⊕ 10.00–15.00 Mon–Wed & Fri, noon–15.00 Thu, 10.00–16.00 Sat–Sun; A$8/4 adult/child), the largest local history museum in WA, owned by the Kalamunda and Districts Historical Society, which has open-air exhibits that illustrate how life developed in the Perth Hills alongside the then-nascent fruit and timber industries that were the backbone of the area in the late 1800s and early 1900s. The two Heritage-listed passenger railway stations and platforms on site – which operated until 1927 and 1948, respectively, with a G-class locomotive – were relocated here and are a centrepiece of the exhibit; other touches include a post shop (with bottles, jars and an old-time cash register), a school (in use until 1970) with period furnishings, the carriage shed, housing old transport including horse-drawn carriages, and the orchard shed, with period equipment. The impressive details here offer breadth and depth to the village that help make it stand out from historical displays elsewhere in the state that focus more on cottages and housing (though there are some of those here too, including McCullagh Cottage, which you can pass through).

Also run by the Kalamunda Historical Society is the 1881 Heritage-listed **Stirk Cottage** (12 Kalamunda Rd; w kalamundahistoricalsociety.com; ⊕ 13.00–16.00 Sun; A$8/4 adult/child), the town's first dwelling, home to Frederick and Elizabeth Stirk and their nine children. The Stirks built the cottage by using material they found on their 6ha property – bear in mind that in 1881 the Perth Hills were considered very isolated. The house has three rooms – the entire family shared one bedroom – though they moved to bigger digs in the late 1890s. After that the cottage had a series of renters, until the cottage and landholding were bought by the local government in 1949 for public purposes – with the historical society taking on management in 1969.

A number of self-guided **heritage walking trails** run across Kalamunda, linking together the town's historical buildings and points of interest including Stirk Cottage, Town Square Hall and the Darling Range Roads Board Office, which is now a Dome café. The hill setting also makes for good **cycling**; the Kalamunda Mountain Bike Collective (w kmbc.org.au) is one of WA's go-tos for serious cyclists, and the Kalamunda Mountain Biking Park (Paulls Valley) has 40km

MARKETS IN KALAMUNDA

Kalamunda has a couple of excellent markets worth visiting if you're on the hunt for good-quality local souvenirs and gifts. Perth's premier arts and crafts market, **Kalamunda Artisan Markets** (w kalamundaartisanmarket. com.au) show off crafts and local produce from some 170 makers, running on the first Saturday of each month at the Central Mall between 08.30 and 14.00. Also at the Central Mall, the **Kalamunda Farmers' Market** (w kalamundafarmersmarket.com) runs each Sunday from 08.00 until noon, showcasing a huge array of produce from the Perth Hills including local fruit and veg, bread, cakes, juices, honey, olive oil, flowers, natural beauty products and more. Between October and April, the last Friday of the month sees the **Kalamunda Night Markets** (w kalamundanightmarket.com.au) on Haynes Street, featuring a variety of food stalls, local sellers and live entertainment.

of track from beginner to expert; maps are available for download from the collective's website. Kalamunda is also the northern terminus for the Bibbulmun Track (see box, page 109).

For something a little different, the **Calamunnda Camel Farm** (361 Paulls Valley Rd; w camelfarm.com; ⊕ 09.00–14.00 Thu–Fri, 09.00–16.00 Sat–Sun) offers a variety of camel rides in the bush, as well as courses on camel training and handling.

In the northwest of town towards Gooseberry Hill are the peaceful **Patsy Durack's Rose Gardens** (33 Parke Rd, Gooseberry Hill; w patsydurackrosegardens. com; ⊕ 10.00–16.30 Sun, other days/times by appointment), home to hundreds of bushes, with information plaques, and a shop. The summer home of the old Perth Archbishop in 1915, Patsy and her partner bought it in 1988, building it up over time themselves to house over 600 rosebushes – chosen by Patsy for colour, form and longevity. Note the pale pink madame presidents and the lavender angel faces. This is a de facto education centre too – lots of info on offer if you're an amateur grower. Even if you're not, the grounds are lovely – and are a nice spot for one of their Devonshire teas. Another delightful garden is found a 15-minute drive south of Kalamunda: **Melville's Rose n Garden** (105 Tanner Rd, w rosengardenperth. com; ⊕ 10.00–16.00 Tue–Sun), perhaps Perth's foremost specialist on roses and complementary plants, who stock a wide variety. We absolutely love the white-and-red striped candy cane rosebushes we bought here for our own garden.

On the northeast edge of town, the 375ha **Kalamunda National Park** is not considered to be one of the Perth area's headliners, but does have a pair of pleasant walking trails through its woodlands of jarrah, wandoo and butter gum (sometimes known as ghost gum due to its powdery bark). The **Schipp Road Walking Trail** (3.8km loop) follows the Piesse Creek while the **Rocky Pool Walk** (4.5km return) takes you to a beautifully scenic and tranquil water pool, framed by boulders and bushland. A more popular national park lies just north of Kalamunda at **Gooseberry Hill** ✳. The one-way scenic drive through the park – known as the Zig Zag – offers sensational views out to the Perth skyline and magnificent photo opportunities as you head down the hill. From Kalamunda, take Williams Street north, where it turns into Lascelles Parade and then becomes the Zig Zag. It ends on Ridge Hill Road, from where you can head west to Watsonia Road to circle back to Kalamunda.

Lesmurdie Falls ✳
One of WA's best-known waterfalls, partly due to its proximity to Perth, this spectacular 40m cascade is located 3km east of Lesmurdie – take Lesmurdie Road north, and then Falls Road west. Walking trails (the longest of which is the 3km Valley Loop Trail) lead from the top of the falls, where there is a lookout down to the base. There are two access points to the falls: Falls Road takes you to the car park at the top, while Palm Terrace goes to the base (handy if you don't want to do all the climbing).

At Lesmurdie's southern edge along Welshpool Road, the **Lions Lookout** ✳ is a superb place to take in the views over the Perth skyline (especially at sunset). Just southwest of the lookout is the **Kanyana Wildlife Rehabilitation Centre** (120 Gilchrist Rd, Lesmurdie; ☎ 9291 3900; f KanyanaWildlife; ⊕ call for hours), which has a breeding programme for all sorts of threatened animals including echidnas, bandicoots and parrots as well as a wildlife hospital. Tours, including a nocturnal one, can be booked by phone.

Bickley-Carmel Valley
Just east of Kalamunda, this scenic wine region – centred around the nearby towns of Bickley and Carmel – is freckled with cideries and cellar doors, and the hilly, winding drive between them offers many fabulous

vantage points into the valley. The **Bickley Valley Wine Trail** (download the map at w experienceperth.com/page/bickley-valley-wine-trail) starts at La Fattoria in Pickering Brook (page 105) and winds its way first through Carmel and then up to Bickley, taking in a dozen vineyards and two cideries. If you're short on time, concentrate along Aldersyde and Loaring roads in Bickley, which has four cellar doors in close proximity to one another, plus the Vineyard Kitchen restaurant for lunch (page 105). If you have time to visit to only one place, make it **Fairbrossen** ✳ (51 Carmel Rd; w fairbrossen.com.au; ⊕ 11.00–16.00 Fri–Sun), with Spanish- and French-themed platter options to complement the excellent wines – their Tempranillo and Durif are recommended (and personal favourites). The cheeses are also top quality; this is our go-to winery in the Perth Hills.

Perth Observatory (337 Walnut Rd; w perthobservatory.com.au; ⊕ 10.00–16.30 Mon–Fri & 13.00–16.00 Sun) On the state's Heritage Register, this historic observatory has been Perth's link to the cosmos for over a century. Uranus's rings were co-discovered here, as have been over two-dozen planets. Numerous tours, day (2hrs, from A$25) and night (2hrs, A$50), are offered – Night Sky tours show you dying stars, nebulae and other fascinating objects in space, night tours change their focus depending on the state of the moon and day tours focus on equipment and telescopes, as well as the history of the facility. You can also adopt a star – the price depends on brightness, anywhere from A$400 to A$2,000. The observatory also runs astrophotography workshops and 'fairy' afternoon teas. A good stop for something different in Perth.

Beelu National Park Just south Mundaring on Mundaring Weir Road, this popular national park is a favourite with walkers and bikers, home to a range of tracks and trails through its jarrah- and marri-filled woodland. Both the Bibbulmun and the Munda Biddi pass through here (see box, opposite), and the Dell is another popular starting point for mountain biking. Also in the park is the **Perth Hills Discovery Centre** (380 Allen Rd; ☏ 9295 2244), the starting point for a number of walking and cycling trails but also the home of the Parks and Wildlife Service's Nearer to Nature programme (w dpaw.wa.gov.au/get-involved/nearer-to-nature), offering a variety of interactive activities for children themed around the natural environment.

A number of scenic viewpoints are dotted along Mundaring Weir Road including South Ledge, from where you can see the **Mundaring Weir**, a huge dam collecting water from the Helena River. The weir is of huge significance in West Australian history – water from here was pumped in C Y O'Connor's pipeline (see box, page 95) to Kalgoorlie to sustain the Goldfields at the start of the 1900s. The dam can hold nearly 64 billion litres of water, with the dam wall rising for 42m and measuring 308m long.

Armadale On Perth's southeastern fringe, the City of Armadale is the last stop in the metro area if you're getting on to the Albany Highway to go down south. While it is technically part of the Perth Hills, Armadale has developed a culture, heritage and identity very distinct from the likes of Kalamunda and Lesmurdie owing to its distance from those two centres (27km and 23km, respectively), and its location at the base of, rather than in, the hills. Armadale also has a 'gateway to Perth' feel that is different from the other hills' centres, as this is where the Albany Highway and South Western Highway converge and junction at the entrance to the metro area in Perth's far southeast. Today, Armadale is seen as a Perth suburb with a somewhat rough- and-tumble climate and you'll probably raise eyebrows if you say you're taking a long weekend here – better to visit as a day trip, or as a bookend to the rest of the hills.

Two of the world's greatest long-distance trails have their terminus in the Perth Hills. The epic **Bibbulmun Track** (w bibbulmuntrack.org.au) stretches for nearly 1,000km from Kalamunda to Albany, and the northern terminus is well-marked near Kalamunda town centre. The walking trail's identifying marker – the Aboriginal Dreaming Rainbow Serpent, Wagyl, in a yellow triangle – is a well-known sight in national parks and hiking trails throughout the southern part of the state. And what a hike it is. The track passes through parts of the Darling Range, jarrah, karri and tingle forests, the hills of the Blackwood, and then along the beautiful coastline of the south coast from Northcliffe to its end point in Albany. Finishing it is considered prestigious and you become known as an 'End to Ender'. Parts of the track go through fairly isolated stretches of forest, woodland or scarp, so it sadly isn't possible to do the whole thing as a series of day walks, but it's certainly feasible to do just parts of it. Guided and assisted hikes are possible; visit the website for more information and map packs broken down by section.

Not as well known but equally as long, the **Munda Biddi** is a long-distance off-road cycling track that follows a similar trajectory to the Bibbulmun – it's northern terminus is at Mundaring, and it winds south through forest and then east along the coast from Northcliffe. While most of the trail is gentle, there are some challenging parts and preparation and an accurate understanding of your fitness and ability is essential – the Munda Biddi Foundation is a good first-stop resource (w mundabiddi.org.au). Jarrah forests, pristine rivers and tidy towns like Nannup are some of the highlights – a veritable tour-de-force of the South West, followed by the spectacular southern coastline from Walpole to Albany. The ride can be broken up and parts done as day trips as well.

A good way to take in the city's main sights is the 34km **Armadale Hills Scenic Drive** (map available to download at w perthhillsarmadale.com.au), which runs in a zig-zaggy semi-circle through the hills behind town and to the east, ending up in Kelmscott on the Albany Highway north of Armadale. You'll pass a great old English-style pub in the **Last Drop Elizabethan** (25 Canns Rd, Bedfordale; w lastdropelizabethan.com; ⊕ 11.00–23.00 Mon–Sat, 11.00–22.00 Sun) with good burgers and handcrafted beers. The route then winds past **Phillips Galleries & Pottery** (20 Wymond Rd; ✆9397 5394; ⊕ call for hours), run by Jill Phillips, who produces a collection of pots, ornaments, baskets, scarves, cushions and more. Continuing on, you'll pass the entrance to **Araluen Botanic Park** (362 Croyden Rd, Roleystone; w araluenbotanicpark.com.au; ⊕ Aug–Apr 09.00–18.00 daily, May–Aug 09.00–16.00 daily; A$10/5 adult/child), 14ha of developed gardens in the hills, with terraces, stone pathways and old cabins. The park is particularly noted for its roses (the state's biggest collection) as well as its tulips – 150,000 bulbs in springtime. Being in the hills, the up-down walking can be a chore if you're expecting another flat Kings Park, but it's a cool retreat from the city and a beautiful spot. There's also a café.

Another refreshment stop on the trail is the **Naked Apple Cider House** (1088 Brookton Hwy; w nakedapple.com.au; ⊕ 11.30–15.30 Wed, 11.30–21.00 Thu, 11.30–22.00 Fri, 11.30–22.00 Sat, 11.00–19.00 Sun), which along with its creative ciders like Green Caviar has an extensive food menu with things like three-cheese croquettes and buttermilk chicken burgers. Not too far away is **Raeburn Orchards** (4 Raeburn Rd, Roleystone; w raeburnorchards.com; ⊕ 09.00–17.00 daily) with its huge range of apples, pears, stonefruits and citrus – however, there is an A$5 charge to access the property.

For wildlife lovers, there are a couple of other noteworthy stops around Armadale. The **Armadale Reptile and Wildlife Centre** (308 South Western Hwy; w armadalereptilecentre.com.au; ☺ 10.00–16.00 Thu–Tue; A$20/8 adult/child) houses a variety of different native snakes, lizards and mammals, including marsupials like wombats and possums, and is also a rescue centre, while the **Kaarakin Black Cockatoo Conservation Centre** (322 Mills Rd E; w blackcockatoorecovery. com; ☺ by appointment, tours from A$50pp) is a rehabilitation centre that rescues wild black cockatoos that have been injured or attacked.

THE SUNSET COAST: SCARBOROUGH TO TWO ROCKS

Often referred to as Northern Beaches or the Sunset Coast, this stretch of suburban coastline extending 50km from Scarborough Beach to Two Rocks at Perth's northern boundary, which also takes in Hillary's Boat Harbour and Yanchep National Park, is home to over two-dozen beaches. There is some great swimming, snorkelling and surfing here and, though geared towards the local suburbanites, there are also some quality shopping and accommodation options as well.

GETTING THERE AND AROUND   The quickest way to access the beaches is to take the Mitchell Freeway north, and then exit at the cross-street closest to the beach you want to visit. The Mitchell ends just north of Clarkson and Mindarie – you can either head to the coast and take Ocean Drive or Marmion Avenue north, or go inland and take Wanneroo Road north. Alternatively, access West Coast Highway from Cottesloe, which hugs the Indian Ocean coast northbound to Trigg Beach – then branch off on to West Coast Drive to continue north along the coast.

TransPerth's Joondalup Line has several stations that, while off the coast, can be used to access the beaches if you're up for a long walk (5km or so one-way), or if there is a connecting bus to the station you need. Bus 990 goes to Scarborough Beach and bus 423 to Hillary's Marina.

🏠 WHERE TO STAY

🏠 **Hillarys Harbour Resort** (31 apts) 68 Southside Dr, Hillarys; 📞9262 7888; w hillarysresort.com.au. At the boat harbour, this complex features self-contained 1-, 2- & 3-bed apts with full kitchens & living areas. **$$$$**

🏠 **Ramada VetroBlu Scarborough Beach** (52 apts) 48A Filburn St, Scarborough; 📞6248 7000 w ramadavetrobluscarboroughbeach. com. Serviced apts near Scarborough Beach with kitchenettes & stoves. Discounts sometimes offered for advance bookings – worth asking. **$$$$**

🏠 **Indian Ocean Hotel** (59 rooms) 23 Hastings St, Scarborough; 📞9341 1122; w indianoceanhotel.com.au. Partly modelled on Las Vegas's Sands Hotel, rooms here do feel a bit retro but it has a good location only a few mins' walk to Scarborough Beach. There's a bar & a restaurant featuring toasties too. **$$**

🏠 **Yanchep Inn** (36 rooms) 3499 Wanneroo Rd, Yanchep National Park; 📞9561 1001; w yanchepinn.com.au. Heritage-listed rustic building with various accommodation options from superior rooms (with spa baths) to backpacker dorms. Restaurant & garden terrace. **$$**

✗ WHERE TO EAT AND DRINK

✗ **D's Authentic Japanese** 13/1 Glenelg Pl; 📞6209 9169; w dsauthentic.com; ☺ 17.30–20.45 Tue–Sat. Classic Japanese dishes done very

well; the hot pots are an excellent antidote on a cold day. Sushi, sashimi, tempura & teriyaki all recommended. **$$$**

✗ **La Capannina** L1/171 The Esplanade; 📞0455 865 586; **w** lacapanninaperth.com.au; 🕐 11.30–15.00 & 17.00–20.30 daily. Another fine Italian restaurant with dishes; the pizza & pasta here are top-notch– I usually get the 4 formaggi, but the marinara is good too, as is the squid ink tagliolini with crab meat. A good mix of Italian & Australian wines are on offer as well as a robust spirit & cocktail list. **$$$**

✗ **Sandbar** 1 Scarborough Beach Rd; 📞9245 2001; **w** sandbar.com.au; 🕐 07.00–22.00 daily. Relaxed & popular beachside eatery serving 3 meals a day. Sometimes runs quirky theme nights like Nutella Day (featuring Nutella pizzas) & Pisco Sours Day. For lunch the watermelon & quinoa salad is a winner, as are the chilli mussels & prawn linguini. A good place to wind up at after strolling along the beach. **$$$**

✗ **Moments Café** 3/47 Davidson Tce, Joondalup; 📞9301 4800; **w** momentscafe.com.au;

06.30–15.00 Mon–Fri. Quirky little café serving great all-day b/fasts & bagels (bacon & egg is my favourite), along with rolls & burgers. Good coffee too, not least because of the unique froth art atop each cup. **$$**

✗ **Pickled Herring** 5 Enterprise Av, Two Rocks; 📞9561 1096; 🕐 11.30–20.00 daily. Wonderful Korean-run seafood restaurant perched overlooking the Indian Ocean at Perth's outer boundary. Serves classics like fish & chips, salt-&-pepper squid & grilled barramundi, as well as Korean fried chicken & bao. **$$**

✳ ✗ **Wild Fig** 190 The Esplanade, Scarborough; 📞9245 2533; **w** thewildfig.com.au; 🕐 06.00–17.00 Mon–Tue, 06.00–21.30 Sun, Wed–Thu, 06.00–22.00 Fri–Sat. Inventive dishes like 'eggs on fire' – with harissa, chilli jam & chorizo – kimchi chicken burgers & lamb & halloumi skewers make this place a winner. Huge smoothie menu is also a hit. **$$**

ENTERTAINMENT AND NIGHTLIFE

♀**El Grotto** 5/148 The Esplanade; 📞1300 919 557; **w** elgrotto.com; 🕐 11.30–midnight Tue–Thu, 11.30–01.00 Fri–Sat, 16.00–midnight Sun. Mexican cocktails, street food & live music inside the Rendezvous Hotel. It won Australian Tequila Bar of the Year in 2018.

♀**The Lookout** 1–2/148 The Esplanade; 📞9245 4091; **w** thelookoutscarbs.com.au; 🕐 11.00–midnight Sun–Thu, 11.00–01.00 Fri–Sat. In the Rendezvous Hotel, this bar/bowling alley has interesting drinks like watermelon martinis &

bubblegum (vodka) sours. Plenty of burgers & pizzas as well; 10-pin bowling can be reserved online, including bowling brunches that come with prosecco.

♀**Scarborough Beach Bar** 1 Manning St; 📞9205 1200; **w** scarboroughbeachbar.com.au; 🕐 11.00–22.00 Mon–Thu, 11.00–midnight Fri, 08.00–midnight Sat, 08.00–22.00 Sun. Popular & relaxed spot for beach vibes & cocktails. The fish tacos are winners.

ACTIVITIES

Scarborough Beach Surf School Suite 8, 23 Scarborough Beach Rd; **w** surfschool.com. Longstanding operator (since 1986), with courses tailored to beginners & more advanced. They also do courses for kids & teenagers & hire boards; book on the website.

SCOOTZ Jet Ski Hire 200 West Coast Hwy; **w** scootzjetskihire.com.au. Sea-Doos available from A$450/day; tubes also from A$15.

WHAT TO SEE AND DO Between Scarborough in the south and Two Rocks in the north, there are over two-dozen beaches along this stretch of coast. With so many in such close proximity, it can be difficult to choose which to visit, and there is only so much difference between the soft sand and clear water at one versus another. Some word association may be helpful: Scarborough – history; Hillarys – shopping; Yanchep – koalas and lagoons; and Two Rocks – well, rocks.

Scarborough Beach Named after the English beach resort, the stretch of sand here – backed by trendy cafés and restaurants, fronted by clear waters that are great

Following the coast for 8km from Scarborough to Hillarys, West Coast Drive (not to be confused with West Coast Highway – you turn off the highway on to West Coast Drive at South Trigg Beach) is a truly stunning road, with excellent views and vantage points past some of Perth's best-known beaches. After Scarborough, the first stop is **Trigg Beach** – one of the city's best surfing spots. Check the waves before visiting though the Trigg Beach Surf Cam at w surfline.com. A few hundred metres north is **Bennion Beach**, which is often overshadowed by Trigg and is usually much quieter – ideal for taking in the views over the Indian Ocean from its lookout area.

Next up is **Mettams Pool**, a beautiful, sheltered lagoon with varying shades of green, turquoise and dark blue, popular with families due to the calm and shallow waters and considered to be one of the best snorkelling spots in the city – look out for starfish. You'll then pass **Hamersley Pool**, another reef-enclosed protected spot, on your way to **North Beach**, a vibrant, buzzing suburb with plenty of eateries and a sweep of white sand sloping down to azure blue waters. After 1.5km you'll pass the blink-and-you'll-miss-it **Waterman's Bay Beach**, which has a playground that complements the generally calm and shallow waters – it's hidden away out of sight, so offers plenty of privacy and solitude for families. Nudging it to the north is **Marmion Beach,** from where the Marmion Angling and Aquatic Club (MAAC) dive and snorkel trail starts – 400m long, in water ranging from 2m to 6m, with 20 information markers on the sea bottom; you can see rays, blue devils and sweeps here. The final beach on West Coast Drive is **Sorrento Beach**, just south of Hillarys, which is known for its particularly soft sand and calm conditions, due to an offshore reef.

for swimming and surfing – has been a place to see and be seen for over a century. Some consider this to be the finest beach in Perth. Supposedly, a Sydney reporter visiting the area in the late 1800s remarked on the beach's high quality, which initially put it on the radar; however, before sealed roads it was difficult to reach, and large-scale development didn't really get off the ground until after World War II. The beach was one of the first to allow men to take their shirts off in 1935; in the early 1900s, bathers, including men, had to be clothed neck to knee and in some grainy photographers you can see men lounging on the sand in full suit and tie. Today, development has swallowed it up – a heated, A$50m beachfront swimming pool opened in 2018 as part of a A$100 million redevelopment of the Esplanade – and it's packed with surfers and Perth's teens, but squint and you can see the history.

Hillarys Boat Harbour (86 Southside Dr; w hillarysboatharbour.com.au) Developed in the 1980s as the first major marina in the Perth's north metro, this major tourism and shopping precinct (four million annual visitors) features **Hillarys Boardwalk** and **Sorrento Quay**, both popular family destinations with their protected beach, cafés and restaurants. You can also book helicopter rides for scenic flights down the coast, whale-watching cruises (this is a major humpback migration area) and deep-sea fishing charters from here.

The harbour is also home to **AQWA – Aquarium Western Australia** (91 Southside Dr; w aqwa.com.au; ⏱ 09.00–16.00 daily; A$30/18 adult/child). Themed as a journey along the state's coast and broken up into representative sections, the coral reef exhibit, one of the world's biggest and using local corals, is stunning in its colour. The 'danger zone' showcases seemingly everything in the water in Western Australia that can kill you – which, it turns out, is quite a lot from stonefish and lion fish to box jellyfish and cone shells. They also organise dive and snorkel experiences with sharks (from A$195).

Yanchep National Park and Yanchep Beach ✳

Koalas are not endemic to WA, and **Yanchep National Park** – where a small colony has lived since the 1930s – is one of the only places in the state to see them. Strolling along the 240m Koala Boardwalk, they are usually spotted sleeping lazily in eucalyptus trees, though they occasionally drop down to chomp on a few leaves, delighting children and adults alike. Nine other walking trails criss-cross the park, ranging from 500m to 46km, each individually designed to showcase a certain aspect of the area's biodiversity. If you're here early in the morning or late in the day, you might spot one of the many Western grey kangaroos, while cockatoos can be seen throughout the day.

Dotted around the park are some 400 caves, and this is one of the best places outside the South West Region to see stalactites, among other geological processes and formations (enquire at the visitors centre about guided tours). The Cabaret Cave used to be the site of a secret party club nearly a century ago, and today can be rented as an event venue.

The park hosts **Wangi Mia** (🕐 Sun & public holidays only), an Aboriginal cultural experience showcasing Noongar life, including language and oral traditions. There is a digeridoo demonstration, and you will be taught about the six seasons and their impact on Aboriginal life (see box, page 30), and how knowledge is passed down from generation to generation.

Around 8km west of the park is **Yanchep Beach**, one of our favourite beaches in the Perth Metropolitan Area; a reef-sheltered lagoon with good snorkelling that opens up to a wider beach with a fair amount of chop for wave action. The car park looking out to the ocean is framed with green palms, presenting a picture-postcard view against the golden sand and turquoise water, with the greys of the reef poking up.

Two Rocks

This is the Perth Metro Area's northern border, named after – you guessed it – two massive rocks jutting out of the sea near the marina, a little reminiscent of the 12 Apostles on the Great Ocean Road in Victoria. The drawcard here, aside from the rocks, is beach's solitude – it's also a good swimming beach, and the rocks are bird sanctuaries. The town's location, 60km north of the CBD, means that not many weekenders venture this far. The hulking Heritage-listed King Neptune statue in the centre has also been restored and is a town icon.

GUILDFORD AND THE SWAN VALLEY

Wine and the Swan Valley go hand-in-hand, but few people realise that viticulture in this part of Perth actually dates to 1829, making it the state's oldest wine region – easily beating the South West and Great Southern by over a century. The area has been associated with agriculture since European settlement and small-scale wine production began here almost immediately when the British arrived, though it wasn't until the 1900s that it became a major industry. Today Chenin Blanc and Shiraz tend to be the most favoured varieties, though others like Verdelho can be found and there is a strong selection of sparkling and fortifieds. Guildford, the area's main town, was one of the original trio of settlements in this part of the state and is classified as a 'Historic Town' by the National Trust and is on the State Register of Historic Places. It's a popular weekend escape with Perth residents; the preserved colonial buildings give the town a charming character that invite visitors to meander before heading out to taste the wines in the valley just north.

GETTING THERE AND AROUND By car, it's about 15km from Perth CBD northeast along the Swan River to Guildford. The town is just north of Perth Airport – the planes descend low overhead on final approach. On public transport, Guildford is on TransPerth's Midland Line and bus 955 goes to Ellenbrook. However, if you're planning a wine tour consider hiring a car or joining an organised tour.

TOURIST INFORMATION AND WINE TOURS

🅘 Swan Valley Visitor Centre Meadow St & Swan St, Guildford; 📞9207 8899; w swanvalley. com.au; ⏰ 09.00–16.00 daily
Out & About Wine Tours w outandabouttours. com.au. Half- & full-day winery tours (from 10.00 to 17.00, A$85/125pp) showcasing reds, whites & fortifieds, as well as beers & spirits. Includes lunch & a cheese platter. The Swan River cruise (from A$169pp) can be done as either morning vineyard/

afternoon cruise or vice-versa, with visits to 2 wineries. They can pick-up/drop-off in the CBD.
Swan Valley Tours w svtours.com.au. A true gourmet experience with wine, beer, cider, chocolate & cheese, the Indulgence coach tour (from A$130pp) takes in 4 wineries, plus lunch & a chocolate tasting. They also do a Swan cruise (from A$165pp) with 3 wineries & a cheeseboard.

WHERE TO STAY *Map, opposite*
Hotels & B&Bs
🏠 **Novotel Vines Resort** (103 rooms) Verdelho Dr, The Vines; 📞9297 3000; w vines. com.au. With a relaxed, exclusive feel, rooms have full-length windows & wonderful views of the surrounding bush, & executive suites have spa baths. Apts & villas also available. The grounds also host a day spa, outdoor pool, tennis academy, 18-hole golf course & an upscale restaurant & café. This is a place to go to escape. **$$$$**
🏠 **Swan Valley Retreat** (2 rooms) 79 Irwin St, Henley Brook; 📞6118 4566; w swanvalleyretreat. com.au. Featuring their own private outdoor spas (with jacuzzi), freestanding bathtubs & modern kitchenette, rooms at this peaceful retreat are the height of luxury. There is an on-site day spa offering massages, facials & hydrotherapy, a Canadian-style cedar sauna & an outdoor fire pit. Continental b/fast inc; grazing-style dinner platters & hampers can be organised. **$$$$**
🏠 **Guildford River Retreat** (3 rooms) 18 Victoria St, Guildford; 📞9379 1728; w guildfordriverretreat.com.au. This elegant Heritage-listed cottage, within walking distance from Guildford's restaurants & shops, has a library,

leafy terrace & inviting saltwater pool to go with the richly appointed rooms (featuring Nespresso machine). **$$$**
✳️ 🏠 **Nivalis B&B** (3 rooms) 78 Park St, Henley Brook; 📞0438 803 630; w nivalisbedandbreakfast.com. Our favourite place to stay in the Swan Valley. Owner Yvonne is a professional chef & serves cooked-to-order homely

PERTH *Guildford & the Swan Valley*
For listings, see from above

🛏️ **Where to stay**
1 Acclaim Swan Valley Tourist Park
2 Discovery Parks – Swan Valley
3 Guildford River Retreat
4 Nivalis B&B
5 Novotel Vines Resort
6 Rose & Crown
7 Stirling Arms
8 Swan Valley Retreat
9 Swan Valley Sisters

✖️ **Where to eat and drink**
10 Black Swan Winery
11 Cottage Tea Rooms
12 Duckstein German Brewery
13 The King & I
14 Mimmo's Gourmet Gelato
      The Posh Convict & The 1841 (see 6)
15 Old Fig Tree
16 Sandalford
17 Sitella Winery & Café

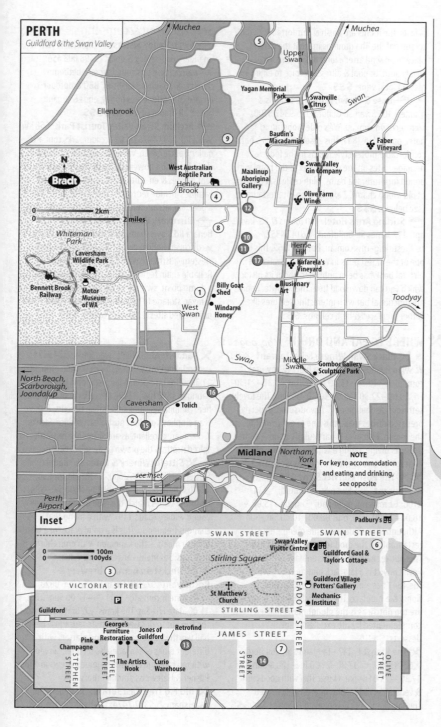

PERTH
Guildford & the Swan Valley

N

Bradt

0   2km
0   2 miles

Muchea

Muchea

Upper
Swan

Swan

Ellenbrook

Yagan Memorial
Park

Swanville
Citrus

Baudin's
Macadamias

Faber
Vineyard

West Australian
Reptile Park

Maalinup
Aboriginal
Gallery

Swan Valley
Gin Company

Henley
Brook

Olive Farm
Wines

Whiteman
Park

Caversham
Wildlife Park

Herne
Hill

Kafarela's
Vineyard

Bennett Brook
Railway

Motor
Museum
of WA

Illusionary
Art

Toodyay

Billy Goat
Shed

Windarra
Honey

West Swan

Swan

North Beach,
Scarborough,
Joondalup

Middle
Swan

Gomboc Gallery
Sculpture Park

Caversham

Tolich

Midland

Northam,
York

NOTE
For key to accommodation
and eating and drinking,
see opposite

see inset

Perth
Airport

Guildford

Inset

0   100m
0   100yds

Padbury's

SWAN STREET   SWAN STREET

Swan Valley
Visitor Centre

Guildford Gaol &
Taylor's Cottage

Stirling Square

VICTORIA STREET

St Matthew's
Church

Guildford Village
Potters' Gallery

Mechanics
Institute

Guildford

STIRLING STREET

George's
Furniture
Restoration

Jones of
Guildford

Retrofind

Pink
Champagne

JAMES STREET

The Artists
Nook

Curio
Warehouse

STEPHEN STREET

ETHEL STREET

BANK STREET

MEADOW STREET

OLIVE STREET

b/fasts; the rooms are plush & comfortable, & the serenity of the 4ha grounds make it the perfect place to unwind after a long drive into town. Lovely outdoor pool & alfresco terrace to enjoy a glass of local wine. **$$$**

☀ 🏠 **Rose & Crown Hotel** (28 rooms & 4 suites) 105 Swan St, Guildford; 📞9347 8100; **w** rosecrown.com.au. WA's oldest operating hotel, opened in 1841, this absolute gem has both comfortable motel-style rooms in the lodge & heritage suites on the upper level of the hotel with period furniture, spa baths, high ceilings & plenty of old-world charm. 2 excellent on-site restaurants (see below). **$$$**

🏠 **Stirling Arms Hotel** (10 rooms & 1 3-bed apt) 117 James St, Guildford; 📞6142 4352; **w** thestirlingarms.com.au. Built in 1852, this is one of the oldest pubs in Western Australia – a pictoral book has been published about its history, which you can download from the website. Rooms are functional but with interesting features like corner fireplaces & high ceilings. **$$**

Self-catering & camping

🏠 **Swan Valley Sisters** (4 chalets) 1715 Gnangara Rd, Henley Brook; 📞0498 008 656; **w** swanvalleysisters.com. Large, 3-bedroom chalets with laundry facilities, BBQ & outdoor terrace. The café serves honey, eggs & organic bread, all produced on site. **$$$$**

🏠 **Acclaim Swan Valley Tourist Park** 6581 W Swan Rd; 📞9274 2828; **w** acclaimparks.com.au/gallery/perth/swan-valley-tourist-park. National chain featuring powered & unpowered sites, tent pitches & en-suite cabins with full kitchens. Facilities include rec rooms, laundry, dump point & a pool. Can accommodate large motorhomes. **$$**

🏠 **Discovery Parks – Swan Valley** 91 Benara Rd, Caversham; 📞9279 6700; **w** discoveryholidayparks.com.au/caravan-parks/western-australia/swan-valley-swan-valley. Reliable chain featuring the usual facilities plus a dump point, swimming pool, playground & caravan storage to go with their powered & unpowered sites & en-suite cabins. **$$**

🍴 **WHERE TO EAT AND DRINK** *Map, page 115*

☀ 🍴 **Black Swan Winery & Restaurant** 8600 W Swan Rd; 📞9296 6090; **w** blackswanwines.com.au; ⏱ 10.30–15.30 Mon–Thu, 10.30–21.30 Fri, 10.00–22.30 Sat, 09.30–16.30 Sun. The lovely setting, seasonal menu & flavoursome, expertly prepared dishes make this one of our favourites in the region. Fish here is particularly good – & the desserts divine. Being a winery, there are plenty of drops for you to choose from as well. **$$$$**

🍴 ☀ **The Posh Convict & the 1841 Restaurant** 105 Swan St, Guildford; 📞9347 8100; **w** rosecrown.com.au; ⏱ noon–15.00 & 18.00–21.00 daily, plus 08.00–10.30 Sat–Sun. Although they share the same menu, these 2 restaurants in the grounds of WA's oldest hotel (see above) have very different vibes – the Posh Convict is a laidback lounge & bar, while the 1841 has a more classical feel, wooden floors & a fireplace. The steaks & Wagyu burgers are top notch, as is the ploughman's platter, complemented by the excellent wine list & desserts. **$$$$**

🍴 **The King & I** 147–149 James St, Guildford; 📞6278 3999; ⏱ 17.30–21.30 Tue–Thu & Sun, 17.30–22.00 Fri–Sat. Classic Thai with good curries & vegetarian dishes, plus interestingly named specials like 'Health & Longevity' & 'Spice I Am'. **$$$**

🍴 **Sandalford** 3210 W Swan Rd; 📞9374 9374; **w** sandalford.com; ⏱ 11.30–16.00 Mon–Thu, 11.30–21.00 Fri–Sun. A long-standing winery dating to 1840 (page 119), the cellar door restaurant here combines Australian & Italian flavours, & there is an emphasis on West Australian produce. Steaks & pizzas are excellent, as are dishes like figs with spiced ricotta & the prawn pasta salad. **$$$$**

☀ 🍴 **Sittella Winery & Café** 100 Barrett St, Herne Hill; 📞9296 2600; **w** sittella.com.au; ⏱ 10.00–16.00 Tue–Fri, 09.30–16.00 Sat–Sun. Beautiful wines match the food at this relatively young winery (page 119), with a menu that changes frequently. This is a good place for a taste of bush meats – the kangaroo with emu chorizo is delicious. Set menus are excellent value. **$$$**

☀ 🍴 **Duckstein German Brewery & Restaurant** 9720 W Swan Rd; 📞9296 0620; **w** duckstein.com.au; ⏱ 11.00–17.00 Sun–Thu, 11.00–late Fri–Sat. The kransky & bratwurst make the trip out to this German-style sausage & beer hall worthwhile. Hearty sharing platters with different types of sausage also on offer, served with red cabbage & crispy potatoes. Brews include Pilsner & Hefeweiss among others. **$$**

🍴 **Old Fig Tree Restaurant** 55 Benara Rd, Caversham; 📞9377 7474; **w** theoldfigtree.com.

THE BOUNTY OF THE SWAN VALLEY

Though the Swan Valley is best known for its wine, it spent its early years as an all-round agricultural producer – with its table grapes, rather than its wine grapes, often taking centre stage. A few of my favourite produce shops are listed below, but the **Fresh Seasonal Produce Trail** (available from the visitors centre or to download from their website: w swanvalley.com.au/ See-and-Do/The-Swan-Valley-Trails/Fresh-Seasonal-Produce-Trail) lists many more, which you can then match to the four-season calendar to see what is available. An easy circuit (which works for wine too) is to take West Swan Road north from Guildford until the T-junctions with the Great Northern Highway, head south on the highway and then at Midland take the Great Eastern Highway back to Guildford.

Baudin's Macadamias 85 Memorial Av; 0412 298 665; ⊕ by appointment. Pick your own macadamias from Paula & Andy's 150-tree orchard. Also offers year-round orchard tours, as well as farm gate stalls with pre-packaged nuts from May to Dec.

Billy Goat Shed 6540 W Swan Rd; ⊕ 09.00–17.00 Sat–Sun. Roadside shed that's great for homegrown melons & grapes.

Kafarela's Vineyard 706 Great Northern Hwy, Herne Hill; 9296 0970; ⬚ kafarelasvineyard; ⊕ 10.00–17.00 Sat–Sun. This 7ha vineyard has been run by the Kafarela family since 1944, & today they specialise in non-alcoholic wines & local fruits (including pick-your-own grapes), & more recently have diversified into dolls & quilts.

Swanville Citrus 15 Nolan Av; 9296 4110; ⊕ 10.00–17.00 Fri, 09.00–17.00 Sat–Sun, noon–17.00 Mon. Just off the Great Northern Highway, this family-run orchard is a must-stop for citrus fruits, especially mandarins.

Tolich 2540 W Swan Rd; 0437 151 917; ⊕ 07.30–16.00 Fri–Sun. Varied roadside stall selling strawberries, citrus & avocados, plus vinegar & jams made by a local *nonna* (Croatian for grandma).

Windarra Honey 5 George St; 9274 6649; w windarrahoney.com; ⊕ 09.00–17.00 daily. Sells all sorts of honey from clover to creamed to jarrah, as well as honey-based products like lotions & soaps.

3

au; ⊕ 11.00–15.00 & 17.00–21.00 Wed–Sat, 11.00–15.00 Sun. You might feel like you've been transported to the Mediterranean at this homely restaurant, with exposed-brick arches & a vine-covered terrace. Classic mains like scotch fillet & barramundi are done well, plus American-influenced dishes like baby back ribs.

The fig pudding with butterscotch for dessert is excellent. **$$**

✳ ✕ **Mimmo's Gourmet Gelato** Unit 9/121 James St, Guildford; 0419 004 926; w mimmosgourmetgelato.com.au; ⊕ noon–20.00 Tue–Sun. Award-winning gelato with incredible flavours like red velvet & tiramisu. A must-try. **$**

SHOPPING

Antiques Antiquing is one of Guildford's major draws & shopping here is like poking through Perth's old basement. A stroll up & down James St, the main thoroughfare, takes you past numerous dealers & bric-a-brac shops.

Curio Warehouse 4/175 James St; 9379 3883; ⊕ 10.30–16.00 Thu–Mon. Eclectic range of used media props, old lamps & vintage ware.

George's Furniture Restoration 179 James St; 9279 4755; w georgesfurn.com; ⊕ 10.00–17.00 daily. Vast array of restored cabinets, mirrors, drawers, glassware & collectables.

Jones of Guildford 165 James St; 9378 2065; ⊕ 09.30–17.00 Wed–Mon. Long-standing operator & one of the biggest shops on the strip, with heaps of vinyl records, glassware, old furniture & more.

Pink Champagne 205 James St; ☎9378 2737; ⏱ 10.30–16.30 Tue–Sat, Sun 11.00–15.00 Sun. The go-to spot for vintage clothing.
Retrofind 167 James St; ☎0432 914 980; ⏱ 11.00–15.00 Wed–Fri, 10.00–16.00 Sat–Sun. Furniture & homeware from the 1950s, '60s & '70s – very kitsch.

Arts & crafts

In addition to antiques, the Swan Valley is something of an artists' haven in Perth & galleries abound, though they are dotted around the region rather than concentrated on a particular street.

The Artists Nook 175–179 James St; ☎0439 860 222; w theartistsnook.com; ⏱ 10.00–15.00 Wed–Fri, 11.00–16.00 Sat–Sun. Guildford-based collective with macrame, abstract art, jewellery & sketches from local artists; they also run printmaking workshops.
Gombuc Gallery Sculpture Park 50 James Rd; ☎9274 3996; w gomboc-gallery.com.au; ⏱ 10.00–17.00 Wed–Sun; free. Opened in 1982 & over 2ha, this is the largest privately owned

gallery in WA. A new exhibition opens every month; the outdoor sculpture gallery hosts local & international artists – the works change as art gets sold.
Guildford Village Potters' Gallery 22 Meadow St; ☎9279 9859; w guildfordpotters.webs.com; ⏱ 10.00–16.00 daily. Local collective with nearly 2 dozen artists producing ceramics & pottery. The artists are quite happy to chat with visitors about their work.
Illusionary Art 633 Great Northern Hwy, Herne Hill; ☎0414 319 769; ⏱ 10.00–16.00 Wed–Sun. Thomas Maurer specialises in unique optical illusions & 3D pieces, all created using an angle grinder & aluminium. Pieces are available to buy from his on-site studio shed, & Thomas also takes bespoke requests.
Maalinup Aboriginal Gallery 10070 W Swan Rd, Henley Brook; ☎9296 0711; w maalinup. com.au; ⏱ 10.00–17.00 daily. Meaning 'Place of the Black Swan' in Wardandi, Maalinup features work by Aboriginal artists from the South West. Bush tucker is also available as well as educational talks.

WHAT TO SEE AND DO

Guildford Founded in 1829, Guildford's preserved Victorian and Federation architecture, compact area and cluster of cafés make it a joy to explore on foot. The **visitor centre** on the corner of Meadow and Swan Street is a good place to start your ramblings, from where you can pick up a copy of *Glorious Guildford* (or download it from the website; w swanvalley.com.au/See-and-Do/ Historic-Attractions/Glorious-Guildford) to discover four heritage walks around town, but it's easy enough to explore on your own steam. The centre is housed in the old **Guildford Courthouse**; originally the courthouse was held inside a room at the gaol but got its own dedicated facility courtesy of convict labour in 1866. Some reports say the courthouse's construction was spurred by the widespread knowledge that convict transportation – and with it, easy construction labour – was going to end imminently (which it did in 1868). The clock tower was added in 1901. Next door is the **Guildford Gaol**, dating from 1840, which was constructed by a local settler to deal with the problem of public drunkenness in Guildford. The initial facility was small (only two cells) but when convict labour arrived, significant extensions were added, including quarters, more cells and horse stables. Moondyne Joe (see box, page 248) was once held here. By the end of World War II, the gaol was no longer in use but has been preserved and is listed on the National Trust – visitors can enter with one of the Historical Society's (see below) guides.

Also nearby is to **Taylor's Cottage** (24 Meadow St; ⏱ 10.00–14.00 Tue–Sat), a beautifully preserved worker's house that provides a fascinating look into life in the late 1800s, detailed all the way down to the toilet facility. Today it is home to the Swan Guildford Historical Society (w swanguildfordhistoricalsociety.org. au), who offer guided and group tours of Guildford. At the end of Meadow Street, at the junction with Stirling Street, is the **Mechanics Institute**, opened in 1868 as a library and gathering hall for public events, and it is still used today used as a meeting space.

On the opposite side of Meadow Street is **Stirling Square**, constructed to be the focal point of the colonial town. It is dominated in the centre by **St Matthew's Church** (w stmatthewschurch.org.au), built in 1860 and one of WA's most impressive surviving examples of Gothic Revival architecture. A war memorial and two powder guns, reflecting Guildford's connections to military service, are also in the square.

A final building of note is State Register-listed **Padbury's** (114 Terrace Rd), one of the original department and general stores in the area. Walter Padbury had an impressive rags-to-riches life story – he arrived in Swan River as a nine year old in 1830 and was an orphan within a year. Slowly accumulating funds throughout his early adulthood, he opened his Guildford store in 1865 and became the Guildford Council's first mayor – he eventually ended up elected to State Parliament, and even grew his wealth enough to own a boat fleet. He died in 1907 but had no heirs, leaving his fortune to religious groups and charities. The store is now a popular café (w padburys.com; ⊕ 07.00–14.30 daily, dinner from 17.30 Fri–Sat) – a good place to stop in for a coffee or lunch and take in the historical surrounds.

Wine tours Any visit to the Swan Valley undoubtedly revolves around wine, and today the state's oldest wine region is home to several dozen cellars. The **Swan Valley Fine Wine Trail**, available from the visitor centre or to download from their website, is a great way to sample some top drops; one of the joys of this region is just picking a winery that looks interesting and dropping in to see what's going on – have a look at the map and point. There are also a number of distilleries in the area, including the award-winning **Swan Valley Gin Company** (1050 Great Northern Hwy; w swanvalleygincompany.com.au; ⊕ 11.00–17.00 Fri–Sun), which produces a wide array of gins, including varieties such as kumquat, strawberry and salt bush. Otherwise, my winery recommendations are:

Faber Vineyard 233 Haddrill Rd; ☏ 9296 0209; w fabervineyard.com.au; ⊕ 11.00–16.00 Fri–Sun. 'Faber' means 'craft' in Latin, & owners John Griffiths & Jane Micallef have been perfecting the art of winemaking since 1997. The Chardonnay Blanc de Blanc is recommended; also serves lunches.
Olive Farm Wines ✳ 920 Great Northern Hwy; ☏ 9296 4539; w olivefarmwines.com.au; ⊕ 11.00–16.00 Mon–Fri, 11.00–17.00 Sat–Sun. Established alongside European settlement in 1829, this historic estate has been in the Yurisich family for 4 generations. Try the Cabernet Franc, though the usual Swan Valley stalwart varieties

are also excellent. No advance booking required for groups of up to 9.
Sandalford Wines ✳ 3210 W Swan Rd; ☏ 9374 9374; w sandalford.com; ⊕ 10.00–17.00 daily. Opened by John Septimus Roe (WA's first Surveyor General) in 1829, this 1,600ha site is one of the region's wine powerhouses. Be sure to try some of their fortifieds, including the Sandelera. There's also a top-class restaurant (page 116).
Sittella ✳ 100 Barrett St, Herne Hill; w sittella. com.au; ⊕ 10.00–16.00 Tue–Fri, 09.30–16.00 Sat–Sun. Relatively young in Swan Valley terms (established 1997), but has top-flight Verdelho & Shiraz (& is a wonderful lunch stop, page 116).

Wildlife parks If you're interested in Australia's poisonous snakes, the **West Australian Reptile Park** (92 Henley St, Henley Brook; w wareptilepark.com.au; ⊕ call for hours) has a vast showcase of death adders, brown snakes and tiger snakes, as well as non-venomous pythons, monitor lizards and bush animals like dingo and emu. You can hold some of the reptiles (although not the death adders…), and there's also occasional talks and lectures. Elsewhere, the acclaimed **Caversham Wildlife Park** (233B Drumpellier Dr; w cavershamwildlife.com.au; ⊕ 09.30–16.00

daily; A$30/14 adult/child) has a broader focus with koalas, penguins, kangaroos, wombats and echidnas, plus a variety of birds including kookaburras, tawny frogmouths and cassowaries. You can feed the kangaroos and penguins, and have interactive experiences with some of the other animals – great for kids.

Caversham is part of **Whiteman Park** (2 entry points; Drumpellier Dr & at Beechboro Rd North; w whitemanpark.com.au; ⊕ 08.30–18.00 daily; free to the grounds), a 4,000ha bushland reserve. The bush trails lead to the park's numerous fauna – including bandicoots, echidnas, quendas and kangaroos, as well as long-neck turtles and goannas – and orchids (like pink fairies and cowslips). Rides on Heritage electric trams (A$6/3 adult/child) take a 5km return route through the park every 30 minutes, while a trip on the **Bennett Brook Railway** (A$10/5 adult/child) explores the park's banksia woodlands. Whiteman is also the home of the **Motor Museum of WA** (motormuseumwa.com.au; ⊕ 10.00–16.00 daily; A$16.50/7 adult/child), where the star attraction is Daniel Ricciardo's Red Bull F1 car.

4

Mandurah & the Peel Region

Driving south from Perth, the state capital's urban sprawl slowly gives way to ample waterways, surf beaches, jarrah forests and bucolic cattle, dairy and sheep farms that define the Peel Region – there are even thrombolites here (rock-like structures built by tiny microorganisms that are related to some of the oldest living things on earth). Perhaps no other region in the state packs such a diverse portfolio into such small area as Peel. Its biggest city, Mandurah, makes full use of its location at the head of the Peel Inlet and next to the Indian Ocean to be one of the country's boating and seafood capitals, and is famous for the bottlenose dolphins that love plying the waters around town.

The rest of the region is a playground for lovers of the outdoors: the jarrah forest walkway at Dwellingup and the waterfalls around Serpentine National Park offer some fantastic walks and the hills around Dwellingup and Boddington make for truly scenic drives. The state's biggest annual rodeo is at Boddington, and some of the state's deepest – and most tragic – history is on display in Pinjarra. For food lovers, one of the state's top country pubs is found at Quindanning, while Peel's seafood – particularly its blue manna crabs, celebrated each year at the Mandurah Crab Fest – are making their way into shops across Australia.

SHIRE OF SERPENTINE-JARRAHDALE

Contrasting sharply with Perth's beaches, surf and urban hustle, the forests, tranquil waterfalls and hiking trails of the Shire of Serpentine-Jarrahdale feel a lot further away from the city than just 50km. Serpentine and Jarrahdale have been tied together for over 100 years, when their respective road boards – then the effective governing bodies of many West Australian towns – were amalgamated, and then combined into a joint shire when the road boards were abolished in 1960. The shire, anchored by Serpentine Falls, is one of the oldest tourist attractions in the state and has been a spot for bathers, picnickers and hikers seeking natural pursuits almost since the first European settlers arrived in the Perth area. Today, the shire has become popular for Perth families wanting a 'tree change' – an escape from the city's urban sprawl to a forested country retreat – and a bit more space, land and nature, but still within easy commuting distance of the city. The shire also has multiple sites listed on the State Register of Heritage Places – a wander through Jarrahdale's townsite can feel like a trip back to the early 20th century.

GETTING THERE AND AWAY By **car**, the shire is less than an hour from Perth. The South Western Highway travels down the spine of the shire, passing Armadale and down through Byford, Mundijong (the shire seat) and Serpentine; the entrance to

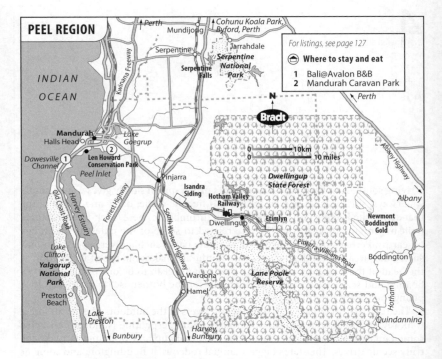

For listings, see page 127

PEEL REGION

🏠 **Where to stay and eat**
1 Bali@Avalon B&B
2 Mandurah Caravan Park

INDIAN OCEAN

Bradt

Serpentine Falls is also along the highway. To reach Jarrahdale, take the Jarrahdale Road off the South Western Highway just after passing Mundijong. Travelling north from Mandurah, the quickest route is to take the Kwinana Freeway to Karnup Road, and then head east on to the South Western Highway. Altogether, Mandurah to Mundijong is 45km.

Transwa's *Australind* **train** passes through several stations in the shire on its way between Perth and Bunbury – at Byford (37mins), Mundijong (44mins) and Serpentine (51mins). TransPerth's **bus** routes 251 to 254 service the shire, and connect Byford, Mundijong and Jarrahdale to Armadale, from which you can catch TransPerth trains.

WHERE TO STAY

🏠 **Tasman Holiday Parks – Serpentine Falls** 2489 South Western Hwy; 🌙 9525 2528; e info@serpentinepark.com.au; w serpentinepark. com.au. Less than 2km from Serpentine Falls, this holiday park consists of bright & modern cabins, holiday homes with private terraces & dog-friendly powered & unpowered sites. Kitchen, ablution block & laundry on site. **$$**

✗ WHERE TO EAT AND DRINK

✗ **Millbrook Winery Restaurant** Old Chestnut Ln; 🌙 9525 5796; w millbrook.wine; 🕐 10.00– 17.00 Thu, Sun & Mon, 10.00–15.00 Fri–Sat. Well-regarded, award-winning winery just south of Jarrahdale with a smart, innovative restaurant showcasing their own produce. Try ordering one of their picnic baskets (advance notice required) from A$45. **$$$**

✗ **Jarrahdale Tavern** 640 Jarrahdale Rd; 🌙 9525 5015; f jarrahdaletavern1; 🕐 11.30– 21.00 Sun–Thu, 11.30–midnight Fri–Sat. Classic pub fare like steak sandwiches, fish & chips & chicken parmi at this local favourite. **$$**

✗ **Lemas** 861 South West Hwy; 🌙 9526 8272; w lemasrooftopbar.com.au; 🕐 11.00–22.00 Wed–Thu & Sun, 11.00–midnight Sat–Sun. In a striking building in Byford, the floor-to-ceiling wraparound glass windows upstairs & the rooftop bar overlooking the town's main thoroughfare give this place a chic vibe. Though the menu is a bit standard, the steaks here are worth visiting for – but vegetarians won't find much for them. $$

✕ **Jarrahdale General Store** 701 Jarrahdale Rd; 📞 9525 5114; 🕐 08.00–16.00 Mon–Fri, 08.00–17.00 Sat–Sun. Rustic roadside café serving filling b/fasts & burgers. The coffee is a great pick-me-up after a bushwalk through the forest. $

THOMAS PEEL

The Peel Region is named after Thomas Peel, an early European settler. Born in England in 1793, Peel became a lawyer there and intended to migrate to New South Wales, until he read about the new Swan River Colony. Known for his prickly and grouchy personality and volcanic temper, there were plenty of friends and family in London who were quite happy to wish him well on his way to Swan River; some reports even say that his father gave him an early inheritance to make the move happen. Peel – along with a few partners – negotiated with the British Colonial Office for several million acres of land; eventually, the partners withdrew, and Peel was conditionally granted one million acres, over a period of time, provided he supplied 400 settlers by the 1 November 1829.

The settlers arrived on three ships – but six weeks after the deadline. Instead of recognising the difficulties of transporting hundreds of settlers by boat from England to what is now Western Australia, and cutting some leeway for being a few weeks late, the British Colonial Office instead made Peel forfeit the grant. Peel threatened to bolt back to England with his settlers, but as the Swan River needed colonists, a compromise was brokered where Peel received 250,000 acres, but to the south, much of which in the region that now bears his name.

The land was unsuitable for farming and conditions terrible, which made Peel's temper all the more ferocious. He was an incompetent farmer, often clashing with Aboriginal peoples who lived in the region, and an even worse administrator. Conditions were so dire that Governor James Stirling untethered the settlers from Peel and allowed them to leave, forcing Peel to move further south to what is now Mandurah. His wife left him and returned to England in 1839, taking their two daughters with her. Peel's run of bad luck became global fodder, and even Karl Marx wrote in *Das Kapital* about him and his struggles to retain settlers in Western Australia.

Peel was also front and centre at the Pinjarra Massacre. Along with Stirling, his desire to make a public demonstration of improved security in the Peel area in order to attract and retain settlers played a role in his participation in the massacre, as did his desire for revenge after an earlier raid on his property killed one of his servants. The battle – which featured settlers armed with firearms and Aboriginals armed with spears – resulted in upwards of 80 Aboriginal deaths (see box, page 133).

The massacre had the opposite effect on the ability to recruit settlers to the Peel Region, as many began fearing Aboriginal reprisals. Peel's financial hardships continued and got worse later in life, when he sank into debt and had to unload some of his land to pay it off. He died broke on 22 December 1865. His grave is at Christ Church Anglican Cathedral in Mandurah (Pinjarra Rd & Sholl St; w anglicanchurchmandurah.org.au).

Mandurah & the Peel Region   SHIRE OF SERPENTINE-JARRAHDALE

4

WHAT TO SEE AND DO

Byford Sculptures Trail While walking or driving along the South Western Highway through Byford, lookout for sculptures of historical people created by internationally renowned local artist Len Zuks, who has had paintings exhibited in the Louvre and at the London Olympics. Developed after consulting Byford's residents, the nine sculptures represent local figures; the traffic inspector Charlie Knox at Jessie Street and the South Western Highway is a personal favourite.

Cohunu Koala Park (Lot 103 Nettleton Rd, Byford; ☎9526 2966; w cohunu.com. au; ⊕ 10.00–16.00 daily; A$15/5 adult/child) Koalas are not native to Western Australia meaning an encounter in the wild is not possible, so this park, along with Yanchep (page 113), is one of the best places to see them in the state. The colony here has more than two-dozen of the eucalyptus-loving marsupials, whose 20 hours of sleep a day put a housecat to shame. You can hold a koala here, as well as chat with the talking parrots, and see other native animals like kangaroos and emus. A good place to spend an afternoon.

Jarrahdale Founded as a timber-milling town in the late 1800s, this historic holiday spot is surrounded by forest, giving its setting in the Darling Range a little extra touch of magic. Classified by the National Trust, Jarrahdale has retained most of its timber-town history through its still-standing buildings. One of the most notable is the **Old Post Office** (631 Jarrahdale Rd; ☎9525 5358; w jarrahdale.com; ⊕ Mar–mid-Dec 10.00–14.00 Sat, 10.00–16.00 Sun), built in 1896 and restored in 1997, and today a much-loved sentimental centrepiece to locals. Its white weatherboard, steeply sloped roof and simple green columns bounding its veranda evoke the tranquil character of a quiet mill town... though legend has it the ghost of a past postworker still resides there! Concern over its fate in the 1990s led to the formation of the **Jarrahdale Heritage Society**, also housed in the building, where there is also a well-regarded museum showcasing high-quality old photographs of what Federation-era mill towns were like.

Horseriding With more horses registered here than in any other shire in the state, Serpentine-Jarrahdale is Western Australia's equine centre. **Jarrahdale Equestrian** (162 Jarrahdale Rd; ☎ 9525 5025; w jarrahdaleequestrian.com.au; ⊕ 10.30–18.30 Mon–Fri, 08.00–18.00 Sat) offers 1- and 2-hour rides through the gentle rolling hills and farmland of the Darling Scarp, culminating with glorious summit views from Bald Hill out over the Perth CBD – capped off with a picnic 'grazing platter' and local wine after in the stables (from A$227pp). They also provide lessons for all ages.

Serpentine National Park (⊕ 08.30–17.00 daily, best to arrive before 10.00 to avoid being turned away; A$15 per vehicle) Stretching along a cleft at the foot of the Darling Scarp between Serpentine and Jarrahdale, this 4,300ha national park has been popular with outdoor lovers for almost a century. Kangaroos, echindas, possums and wallabies are common in the park, as are some 70 species of bird including cockatoos and red-capped parrots. Its star attraction, **Serpentine Falls**, is perhaps the jewel in the shire's crown – a gorgeous raft of water tumbling 15m down a light-brown granite rockface into a pool, deep enough for swimming; on a hot day, the light reflecting off the rockwalls gives the water a blue-green shimmer that makes it extremely inviting. Access is via the 400m return **Falls Walk Trail**, which takes you to a viewing platform or the pool itself. Various other trails criss-cross the park's jarrah and marri woodland, with brilliant views over the Swan Coastal Plain. From the Jarrahdale side of the park, **Kitty's Gorge Walk Trail** (Class 4, 14km return) is the pick of the bunch, passing several falls on Gooralong Brook and numerous granite outcrops. On the southwest edge of the park, **Serpentine Dam** is a major water supplier for the Perth area; it's a good place for spotting kookaburras, cockatoos and parrots, and there's a café overlooking the water. Access is along Kingsbury Drive.

MANDURAH AND PEEL INLET

Mandurah's growth in the last 70 years has been explosive. From a fairly isolated village in a sparkling seaside setting, it first became a retiree haven and industry-worker town with the establishment of the Kwinana industrial complex in the 1950s, before being swallowed up by Perth's urban sprawl and transforming quickly into a middle-class bedroom community as Perth's young adults and country folk migrating to the Big Smoke sought a cheaper yet still-commutable alternative to the capital's ever-increasing house prices. While this growth has resulted in an emerging strip-mall suburban feel, water is still the overwhelming signature feature here, as it was in the city's village days – aside from the string of Indian Ocean beaches, there is Peel Inlet, dolphin-loving canals and the Murray and Serpentine rivers flowing inland. While the occasional marketing comparison of Mandurah's canals to Venice is wildly overblown, the 'relaxed by nature' pun-slogan you will see on highway billboards as you roll into town is an embraced ethos here. Perhaps nowhere in the state is better for grabbing a kayak, pedal-boat or paddleboard and heading out into the deep blue.

With a population of 81,000 – busy by West Australian standards – Mandurah (which means 'meeting place of the heart' in Noongar) is considered to be the most southerly town of the Perth Metropolitan Area. Sitting directly north of Peel Inlet and east of the Indian Ocean, its an easy day trip from Perth by public transport and is gaining in popularity with Perth residents looking for weekend breaks. Its known primarily for its dolphins, crabs and variety of waterways – the Mandurah Crab Fest towards the end of March gets over 100,000 visitors each year, and the term 'Mandurah crabs' gets scrawled on seafood restaurant and shopfront chalkboards statewide. Scooping up your own crabs in Peel Inlet's shallow waters is an iconic local past time.

GETTING THERE AND AROUND Mandurah is 72km south of Perth, more-or-less an hour's **drive** along the Kwinana Freeway, depending on traffic (which can be heavy, even outside rush hour). Exit the Kwinana at Mandjoogoordap Drive, which turns into Mandurah Road near town. The drive from Bunbury, 107km south of Mandurah on the Forrest Highway, takes about 1 hour 15 minutes.

On public transport, the easiest way to get from Perth to Mandurah is on a TransPerth **train**; the Mandurah Line takes just 56 minutes from the CBD (from A$4.90 one-way). **Bus** routes from the CBD are not competitive with the train, taking more than three times as long, but Transwa buses to Bunbury leave from Mandurah train station and take 1 hour 20 minutes (from A$9.25 one-way).

The train station is around 3km from Dolphin Quay and the marina and 17km from Dawesville, but TransPerth has a plenty of bus services to help you get around. From the train station, routes 588 and 589 will take you to the shores of Mandjar

4

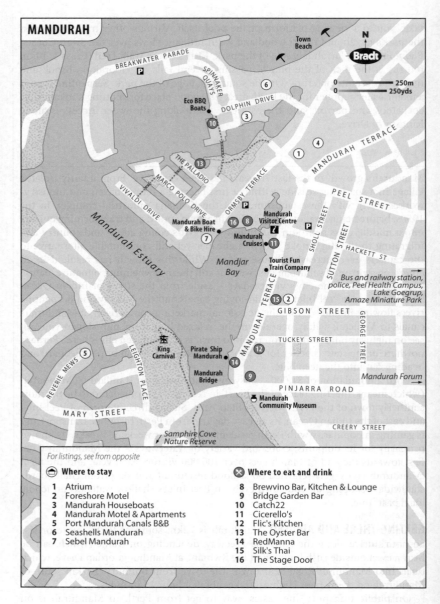

Town
Beach

N

0   250m
0   250yds

BREAKWATER PARADE

SPINNAKER QUAYS

P

6

Eco BBQ
Boats

DOLPHIN DRIVE

3

10

4

1

MANDURAH TERRACE

THE PALLADIO

13

MARCO POLO DRIVE

VIVALDI DRIVE

ORMSBY TERRACE

PEEL STREET

Mandurah Estuary

P

Mandurah
Visitor Centre

16   8

SHOLL STREET

SUTTON STREET

P

Mandurah Boat
& Bike Hire

7

Mandurah
Cruises

11

HACKETT ST

Mandjar
Bay

Tourist Fun
Train Company

MANDURAH TERRACE

Bus and railway station,
police, Peel Health Campus,
Lake Goegrup,
Amaze Miniature Park

15   2

GIBSON STREET

GEORGE STREET

King
Carnival

5

REVERIE MEWS

LEIGHTON PLACE

Pirate Ship
Mandurah

TUCKEY STREET

12

14

Mandurah
Bridge

9

Mandurah Forum

PINJARRA ROAD

MARY STREET

Mandurah
Community Museum

CREERY STREET

Samphire Cove
Nature Reserve

For listings, see from opposite

⊖ **Where to stay**

1   Atrium
2   Foreshore Motel
3   Mandurah Houseboats
4   Mandurah Motel & Apartments
5   Port Mandurah Canals B&B
6   Seashells Mandurah
7   Sebel Mandurah

⊗ **Where to eat and drink**

8   Brewvino Bar, Kitchen & Lounge
9   Bridge Garden Bar
10   Catch22
11   Cicerello's
12   Flic's Kitchen
13   The Oyster Bar
14   RedManna
15   Silk's Thai
16   The Stage Door

Bay, routes 591 to 594 to Halls Head (with 592 continuing to the southern end of
Avocet Island, and 593 and 594 crossing the Dawesville Channel) and route 598 to
Goegrup Lake. **Mandurah Taxis** (4 Harlem Pl; ☏ 131 008; w 13cabs.com.au) can also
provide charter vehicles for larger groups.

TOURIST INFORMATION

☐ **Mandurah Visitor Centre** 75 Mandurah   w visitmandurah.com; ⊕ 09.00–16.00 daily
Tce; ☏ 9550 3999; e visitor@visitmandurah.com;

WHERE TO STAY *Map, opposite, unless otherwise stated*

Mandurah is easily done in a day from Perth, but there are a couple of good options if you want to linger a little longer and explore the rest of the Peel Region – although it's worthwhile booking in advance.

Mandurah Houseboats 13a Dolphin Dr; 9535 9898; e info@houseboatsmandurah. com.au; w houseboatsmandurah.com.au. Explore Mandurah's waterways at your own pace on a fully equipped houseboat. Choose the boat yourself (take a 3D tour of the fleet on the website) & after a tutorial on safety & moorings, simply head off & drop anchor whenever the mood takes you. Bookings are for a minimum number of nights & other conditions apply. **$$$$**

Seashells Mandurah 16 Dolphin Dr; 9550 3000; w seashells.com.au/resorts/ mandurah. One of Mandurah's premier options, the 4.5-star resort on the waterfront at Dolphin Quay offers spacious 1-, 2- & 3-bed apts with spa baths, kitchen & docking stations, as well as luxurious beachfront villas. Facilities include eco-spa, tennis courts, Pilates classes & an infinity pool with BBQ terrace; it's not cheap here, but it is worth it. **$$$$**

Bali@Avalon B&B [map, page 122] (2 rooms) 30 Yeedong Rd, Avocet Island; 0406 534 696; e hosts@baliavalon.com.au; w baliavalon. com.au. The clue is in the name – this peaceful, Indonesian-inspired B&B really does feel like a slice of Bali. Exquisitely appointed villa-style rooms come with Nespresso machine & fridge; 4-poster beds are very comfortable. Outside, the tropical gardens are centred around a solar-heated pool, & there's a fully equipped outdoor kitchen if you don't feel like heading into town for dinner. **$$$**

Sebel Mandurah (89 rooms) 1 Marco Polo Dr; 9512 8300; w thesebel.com/ western-australia/the-sebel-mandurah. Relaxing waterfront hotel; the spacious king rooms overlooking the marina are worth the money. The on-site café does good b/fast & coffee, & the Peninsula Restaurant (11.00–22.00 Sun–Thu, 11.00–23.45 Fri–Sat) has a great range of starters & cocktails. **$$$**

Atrium Hotel (117 rooms) 65 Ormsby Tce; 9535 6633; e reservations@atriumhotel. com.au; w atriumhotel.com.au. These light & modern studios, apts & suites make good use of space (some with kitchenettes & balconies), while loft apts have spiral staircases. Facilities are top-notch – spa, sauna & a heated lagoon pool, plus restaurant & bar. **$$**

Foreshore Motel (17 rooms) 2 Gibson St; 9535 5577; w foreshoremotel.com.au. No-frills en-suite rooms with microwaves & tea/coffee facilities get the job done if location is your priority. Laundry on site. **$$**

Mandurah Motel & Apartments (40 rooms) 110 Mandurah Tce; 9582 9488; w mandurahmotelandapartments.com.au. Good-value motel set within palm-filled grounds; rooms have mini-fridges, while spacious apts have self-contained kitchens. **$$**

Port Mandurah Canals B&B (2 rooms) 3 Reverie Mews, Halls Head; 9535 2252; w portmandurahcanals.com.au. One of the best-value options in town, right on the water. Comfortable rooms, meals by arrangement, BBQ facilities & a pick-up service from the train station. Non-guests can enjoy the Fri morning 'Teapots & Tiaras' high tea overlooking the water (from A$18pp). **$$**

Mandurah Caravan Park [map, page 122] 522 Pinjarra Rd; 9535 1171; e reception@mandurahcaravanpark.com. au; w mandurahcaravanpark.com.au. Well-regarded park with cabins, chalets & powered & unpowered tent sites. The 3-bedroom 'brick villa' is a great, cost-conscious alternative for family accommodation. Facilities include a crab cooker, BBQs, swimming pool, dump point & plenty of games for the kids. Pet-friendly if staying in a caravan or at the campsite. **$**

WHERE TO EAT AND DRINK *Map, opposite*

Mandurah boasts an abundance of riches when it comes to dining, inspired by the fantastic local produce and emerging foodie scene in the wider Peel Region. Listed are just a few of my favourites, but you'll find plenty of places on and around Mandurah Terrace.

127

✖ Brewvino Bar, Kitchen & Lounge
75 Mandurah Tce; ☏0408 789 820; w brewvino.
com.au; ⏰ 11.30–late. Trendy boardwalk spot
with lovely waterside views. Fresh fish, good pizzas
& happy hour 18.00–19.00, plus live music & beer
& wine tastings. $$$
✖ Bridge Garden Bar & Restaurant
2 Pinjarra Rd; ☏9535 1004; w thebridgebar.com.
au; ⏰ 11.00–22.00 Sun–Thu, 11.00–midnight
Fri–Sat. Joining together 2 historic buildings –
Granny's Cooper Cottage from 1869 & Sutton's
Corner Store, run by Granny Cooper's daughter,
from 1929 – on the foreshore, the 'Street Eats'
menu here is worth a go with its Korean-style
chicken, vegan nachos & pork belly bites. $$$
✖ The Oyster Bar The Palladio, Dolphin Dr;
☏9535 1880; w oysterbar.com.au; ⏰ 11.00–
midnight Mon–Sat, 11.00–22.00 Sun. Oysters
served every which way, even with caviar, are the
feature here, but there is enough for non-oyster-
lovers to enjoy too like octopus salad. $$$
✳ **✖ RedManna** 5/9 Mandurah Tce; ☏9581
1248; w redmanna.com.au; ⏰ 17.30–21.00
Wed, 11.30–14.30 & 17.30–21.00 Thu–Sun.
Fantastic award-winning seafood restaurant. The
local crayfish in cheesy mornay is a real champion,
as is the crab bruschetta as an entrée. Plenty
of meat options (including kangaroo) too. The
peach & grapefruit dacquoise for dessert is highly
recommended. $$$
✖ The Stage Door 9 James Service Pl; ☏9586
3733; w thestagedoor.com.au; ⏰ 11.30–20.30
Wed–Thu, 11.00–21.00 Fri–Sat, 11.00–16.00 Sun.
Highly regarded waterfront restaurant with an
eclectic menu – the traditional laksa is tasty, as is

the Portuguese chicken, though the pub classics
like the steak sandwich are also top notch. $$$
✖ Catch 22 1/4 Zephyr Mews; ☏9582 7611;
w catch22mandurah.com.au; ⏰ 17.00–21.00
Wed–Thu, 11.00–21.00 Fri–Sat, 11.00–15.00 Sun.
Kitschy tapas & cocktail bar serving everything
from pulled pork cigars to Mexican potato skins &
sesame beef. The prawn gyozas are a headliner.
$$
✖ Cicerello's 2/73 Mandurah Tce; ☏9535
9777; w cicerellos.com.au; ⏰ 10.00–19.00 daily.
Though fish & chips is their bread & butter, this
iconic restaurant – the Fremantle location has
been operating for over a century (page 93) – has
a huge variety of seafood & 80,000 litres worth of
aquariums for diners to gaze at as they dine. Grilled
& fried options available, plus seafood pastas. $$
✖ Flic's Kitchen 3/16 Mandurah Tce; ☏9535
1661; w flicskitchen.com; ⏰ 11.00–15.00
& 17.30–21.00 Wed–Thu, 11.00–15.00 &
17.00–21.00 Fri, 08.30–15.00 & 17.00–22.00
Sat, 08.30–15.00 Sun. Sophisticated eatery with
beautifully presented, arty plates showcasing
local fare like Rottnest Island scallops, Shark Bay
tiger prawns, blue manna crab & Abrolhos Island
octopus. Their bottomless brunch with an hour of
unlimited prosecco is also a winner. $$
✳ **✖ Silk's Thai Restaurant** 52 Mandurah Tce;
☏9536 2373; w silkthai.com.au; ⏰ 11.30–14.00
& 17.00–20.30 Sun & Tue–Thu, 11.30–14.00 &
17.00–21.00 Fri–Sat. This classic Thai does a great
jungle curry & is a top spot for your Asian food fix,
with friendly staff who can talk you through the
options on offer. $$

SHOPPING Australia's two giants, Coles and Woolworths, are both represented in
the **Mandurah Forum** (330 Pinjarra Rd; ☏9535 5522; w mandurahforum.com.au;
⏰ 08.00–18.00 Mon–Sat, 10.00–17.00 Sun), which also has substantial food court,
take-away and café options.

OTHER PRACTICALITIES
Peel Health Campus 110 Lakes Rd; ☏9531
8000; w peelhealthcampus.com.au

Police 333 Pinjarra Rd; ☏9581 0222

WHAT TO SEE AND DO
Dolphin spotting Mandurah may sometimes compare itself to Venice – a
dramatic oversell – but its waterways are nevertheless lovely, teeming with marine
and birdlife. Its most famous residents are the Indo-Pacific bottlenose dolphins,
often seen travelling in pods of as many as 15 in Peel Inlet and Harvey Estuary.
Their modern history here begins in 1990, when ten were found stranded in Lake

Goegrup; they kept returning, as the inland waterways provide good food and protection. The Mandurah dolphins are noted for being particularly social and love to show off their presence – thus firmly embedding themselves into the hearts of locals. The website w mandurahdolphins.com has a lot of information about the resident dolphins, including about their unfortunate history of strandings – common as the waters are shallow, and dangerous given Australia's microwave sun (dolphins are also at risk of sunburn).

Summer and autumn are probably the optimum time for sightings, although they can be seen year-round. The best place on land to try and spot them is probably around Dawesville Cut, Mandurah Ocean Marina and along the banks of the Mandurah Estuary; however, taking a dolphin cruise is your best bet for sightings, and a relaxing way to spend a morning or afternoon. Plenty of operators know where to go on Mandurah's expansive waters; **Mandurah Cruises** (73 Mandurah Tce; ☏9581 1242; e info@mandurahcruises.com.au; w mandurahcruises.com.au) offers a 90-minute dolphin-watching trip, as well as scenic half-day waterway cruises down the Murray River, crabbing and seafood tours.

Canoeing, kayaking and SUPing

If you want to go in search of dolphins on your own, there are numerous popular canoe, kayak and SUP trails in Mandjar Bay and Mandurah Estuary, many with landing points along the way (though not in the canals). From the estuary, a short route (1.5km) goes south to the wetlands or **Samphire Cove Nature Reserve**, where you can park your watercraft and walk along a boardwalk to a pair of bird hides to spy black swans, Australian white ibis, great cormorants, ospreys, kites and even possibly white-bellied sea eagles. There's a longer route (20km) from the estuary to the shallow, sandy **Lake Goegrup**, where you'll find swans, quendas and even the occasional dolphin. But this is also prime paddling country – Goegrup is connected by channel to the deeper Black Lake, which is actually multiple lakes connected together, where you can see ibis, heron and even the occasional kingfisher from the boardwalks. The channels can be a bit difficult to spot at first but once you have found them once, it gets much easier to navigate on subsequent visits. If that sounds a bit too taxing, there is an upstream launch on the Serpentine River into the lake that is only 500m long. From the estuary, you can also head into the canals – an added bonus is that these are usually sheltered and therefore provide calm waters to paddle through.

Salt and Bush Eco Tours (☏ 0414 174 415; w saltandbush.com.au) are go-to specialists for Peel's inland waterways – 2½-hour guided kayak tours (foot- or hand-pedalled) through the Ramsar-protected estuary start at A$175pp, but they also offer nocturnal wildlife walks where you are likely to see marsupials from A$80pp. For equipment, **Mandurah Boat and Bike Hire** (20A Ormsby Tce; ☏9535 5877; e mandurahboathire@westnet.com.au; w mandurahboatandbikehire.com.au) provides powered craft, dinghies and kayaks and can advise on routes. **WhatSUP Board Hire** (☏0410 544849; e hello@whatsupboardhire.co.au; w whatsupboardhire.com.au) offers SUP boards, lessons and day trips.

Fishing

Aside from dolphins, Mandurah is also synonymous with blue manna crabs – sometimes called blue swimmer crabs. Catching them yourself is an enormously popular activity between December and August, in particular in the shallow waters of the Harvey Estuary – taking out a scoop net and raking in your own catch is great fun; crabbing – and all things crab – are immortalised in Mandurah's annual Crab Fest (see box, page 130).

CRAB FEST

Founded in 1998, Mandurah Crab Fest (w crabfest.com.au) is the city's biggest annual event and attracts over 100,000 people each March to celebrate all things blue manna crab. Its showpiece is the cooking stage, where demonstrations seek to make the most of the event's star, as well as other local produce. Dishes like crab cakes, crab sliders, crab paella, crab arancini and crab quiche are served, while museums also get in on the act with informational displays on crabs and the marine environment.

Take your pick when it comes to fishing; Mandurah Estuary, Peel Inlet and around Dawesville are popular. Mandurah Cruises (page 129) run guided seafood cruises and excursions, and Mandurah Boat and Bike Hire (page 129) also hires out fishing and crabbing gear. For something a little different, **Eco BBQ Boats** (1 Spinnaker Quays; ◊9581 1242; e hello@ecobbqboats.com; w ecobbqboats.com) hires out boats (no license necessary) kitted out with barbecues, so you can grill your catch right away and enjoy lunch on the waterways.

Walking trails Mandurah's location on the Swan Coastal Plain bounds it by dune systems along the coast and the Darling Scarp to the east, meaning coastal walks can have some steep terrain to navigate, but inland sections will be relatively flat. Starting at Doddi's Beach on Halls Head Parade, the 12km **Halls Head Coastal Trail** takes in the beautiful coastline (with possible dolphin sightings), with plenty of seating and boardwalks en route. The shorter **Riverside Heartwalk** (2km) also has good dolphin-sighting chances as it follows the Serpentine River – there is also a boardwalk that goes out to the water. Birdwatchers will want to visit **Len Howard Conservation Park** on the Avocet Island side of Peel Inlet, where a 6km path through the wetlands, swamp paperbark and coastal woodland offers bird hides and plenty of sightings of splendid wrens, golden whistlers, white-face herons and black swans. For guided walks, **Ways to Nature** (◊0439 264 942; e hello@waystonature.com.au; w waystonature.com.au) offers tours led by zoologist Sarah Way in Len Howard Conservation Park, Samphire Cove and the Creery Wetlands, plus a nocturnal wildlife tour.

Mandurah is also home to two interconnected **art trails** (downloadable at w mandurah.wa.gov.au/explore/heritage-museum/Mandurah-Heritage-Trails). Highlights include the message stick, which symbolises the cooperation of the Aboriginal community – the Bindjareb people of the Noongar and the City of Mandurah, the Bindjareb Fishing Site, illustrating the cultural significance of the waterways for the local Aboriginal people, and the poignant war memorial, commemorating those who gave their lives for Australia.

Beaches With some 60km of coastline, Mandurah boasts some wonderful white-sand beaches. **Falcon Beach,** on Avocet Island, is a local favourite – a great place for swimming and paddling, with a reef here that offers some interesting snorkelling where you can look for starfish, lionfish and crabs. South of the Dawesville Channel, **Pyramids Beach** is popular with surfers thanks to its great swell, while **Town Beach** on Dolphin Quay is a favourite with families and less-visited **Blue Bay** at Halls Head has good snorkelling.

Aboriginal Mandurah The Bindjareb, a society of the Noongar, were the first peoples and Traditional Owners of the Mandurah area. They believe that the waterways around Mandurah (which they called Mandjoogoordap, meaning 'meeting place of the heart') were originally dry, and that the subsequent droughts caused intense hardships for their people. The Bindjareb went to the beach to ask for Wagyl Maadjit (the rainbow serpent), who responded and created a path by pushing through the sand dunes, creating the Mandurah Inlet. Wagyl then created a hollow – Lake Clifton – in which to lay her eggs (the thrombolites), and when hatched she sent her babies to create the rivers of the region – their paths forming the Harvey, Serpentine and Murray rivers. The babies, however, soon tired, which is why the rivers began to narrow as they headed towards the hills; they eventually starved and died, returning to their heaven (the ocean). Wagyl went to look for her babies, popping up at what is now Lake Clifton, Lake Preston and the Leschenault Inlet. She is still there today – a spring of water representing where her mouth is.

A good place to start to explore Mandurah's Aboriginal history is the free **Mandurah Community Museum** (3 Pinjarra Rd; ☎ 9550 3682; w mandurah. wa.gov.au/explore/heritage-museum; ⏰ 10.00–16.00 Tue–Fri, 11.00–15.00 Sat–Sun), which traces Mandurah's development from its indigenous origins to the present day through a wide collection of historical source documents, photographs and stories. The museum offers a free guided heritage walk along the foreshore as a loop from the museum – the tour takes about an hour and departs on Friday and Saturday at 11.00 in spring and summer. Also offering excellent insight into Mandurah's Aboriginal culture, heritage and history is

MANDURAH FOR KIDS

Though not at the forefront to local consciousness as a kid-friendly destination, Mandurah does not disappoint children. Amusement parks, sheltered waterways, dolphin wathching and railways all make Mandurah a fun day trip, and the town's easy accessibility by car and public transport makes it a convenient option for parents too.

Amaze Miniature Park 24 Husband Rd; ☎ 9595 1299; w amazeminiaturepark.com. au; ⏰ 10.00–16.00 Fri–Mon; A$15/12 adult/child. This delightful miniature village is modelled in part on the Oxfordshire town of Abingdon, UK & includes many replica scale-model buildings, canals & a tiny railway. The hedge maze & mini-golf are a real hit with kids.

King Carnival 25 Leighton Pl, Halls Head; ☎ 0418 444 583; w kingcarnival.com; ⏰ 10.00–17.00 weekends & school holidays, mini-golf 10.00–17.00 daily. One of the oldest amusement parks in Western Australia, King Carnival has a variety of rides such as Tilt-a-Whirl, dodgems & a Ferris wheel, as well as a video game arcade. Entry is free, but rides are A$6 each & mini-golf is A$15/12 adult/child.

Pirate Ship Mandurah Eastern Foreshore Jetty; ☎ 6117 5803; w pirateshipmandurah. com.au; tickets from A$24/12 adult/child. Specifically built for Mandurah's waterways, this pirate-themed vessel is a hit with kids as it tours Mandurah's canals, estuaries & the inlet. Passengers are encouraged to dress as pirates & kids can take a pirate wheel.

Tourist Fun Train Company 73 Mandurah Tce; ☎ 0410 099 075; w touristfuntrain.com; tickets from A$15/6 adult/child. This trackless train is a touristy yet fun way to get around, & great for small kids. The 'Big Toot' makes 10 stops from the marina, down the Foreshore & across to Halls Head, while the 'Mini Toot' just goes down the Foreshore (stopping at a children's play area en route).

Mandjoogoordap Dreaming (📞 0408 952 740; w mandurahdreaming.com.au), who run excellent tours to the waterways and coastal plain tied in with cultural knowledge and stories. The tour of the thrombolites and their interpretation is a highlight.

The organisation Our Knowledge, Our Land (w ourknowledgeourland.com. au) publish a free guide and interactive map to the **Bilya Country Story Trail**, a driving route centred on 13 places of significance to the Bindjareb community around the Mandurah/Peel Inlet area, from George Windjan's camp in Halls Head (a key leader in the 1830s) all the way out to Goegrup Lake. As this drive covers quite a bit of ground in the Mandurah area – Harvey Estuary to Goegrup Lake is about 20km – it's a good idea to combine it with some birdwatching and bushwalking at Goegrup Lake, a bit of crabbing at the Inlet and maybe some dolphin-watching for a full-on cultural and nature experience. Their website also features several Bindjareb individuals like Frank Nannup sharing stories and history of the people.

PINJARRA

One of the oldest European settlements in WA, Pinjarra is a town of historical contrasts – home to graceful, Heritage-listed buildings and homesteads, but also the site of the Pinjarra Massacre, one of the most brutal Aboriginal killings in Western Australian history. Its bucolic setting on the Murray River belies its tragic past, although walking alongside the ghosts on the main street makes for a poignant afternoon.

GETTING THERE AND AWAY By **car**, Pinjarra is about halfway between Perth and Bunbury along the South Western Highway; the drive takes approximately an hour from Perth, depending on traffic, and slightly longer from Bunbury. The *Australind* **train** stops here en route from Perth to Bunbury (1hr 10mins from both), while TransPerth's Route 600 **bus** runs between Mandurah and Pinjarra (30mins).

 WHERE TO STAY AND EAT

✱ 🏠 **Lazy River Boutique B&B** (4 suites) 9 Pinjarra Rd; 📞9531 4550; e unwind@lazyriver. com.au; w luxuryaccommodationmandurah.com. au. Hotel veterans Steve & Liz have crafted this B&B from their life's work in upmarket hospitality overseas; Steve's gourmet dinners are a thing of beauty. Plasma TVs, relaxing grounds & direct access to the Murray make this a perfect spot for a weekend away, though you do pay for the pleasure. **$$$$**

🏠 **Pinjarra Motel** 55 McLarty Rd; 📞9531 1811; e pinjarramotel@westnet.com.au; w pinjarramotel.com.au. A good option if you want to be in town; standard, deluxe & spa rooms here are clean, well-appointed & good value though nothing special. **$$$**

🏠 **Pinjarra Caravan Park & Cabins** 1716 Pinjarra Rd; 📞9531 1374; e oliver.gillbard@

bigpond.com; w pinjarracaravanpark.com.au. A variety of cabins on offer here, some with disabled access, plus 2 multi-bedroom houses. Powered & unpowered sites with camp kitchen, BBQ, games room & swimming pool available. **$**

✕ **Edenvale Tea Rooms** 2 Henry St; 📞0437 791 531; f edenvaletearooms; ⏰ 08.00–16.00 daily. Hearty b/fasts are served here inside Edenvale Heritage Precinct, including eggs benedict, bruschetta with bacon, as well as pastries & substantial lunches. **$$**

✕ **Jarra Infusion** 28 George St; 📞9518 7225; w jarrainfusion.com; ⏰ 08.00–14.00 daily. Handily located, excellent little café with vegan options, including a chilli non carne with cashew cream. The beef lasagne is particularly good, though there are also burgers & pizzas. **$$**

WHAT TO SEE AND DO It can seem like every country town in WA has a historic main street, but what separates **George Street** in Pinjarra is how old it is – with the townsite dating from 1830, just a few years after the establishment of WA – and its proximity to the town's other main sites, which are packed within 1km of flat, easy terrain. What also differentiates it is that the road also doubles as the South Western Highway – mixing such a historical backdrop with the heavy, rumbling traffic means you won't *quite* be able to imagine you are back in the days of Swan River Colony, but almost.

Of the 19 sites, **Edenvale Homestead** (1 George St; ☏ 9531 7777), built in 1888, is a good place to start. For decades it was the residence of the major local powerbrokers, the McLarty family, whose many businesses had a major impact on the development of early European Pinjarra. It's a massive complex – the homestead has 18 rooms, and there is also a dairy and barns – and the bricks were locally produced. Duncan Ross McLarty, Premier of Western Australia in 1947–53, also lived here. Other standouts are the Heritage-listed, 1934 Georgian Revival **courthouse** (22 George St), whose Art Deco detailing contrasts with the overall modesty of the building – an understated

THE PINJARRA MASSACRE

The Pinjarra Massacre is one the deadliest and most notorious attacks on Aboriginal peoples in Australian history. It was the culmination of tensions and violence between the European settlers and Bindjareb Noongar people, who had inhabited the Peel Region before Thomas Peel took control of the area in the 1830s. He encouraged other Europeans to fence off land and establish farms, encroaching on the Bindjareb's traditional hunting areas and forcing them to spear settlers' cattle and take their crops as a source of food. The settlers repeatedly requested military and police intervention from Swan River Governor, James Stirling, as the situation escalated, but in April 1834 the Bindjareb attacked a flour mill, and the settlers captured and beat three Bindjareb in retaliation, including their leader, Calyute.

Stirling promptly took action in response, forming a 25-strong group of police and soldiers to head to Pinjarra and deliver punishment to the Bindjareb for previous attacks (though some believe another goal was to assist Peel in attracting settlers to Mandurah – tough going in any event, but made worse by conflict with the Bindjareb). On 28 October, the party approached the Murray River and came across around 70 Aboriginal Bindjareb. They attempted to encircle them, and when the Bindjareb fought back, the settlers opened fire – guns were no match for the Bindjareb's spears. The number of dead is disputed – only one man was killed from the attacking side, but at least 15 Bindjareb men, women and children were killed, if not double that.

The attack backfired; far from bringing security to the area, paranoia set in among the settlers that the Aboriginal groups would band together in revenge to eject the settlers once and for all. For the next 170 years, the Aboriginal perspective on the massacre was ignored; as recently as the late 1990s, the Shire of Murray still declined to label what happened as a massacre. However, changing attitudes in contemporary times, and a greater and emerging understanding of perspective, has led to a rethink and a more sobering analysis of events. A memorial was approved in-principle by the Shire of Murray in 2018, on McLarty Road next to Murray District Hospital.

yet elegant distinction to many of the more grand structures of the era. Nearby, the 1896 **post office** (20 George St), also Heritage-listed, was built as both a mail facility and a residence for the postmaster – its stately bricks and gables making an excellent preserved example of late 1800s architecture. The 1861 **St John's Church** (Cnr Henry St & George St) – one of the oldest buildings in the state – is no longer a working church and is on the National Trust, but its rustic Victorian architecture and wooden bell tower make for a quaint and scenic photo along the highway. The grounds also contain the graves of many early pioneers. The Heritage Walk Trail is available to download from w pinjarra.destinationmurray.com.au/culture-history/pinjarra-heritage-walk-trail, which links these sites together in a well-organised walk.

Horse racing Horses and equestrian are very popular in the Peel Region, and the Pinjarra Race Club based at **Pinjarra Park** (Racecourse Rd; \ 9531 1956; w pinjarrapark.com.au) has been holding races for over 100 years. The season here is robust, with about two-dozen events annually; check their website for a calendar. The **Pinjarra Paceway** (7 Paceway Ct; \ 9531 1941; w pinjarrapaceway.com.au), home of the Pinjarra Harness Racing Club, also operates several dozen harness races a year.

Ranger Red's Zoo and Conservation Park (Sanctuary Dr; \ 9531 4322; w redzzoo.com.au; ⏰ 10.00–16.00 Mon–Fri, 09.00–17.00 Sat–Sun; A$23 adult/child) Formerly the Peel Zoo, this attraction features animal interactions and hand feedings, and when combined with a walk along George Street, bush tucker at Bindjareb Park and a stroll across the suspension bridge, would cap a good afternoon for kids too. Koalas and squirrel gliders can be interacted with, and there's a massive walk-through aviary – a great treat for kids and adults.

DWELLINGUP

Synonymous with jarrah forest, Dwellingup's timber houses and cottages make a charming first impression as you drive into town. This is Perth's forest hideaway – both the Munda Biddi and the Bibbulmun Track pass through here (see box, page 109), and there are plenty of other hiking and mountain-biking options to boot. Pretty Lane Poole Reserve, 7km south of town on Nanga Road, is the focal point of such activities, with trails winding past its many enchanting pools and meandering waterways.

GETTING THERE AND AWAY Dwellingup is 109km from Perth and 112km from Bunbury (90 minutes from both) and 42km or a 25-minute drive from Mandurah. The Pinjarra–Williams Road is the best route to take, though heading south you can also access the town from Del Park Road, turning off the South Western Highway at North Dandalup (27km south of Mundijong). Unfortunately public transport does not reach Dwellingup, so you'll need your own wheels.

TOURIST INFORMATION

ℹ️ **Dwellingup Trails and Visitor Centre** Marrinup St; \ 9538 1108; w dwellingup. destinationmurray.com.au; ⏰ 09.00–16.00 daily. An ideal orientation point when you arrive, with comprehensive information & maps on surrounding attractions.

🏠 **WHERE TO STAY AND EAT** There are a handful of options in Dwellingup itself, though if you'd rather stay in the forest then Lane Poole Reserve has nine **campsites**

($) of varying sizes – the largest being Nanga Mill and Nanga Townsite. See w parks.dpaw.wa.gov.au/park/lane-poole-reserve for details.

🏠 **Dwellingup Forest Lodge** (8 chalets) 55 Helio Rd; ☎ 9538 0333; e relax@dwell.com.au; w dwell.com.au. A short drive west of town, these self-contained chalets overlooking a small but pretty lake feature private deck, kitchen, TV & DVD player, & there is also a guest laundry. **$$$$**

🏠 **Dwellingup Chalet and Caravan Park** 23 Del Park Rd; ☎ 9538 1157; e enquiries@dwellingupcaravanpark.com.au; w dwellingupcaravanpark.com.au. Not just a caravan park, this picturesque site just north of town also offers cabins with full kitchens & larger chalets (some en suite) with campfire facilities. The park sells firewood. **$$$**

🏠 **Dwellingup Hotel** (13 rooms) 11 Marinup St; ☎ 9538 1000; ☐ @Dwellinguphotel. Known as the 'Dwelly Pub,' this town icon offers adequate but clean motel- & hotel-style rooms (some with shared facilities) to go along with its hugely popular pub. It can get insanely busy; the restaurant menu doesn't have much innovation from other country pubs (steak, fish & chips etc) but the meals are prepared well. Both hotel & pub are popular with hikers for its dependability

& convenience – deposit required when booking, however. **$$$**

✖ **Longriders Woodfired Pizza Café** 41 McLarty St; ☎ 9538 1159; 🕘 09.00–14.00 Wed–Thu, 09.30–19.30 Fri-Sat, 09.00–15.00 Sun. This cosy pizza joint serves a great range of wood-fired pizzas plus burgers & chicken. A filling way to end an exhausting day out on the trails. **$$**

✖ **Wine Tree Cidery** 46 Holyoake Rd; ☎ 9538 1076; w winetreecidery.com.au; 🕘 11.00–18.00 Sat–Sun. An outstanding range of fruit wines complement the house ciders at this bijou cidery including quince, raspberry & an apple sparkling wine. Something different in a wine-growing area where a lot can seem the same; the sampler paddles go well with the ploughman's platter. **$$**

✖ **Blue Wren Café** 53 McLarty St; ☎ 9538 1234; ☐ DwellingupBlueWrenCafe; 🕘 08.00–15.00 Mon–Fri, 07.30–15.30 Sat–Sun. A quaint local favourite with fantastic strudels, cakes, sausage rolls & scones made on site. B/fast & lunch are the real deal – try the chilli con carne or Thai beef salad. **$**

THE DWELLINGUP BUSHFIRE

Bushfires are a fact of life in WA, but one of the most impactful and historically significant occurred in Dwellingup from 20–24 January 1961. Dry lightning strikes started multiple fires around the townsite, aided immensely by hot, dry weather, strong winds and heavy fuel loads in the forest. These resulted in an out-of-control burn that, at its height, reached 150,000ha. Over 1,000 firefighters battled the blazes and, miraculously, nobody was killed, but over 100 homes were destroyed and 800 people were left homeless – of the five towns destroyed, only Dwellingup was rebuilt.

In the post-fire review, maintaining low fuel loads in the forests were identified as a key to preventing a repeat of the tragedy. WA's fuel reduction burning programme became a template for fire management – the high fuel loads around Dwellingup had guaranteed that fighting a major bushfire under those conditions would be hopeless. The second lesson was a reflection on the miracle that no lives were lost – highlighting the importance of community education and evacuation preparation, which the population of Dwellingup, as a forest town, had in abundance. WA's bushfire education and awareness programs are top-notch; if you are here during bushfire season, you are likely to see and hear public service announcements, alerts, billboards and signs near daily.

WHAT TO SEE AND DO Your first port of call for all things forest-related should be **Dwellingup Forest Discovery Centre** (1 Acacia Rd; ✆ 9538 1395; w forestdiscoverycentre.com.au; ⊕ 10.00–16.00 Sat–Sun; A$5/3 adult/child), which runs guided bushwalks in the surrounding jarrah forest, as well as self-guided walking trails emphasising education about the forest, its inhabitants and its resources. There is also a treetop canopy viewing platform. Informative workshops for both adults and children focus on making art from wood, and the retail gallery showcases the likes of sculptures and tables, crafts and carvings and more eclectic items like birdhouses. If you want to explore the surrounding forest on your own, **Dwellingup Adventures** (21 Newton St; ✆9538 1127; w dwellingupadventures.com. au; ⊕ 09.00–16.00 Sat–Sun) have all sorts of equipment available for hire, from canoes to kayaks to rafting gear.

Lane Poole Reserve (Banksiadale Rd; w parks.dpaw.wa.gov.au/park/lane-poole-reserve; A$12 per vehicle) At a massive 50,000ha, this reserve (actually in the Shire of Waroona, 7km of Dwellingup) is arguably the crown jewel of the Peel's jarrah forests and is where Dwellingup's reputation as a hiking and biking paradise comes into full bloom. The terrain here varies significantly from steep and sloping forest carpets to more open jarrah woods with heaps of grass trees, blackbutt and marri. There are over 500 plant species here, and you may come across quokka, chuditch or Carnaby's cockatoo. As you explore, you will pass a few idyllic swimming spots that look like they were lifted out of a stereotypical kids' summer camp: the rocky **Scarp Pool**, surrounded by woodland, with the branches and rocks reflecting up between the water's gentle ripples, and **Island Pool**, which has a wider, more open and river-like feel about it – there are steps down to the water where you are more likely to see paddlers. You'll also come across the remains of the old timber mill town of Nanga – which capped out at a population of about 100 during the mid 20th century, but did not survive the 1961 fire (see box, page 135) – the area now has more recognition as a campground (A$11 per night).

For mountain bikers, there are over a dozen easy (green) and moderate (blue) trails, as well as one difficult (black) trail. The most popular of the walking routes is the 18km loop **King Jarrah Trail**, which leads through some very pretty valleys to a 600-year-old jarrah tree (which, in my opinion, is not as impressive as many claim, so you might feel a bit let down). The park is also home to WA's first treetop canopy and zipline course; run by **Trees Adventure** (✆9463 4063; w treesadventure. com.au; ⊕ 09.00–17.00 daily), the 2½-hour sessions include training before exploring the 25m-high ropeway through the pine and jarrah trees.

Facilities at Lane Poole are basic – just some toilets, barbecues and picnic tables. There are nine campsites, but each vary considerably with who they cater for – check DPaW's website for details and to book.

Hotham Valley Railway (✆ 6278 1111; e hvr@hvr.org.au; w hothamvalley railway.com.au) Departing from Dwellingup Station in the centre of town, these nostalgic diesel and steam trains have been offering memorable rides through the forest since 1974. The diesel-powered *Forest Train* (⊕ 10.30 & 14.00 Sat, Sun & public holidays) goes 8km southeast to Etmilyn, where you can take a 1km loop trail through the jarrah forest before boarding the train back to Dwellingup, while the *Steam Ranger* (⊕ May–Oct 10.30 & 14.00 Sun, also Sat & Wed in school holidays) travels 14km northwest to Isandra Siding through the magnificent scenery of the Darling Scarp. There is also a *Restaurant Train* operating on

Saturday nights with vintage 1919 and 1884 cars – the five-course dinner is a unique and memorable experience.

SHIRE OF BODDINGTON

As you head east from Dwellingup, the landscape gradually starts to change as the jarrah forests of the Central Peel start to fade into stark green hills and sheep farms. The winding roads here are all under a big, open sky, and the route through the hills, forests and farmland has given the area a reputation for being 'scenic drive' country. Top off your visit here with lunch at one of the state's signature pubs in Quindanning. Continuing the Peel Region's love of riding animals, the shire hosts the state's biggest rodeo (see box, page 139). This is also mining country; the Boddington Gold Mine recently surpassed Kalgoorlie's Super Pit (page 233) as the largest in the state.

If you aren't a FIFO worker or here for the rodeo, however, Boddington works best for the visitor as a day-trip from Mandurah or the South West.

GETTING THERE AND AWAY At the eastern edge of the Peel Region, Boddington is only accessible by car – there are no public transport links. It's about a 90-minute drive from Perth; from the Albany Highway, which forms part of the shire's border, you can turn-off at either Bannister (16km) or Crossman (8km). From Bunbury (160km) or Mandurah (92km), head to Dwellingup and then take the Pinjarra–Williams Road from there.

TOURIST INFORMATION

🅘 **Visitor centre** Town library, Wuraming Av;
☏ 9883 4999 ⏱ 09.30–16.00 Tue & Thu, 10.00–16.00 Wed & Fri, 09.00–13.00 Sat

WHERE TO STAY AND EAT

🏠 **Boddington Motel** (9 rooms) 55 Bannister Rd, Boddington; w boddingtonmotel.com.au. Clean & spacious en-suite rooms with microwave & tea/coffee facilities, but no Wi-Fi. Decent continental b/fast served. **$$**

🏠 **Boddington Caravan Park** 32 Wuraming Av, Boddington; ☏ 9883 4999; e caravanpark@ boddington.wa.gov.au; w boddington.wa.gov. au/caravan-park.aspx. Pretty dog-friendly caravan park across from the river with powered & unpowered sites & good rates. Free Wi-FI, a dump point & access to town water. Also on site is the **Old Police Station** (**$$$**), the town's small, renovated old jail which now offers family accommodation sleeping up to 6. Some original features have been retained, with somewhat kitschy bedrooms, but a modern living room, large bathroom & kitchenette have been added. **$**

✳ ✗ **Quindanning Hotel** (16 rooms) Pinjarra-Williams Rd; ☏ 9885 7053; w quindanninghotel. com.au. One of the best country pubs & hotels in WA, located in Quindanning, 35km south of Boddington, it has an olde-English feel with open fires, dark-wood paneling & blackboards detailing what's on offer. The menu offers classic pub fare done well, with great burgers & steaks. There is also a pool room & beer garden. Upstairs, the accommodation is simple & clean but does not match the grandeur of the pub. **$$**

WHAT TO SEE AND DO Boddington itself is an attractive town with a workaday population based in the agriculture and mining industries – it is named after Henry Boddington, who was a shepherd, which gives you an idea of the basis for the town's founding. Nestled on the banks of the Hotham River and surrounded by lush hills, it is a great place to stop for a picnic, and you might spot black cockatoos, purple swamphens and red wattlebirds as well as a variety of ducks and cormorants on the water. Walking trails lead along the banks of the river; one of the most popular is along the town's old railway line to **Ranford Pool**, a deeper part of the Hotham River that has formed a swimming hole. A lengthier walk (16km return) leads west through some wonderfully scenic pasture and timber land to **Tullis Bridge**, a 1912 trustle-style railway bridge once used by the timber industry. While only parts are still there due to an arson attack in the 1990s, it still provides a scenic accent to the riverbank.

Just northwest of town is **Newmont Boddington Gold**, Australia's biggest gold mine (and the world's seventh largest), producing around 700,000 ounces of gold per year as well as copper. Large-scale gold mining does not have a long history in Boddington – it did not become a significant commercial operation until the opening of this mine in 1987. Though the mine is one of the world's biggest operations, Boddington is still not associated with gold in the West Australian psyche the way Kalgoorlie-Boulder is. The mine shuttered in the early 2000s before restarting with Newmont as sole owner in 2009. **Go West Tours** (✆ 9791 4143; w gowesttours.com.au; from A$45) take you behind the scenes of the mine, where

---

THE HOTHAM WAY

Linking Pinjarra and Pingelly in the Wheatbelt, the 160km Hotham Way drive was created in 2003 as a way to draw tourists off the coastal strip and raise awareness of the inland charms of the Peel and Wheatbelt. The most attractive sections of the route are Dwellingup–Boddington (66km) and Boddington–Wandering (24km), both of which encapsulate the area's magnificent scenery – tall jarrah forests, stark, barren rolling hills punctuated with rocky outcrops, thousands of grazing sheep oblivious to the world around them, and a landscape dotted with abandoned, century-old crumbling farmhouses that seem to be screaming for restoration. The main attraction lies in the 'Sunday drive' feel than for specific sights, though there are a few craft artisans and wineries (mostly around the town of Wandering in the Wheatbelt but also the Wine Tree in Dwellingup, page 135).

When you get to Boddington, instead of crossing the Hotham and continuing to Crossman, there's an option to take a 16km detour north to Bannister, home to the **Bannister Riverside Roadhouse** (6390 Albany Hwy; ✆ 9883 8035); ⊕ 06.30–17.00 daily). This attractive roadside pitstop has gained a cult following among Wheatbelt and Peel locals thanks to the delicious bread and fluffy croissants baked on site. From here you can continue along the Bannister Road for 18km to Wandering, passing **Tanglefoot Winery & Café** (2507 N Bannister-Wandering Rd; ✆ 0427 988 415; f TangleFootWine; ⊕ 09.00–17.00 Fri–Mon) just before you reach the town.

Along the route, you will likely spy frog and snake emblems on signage. The Hotham River, as a water source, was very important historically to the local Aboriginal peoples. The frog represents the Aboriginal people of the Pingelly region – frogs appear in many creation stories and some societies believe they were created to rule inland waterways – while the snake is actually Wagyl, important to the Noongar, and believed to be responsible for the creation of the Peel's rivers and in charge of their protection (page 131).

BODDINGTON RODEO

Founded by the Lions Club in 1976, the largest rodeo in WA takes place on the first weekend of November in the rodeo complex in the centre of town. The event starts with a Friday Night Festival, featuring a variety of local food, music and entertainment, followed by a Saturday morning Rodeo Street Parade through Boddington, with mounted police and a themed float – past parades have had taken wide-angle themes such as 'anything goes'. The main rodeo event usually takes place in the early afternoon. Bull riding – where someone has to stay on a bull for eight seconds – is the best-known event, but there are other activities on display such as steer wrestling (attempting to grab a steer by the horns and wrestling it to the ground), roping (attempting to rope and capture a steer), and barrel racing (attempting to ride a cloverleaf pattern around a series of barrels). The Bushman's Ball starts in the early evening, and there is a recovery breakfast Sunday morning (cash only) served at the rodeo grounds.

on a 90-minute tour you can watch the haulage trucks transport the ore back and forth and the grinding process – the ore is fed into the processing plant and the gold is separated out, before being melted in the furnace and poured into moulds. As this is a working mine, you will be kitted out in safety gear for the tour and must have closed-in shoes.

One of the true pleasures of the exploring the area is simply hopping in your car and going for a **drive**. The Hotham Way (see box, opposite) passes through Boddington, while Marradong Country (w marradongtrails.com/tours) has created a series of five multi-day self-drive trails in and around the Boddington/Hotham Valley region, each reflecting a particular aspect of the area's geography – from food and wine to farming and rural life. See the website for maps and comprehensive itineraries.

SHIRE OF WAROONA

The most southerly shire in the Peel Region, and the last before you enter the South West, Waroona's star sights are Lake Clifton and Preston Beach, but aside from them most people just pass through quickly from Perth on their way to Bunbury or the South West. In recent times, the shire is most noted for a 2016 bushfire, impacting both the towns of Waroona and Yarloop, burning through nearly 70,000ha, destroying more than 160 houses and killing two people over a four-day period. Lake Clifton and Preston Beach are easily accessed from the Forrest Highway, but Waroona townsite, being on the South Western Highway, gets less traffic passing through.

GETTING THERE AND AWAY By **car**, the South Western Highway passes directly through Waroona, 45km from Mandurah and 25km from Pinjarra. On the coast, Preston Beach, Lake Clifton and Yalgorup National Park are accessed from the Forrest Highway if coming from Perth, Mandurah or Bunbury – from Waroona, take Coronation Road east as it turns into Peppermint Grove Road.

By **train**, the *Australind* stops in Waroona – it is 90 minutes from Perth, and 55 minutes from Bunbury.

WHERE TO STAY AND EAT

Footprints Preston Beach (71 apts)
56 Mitchell Rd, Preston Beach; ✎9739 1111;
e info@footprintsprestonbeach.com.au;
w footprintsprestonbeach.com.au. Townhouses
& modern twists on the Aussie classic beach
shack are on offer here with AC, TV & kitchenette.
Swimming pool, tennis courts, playground & bike
hire are available; the on-site café has good meals
but limited opening times. **$$$$**

Drakesbrook Hotel Motel (32 rooms)
8222 South West Hwy, Waroona; ✎9733
1566; e info@drakesbrookhotel.com.au;
w drakesbrookhotel.com.au. Good-value motel-
style & donga rooms here are clean & comfortable,
with tea/coffee facilities, TV, AC & heating, though
décor is standard. The on-site restaurant does bar
meals & pizzas & there is also a bottle shop. **$$**

The Hairy Lentil 61 South West Hwy,
Waroona; ✎0460 969 474; **f** HairyLentil;
🕐 09.00–15.00 Tue, Sat–Sun, 09.00–18.00 Wed–
Fri. Specialising in vegetarian & vegan options, this
vibrant café is highly recommended for coffee &
lunch– if their marshmallow delight or black forest
scrolls are available, they go well with a coffee.
Worth stopping in if you are in town. **$$**

WHAT TO SEE AND DO

Lake Clifton and Yalgorup National Park (w parks.dpaw.wa.gov.au/park/
yalgorup) Nestled between the Forrest Highway and the Indian Ocean, the 12,000ha
Yalgorup National Park is the largest national park in the Swan Coastal Plain. Part of
a large wetlands system, it is dotted by ten lakes – most notably **Lake Clifton**, known
for its **thrombolites** (rock-like structures built by microorganisms (too small to see)
that are related to some of the oldest living things on earth). Thought to be 2,000
years old and the largest example of thrombolites in the southern hemisphere,
they are best viewed from the shoreside boardwalk as you can get up close to the
thrombolites without damaging them. Mandjoogoordap Dreaming (page 132) offer
guided tours to the thrombolites and their place in creation stories and Aboriginal
culture and history.

Other activities in the park are limited due to the fragile nature of the ecosystem
– walking is permitted, but use of the lakes for swimming, boating, canoeing and
fishing is not. While the trails through the woodlands are perfectly pleasant, this is
not considered to be one of WA's showcase national parks – indeed, many visitors
have never heard of it until they pass the sign for it on their way from Perth to
Bunbury along the Forrest Highway.

Preston Beach On the coast just west of Yalgorup, this very popular fishing spot
for locals has grown into something of a small resort town, anchored by its top-
notch swimming and surfing beach. The beach is 4x4 friendly and many enthusiasts
drive along the sand to find the perfect fishing spot. Its relative seclusion off the
Forrest Highway and behind the lakes off the Forest Highway means it is usually far
from overrun and it's a good spot to get away from the crowds – indeed, the town
itself only has about 200 year-round residents.

Waroona If you do find yourself taking the inland highway down south rather
than the coastal road, there isn't a whole lot to detain you in Waroona itself. But
do take a minute to check out the **Memorial Hall** (86 South West Hwy), a beautiful
brick-and-stone building which stands out because of its bright contrasting colour
scheme – white and red – and decorative arched entryway. It was built to honour
those who served in World War I and opened in 1932.

Hamel Just 7km south of Waroona, Hamel has a few points of interest if passing
through. The **town hall** (Cornucopia St) was built by convict labour around the

turn of the 20th century and was originally a prison, before being relocated to its current location and repurposed as an exhibition space that remains in use today. Frog lovers will enjoy the **Hamel Wetlands**, accessed from Cornucopia Street, with its 550m nature walk and numerous species of amphibian (including over a dozen types of frog) and bird. The memorably named motorbike and banjo frogs – so-called because of the resemblance of those sounds to their calls – are common here, though often will be heard rather than seen.

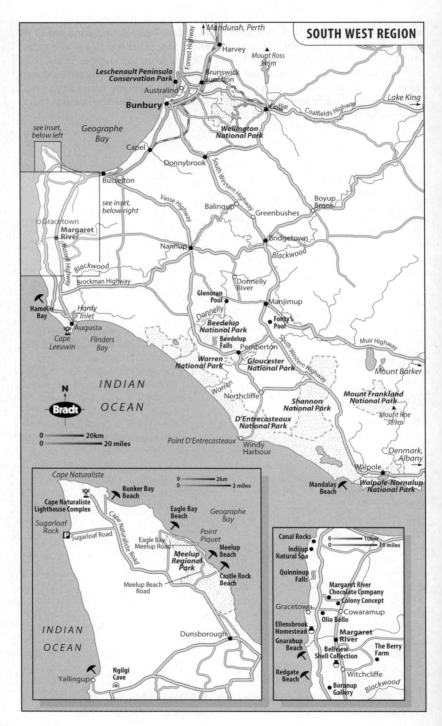

Mandurah, Perth

Forrest Highway

Harvey

Mount Ross
346m

Leschenault Peninsula
Conservation Park

Brunswick
Junction

Australind

Bunbury

Collie

Coalfields Highway

Lake King

*Geographe
Bay*

see inset,
below left

Capel

Donnybrook

South Western Highway

**Wellington
National Park**

Busselton

see inset,
below right

Vasse Highway

Balingup

Greenbushes

Boyup
Brook

O Gracetown

**Margaret
River**

Busselton Highway

Blackwood

Nannup

Bridgetown

Blackwood

Brockman Highway

Donnelly
River

Glenoran
Pool

Manjimup

**Hamelin
Bay**

Hardy
Inlet

Augusta

Donnelly

**Beedelup
National Park**

*Fonty's
Pool*

Cape
Leeuwin

Flinders
Bay

Beedelup
Falls

Pemberton

**Warren
National Park**

**Gloucester
National Park**

Muir Highway

South Western Highway

Mount Barker

N

INDIAN

Warren

Bradt

OCEAN

Northcliffe

**Shannon
National Park**

**Mount Frankland
National Park**

Mount Roe
389m

0 ——— 20km
0 ——— 20 miles

**D'Entrecasteaux
National Park**

Point D'Entrecasteaux

Windy
Harbour

Denmark,
Albany

Walpole

Mandalay
Beach

**Walpole-Nornalup
National Park**

Cape Naturaliste

**Cape Naturaliste
Lighthouse Complex**

**Bunker Bay
Beach**

0 ——— 2km
0 ——— 2 miles

*Sugarloaf
Rock*

P Sugarloaf Road

Cape Naturaliste Road

**Eagle Bay
Beach**

*Geographe
Bay*

*Point
Piquet*

Eagle Bay-
Meelup Road

**Meelup
Regional
Park**

**Meelup
Beach**

Meelup Beach
Road

**Castle Rock
Beach**

Canal Rocks

0 ——— 10km
0 ——— 10 miles

**Indijup
Natural Spa**

**Quinninup
Falls**

INDIAN

OCEAN

Dunsborough

**Margaret River
Chocolate Company**

Colony Concept

Gracetown

Cowaramup

Olio Bello

**Ellensbrook
Homestead**

**Margaret
River**

Yallingup

**Ngilgi
Cave**

**Gnarabup
Beach**

**Bellview
Shell Collection**

**The Berry
Farm**

**Redgate
Beach**

Witchcliffe

**Boranup
Gallery**

Blackwood

5

The South West

Long Western Australia's favourite holiday playground, the towering forests, world-class beaches and verdant vineyards of the South West stand in stark contrast to scrub terrain often found in the state's interior. There are plenty of options to enjoy the coast: go dolphin-spotting in Bunbury, explore Busselton's iconic jetty, laze on Cape Naturaliste's world-class beaches or take a surf lesson in Yallingup or Margaret River. And for food and wine lovers, there are ample opportunities to sample the region's gourmet produce in the Blackwood Valley, before walking it off with a stroll through the giant karris and tingles in Pemberton and Walpole.

TOWARDS BUNBURY: HARVEY AND BRUNSWICK JUNCTION

Running south from Perth, the inland South Western Highway passes low-rise hills, haybale-dotted farmland and woodlands as it heads down to Bunbury. While most people just zip through on their way to the state's second city, the towns of Harvey and Brunswick Junction are good stopping-off points to break up the drive.

Surrounded by vineyards, citrus groves and cattle farms and the hub of WA's dairy industry, **Harvey** is home to some of the state's best-known brands: Harvey Fresh (juice), Harvey Beef and Harvey Cheese are all staples in West Australian supermarkets. You can pick up some of the latter in the main **retail store** (11442 South Western Hwy; ℡ 9729 3949; w harveycheese.com.au; ⏰ 09.30–17.00 daily) – try one of the many complimentary samples before deciding which to take home. Afterwards, head to the local cellar door, **Harvey River Estate** (163 Third St; ℡ 9729 2588; w harveyriverestate.com.au; ⏰ 10.00–16.00 daily). It's known for its Chardonnay and Shiraz, and the evening platters are perfect to enjoy while watching the sunset over the Darling Scarp. The visitor centre on the grounds of **Stirling Cottage** (283 South Western Highway; ℡ 9729 1096; ⏰ 09.00–16.00 daily), built by convict labour for Western Australia's first governor, James Stirling, can advise which farm gates are open.

A 15-minute drive south along the South Western Highway from Harvey brings you to **Brunswick Junction**, synonymous with West Australian dairy giant, **Peters Creameries**. The 'Detroit chic' industrial-style, faux-derelict façade of the historic main factory has become a sight in itself – although it looks abandoned, it is still operating (though not open to visitors). **Daisy**, a huge statue of a Friesian cow, sits in the town's main park as a testament to the importance of dairy in Brunswick.

BUNBURY

Driving into WA's second city, you would be forgiven for thinking that Bunbury lives up to the 'gritty port town' tag West Australians have long given it. Heading towards the centre on Sandridge Road and Blair Street – the two main thoroughfares

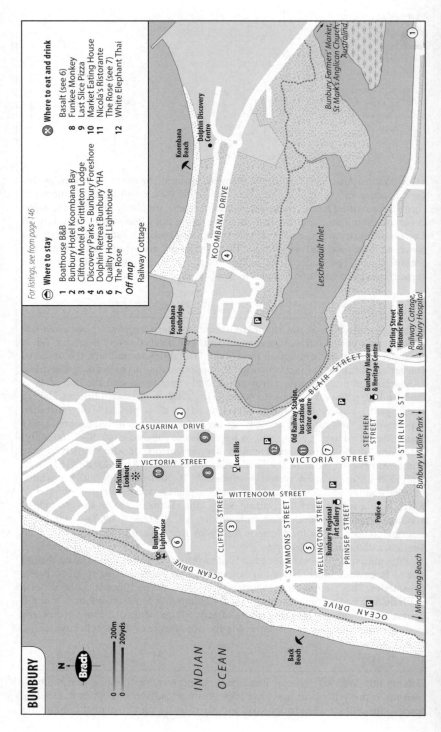

BUNBURY

N

Bradt

0   200m
0   200yds

INDIAN OCEAN

Back Beach

Bunbury Lighthouse

Marlston Hill Lookout

Lost Bills

Koombana Footbridge

Koombana Beach

Dolphin Discovery Centre

Leschenault Inlet

OCEAN DRIVE

VICTORIA STREET

CASUARINA DRIVE

KOOMBANA DRIVE

CLIFTON STREET

WITTENOOM STREET

SYMMONS STREET

WELLINGTON STREET

PRINSEP STREET

STEPHEN STREET

STIRLING ST

BLAIR STREET

VICTORIA STREET

Bunbury Regional Art Gallery

Police

Old Railway Station, bus station & visitor centre

Bunbury Museum & Heritage Centre

Stirling Street Historic Precinct

Railway Cottage, Bunbury Hospital

Bunbury Wildlife Park →

Mindalong Beach →

For listings, see from page 146

Where to stay

1   Boathouse B&B
2   Bunbury Hotel Koombana Bay
3   Clifton Motel & Grittleton Lodge
4   Discovery Parks – Bunbury Foreshore
5   Dolphin Retreat Bunbury YHA
6   Quality Hotel Lighthouse
7   The Rose

Off map
    Railway Cottage

Where to eat and drink

    Basalt (see 6)
8   Funkee Monkey
9   Last Slice Pizza
10   Market Eating House
11   Nicola's Ristorante
    The Rose (see 7)
12   White Elephant Thai

Bunbury Farmers' Market, St Mark's Anglican Church, Australind →

connecting the CBD to the Bussell Highway – takes you past rows of tyre shops, big box chain stores and the usual familiar take-aways, and you may think to yourself that's there 'nothing to see here, move along'. But press on. Bunbury today is not the Bunbury of 50, 20 or even five years ago. Once past the outer industrial zone, the town centre has transformed itself into a coastal showpiece, with great beaches, surfing, boating, hands-on museums, urban nature trails, a lively restaurant strip and a showstopping farmers' market. Far from just a jumping-off point for a South West excursion, Bunbury is now a substantial destination in its own right. Two to three days would be enough time to explore the city and the surrounding natural playgrounds of the Ferguson Valley and Wellington National Park.

HISTORY The original inhabitants of the area are the Noongar, who have lived on the land around Bunbury for tens of thousands of years. The Dutch were the first Europeans to explore the area along the coast in the 1600s, and in the early 1800s the French and Nicolas Baudin came ashore from their ships, the *Geographe* and the *Naturaliste*, during their 1800–04 expedition to Australia that charted nearly two-thirds of the coast. The expedition was also carrying botanist Jean Baptiste Louis Claude Theodore Leschenault de Tour, after which the Leschenault Inlet is named. In 1829, a British expedition from Perth arrived, led by Dr Alexander Collie and Lieutenant Preston – both of whom gave their names to the rivers that flow through the town.

Bunbury was officially founded in 1843 and is named after Lieutenant Henry William St Pierre Bunbury, who was one of the first Europeans to explore the South West – his team charted an inland road to Pinjarra. The town quickly established itself as a major seaport and whaling station. Timber from the South West's forests was exported to England from Bunbury's port, which was often used to make sleeper train carriages in Europe. Convict labour built key infrastructure such as roads and the jetty, and by the end of the 1800s Bunbury was the South West's key service centre, with a port, hospital and other important facilities.

For most of the 20th century, Bunbury's growth was closely tied to the port. At the start of World War I, operations expanded to include the shipment of wheat, which was becoming a key driver of the West Australian economy. The town industrialised after World War II, and mining mineral sands, the opening of a chemical plant and continued storage expansion underpinned the economy. The port's exports have reflected that, with alumina now being the largest export out of Bunbury's port. Today Bunbury is a fast-growing city with a population of about 75,000, making it WA's second-largest metro area, and the biggest outside the Perth–Mandurah corridor. In 2015, the state government announced the multi-stage Transforming Bunbury's Waterfront project, which included a A$22 million facelift for Koombana Beach, upgrades to waterfront roads plus construction of additional retail and marine facilities, and has been a key spur in the town's rejuvenation.

GETTING THERE AND AWAY Bunbury sits on an important highway junction: the Forrest Highway travels north to Perth and Mandurah; the Bussell Highway leads south to Busselton, Margaret River and Augusta; the South Western Highway travels south to Donnybrook, Bridgetown, Manjimup and Pemberton, and north through Brunswick Junction and Harvey to Perth; and the Coalfields Highway goes east to Collie, Arthur River, Wagin and terminates at Lake King at the edge of the Outback. By **car**, average driving times from Bunbury are about 2 hours to Perth, an hour to Mandurah, Margaret River and Bridgetown and 30 minutes to Busselton and Collie.

Transwa offers two daily **train** services between Perth Station and Bunbury Terminal (Picton St) on the *Australind* (2½hrs). Transwa and South West Coast Lines also offer **coach** services from Perth to Bunbury (3hrs), and there are onward connections to Albany, Augusta, Donnybrook and Pemberton. South West Coach Lines also offers express services from Bunbury to both the domestic and international terminals at Perth Airport.

GETTING AROUND Transwa operates TransBunbury: Bunbury's answer to TransPerth. There are ten bus routes, covering the area from Australind down to Dalyellup. There are two 'zones' in Bunbury – a two-zone fare is A$4.90 while a one-zone fare is A$3.20. The most useful routes for visitors are the 825 and 826, which run from Bunbury to the Dolphin Discovery Centre and the Bunbury Passenger Terminal, respectively. Information on schedules can be found at w pta.wa.gov.au/our-services/transregional.

The Bunbury CBD is compact and easy to navigate; walking west–east from Bunbury Lighthouse near Back Beach to the Dolphin Discovery Centre is only 2km on flat terrain, and north–south through the CBD on Victoria Street is about 1km.

TOURIST INFORMATION
Bunbury Visitor Centre Haley St; 📞 9792 7205; w visitbunburygeographe.com.au; ⏱ 09.00–16.30 Mon–Fri, 09.30–16.00 Sat, 10.00–14.00 Sun

WHERE TO STAY *Map, page 144*
Luxury & mid-range
Boathouse B&B (2 suites) 11 Austral Pde; 📞 0400 543 111; w boathousebunbury.com.au. Not a boat, but a well-located B&B on the inlet, 20mins' walk to Victoria St. Rooms have microwaves & mini-fridges & free Wi-Fi. Good-value retreat away from the CBD. **$$$**

Bunbury Hotel Koombana Bay (64 studios) 1 Holman St; 📞 9721 0100; e reservations@bhkb.com.au; w bunburyhotelkoombanabay.com.au. Just a stone's throw from the CBD, these spacious & modern self-contained studios come with microwaves, toasters & AC. On-site spa, heated pool & underground parking. Worth paying the extra for a studio with a view over the bay. Lower prices available with longer-stay packages. **$$$**

Clifton Motel & Grittleton Lodge (48 rooms) 2 Molloy St; 📞 9792 6200; e enquiries@theclifton.com.au; w theclifton.com.au. Billing itself as Heritage-style boutique accommodation, the Clifton (**$$**) offers traditional motel-style rooms from standard to Executive Spa Suites. Rooms have all mod-cons & are just 100m from the ocean & shopping. Grittleton Lodge (**$$$**) – within the Clifton's grounds – is a 2-storey Heritage-listed house with great views

& impeccable Victorian interior décor, including marble & lounge rooms.

Railway Cottage 9 Ednie St; 📞 0408 838 019; w railway-cottage-holiday-accommodation-service.business.site. Heritage award-winning weatherboard cottage from the turn of the 20th century. Fully renovated with character touches like timber floors & pressed tin. Location is a bit of a drawback if you're on foot – behind a big-box retail strip – & it's a 1.5km walk into the CBD, but a short, easy breeze if you have your own wheels. 2-night min stay may apply. **$$$**

Quality Hotel Lighthouse (71 rooms) 2 Marlston Dr; 📞 9781 2700; w lighthousehotel.com.au. With a premier location 2 mins from the CBD & the beach, this business-style hotel has clean rooms with all the mod-cons & complimentary Wi-Fi & parking. Some look out over the lighthouse, ocean & city, while the Lighthouse Suite has a jet spa, dining area & coffee machine. The hotel also has a heated pool & on-site restaurant with fantastic ocean views (see opposite). **$$**

The Rose Hotel (25 rooms) 27 Wellington St; 📞 9721 4533; e info@rosehotel.com.au; w rosehotel.com.au. Dating from 1865, this historic hotel & attached pub on one of Bunbury's busiest shopping streets stands out for its soft-colour design, neon banner signs and the white lattice-metal framing of its 2nd-floor wraparound veranda. Simple rooms come with LCD TVs & standard mod-cons, & bookings will usually include a voucher to use in the downstairs restaurant (see below). **$$**

Budget

🏠 **Discovery Parks – Bunbury Foreshore**   Koombana Dr; ✆ 9791 3900; e bunburyforeshore@discoveryparks.com.au; w discoveryholidayparks.com.au. Next to the beach & a 5min walk to the CBD, this is one of 2 Discovery Parks sites in Bunbury – but its new

Splash Park, slated to open in late 2022, & with over 40 water features, a giant tipping bucket & other amenities, makes it standout. Offers a variety of en-suite cabins plus powered & unpowered sites. **$$$**

🏠 **Dolphin Retreat Bunbury YHA**   (13 rooms) 14 Wellington St; ✆ 9792 4690; e info@dolphinretreatbunbury.com.au; w dolphinretreatbunbury.com.au. Just 100m from the beach & with free b/fast & parking, this is a great option for those on a budget. Dorms, sgls & family rooms available; well-equipped kitchen, games room & lounge on site. **$**

✖ WHERE TO EAT AND DRINK   *Map, page 144*

✖ **Market Eating House**   9 Victoria St; ✆ 9721 6078; w marketeatinghouse.com.au; ⏲ 17.30–late Wed–Thu, noon–late Fri–Sat. Offering a Mediterranean- & Middle East-infused menu of sharers & large mains, this hip eatery is the brainchild of professional restauranteurs Bec & Brenton Pyke. The hummus & stuffed apricots are divine. Book ahead. Brenton also runs cooking classes. **$$$**

✖ **Basalt**   2 Marlston Dr; ✆ 9781 2700; w lighthousehotel.com.au; ⏲ 06.00–09.00 & 16.00–21.00 Mon–Fri, 07.00–10.00 & 16.00–21.00 Sat–Sun. At the Lighthouse Hotel (see opposite), this spacious & good-value restaurant is named after the basalt rocks it overlooks. Scotch fillets, seafood & tempura snapper are the headlines here, all washed down with superb views over the Indian Ocean. The harissa chicken is also recommended, & their cheeseboards & dessert cocktails are a great way to round off your meal. **$$**

✖ **Funkee Monkee**   27 Victoria St; ✆ 9721 1555; w funkeemonkee.net.au; ⏲ noon–14.00 & 17.00–22.00 daily, breakfast from 08.00 Sat–Sun. One of Bunbury's trendiest spots, this Indian fusion restaurant has a creative menu featuring deconstructed samosas, spicy duck tortillas & lamb shank Punjabi, plus classics such as chicken parmi & Wagyu burgers. Also boasts an enormous list of cocktails. Bookings advised. **$$**

✖ **Last Slice Pizza**   1/33 Clifton St; ✆ 9742 1888; w lastslice.com.au; ⏲ 16.30 –21.30 Sun &

Wed–Thu, 16.30–21.30 Fri–Sat. Hand-stretched & baked New York-style pizzas with Australian-style toppings like honey pepperoni & BBQ chicken & pineapple – the 22" are enormous. One of the few places in the state that also serves pizza by the slice. Limited seating inside; take-away & delivery available. **$$**

✖ **Nicola's Ristorante**   62 Victoria St; ✆ 9791 3926; w nicolasristorante.com.au; ⏲ 11.30– 14.00 & 17.00–20.00 Tue–Sat. Bunbury's only classic Italian, the pastas, pizzas & grills at this well-appointed eatery are a favourite with the local business crowd. The crab linguini & five-cheese ravioli are especially good, as is locally sourced scotch fillet from the Stirling Ranges. There is an extensive wine list for pairings. **$$**

✖ **The Rose Hotel**   27 Wellington St; ✆ 9721 4533; w rosehotel.com.au; ⏲ 11.00–21.00 daily. Classic Australian pub fare in atmospheric & lively surrounds at this historic hotel in the CBD (see opposite). Steaks, steak sandwiches, roast lamb & fish & chips are reliable mains & there is an expansive starters menu of wings, squid & tacos. **$$**

✖ **White Elephant Thai Restaurant**   38 Victoria St; ✆ 9721 6522; ⏲ 17.30–21.00 Sun & Tue, 11.30–14.00 & 17.30–21.00 Wed–Sat. Highly recommended Thai serving all the usual fare – the pad Thai is particularly good, as are the soups, stir-fries & satays. Service is attentive & the place is usually busy. **$$**

ENTERTAINMENT AND NIGHTLIFE   Bunbury does not have a great reputation for nightlife, and the drinking scene tends to be pub-style and concentrated at the hotels and restaurants on Victoria Street. One recommendation is **Lost Bills** (41 Victoria St; w lostbills.com; ⏲ 17.00–20.00 Wed–Thu, 16.00–midnight Fri–Sat), a tiny bar with an excellent range of West Australian wine, plus gins, whiskeys, rums and cocktails like espresso martinis. Food is BYO, though they do have some hash browns and American snacks like Pop Tarts and Twinkies.

SHOPPING Bunbury Farmers' Market (2 Vittoria Rd; ✆ 9724 2999; w bunburyfarmersmarket.com.au; ⏰ 07.30–18.30 Mon–Fri, 07.30–17.30 Sat, 08.00–17.30 Sun) is one of the finest in Australia and people are known to drive from all over to shop here. Far from a couple of stalls in a park, this large supermarket-style market with over 300 staff sources 90% of its produce from West Australian producers. Over 150 growers are represented here, catering to all your picnic lunch or self-catering needs. Fish and butcher meats are also for sale and platters can be ordered. When I drop in, I tend to go for the citrus fruits and berries and the locally produced fruit jams and honey – but they have quite a large selection of cheeses as well.

OTHER PRACTICALITIES

Western Australia Police Force 76–78 Wittenoom St; ✆ 13 14 44

Bunbury Hospital at South West Health Campus Bussell Hwy, cnr Robertson Dr; ✆ 9722 1000; ⏰ 24hrs

WHAT TO SEE AND DO

Bunbury Museum and Heritage Centre (1 Arthur St; ✆ 9792 7283; w bunburymuseum.com.au; ⏰ 10.00–16.00 Tue–Sun; Gold Coin donation) This colourful museum shines a light on the people of Bunbury, highlighting key events and individuals in the town's history – from shipwrecks and convicts to early settlers and the development of the port. A highlight are videos of Noongar people talking about their lives in the Noongar language, as well as what the museum calls 'stories' – personal recollections of people in Bunbury's history, which the museum encourages patrons to use as a historical basis and reference point to reflect on how the town has changed in modern times.

Bunbury Regional Art Gallery (64 Wittenoom St; ✆ 9792 7323; w brag.org.au; ⏰ 10.00–16.00 daily; free, although voluntary donation requested) After World War II, philanthropist Sir Claude Hotchin began donating numerous works of art to regional West Australian towns as a way of bringing art to country areas and to encourage local artists. Bunbury received his first donation of nearly two-dozen artworks, which formed the historical foundation of what is now the Bunbury Regional Art Gallery. Today housed in the old Convent of Mercy, the two-floor gallery has expanded to over 800 works from West Australian artists as well as Noongar art, and strives to encourage indigenous expression.

Bunbury Lighthouse (6230/3 Marlston Dr) At 25m tall, this iconic lighthouse casts a light that can supposedly be seen almost 20km away. Bunbury's original cast-iron lighthouse was built on Marlston Hill in 1903 and updated over the years, before parts of it were moved and attached to the base of the new lighthouse structure at the present site in 1971 – look about 10m up and you can see where it has been joined. It was moved because, as Bunbury grew, sightlines from the sea to the lighthouse at its old location became obscured. Its chequerboard pattern is unique – it was chosen by Captain Robert Allsop, Port of Bunbury Harbour Master 1963–88, because he purportedly liked Black and White Whisky and black and white Scotch terriers. Allsop also researched lighthouse designs across Australia to ensure that Bunbury's was unique, and it. was he who reportedly first noticed that the lighthouse's original location had an obstructed view.

The lighthouse can only be admired from the outside – it is not open to the public. However, 360-degree views of the city, Indian Ocean and Darling Scarp can be enjoyed from nearby **Marlston Hill Lookout** (10A Whale View), built on the site of the original lighthouse. It takes only a few minutes to climb to the top, but there is no wheelchair access.

Old Railway Station (Wellington St; ☏9792 7205; w visitbunbury.com.au; ⊕ 09.00–17.00 Mon–Fri) This Heritage-listed brick building was Bunbury's main train station for almost 80 years and is still in daily use today as home of the visitor centre and the main bus station. A great example of Federation Free Classical architecture, it has been restored with only minor alterations. Nearby is the **Stirling Street Historic Precinct**, between Blair Street and Albert Road, which is also Heritage-listed. This area sits on the land first granted to James Stirling back in 1830 and contains some of the state's finest examples of period residential architecture, much of it painstakingly restored and maintained by the current owners.

Beaches Bunbury's premier beach, **Back Beach** is noted for its 130-million-year-old, jet-black basalt rocks, the result of ancient lava flows occurring during the latter stages of the break-up of the Gondwana supercontinent when what is now India separated from what is now WA. The colour is intense and provides a scenic contrast with the golden sand and turquoise water. Surfing and bodyboarding is popular, and most days you can see tanker ships in the distance lining up for the port. Just north of Back Beach is **Wyalup**, which holds substantial significance to the Noongar people as a burial ground – 'Wyalup' means 'place of mourning'. Further south along the coast, and backed by the sand dunes of Maiden's Reserve, **Mindalong Beach** is Bunbury's designated nude beach. There have been some assaults here, so do take precautions.

Mangrove Boardwalk and Koombana Bay A 5km circuit around Leschenault Inlet, the **Mangrove Boardwalk** winds its way through WA's southernmost white mangroves and provides opportunities to watch over 60 species of waterbird. The mangroves are ancient – by some accounts, the colony is 20,000 years old. If you aren't up for the full 5km walk, there is a shorter (200m), wheelchair-accessible section of the boardwalk on Koombana Drive, directly opposite the Dolphin Discovery Centre. There is also a lookout tower that was completed in 2019.

Just north of the mangroves is **Koombana Beach**, next to the Dolphin Discovery Centre. The sheltered calm water makes it a good choice for kids – though the surrounding industrial scenery is less than alluring. A short walk west brings you to the 1km-long **Koombana Footbridge**, which connects the connects the Bunbury CBD to the Bunbury Foreshore. Architecturally designed to resemble a ship's hull, it pays tribute to those who have lost their lives in the area's many shipwrecks; the materials used were recycled from an old bridge.

Dolphin Discovery Centre (Anchorage Cove, off Koombana Dr; ☏9791 3088; w dolphindiscovery.com.au; ⊕ 07.00–17.00 daily; A$18/12/10 adult/concession/child) Billing itself as 'Australia's premier wild dolphin experience', this part-museum, part-education centre offers an opportunity to swim with Koombana Bay's famous resident dolphins (from A$165) or take an ecocruise (90mins; from A$54) to sight them from the comfort of a boat. A pod of about 50 bottlenose dolphins live year-round in Koombana Bay and have been resident there for decades; nobody fully understands why they came here or why other dolphins (estimated at about 100 per year) come and visit before moving on. The interpretation centre includes a showstopping 360-degree dolphinarium, as well as interactive exhibits on the wider ecosystem of the region.

The centre is a non-profit and its 'Environment Fund' is dedicated to protecting animals through conservation programmes devoted to dolphin rescue (whether caught in nets or stranded on sand, etc), whale stranding, turtle rehabilitation and a variety of research and education programmes – over A$300,000 per year is required to fund the centre's support. The centre does look for volunteers, including visitors in Bunbury for shorter periods of time – though the time commitment is intense (minimum 25hrs/week for six weeks). Volunteers help educate visitors on what the centre does and help maintain the physical areas, and also help input research data into systems – the centre estimates that about 80% of a volunteer's time is spent with visitors. If you can't make a time commitment but still want to help out, you can download a dolphin survey from the website to help catalogue dolphin sightings around the Bunbury area, or engage in their adopt-a-dolphin or turtle programmes – with the money from your 'adoption' going to marine conservation.

Bunbury Wildlife Park (Prince Philip Dr; ☏9721 8380; w bunburywildlifepark. com.au; ⊕ 10.00–17.00 daily; A$11/8.50/5.50 adult/concession/child) Pet kangaroos, chat with cockatoos and feed all kinds of native birds at this interactive facility that is a favourite with adults and kids alike. It's also home to Big Swamp Parkland, a wetland reserve that is a popular breeding site for black swans. A 2km path loops around the lake, from where visitors can spot some 70 bird species as well as long-neck turtles.

St Mark's Anglican Church (41 Flynn St; ☏9721 7922) In the suburb of East Bunbury, this Heritage-listed weatherboard church opened in 1842 (and by some accounts is the state's second oldest) is a good surviving (though heavily restored) example of early West Australian church design, with its timber-shingled roof and graveyard of pioneer settlers. The church has a lovely setting, with a grand Moreton Bay fig tree, near the Preston River.

AROUND BUNBURY
Australind and Leschenault Peninsula Conservation Park Bunbury's northernmost suburb, Australind takes its name from a cross of 'Australia' and 'India' – the land was initially bought by the Western Australian Land Company, with the idea that horses could be bred here and then sold and exported to India. The idea was poorly conceived, however, and failed miserably, though a few settlers stayed on and a tiny settlement with minimal services persisted for decades, with construction of the railway inland through Pinjarra and Harvey further isolating the settlement. The town grew slowly, and eventually Bunbury's growth gobbled it up – today Australind is primarily a residential suburb. If in town, take a peek inside Heritage-listed **St Nicholas Church** (11 Paris Rd; ☏9725 8236; w stnicholasaustralind. org.au; ⊕ 10.00–16.00 Mon–Fri, 09.00–noon Sat, 08.00–09.45 & 10.30–12.30 Sun). Built in 1840, it is reputed to be the smallest church in the country, at 3.6m wide and 8.2m long. One of the early reverends from the 1800s, Andrew Buchanon, used to walk 10km from Bunbury to Australind each Sunday to deliver the sermon (and

then walk back to Bunbury the same day!). The congregation is still active and services are held here on Sundays at 09.00.

Australind also marks the start of the Heritage-listed Cathedral Avenue, once part of an 1800s mail road from Perth to Bunbury that today leads through a gallery of paperbark trees along the Leschenault Inlet, terminating at Buffalo Road. This is the jumping-off point for the **Leschenault Peninsula Conservation Park**, a narrow stretch of sand dunes, tuart and peppermint woodland, bounded by the inlet to the east and the Indian Ocean to the west. The peninsula is home to over 60 species of bird, western ringtail and brushtail possums, and the occasional dolphin pod can be spotted off the coast. The estuary also hosts white mangroves, believed to be descendants of a colony around 2,500 years old. Three walking trails meander through the park, the longest of which – the 18km return Harris Track – makes its way down to The Cut, a thin, manmade channel completed in 1950 that connects the estuary to the Indian Ocean. **Buffalo Beach** and **Belvidere Beach** are good for beach fishing – whiting, herring, mulloway and salmon – though neither is particularly scenic.

For those short on time, **Leschenault Waterways Discovery Centre** (187 Old Coast Rd; ⊕ 24hrs daily), just south of Australind, has interpretive paneling teaching about the waterways. The nearby jetty leads across to one of the estuary islands, where the waters are shallow and teeming with crabs – this is a good place to catch them.

Donnybrook   Situated 37km south of Bunbury on the South Western Highway, Donnybrook is a town synonymous with apples and it's worth visiting some of its farm gate orchards. Aside from those mentioned here, numerous other farms sell by the roadside but these can be irregular and often unadvertised (we usually find these by accident, often slamming on the brakes as we drive by and notice it!). The Visitor Centre in Donnybrook (South Western Hwy; ☎ 9731 1720; w donnybrookwa. com.au; ⊕ 10.00–16.00 Mon–Fri, 10.00–14.00 Sat) will know who is selling what and where.

The Fruit Barn   7 South Western Hwy; ☎ 9731 1198; ⊕ 07.00–19.00 daily. Has an orchard & is stocked with local fruit from around the area.
Karintha Orchards   South Western Hwy; ☎ 0427 316 277; ⊕ 08.00–18.00 daily. Sells to the public directly from their orchard – Pink Ladies, Sundowners & Granny Smiths, as well as multiple varieties of pear.

Spring Valley Orchard   19724 South Western Hwy; ☎ 9731 6214; w organic-orchard.com.au; ⊕ Jan–Jun, call for hours. Their 'pick your own' orchard features pink lady & sundowner apples, as well as plums. Also educates about organic farming & production & frequently holds seminars for small & hobbyist organic farmers.

Capel   Halfway between Bunbury and Busselton, Capel is most famous for **Peppermint Grove Beach** (though its reputation is perhaps oversold). Locals come here for the striking sunsets, but it's also good for swimming, has designated beach fishing areas and a large playground area for kids.

Some 19km southeast of Capel along Goodwood Road, towards Donnybrook, are **Ironstone Gully Falls**, which in winter have a drop of over 9m and a series of small rapids; cockatoos are also a common sight.

COLLIE AND WELLINGTON NATIONAL PARK

Boom-and-bust Collie has been a hub for WA's coal and timber industry since the 1880s – the ABC once said that 'Collie and coal go hand-in-hand'. A lot of the state's

Plan on taking a whole day for this forest excursion. From Collie, head south for about 3km on Mungalup Road until you reach **Minninup Pool** – a beautifully calm swimming and fishing spot at a wide point on the Collie River. Try to get here in the morning – in winter, the mist gives the scenery a dramatic feel and the site is a favourite for photographers. From Minninup, continue south on Mungalup Road for about 30km, and then make a left on to the unsealed King Tree Road. This will take you to a boardwalk leading to the 36m-tall **King Jarrah Tree**, which scientists estimate may be as much as 500 years old.

Continuing on King Tree Road, the very last section becomes sealed and ends at the T-junction for Wellington Mill Road. A left here takes you to **Gnomesville** (w gnomesville.com.au), just 1km away. This very quirky place is home to more than 10,000 gnome statues, many of which have been painted in various uniforms, national colours or whatever their owners imagined before leaving them behind. Such a tradition just started of its own – some local landholders put a few out one day, and it grew from there as passers-by began leaving their own. You are welcome to bring your own to leave, or you can buy one at the Ferguson Valley Visitor Centre in Dardanup.

Retrace your steps on Wellington Mill Road, pass King Tree Road and then make a right on to the unsealed Wellington Forest Road. After 4km this will take you to the **Wellington Discovery Forest**, where you can learn about the surrounding jarrah on two educational walking trails. Continue for roughly 4km, turn left at the Falcon Road junction, and after another 5km you reach **Lennard Drive** – a sealed, one-way scenic road through a deep river valley. Along the way you pass several other swimming, canoeing and kayaking spots, such as **The Rapids**, **Big Rock**, **Little Rock** and **Long Pool**. There are also mountain biking trails from here. A right turn after Long Pool on to River Road leads to **Honeymoon Pool** (see opposite).

Around 5km down the road from the pool is the T-junction for Wellington Weir Road. Turn right and after 4km you reach **Potters Gorge** – a popular swimming and fishing site at **Wellington Dam** – and then after another 3km, **The Quarry**, where abseiling is popular.

From there, turn back and head north on Wellington Weir Road, which after 12km will T-junction at the Coalfields Highway. A right turn takes you back into Collie, but you may want to consider taking the 38km route from Gnomesville to Bunbury through Dardanup, as the winding hills through the **Ferguson Valley** are quite scenic and pass numerous galleries, studios, wineries and a craft brewery. They also pass near **Crooked Brook Forest**, which has four walking trails, including one that is wheelchair-accessible and made from rammed earth.

electricity is produced here and Collie has long been perceived as being a hardscrabble mining town, though in recent years has worked hard to change its image. In 2006 those efforts paid off when Collie won the Australian Tidy Towns Competition. Still, pressure from renewable energies, combined with declining demand for coal, have led to job losses and an increasing sense of uncertainty for the town's future.

The town and its namesake river are named after Dr Alexander Collie, a surgeon who was one of the first Europeans to explore the area in 1829. Today the town has a population of around 9,000 and is a service centre for the surrounding area, and a jumping-off point for exploration into the forests and Wellington National Park.

GETTING THERE AND AWAY By **car**, Collie is 50km east of Bunbury along the Coalfields Highway (Highway 107) and the drive takes about 30 minutes. Once past Collie, the road continues to Arthur River and Wagin in the Wheatbelt.

Transwa has a daily **coach** to and from Bunbury (1hr). There is also a Transwa service from Collie through the Blackwood River Valley to the Southern Forests, as part of its Perth–Pemberton service on the SW3 route – it's 40 minutes from Bunbury to Collie. South West Coach Lines run to Perth and Perth Airport via Bunbury, taking 4 hours from Elizabeth Quay and 55 minutes from Bunbury Bus Station.

WHAT TO SEE AND DO Although most people pass through Collie on the way to Wellington National Park, there are a couple of sights in town showcasing its history. Housed in the old Road Board buildings, **Coalfields Museum and Historical Research Centre** (161 Throssell St; \9734 1852; ⊕ 10.00–15.00 Thu–Mon; A$5/free adult/child) houses memorabilia and artefacts from Collie's early days. Its signature artefact is a restored Italian barrel organ, which used to keep drinkers entertained while in one of the town's old saloons.

Attached to Collie Visitor Centre (156 Throssell St; \ 9734 2051; w collierivervalley.com.au; ⊕ 09.00–16.00 Mon–Fri, 10.00–15.00 Sat, 10.00–14.00 Sun), the **Replica Underground Coal Mine** gives a period example of what life in the coalface was like for the early miners in the area. Tour guides are retired miners themselves whose stories and explanations of the conditions have a real authenticity to them.

Wellington National Park Only 10km from Collie, the beautiful jarrah and marri forests, clearwater swimming holes and picturesque valleys of this 17,000ha national park make it one of the region's gems, and it's popular year-round. The highlight is **Honeymoon Pool**, a spectacular swimming hole set against a forest backdrop with water so clear you can see straight down to the marrons at the bottom. Peppermint trees line the banks, and a deck provides access for swimmers, canoers and kayakers. This is one of the most popular bush swimming and camping spots in WA (contact DPaW for details), so it does get crowded.

Walking trails abound and many lead to less-crowded waterholes. The easy, 12km **Jabitj Trail** tracks the Collie River through forest, rapids and pools, while the steeper, 10km **Sika Dual Use Trail** (for hikers and cyclists) offers lovely views over the valley.

BUSSELTON

The high-school graduation party ('Schoolies' in Australian slang) capital of WA, Busselton's sheltered, alluring crystal-clear waters, long stretches of unbroken white sand and 1.8km-long jetty (the longest in the southern hemisphere) have long made it a favourite for travellers, and it's a consistent winner of WA's 'top tourist town' award.

Busselton was first established as a cattle station by the Bussell family in the 1830s – hence the name. So successful was the station, that it became a spur for population growth in the South West, while the forests around the settlement did the same thing for millers. The town's famous jetty was built in 1865 and the state's

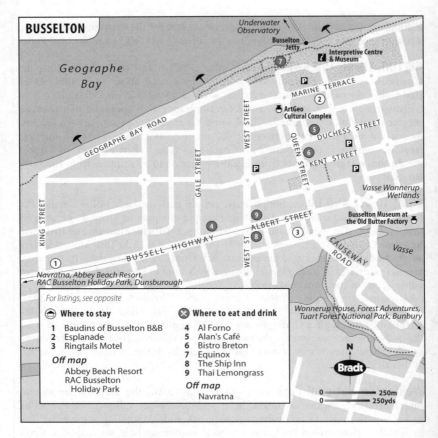

BUSSELTON

Geographe Bay

Underwater Observatory

Busselton Jetty

Interpretive Centre & Museum

MARINE TERRACE

ArtGeo Cultural Complex

DUCHESS STREET

KENT STREET

WEST STREET

GALE STREET

QUEEN STREET

KING STREET

Vasse Wonnerup Wetlands

Busselton Museum at the Old Butter Factory

ALBERT STREET

WEST ST

BUSSELL HIGHWAY

CAUSEWAY ROAD

Vasse

Navratna, Abbey Beach Resort,
RAC Busselton Holiday Park, Dunsburough

For listings, see opposite

⊖ **Where to stay**
1 Baudins of Busselton B&B
2 Esplanade
3 Ringtails Motel
Off map
   Abbey Beach Resort
   RAC Busselton
      Holiday Park

⊗ **Where to eat and drink**
4 Al Forno
5 Alan's Café
6 Bistro Breton
7 Equinox
8 The Ship Inn
9 Thai Lemongrass
Off map
   Navratna

Wonnerup House, Forest Adventures,
Tuart Forest National Park, Bunbury

N

Bradt

0 ——— 250m
0 ——— 250yds

first railway connected it to the forests, for easy shipment of logging and timber. By the early 1900s, Busselton had also become well established as a resort town and was the 'sanatorium of Western Australia'. An extended railway allowed easy access from Perth and Bunbury, and the discovery of caves along the coastline near what is now Yallingup and all the way down to Augusta was an early drawcard for visitors and further spurred tourism development. The establishment of wine in Margaret River further cemented Busselton's economy as tourism-centric, and by the latter part of the 20th century, the port had closed. Today roughly 35,000 people live in the area, though that number expands significantly in the summer.

GETTING THERE AND AROUND Transwa and South West Coach Lines offer **buses** to Perth (4hrs), Bunbury (45mins) and Perth International Airport (South West Coach Lines only – 3hrs 30mins). By **car**, Busselton is on the Bussell Highway, 50km from Bunbury to the northeast, 26km from Dunsborough to the west, 50km from Margaret River to the southwest and 57km from Nannup to the south. It takes about 2½ hours to reach Perth by car, and 30 minutes to Bunbury and Margaret River.

TransBusselton offers buses from the Albert Street/Queen Street intersection to Dunsborough and intermediate points along the Bussell Highway. There is also a circular town route. While Busselton extends about 10km east–west, the main CBD strip, visitor sites and jetty are all in a compact, highly walkable area.

WHERE TO STAY *Map, opposite*

A string of beach resorts line the Bussell Highway west of town.

Abbey Beach Resort (213 rooms) 595 Bussell Hwy; ☎9755 4600; e reservations@ abbeybeach.com.au; w abbeybeach.com.au. The largest resort in the region has indoor & outdoor pools, multiple restaurants & bars & sports equipment for hire. Stylishly appointed rooms range from spa suites to serviced apts. **$$$$**

Esplanade Hotel (39 rooms) 30–38 Marine Tce; ☎9752 1078; e enquiries@ehb.net. au; w esplanadehotelbusselton.com.au. Set just behind the foreshore & within easy walking distance to Queen St, spacious motel units have bathtubs, toasters, kettles & kitchen sinks. On-site bar & restaurant. **$$$$**

✱ **Baudins of Busselton B&B** (4 rooms) 87 Bussell Hwy; ☎9751 5576; e baudins@iinet. net.au; w baudins.com.au. Immaculate, spacious rooms with cooked b/fasts in the morning await

you at this wonderful B&B. Walking distance from the beach (5mins) & town (10mins). Do not be put off by the busy highway, you will not hear a thing in your room. **$$$**

RAC Busselton Holiday Park 97 Caves Rd; ☎9755 4241; e reservations@ racbusseltonholidaypark.com.au; w parksandresorts.rac.com.au/busselton. 300m from the beach, this complex features an assortment of apts, cabins, powered & unpowered sites, as well as pet-friendly & 'Big Rig' sites for large vehicles. Facilities include a variety of sport pitches, games room & minigolf. **$$$**

Ringtails Motel (9 rooms) 6 Pries Av; ☎9752 1200; e admin@ringtailsmotel.com.au; w ringtailsmotel.com.au. Centrally located motel with softly toned rooms & microwaves. Guest laundry, BBQ & outdoor pool. **$$**

WHERE TO EAT AND DRINK *Map, opposite*

Queen Street is the town's main café and shopping area, while there is the usual assortment of fast-food outlets on the Bussell Highway.

✱ ✗ **Alan's Café** 63 Duchess St; ☎9751 1037; w alanscafe.com.au; ⊕ 07.00–14.30 Wed–Fri, 07.00–13.30 Sat–Sun. An immediate hit from the day it opened, serving tasty, filling b/fasts – the Outback B/fast with spiced sausages & the Cowboy Hash with crispy potatoes is a real treat. **$$**

✗ **Al Forno** 19 Bussell Hwy; ☎9751 3775; w al-forno.com.au; ⊕ 17.00–20.00 Wed–Sun. One of the South West's leading Italian eateries, this popular place makes gourmet pizzas, pastas & casseroles. The lasagne is particularly good. **$$**

✱ ✗ **Bistro Breton** 49 Queen St; ☎9754 6217; w bistrobreton.com.au; ⊕ 08.00–14.00 Wed– Mon. This popular crêperie serves savoury & sweet crêpes to go with its range of coffees. They also serve scrumptious croque-monsieurs & salads. It's a great concept, wonderfully executed & is usually very busy. **$$**

✗ **Equinox** 1 Foreshore Pde; ☎9752 4641; w theequinox.com.au; ⊕ 09.30–20.00 daily. With a nice setting on the foreshore, this relaxed

eatery has a number of seafood dishes like chowder & fish & chips to go with burger options. It is on the expensive side, but you are paying for the location. **$$**

✱ ✗ **Navratna** 174 Bussell Hwy; ☎9752 3466; w navratna.com.au; ⊕ 17.00–late daily. Outstanding & well-priced Indian food, with particularly good beef & lamb dishes & samosas. The sides are varied & tasty & the service is excellent. This is one of our go-tos in the area. **$$**

✗ **The Ship Inn** 8 Albert St; ☎9752 3611; w shipinnbusselton.com.au; ⊕ 10.00–22.00 Sun–Thu, 10.00–midnight Fri–Sat. A Busselton institution, dating from the 1840s, with a solid menu of burgers, steaks & fish & chips. Sports bar & beer garden; they also offer accommodation. **$$**

✗ **Thai Lemongrass** 3/1 Albert St; ☎9754 7618; w thailemongrassbusselton.com.au; ⊕ 11.30–14.00 & 17.00–20.30 Tue–Fri, 17.00– 20.30 Sat–Mon. Popular eatery with decent pad Thais & stir-fries. **$$**

WHAT TO SEE AND DO

Busselton Jetty and Foreshore On a good-weather day Busselton simply looks spectacular. The seemingly endless stretches of sugar-white sand, the

The cold, southerly waters of the South West don't usually lend themselves to cyclones. But in late March 1978, Cyclone Alby stunned forecasters when, after making a turn away from WA's northern coast into open waters – where it was expected to weaken and disband – it instead turned back and headed to the South West, and more than doubled its speed in the process. The cyclone passed through the South West on 4 April 1978, packing a wallop of 150kph winds. The region was unprepared and five people died – the carnage extended all the way to Albany. Some estimates say Busselton recorded wind gusts of up to 175kph.

The cyclone wiped out a 700m section of Busselton Jetty, not yet a tourism icon in those days. But the outpouring of community grief at the jetty's destruction helped spur the development of the Busselton Jetty Preservation Society – which worked to spare the jetty from dismantling and removal by the government. Community efforts to preserve the jetty continued through decades, raising several million dollars, and in 2011 the final piece – A$27 million in restoration funding, mostly from the West Australian Government but also from the City of Busselton – was completed, 33 years after Cyclone Alby.

tranquil turquoise and dark blues of Geographe Bay and the pine tree backdrop make walking the foreshore and swimming at its beaches feel like a postcard come to life. The star attraction here is undoubtedly the **jetty** (w busseltonjetty.com.au) – which, at 1.8km long, is the longest timber jetty in the southern hemisphere. Buy your entry ticket (A$4/free adult/child) at the **Interpretive Centre and Museum** (☉ 09.30–16.15 daily) at the jetty's base. The museum features interactive displays covering the jetty's history from its inception in 1853, to its closure as a port in 1972, to its near destruction and final restoration to a premier tourist facility in the early 2000s (see box, above). The centre also offers information on the jetty's seasonal activities such as canoe and night tours, whale watching and scuba diving.

Walking the length of the jetty is a pleasure as it is lined with art, interpretive panels, plaques, memorials and more, plus you get to see the catches of the many fishermen who cast their lines off the sides. If you aren't up for walking all the way, the **Jetty Train** (A$14/8.50 adult/child) carries visitors to the end and back every 15 minutes.

You are encouraged to swim at the jetty's end – the bottom of Geographe Bay at that point is about 8m down – and it can be an exhilaratingly disorienting experience if you are not used to swimming in water that deep. The **Underwater Observatory** (A$34/20 adult/child) is found here, where a spiral staircase takes you to the bottom of the bay for a closer look at the various sealife – all manner of fish and crabs. The timber pylons form an artificial reef, and the colours of the corals that have grown on it are mesmerising. Dolphins call in here too – it is not unheard of for them to come close to the jetty and study the people passing by. There are swimming decks at various stages, though, so you don't need to walk all the way to the end if you want to swim away from the beach.

Other beaches About 1km west from the jetty, near the Yacht Club at the intersection of Geographe Bay Road and King Street, is another popular white-sand beach with calm waters, but without an enclosed children's playground. Further west along the Bussell Highway are three other popular beaches: **Dolphin Road Beach**, **Alan Road Beach** and **Holgate Road Beach** (although be wary of stingers at all). A pleasant walking trail connects the latter two.

ArtGeo Cultural Complex (4 Queen St; ☏9751 4651; w artgeo.com.au; ⊕ 10.00–16.00 daily)

Housed in a complex of Heritage-listed buildings on the foreshore, this is the town's premier creative hub. Built in 1931, the Neoclassical Agricultural Bank of Western Australia, with its archways and tiled veranda, now houses the **ArtGeo Gallery** whose signature event, the City of Busselton Art Award, attracts entrants from all over the state competing for a A$10,000 prize and a solo exhibition. At other times of year, it hosts temporary artist exhibitions and workshops. Across the street is the old **Busselton Courthouse and Police Precinct**, which contains fine Victorian- and Federation-period buildings as well as the old courtroom (complete with original furniture), nine goal cells, the post office and bond store, which today is a retail outlet for locally produced arts and crafts. The **Weld Theatre**, home of the Busselton Repertory Club, hosts numerous performances throughout the year, plus a pantomime. The **Merenj Boodja Bushfood Garden** was designed in the Noongar six seasons (see box, page 30) and is filled with native bushfood plants like emu plums, sea celery and salt bush.

Busselton Museum at the Old Butter Factory (Peel Tce; ☏ 9754 2166; w busseltonmuseum.org.au; ⊕ 10.00–16.00 Wed–Mon; A$10/5 adult/child)

Transport aficionados will love this museum, which features a paddle steamer, horse-drawn vehicles and a variety of engines and tractors. Originally a butter factory until 1952, it still houses the old butter-making equipment, and there are other exhibits about Busselton's history, including a fully restored one-room school.

Walking and cycling trails

Busselton has over 200km of walking and cycling paths. The City of Busselton's 'Walk, Ride, Discover 2020' map can be downloaded from its website, provides a comprehensive list of trails and also gives information on where to hire a bike, what cycling clubs are around the area and where to have a bike repaired. For history and art buffs, the 2.5km **Busselton Heritage Trail** traces the town's history through historical buildings from the old railway house at the base of the jetty to the Old Butter Factory on Peel Terrace – 14-day subscriptions can be bought through the heritage trail's website (w busseltonheritagetrail.com).

AROUND BUSSELTON

Vasse Wonnerup Wetlands (Layman Rd)

Just east of town, these 18km² wetlands are classed as being of 'International Importance' by Ramsar as they provide habitat for numerous rare birdlife like Caspian terns, marsh sandpipers and red knots (all protected by international agreement); some 33,000 birds across 60 species have been recorded here at one time. The wetlands change profoundly from season to season and are best explored on the walking trail accessible off Layman Road – the largest breeding colony of black swans and ibis are also here, as well as herons, spoonbills and egrets. Summer is the best time to visit when the number of migratory birds is at its highest.

Forest Adventures (12 Ludlow Park Rd; ☏9780 5908; w forestadventures.com.au; ⊕ 09.00–17.00 Thu–Mon)

Grab a safety harness and ascend to the high ropes in the tuart trees at this facility in Ludlow State Forest, 17km northeast of town. Six rope courses of different difficulty levels will get your adrenaline brewing; book in

2-hour blocks. Expert instructors provide an introduction and orientation to the equipment before you set off, as well as a low-altitude practice run. Great for kids, and plenty of adults love it too.

Tuart Forest National Park (Layman Rd; w parks.dpaw.wa.gov.au/park/tuart-forest) Just 15km northeast of Busselton is the largest remaining stretch of tuart forest in the world, though today it is just a fairly narrow slab. Some trees are over 300 years old, 30m tall and 10m in circumference. Also at the park is the fantastic Possum Spotlighting Trail, a self-guided, 1.5km trail offering plenty of opportunities to see nocturnal marsupials such as the western ringtail possum and brushtail possum. Red reflectors guide the way, but bring a torch.

Nearby is **Wonnerup House** (935 Layman Rd; ℡9752 2039; w nationaltrust.org.au/places/wonnerup; ⊕ 10.00–16.00 Thu–Mon; A$10/5 adult/child), a Heritage-listed schoolhouse and homestead owned by the Layman family (the last one of whom died in 1962). It stands out for its presentation – it actively encourages visitors to consider the arrival of settlers in the South West from both a European and an Aboriginal perspective – and that is evident immediately upon entering the grounds, when you pass the sign reading: 'What happens when two worlds collide?' Though the house itself can seem quite cookie-cutter with those elsewhere in the state, and at times even a bit bare-bones, its ethos to deliberately encourage visitors to think about early settlement from multiple perspectives makes it worth the visit.

DUNSBOROUGH AND CAPE NATURALISTE

Beaches, beaches and more beaches – this is what has drawn visitors to Dunsborough for nearly 100 years. As late as the 1950s, the townsite consisted of just a few shops and beach shacks but when surfing became popular a decade later, tourism really took off. That continued with the establishment of wine tourism in the 1980s and later development of resorts and the Cape-to-Cape Track (see box, opposite). The area is immensely popular with holiday homers and Perth long weekenders.

Dunsborough sits on Geographe Bay, at the right-hand base of Cape Naturaliste; the cape itself forms almost the shape of a shark fin. Some of WA's best and most popular beaches are found on Cape Naturaliste and its namesake lighthouse – which was manned until 1996 – is a state icon. Beach-hopping along the cape spoils you, and the sands here are so regularly breathtaking that you can actually begin to shrug your shoulders at places that would be brochure-cover worthy in many other destinations but don't even make the top-ten list in the South West.

GETTING THERE AND AWAY By car, Dunsborough is 24km west of Busselton along the Bussell Highway and Caves Road. Be mindful that, if heading from Busselton, the Bussell Highway breaks off and veers left to Margaret River and bypasses Dunsborough, so you need to go straight on Caves Road.

Both Transwa and South West Coach Lines offer **coaches** to Perth (4½hrs). TransBusselton buses offer services to Busselton (45mins).

 WHERE TO STAY AND EAT

Dunsborough Central Motel (47 rooms) 50 Dunn Bay Rd; ℡9756 7711; e reservations@dunsboroughmotel.com.au; w dunsboroughmotel.com.au. Major complex in town with a variety of rooms from standard motel to spa suites. All rooms have flatscreen TVs with free in-house movies; spa & superior rooms have kitchenettes with hobs. **$$$**

Dunsborough Tavern 2 Dunsborough Pl; ℡9755 3657; w thedunsborough.com.au;

THE CAPE-TO-CAPE TRACK

Extending for 125km from Cape Naturaliste near Dunsborough to Cape Leeuwin near Augusta, the Cape-to-Cape Track is one of Australia's best long-distance hikes. The trail takes about five to seven days and can be done in either direction, and it's particularly scenic in wildflower season. The track mostly follows the coast, providing spectacular views out over the Indian Ocean and nearby rock formations (like Canal Rocks and Sugarloaf Rock), but it also passes Quinninup and Meekadarabee Falls, the giant karris of Boranup Forest, dozens of beaches that string along the coast like Yallingup, Foul Bay and Cosy Corner, surf spots galore (like Three Bears) and plenty of magnificent clifftop lookouts. If you are new to long-distance hiking, there is probably no better track in the state to cut your teeth on than this one.

The route is split into five sections, and there are plenty of access roads from which the track can be chopped up into smaller bits. Camping is possible but it isn't necessary – there are plenty of hotels and restaurants along the route, but you do have to organise your own transport to/from a drop site. The Friends of the Cape-to-Cape Track website (w capetocapetrack. com.au) is a good place to start for more details.

⌚ 11.00–22.30 Tue–Thu, 11.00–midnight Fri, 10.00–midnight Sat, 10.00–22.30 Sun–Mon. Bright & cheerful tavern with a sports-bar vibe. The steak sanga & cheeseburgers are well done, as are the desserts. $$

❋ ✖ **Pedro's** 15/34 Dunn Bay Rd; ☎ 9759 1828; w pedrosmexican.com.au; ⌚ 17.00–20.00 daily. Great Mexican food with a hip vibe at this cool eatery – one of our favourites. Everything is well done here but the burritos & fajitas are particularly good. Start your meal with the nachos & wash it

all down with a cocktail. They show Road Runner cartoons on the wall in the dining room. $$

❋ ✖ **Simmo's** 161 Commonage Rd; ☎ 9755 3745; w simmos.com.au; ⌚ 10.00–17.00 daily. Legendary ice cream parlour with over 60 flavours – you will see restaurants all over Perth & WA advertising that they sell Simmo's ice cream. Kids justifiably love this place & adults will too, especially creative flavours like liquorice. Don't be deterred if there's a huge queue – it moves quickly. $

WHAT DO SEE AND DO Dunsborough's main street has a bright and quirky eating and shopping scene that gives an air of a town perpetually on holiday. There isn't much to do other than eat, drink and be merry – even the town beach pales in comparison to those up the road – and most visitors just use it as a base from which to take a spin around Cape Naturaliste.

A few kilometres north of Dunsborough on Cape Naturaliste Road is the 577ha **Meelup Regional Park** (w meeluppark.com), Meelup meaning 'place of moon rising' in Wadandi. The park is a biodiversity hotspot – the endemic Meelup mallee tree (*Eucalyptus phylacis*), of which there are fewer than 50, exists only here, and the critically endangered Cape spider orchid is also present. One partial hypothesis for the region's biodiversity is that the granite outcrops served as a kind of 'refuge' or 'shelter' for plant species over millions of years as the Australian climate fluctuated – which also led to genetic divergence. The variation in plant coverage is also quite striking as you travel the cape – scrublands give way to jarrah forests. This is also an important place for the South West's fauna – quendas (a type of bandicoot), Western pygmy possums and Carnaby's cockatoos are just some of the species you will spot.

Turning into the park, and then on to Castle Rock Road, takes you to the cape's first glorious beach – **Castle Rock**. The water here is sheltered, and some of the clearest in WA. The beach's namesake, the hulking Castle Rock, lords over the bay from the eastern side – climbing to the top affords grand views.

Returning to Meelup Beach Road, 3km further is **Meelup Beach**, arguably the most famous of Dunsborough's beaches and typically the busiest on any long weekend. There's plenty of shade, making it ideal for picnics and families. Continuing north for 1.5km takes you past **Point Picquet**, a slight but magical stretch of sand sandwiched between ochre rocks and azure water. Getting to the beach here does require a rock scramble, so better to continue on for another 2km to magnificent **Eagle Bay Beach** ✳, with its brilliant white sand and dazzling clear waters. There is also a small residential community tucked back behind the beach's dunes. From here, Meelup Beach Road ends and takes you back inland to Cape Naturaliste Road; a right turn there, to Bunker Bay Road, will take you to **Bunker Bay Beach** – the closest beach to the tip of Cape Naturaliste.

At the end of Cape Naturaliste Road is the **Cape Naturaliste Lighthouse Complex** (1267 Cape Naturaliste Rd; ☏ 9780 5911; ⊙ 09.00–17.00 daily; A\$15/7.50 adult/child), one of the most iconic sights in the region. The complex details the area's fascinating maritime history, including the shipwrecks, physical geography, ocean currents and life as a lighthouse keeper – the keeper's old cottage has been restored into a lovely café. The lighthouse itself is 20m tall, built with limestone in 1904 and situated on a 100m-high bluff; there are 59 steps leading to the top (accessible only by organised tour). This was the last manned lighthouse in WA – the last keeper departed in 1996 – and today maintenance is done by the Australian Maritime Safety Authority. At least 14 ships have met their end off Cape Naturaliste.

The complex has an observational platform providing grand vistas of the Indian Ocean and there are a couple of walking trails (note the whale-watching lookout points; the season is September to November). A 3km (one-way) wheelchair-accessible track leads south to **Sugarloaf Rock**, jutting out of the shallow waters across a narrow channel from the mainland. Once the cover of *Australian Geographic*, the rock is home to the rare red-tailed tropicbird (*Phaethon rubricauda*) – though count yourself lucky if you see one, as they spend most of their lives at sea. An elevated platform on the mainland provides excellent views (as does the descending road if you choose to drive in).

YALLINGUP AND THE COAST

One of the best-known towns in Australian surfing, beautiful Yallingup – which means 'place of love' in the local Wardandi language – is perhaps the most prime area of real estate in the Capes. The beach here is spectacular – progressing from south to north from part rockpool, part reef-protected sheltered snorkelling spot to surfing territory with rip-roaring waves. Some of the world's best breaks are near here, as is WA's first surfing museum at Aravina Estate Winery. The tiny town does have an exclusive vibe about it, and accommodation and restaurants can be priced to match. South from here along Caves Road is where some of the Margaret River region's most famous surf breaks, wineries and snorkelling spots hug the coastline.

GETTING THERE AND AWAY By **car**, Yallingup is 12km from Dunsborough on Caves Road, and 37km north of Margaret River on the same road. Transwa **coaches** stop here on their way from Bunbury to Augusta (1hr 20mins from Bunbury, 1hr 10mins from Augusta).

WHERE TO STAY AND EAT

Caves House Hotel (32 rooms) 18 Yallingup Beach Rd; 9750 1888; e reception@ycch.com.au; w caveshousehotelyallingup.com.au. One of the oldest accommodations in the region, opened in 1903, now a luxury hotel featuring spa rooms, apts & heritage rooms. Restaurant does buffet b/fasts, high teas & pub classics. A great option if you want to be near Yallingup Beach. **$$$$**

Empire Spa Retreat (11 rooms) 9755 2065; e retreat@empireretreat.com; w empireretreat.com. Designed to be a relaxation retreat, exquisite rooms here with massage facilities on site provide a true escape. Hampers are available for lunch & dinner at a cost; b/fast inc. Pricey, but worth it if you want to be away from the crowds. **$$$$**

Aravina Estate 61 Thornton Rd; 9750 1111; w aravinaestate.com; 11.00–17.00 daily. Winery offering top-notch Cabernet Sauvignon & Chardonnay, plus fine (& pricey) dining – try the lamb backstrap if it's on offer (they also have gourmet pizzas). It's also home to the **WA Surf Gallery** – WA's first official surfing museum – with 1950s surfboards & historical images. **$$**

Yallingup Gugelhupf 18 Yallingup Beach Rd; 0477 427 770; 07.30–17.00 Wed–Mon. *Gugelhupf* is a small, donut-shaped cake common in German-speaking Europe. This small shop right at the entrance to town does them well, with savoury & sweet options, as well as coffee. Worth trying & taking with you as a snack. **$**

WHAT TO SEE AND DO

Yallingup Beach * One of WA's most dazzling beaches stretching north from town, there is both sheltered swimming and substantial surfing on offer here. The water simply sparkles, and the colour contrasts – light and dark blues mixed with the silver, grey and black speckles of the reef system – are remarkable. The swimming lagoon is sheltered by a reef and gets to around 3m deep, with plenty of fish and other sea creatures to gaze at through your mask. The water here is very calm and suitable for children. Slightly further south along the beach are a series of shallow rockpools that are popular for shell- and rock-hunting. Towards the north end, the surf challenges even experienced surfers (and some swimmers). If you do swim at the break, be warned there can be a ferocious tow. The beach is popular with surfing schools; **Yallingup Surf School** (Yallingup Beach Rd; 0429 881 221; w yallingupsurfschool.com) offers individual and group lessons from A$100, along with multi-day courses.

Ngilgi Cave (76 Yallingup Caves Rd; 9757 7411; 09.00–17.00 daily; A$22.50/11.50 adult/child) Caves were the early drawcard of this region, and a guided tour of Ngilgi Cave – a 5-minute drive from Yallingup – offers the opportunity to view stalactites, touch crystals and view geological marvels. The cave's temperature is roughly 20°C year-round – a great place to retreat to on a hot summer day. Early tourists used to explore the cave in their Sunday Best – difficult as it is to imagine now, this was the expected social etiquette at the time – and due to the great acoustics here, Dame Nellie Melba – whose image is on the A$100 note – had her grand piano lowered down in here in the early 1900s for an opera concert.

Smith's Beach Another excellent swimming and surf beach just south of Yallingup, this is near the famed Supertubes surfing spot known for its ability to hold huge swells. While unprotected, the parts of the beach close to the car park provide good swimming without huge breaks. Beginner surfers often come here to train; and it's a popular local's choice when Yallingup is overcrowded.

Canal Rocks * The constant heave-ho of the rough Indian Ocean surf over millennia has opened up a channel inside these granite rocks at the coastline, creating a picturesque geological 'canal'. A narrow boardwalk takes you through the rocks and across the canal to more rocks, which you can scramble around for better views.

Nearby is **The Aquarium** ✳, a magnificent, sheltered snorkelling channel. It requires a bit of a hike (around 1km on a dirt and sand path) and it isn't signposted, but is worth the effort if you can find it. Driving in, proceed like you are going to Canal Rocks, but stop at the car park about 500m before reaching them. Exit the car to the right and follow the path for about 500m; at that stage, another dirt path will open up down to the shore.

Injidup Beach
The dune-and-cliff setting of this beach frequently sees it grace the cover of many tourist publications about the Capes. The long bay gives plenty of space for crowds to thin out, though take care if swimming here; the current has a reputation. The **Injidup Natural Spa** sits at the beach's northern end, a rockpool filled with waves crashing over the rocks, creating a spa-like 'bubbles' effect, and is a popular place for people to sit and relax. Note it isn't signposted and requires a rock scramble to get to. Don't confuse the natural spa with **Injidup Spa Retreat** (Cape Clairault Rd; ☏ 9750 1300; e stay@injidupsparetreat.net.au; w injidupsparetreat.com.au; **$$$$**), just inland from the beach, which offers gorgeous villas and spa treatments from A$680 per night, with minimum stay requirements.

Quinninup Falls
Although a bit tricky to find, the hike to these falls along a section of the Cape-to-Cape Track (you can't drive to them) is a nice afternoon activity when there has been enough rainfall in winter to make the water flow. Plunging 10m into a small pool (not suitable for swimming), the falls attract plenty of frogs and gooey algae is also around when there's enough water. In summer check with the Dunsborough or Margaret River visitor centres to see if the falls are flowing before setting off. From the car park at the end of Moses Rock Road, take a right and head up the log steps following the Cape-to-Cape Track for around 45 minutes to an hour.

Gracetown and Cowaramup Bay
Some 12km north of Margaret River, Gracetown is holiday home country, and there is little in the townsite itself to interest visitors except Cowaramup Bay Beach – also called Gracetown Beach, though the road here from Caves Road is confusingly called Cowaramup Bay Road. The beach has magnificent, sheltered swimming, with lots of underground rocks and all manners of marine life, and is justifiably popular with families and children. The drive in is postcard worthy, offering a gorgeous panorama of Gracetown where the beach unfolds right in front of you as you come over the last small hill into the settlement. At either end of Cowaramup Bay, two high-level surfing spots – North Point and South Point, named for obvious reasons – beckon for experienced surfers. North Point, in particular, can have huge swells; South Point is a bit gentler. Huzzawouie (just call it Huzzas) is next to South Point, southeast along the curved bay, and gentler still – suitable for beginners. Don't confuse Cowaramup Bay with Cowaramup; the latter is an inland town 13km east of the beach on the Bussell Highway.

MARGARET RIVER AND AROUND ✳

It seems difficult to believe that in the 1950s and 1960s, Margaret River was considered one of the poorest regions in WA, and the epitome of a backwater. How times change. Today it is one of the world's capitals of wine and surfing, and no trip to WA would be complete without at least a weekend call-in here.

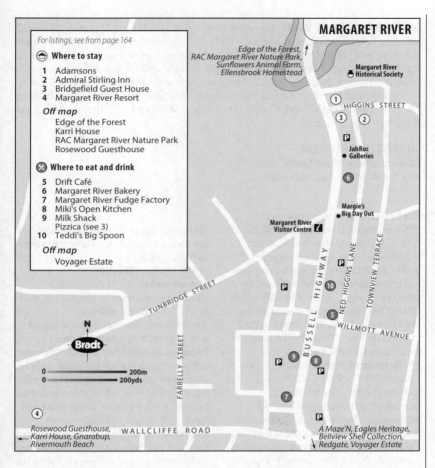

MARGARET RIVER

For listings, see from page 164

🛏 **Where to stay**
1 Adamsons
2 Admiral Stirling Inn
3 Bridgefield Guest House
4 Margaret River Resort

Off map
Edge of the Forest
Karri House
RAC Margaret River Nature Park
Rosewood Guesthouse

✗ **Where to eat and drink**
5 Drift Café
6 Margaret River Bakery
7 Margaret River Fudge Factory
8 Miki's Open Kitchen
9 Milk Shack
 Pizzica (see 3)
10 Teddi's Big Spoon

Off map
Voyager Estate

Edge of the Forest,
RAC Margaret River Nature Park,
Sunflowers Animal Farm,
Ellensbrook Homestead

Margaret River
Historical Society

HIGGINS STREET

JahRoc
Galleries

Margie's
Big Day Out

Margaret River
Visitor Centre

NED HIGGINS LANE

TOWNVIEW TERRACE

BUSSELL HIGHWAY

WILLMOTT AVENUE

TUNBRIDGE STREET

N

Bradt

0 ———— 200m
0 ———— 200yds

FARRELLY STREET

Rosewood Guesthouse,
Karri House, Gnarabup,
Rivermouth Beach

WALLCLIFFE ROAD

A Maze'N, Eagles Heritage,
Bellview Shell Collection,
Redgate, Voyager Estate

The South West   MARGARET RIVER AND AROUND

5

Backed by forest on one side and beaches on the other, the Margaret River region has been home to the Noongar people for around 50,000 years. European pioneers arrived in the 1850s, and the town was gazetted in 1913. Dairy farming took off and became an entrenched part of the early economy, as with many other areas of the South West. It was in the 1960s, however, when the seedlings were planted for the area to become a wine region. The region received favourable reports about its suitability for viticulture, and in 1967 Dr Tom Cullity planted the first vines at what would become Vasse Felix. Other wineries such as Cape Mentelle, Cullens and Sandalford also appeared and still form the backbone of the Margaret River wine region today. Surfing also became popular in the 60s, at a time when it was beginning to enter the mainstream in WA, and the huge swells off the Margaret River coast were an obvious attraction; the 1969 Australian National Titles cemented Margaret River as a surfing capital in the national psyche. The economy of the area changed rapidly and now is firmly anchored in tourism.

Today, you will find people who claim that growth and development have 'changed' Margaret River. That it has – it has made it a more special, much more mature destination with a much wider array of attractions, yet outside the main road in town still feels wonderfully relaxed and unhurried.

163

GETTING THERE AND AWAY Margaret River is on the Bussell Highway, 50km/35 minutes southwest from Busselton, 100km/1 hour 15 minutes southwest from Bunbury and 42km/30 minutes north of Augusta. Caves Road runs parallel to the highway along the coast (but no water views), while Mowen Road connects Margaret River to Nannup, 70km/50 minutes east, and the Blackwood River Valley.

Transwa **coaches** stop here on their way to/from Bunbury (2hrs) and Augusta (30mins), and South West Coach Lines offers services to Perth (4½–5hrs) via Busselton (1hr 15mins).

TOURIST INFORMATION

⁊ Margaret River Visitor Centre 100 Bussell Hwy; ☏ 9780 5911; w margaretriver.com; ⊕ 09.00–17.00 daily

⌂ WHERE TO STAY *Map, page 163*

⌂ Karri House (3 rooms) 20 Karri Loop; ☏ 0411 745 221; e stay@karrihouse.com.au; w karrihouse.com.au. Surrounded by peaceful gardens, this characterful property with charming wooden veranda offers tastefully appointed rooms with TVs & private bathrooms. Other little touches include a bocce court, an orchard where you can pick fruit, & eggs for b/fast that come from the property's chickens. It is expensive, but you pay for the ambience & setting. **$$$$**

⌂ Rosewood Guesthouse (6 rooms) 54 Wallcliffe Rd; ☏ 9757 2845; e info@rosewoodguesthouse.com.au; w rosewoodguesthouse.com.au. High-end accommodation featuring touches like Devonshire teas, cheese platters & optional private tours (for a fee) in the owners' 1956 Rolls Royce. Beds are very comfortable. Cooked b/fast can cater to vegans. **$$$$**

⌂ Edge of the Forest (6 rooms) 25 Bussell Hwy; ☏ 9757 2351; e info@edgeoftheforest.com.au; w edgeoftheforest.com.au. Excellent-value motel-style rooms, all with decked patio/balcony & some with views to forest. BBQ area & DVD library; continental b/fast option. **$$$**

⌂ Margaret River Resort (25 rooms) 40 Wallcliffe Rd; ☏ 9757 0000; e stay@theriverhotel.com.au; w mrresort.com.au. Not to be confused with the Margaret River Hotel, this comfortable place just outside the centre of town has light-

filled suites & homey, Old-English-style rooms. Spa apts & self-contained villas available; there's also a bottle shop. **$$$**

❋ ⌂ Margaret Riverside Accommodation ☏ 9757 2013; e info@margaretriverside.com.au; w margaretriverside.com.au. This is actually 3 different accommodations close to each other, all booked from the same phone number & website. **Adamsons** (71 Bussell Hwy; 10 rooms) offers very comfortable queen rooms with a garden, while the character-laden **Admiral Stirling Inn** (Ned Higgins Lane; 11 rooms) has jarrah weatherboard, leadlights & timber furniture. **Bridgefield Guest House** (73 Bussell Hwy; 6 rooms) is an eye-catching landmark on the northern entrance to town, with its verandas & gazebo. An added bonus – whichever you stay at, you're next to 2 of the best Italian restaurants in the state. **$$$**

⌂ RAC Margaret River Nature Park Carters Rd; ☏ 9758 8227; e reservations@margaretrivernaturepark.com.au; w parksandresorts.rac.com.au/margaret-river. Huge range of options from cabins & eco-lodges to safari tents & dorm rooms, plus powered sites & bush camping. The park makes use of its forested surroundings just 2km north of town in Wooditjup National Park – there is an old mill used for activities, along with a climbing forest & plenty of games for kids. **$$**

✗ WHERE TO EAT AND DRINK *Map, page 163*

❋ ✗ Voyager Estate 41 Stevens Rd; ☏ 9757 6354; w voyagerestate.com.au; ⊕ 10.00–17.00 daily. Although not cheap, the seasonal 7-course Discovery Menu is an exceptional delight to

the palette & the estate advises to not look at the menu until you arrive. At the risk of being a spoiler, you can expect things like rock lobster & aged duck – there are also vegetarian menus. A shorter, 4-course Terroir menu offers the likes of line-caught fish & lamb. The wine pairings are what you would expect from one of the state's best vineyards. $$$$

✕ Miki's Open Kitchen 131 Bussell Hwy; ☏9758 7673; w mikisopenkitchen.com.au; ⏲ 18.00–21.30 Tue–Sat. A unique Japanese-inspired restaurant run by Miki, who uses local ingredients. There are 4 degustation menus – including a 6-course sake discovery & 1 for kids. You can also opt to 'trust Miki' or create your own degustation. Dishes change daily but include the likes of tuna sashimi with wasabi oil, sesame-crusted lamb scotch & asparagus with wasabi goat cheese. The open kitchen is a theatre itself – watching is part of the dining journey. An interesting experience worth trying. Book well in advance. $$$

✕ Drift Café 1/72 Willmott Av; ☏9757 2237; w driftcafe.com.au; ⏲ 08.00–14.00 Mon–Fri, 07.30–14.00 Sat–Sun. Very popular hip café with good b/fasts & lunches & an array of juices & smoothies. A good place to fuel up for the morning. $$

✳ ✕ Pizzica 73 Bussell Hwy; ☏9758 7361; w pizzica.com.au; ⏲ 17.00–22.30 daily, 21.30 last orders. This may be WA's best pizza joint – Italian owned & operated, with native Italian staff,

you can't go wrong with any of the pizzas (or the drinks menu, with negronis & limoncello). The *ascolane* (stuffed olives) are a great way to kick off the meal. We're regulars when in town. $$

✕ Teddi's Big Spoon 113A Bussell Hwy; ☏9758 8443; ⏲ 11.00–20.00 Wed–Sun. Quality Korean food at this little restaurant on the main strip. Highlights include bulgogi & glass noodles. The fruit teas & seafood pancakes are also good. $$

✳ ✕ Margaret River Bakery 89 Bussell Hwy; ☏9757 2755; w margaretriverbakery.com.au; ⏲ 07.00–14.00 Mon–Sat. One of our favourites, this outstanding bakery has great sandwiches, croissants, cinnamon rolls, meringues, pies & pastries. Some items can sell out before the day is done. An excellent choice for b/fast or lunch. $

✕ Margaret River Fudge Factory 152 Bussell Hwy; ☏9758 8881; w fudgefactory.com.au; ⏲ 10.00–16.00 Mon–Wed, 10.00–16.30 Thu–Sat, 10.00–14.00 Sun. Award-winning factory with hundreds of selections available, including candies & chocolates. We often stop here for dessert after lunch elsewhere. $

✕ Milk Shack 140 Bussell Hwy; ☏9757 3535; w millersicecream.com.au; ⏲ 10.30–17.00 daily. Our go-to place for dessert. Ice cream made from locally sourced dairy – high-quality ingredients & high-quality products. $

SHOPPING The Margaret River region's shopping scene tends to revolve around gastronomy, with heaps of venues strewn north and south of the townsite.

Berry Farm 43 Bessell Rd; ☏9757 5054; w theberryfarm.com.au; ⏲ 10.00–16.00 daily. This local institution on the road east towards Rosa Brook & Nannup sells a variety of boutique jams, condiments, wines, ports & liqueurs – the apricot & almond jam is a personal favourite, as is the liquorice liqueur. They have good olive tapenades too.

Boranup Gallery 7981 Caves Rd; ☏9757 7585; ⏲ 10.00–noon daily. Huge collection of artistic works from wood furniture to metalwork sculptures, as well as glass & ceramics, from West Australian artists. Note the short opening hours.

Colony Concept 62 Harmans Mill Rd; ☏9755 7777; w southernforestshoney.com.au. Home of Southern Forests Honey, this shop celebrates all things honey from raw to creamed, including marri & jarrah honeys, honeycomb & several types of mead alongside honey-infused salad dressings, soaps & body lotions.

JahRoc Galleries 83 Bussell Hwy; ☏9758 7200; w jahroc.com.au; ⏲ 10.00–17.00 daily. This gallery features designer furniture made from West Australian timber & Australian art. Additionally, ceramic art, glass art & even diamonds are for sale.

Margaret River Chocolate Company 415 Harmans Mill Rd; ☏9755 6555; w chocolatefactory.com.au; ⏲ 09.00–17.00 daily. Over 200 types of chocolate items are on sale here – truffles, sauces, drinking chocolate & chunky chocolate bars (try the cookies & cream). The white malt drinking chocolate is a wintertime favourite of mine.

Olio Bello 36 Armstrong Rd; ☏9755 9771; w oliobello.com; ⏲ 10.00–16.30 daily. Organic producer of extra-virgin olive oil, alongside plenty of health & beauty products like soaps, shave bars & essential oils.

Margaret River wine is some of the best in the world. The region's Cabernet Sauvignon and Chardonnay are particularly well renowned, and no visit to the South West would be justified without a trip to some of its wineries. Though the region produces just 2% of Australia's wine, it holds a significant spot in the premium wine market.

Dr Tom Cullity is widely credited as being the 'father' of Margaret River wine in the 1960s, but the establishment of a world-class industry here was the result of many others. Dr John Gladstones at the University of Western Australia followed up early work on viticulture and felt the Margaret River region in particular would be an excellent area to produce wine due to its climate and soil, and was influenced by earlier favourable reports about the wine-making capacity of the Great Southern. Gladstones also felt that as long as the soil was drained enough, the Margaret River region's high annual rainfall would not impinge upon wine production. Gladstones' work, with support from the state government, who saw potential for economic growth, led directly to the establishment of the initial vineyards in the late 1960s and early 1970s, with the region coming into its own with several award winners in the 1980s.

The 'Founding Six' wineries were Vasse Felix (the first), Cape Mentelle, Sandalford, Cullen, Moss Wood and Leeuwin, but today there are over 210 wineries with 85 cellar doors – with 72 winning a five-star rating from the prestigious 2021 Halliday Wine Companion by guru James Halliday, one of Australia's foremost experts on wine (w winecompanion.com.au/wineries/western-australia/margaret-river). Cabernet Sauvignon and Sauvignon Blanc are the two most harvested varieties here, with Semillon and Chardonnay not far behind. Shiraz is also well represented. US-based wine legend Robert Mondavi took an interest in the region in the early 1970s – it was supposedly his advice in the early 1970s to plant Chardonnay.

The biggest concentration of wineries is dotted in a loop north of Margaret River near Gracetown, and the following list offers a sample tour. Winery maps can be picked up at the Margaret River Visitor Centre. You can also take an organised tour – both **Margie's Big Day Out** (\0416 180 493; w margaretrivertourswa.com.

WHAT TO SEE AND DO

Beaches Aside from wine tours (see box, above), Margaret River is a good base from which to enjoy some of the region's best swimming and surfing beaches. **Gnarabup** is the longest and most popular, located 9km west of town close to the small township of Prevelly. The far southern end is sheltered and provides great snorkelling, although it gets steep quickly. The reefs are about 500m out, from where you can find a few of the world's great left-handed breaks – Boat Ramp, Bombie and Suicides. Walking north along the beach takes you to **Surfer's Point** – frequently considered the premier surfing spot in the South West, home of the Main Break and the Margaret River Pro, attended by thousands of spectators each year. **Rivermouth Beach**, where the Margaret River meets the Indian Ocean, is accessed nearby.

South of Gnarabup, **Redgate** is a good family beach with easy surf breaks, partially sheltered between granite rocky outcrops due west of Witchcliffe. There are plenty of rockpools to explore and walking along the sand brings more coves and bays. The **Margaret River Surf School** (\0401 616 200; w margaretriversurfschool.com) au) and **Harvest Tours** (\ 0429 728 687; w harvesttours.com.au) offer half- and full-day trips.

THE FOUNDING WINERIES

Cape Mentelle 331 Walcliffe Rd; \ 9757 0888; w capementelle.com.au; ⊕ 10.00–17.00 daily. Their Cabernet Sauvignon & Zinfandel are known Australia-wide.

Cullen Wines 4323 Caves Rd; \ 9755 5277; w cullenwines.com.au; ⊕ 10.00–16.30 daily. Renowned Cabernet Merlot & Chardonnay are well noted.

Leeuwin Estate Stevens Rd; \ 9759 0000; w leeuwinestate.com.au; ⊕ 10.00–17.00 daily. The winery has a reputation for terrific Chardonnays.

Moss Wood Wines 926 Metricup Rd; \ 9755 6266; w mosswood.com.au; ⊕ by appointment. Wine journalist Ray Jordan – one of Australia's most trusted –gave their 2014 Cabernet Sauvignon a rating of 99/100, his highest ever score.

Vasse Felix 4357 Caves Rd; \ 9756 5000; w vassefelix.com.au; ⊕ 10.00–17.00 daily. Vasse Felix offers a simply named 'Classic Red' & 'Classic White,' & the on-site museum is well worth a look, with newspaper reproductions of early media stories about the local wine industry & bottles of vintages of each year of the winery's existence.

OTHER WINERIES

Evans & Tate Metricup & Caves Rd; \ 9755 6244; w evansandtate.wine; ⊕ 10.30–17.00 daily. Their Semillon Sauvignon Blanc is a best-seller, & their Chardonnays are highly marked.

Fermoy 838 Metricup Rd; \ 9755 6593; w fermoy.com.au; ⊕ 11.00–17.00 daily. Noted for its outstanding whites, particularly Semillon & Chardonnay.

Grace Farm 741 Cowaramup Bay Rd; \ 0438 514 831; w gracefarm.com.au; ⊕ 11.00–16.00 Wed–Sun. Small boutique winery with an emphasis on sustainability. Try the Malbec.

Gralyn Estate 4145 Caves Rd; \ 9755 6245; w gralyn.com.au; ⊕ 10.30–16.30 daily. Stars with its ruby-chocolate, white-chocolate & coffee ports.

McHenry Hohnen 5962 Caves Rd; \ 9757 9600; w mchenryhohnen.com.au; ⊕ 10.30–16.30 daily. Their Chardonnay is excellent, & they also sell terrific meats & sausages (we love the merguez) that will star in any beach barbecue.

Sandalford 777 Metricup Rd; \ 9755 6213; w sandalford.com; ⊕ 10.00–17.00 daily. Sandalford started 180 years ago in the Swan Valley, before expanding into Margaret River. They produce an exquisite Chardonnay.

is based here, offering lessons from beginner to advanced, plus equipment hire and personal 'surf guides'. The water here can be treacherous – some 80 shipwrecks are said to have occurred here in the 1800s, including that of the *Georgette*, which can be seen from the beach in favourable conditions. When the *Georgette* wrecked in 1876, Aboriginal stockman Sam Isaacs led a rescue that ultimately saved dozens of lives. On the way back to Margaret River, it's worth stopping in at **Bellview Shell Collection** (10291 Bussell Hwy; \ 9757 6342; ⊕ 09.00–17.00 Sat–Wed; A$8/4 adult/child), one of the largest private collections of shells and coral in the world, with over 30,000 items on display.

Historical sights For a window into 19th-century life in Margaret River, the **Margaret River Historical Society** (69 Bussell Hwy; \ 0439 508 844; w mrdhs.com.au; ⊕ 10.00–12.30 Tue, 13.00–16.30 Thu, 10.00–15.00 Sat–Sun), housed in a 95-year-old school building, is home to displays and artefacts from the 1920s like blacksmith tools and an old dairy. Elsewhere, the 160-year-old, Heritage-listed **Ellensbrook Homestead** (Ellen Brook Rd; \ 9755 5173; w nationaltrust.org.au/

A Maze'N 9978 Bussell Hwy; 9758 7439; w amazenmargaretriver.com.au; ⏰ 09.00–17.00 Thu–Mon; A$24/16 adult/child. This 3m-high hedge maze, 2km south of Margaret River, also has outdoor games & puzzles, an 18-hole mini-golf course (A$15/12 adult/child) & 2ha of botanical gardens, brimming with birds & butterflies. There is a café on site.

※ **Eagles Heritage** 341 Boodjidup Rd; 9757 2960; w eaglesheritage.com.au; ⏰ call for times. This raptor centre helps to rehabilitate & release birds of prey that are permanently disabled or have been transferred in from elsewhere, & you can see the birds on the 1km self-guided walking trail through the grounds. The tawny frogmouth, which uses its colour to blend into branches to hide from predators, is a personal favourite. Highly informative & educational & recommended for children.

Sunflowers Animal Farm 5561 Caves Rd; 9757 3343; w sunflowersfarm.com; ⏰ 09.00–17.00 daily; A$14.50 adult/child. Over 350 animals live at this 127ha cattle farm, 7km north of Margaret River – everything from pigs, llamas & emu to Shetland ponies, grey galahs & Pommy, the long-billed corella. Interaction between visitors & animals is encouraged, with feedings twice daily at 10.00 & 16.00. Tractor rides also on offer.

places/ellensbrook; ⏰ 10.00–16.00 Thu–Sat; A$10/5 adult/child), located 13km northwest of town, offers a chance to relive life on an old working farm through the room-by-room stories of its settlers (the Bussell family) and those of the local Noongar who refer to this place as Mokidup. A 2km walking trail behind the homestead leads to Meekadarribee Falls (meaning 'the place where the moon bathes').

SOUTH OF MARGARET RIVER: CAVES ROAD The southern part of the non-contiguous Leeuwin-Naturaliste National Park features karri forest and even more spectacular beaches. There are at least 350 caves in the area, a few of which have been safely opened up to visitors. The following sights are dotted along Caves Road south from Redgate, and can be combined for an enjoyable day trip from Margaret River or as stop offs en route to Augusta.

Heading south on Caves Road, the first show cave you come to is the 300m-long **Calgardup Cave** (⏰ 09.00–16.15 daily; A$19/9.50 adult/child), with boardwalk and stairs suitable for children. Its chambers are a stream of colour and from winter to spring, water flows through the cave, creating an amazing reflection effect. Just 1km south is **Mammoth Cave** (⏰ 09.00–17.00 daily; A$22.50/11.50 adult/child), which has been open to visitors for more than a century. Paleontology is the big focus here; fossils of several extinct mammals have been found, including the thylacine (Nannup or Tasmanian tiger). There is wheelchair access into the first chamber of the cave, and an audio guide is available for self-guided tours.

Another 3km further along Caves Road, **Lake Cave** (⏰ call for hours; A$22.50/11.50 adult/child) has a rather dramatic entrance – down 300 or so steps, past giant karris – and inside is an internal cave lake that is crossed by a footpath. The showstopper is the 'Suspended Table' – a huge, 10m² piece of calcite. The CaveWorks Eco-Centre (9757 7411; ⏰ 09.00–17.00 daily) is located here, with a cave crawl for kids, true-size cave model and various multi-media displays. They can also organise activities like abseiling and rock climbing. The final cave along this stretch is also the deepest in the national park – **Giants Cave** (⏰ 09.00–16.00 daily, school holidays & public holidays 09.30–15.30; A$19/9.50 adult/child), with a depth of 86m. There is about 500m of chamber to explore; however, negotiating this cave requires navigating vertical ladders and rock scrambles, and children under six are not permitted.

Around 1.5km south from Giants Cave is the turn-off for **Boranup Forest Scenic Drive**, a 12km, 2WD-suitable loop through Boranup Forest. Karri trees, some 60m tall, spread across the valley, and wildflowers, orchids and mushrooms on the forest floor. At the edge of the forest, just off Caves Road where the scenic drive ends, the **Boranup Forest Maze** (6 Maze Rd; ☏0467 271 596; ⊕ 05.00–20.00 daily; A$5/2 adult/child), grown from native shrubs, is a good place for kids to run around.

A 5-minute drive south from the maze brings you to the turn-off for **Hamelin Bay** ※ (Hamelin Bay Rd), a sensational beach offering sheltered swimming and set against a beautiful dune backdrop. Friendly and curious stingrays can be seen only inches from the shoreline here and tend to congregate to the left of the derelict jetty as you face the water. They have been present here for years; according to local legend, they became accustomed to humans after eating scraps of fish carcasses fed to them in the mornings by fishermen. They have been known to 'kiss' humans by sucking on a leg – this is how they take in food in that way, and though this supposedly does not hurt you should not allow them to get that close to you. Stingrays are not naturally aggressive to humans – as of 1996, there had only been 17 fatal attacks worldwide – but they can and will defend themselves if they feel threatened, so look, but don't touch, approach or feed them. **Hamelin Bay Caravan Park** (95 powered sites, 25 unpowered sites; Hamelin Bay Road W; ☏9758 5540; w hamelinbayholidaypark.com.au; **$$**) is the place to stay here, with a spectacular sheltered beachfront location.

South of Hamelin Bay are two other magnificent beaches: **Foul Bay** and **Cosy Corner**. Foul Bay's long, lazy coastline makes it popular with families; Cosy Corner involves a 500m hike down a sand dune, but the water is partially reef-sheltered and the view across to the rocky outcrops is sensational.

Shortly before Caves Road joins the Bussell Highway, there is one more show cave of note: **Jewel Cave** (⊕ 09.00–17.00 daily; A$22.50/11.50 adult/child), so-

MARGARET RIVER REGION'S SURFING SPOTS

With over 100 beaches from Cape to Cape, there are plenty of acclaimed surfing spots in the Margaret River region. The following is just a selection, going from north to south. Note that some of these are not accessible with conventional vehicles – you will need a 4x4.

Windmills North of Sugarloaf Rock; has some small lefts & rights.

Three Bears Some serious rights & lefts – among the best surfing spots in the Capes. Not accessible with a 2WD. The name comes from the tendency to have 3 surf peaks of varying intensity – named Papa Bear, Mama Bear & Baby Bear.

Honeycombs Medium-size swells.

Gallows Very big lefts, usually not busy.

Guillotines A big reef break that really sets up in summer.

North Point A spectacular long right that challenges experienced surfers.

South Point Like North Point, though this one is a left.

Lefthanders Another famous left that is for serious surfers; it can attract a crowd.

Grunters A major right-hander, though it is quite a way out from the shore.

Conto's Good for beginners & swimmers. Lovely spot & easily accessible.

called because of its extensive decorations. Its helictites, cave coral and flowstone have nicknames like the 'Karri Forest', 'Frozen Waterfall' and 'Organ Pipes', and one of the biggest straw stalactites in the region is also found here. The grounds host a café, visitor centre and museum – however, entrance to the cave is by guided tour only.

AUGUSTA AND CAPE LEEUWIN

The southwesternmost settlement in Australia, bottom-of-the-world Augusta has retained its small fishing village charm and yesteryear feel. Founded in 1830, when a party of settlers arrived looking for good land, it was one of the earliest European settlements in the state (after Albany, Perth, Fremantle and Guildford). The wider region was settled a bit earlier, in 1801, by Matthew Flinders, who named it after the *Leeuwin*, a Dutch East India Company ship that mapped the region in 1622. Today the area's rough, windswept coastal beauty and less frenetic pace than Margaret River make it a nice alternative base for a quieter holiday.

GETTING THERE AND AWAY Augusta is the southern terminus of the Bussell Highway, 42km/30 minutes south of Margaret River. The junction for the Brockman Highway is around 15km north of town and leads to Nannup (88km/1hr) and Pemberton (122km/1hr 30mins).

Daily Transwa coaches run to/from Bunbury (2hrs 30mins via Margaret River and Busselton), with thrice-weekly services to/from Nannup (1hr 5mins).

WHERE TO STAY AND EAT

⌂ Augusta Hotel Motel (50 rooms) 53 Blackwood Av; ☎ 9758 1944; w augustahotel. com.au. The century-old hotel boasts fine views of the Blackwood River & Hardy Inlet; queen rooms & studios also have a view. A big range of accommodation is offered from luxury apartments to backpacker dorms. The bistro has good specials. **$$**

⌂ Georgiana Molloy Motel (16 rooms) 84 Blackwood Av; ☎ 9758 1255; w augustasmolloymotel.com.au. High-quality motel – all rooms have full cooking facilities, including ovens, & en suites – as well as access to laundry facilities. Right in the centre of town, it's great value. **$$**

⌂ Flinders Bay Caravan Park Albany Tce; ☎ 9780 5636; w flindersbaypark.armshire.wa.

gov.au. 3.5km south of town on Flinders Bay, this dog-friendly site has laundry facilities, amenity blocks, car storage if you're doing the Cape-to-Cape, & free 500mb Wi-Fi. It's walking distance to Granny's Pool. **$**

✕ Blue Ocean Fish & Chips 37 Blackwood Av; ☎ 9758 1748; ⏰ 11.30–14.00 & 17.00–20.00 daily. Terrific, fresh fish & chips, perfectly battered. **$**

✕ Colourpatch 98 Albany Tce; ☎ 9758 1869; w thecolourpatchaugusta.com; ⏰ 08.00–16.00 Sun–Tue, 08.00–20.00 Wed–Sat. High-quality seafood – scallops, whiting, braised squid & king prawns – alongside a fairly standard pizza & burger selection. Big wine list & they serve cocktails. **$**

WHAT TO SEE AND DO Augusta's appeal lies in its geography – its rugged coastline where two oceans meet, and its isolation at the far southern tip of the Capes, which has sheltered it from a lot of the development in the north and allowed it to retain its sleepy feel.

The town sits on the Blackwood River, which flows for almost 300km from its source in the Wheatbelt before meeting the coast at Augusta's Hardy Inlet. Along Albany Terrace, the river's **foreshore** has a narrow strip of sand with a large grassy area and picnic tables – the panoramic views across to East Augusta, down the

Hardy Inlet and into Flinders Bay, offer a beautiful backdrop; look for Caspian terns and sooty oystercatchers around here. The swimming is sheltered and good for children, and **Augusta Boat Hire** (1 Ellis St; ✆0499 600 401; ⊕ 08.00–17.00) rents canoes, kayaks, SUPs and snorkelling gear. Also on the river, just behind the Yacht Club, **Donovan Street Reserve** – sometimes referred to as Augusta's Kings Park – is a wildflower hotspot with over 200 species, known for its orchids, including vibrant yellow donkeys, white spiders and cowslips. Flat Rock is a particularly good area to look for them. Outside wildflower season, you may come across bandicoots and kangaroos.

From May to September, hundreds of humpback and southern right whales migrate just off the coast here. **Flinders Bay** (Davies Rd) is probably the best place to see them – this scenic, sheltered beach also has a small jetty for jumping off, and the waters are good for snorkelling. Whale-watching cruises also depart from Augusta Boat Harbour – try **Whale Watch Western Australia** (✆1300 388 893; e contact@ whalewatchwesternaustralia.com; w whalewatchwesternaustralia.com).

One of the South West's most popular attractions lies 6km from town: **Cape Leeuwin Lighthouse** (Leeuwin Rd; ✆9757 7411; ⊕ 09.00–17.00 daily; A$20/10 adult/child). Opened in 1896 and built from local limestone, this is one of the tallest lighthouses in Australia (39m) and the country's southwesternmost point. The climb to the top is 176 steps (guided tour only – this is still a working lighthouse, and one of the busiest sea lanes in Australia), and the light can be seen for nearly 45km. The grounds are Heritage-listed and also feature three old keeper's cottages as the lighthouse was manually operated until 1982. Behind the lighthouse is a lookout from which you can see the point where the Indian and Southern oceans meet. One of the cottages is now an interpretive exhibition, where you can practice morse code and learn about previous lighthouse keepers and their families. One of the most poignant things about the cottages is imagining the complete isolation of the area at the time, and how difficult life must have been for those who lived there. The Cape-to-Cape Track (see box, page 159) also ends here.

BLACKWOOD RIVER VALLEY

Gently winding southwest from Arthur River in the Wheatbelt, the Blackwood River stretches for nearly 300km through most of the South West before ending at Augusta. This is the South West's Hill Country, a place for leisurely drives on country roads, strolls through karri and jarrah forests and visits to local wineries, while basing yourself in the quaint towns of Nannup, Bridgetown and Boyup Brook. This is also one of the coldest places in WA and can experience four seasons in one day, though autumn is a particularly charming time, with morning mists partially shrouding the hills and the foliage changing colour on the main streets in front of rustic Federation-style buildings. The Blackwood is also known in winter as a place for canoeing and kayaking. The economy here has been historically based on timber milling and fruit farming, and is in transition as tourism takes on a greater role.

NANNUP Gazetted in 1890, this 'Garden Village' is best known for its main street, which has an almost perfectly preserved, 1970s country-town feel and represents one of the best examples of living architecture from that period in Australia. Indeed, the 2013 surfing movie *Drift*, set in the 1970s, was filmed here. Being a small, inland town – the shire has a population of 1,200, and timber and agriculture still drive the economy – Nannup did not have the same influx of growth and development that Busselton and Margaret River did – and this has helped to preserve the charming, old-timey character of the main street that is now the town's calling card. August is a particularly good time to be here – the Nannup Flower and Garden Festival (formerly the Tulip Festival) brings the town alive in a blaze of floral colour and open gardens. The town is also famous for the Nannup Music Festival – one of the biggest in the South West – which takes place each Labour Day weekend (first weekend in March).

Getting there and away Nannup is a central transit junction in the South West. Mowen Road goes west to Margaret River (68km/50mins); the Brockman Highway goes east to Bridgetown (45km/35mins) and south to Augusta (100km/1hr); and the Vasse Highway goes north to Busselton (60km/40mins) and south to Pemberton (76km/1hr).

Transwa **coaches** run from Nannup to Pemberton (1hr) and along the coast to Perth (7hrs; via Augusta, Margaret River, Busselton and Bunbury).

 Where to stay and eat

Holberry House (7 rooms) 14 Grange Rd; 9756 1276; e info@holberryhouse.com. au; w holberryhouse.com.au. Set just behind Nannup's main road, this tranquil property in 1.6ha of open gardens is full of country charm, accentuated in winter with the open fireplace. Cooked b/fast (recommended) available for an extra cost. **$$$**

NANNUP'S FARM GATE PRODUCE

Nannup produces an agricultural bounty. Stonefruits are the stars here, but producers have branched out into wines, cheeses and other gourmand fare. A spin through the hills to a couple of farm gates is a relaxing way to spend an afternoon.

A Taste of Nannup 16 Warren Rd; 9756 1901; w atasteofnannup.com.au; 09.30–16.00 daily. This shop & visitor centre is a great orientation stop in town. Stocks plenty of South West produce & wares from local artisans, plus guides & maps.

Cambray Cheese Vasse Hwy; 9756 2047; w cambraycheese.com.au; 10.00–16.00 daily. Signposted 11km north of town, this husband-&-wife team offer a delectable range of handmade sheep cheeses. Their boursan & 'camembray' are recommended.

Chestnut Brae 106 McKittrick Rd; 0409 104 120; w chestnutbrae.com.au; 10.00–16.00 Thu–Mon. Off the Vasse Highway around 10km south of town, this 28ha farm produces 12 tonnes of chestnuts each autumn – in Apr & May, visitors are encouraged to come & pick their own. Other products are available – like chestnut flour, chestnut honey & chestnut-fed pork, which the owners try to model after Italian prosciutto.

Nannup Lavender Farm 4365 Graphite Rd; 0428 302 370; w nannuplavenderfarm. com; 10.00–16.00 Fri–Sun. Just a 10-min drive south of Nannup, this farm shop produces a range of sweet-scented & decorative homewares & preserves from its lavender fields, in full bloom Dec–Jan. If the gate is not open – call ahead before you drive out – A Taste of Nannup also stocks its products.

Whimwood Wines 2581 Balingup-Nannup Rd; 0417 003 235; w whimwoodestatewines.com.au; 11.00–16.00 Sat–Sun. Award-winning winery; James Halliday rated. Their Shiraz & Chardonnay are first-rate. Tours, tastings & light lunches available.

🏠 **Jarrah Glen Cabins** (5 cabins) Rodda Rd, Jalbarragup; 📞 9756 0390; ✉ jarrahglen@ westnet.com.au; 🌐 jarrahglen.com.au. Tranquil bush retreat 17km south of town, with plenty of kangaroos & emus roaming the grounds. The 2 cottages have kitchens while the 3 cabins have kitchenettes. Good for groups or big families – the Vine Cottage can sleep 10 – & a great option if you want to get away from it all. **$$$**

🏠 **Black Cockatoo** (5 units) 27 Grange Rd; 📞 9756 1035; ✉ info@nannuplodge.com;

🌐 nannuplodge.com. A well-priced option, with a self-contained apartment & 'safari tents' with shared bathrooms & cooking facilities. Easy walking distance to the main street. **$$**

✖ **Nannup Brewing Co** 1 Warren Rd; 📞 9700 9011; 🌐 nannupbrewingco.com.au; ⊕ 17.00– 20.30 Wed, 11.00–20.30 Thu & Sun, 11.00–22.00 Fri–Sat. Small micro-brewery with a decent range of brews to choose from, as well as a food menu with pulled beef burgers, vegan open sandwiches & spring rolls. **$$**

What to see and do The architecture of Nannup's compact townsite is easily explored on foot, mostly clustered in a 650m stretch of Warren Road, which is Nannup's main street. While some Heritage towns in WA can take on a samey-ness, town after town, Nannup stands out thanks to the timber influence on many of the buildings, as well as the dense concentration of sites in such a small leafy area – the entire street feels like a place where time has stood still, rather than just a series of individual historic buildings.

One of the town's dual centrepieces is the **Nannup Hotel** (12 Warren Rd; 📞 9756 1080; ⓕ thenannuphotel; ⊕ 17.00–21.00 Mon–Fri, 11.00–15.00 & 17.00– 21.00 Sat–Sun), built in 1898, replaced in 1909, and with the second storey added in 1924. Its green-and-white trim veranda overlooks the main street, with a small pyramid on the roof bearing its name. Across the street is the 1930 **Bowling Club**, whose lush green field with bush backdrop reminds visitors that they are in a small country town, and the white timber main building perfectly complements its next-door neighbour, **Nannup Town Hall**. Built in 1903, the jarrah-weatherboard and gable-roofed building has a large jacaranda tree next to it, which is particularly striking when in flower and its purple leaves litter the footpath underneath.

At the entrance to town, across Warren Road from the Town Hall, is the **Nannup Roads Board building**, opened in 1926, which now houses the **Nannup Historical Society** (1 Warren Rd; 📞 0414 986 525; 🌐 nannuphistory.org). The structure stands out for its contrast – a beautiful concrete block construction, with the blocks standing out prominently with gabled front portico and timber sash windows. The Historical Society also publishes a cheap (A$3) guidebook for the **Nannup Heritage Trail**, which explores 51 historical sites across the town, mostly in close proximity on Warren Road. Buy the book at A Taste of Nannup (see box, opposite).

Otherwise, the joys of a stay in Nannup are the bountiful opportunities to reconnect with nature. In town, the 5km **Blackwood River Trail** starts from the old railway bridge and follows the river, providing numerous birdwatching opportunities – look for western rosellas, red-eared firetails, splendid fairy-wrens and cormorants. Numerous wildflower walks – year-round, though spring is by far the best time – can be enjoyed in **Kondil Wildflower Park**, on the town's northwest fringe, a terrific place to see kangaroo paws, white spider orchids and the fringe lily.

The 22km **Old Timberline Trial**, done over two days, helps trace the timberline history of the region. In the early 1900s, the forested area between Jarrahwood and Nannup was a hive of timber and logging activity, with a mill at Barrabup – most of the workers lived in Jarrahwood and Nannup, but if they were cutting

The South West BLACKWOOD RIVER VALLEY

5

Don't let the Blackwood's gentle-looking demeanour fool you. The river has a nasty streak and has flooded catastrophically several times. The most severe was in summer 1982, after the dying bits of a cyclone inundated the South West with unseasonal rainfall. In Nannup, the Blackwood rose 11.6m above its normal levels; boats were tethered to stop signs and the town of only a few hundred people lost 50 houses. A tree behind the caravan park in Nannup records the height of the town's various floods through the 1900s – replacing an old tree that used to have those markers, but which fell in 2009. The markers are a breathtaking, and sobering, reminder of the power of Mother Nature.

trees in the woods, many stayed in simple, hastily constructed 'sleepers huts' that dotted the forest. The Old Timberline Trail, together with the Sidings Rail Trail (26km; they connect and can be combined into a 37km loop, if you cut off the last portion of Youngs Siding), pass alongside the old, no-longer-operational railway line and have interpretive signage about the industry and life as an early 1900s mill worker. The routes wind through state forest, and over a couple of picturesque old railway bridges. Two secluded swimming spots lie just 10km from town off Mowen Road, on the Old Timberline Trail: **Barrabup Pool** and **Workmans Pool**, both of which have been used for decades by mill workers for rest and recreation and have a glorious backdrop of tall forest overlooking and reflecting off of the calm, placid water. A wooden deck at Barrabup is a great jumping-off point for kids and an excellent vantage point for photographs, especially on misty mornings.

An excellent scenic drive is the 114km '**Golden Triangle**' (Route 251), which stretches from Nannup to Balingup to Bridgetown and back to Nannup. There are no towns in between the three points of the triangle, but leaving Nannup you pass through orchards, farmland and pastures at the base of the hills, winding through forest until arriving at the Balingup (41km) end of the road. The route from Balingup to Bridgetown (26km) is on the South Western Highway; the Bridgetown to Nannup part (45km) is a windy ascent through stark hills and farmland, past a roadside windmill and into dense karri forest, before exiting the forest just a few kilometres before Nannup on a ridge that has a jaw-dropping view out towards the horizon over the bush. You then descend in a sharp twist into Nannup itself. The 'triangle' is popular with cyclists and motorcyclists – it is a slow road due to the curves and bends so allow plenty of time.

BRIDGETOWN AND AROUND The only town in the South West to be granted 'Historic Town' status by the National Trust, lovely Bridgetown draws visitors for the old-style charm on its main street, its setting in the rolling hills, nestled along the Blackwood River, and its delectable local wine and produce. Bridgetown personifies the idea of a tranquil country escape in every nook and cranny and, as the biggest town in the Blackwood River Valley, makes a lot of sense as a base for a stay in the region. A good time to visit is during the three-month **Fridgetown Fest** (w fridgetownfest.com.au), when shops string blue lights along their fronts and events include everything from live music concerts and jigsaw puzzle competitions to quiz nights, theatre performances and pottery making.

Getting there and away Bridgetown is on the South Western Highway, 35km/25 minutes north of Manjimup and 95km/1 hour 10 minutes south of Bunbury. Nannup is 45km/35 minutes west on the Brockman Highway and Boyup Brook 28km/30 minutes east on the Bridgetown–Boyup Brook Road.

South West Coach Lines and Transwa offer **coaches** to Perth (4hrs 15mins), Bunbury (1hr 15mins) and Manjimup (30mins), and the latter also serves Pemberton (1hr 25mins), Boyup Brook (30mins) and Collie (1hr 20mins).

Tourist information

🛈 **Bridgetown-Greenbushes Visitor Centre** 154 Hampton St; ☎ 9761 1740; w bridgetown.com.au; ⏱ 10.00–16.00 Mon–Fri, 10.00–13.00 Sat–Sun

Where to stay and eat

✻ 🏠 **Innkeepers House** (2 suites) 20164 South Western Hwy, Mullalyup; ☎ 9764 1138; w innkeepershouse.com.au. Located 5km north of Balingup, this historic property has large, luxuriously appointed suites with spa baths & tasteful furniture. The on-site private restaurant for guests only – order in advance – has steaks that are cooked to absolute perfection & the piano music adds to the ambience. A destination in its own right. **$$$$**

🏠 **Bridgetown Hotel** 157 Hampton St, Bridgetown; ☎ 9761 1034; e nelsons@westnet. com.au; w bridgetownhotel.com.au. Located in one of the town's signature buildings – a 1920's Federation-style property – rooms feature spa-style rainhead showers & wide verandas overlooking the town. Continental b/fast inc; on-site bar & café serves respectable pub mains, inc burgers, pizzas & pastas. **$$$**

🏠 **Ford House** (9 rooms) Lot 56 Eedle Tce, Bridgetown; ☎ 9761 1816; w fordhouse.com.au. Set among 2ha of glorious gardens, this country-style B&B offers individually designed rooms across 4 buildings, including a 120-year-old homestead – think bay windows, wood floors, fireplaces, floral bedspreads & high ceilings. The on-site Wag Walters Emporium showcases a number of unique houseware items like locomotive clocks, as well as brightly coloured & eccentrically designed vases, plates & cups. Excellent b/fast. **$$$**

🏠 **Tweed Valley Lodge** (8 suites) 171 Tweed Rd, Bridgetown; ☎ 9761 2828; e info@ tweedvalleylodge.com.au; w tweedvalleylodge. com.au. On the banks of the Blackwood just south of town, this adults-only retreat offers spacious suites with fully equipped kitchenette, living/ dining area & private veranda. Outside among the

PADDLING THE BLACKWOOD RIVER

The Blackwood River is known for excellent canoeing, but in winter when the rains arrive, rapids form and whitewater rafting is also possible. Some sections of the river are gentle and easy, while others are difficult and treacherous; even experienced kayakers can run into trouble, and one died in 2016 in the rapids near Bridgetown – branches and debris in the river can create traps if your canoe or kayak overturns. A grading system ranges from a grade of 1 (easy) to 6 (extreme). Between Boyup Brook and Nannup, the river generally grades as a 1 or a 2 (medium), but grades and rapids as high as 4 (advanced) can also be found between Boyup Brook and Bridgetown. Sections suitable for novices tend to be the area just west of Boyup Brook and the area to the west of Nannup; substantial experience is required for the area to the east of Bridgetown. Contact **Blackwood River Canoeing** (Poison Swamp Rd, Nannup; ☎ 9756 1209) for a range of experiences, from 1-hour rides to multi-day expeditions, and they can point you to the best sections for canoeing, kayaking and white-water rafting based on your experience and skill.

marri trees is a BBQ decking area, from where you can spot some 70 species of bird – daily afternoon feedings are also a highlight, attracting Australian ring-necks, red cap parrots & western rosellas. **$$$**

✕ Barking Cow 88 Hampton St, Bridgetown; 📞9761 4619; **w** barkingcow.com.au; ⏱ 08.00–14.00 Mon–Sat. Popular café offering large & filling b/fasts – the banana & coconut bread is worth trying & the coffee is some of the best in the Blackwood region. **$$**

✕ The Cidery 43 Gifford Rd, Bridgetown; 📞9761 2204; **w** thecidery.com.au; ⏱ 11.00–16.00 Sat–Thu, 11.00–20.00 Fri. Popular with the locals, this boutique cidery situated among flower-filled gardens produces nationally renowned ciders (alcoholic & non-alcoholic), beers & wines. A good lunch spot too – ploughman's & platters complement the perry. **$$**

✕ The Treehouse 66 Abel St, Boyup Brook; 📞9765 2888; 🅵 boyupbrooktreehouse; ⏱ 07.00–15.00 Mon–Fri, 07.00–14.30 Sat. This funky coffee lounge serves great homemade muffins & pastries. **$$**

✳ ✕ F.A.T.S. 179 Hampton St, Bridgetown; 📞9761 2313; 🅵 FATS.bridgetown; ⏱ 09.00–16.00 Wed–Mon. Bagel joint meets Christmas shop at this unique store (the initials stand for Food, Art, Toys, Santa). A choice of creative bagels, both filled & topped, with interesting names – try the Holmes & Watson or Batman & Robin. Clever presentation & good coffees too. **$**

✕ Mushroom @ No. 61 61 South Western Hwy, Balingup; 📞9764 1505; ⏱ 08.00–15.00 daily & 17.00–19.30 Fri. Award-winning pie bakery with a range of fillings inc veggie & gluten-free. Has a dining area for lunch, & also serves chips, cakes & coffees. Good for take-aways to eat later on your hike or drive. **$**

What to see and do One of the biggest attractions of visiting Bridgetown is simply walking up and down Hampton Street, the main road, and taking in its quaint historic buildings and interesting shops. Gazetted as a town in 1868 and originally known as Geegelup – a Noongar name for the freshwater crustaceans found in the water here – the town was renamed Bridgetown after a ship of the same name that called in at Bunbury to take wool from here. Some of the first buildings erected in town back in the 1860s still stand, which help give the main street its historical character – the National Trust awarded Bridgetown historic town status in 2000. Highlights include the 1912 **Bridgetown Post Office** (142 Hampton St), a Federation Free-style building, with a double-arched entrance way to the porch, arched windows and steep roof. The Art Deco-style 1936 **Town Hall** (1 Steere St), at the town's most prominent intersection (with Hampton St), has differing shades of yellow and off-white with a red-brick base – a significant contrast to neighbouring buildings. The 1911 **Bridgetown Hotel** with gabling, highly detailed veranda and jarrah staircase inside is another showpiece as you enter town from the north.

Inside the visitor centre, **Brierley Jigsaw Gallery** is one of only two jigsaw puzzle galleries in the world and has the largest collection in the southern hemisphere. Puzzles have been mounted and hung, but there is an area for you to do your own jigsaw – the visitor centre also sells jigsaws of places in town.

West of town on the road to Nannup is **Donnelly River** – an old, now abandoned, tiny timber mill town. Milling began around the site in 1909, with the cutting of karri and jarrah to produce telegraph poles, and the present mill opened in 1951 – operated by the Bunnings brothers of Bunnings store fame. A settlement grew to include a primary school, housing, post office and store, but the mill was not very efficient and closed in 1978 – with Bunnings donating the mill and land to the Crown. It's now Heritage-listed and the cottages have been turned into accommodation (📞9772 1244; **w** donnellyriver.com.au). Guests and non-guests are welcome to wander around the town – there are always kangaroos and emus about – and there is a small general store and café.

Bridgetown also boasts a handful of decent wineries: **Shedley Wines** (Dalmore Rd; ☏9761 7512; w shedleywines.com.au; ⏰ call) is long-standing in the Blackwood, hand-picks its grapes and makes nice reds; **Sunnyhurst** (16 Doust St; ☏0437 846 610; w sunnyhurst.com.au; ⏰ 11.00–17.00 Thu–Sun) is the place for whites; and **Bridgetown Winery** (10891 Brockman Hwy; ☏0448 810 960; w bridgetownwinery. com.au; ⏰ 11.00–17.00 Sat–Sun) is my go-to for ports and fortified wines.

Around Bridgetown

Greenbushes This tiny town, 17km north of Bridgetown on the South Western Highway, has a lengthy mining history, dating from tin exploration in 1888. Lithium operations began in 1983, and it is now the largest lithium mine in the world – Talison holds open days where visitors can tour the mine. Elsewhere, the **Greenbushes Eco-Discovery Centre** (38 Blackwood Rd; ☏ 9764 3883; f greenbushesecodiscoverycentre; ⏰ 10.00–14.00 Wed & Fri–Sun) has an interactive timber display, replica underground tunnel and 'Heritage Amble' walk trail, while the **public mine lookout**, on Telluride Street at the edge of town, provides a good viewpoint of Talison's open-cut mining operations.

Balingup This small but colourful village, a further 11km north of Greenbushes on the South Western Highway, has long attracted artists from across the region due to its superb leafy setting – come in autumn to see it as its best, when the trees are a kaleidoscope of reds and golds. One of its most popular attractions is the Heritage-listed **Golden Valley Tree Park** (Old Padbury Rd; w goldenvalleytreepark. org.au), the state's largest (60ha) arboretum with maples, sequoias and redwoods. The **Packing Shed**, on Balingup's main road, has a fantastic fruit winery.

Boyup Brook A 30-minute drive east from Bridgetown (also served by Transwa coaches), this farming town is known as the 'Country Music Capital of Western Australia' thanks to its annual **Boyup Brook Country Music Festival** each February (w countrymusicwa.com.au) – a celebration of local country music held among the town's majestic gum trees. If not in town for the festival, stop by **Harvey Dickson's Country Music Centre** (☏ 9765 1125; w harveydickson.com.au), 5km east on the Boyup Brook–Arthur River Road. This awesome museum of memorabilia, some of it 100 years old, has a focus on Elvis but there are all sorts of records, posters and T-shirts and other things – Harvey is a walking music encyclopedia. For A$10 he will give you a tour (blow the horn when you arrive) and happily play his records for you while you chat about all things country music.

MANJIMUP, PEMBERTON AND THE SOUTHERN FORESTS

WA's Southern Forests cover a huge area from the central inland South West down to the Southern Ocean coast – roughly encompassing the entirety of the immense (7,100km²) Shire of Manjimup, which contains the towns of Pemberton, Walpole and Northcliffe in addition to its namesake townsite. The Southern Forests are home to jarrah, marri and karri trees – the kings of the forest. Among the tallest trees in the world, karris can grow up to 90m tall and live upwards of 300 years. Ferns, mosses, fungi, wildflowers and other plants form the undergrowth and understory, with streams and swamps dotted around the land. There are nearly 100 species of plant growing here that are found nowhere else in the world.

The history of the Southern Forests stretches back to Gondwana, the ancient supercontinent from which the seven current continents separated from over time.

Australia was covered in rainforest, but as continents separated and the climate dried, the forests shrunk and the environment in what is now the Southern Forests began to evolve differently from that in the rest of Australia, creating conditions for the unique life we see here today. Visitors come here for forest retreats and, in increasing numbers, the growing gourmet food and wine scene.

MANJIMUP The largest settlement in the Southern Forests, Manjimup used to be seen as a gritty logging town but has somewhat reinvented itself into a foodie destination. It is the leading producer of black truffles in mainland Australia and is also famous for its cherries – both of which are celebrated at respective festivals in June and December.

Getting there and away On the South Western Highway, Manjimup is midway between Bridgetown and Pemberton – 35km/25 minutes from both. Both Transwa and South West Coach Lines run coaches to/from the town.

Where to stay and eat

Kingsley Motel & Restaurant (30 rooms) 74 Chopping St; 9771 1177; e kingsley@ kingsleymotel.com.au; w kingsleymotel.com.au. Clean, recently renovated motel. On-site restaurant has good steaks. **$$$**

Tall Timbers 88 Giblett St; 9777 2052; w talltimbersmanjimup.com.au; ⏱ 11.00–21.00 Mon–Thu, 11.00–23.00 Fri–Sat, 09.00–15.00 Sun. Celebrates the produce of the Southern Forests

with seasonal menus & a huge choice of local wines. The steaks are particularly good. **$$$**

Southern Roasting Co 94–96 Giblett St; 0491 048 058; w southernroasting.com; ⏱ 06.30–17.00 Mon–Fri, 07.00–13.00 Sat–Sun. Speciality roasters serving a range of local brews alongside sandwiches & light bites; also ground beans to take home. **$**

What to see and do The main draws of a visit to Manjimup are in the surrounding forests. A couple of impressive trees lie not far from town: the 600-year-old, 47m-tall **King Jarrah Tree**, just off the road to Perup, is worth a look, as is the 51m-tall **Diamond Tree Lookout**, on the South Western Highway between Manjimup and Pemberton. The latter was once used as a lookout for bushfires, with a cabin constructed at the top, but this closed to tourists in 2019 after engineers determined the base was no longer safe. There is, however, a short loop trail around the forest and an interpretive booth detailing the history of the area.

On the way to Nannup, just off Graphite Road, is beautiful **Glenoran Pool**, a popular swimming spot which, when the water is still, gives a perfect reflection of the surrounding trees. A walking path connects the pool to **One Tree Bridge**, a suspension bridge over the Donnelly River, and then a further 1km or so across the road (there is an underpass) takes you the **Four Aces** – four centuries-old karri trees, grown from seedlings from the same fallen tree, and today lined in a perfect row.

A 10-minute drive southwest of town, freshwater **Fonty's Pool** (699 Seven Day Rd; 9771 2105; w fontyspool.com.au; ⏱ 09.00–17.00 daily) is a National Trust-listed swimming spot popular with campers staying in the nearby caravan park. Also nearby is **A Guadagnino & Co** (595 Seven Day Rd; 9771 2153; AGuadagninoCo), a massive farm gate (you can't miss the Australian and Italian flags) selling produce out of their large shed – apples, cherries and stonefruits star. **Truffle Hill** (490 Seven Day Rd; 9777 2474; w trufflehill.com.au; ⏱ 10.00–16.00 daily) showcases all manner of truffle products from oil to honey at the shop on their farm; boxes make excellent gifts to take home.

In town, the 12ha **Maniimup Heritage Park** (33 Edwards St; ✆ 9771 7777; w manjimupheritagepark.com.au) is a good options for families, with walking trails, adventure playground and museums showcasing the likes of timber and steam. The highlight is the **Power Up Electricity Museum** (🕐 09.00–17.00 Mon-Sat, 09.00–15.00 Sun; A$14/8 adult/child), which displays early electrical appliances, generators and vehicles, and demonstrates how the usage and production of electricity in WA has evolved during the state's existence.

PEMBERTON Off all the towns in the South West, Pemberton is the place most inexorably linked in the West Australian psyche to the state's majestic forests, effectively fenced in by national parks. Its timber architecture and proximity to gorgeous forest make it a great base point from which to explore the wider region.

Getting there and away Pemberton is 35km/25 minutes south of Manjimup; turn off the South Western Highway at the Vasse Highway. Transwa run **coaches** from Pemberton to Perth (5hrs 10mins) along the Bussell Highway, stopping at all the major towns en route.

Where to stay and eat

🏠 **Forest Lodge Resort** (18 rooms) 13626 Vasse Hwy; ✆ 9776 1113; w forestlodgeresort. com.au. Well-appointed rooms on secluded grounds (5ha) just outside town. Some rooms have spas & private terraces, & all have en suite – you do pay for the privileges, though. **$$$**

🏠 **RAC Karri Valley Resort** (62 cabins) 11342 Vasse Hwy, Beedelup; ✆ 9776 2020; e reservations@karrivalleyresort.com.au; w parksandresorts.rac.com.au/karri-valley. This well-known & venerable facility has its ace-in-the-hole location near Beedelup Falls, 20km west of Pemberton. Some chalets have lake & forest views, where there are lots of kangaroos hopping about, & there are powered & unpowered sites too. The

setting here alone is worth it – if you are looking for a forest escape, this is it. **$$$**

🏠 **Gloucester Motel** (51 rooms) Lot 1 Ellis St; ✆ 9776 1266; w gloucestermotel.com.au; e reception@gloucestermotel.com.au. Functional en-suite motel rooms, shared dorms & a communal kitchen. Local orchards advertise for farm work here. **$$**

✳ ✖ **Treehouse Tapas** 50B Brockman St; ✆ 9776 1654; w treehousewinebar.com.au; 🕐 17.00–22.00 Thu, 16.00–22.00 Fri–Sat, 16.00–21.00 Sun. Surprisingly filling Spanish-inspired tapas plates, made using local ingredients – the pinchos & cheeses are good value. Extensive wine list from the surrounding area. Walk-ins only. **$$$**

What to see and do Given its blessed forested setting, surrounded by national parks almost on all sides, it's no surprise that Pemberton is a hive of natural activity. A great way to explore the surrounding area is on the 86km **Karri Forest Explorer** drive (w parks.dpaw.wa.gov.au/site/karri-forest-explorer; 2WD suitable, but parts are unsealed), which takes in several of the nearby national parks and is an ideal introduction to the area's karri forests. The following sights are all included on the drive.

A 5-minute drive north from town is **Big Brook Dam**, a relatively new construction (built in the 1980s) that provides a picturesque setting for swimming and other water activities. Another 3km further is the **Big Brook Arboretum**, featuring several different species of tree (American redwoods, Warren River cedars and eucalypts) that were planted to see how they would grow in Pemberton's soil and climate in the 1930s.

Some 20km off the Vasse Highway, **Beedelup National Park** is one of the jewels of the area – its centrepiece being the 100m-high **Beedelup Falls**. A suspension bridge crosses the brook at the base of the falls, and a trail (steep in sections) with viewing platforms loops around them. A longer 4.5km walk goes to the RAC Karri Valley Resort (page 179) through the forest.

Gloucester National Park, on the town's western edge, is home to one of Pemberton's two famous fire-lookout trees: the 53m-high **Gloucester Tree**. Climbing pegs go to a viewing platform at the top, from where there are astounding views of the surrounding karri forests. On the park's southern edge are the **Cascades**, where Lefroy Brook spills over a series of rocks creating the visual effect of a rapid.

To the southeast of town is **Warren National Park**, a 3,100ha carpet of virgin karri forest home to Pemberton's other, taller fire-lookout tree: the 68m-high **Dale Evans Bicentennial Tree**, pegged in 1988 to celebrate the country's bicentennial. On clear days, you can see the coast from the top. Another highlight is the **Marianne North Tree**, a large, oddly shaped karri whose image is displayed at the Marianne North Gallery at Kew Botanic Gardens in London – Marianne North was an artist who painted plans and trees around the world, and painted this tree on her 1880s trip to Australia. Within the park, the 10.5km, moderately difficult **Warren River Loop Walk** passes through the valley and along the river, in which paddling and canoeing is possible – launches can be found at Maiden Bush, Warren Camp and Blackbutt.

NORTHCLIFFE AND AROUND

Blink-and-you'll-miss-it Northcliffe is best known as the jumping-off point for D'Entrecasteaux National Park. In 2015, one of the biggest bushfires in Australian history occurred here – burning through nearly 100,000ha – though miraculously the town was largely spared, suffering no loss of life and only minimal property damage. The **Visitor Centre** (Muirillup Rd; ☏ 9776 7203; w northcliffe.org. au; ⊕ 09.00–16.00 daily) has plenty of good local information, but the town's highlight is undoubtedly the **Understory** (w southernforestarts.com.au/ understory; ⊕ 09.00–16.00 daily; A$10 adult/child), a 1.2km art trail through the forest, exploring Northcliffe's connection to a 'spirit of place'. Various sculptures, poems and stories from local artists line the trail; acclaimed South West artist Kim Perrier's *Rising from the Ashes*, a series of 50 sculptures commemorating the bushfire, is a must-see.

Named after French explorer Bruny D'Entrecasteaux, the first European to sight the area in the 1700s, **D'Entrecasteaux National Park** is enormous – nearly 119,000ha, and extending for about 130km in a narrow coastal band all the way from near Augusta to Walpole. One of the park's unique attractions are the massive, 40m-high **Yeagarup Dunes**, which look like scoops of vanilla ice cream out on the bushland. You can drive through them on 4x4 designated tracks, but if you only have a 2WD, a scramble up **Mt Chudalup** (187m), a granite outcrop about 10km north of the park's entrance, will give you a good view – as Australia's coastline changed over millions of years due to rising and falling sea levels, this bushland was once underwater. For wildlife, head to D'Entrecasteaux Drive, 27km south of Northcliffe – dolphins and whales can be seen from the various lookouts over the Southern Ocean, especially Tookulup Lookout. Wander down to shores of Salmon Beach for great views of the waves slamming into the sea cliffs; I have seen (and been approached by) penguins here though I must have been lucky – it is a relatively rare occurrence.

Surrounded by the park, around 27km south of Northcliffe, **Windy Harbour** is a tiny fishing and holiday village on Crown land and the 230 cottages here are on leasehold, though some are now hired out to tourists – indeed, one of the settlement's raisons d'être was to provide cheap holidays for timber workers in the Southern Forests. The sheltered water here is very popular for fishing.

Some 30km east of Northcliffe, just off the South Western Highway en route to Walpole, **Shannon National Park** is home to some of the state's finest jarrah, marri and karri forest. The 48km, unsealed **Great Forest Trees Drive** is a fantastic way to explore the park, and there are plenty of jumping-off points where you can get out and stretch your legs. The 2.5km Rocks Walk Trail starts at Shannon Dam, which once supplied the water for the town of Shannon and its thriving timber mill, and goes to Mokare's Rock from where there are splendid views of the valley.

GETTING THERE AND AWAY Northcliffe is 31km south of Pemberton, on the Pemberton–Northcliffe Road. Transwa **coaches** stop here en route from Bunbury (3hrs) to Walpole (1hr 15mins) and Albany (3hrs).

Most people visit Northcliffe as a day trip from the bigger bases in Pemberton, Manjimup or Walpole. There is a general store in Northcliffe, but consider packing lunch.

WALPOLE

Forest scenery, granite outcrops, quiet rivers and inlets and a sense of seclusion are what draw visitors to Walpole. The surrounding national parks and forests are collectively known as the Walpole Wilderness, and the town itself sits on the northern end of the Walpole and Nornalup inlets, connected to each other north–south by a narrow channel. Nornalup Inlet, by far the larger of the two, also connects to the Southern Ocean through a narrow channel.

Nornalup is an anglicisation of 'nor-nor-nup', which in Noongar for 'the black snake'. The area around Walpole was declared a national park by the state government in 1910 – which was also the year European settlement started, with land opened up for agriculture. Farming and tourism have remained the mainstays of the town.

GETTING THERE AND AWAY Walpole is the last town on the South Western Highway before it becomes the South Coast Highway, en route to Denmark (65km/50mins). Transwa **coaches** call here from Bunbury (4hrs 30mins) to Albany (1hr 45mins). Manjimup is 119km away (1hr 15mins).

The town's small size and distance from Denmark and Manjimup lend to an almost surprising sense of seclusion and isolation that sneaks up on you.

WHERE TO STAY AND EAT Accommodation options in Walpole are limited to two basic but comfortable motels, both with decent restaurants: **Tree Top Walk Motel** (35 rooms; 45–50 Nockolds St; ☎ 9840 1444; e treetopmotel@ westnet.net.au; w treetopwalkmotel.com.au; **$$$**) and **Walpole Hotel-Motel** (22 rooms; South Western Hwy; ☎ 9840 1023; e walpolehotelmotel@bigpond.com; w walpolehotelmotel.com.au; **$$**).

WHAT TO SEE AND DO Surrounded by hills and eucalypt forest, the tranquil Walpole and Nornalup inlets are a fishing, paddling and swimming paradise. On the northern edge of Nornalup Inlet, **Coalmine Beach** – named after the traces of coal that can be found in its sand – is a particular highlight, though the water can stay shallow a long way out. West of this, the short (5km), circular **Knoll Drive** on the peninsula between the two inlets provides a sweeping panorama of the channel.

At 20,000ha and surrounding the town on all sides, **Walpole-Nornalup National Park** – with its gentle waterways and stately tingles and karris – is the reason people fell in love with this area and was declared a national park in 1957. The 10km **Hilltop Drive** (gravel), 2km to the east of Walpole, through the giant tingle and karri forest north of Walpole, takes in the **Hilltop Lookout** – with views to the inlets and the ocean – the **Giant Tingle Tree**, and an 800m circular boardwalk around this massive tree and its hollow. The drive then continues on to **Circular Pool**, a quiet canoeing and marron spot in the forest.

Walpole is also a good base to explore **Mt Frankland National Park**, covering around 31,000ha of karri, jarrah and tingle forest. The park's centrepiece is undoubtedly Mt Frankland, a 411m granite peak atop which is a metal lookout, accessed by the Summit Trail. The route to the top might only be 1.2km, but the walk is strenuous – although your efforts are rewarded by sensational 360-degree views of the Walpole Wilderness. For those seeking a more accessible route, the Mt Frankland Wilderness Lookout is wheelchair-friendly and provides an equally impressive bird's-eye view of the forest below.

Other highlights include the cascading **Fernhook Falls** on the Deep River, its foam and bubbles naturally caused by saponin, a compound that comes from the breakdown of plants in the water. To access the falls, head west on the unsealed Beardmore Road for about 20km.

Closer to Walpole, around 8km from town on North Walpole Road, is the **Swarbrick Art Trail**, a 700m loop exploring artwork designed to illustrate how the area has evolved over time and how interconnected people are with nature. The most impressive of the pieces is the 39m-long 'Wilderness Wall of Perceptions', with pertinent quotes about forests and a timeline about forest management and politics over the last 100 years.

Though too rough to swim at, spectacular **Mandalay Beach**, at the eastern end of D'Entrecasteaux National Park 12km from Walpole, occasionally offers views of the shipwrecked *Mandalay* that gave the beach its name.

6

Albany & the Great Southern

The first time my wife and I visited Albany in 2014, we arrived in the evening. After passing the rows of chain shops on the long drive into the CBD – and navigating the notorious five-road roundabout – we dropped our bags at the hotel and promptly set out for a nature walk. It was dark by then, and made a wrong turn and found ourselves at the silos in the industrial zone by the port. Back at the hotel, my wife told me that she thought Albany was the worst, most unsightly place in Western Australia and that she wanted to cut our trip short and leave there and then.

She agreed to give it another go the next morning, and by the end of that day – having explored the surrounding national parks, beaches (some of the best in the country), mountains, wineries, spectacular coastal drives (reading the map correctly this time) and soaking up the historic and increasingly energetic vibe of Albany itself – she wanted to move here. I was back a few months later to check out the real estate market; and although we didn't end up buying a property here, the thought has never left the back of our minds. Now we understand the bumper stickers on cars rolling around town emblazoned 'Amazing Albany' – they are just stating the obvious.

Albany anchors the Great Southern region, and its location on WA's south coast – just far enough away from Perth to make weekend trips unfeasible – have kept the tourist hordes diverted towards Busselton and the South West, leaving the area with very manageable crowds. It is the oldest European settlement in WA, and with a population of around 25,000, one of the biggest regional towns in the state. A half-hour drive north near the town of Mount Barker are the stark, granite-faced Porongurup hills and another 30 minutes further north is the Stirling Range, with its lavender and purple hues. From there, the landscape transforms into wheat and sheep farming as you head towards Katanning. The funky town of Denmark, with its forest and spectacular coastline, is 30 minutes' west of Albany while the east is home to wide open farmland and more glorious coastline. The region's food and drink has exploded on to the national scene in recent years; Great Southern wines compete ferociously for awards with those from Margaret River and the South West.

KOJONUP, KATANNING AND THE UPPER GREAT SOUTHERN

Wheat, sheep and magpies are the bywords of this powerhouse farming area, whose raison d'être becomes abundantly clear driving past the endless acres of rolling paddocks and their white fluffy occupants. While most people just blow through en route to Albany, there are a couple of sites that are worth lingering an afternoon here. If you are only going to the Stirling Range and no further south, Katanning also makes sense as an alternative base to Albany – it is the same distance to the mountains, but you'll cut 90 minutes off the drive back to Perth.

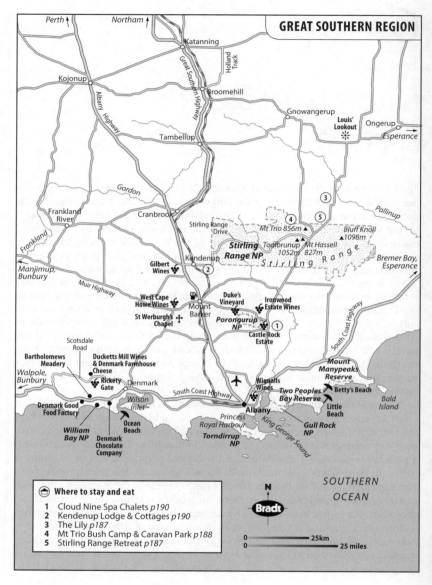

Perth ↑ Northam ↑

Katanning

Kojonup

Broomehill

Gnowangerup

Louis' Lookout

Ongerup

Esperance

Tambellup

Gordon

Frankland River

Cranbrook

Stirling Range Drive

Mt Trio 856m ▲

Bluff Knoll ▲1098m

Pallinup

Stirling Range NP

Toolbrunup 1052m

Mt Hassell 827m

Stirling Range

Bremer Bay, Esperance

Kendenup

Gilbert Wines

Manjimup, Bunbury

Muir Highway

West Cape Howe Wines

Mount Barker

Duke's Vineyard

Ironwood Estate Wines

South Coast Highway

St Werburgh's Chapel

Porongurup NP

Castle Rock Estate

Scotsdale Road

Bartholomews Meadery

Ducketts Mill Wines & Denmark Farmhouse Cheese

Rickety Gate

Denmark

Walpole, Bunbury

South Coast Highway

Wilson Inlet

Wignalls Wines

Mount Manypeaks Reserve

Betty's Beach

Denmark Good Food Factory

Ocean Beach

William Bay NP

Denmark Chocolate Company

Two Peoples Bay Reserve

Little Beach

Bald Island

Princess Royal Harbour

Albany

King George Sound

Gull Rock NP

Torndirrup NP

SOUTHERN OCEAN

N

Bradt

⊜ **Where to stay and eat**

1 Cloud Nine Spa Chalets *p190*
2 Kendenup Lodge & Cottages *p190*
3 The Lily *p187*
4 Mt Trio Bush Camp & Caravan Park *p188*
5 Stirling Range Retreat *p187*

0 ———— 25km
0 ———— 25 miles

KOJONUP As you head south along the Albany Highway, Kojonup is the first town of note as you arrive in the heart of WA's wheat and sheep country. It's best-known for being the home of **Kodja Place** (143 Albany Hwy; ☏9831 0500; w kodjaplace. com.au; ⊕ 09.00–16.00 daily; A$10/5 adult/child for the gallery), an award-winning exhibition and gallery documenting local Aboriginal culture, heritage and ways of life – a groundbreaking collaboration between indigenous and European local cultures. A highlight is the rose maze, where the stories of three 20th-century women from three cultures (Noongar, English and Italian) are interspersed throughout the beautiful rosebushes (over 100 varieties are represented), giving a

Top   The state is well known for its high-quality wines, with superb vineyards in the South West, Great Southern and Peel regions (VE) page 59

Above left   The Chittering Valley is an excellent place to explore WA's farm gates, with produce ranging from citrus and stonefruits to asparagus (APP) page 263

Above right   'Bush tucker' — any food native to Australia — has sustained human life here for tens of thousands of years (NT)

Below   Found only off Australia's west coast, western rock lobster is extremely valuable; head to the Lobster Shack in Cervantes to try some for yourself (TA) page 268

Above At 1.8km long, Busselton Jetty is the longest in the southern hemisphere (TA) page 155

Below left Bunbury's chequerboard lighthouse is unique – the pattern was supposedly chosen because the architect liked Black and White whisky (AY/S) page 148

Bottom left The height, steepness and variety of Lancelin's sand dunes have led some to claim that the town is Australia's premier sandboarding destination (JC/S) page 265

Below right Lake Clifton is home to one of the world's largest groupings of thrombolites, thought to be 2,000 years old (MM/S) page 140

Above	With its awe-inspiring red and orange dunes, Francois Peron National Park is one of Shark Bay's most popular destinations (NTH) page 298
Below left	WA has a handful of mesmerising pink lakes, the most accessible of which is Hutt Lagoon en route to Kalbarri (HA/S) page 284
Below right	On the south coast, Bremer Bay is one of the state's premier whale-watching destinations (NC) page 203
Bottom right	In the Kimberley, Cable Beach is WA's signature stretch of sand, where camel safaris are a popular pastime (TA) page 343

Above   With its distinctive 'surf wave' shape, Wave Rock is the most famous of the Eastern Wheatbelt's granite outcrops (MH/S) page 254

Left   A highlight of a trip to Purnululu National Park is Cathedral Gorge, a vast natural amphitheatre with sensational acoustics (DD/AWL) page 355

Below   Emus roam the desert plains of Nambung National Park, where the limestone Pinnacles create a landscape fit for a science-fiction film (m/S) page 268

Top left   Anthony Gormley's award-winning *Inside Australia* figures reside on Lake Ballard, a remote 4,900ha salt lake (D/S) page 238

Above left   Isolated Kennedy Range National Park is best known for its remarkable honeycomb-like gorges (MW/S) page 302

Above right   Crossing the Nullarbor is an iconic Outback experience; the '90 Mile Straight' is a 146.6km stretch of highway without a single turn or bend (KH/S) page 219

Below   The north Kimberley is home to a handful of incredibly remote but beautiful national parks, such as Mitchell River (SDP) page 361

Above   The centrepiece of Lake Kununurra is known as either Elephant Rock or Sleeping Buddha, depending on which way you look at it (TA) page 359

Left   There are at least 350 caves in Leeuwin-Naturaliste National Park; dramatic Lake Cave houses a dramatic 10m² piece of calcite (TA) page 168

Below   The 600m Tree Top Walk weaves through the vast tingle forest of the Valley of the Giants (TA) page 202

Top left   The Hotham Valley Railway has explored the jarrah forests of Dwellingup since 1974 (IB/A) page 136

Above left   Stretching for 125km, the Cape-to-Cape Track is one of the state's best long-distance hikes (WIL) page 159

Above right   Although not the tallest mountain in WA, Bluff Knoll in the Stirling Range is certainly the best known (O/IS) page 187

Below   The ancient granite hills of the Porongurups are best viewed from the suspended Granite Skywalk atop Castle Rock (TA) page 189

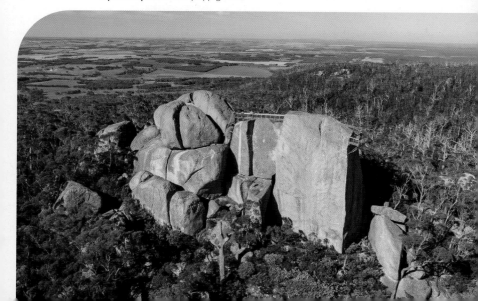

Above   Coalseam Conservation Park is one of the state's premier wildflower hotspots (IGJ/S) page 289

Below left   The endemic royal hakea is an emblem of Fitzgerald River National Park (at/S) page 209

Below right   The elusive wreath flower is one of WA's most sought-after species (I/S) page 290

Bottom right   Some 60 banksia species occur in the South West, including the scarlet banksia (iSD/S) page 290

taste of what country life was like for a group of people often brushed over in formal histories. The attached **Black Cockatoo Café** (⏰ 09.00–15.00 Mon–Fri, 08.00–15.00 Sat–Sun) offers hearty meals, coffees and cakes and is the best place to stop for a snack in town.

If you don't have a car, Transwa services Kojonup to/from East Perth (4hrs; A\$87 return) and Albany (2hrs; A\$56 return).

KATANNING Those heading south along the Great Southern Highway will want to stop off at Katanning, the area's main town. The turn-of-the-century buildings lining Clive Street, many featuring old verandas, along with flocks of pink-and-grey galahs, make a striking first impression. The town is also revered as an example of cultural integration and harmony; a large Malay Muslim community from Christmas Island and the Cocos Islands started forming in 1974, due to a labour shortage at the nearby halal abattoir. In 1980, the **Katanning Mosque** opened. The Islanders have since become an integral part of the town's fabric; imam Alep Mydie, who is also a Shire Councillor, has implemented an 'open-door' policy to the mosque to encourage other townspeople to better understand the culture and faith. At Katanning's entrance, **All Ages Playground** (Cnr Clive St & Great Southern Hwy) has a 10m spiral slide as its centrepiece (thanks to a recent A\$5 million upgrade) and the huge play equipment encourages adult use

THE HOLLAND TRACK

Created in 1893 by John Holland as a way for prospectors from the Eastern States to reach the Goldfields, the 680km Holland Track is the longest cart road in Australia, connecting Broomehill (20km south of Katanning on the Great Southern Highway) and Coolgardie in the Goldfields. Those looking to strike their fortune would sail over from the east, rather than take the arduous land trip across the Nullarbor. The boats would dock at Albany, and then men would make their way up to Broomehill (by wagon or on foot) and cut across to the Goldfields from there. Although there are not a whole lot of sights here, the appeal lies in the experience of real isolated bush driving.

The track is actually made up of two separate roads – the 2WD-suitable John Holland Way, and the 4x4 John Holland Track. The drive usually takes three days, whichever path you choose. Both the Way and the Track follow the same path for the first 200km, heading northeast from Broomehill to the small town of Newdegate, where there is accommodation. This is where the two roads separate; the Way leads for 280km to the orange and white cliffs of Buckley's Breakaway, a colour masterstroke of natural erosion in laterite, where there is a campground. It's then another 200km to Coolgardie the next day. If you need your comfortable bed and restaurant dinner, it's only 30km from Buckley's Breakaway to the town of Hyden (page 252).

The Track, instead, goes 280km to Sandalwood Camp, which is where you'll pitch a tent for the night – a real 4x4 experience with plenty of mud, sludge, chopped-up road and pure bush, before continuing on the track another 200km to Coolgardie.

Generally, anytime but summer (due to unbearable heat) is OK to do the drive; avoid right after heavy rains, however, which can result in substantial mud. Carry some reserve fuel if you are doing the 4x4 track; though, if you fill up on the 2WD section, you shouldn't have any problems.

as well as that of kids. There is also miniature railway that operates on alternating Sundays (⏰ 11.00–16.00).

For those without a car, Transwa coaches leave from the Katanning Shire Office for Albany (2½hrs; A$62 return) and East Perth (5½hrs; A$99 return).

Where to stay and eat

🏠 **Premier Mill Hotel** (22 rooms) Cnr Austral Tce & Clive St; ✆6500 3980; w premiermillhotel. com. This is not your usual country town hotel. Located in an 1890s flour mill, this luxury accommodation has been repurposed in keeping with the building's history. Some of the old areas of the mill, like the packing rooms, have been turned into rooms with reminders of their original uses inside, like pulley wheels or, in the purifying rooms, grain chutes. The street-level Dome Café (⏰ 06.00–21.00 daily) has taken over the old mill, serving casual light bites across the day, while the low-lit basement Cordial Bar (⏰ from 15.00) serves a strong local wine list alongside spirits & sharing platters. **$$$$**

✖ **Daily Grind Café** 90 Clive St; ✆9821 7779; ⏰ 06.00–16.30 Mon–Sat, 06.00–14.00 Sun. A long-running local favourite, with a mix of Australian classics & Malay-infused dishes (the satays are particularly good). **$**

A UNIQUE BIRD

Located in head-of-a-pin-small Ongerup – 116km east of Katanning, and 150km north of Albany – the Yongergnow Australian Malleefowl Centre (Lot 260, Jaekel St; ✆9828 2325; w yongergnow.com.au; ⏰ 09.00–16.00 Tue–Sun) is dedicated to preserving the malleefowl (*Leipoa ocellata*), a bird unique to southern Australia. Classed as a rare animal threatened with extinction by the state, and as vulnerable nationally by the Commonwealth, the chicken-sized bird's numbers have declined precipitously over the last 100 years, with some estimates being that their range has decreased by half; there are only about 100,000 left across Australia today. The bird, which weighs between 1.5kg and 2.5kg, is typically brown, with a grey head and grey, white and cream striping across the bulk of its back and wings – which makes it difficult to spot as it camouflages quite well in the bush.

Why exactly is the malleefowl so endangered? Alongside the usual factors that pop up whenever an animal becomes seriously threatened, another issue for the malleefowl is that the bird is *slow*, making it vulnerable to being hit by cars, since it has trouble getting out of the way in time. Another problem is that it prefers being on the ground to flying, making it an easy mark for a whole bunch of predators, particularly introduced animals like foxes and cats. It even builds its nests and lays its eggs on the ground – again an easy target – leaving the chicks on their own for survival after hatching. The long-term survival of the species is very much in question; predation and competition for food from introduced species has been the swan song for many native Australian animals.

The centre engages in captive breeding and raising of the birds, and over the last decade has been able to release 13 back into the wild. The aviaries for the malleefowl were purpose-built and you can walk among the 5ha grounds to see them. There's also a café and shop on site. It's worth stopping if you're heading out to Esperance from the Great Southern.

Around 20km before the centre, be sure to stop at **Louis' Lookout**, on the Gnowangerup–Jerramungup Road just past Chester Pass Road, to take in the views of the Stirling Range.

STIRLING RANGE NATIONAL PARK

Rising out of gentle farmland, the striking blue and purple hues of the 65km-long Stirling Ranges are almost majestic. The beauty of the area was recognised very quickly; the national park was one of the first in the state, gazetted in 1913. Its centrepiece is Bluff Knoll, which at 1,098m is often incorrectly claimed to be the tallest peak in WA – that honour actually belongs to 1,241m Mt Meharry in the Pilbara – but it is certainly the most well known, and a well-worn (though intense) hike trail leads to the top. The summit hosts occasional snowfall – on days when snow is predicted, parking often overflows so much that cars will line up along the sides of Chester Pass Road, full of hikers wanting to ascend to the top and get their photos taken in the white exotica.

It's worth nothing that these aren't the Alps or the Rockies, and there are no lodges nor skiing to be had. Judge the range on its own merits, not in comparison to others, and you will be more than rewarded. One of the best times to visit is in late winter, when the canola is out – their bright-yellow frame contrasting against the light blues of the mountains and the brown timber of ramshackle farm sheds is one of the most memorable natural sights in the state.

The park itself is known for its huge range of flowers, including several types of mountain bell – so named because their upside-down hangings create the appearance of a bell – as well as banksias and orchids, with the elusive Queen of Sheba being the most famous (see box, page 188). You are very likely to come across heaps of kangaroos here and, if very lucky, maybe even a quokka. The main reason to come if you are not a plant enthusiast, however, is for the range's visual beauty, best accessed through hikes and scenic drives.

GETTING THERE AND AWAY To visit the Stirlings you will need your own vehicle. The Stirling Range lies 100km north of Albany, and access is along Chester Pass Road. The eastern end of the park (where most of the attractions are) is the busiest. You can also access the park from the north, from Gnowangerup (75km) along Formby South Road, and from the west using Salt River Road from Cranbrook (89km). Mount Barker is 85km away on Woogenellup Road, which connects to Chester Pass Road. Multiple communities claim to be the 'Gateway to the Stirling Ranges'.

Visitors with a 2WD will have no problem at all accessing the sights here – however, if in a hire car, ensure that your contract allows you to drive on unsealed roads inside national parks (as Stirling Range Drive is unsealed).

WHERE TO STAY AND EAT *Map, page 184*

The Lily (5 accommodations) 9793 Chester Pass Rd, Amelup; 9827 9205; e thelilydutchwindmill@bigpond.com; w thelily.com.au. Home to a 16th-century replica, 5-storey Dutch windmill (the only operational flour mill in mainland Australia), the Lily is one of our favourite places to stay in the Upper Great Southern. You can choose to stay in the adjacent Dutch houses, the 'millers quarters' housed in the milling shed & windmill workshop, the 'winery quarters' in the same building as the on-site winery, or in the cabin of a refurbished Dakota DC-3 aircraft, with en-suite facilities in front of the cockpit (which you can see but can't enter). The accommodation also has a private airstrip & reception is housed in a 1924 railway station. Consider packing your dinner & ordering a breakfast basket for the morning. **$$$$**

Stirling Range Retreat 8639 Chester Pass Rd; 9827 9229; e info@stirlingrange.com.au; w stirlingrange.com.au. The closest accommodation to Bluff Knoll, this offers a range of options from motel rooms & 2-bedroom chalets to powered & unpowered sites. Camp kitchen, BBQ,

Albany & the Great Southern   STIRLING RANGE NATIONAL PARK   **6**

187

swimming pool, laundry; guided flower & bird walks also available. **$$$**

🏠 **Mt Trio Bush Camp & Caravan Park** 4850 Salt River Rd; \0419 751 801; e enquiries@mttrio. com.au; w mttrio.com.au. Huge, popular park with powered & unpowered sites & tent pitches, plus camp kitchen, lounge & showers. Bush walks & guided wildflower walks on site. A great base for Stirling Range exploration. **$**

WHAT TO SEE AND DO Hiking is the big draw here – walks in six of the peaks are graded Class 4 or above. It's difficult to find, but if you are planning on doing some serious hiking here, *Mountain Walks in the Stirling Range* (two parts) by A T Morphet is one of the most comprehensive guides to the area. Occasionally the Mount Barker Visitor Centre (page 190) has stray copies.

The signature hike in the Stirling Range, and one of the best-known day hikes in WA, the path to **Bluff Knoll** (Class 4; 6km return) is easy to follow but strenuous; allow 4 hours, and reasonable fitness is required. There is a small waterfall en route, but the views out over the rest of the mountains and the farmland beyond are spectacular; not to mention the everlasting sense of accomplishment when you do reach the summit. Rare yellow mountain bells can be found towards the summit, and along the track you'll find the more common pink mountain bells. You do need to plan according to the weather; the cloud cover can be low, and there is no real point in doing the hike if the views are going to be fogged out. If you aren't up for walking, it's worth driving the 7km of Bluff Knoll Road up to the car park (the 'Eastern Lookout') at the start of the route – there are some nice views out to the mountains and information boards about the area.

Although not as tall as Bluff Knoll at 1,052m, **Toolbrunup** (Class 5; 4km return) is accessed by a shorter, tougher hike, starting in woodland and getting steeper from there. Access is along Toolbrunup Road, which you turn on to from Chester Pass Road. Another option is **Mt Magog** (Class 5; 7km return), which is frequently overlooked, partly because of its location in the centre of the park and that it is set back off Stirling Range Drive (though that is the access road to get there). This is a long day hike and quite challenging – I have on occasion lost the trail and taken a few tumbles down its steep, rocky slopes (and I've also had an eagle circle me at the summit). However, the first half-hour is through flat open country which, if you go in September, is absolutely ablaze in wildflowers and probably the main reason to do this hike – the views from the summit aren't as grand as the other peaks.

THE QUEEN OF SHEBA

With its six purple leaves fringed with gold and red and covered in dark violet specks, the spectacular Queen of Sheba orchid (*Thelymitra speciosa*) is as rare as it is beautiful – truly the holy grail for orchid lovers. They are very hard to find as they look like any other orchid when they aren't flowering, and it can be difficult to tell them apart from various grasses. But the Stirling Range is one of the best places to hunt for them – sightings have been had on Bluff Knoll and Mt Trio. However, if you are looking for a map to tell you where they are, don't – one of the 'unwritten codes' among orchid hunters is that if you find a Queen of Sheba, you don't tell anyone where you found it. But if you can keep a secret … **Tozer's Bush Camp** (Lot 52 Ocomup Rd; \0428 371 015), an hour's drive west of the national park, just north of Bremer Bay and west of Fitzgerald River National Park, has them on their property and you can take a tour to see them. Call for details.

For a real challenge, the **Stirling Range Ridge Walk** (Class 5; 23km one-way) is seen as one of the most difficult hikes in WA. From the starting point at Ellen Peak to the finish at the Bluff Knoll car park, the trail is effectively unmarked, does not follow a straight line and involves a lot of climbing – it is takes two to three days to complete. You will need to be self-sufficient, and should contact the park ranger before you start – it's a great idea to carry a personal locator beacon and emergency communications equipment as well.

Those seeking an easier hike should consider the 827m-high **Mt Hassell** (Class 4; 3km return; access along Stirling Range Drive) or the 856m-high **Mt Trio** (Class 4; 3.5km return), comprised of three separate peaks joined by a plateau. The first section is quite rugged but it gets progressively easier, so you cover the tricky bit while your legs are still fresh. Lots of wildflowers are here in season and it's a great place to see mountain bells and banksias. Access is from Formby South Road at the northern end of the park.

Often overshadowed by the park's other peaks, the hike to **Talyuberlup** (Class 5, 2.6km return) may seem like a short distance but it's tough going. The difficulty here, despite not being as high (783m) as the better-known peaks, means you might want to keep this one towards the bottom of your bucket list.

Stirling Range Drive is a 42km (one-way) unsealed road along the spine of the park. If you do it westbound (from Chester Pass Road towards Cranbrook) at dusk, you may witness one of the most glorious sunsets you've ever seen. The drive passes two of the park's three lookouts – the Central Lookout and the Western Lookout – however, there are views of the mountains and farmland throughout the drive and the road's surface is in good condition, though it can get a bit slippery and muddy after rains. Another option is to take a half-circle loop around the outer boundary of the eastern end of the park, following Chillinup Road to Gnowellen Road and then left on to Sandalwood Road, which takes you back to Chester Pass Road. Though not part of the national park, this drive does offer magnificent views behind the Bluff Knoll section of the park.

MOUNT BARKER AND THE PORONGURUP RANGE

Nestled between the Stirling Range and Albany, the Porongurup Range – usually just called 'the Porongurups' – is smaller and gentler than its cousins to the north, stretching for about a dozen kilometres. Think bald Wheatbelt granite rather than Irish rolling green hills. Often likened to domes, the Porongurups are ancient granite hills formed over millions of years as erosion weathered away the granite into its current shapes – exposed in many parts but interspersed with some vegetation. They may not be as high or as rugged as the Stirlings, but there is some excellent walking and hiking in the Porongurups – the suspended Granite Skywalk at Castle Rock is a regional icon, and there is karri forest if you can't make it to the South West – and their proximity to Albany (45km) and Mount Barker (22km) make a visit here a very easy day trip. This is also one of Australia's great wine regions; Porongurup Riesling has a string of awards to its name, and cellar doors line nearly the entire length of the range, providing a gourmet alternative to the isolation of the Stirlings. The area also packs in a huge amount of biodiversity, with some surveys indicating over 700 species of flora are present here – orchids are particularly noteworthy with pink fairy, purple enamel, cowslip, shy sun and blue lady prominent. This is also a good place to see cockatoos, and I have seen the occasional echidna.

The contrasts between the Stirlings and the Porongurups – and their proximity to one another – mean that they complement each other well; make time for both.

GETTING THERE AND AWAY Mount Barker is 50km/30 minutes north of Albany on the Albany Highway; it's about 260km/4 hours from Perth on the same road. Transwa coaches between East Perth and Albany stop at Mount Barker (6hrs/A$161 return from Perth; 40mins/A$21 return from Albany); there is also a coach from Bunbury (6hrs; from A$140 return).

To get to the Porongurups from Albany, you're better off taking Chester Pass Road – Castle Rock is 44km north. You'll turn off on to Porongurup Road. Incoming from Mount Barker, Porongurup Road connects to the Albany Highway at the southern end of town; from there, it's 28km to the Granite Skywalk.

TOURIST INFORMATION

⚡ Mount Barker Visitor Centre 622/6 Albany Hwy; ☏ 9851 1163; w mountbarkerwa.com.au; ⏱ 09.00–16.00 Mon–Fri, 10.00–15.00 Sat–Sun

 WHERE TO STAY AND EAT Mount Barker and the Porongurups are close enough to Albany that it makes sense to base yourself there and make use of the ample facilities and services. However, there are a few options in the area worth considering.

✳ 🏠 **Cloud Nine Spa Chalets** [map, page 184] (2 chalets) 278 Moorialup Rd; ☏ 9853 1111; e rod-mel@bigpond.com; w cloudninespachalets.com.au. Beautiful chalets set within 40ha of bushland a stone's throw from the national park, just east of Chester Pass Road. The accommodation is very private; 1 chalet has a spa bath & the other an indoor jacuzzi, & both come with a free bottle of bubbly. Picnic sets & toiletries are also included, guided bushwalks are offered & galahs, parrots & kangaroos can be spotted in the grounds. **$$$**

🏠 **Porongurup Range Tourist Park** (35 powered sites, 15 unpowered sites) 7 Boxhill Rd, Porongurup; ☏ 0404 062 943; w porongurupprangetouristpark.com.au. You can't get any closer to the Porongurups than this caravan park right across from the park's main entrance. Camp kitchen, gas BBQs & laundry facilities also

available, as are chalets with fridges (2-night min stay applies). **$$$**

🏠 **Kendenup Lodge & Cottages** [map, page 184] (11 accommodations) 217 Moorialup Rd, Kendenup; ☏ 9851 4233; e kendenupcottages@hotmail.com; w kendenup.com. A 10min drive from Mount Barker just outside Kendenup, these homey en-suite units boast earthy tones, AC & flatscreen TVs. There is an on-site restaurant & bar (⏱ Fri & Sat evenings) which comes in handy in the small town, as does the communal pizza oven. **$$**

✳ ✗ **Mount Barker Country Bakery** 18 Mondurup St, Mount Barker; ☏ 9851 1000; ⏱ 05.00–18.00 daily. A multi-award-winning bakery that has some of the best gourmet pies in the state – I'd recommend the garlic prawn & rice. A must-stop if you're in town. **$**

WHAT TO SEE AND DO

Mount Barker The seat of the Shire of Plantagenet, Mount Barker – don't abbreviate the Mount – is more of a base to explore the Porongurups, Stirlings and the wine regions than a destination in itself. On the Albany Highway through town, the **Mount Barker Old Police Station Museum Complex** (f mtbarkermuseum; ⏱ 10.00–15.00 Sat–Sun) was built by convicts in 1868 and today hosts its namesake plus the old courthouse, a house from the 1870s, an old one-teacher school and many artefacts. It's a great place to get a glimpse of what pioneer life was like in the late 1800s and early 1900s, in what was then the West Australian frontier. A short drive southwest from town, **St Werburgh's Chapel**, built in 1872, is Heritage-listed due to its rural Gothic style. It has never had electricity; the cemetery is still active, and there are limited services – the fifth Sunday of months that have five Sundays.

A MOUNT BARKER AND PORONGURUP WINE TOUR *

Though they are only about 20km apart, the Mount Barker Wine Region and Porongurup Wine Region are classed as distinct because of their different climactic conditions – there is more average rainfall in Mount Barker, and the big granite hills in the Porongurups and their valley floors allow cool air to settle more easily. Though Mount Barker Rieslings are great, this wine region also produces very good Shiraz and Cabernet Sauvignon, and there are many well-known vineyards. The Rieslings here are sensational – though the Chardonnay and Pinot Noir are also excellent.

MOUNT BARKER

Gilbert Wines 30138 Albany Hwy; 9851 4028; w gilbertwines.com.au; 10.00–17.00 Fri–Mon. If you are driving down from Perth, this will be one of the first wineries you see, located near Kendenup, 18km north of Mount Barker. I come here when I am in the mood for rosé, but the Rieslings are great too. The café has good lunches but also does wine pairings with cheese & chocolate.

Plantagenet Wines Lot 45 Albany Hwy; 9851 3111; w plantagenetwines. com; 10.00–16.30 daily. With a very prominent location on the Albany Highway in Mount Barker, this produces really good fortifieds & I always pick up a bottle of their Old Tawny when I visit. The sample platter with ham, free-range chicken & local cheeses here is nice & they rotate their menu frequently.

West Cape Howe Wines 14293 Muir Highway; 9892 1444; w westcapehowewines.com.au; 10.00–17.00 Mon–Fri, 11.00–16.00 Sat–Sun. 10km west of Mount Barker, this locally well-regarded winery is a great choice, particularly for a range of whites. They don't have a café but do stock things like olive oil.

PORONGURUP

❋ **Castle Rock Estate** 2660 Porongurup Rd; 9853 1035; w castlerockestate.com.au; 10.00–17.00 daily. Next to its namesake (page 159), this multi-award winner is our go-to cellar door. This part of the Great Southern is mostly known for its Rieslings – Castle Rock produces a European-style & an

Australian-style – & the Pinot Noirs here are also top-notch. Buy a bottle of both.

Duke's Vineyard 1328 Porongurup Rd; 9853 1107; w dukesvineyard.com; 10.00–16.30 daily. Another award winner with excellent Rieslings.

Ironwood Estate Wines 2191 Porongurup Rd; 9853 1126; w ironwoodestatewines.com.au; 11.00–17.00 Wed–Mon. Long-standing winery named after the town in Michigan, US where one of the owners is originally from. The Rieslings here are standout, & the Shiraz is excellent too. Excellent on-site café; the cheeseboards & platters are hearty.

FRANKLAND RIVER This village,
76km west of Mount Barker, is another distinct wine region within the Great Southern – though the most isolated. It's a lonely drive here, but the whites make it worth the effort.

❋ **Alkoomi Wines** 1141 Wingebellup Rd; 9855 2229; w alkoomiwines.com. au; 10.00–16.30 daily. The area's best-known winery has (of course) excellent Rieslings, but the Chardonnay & Pinot Noir are good too.

Ferngrove Wines 276 Ferngrove Rd; 9855 2378; w ferngrove.com.au; by appt 10.00–16.00 weekdays. Good Sauvignon Blancs.

Frankland Estate 530 Rocky Gully-Frankland Rd; 9855 1544; w franklandestate.com.au; 10.00–16.00 Mon–Fri. Does a fantastic Riesling but also a variety of exotic small-batch releases.

6

Porongurup National Park ✳ (Entry: A$15/vehicle) The star attraction of the park is the **Granite Skywalk**, a suspended walkway on the huge granite outcrop of Castle Rock situated towards the eastern end of the park near Chester Pass Road. The walk begins at the car park; after ascending through jarrah, marri and karri forest you arrive at Balancing Rock – a large boulder perpetually and precariously balancing on a small granite peak – before reaching the Skywalk, which requires scaling a 6m-tall vertical ladder and scrambling some rocks (they have handles drilled and bolted into them to assist you). The walkway provides wonderful views out to other peaks in the range as well as the Stirlings, but is equally impressive as a feat of the engineering in its own right.

A number of hiking trails criss-cross the park, including the circular **Hayward Peak and Nancy Peak Walk** (Class 4; 5.5km) – you first pass Hayward Peak before reaching Nancy Peak and then returning through karri forest. Through this walk you can also access the lookout at Morgan's Peak. Two other trails explore the karri forest; the **Bolganup Trail** (Class 2; 600m return) and the **Wansborough Walk** (Class 4; 4km one-way), which passes through the part of the park between Nancy Peak and **Devil's Slide** ✳, the tallest peak in the Porongurups at 670m. This is accessed by a rugged walk (Class 4, 5km return) and the views over the landscape and neighbouring mountains are sensational – the panorama from the summit is the best in the Porongurups.

The 23km (signposted) **Porongurup Scenic Drive** effectively circumnavigates the park, on a mix of sealed and unsealed (but 2WD-suitable) roads. There are views out to the Stirlings and good close-ups of the Porongurup's granite hills.

ALBANY

The Great Southern's largest town, Albany offers a wealth of historic sites to go with its incredible coastal scenery and some of the best beaches in the state. Albany sits on three main bodies of water – the deep-water Princess Royal Harbour, which the CBD fronts to the south; Frenchman Bay, which it fronts to the east; and Oyster Harbour, which is to the northeast and empties into Frenchman Bay. Collectively the waters are known as King George Sound, named after King George III by Commander George Vancouver in 1791, and where the Brig *Amity* arrived in 1826, establishing Albany as a convict settlement and making it the first permanent European settlement in WA.

However, Aboriginal peoples were here well before the British. The Menang Noongar call this area 'Kinjarling', meaning 'place of rain', and have been in southwestern Australia for 50,000 years, and archaeological evidence has been found in Albany going back at least 18,000 years. There is some evidence that the Menang Noongar lived on the coast during the summer months and then headed inland during winter – fish traps and other artefacts indicate that the natural harbour sustained a large population of Aboriginal peoples pre-European settlement. When the British arrived, the Menang Noongar were led by a man named Mokare, and relations started more positively than elsewhere;

ALBANY
For listings, see from page 195

🛏 **Where to stay**
1 1849 Backpackers Albany
2 BIG4 Middleton Beach Holiday Park
3 Dog Rock Motel
4 Pelicans Albany Middleton Beach
Off map
  Albany Apartments

✖ **Where to eat and drink**
5 Bay Merchants
6 Dylan's on the Terrace
  Garrison (see Princess Royal Fortress)
7 Hybla Tavern
8 Joop Thai
9 Ocean & Paddock
10 Rustler's
11 Three Anchors

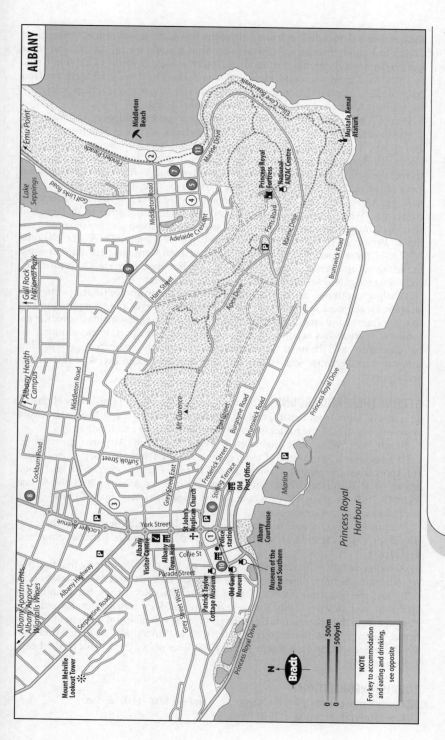

ALBANY

Emu Point

Lake
Seppings

Gull Rock
National Park

Middleton Beach

Finders Parade

Golf Links Road

Middleton Road

Adelaide Crescent

Middleton Road

Albany Health
Campus

Hare Street

Suffolk Street

Marine Drive

Apex Drive

Mt Clarence

Park Street

Burgoyne Road

Brunswick Road

Fort Road

Princess Royal Drive

Princess Royal Drive

Princess Royal
Harbour

Marina

Museum of the
Great Southern

Old Gaol
Museum

Albany Courthouse

Patrick Taylor
Cottage Museum

Parade Street

Collie St

Police
station

St John's
Anglican Church

Albany
Town Hall

Albany
Visitor Centre

York Street

Grey Street East

Grey Street West

Frederick Street

Stirling Terrace

Old
Post Office

Cockburn Road

Locker Avenue

Albany Highway

Serpentine Road

Albany Apartments,
Albany Airport,
Wignalls Wines

Mount Melville
Lookout Tower

Brunswick Road

Princess Royal
Fortress

National-
ANZAC Centre

Mustafa Kemal
Ataturk

N

Brad†

0   500m
0   500yds

NOTE
For key to accommodation
and eating and drinking,
see opposite

Mokare was a skilled diplomat and he and the first government resident, Alexander Collie, had good chemistry – Mokare served as a guide for the British and there was no competition for land or hunting. However, Mokare died in 1831 and Collie in 1835. As Albany grew and expanded, competition and encroachment for land erupted, disruptions to Noongar traditional life intensified and practices to 'civilise' and convert Aboriginal peoples to Christianity also began.

Part of Albany's growth was that it became an important shipping and transport centre in early colonial days – it took roughly six weeks to sail here from Sydney, and it was a well-worn disembarkation point for travel to Kalgoorlie and the Goldfields during the Gold Rush. The emergence of the port at Fremantle at the turn of the 20th century had a significant negative impact on the area as it siphoned away shipping, and the economy turned to agriculture, timber and even more whaling. Albany was also the departure point in 1914 for a pair of Australian troop convoys in World War I; over 40,000 ANZAC soldiers departed from here, and were instrumental in the formation of an Australian national identity separate from that of Britain. ANZAC culture and history is part of Albany's DNA –the National ANZAC Centre opened here in 2014. Noongar men were not permitted to enlist in the army, though many did anyway by concealing their heritage. On return they were not recognised for their efforts like white Australians were.

Whaling continued in Albany until 1978; and the town continued, somewhat sleepily, for the next several decades – in the process developing a reputation as a tourism centre for its natural gifts, and also as a favoured retirement destination for farmers. Tourism has become an increasingly important part of the economy, as has viticulture, and the town vibe is changing accordingly – embracing a new, edgy, innovative and creative feel evidenced in the many new and excellent restaurants and shops.

GETTING THERE AND AROUND Albany is the end of the road for the Albany Highway, 413km/4½ hours from Perth. Transwa **coaches** can make the run in 6 hours (from A$66 one-way); take the route that runs through Williams and Kojonup.

By **air**, Rex offers daily flights from Perth to Albany Airport (1hr 10mins; A$183 one-way), 7km north of town on the Albany Highway. There is no public transport from the airport – you will need to take a taxi (about A$30) and book ahead, as it is unlikely there will be any waiting; try **Albany City Cabs & Taxi** (❧ 9841 7000; w albanycitycabs.com.au) or **Rainbow Coast Taxis** (❧ 9844 1115; w rainbowcoasttaxis.business.site).

Within Albany, TransAlbany operates six public circular **bus** routes. The most useful for visitors is the 803, which runs to Middleton Beach, Lake Seppings and Emu Point.

Arriving in town by **car**, when you get to the city's notorious five-fingered roundabout, continue down the Albany Highway to York Street – the heart of the CBD and the historical district. Taking Chester Pass Road from the roundabout will lead you down a long commercial strip and eventually out towards the Porongurups; the other South Coast Highway exit will take you to Denmark. York Street ends at a T-junction along the waterfront, at Princess Royal Drive. Middleton Road connects Middleton Beach to the CBD – it's only a 3km drive to the beach from York Street.

TOURIST INFORMATION
🄵 **Albany Visitor Centre** 221 York St; ❧ 6820   Mon–Fri, 10.00–14.00 Sat–Sun
3700; w amazingalbany.com.au; ⊕ 10.00–16.00

WHERE TO STAY *Map, page 193*

🏠 **Dog Rock Motel** (80 rooms) 303 Middleton Rd; ☎ 9845 7200; e info@dogrockmotel.com.au; w dogrockmotel.com.au. Venerable motel that gets its name from the dog-shaped rock nearby. Rooms do appear dated (& sometimes very dated) – but I often stay here when I'm climbing the Stirlings because, even so, it's a clean & serviceable option that is well located & has a good b/fast buffet in the on-site restaurant. Recommended if you want to be fairly central. **$$$**

🏠 **Pelicans Albany Middleton Beach** (22 apartments) 3 Golf Links Rd; ☎ 9841 7500; w pelicansalbany.com. One of the premier options in town, just off Middleton Beach, apartments & villas here have kitchens & are tastefully decorated & furnished – very good value for money. **$$$**

🏠 **BIG4 Middleton Beach Holiday Park** (37 accommodations) 28 Flinders Pde; ☎ 9841 3593; e holiday@holidayalbany.com.au; w holidayalbany.com.au. Right on Middleton Beach with wonderful ocean views, this resort offers 3-bedroom beach houses, 2-bedroom spa villas, chalets, caravan sites & general pitches. There are a whole range of facilities on offer including solar-powered swimming pool, indoor spa, BBQ areas, mini theatre, camp kitchen & a fish cleaning station. *Cabins* **$$$**, *campsites* **$**

🏠 **Albany Apartments** (8 rooms) 278 Albany Hwy; ☎ 9841 5259; e traceymelrose@bigpond. com.au; w albanyapartmentsmotel.com. On the highway as you come into town, these spotlessly clean & spacious rooms & apartments with very comfortable beds are very good value. **$$**

🏠 **1849 Backpackers Albany** (23 rooms) 45 Peels Pl; ☎ 9841 1574; e 1849albany@gmail.com; w 1849backpackers.com.au. Centrally located hostel with free Wi-Fi & free pancakes for b/fast. Rooms (dorms & private rooms) are basic, but everything in the CBD is walkable from here. Guest kitchen, laundry, TV room, table tennis & darts, & outdoor area with BBQ. **$**

WHERE TO EAT AND DRINK *Map, page 193*

✕ **Garrison** 7 Forts Rd; ☎ 9842 6654; w garrison.net.au; ⏰ 11.30–15.00 & 17.30–22.00 Tue–Fri, 08.00–15.00 & 17.30–22.00 Sat, 08.00–15.00 & 17.30–21.00 Sun. At the National ANZAC Centre, this stylish eatery focuses on Middle Eastern-inspired sharing plates & sourdough pizzas – the lamb is good, but so are the hummus & labneh dishes. B/fasts of eggs & pancakes; take-away also available. Book ahead. **$$$**

✕ **Hybla Tavern** 11 Flinders Pde; ☎ 9841 1120; w hybla.com.au; ⏰ 15.00–21.30 Wed–Thu, 15.00–22.30 Fri, 11.00–22.30 Sat, 11.00–21.30 Sun. A good place for pub grub – the burgers are quality, as are the onion rings. Good cocktails too. **$$$**

✳ ✕ **Rustlers** 222 Stirling Tce; ☎ 9800 9191; w rustlers.com.au; ⏰ 11.30–14.00 & 17.00–20.30 Sun–Mon & Wed–Thu, 11.30–14.00 & 17.00–21.00 Fri–Sat. One of Albany's signature restaurants. Dinner here on my first night in town is a personal tradition. With its name you can guess that it specialises in steaks – the variety & quality is terrific, as are the sides. My go-to is usually the kangaroo loin, but you can't go wrong with almost any other choice here. Book ahead. **$$$**

✕ **Dylan's on the Terrace** 82 Stirling Tce; ☎ 9841 8720; w dylans.com.au; ⏰ 07.00–16.00 Tue–Thu, 08.00–20.00 Fri, 08.00–16.00 Sat–Sun. Right off York St in the CBD, this laidback restaurant serves cooked b/fasts, burgers & sandwiches but done very well. Walk-ins only, but it gets busy. The building itself dates from the 1800s – originally a warehouse & woolstore – but has had many incarnations since then, including at one point in the 1960s as home to an opera company. Dylan's opened in 1987. **$$**

✳ ✕ **Joop Thai** 130 Lockyer Av; ☎ 9841 5377; 🅵 JoopThai; ⏰ 17.00–21.00 Tue–Sun. Offering some of the best Thai in the state, this legendary restaurant serves out-of-this-world pad Thais, stir-fries, soups & curries. A must-visit. **$$**

✕ **Ocean & Paddock** 116 Middleton Rd; ☎ 9842 6212; w oceanandpaddock.com.au; ⏰ 11.00–21.00 Tue–Sun. Multi-award-winner specialising in locally caught fish & chips, though there are things like pork & chicken tacos too. **$$**

✕ **Three Anchors** 2 Flinders Pde; ☎ 9841 1600; w threeanchors.com.au; ⏰ 06.30–20.30 Sun–Tue, 06.30–17.00 Wed–Sat. You'll come across this place as you're strolling Middleton Beach. Good b/fasts, as well as coffee & beignets (a type of square donut topped with powdered sugar – popularised in New Orleans) – I nearly fell over when I walked in & saw that unique gem on the menu one

afternoon! Lunches are a fairly standard, though well-done, collection of steaks, burgers & pastas. $$
X Bay Merchants 18 Adelaide Cres; ✎9841 7821; f baymerchants; ⏰ 06.00–14.00 Mon–Fri,

07.00–noon Sat–Sun. Having been a shop for over a century, this establishment relishes its history, its coffee & its location in Middleton Beach. Also a wine merchant. Terrific for a morning stop. $

OTHER PRACTICALITIES

Albany Health Campus 30 Warden Av; ✎9892 2222; ⏰ 24hrs. The newly opened A$170 million medical centre is in Spencer Park, northeast of the CBD.

Western Australia Police Force 210 Stirling Tce; ✎9892 9300; ⏰ 24hrs

WHAT TO SEE AND DO Albany's utility is that of a comfortable central base to explore the surrounding natural attractions – the Porongurups, the Stirlings and the proliferation of superlative beaches and national parks to the east and west of town. That being said, the CBD is a charismatic historical quarter, and the National ANZAC Centre and Museum of the Great Southern are both substantial attractions worth your time.

The CBD Being the oldest European settlement in WA, Albany has some wonderful colonial buildings, clustered around **York Street** – the CBD's main thoroughfare. The self-guided **Albany Heritage Walk Trail** connects many of these – ask at the visitor centre for details, or enquire about a guided Heritage Walking Tour at the Museum of the Great Southern (see opposite). The most recognisable building in town is probably the 1888 stucco-and-granite **Albany Town Hall** (217 York St), notable for its cobblestone side wall and four-sided clock tower. The building has a long history of being at the centre of Albany's cultural life; the first event held here was a ball, on the same day that it opened, and the building was even used as an early cinema in 1911. It has continued to host performances off and on through its history – most recently reopening in 2020 after extensive renovations saw the opening of an art gallery with temporary exhibitions. A few doors down, the stone and gabled **St John's Anglican Church** was the first church consecrated in WA, completed in 1848 and today listed on the National Trust – services are daily at 08.00.

Built in 1896, the red-brick and granite **Albany Courthouse** (184 Stirling Tce), with its distinctive round front corners and convolute arched entryway, is still in use today. Nearby, the 1852 **Old Gaol Museum** (255 Stirling Tce; ✎0457 895 700; ⏰ 10.00–16.00 daily; adult/child A$5/2.50) was originally established for skilled convict labour from Britain but was expanded to be an all-purpose prison in 1873. Further expansions were made to imprison women and Aboriginals – it was seen as a more secure (ie: escape-proof) facility than the one in Lawley Park. Aboriginal prisoners were held in a separate timber cell – you can wander through cell blocks and see their cell carvings. The gaol was closed in 1941 and it reopened as a museum in 1996. Though not open to the public, the 1869, National Trust-listed **Old Post Office** (31–39 Stirling Tce) has a 25m clock tower; it was originally also used as a customs house and a telegraph office in addition to being a post office and is now the Albany campus for the University of Western Australia and Curtin University.

The 1832 **Patrick Taylor Cottage Museum** (37 Duke St; ✎0457 329 944; ⏰ 11.00–15.00 daily; A$6/2.50 adult/child) is the oldest surviving house in WA. Its wattle-and-daub construction is typical of the early European settlers. This became Albany's first museum in 1964 and is home to some 2,000 artefacts like silverware, clocks and so on, but the real attraction is its historical value. There is talk the cottage is haunted by the ghost of a military veteran from the Boer War who lived here, and who returns once a year on the anniversary of his death in September.

For a great introduction to the town's history, visit the **Museum of the Great Southern** (Residency Rd; ✎ 9841 4844; w museum.wa.gov.au/museums/museum-of-the-great-southern; ⊕ 10.00–16.00 daily; free, donations welcome), the Albany branch of the Western Australian Museum. Overlooking Princess Royal Harbour, it is anchored by a replica of the Brig *Amity* (adult/child A$5/2), which you board via a gangplank – informative volunteers detail what life was like for the crew, convicts and soldiers aboard the original ship some 200 years ago. Other permanent exhibits include a one-room period school – complete with holes for ink jars in the desks – and a gallery featuring stories of the Menang Noongar people, as well as a lighthouse exhibition and marine discovery centre, both in the Eclipse Building.

A short walk northwest of the CBD along Serpentine Road, the **Mount Melville Lookout Tower** – atop 152m Mount Melville – provides great views down over Albany, King George Sound and, on clear days, as far as the Porongurups.

National ANZAC Centre (67 Forts Rd; ✎6820 3500; w nationalanzaccentre.com. au; ⊕ 09.00–17.00 daily; adult/child/additional child A$25/11/6) Telling the war through the stories of the ANZACs themselves, rather than through historical or documentary narrative, the centre – on Mount Clarence, providing a view of where the ships carrying the ANZACs departed – is a multi-award winner. You take the identity of one of 32 actual servicemen or servicewomen during the war, and follow their journey and experience – from recruitment and enlistment to theatre – through a variety of multimedia exhibits. At the end you find out if your person lived or not and, if they did, what happened to them post-conflict. A truly moving experience.

The centre is located inside the 1893 **Princess Royal Fortress**, also known as the Albany Forts. Complete with original gun emplacements, barracks and batteries, the fortress was built to protect trade coming into Australia's eastern colonies – losing control of the sea lanes around WA's southern coast was seen as a security risk by all the colonies, and so construction of the fort was financed by everyone, with the guns supplied by the British. In World War I, the forts were the last port of call before departure for Australian and New Zealander troops heading to Europe, and thus has an instrumental place in the formation of the ANZAC legend and Australian national identity. This was the last piece of Australia many of these troops ever saw. The fort sits within the 250ha **Albany Heritage Park**, which includes the Desert Mountain Corps Memorial at the summit of Mt Clarence – a 1964 recast of the original 1932 statue at Suez, which was damaged and then brought to Australia.

Middleton Beach Stretching for 5km along Frenchman's Bay, Albany's town beach is a popular swimming, windsurfing and fishing spot, somewhat sheltered by two granite islands, Michaelmas and Breaksea. The Norfolk pines behind the sand have become iconic and a furor erupted in 2020 when the city removed a few for infrastructure reasons. An upgraded shark enclosure was installed in 2020, making the area safe for swimming. Another 4km north, **Emu Point** is the site of a narrow channel separating Oyster Harbour from King George Sound – the harbour side of the water is sheltered and very good for swimming. The views across the channel to Gull Rock National Park (page 198) are grand, and there is a shop selling live blue crabs at the neighbouring marina.

Linking Middleton Beach with Brunswick Road, the 5km **Ellen Cove Boardwalk** around Ellen Cove provides stunning views out into King George Sound, as well as a whale-watching lookout (migrating humpback and southern right whales visit between May and November). We have also seen bandicoots on this trail. About halfway along, there is also a life-size statue of Mustafa Kemal Ataturk, first President of Turkey in 1923–38, and commander of the forces that opposed the ANZAC troops at Gallipoli during World War I. He is carrying a speech he made to the first Australians and New Zealanders who visited the Gallipoli battlefield in 1934, laying down the foundation of a spirit of kinship between the Turks and the ANZACs even though they had been on opposite sides at Gallipoli. The statue was unveiled on ANZAC Day 2001 and overlooks Ataturk Channel, which was renamed at the same time Turkey officially christened 'ANZAC Cove'.

Just behind Middleton Beach, **Lake Seppings** is a freshwater birdwatching haven home to over 100 species of bird, such as black swan, white ibis and purple swamphen. A 3km walkway circumnavigates the lake.

Gull Rock National Park ✻
Across Oyster Harbour from Emu Point, this highly scenic but somewhat underrated national park is great for swimming and views; the white sand tumbles down the green scrub-covered hills to the beach like a bag of spilled sugar. Beautiful Ledge Beach has a shipwreck that you can swim out to, while Nanarup Beach – technically not part of the national park, but on its eastern boundary – has a long, wide stretch of sand and a secluded cove.

AROUND ALBANY
Little Beach ✻
Perched on Two Peoples Bay 40km east of Albany, this is our favourite beach in all of Australia. If it was anywhere else in the world it would be sardine-packed with people, but it rarely is. The elevated car park gives you a great view of the curving white sands, complete with granite boulder, sandwiched between exquisitely blue water and green hills. Climbing over these leads to a sheltered swimming area, and behind the granite rocks there is a walking trail to a boardwalk that has a natural wading pool. The highly endangered Gilbert's potoroo was thought to be extinct for decades until it was rediscovered here in 1994; about 30cm long and weighing 10kg, it is arguably the world's rarest marsupial.

Betty's Beach ✻
Some argue that this safe-for-swimming semi-sheltered beach, 50km east of Albany, is nicer than Little Beach – and although I don't buy it, Betty's Beach is certainly in the same category. A zillion shades of blue and white converge here, and Mount Manypeaks Reserve provides a stunning backdrop to the east.

Torndirrup National Park ✻
Made up of three interconnecting peninsulas – Flinders, Torndirrup and Vancouver – south of Albany, this 3,906ha national park is known for its dramatic granite coastal scenery. As you head into the park along Frenchman Bay Road, turn on to The Gap Road for one of the first landmarks – **The Gap**, a rectangular hole in the granite cliff-face that causes explosive wave crashes, sometimes upwards over 40m. A viewing platform, partially hanging over The Gap, was recently opened – despite being that high up, sometimes visitors do get splashed. A short walk away over the granite is **Natural Bridge**, a large natural granite arch that forms a gateway down the rocks into the water. Driving back towards Frenchman Bay Road, you can see

Cable Beach, highlighted by a massive marble-shaped boulder weighing several tons that was thrown up on to the beach by the sea – a reminder of how powerful the ocean is.

Continuing south on Frenchman Bay Road, the next left turn leads to the **Blowholes**, where water gets pushed up through the cracks in the granite, creating a visual phenomenon similar to a whale spouting. The walk from the car park is 1.6km return. Further south is the superlative **Jimmy Newells Harbour**, an earplug-shaped blue and turquoise tiny, sheltered harbour, in between two densely brush-covered hills. The colour contrasts here are remarkable and it's one of the most scenic parts of the park, although it's visible only from a viewing platform. Frenchman Bay Road then curves north, from where a side road leads to **Salmon Holes**, a wild and rough beach famous for its dangerous rock fishing (people can and do die here – if you are going to rock fish, do not blow off the precautions), before finally the road ends between two beaches on Frenchman Bay.

Just east of this is **Whale World, Albany's Historic Whaling Station** (81 Whaling Station Rd; ✆ 9844 4021; w discoverybay.com.au; ⊕ 09.00–17.00 daily; A$32/12 adult/child) – the world's only complete whaling station tourist attraction, which documents the history and significance of whaling in the area. When the whaling station closed in 1978, the equipment was left in place – allowing for preservation. You can explore the whale chaser, the processing station and the whale oil tank theatres, among others. There's also a skeleton of the last sperm whale harpooned in the waters off the Great Southern. Next door is the **Australian Wildlife Park** (entry included in Whale World ticket, or A$15 for just the park in school holidays) with kangaroos, possums and birds like Major Mitchell's cockatoos, and a regional wildflower garden with a wetlands area.

From Whale World, **Bald Head bushwalk** (Class 5; 12.5km return) leads to Bald Head at the end of the Flinders Peninsula. This day hike, though difficult with steep ascents (take lots of water), largely follows a ridge along the peninsula and has gained significant popularity in recent years due to its incredible 360-degree views of beaches like Salmon Holes and, in spring, colourful wildflowers. Plan on this taking about 8 hours.

DENMARK

Long associated with counterculture and the home of an arty, alternative community, Denmark makes the most of its location within one of WA's most scenic coastal national parks, and as the gateway to the giant tingle forests further east. There isn't much for visitors in the townsite itself; most use it as a base to explore the incredible surrounding natural setting.

The area and river were named in 1829 by surgeon Thomas Wilson, who named it after one of his colleagues – Alexander Denmark. The town's first settlers did not arrive until 1895; however, it developed along the usual Great Southern and South West lines of cattle, dairy, timber and fruit, until after World War II when tourism began to develop. In the 1970s, artists, writers and creatives who enjoyed the town's peaceful setting and nearby forests began arriving in droves, as did retirees. The first vineyards were planted and Denmark quickly became one of the Great Southern's five distinct wine regions. Since then, the area has also developed a strong foodie culture, anchored by establishments on and around Scotsdale Road just north of town, with shops producing fudges, cheeses and mead.

Today, Denmark is no longer the hippie haven it once was, as the region and its economy has changed. It still attracts an eclectic group of people, but these days they are far more diversified; photographer Nic Duncan captured some of Denmark's unique character for the ABC in 2015. You can find his photos and the accompanying story at w abc.net.au/local/photos/2015/07/22/4278643.htm.

GETTING THERE AND AWAY Denmark is on the South Coast Highway, 55km/40 minutes west of Albany and 65km/45 minutes east of Walpole. Transwa coaches run to/from Albany (40mins; A$10.40 one-way), Walpole (1hr; A$15 one-way) and Bunbury (5½hrs; A$55 one-way).

TOURIST INFORMATION
Denmark Visitor Centre 73 South Coast Hwy; ☏ 9848 2648; w denmarkchamber.com.au/ discover-denmark; ⏱ 09.00–15.00 Mon-Sat

---

WHERE TO STAY AND EAT

Chimes Spa Retreat (10 suites) 467 Mount Shadforth Rd; ☏ 9848 2255; w chimes.com.au. Relaxation & tranquility are the main focus of this adults-only retreat, situated in a quiet, rural location west of town. Garden- & ocean-view suites all feature in-room jacuzzi & balcony, while the multi-level Tower Suite & Best Room in the House have dedicated spa areas. Massages & waxes also on offer at the day spa, & there's an outdoor pool set among tropical gardens. **$$$$**

Sensational Heights (4 suites) 159 Suttons Rd; ☏ 9840 9000; e info@sensationalheights.com. au; w sensationalheightsbandb.com.au. Off the Scotsdale Rd, this secluded & tranquil B&B offers spacious & bright suites, some with spa. Panoramic views abound of the surrounding pastures & karri forest. Cooked b/fast inc. **$$$$**

Denmark Hotel & River Rooms Motel 36 Hollings Rd; ☏ 9848 2206; e denmarkhotel@ westnet.com.au; w denmarkhotel.net. The local pub since 1926, motel rooms here are standard but come as sgls, dbls, trpls & family size. The on-site restaurant is popular & serves the likes of Korean beef bulgogi, lamb shanks & steaks. **$$$**

Karrak Reach Forest Retreat (4 chalets) 103 Silver Rd; ☏ 9840 9993; w karrakreach.com. au. Good, secluded option nestled among the karri forest of the Scotsdale Valley. Fully equipped chalets (3 named after types of forest) are superbly kept & stylishly furnished, & this is a point of pride for the owners. Pets can stay here on request. **$$$**

William Bay Cottages (7 cottages) 65 Rice Rd; ☏ 9840 9221; e info@williambaycottages. com.au; w williambaycottages.com.au. You can't get any closer to William Bay National Park than these timber & stone cottages, run by a long-

standing Denmark family, scattered among 133ha of karri & peppermint forest with a private track to Mazzoletti Beach. The 1-, 2- & 3-bedroom cottages have a wonderful farmhouse-style character about them, featuring plenty of exposed beams & brickwork, & take full advantage of the landscape. **$$$**

Boston Brewing Co 678 South Coast Hwy; ☏ 9848 1555; w bostonbrewing.com.au; ⏱ 11.00–21.00 Tue–Thu & Sun, 11.00–22.00 Fri–Sat. Fast becoming a local institution, this brewpub on the way to Albany specialises in handcrafted beer produced on site, though there is also plentiful wine. An extensive wood-fired pizza list joins burgers & sharers on the menu. Consider booking ahead. **$$$**

Pepper & Salt 1564 South Coast Hwy; ☏ 9848 3053; w pepperandsalt.com.au; ⏱ noon–15.00 Thu, Sat & Sun, noon–22.00 Fri. At the Forest Hill Winery, this rustic but elegant restaurant offers a seasonal, local menu, with dishes like Stirling Range beef eye-fillet & local asparagus. A 'trust the chef' 4-course option with champagne is good value at under A$100. Great views of the surrounding countryside. **$$$**

Denmark Gelato Co 5B Strickland St; ☏ 0482 525 551; ⏱ noon–17.00 Thu & Sun, noon–19.00 Fri–Sat. Sorbets & gelatos made on site, with a variety of other sweets & waffles too. Great place to stop after dinner. **$**

Ravens 1/7 South Coast Hwy; ☏ 9848 1163; w ravenscoffee.com; ⏱ 07.00–15.00 daily. This is perhaps Denmark's signature coffee joint – its location at the entrance to town (Albany side) makes it unmissable. Range of good blends & pastries available. **$**

SHOPPING

Denmark is renowned across WA for its gourmet produce, and this industry is centred on the scenic Scotsdale Road just north of town. A leisurely drive along its entire length, stopping at one delectable farmgate, winery and shop after another, is a must while in the area. In terms of wine, the Rieslings and Chardonnays are very good.

✳ **Bartholomews Meadery** 2620 South Coast Hwy; ☏ 9840 9349; w honeywine.com.au; ⏱ 09.30–16.30 daily. Family-run shop producing a range of honeys, honey ice creams & mead, plus beeswax candles & a host of bee-themed merch. There is an active colony inside the shop that you can view through glass. The ice cream is a must-try & I always buy a few bottles of the mead when I'm in the area.

✳ **Dark Side Chocolates** Shop 1, 19 South Coast Hwy; ☏ 0407 984 820; w darksidechocolates. com.au; ⏱ 09.00–14.00 Wed–Mon. Sells vegan chocolates as well as chocolates with bush flavours like wattleseed, finger lime & lemon myrtle.

Denmark Chocolate Company 2023 South Coast Hwy; ☏ 9840 9708; w denmarkchocolate. com.au; ⏱ 10.00–16.30 Wed–Sun, closed May & Nov. Gourmet chocolates paired with a variety of beers, wines & liqueurs, plus hot chocolates. They have some exotic flavours, like sambuca truffle, lime & mango ganache, & 'tigers' – chocolate, rum & orange.

Denmark Good Food Factory 2927 South Coast Hwy; ☏ 9840 9900; w denmarkgoodfoodfactory.com.au; ⏱ 10.00–16.00 daily. As you head west towards Walpole, you'll come to this factory specialising in traditional English toffees but which has also expanded into a range of other products including brittles, sauces, jams & dressings.

Ducketts Mill Wines & Denmark Farmhouse Cheese 1678 Scotsdale Rd; ☏ 9840 9844; w duckettsmillwines.com.au; ⏱ 09.00–17.00 daily. Notable for its array of fudges & cheeses, in addition to wines & ports. They also serve cheese tasting platters & toasties.

Wine

Rickety Gate 1949 Scotsdale Rd; ☏ 9840 9503; w ricketygate.com.au; ⏱ 11.00–16.30 Sat–Sun. One of the finest wineries on the Scotsdale Rd, they do outstanding sparklings as well as high-quality Rieslings.

Rockcliffe 18 Hamilton Rd; ☏ 9848 1951; w rockcliffe.com.au; ⏱ 11.00–17.00 daily. James Halliday has awarded this outstanding winery 5 stars for 7 consecutive years. For reds, try their Shiraz & Cabernet Sauvignon; their 2018 Shiraz was rated particularly highly by Ray Jordan.

Singlefile 90 Walter Rd; ☏ 1300 885 807; w singlefilewines.com; ⏱ 11.00–17.00 daily. This highly respected winery does excellent whites; their Semillon Sauvignon Blanc is first-rate, as is their Fiano. It was founded by a couple who were geology & mining consultants; their daughter & son-in-law oversee the day-to-day operations & draw on their experiences of having lived in Europe.

WHAT TO SEE AND DO

Beaches A short drive south of town, **Ocean Beach** is effectively Denmark's town beach. It's enormously popular; this is where Wilson Inlet empties out into the sea, and so you can choose from the more tranquil waters of the inlet itself or the surf conditions out in the sea – **South Coast Surfing Lessons** (☏ 0401 349 854; w southcoastsurfinglessons.com.au) will teach you what you need to know. The **Lions Lookout** here is a good vantage point from which to whale-watch.

Between Ocean Beach and the Greens Pool area are three separate beaches, which in the local lexicon are referred to as **Lights Beach**. The eastern beach is home to Princess Pool, which creates a waterfall as it continually fills and empties with the waves. The central of the three beaches has wonderful views, but is not great for swimming due to rough surf and strong currents. Lights Beach West is another beautiful spot but requires a hike along the Bibbulmun (see box, page 109).

William Bay National Park ✳ A 15-minute drive west of Denmark just off the South Coast Highway, this is one of the showcase national parks on the South Coast. Its centrepiece is the fabulous **Greens Pool**, sheltered by scattered granite outcrops that form a break. There is plenty of safe swimming and snorkelling here, in the clear, dazzling waters that fringe the white sandy beach stretching down the coast. A short walking trail, with great views over the Southern Ocean, leads from Greens Pool to **Elephant Rocks**, a cluster of giant granite boulders (the 'elephants') sitting in a narrow channel, which leads out to the Southern Ocean. The boulders break up the current and create ideal sheltered swimming conditions. The trail leads up and over an outcrop, from where there are spectacular views down to the rocks before you descend to the beach. A climb up **Tower Hill** offers great views down towards Elephant Rocks and Greens Pool – it is hard going, however, and part of the Bibbulmun Track (see box, page 109), so if you want to give that a go, plan for this to be a serious outing in itself. Access is before you get to the Greens Pool car park.

A few kilometres east of Elephant Rocks is **Madfish Bay**, where at low tide there is a sandbar crossing the water to an island on the other side, to which you can walk across. Just north of Madfish is **Waterfall Beach**, another popular swimming spot, named after the waterfall that tumbles down the granite and into the ocean – especially prominent in winter, which is the rainy season on the South Coast. You can walk from Greens Pool and Elephants Rock to Madfish Bay, but you are better off taking the 2WD-suitable path.

Stretching to the west of Greens Pool for 9km is **Mazzoletti Beach**, which in turn leads to the 5km-long **Parry Beach**, which has good surfing.

WEST FROM DENMARK Although these sights are closer to Walpole (page 181), most people visit as a day trip from Denmark or Albany.

Valley of the Giants ✳ (Valley of the Giants Rd; ☎9840 8263; w valleyofthegiants. com.au; ⏰ 09.00–17.00 daily; adult/child A$21/10.50) This tingle forest hosts an acclaimed and iconic West Australian attraction, the 600m **Tree Top Walk**. This suspended metal boardwalk ascends 40m into the canopy of centuries-old giant tingle trees, providing some of the most spectacular forest views in Australia. Adjacent is the 450m **Ancient Empire Walk**, a sealed path on the forest floor that weaves among 400-year-old red tingles, which can have a base circumference of 20m and are only found in this small section of the state. Yellow tingles are also seen on the walk; much shorter, at only about 35m tall, their timber has a yellowish tinge.

Peaceful Bay ✳ This hamlet, accessed via Peaceful Bay Road, just 1km or so past the eastern Valley of the Giants turn-off, is home to an excellent sheltered pool offering great swimming and snorkelling. I have seen dolphins come into the shallows to ask for fish from beach fishermen here, and then sulk away, disappointed, when the answer was no. **Peaceful Bay Caravan Park** ✳ (East Av; ☎9840 8060; w peacefulbaywa.com.au; ⏰ 10.00–18.00 Sun–Fri, 09.00–18.00 Sat) has some of the best fish and chips in the state – they catch the fish (dhufish, hapuka, nannygai to name a few) themselves from their deep-sea boat – and it is worth the drive out here just for lunch. They also have a range of powered and unpowered sites plus a general store.

Esperance & the Outback Riviera

Many visitors to Western Australia bypass Esperance because of its distance from Perth (some 700km), but this is a real shame. I believe this well-equipped Outback town is the undisputed heavyweight champion when it comes to beaches. Once you've visited, you'll forever be comparing every future stretch of sand you encounter to the ones here – the colours, water clarity and lack of crowds converge in this region like nowhere else.

The area also boasts two of WA's finest drives. The first is the state's most underrated 2WD-suitable track, which cuts right through the Great Western Woodlands – at 16 million hectares, these are the largest temperate woodlands on earth and an incredible store of biodiversity. The second is the epic 700km trip to 'cross the Nullarbor' from Norseman to Eucla on the border with South Australia. Following the country's longest straight road, this is the trip of a lifetime for many Australians.

BREMER BAY, HOPETOUN AND FITZGERALD RIVER NATIONAL PARK

On the coast between Albany and Esperance, the tiny communities of Bremer Bay and Hopetoun have a relaxed-yet-isolated feel, which is the real appeal – but don't expect much in the way of services. Beachcombing, fishing and whale-watching are the major draws, while Fitzgerald River National Park has been recognised by UNESCO as a biodiversity hotspot with over 2,500 flora species – headlined by the endemic royal hakea.

BREMER BAY Sitting on the Wellstead Estuary, where it meets the sea, Bremer Bay is a longstanding West Australian holiday favourite – so much that, at times, it can feel like half the farmers in the state have holiday homes here. Beaches are the main draw, but it's also popular for fishing and whale watching, and is the gateway to the western end of Fitzgerald River National Park.

Getting there and away Bremer Bay is effectively the end of the line; the only access is via the Borden–Bremer Bay Road, which runs for 60km from the South Coast Highway. It's 181km/2 hours to/from Albany and 380km/4 hours to/from Esperance.

⫟ Where to stay and eat

🏠 **Bremer Bay Resort** (21 rooms) 1 Frantom Way; \ 9837 4133; **w** bremerbayresort.com.au. 4-star resort offering a mixture of motel rooms, spa apartments & a 2-bedroom villa. The on-site Mt

Barren Restaurant serves 3 meals a day (plus room service); the crab linguini is a winner. There is also a bar & bottleshop. **$$$**

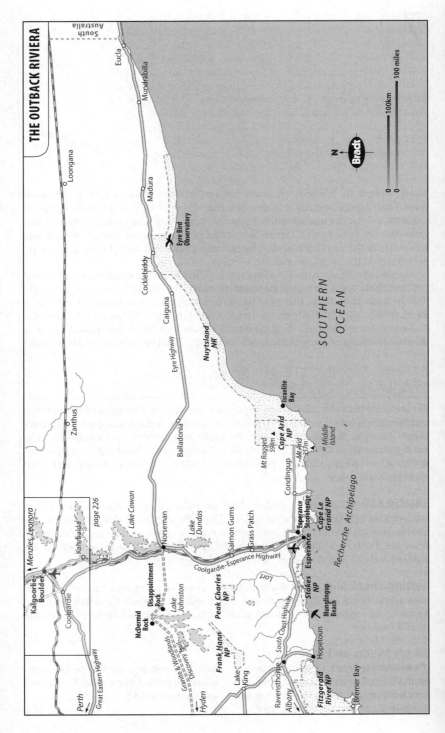

THE OUTBACK RIVIERA

South Australia

Eucla

Mundrabilla

Loongana

Madura

Cocklebiddy

Caiguna

Eyre Highway

Eyre Bird Observatory

Nuytsland NR

Zanthus

Balladonia

Lake Cowan

Norseman

Lake Dundas

Salmon Gums

Grass Patch

Condingup

Israelite Bay

Mt Ragged 594m ▲

Cape Arid NP

▲ Mt Arid 357m

∞ Middle Island

SOUTHERN OCEAN

Esperance Stonehenge

Esperance

Cape Le Grand NP

Recherche Archipelago

Coolgardie–Esperance Highway

Lort

Stokes NP

Munglinoup Beach

Peak Charles NP

McDermid Rock

Disappointment Rock

Lake Johnston

Frank Hann NP

Granite & Woodlands Discovery T

Lake King

Hopetoun

South Coast Highway

Fitzgerald River NP

Ravensthorpe

Albany

Bremer Bay

Menzies, Leonora ↑

Kalgoorlie, Boulder

page 226

Kalgoorlie Boulder

Coolgardie

Great Eastern Highway

Perth ↗

Hyden

N

Bradt

0   100km
0   100 miles

✕ Bremer Bay Brewing Company

1 Seadragon Av; ⓕ BremerBayBrewingCompany; ⏲ 11.30–21.00 daily. A welcome newcomer to town, with pizzas, nachos, burgers & plenty of award-winning beers on tap, many of which are making their way to menus across the state. Walk-ins only. $$

What to see and do It's almost always whale-watching season in Bremer Bay, with the southern rights arriving to give birth and rear their young between July and November, and in summer the orcas come – the only place in Australia where you are guaranteed to meet them. During a six-week summertime period, **Bremer Bay Canyon**, 70km offshore, is filled with nutrients by a current from the Antarctic, attracting all sorts of marine life – and their predators, such as the orcas. The discovery of the marine significance here is new; expeditions to the canyon started only in 2014. Two companies can organise excursions (roughly 8hrs, starting from A$385), although neither are based in Bremer Bay: **Naturaliste Charters** (Dunsborough; ☎9750 5500; w whales-australia.com.au) and **Whale Watch Western Australia** (Fremantle; ☎1300 388 893 w whalewatchwesternaustralia.com).

There are plenty of great beaches for swimming, surfing and fishing. Probably the most famous of these is **Blossoms Beach**, to the south of town, with a glorious setting backed by vegetation, sugar-white sand and water that is shallow for quite a way out. Just north of here is **Native Dog Beach**, which is popular with surfers, while **Fishery Beach**, **Bremer Beach** (the town beach) and **John Cove** are all considered good swimming beaches.

Fishing is extremely popular in Bremer Bay, with herring, salmon, groper, black bream, millet and snapper commonly caught. The Bremer River, Short Beach (which has a reef) and Fishery Beach are all good spots, but really you are spoiled for choice. There are bait and tackle shops in town.

HOPETOUN Tiny Hopetoun retains an under-developed, lazy beach-shack vibe that is instantly appealing, and its position 50km south of the South Coast Highway helps it remain largely undiscovered – most travellers tend to zip past it en route to Albany or Esperance. Though infrastructure is not what you'll find in bigger towns, there are quality services around and some spectacular beaches too – probably a notch below those in Esperance, but still world class. It's also the gateway to the eastern side of Fitzgerald River National Park.

The town is divided over whether its 'undiscovered' status is a good or bad thing. More visitors means more economic development, but at the same time there are serious local concerns over the impact that increased tourism will have on the fragile biodiversity of Fitzgerald River National Park.

Getting there and away Hopetoun is 50km from the South Coast Highway along the Hopetoun–Ravensthorpe Road. It's 182km/2hrs from Esperance, and 331km/3½hrs from Albany. Transwa coaches run to Ravensthorpe (45mins; A$10 one-way), with connections to East Perth and Albany (5hrs; A$58 one-way).

🛏 Where to stay and eat

🏠 **Hopetoun Motel & Chalet Village** (14 units) 49 Veal St; ☎9838 3219; w hopetounmotel. com.au. In a rammed-earth building that helps with climate control year-round, the rooms here are spacious, comfortable & walking distance to town. If you want to cook, upgrading to the self-contained motel units that have an oven, hob & fridge is worth it; the chalets, which have 2 bedrooms & bunks as well as cooking facilities, are good value if you have a group or family & want to self-cater. $$$

Wavecrest Village & Tourist Park (16 accommodations) 279 Hopetoun-Ravensthorpe Rd; 9838 3888; w wavecrestvillage.net.au. Multiple caravan options plus self-contained cabins, as well as extra-large places for motorhomes & wide vehicles. Excellent facilities including swimming pool, tennis court & on-site bistro, known for its theme nights & good pizzas & burgers. The rocky road sundae is a hit. **$$$**

Hopetoun Beachside Caravan Park 14-30 The Esplanade; 9838 3096; w hopetounbeachside.com.au. Just a few hundred metres from the beach at the foot of town, with campsites, caravan sites, cabins & self-contained units. Facilities include coin laundry & camp kitchen. **$$**

Port Hotel 11 Veal St; 9838 3053; e porthotel1@bigpond.com.au; f PortHotelHopetoun. This prominent 1901 building at the base of town offers great views of the ocean. Rooms have shared facilities. The restaurant is the best place to eat in town & gets packed – excellent takes on pub classics, try the garlic prawns & rice. *Cabins* **$$**, *sites* **$**

Christine's Kitchen 32 Veal St; 0474 181 515; 07.00–19.00 daily. Good place for pies, wraps & smoothies. **$**

What to see and do The groyne lies at the end of town, to the right (west) of which are two popular swimming beaches: **Mary Ann Haven**, which was the original name of the area before it was gazetted in 1901 as Hopetoun (named after the first Governor-General of WA, the Earl of Hopetoun, John Hope), which connects the groyne to Flathead Point; and around Flathead Point, **West Beach** (not to be confused with the other West Beach in Fitzgerald River National Park).

Some more excellent beaches are to the east of town. The Esplanade turns into Southern Ocean Road, which passes some local favourites. The first part of the drive from Hopetoun is sealed, but it does become unsealed (though 2WD suitable) at Twelve Mile Beach. Of the long string of sands on this drive, **Starvation Bay**, 48km east of town, is probably the locals' favourite swimming beach in the area – in addition to gorgeous colours in the bay, there are small rocky coves that can be waded in. Twelve Mile Beach is also a good spot for fishing (boat).

There is also a long-distance hiking track, the **Ravensthorpe–Hopetoun Railway Track** (Class 2; 39km one-way), which is particularly scenic in wildflower season. The railway track itself was used for gold mining, opening in 1909 to transport materials from Ravensthorpe to the port at Hopetoun, and then later on for farming. However, this stopped in 1935 and the railway has been disused since.

AROUND HOPETOUN Just north of the South Coast Highway, the town of **Ravensthorpe** is a mining centre and transit junction. There is not much in town to interest visitors other than some petrol stations and cafés, but behind town are the **Ravensthorpe Ranges**, part of the Fitzgerald Biosphere, which are widely believed to house some of the largest numbers of eucalypts in the world. Traversing a roughly 40km-long chain of low hills, the 29km, 4x4-only **Range Top Scenic Drive** provides excellent views and wildflower sightings (in season, from August to October), passing Mt Benson (404m) and Mt McMahon (274m); you can get as far as the Archer Drive Lookout in a 2WD. Call into the **Ravensthorpe Visitor Centre** (86 Morgans St; 9838 1191; 10.00–16.00 Mon–Fri, 10.00–16.00 alternating Sats) for detailed brochures on this and other scenic drives in the area.

Back on the coast, 69km east of Hopetoun and 131km west of Esperance, is **Munglingup Beach**, which after lengthy obscurity is fast becoming a visitors' favourite – every time I come back, there are more and more people. Reef protected, around a picturesque, sweeping expanse of beach, this is a good place for sheltered snorkelling and paddling. At times I've even seen horseriding along the sand here. There is a campground (no power or potable water) in the car park, and the **Munglingup Beach**

Holiday Park (Munglingup Beach Rd; 📞9075 1155; w munglinupbeach.com.au; **$$**) has powered/unpowered sites, cabins and caravans. Access to Munglingup Beach is by Springdale Road, from either direction; turn at Munglingup Beach Road.

FITZGERALD RIVER NATIONAL PARK About halfway between Albany and Esperance, the Fitzgerald Biosphere was originally recognised by UNESCO's Man and Biosphere Program in 1978 and is considered to be one of the most important biodiversity spots in the country, with over 2,500 species of flora. About one-fifth of WA's plant species can be found here, and whales and dolphins just *love* the waters off the coast – it is one of the state's most reliable places for sightings.

Though the biosphere is huge, comprising 1.5 million hectares, and includes the townsites of Hopetoun, Ravensthorpe, Jerramungup and Bremer Bay, the focus of it is Fitzgerald River National Park which lies on the coast between Bremer Bay and Hopetoun, and is bounded to the north by the South Coast Highway. The park has two distinct entrances – the western end, accessed near Bremer Bay, and the eastern end, accessed near Hopetoun. The two ends are not connected by road; to go from one to the other, you need to leave the park, get on the South Coast Highway and re-enter at the other end. The western end is the more isolated and difficult to reach but is the most reliable and dependable for whale watching (and Point Ann is simply breathtaking). The eastern end has more accessible beaches, is easier to travel in a 2WD and has Hopetoun as a nearby base.

The western side The western end of the park is headlined by **Point Ann**, one of the state's premier whale-watching spots, complete with lookout point. Aside from a dreamy backdrop of white beaches, blue waters and bluish-purple peaks – reason enough to visit – in whale-watching season (from June to October, but particularly August) the cove becomes a sort of nursery for southern right whales, and it is very common to see multiple mother whales resting with their calves in very shallow water – it can be surprising just how close to the shoreline they actually come. The most mother-calf pairs I've seen at any one time is half a dozen, but I have had others tell me they've seen as many as 30.

Walking routes in this area include the short **Point Ann Heritage Trail** (Class 2; 1.5km return), following part of the original Rabbit-Proof Fence, offing great views out over the bay and more opportunities to spot whales, the **Mt Maxwell Walk** (200m return) which leads to a viewpoint on the eponymous peak, and the **West Mount Barren Walk** (1.7km return), noted for its flora including the pink-and-yellow Qualup bell (*Pimelea physodes*), which resembles something of an upside-down tulip.

If you are up for a long-distance hike, the **Mamang Trail** (Class 4; 31km return; 'Mamang' is Noongar for whale) connects Point Ann with the Fitzgerald River Inlet campsite. This is a remote trail, best covered over two days, with no road access beyond the starting point at Point Ann – there is a 4x4 track to the campsite but it does not pass by Point Ann (and the track is frequently closed due to weather – call ahead to check its status). The first part follows the sand along St Mary's Beach, before sloping up to Lake Nameless, with views of the peaks like West Mt Barren en route. The trail continues through dunes and along ridges to the Point Charles Lookout and Fitzgerald Beach, and after about 1km from there you reach the very basic Fitzgerald River Inlet campsite; you may see woylies and tammar wallabies around. You can return to Point Ann along the trail or take the beach route the entire way back. DPaW's excellent Mamang Walk Trail booklet has detailed information including half-day and one-day options for this walk, and can be downloaded from DPaW's website.

Getting there and away Access to the western end of the park is by the unsealed Devil's Creek Road, possible in a 2WD, but prepare for a lengthy and difficult journey. Sometimes the road is impassable, but it will be noted at the entry gates. If you're coming from the South Coast Highway (heading north towards Jerramungup), turn off on to Devil's Creek Road (which changes its name to Pabelup Drive inside the park) and then take the Point Ann Road turn-off. Altogether, it's 67km from the highway to Point Ann. The West Mt Barren turn-off is before you reach Point Ann Road, and the Mt Maxwell lookout is just at the park boundary on Devil's Creek Road. If you are coming from the South Coast Highway north of the park – that is, east of Jerramungup – take Quiss Road, another unsealed but 2WD-suitable road, and after 50km you will reach the Point Ann Road turn-off. The 4x4 Fitzgerald Inlet Track to Point Charles and the inlet's campsite can also be accessed from Quiss Road.

Where to stay and eat In addition to the DPaW campsites, the Heritage-listed **Quaalup Homestead Wilderness Retreat** (Gairdner Rd; \ 9837 4124; w whalesandwildflowers.com.au; **$$$**), in the western end of the park, has self-catering units, chalets and cabins; dinner can also be arranged if booked well in advance.

The eastern side Primarily accessed just north of Hopetoun, this side of the park is very different from the west. For one, there is a major townsite just kilometres away, and secondly there is a sealed, scenic road (Hamersley Dr) running through this end. **Barrens Beach** is one of the star attractions here – the locals' choice in the park, with various shades of blue, black rocks and white sand providing a beautiful setting for sheltered swimming and snorkelling. **Mylie's Beach**, just west of Barrens, is also a favourite of whales, and sometimes mothers and their calves come almost right up to the shore. A short hop south, **West Beach** is a choice spot for bottlenose dolphins – I have seen them playing and riding the waves very close to the shore.

In terms of walking, **East Mount Barrens Walk** (Class 4; 2.6km return) gives views out to Hopetoun and is accessed from Hamersley Drive. The walk up to the 450m summit offers lovely vistas out to the Eyre and Barrens ranges, Hopetoun and the Southern Ocean. There are two shorter walks: the **Sepulcralis Hill Walk** (Class 3; 600m return), with views out towards East Mt Barren and over violet banksias; and the **Barrens Lookout Walk** (Class 3; 250m return), which has a sensational bird's-eye viewpoint of the narrow isthmus separating the Southern Ocean with its sparkling beach, and the greyer Culham Inlet.

Starting from Cave Point, the **Hakea Trail** (23km one-way) leads through the magnificent Hammersley Dunes to the fantastic beach at Quoin Head, which is accessible only by 4x4 track. If you can do only one long-distance walk in the park, choose this over the Mamang (page 207) – although longer, the Hakea has a more varied landscape and a better selection of lookouts. Swimming is possible at Quoin Head, but always check conditions; the Southern Ocean is unpredictable, and this is a remote location. 4x4 tracks do intersect with the track at the Whalebone Campground and Quoin Head. Note that the campground is at Whalebone, not Quoin Head – once you finish the trail, it will be about a 3km trip back to Whalebone.

Getting there and away Getting to the eastern end of the park is much easier than the west; the turn-off for Hamersley Drive, the sealed road into the park, is about 5km north of Hopetoun and very well signposted. Just on the north edge of town, Hamersley Drive also leads to the park and becomes unsealed just after

FLORA IN FITZGERALD RIVER NATIONAL PARK

The unofficial emblem of the Fitzgerald River National Park, the royal hakea (*Hakea victoria*) may look like a hippie cactus, but this rigid, vertical plant with bursts of neon orange, yellow and red among its otherwise green exterior, is not a cactus – it's a shrub. Endemic to WA and growing up to 3m tall, it loves rocky landscapes, sand and quartz, meaning the area between Albany and Esperance fits the bill perfectly and huge numbers of the plant are clustered in the national park. It does have some small flowers – red, pink and white – but these are often hidden by the large green leaves. The plant is easy to grow from seeds and tolerates frost, but it does need cold weather to form its bright colours, and it doesn't like humidity.

Another iconic native plant you are likely to see here is the scarlet banksia (*Banksia coccinea*). Growing to between 4m and 8m, its red and white flowers are particularly striking and it grows along the roadside in the park. Like the royal hakea, it does not like humid conditions and is clustered mostly in this region of WA.

Miley's Beach when it turns north towards Sepulcralis Hill – you can follow this all the way back to the South Coast Highway, about two-thirds of the way to Ravensthorpe from Jerramungup. This is a 2WD-suitable road – however, it is heavily corrugated and can be in poor condition; the last time I attempted it, I turned back after a few kilometres.

ESPERANCE

Esperance has a spectacular coastal setting and has taken full advantage of it. The seafront promenade in the CBD, lined with the town's famous pines, has a beautiful vista out to the massive granite outcrops in the Bay of Isles. To the west of the CBD, the 40km circular Great Ocean Drive is one of the best coastal roads in Australia, passing postcard-worthy beach after beach after beach, while the national parks to the east of town present even more squeaky, sugar-white sands framed by golden-brown outcrops – most of which you are likely to have all to yourself.

The Ngadju and Esperance Noongar peoples have native title in the Shire of Esperance. The Ngadju have resided in the area between Kalgoorlie-Boulder and Esperance for over 50,000 years and are particularly known for their song and dance, and have native title in (generally) the northern part of the shire; Esperance Noongar country is connected to the mallee landscape, which they believe makes up their country, and have native title in (generally) the southern region.

In 1792, a fierce storm forced two French ships – the *Esperance* ('hope') and the *Recherche* ('research') – to seek shelter, which they found at Observatory Island near Cape Le Grand. Although they named landmarks in the area – the future township taking the name of the *Esperance*, and the archipelago taking the name of the other ship – it was not until 1861 that a party from South Australia led an expedition here, as generous regulations on pastoral leases were enacted to encourage westward migration; and in 1864, the Dempster brothers arrived from Northam and Albany and began pastoral operations. Relations between the European settlers and the local Aboriginal peoples were tension-plagued and resulted in some high-profile tit-for-tat killings in the 1870s and early 1880s.

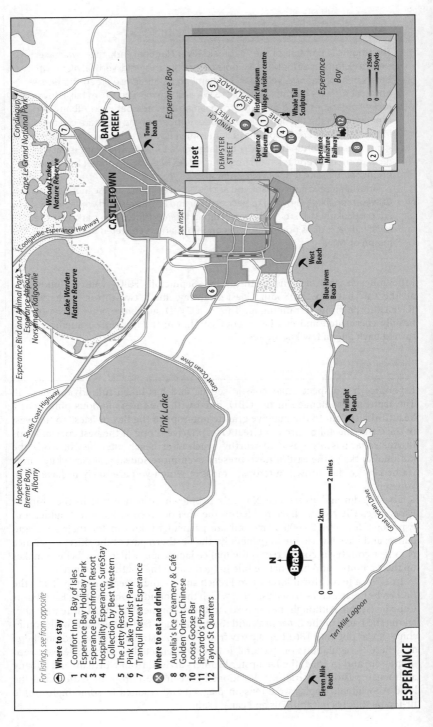

210

ESPERANCE

For listings, see from opposite

Where to stay
1 Comfort Inn – Bay of Isles
2 Esperance Bay Holiday Park
3 Esperance Beachfront Resort
4 Hospitality Esperance, SureStay Collection by Best Western
5 The Jetty Resort
6 Pink Lake Tourist Park
7 Tranquil Retreat Esperance

Where to eat and drink
8   Aurelia's Ice Creamery & Café
9   Golden Orient Chinese
10 Loose Goose Bar
11 Riccardo's Pizza
12 Taylor St Quarters

Inset
Esperance Museum
Historic Museum Village & visitor centre
Whale Tail Sculpture
Esperance Miniature Railway
DEMPSTER STREET
WINDICH STREET
THE ESPLANADE
Esperance Bay

CASTLETOWN
BANDY CREEK
Town beach
Esperance Bay
Cape Le Grand National Park
Condingup
Woody Lakes Nature Reserve
Coolgardie-Esperance Highway
Lake Warden Nature Reserve
Esperance Bird and Animal Park
Esperance Airport, Norseman, Kalgoorlie
South Coast Highway
Hopetoun, Bremer Bay, Albany
Pink Lake
Great Ocean Drive
see inset
West Beach
Blue Haven Beach
Twilight Beach
Ten Mile Lagoon
Eleven Mile Beach
Great Ocean Drive

2km
2 miles
N

After fits and starts, the population finally started increasing as the viability of farming in the region became known. The railway connecting the town to the Goldfields opened in 1927, and the Port of Esperance became a vital transit centre for the Goldfields and mining industry, which still remains today – iron ore, nickel and a whole heap of agricultural products like grain are exported from here.

Today, though an isolated Outback town, Esperance is larger than one might expect, with a population of around 15,000. With multiple national parks and attractions within easy reach, and plenty of accommodation and restaurant choices (plus commercial flights), this is the best place to base yourself when exploring this region.

GETTING THERE AND AROUND Esperance is 700km/8 hours from Perth, 400km/4 hours from Kalgoorlie and 480km/5 hours from Albany. Transwa **coaches** take a bit over 10 hours from East Perth (from A$99 one-way), almost 10 hours to Albany (changing at Wagin; from A$74 one-way) and 5 hours to Kalgoorlie (from A$64 one-way).

Esperance Airport is 22km north of town near Gibson on the Coolgardie–Esperance Highway; Rex flies there from Perth (1hr 35mins; from A$216 one-way). If you don't have a car, you will need to take a taxi into town.

To make the most of Esperance and the surrounding coastline and national parks, you will need your own vehicle.

TOURIST INFORMATION

Esperance Visitor Centre Cnr Dempster & Kent St; ☎ 9083 1555; w visitesperance.com; ⏱ 09.00–17.00 Mon, Tue & Thu, 08.00–17.00 Wed & Fri, 09.00–16.00 Sat, 09.00–14.00 Sun & public holidays

WHERE TO STAY *Map, opposite*

Hospitality Esperance, SureStay Collection by Best Western (50 rooms) 44–46 The Esplanade; ☎ 9071 1999; w esperance. wa.hospitalityinns.com.au. Though well located on the seafront, rooms here are fairly standard & pedestrian. The on-site Seasons Restaurant, however, does good steaks & an excellent cooked b/fast – a wonderful engine-starter for a day of exploration. **$$$**

Tranquil Retreat Esperance (3 rooms) 115 Tranquil Dr; ☎ 9071 5392; w tranquilretreat. com.au. Northeast of town near Woody Lake Nature Reserve, the 6.5ha property offers tastefully decorated en-suite rooms with complimentary port, chocolate & cake. A great option if you want to be away from the hustle & bustle of town. Fantastic b/fast inc. **$$$**

Comfort Inn – Bay of Isles (62 rooms) 32 The Esplanade; ☎ 9071 9000; w comfortinnbayofisles.com.au. Popular, reliable chain right on the seafront; spa rooms are tastefully done & worth the extra money. On-site restaurant Eljay's is also very popular; book ahead. **$$**

Esperance Bay Holiday Park (16 accommodations) 162 Dempster St; ☎ 9071 2237; e info@esperancebayholidaypark.com.au; w summerstar.com.au/caravan-parks/esperance-bay. With chalet units that can sleep up to 6 in addition to camping & caravan sites & only a block back from the seafront, this park has a camp kitchen, playgrounds & dump point. The units & chalets have their own bathrooms & are good choices for families. Pet friendly. **$$**

Esperance Beachfront Resort (10 units) 19 The Esplanade; ☎ 9071 2513; w esperancebeachfrontresort.com.au. One of our go-tos when we're in town; you can't beat the location (right on the seafront), the cleanlinesss & spaciousness of the units (fully self-contained with separate bedroom & living areas) & very competitive pricing. **$$**

The Jetty Resort (32 rooms) 2 Dempster St; ☎ 9071 3333; w thejettyresort.com.au. Near the (now closed & inaccessible) jetty, their attractive balconies are visible as you drive into the CBD. Though interiors can seem dated, they

7

are very good value, clean & comfortable. Hire equipment like kayaks, surfboards & fishing rods are available. A good option. **$$**

🏠 **Pink Lake Tourist Park** 113 Pink Lake Rd; 📞 1800 011 311; w pinklakepark.com.au. Out in Nulsen, 2.5km west of town, this complex offers powered & unpowered sites as well as cabins & villas. Camp kitchen, BBQs, dump point & children's play areas. Competitively priced. Pet friendly. **$$**

🍴 WHERE TO EAT AND DRINK *Map, page 210*

🍴 **Loose Goose Bar & Restaurant** 9A Andrew St; 📞 9071 2320; w loosegooseesperance.com.au; ⏰ 16.00–midnight Tue–Sat. It's hard to miss this lime green shopfront in the CBD. I'd recommend the curried beef & there is a good cocktail menu, but the restaurant is pricey. **$$$**

🍴 **Taylor St Quarters** 1 Taylor St; 📞 0457 232 039; w taylorst.com.au; ⏰ 11.00–21.00 Wed–Sun. Behind the clock tower, this popular spot serves trendy brunches, local fish dishes (Shark Bay prawns, Albany oysters) & stylish sharing platters – the mushroom gnocchi is a winner. Ample drinks list; also a good place to stop for a coffee & a snack mid-afternoon. Book ahead. **$$$**

🍴 **Golden Orient Chinese Restaurant** 49 Dempster St; 📞 9071 3744; ⏰ 11.30–14.00 & 16.30–22.00 daily. A huge variety of dishes from BBQ to garlic to satay; the variety of soups here go down well during Esperance's chilly winters & the Mongolian beef is good. **$$**

🍴 **Aurelia's Ice Creamery & Café** 84–85 The Esplanade; 📞 9072 0002; 📘 aureliasicc; ⏰ 07.00–18.00 Mon & Thu, 08.00–17.00 Tue–Wed, 08.00–18.00 Fri, 08.00–17.30 Sat–Sun. Popular ice-cream parlour with a great number of flavours (my favourite is liquorice); also offers meals. **$**

🍴 **Riccardo's Pizza** 51 The Esplanade; 📞 9072 1244; ⏰ 16.30–20.30 Tue–Thu, 16.00–21.00 Fri–Sat, 16.00–19.30 Sun. Huge variety of pizzas – from traditional to seafood to gluten-free – plus comforting lasagne. Good value. **$**

WHAT TO SEE AND DO The town's famous pines curve around the footpath along Esperance Bay, creating a foreshore that links the bay to the town and provides beach access in front of the CBD. One of the most prominent sights here is the **Whale Tail Sculpture**, created by local artists Cindy Poole and (British-born but now Esperance-local) Jason Wooldridge as part of the foreshore redevelopment project in 2014 – the sculpture represents the southern right whale population in the offshore waters. Though the **town beach** can be accessed anywhere along the foreshore, the main swimming areas are in the suburb of Castletown, north of the CBD, along Castletown Quays Road and at Bandy Creek (take Goldfields Road to Daw Drice), which is also a boat harbour and popular fishing spot.

Black Jack Charters (📞 0429 106 960; w blackjackcharters.com.au) run deep-sea and adventure fishing charters (full-/half-day options starting at A$240/170pp), as well as custom trips for big game in 4,000m-deep waters. They can also be chartered for dives, including at shipwrecks. **Esperance Diving and Fishing** (📞 9071 5757; e info@esperancedivingandfishing.com.au; w esperancedivingandfishing.com.au) offers all-inclusive fishing charters (from A$250pp but with cheaper 'rod-share' options available), plus dives, diving courses and shipwreck dives.

A good place to learn about Esperance's history is the **Esperance Museum** (6 James St; 📞 9083 1580; w esperance.wa.gov.au/esperance-museum; ⏰ 13.30–16.30 daily; A$8/3.50 adult/child), a vast warehouse brimming with some 4,000 objects – including a 19th-century train carriage that you can climb aboard. There is also a model of *Skylab*, the NASA space station that crashed near here in 1979 (see box, page 220), with actual debris (including the oxygen tank) from the wreck. Nearby is the **Historic Museum Village** (Dempster St; free; ⏰ varies by shop), a collection of restored old buildings (including a school, courthouse and chemist) dating from the late 1800s, which have been repurposed into shops and galleries; it is easy to

Esperance Bird and Animal Park 549 Coolgardie–Esperance Hwy; 9076 1067; w esperancebirdandanimalparkcafe.com; 09.00–16.00 Thu–Fri, 08.00–16.00 Sat–Sun. With over 200 birds & native animals, this is a great place for a family day out – you can feed some of the animals (the emus will tuck their long necks into the paper feed bags to peck at what's in there) & there's also a mob of kangaroos roaming about. There is also an on-site café & accommodation.

Esperance Miniature Railway Taylor St; 9083 1555; Oct–Apr & school holidays 10.00–16.00 Sat–Sun. Leaving from in front of the clock tower & Taylor St Quarters, this offers train rides for all ages that go around the surrounding park for A$3.

imagine yourself in the period as you wander through here – though it's worth noting that the buildings were moved here from other parts of Esperance and this is not an intact historical quarter in its original location. The **Museum Village Markets** are held here (usually) on alternating Sundays.

Great Ocean Drive ✳ Starting from the town centre, this 40km circular route west of town is one of the best scenic drives in the state. Starting on Twilight Beach Road at Esperance's southern boundary, the road quickly sweeps westward along the coastline. The views start almost immediately, as you drop down from the first hill towards **West Beach**, when a vista of the Southern Ocean unfolds in front of you. This is the first beach you get to on the drive, 3km from the CBD, and how glorious it is – a sweeping white bay with a reef in front of it and a big granite hill forming a massive natural wall on the eastern side. You can swim here, carefully – note the signs about rips. **Blue Haven Beach** is next, about 4km beyond, and is one of the most popular swimming beaches – with calm conditions close to the shore and a stunning outlook to Chapman Point and West Beach in the distance. Long-distance views and more beaches then follow for about 5km until you reach Esperance's star, **Twilight Beach**, roughly 12km from town and routinely voted one of the best beaches in Australia. While it has the pre-requisite vanilla sands and impeccably turquoise waters, what sets it apart are the unusually shaped outcrops just offshore – one with a massive circular dent in it about two-thirds of the way up – that, when photographed with the seagrasses behind the beach, offer a truly photogenic scene. Though the postcard-worthy landscapes continue after Twilight Beach, both **Ten Mile Lagoon** and **Eleven Mile Beach** are very attractive with sand dunes in the background and a reef bar in the foreground – though the water here can be too shallow for swimming. From there, the road cuts inland towards the centre, passing **Pink Lake** – part of a nature reserve, although the water is normally a milky grey; it used to be pink, but hasn't been in years owing to over-harvesting of salt from the lake – the reduction in salt has meant that the algae and archaea that helped make the lake pink are no longer growing. The Shire of Esperance is, however, considering a trial to put more salt into the lake in the hope it will turn pink again, but this is still in the discussion stage. Don't confuse Pink Lake with Lake Hillier (page 214), which maintains a bright-pink hue and is the darling of travel brochures.

Lake Warden Nature Reserve Recognised as a Ramsar Site of International Importance, this wetland complex is made up of a series of lakes on the north edge of town and can support nearly 30,000 waterbirds including hooded plovers,

The number of shark attacks per year in Australia is increasing. Since 2000, there have been over 25 attacks in WA; the watershed moment being the attack in November 2000 that killed businessman Ken Crew as he swum his morning routine off Cottesloe Beach. In recent years, however, Esperance has seemingly become ground zero for fatal shark attacks, with three events occurring since 2018. In that year, teenager Laeticia Brouwer was killed while surfing at Wylie Bay; Gary Johnson was lost in early 2020 while diving 5km south of Esperance; and surfer Andrew Sharpe was a victim at Wylie Bay in late 2020, an attack that was witnessed by multiple other surfers. Unfortunately, nobody knows why the number of attacks has suddenly spiked upwards.

The issue of what, if anything, to do about sharks has been a hotly debated topic in state government, with proposals including everything from lethal drumlines and non-lethal shark nets and barriers to doing nothing at all. Some companies have started designing and marketing wetsuits with striped patterns to fool sharks into thinking a bather is actually a venomous sea snake. The state government has developed an app called SharkSmart (w sharksmart.com.au), which provides real-time information on shark activity, and has also funded some enclosures, but sadly not in Esperance.

That being said, shark encounters remain very low and the risk is small. However, it is sensible to use apps like SharkSmart to see if there are sightings; avoid swimming or going into the water if there have been carcasses around, as these attract sharks; swim within enclosures, if there are any; and don't swim alone – you will need someone to help you if there is an incident.

grey and chestnut teals and black swans; it is also important as a site of refuge for birds impacted by drought. The **Kepwari Walk** (Class 3; 7km return), which starts/ends at the Lake Wheatfield car park, is a great place to spot birds with hides en route. Birds Australia's *Birdwatching Around Esperance* brochure (pick it up at the visitor centre) is an excellent resource describing the variety of birds you are likely to encounter. You can also canoe or kayak here, but you need to bring your own. The 5.5km **Esperance Lakes Canoe Trail** starts at the Lake Wheatfield car park and has markers every 200m to guide you – though you have to do this trail in winter when the water levels are high enough. There are also launches at Woody Lake and Lake Windabout.

The Recherche Archipelago Also known as the Bay of Islands, this group of 105 granite islands is located just a few kilometres off Esperance's coast. The only inhabited island is **Woody Island**, where there is a visitor centre, café and accommodation (furnished tents and camping sites); **Woody Island Eco Tours** (✆0484 327 580; w woodyisland.com.au) runs ferries and tours to the island. There is decent snorkelling, swimming and walking trails – if you want to get out on to the water and clamber about the granite islands, this is an easy option; day tours leave from the Taylor St Jetty.

The largest in the archipelago, **Middle Island**, near Cape Arid, is home to the bright-pink **Lake Hillier** ✳ – its size, nearly 15ha, differentiates it from some of the state's other pink lakes in places like the Wheatbelt, and the contrast of its white salty shores, the turquoise waters of the surrounding ocean and the green vegetation on the island make it as photogenic in real life as it is in the brochures.

Scientists aren't really sure what makes Lake Hillier pink – generally it's believed to be related to salinity, but Lake Hillier is different from WA's other pink lakes because it stays a vibrant colour all year round rather than fading with the seasons. Salt used to be mined here in the 1800s, but only for a few years, and there was a very small camp settlement associated with the mining venture. Swimming in the lake is not permitted – this is a nature reserve – but **Esperance Island Cruises** (\9071 5757; w esperancecruises.com.au) run trips to the lake as well as a wildlife cruise, taking in multiple islands in search of seals, whales, dolphins and sea lions.

Stokes National Park Known for its 14km² inlet, this 10,667ha national park 80km west of Esperance is a fishing haven where long beaches are fringed by dense bushland (although you will need a 4x4 to make the most of them). Terrific snorkelling can be enjoyed at **Shoal Cape**, while further west **Skippy Rock** is great for diving, snorkelling, swimming and fishing – both have small, basic DPaW camping facilities. Abundant birdlife frequent the inlet's waters – black-browed albatross, white-naped honeyeater and fairy tern are just a few of the 40 species found here – and there is a boat launch at the end of Stokes Inlet Road from which canoeing and kayaking are also popular. Also in the park are the 1870s' ruins of **Moir Homestead**, home of the Moir family who were early pastoralists – the homestead is on the Heritage Register as an example of early pastoral structures in the area. Note it can only be accessed by 4x4 on the way to Shoal Cape.

Access to the national park is from the South Coast Highway on the 2WD-suitable Stokes Inlet Road, which will get you to the inlet. If you want to go to the mouth of the inlet where it meets the Southern Ocean, you will need a 4x4.

CAPE LE GRAND NATIONAL PARK AND DUKE OF ORLEANS BAY ✳

You won't get far into researching your trip to Esperance before you see the image of kangaroos lounging on a beach in front of some impossibly gorgeous bay. Photoshop, you might ask? PR stunt? No – this is all natural, an occurrence that happens near-daily at Lucky Bay in Cape Le Grand National Park, about 40km east of Esperance. The kangaroos come down from the surrounding bush because they like to eat the seaweed that washes ashore. Of my visits to Lucky Bay, there's been only one occasion where I didn't see kangaroos on the beach – and even then I did see them nearby, just a few kilometres down the road on another beach.

As you head east from Cape Le Grand, the 'Outback Riviera' lays out for you in all its glory; 70km down the road is Duke of Orleans Bay – known almost universally here as 'The Duke' – arguably the most popular local beach for its superlative waters, sparkling white sand, glorious swimming and abundant fishing opportunities. Though camping at both is a popular and viable option, Cape Le Grand and The Duke are close and accessible enough to make them an easy day trip from Esperance and most people just do that. You'll want to book ahead in summer, but still, 'busy' here is still going to feel pretty uncrowded. This is, after all, the Outback.

GETTING THERE AND AWAY Cape Le Grand is 40km/25–30 minutes from Esperance; take Fisheries Road to Merivale Road, and then turn south on to Cape Le Grand Road to reach Lucky Bay. To get to Wharton Beach, on the eastern edge of the park around 90km from Esperance, you will find it easier to take Fisheries Road to the village of Condingup (as Merivale is not sealed the entire way), and then turn south on to Orleans Bay Road. The roads are 2WD suitable.

WHERE TO STAY AND EAT There are DPaW campgrounds at Le Grand Beach and Lucky Bay, though they fill quickly and need to be booked in advance.

Duke of Orleans Bay Caravan Park (16 accommodations) Wharton Rd, Condingup; ℡ 9075 0033; w orleansbaycamp.com.au. Just east of the national park not far from Wharton Beach, this complex offers chalets, powered & unpowered sites plus a general store. The advantage of being here, instead of staying in Esperance, is the proximity to the beach. *Chalets* **$$$**, *sites* **$**

✗ Condingup Tavern Cnr Ayre & Parish St, Condingup; ℡ 9076 6024; w condinguptavern. com.au; ⏱ ring for hours. A favourite with Esperance locals, the tavern serves a variety of well-done pub classics. An excellent place to stop for lunch while you are exploring Cape Arid, Cape Le Grand or The Duke. **$$**

WHAT TO SEE AND DO

Cape Le Grand National Park (A$15/vehicle entry fee) At 318km², this sweeping heathland is dotted with light brown granite outcrops and white sandy-beach coves. Jewel of a thousand brochure covers, **Lucky Bay** ❋ – with its impossibly clear water, crystal-white sand and spectacular, sheltered granite backdrop – is unsurprisingly the centrepiece of the national park. It's undeniably popular with visitors but don't worry – even when the beach is 'packed', this is only by Outback standards and you will find plenty of space on the sand for yourself. The swimming here is magnificent – the clarity of the water is such that it feels like you're in a swimming pool. There are also heaps of marsupials – while the kangaroos get the attention here, the park is also home to honey and ring-tailed possums and bandicoots.

For the experienced walker, the 17km (one-way) **Coastal Track** goes from Le Grand Beach to Rossiter Bay, taking in Lucky Bay, Thistle Cove and Hellfire Bay (another popular swimming beach) and providing beautiful headland, coastal and ocean views along the way. Though different sections of the walk have different class ratings, it is a challenging walk; be prepared for Class 4 and Class 5 conditions. All of these beaches can be visited by car.

Away from the coast, the national park is dominated by dramatic granite hills, the best-known of which (though not the highest) is **Frenchman Peak** (262m). There is a Class 4, 3km return hike to the summit that provides great views of the park. **Mount Le Grand**, near Hellfire Bay, is the highest peak in the park at 345m; however, access is difficult and there are no marked trails to the summit. If you are a keen rock climber, Ross Weiter's helpful *Cape Le Grand Rock Climbing Guide* can be downloaded at w climberswa.asn.au/wp-content/uploads/2008/10/Cape-le-Grand-Climbing-Guide.pdf.

If entering the park on Merivale Road, do stop off to visit **Esperance Stonehenge** (℡ 9075 9003; w esperancestonehenge.com.au), a full-size duplicate of the UK original built with 137 locally quarried stones and aligned to the solstices in Esperance so that, on those days, the sun's rays shine through to the altar stone. The person who came up with the idea to build it was going to put it in Margaret River, but then ran into money problems – so Kim and Jillian Beale, owners of the cattle farm next to the quarry providing the stones, decided to step in and put it on their property in 2011. The Beales have since moved on, but the exhibit is still open under new ownership.

To the east of Cape Le Grand National Park is **Duke of Orleans Bay**, a series of beaches also known as 'The Duke'. Immensely popular with Esperance locals, it's accessible only by 4x4 – ample beach tracks lead to isolated sands and coves fantastic for swimming and fishing, which, more often than not, you will have to yourself. Perhaps the best-known is **Wharton Beach**, which is often frequented by youngsters trying out surfboards for the first time. Though it's an unquestionably great beach, I prefer Cape Arid and Lucky Bay.

CAPE ARID NATIONAL PARK *

Some 110km east of Esperance is this gem of a park on the edge of the Nullarbor. Its distance from Esperance and the fact that it is effectively the dead end of a long cul-de-sac means there's limited traffic through here – you'll likely be one of the only visitors. The park itself is immense at 280,000ha, but most of that is inaccessible and you will explore only a tiny part in the southwestern corner. The terrain is mostly scrub and mallee, though as you go further north it turns to woodland. By far the biggest draw for visitors are the lonely, isolated beaches at Yokinup Bay (one of my favourites in the state) and Dolphin Cove – both 2WD accessible and in close proximity to each other.

GETTING THERE AND AWAY This is also the furthest east you can go in the Esperance area with a 2WD. There are no facilities anywhere in or near the park; however, the closest petrol is in Condingup (55km away). But getting here from Esperance is pretty straight-forward: take (sealed) Fisheries Road about 100km or so and turn on to (unsealed) Tagon Road, pass Merivale Road and follow the signs into the park – all in all from Esperance to the Thomas River campground it's about 125km. All of that can be done by 2WD (I have done it many times). The Balladonia Track is a difficult, high-clearance 4x4 shortcut from just past the Tagon Road turn-off on Fisheries Road, to the Eyre Highway near Balladonia – however, it is currently closed indefinitely to all but local traffic.

WHAT TO SEE AND DO The star of Cape Arid is **Thomas River Beach** *, on the western edge of the park, connected to Merivale Road by an unsealed track. This is one of my favourite spots in all of Australia, and maybe the world. You'll get your first glimpses of Mt Arid and Yokinup Bay as you descend towards the Thomas River campsite. Park in the picnic area and then walk the few hundred metres to the beach; if you have a 4x4 you can drive it on to the sand, but walking or driving requires crossing the Thomas River – usually ankle deep at the main crossing point, sometimes knee deep. Once you cross, what a glorious sight awaits: kilometres of wide, sweeping sugar-white sands curving around the striped bay with Mt Arid, in its purple and grey hues, directly in front of you. The beach is good for swimming – not too calm but not too rough – and it stays relatively shallow a long way out. There's wildlife here too; on my last visit an emu and its chicks were patrolling the beach, before disappearing up a granite hill and into the scrub at the southern end of the beach.

The other 2WD-accessible road forks off the park's main road a few kilometres before you arrive at the Thomas River area, signposted for Dolphin Cove. Taking this road will provide you with a sensational vista of Yokinup Bay, before arriving at a car park that has access to two beaches: **Dolphin Cove** to the left and **Little Tagon** to the right. Both require a short (but not necessarily easy) walk – Dolphin Cove also requires a descent down granite. With its bush-covered pyramidal granite hill in the background, Little Tagon reminds me of Little Beach in Albany (page 198). For walkers, the moderately difficult **Tagon Coastal Trail** (Class 4; 15km return) runs across the granite to Tagon Bay from Thomas River.

To get to **Mt Arid** (357m) itself, you will need to drive along Thomas River Beach to the end of Yokinup Bay, where a Class 5, 4km return track leads up to the summit. This is a very challenging, steep, slippery and poorly marked trail, but the views out to the islands and over the park are rewarding. Before attempting this, check the tides and make sure your vehicle is suitable for beach driving. In the northern reaches of Cape Arid, away from the coast, is its tallest peak – **Mt Ragged** (594m), which slightly tops neighbouring **Tower Peak** at 585m. Access to the summit is via the highly challenging and poorly signposted **Mt Ragged Walk** (Class 5; 3km return), leading from the 4x4-only track to Balladonia.

There's a campsite at the summit, from which you can follow the 4x4-only Gora Track to remote **Israelite Bay**, which is technically outside Cape Arid National Park in neighbouring **Nuytsland Nature Reserve**. Ironically, most West Australians will have heard of Israelite Bay even if few have been there – it is often used as a geographic reference point for statewide weather forecasts. There are some remnants of an old telegraph station there, dating from the late 1800s; this was once a small town with a post office and this is listed on the National Trust. If the Gora Track is closed or impassable, you can take the Fisheries Track (4x4 only, it starts where Fisheries Road ends) and go that way from Esperance. From Israelite Bay, a spectacular, 317km track leads east to **Twilight Cove**, passing the 100m-high **Bilbunya sand dunes**, which look like giant scoops of vanilla ice cream. It also passes the 80m-high **Baxter Cliffs**, which stretch for nearly 200km and form part of the Great Australian Bight. Note that this is extremely rugged and isolated terrain, suitable only for experienced and self-sufficient 4x4 drivers who can do their own repairs – and even then, bogging is common. Many people do the track in the reverse, heading along the Eyre Highway to just west of Cocklebiddy, then down to Twilight Cove, Israelite Bay and back into Esperance. Check conditions and feasibility with the shire and park rangers before attempting this drive in either direction.

NORSEMAN AND THE GREAT WESTERN WOODLANDS

Anyone crossing between Western Australia and South Australia by car ends up in Norseman – the small town at the junction of the Coolgardie–Esperance and Eyre highways. But despite its gateway status, the town's facilities and services are fairly limited and it can become overwhelmed when events such as bushfires close the Eyre Highway, leaving travellers stranded. The tin camel sculptures made from corrugated metal around the main roundabout in town recognise the camel trains of the area from pioneering days.

The town was originally founded as a gold mining camp and became a municipality in 1896; there was more gold in Norseman than 7km south in Dundas, where there was also a find, and so Norseman became the principal settlement of the area. Today, the town is quite small – the entire shire has fewer than 600 people – but it has outsized services due to its position as a significant transit junction (the Eyre Highway T-junctions here – north to Kalgoorlie, south to Esperance) and its position as the first town visitors from South Australia and the Eastern States reach when they arrive in WA.

The **Dundas Coach Road Heritage Trail** (**w** dundas.wa.gov.au/Profiles/dundas/Assets/ClientData/dundas_coach_road_heritage_trail.pdf) features interpretive stories of the shire's past, exploring historic mine sites and the original Dundas townsite (very little left) that preceded Norseman by three years – the discovery of more gold at what is now Norseman created a giant vacuum sound for prospectors and Dundas was nearly abandoned almost as soon as it was built. The track follows the path the Royal Mail Coaches took to get to Norseman. Though this is 2WDsuitable, the road is not great and quite rocky in places, and some signage is really all that is left of the old Dundas townsite.

Norseman is also the eastern terminus for the 300km **Granite and Woodlands Discovery Trail** *, an unsealed, 2WD-suitable road connecting the town with Hyden (page 252) that goes right through the Great Western Woodlands. Covering around 16 million hectares (roughly the same size as England), this is the largest remaining Mediterranean-climate woodland left in the world, and one-fifth of all flora species in Australia can be found here. The woodlands are often referred to as 'Australia's lungs' – indeed, US-based charity The Wilderness Society estimates that 950 million tons of carbon are stored here, which is more than Australia emits in a year. The trail is specifically maintained for tourism and is one of the best long-distance unsealed roads I have ever driven.

Pick up the extensive brochure, which outlines the 16 stopping points, from the **Norseman Visitor Centre** (78 Prinsep St; ✆ 9039 0040; w dundas.wa.gov.au; ⊕ 08.30–16.30 Mon–Fri, 08.30–12.30 Sat). While the road can be done as a straight shot in about 4 hours, those with more time should consider camping at the **Breakaways** mid-route – where erosion has formed small, highly colourful cliffs and hills from clay, with chalk white, red, orange, brown and purplish stripes and patterns. Other highlights include **McDermid Rock** and **Disappointment Rock**, both walking trails (1.1km for McDermid and 1.9km for Disappointment) with nice views at the summits out over the woodland, and the tranquil salt lake, **Lake Johnston** (Stop #10), guarded by the picturesque 'Three Sentinels' (three gum trees). The **Gemfields** (Stop #14) are a good place to fossick, particularly for agate and gypsum crystals – ask the visitor centre about permits and tips.

On the way to Norseman from Esperance, you will see the 651m granite summit of **Peak Charles** sticking up out of the ground, some 50km away, like a giant Hershey's Kiss. It's the centrepiece of Peak Charles National Park, located within the Great Western Woodlands; DPaW has not given the Peak Charles hike – 3.4km return – a classification because they say it is more difficult than Class 5, their highest difficulty ranking; however, the climb is broken down into sections and the bottom two (of three) sections are Class 3 and Class 4, respectively. Access to the national park is by 4x4 only; from the Coolgardie–Esperance Highway, take Norseman–Lake King Road and then bear on to Peak Charles Road.

GETTING THERE AND AWAY Norseman is 203km/2 hours from Esperance. Kalgoorlie is 187km/2 hours away, and the South Australian border is 720km/7 hours away.

WHERE TO STAY In an attractive Art-Deco style building, the **Railway Motel & Woodlands Guesthouse** * (106 Roberts St; ✆ 9039 0003; w therailwaynorseman. com.au; **$$**) offers standard motel units and more expensive (but excellent-value) spa rooms – I always look forward to staying here when I'm in town.

THE NULLARBOR

It's just over 700km on the Eyre Highway from Norseman to Eucla, the last stop before South Australia. This border town lies within the Nullarbor, an ancient, treeless plain sprawling across this southern-central part of Australia – the world's largest single exposure of limestone, covering an area of around 200,000km². Formed 20 million years ago when sea levels dropped and huge amounts of limestone accumulated from the shells of small sea animals, much of the Nullarbor is dotted with underground caves and caverns – though exploring them requires a permit from DPaW, which are typically only granted to scientists and specialised caving clubs. It's a geologically stable area where the land has largely been left untouched by tectonic plate dramatics, resulting in the limestone slab being more or less left alone over the millennia, rather than being pushed or pulled into forming mountains or other geological features.

The Nullarbor has a fascinating place in the Australian psyche: somehow synonymous with excitement and adventure and, at the same time, dullness and monotony. 'Crossing the Nullarbor' is one of Australia's iconic road trips, connecting the east with the west, symbolic of the inhospitable landscape, incredible distances,

SKYLAB

Launched in 1973, *Skylab* was the first US space station, designed to facilitate research and data-gathering. The station orbited Earth for around 24 weeks, and was considered a marvel of engineering at the time. What goes up, however, must come down, and it soon dawned on NASA that they had not properly considered that latter part – *Skylab* had been left in a parking orbit in space, but that orbit was decaying quickly. By 1978, it became clear that a crash on Earth was inevitable.

Skylab's impending crash was well known at the time among the public across the world and NASA engineers came up with a plan to use the station's rockets to alter its trajectory and send it into the Southern Ocean, away from land. Confidence was low, however, and people as far away as western Europe made contingency preparations for it to strike there in case NASA's calculations were off. One US newspaper, the *San Francisco Examiner*, even promised a cash reward of US$10,000 to anyone who showed up at their office with a piece of *Skylab* within 72 hours of the crash.

Thankfully, the crash occurred mostly as per NASA's calculations, though those were by no means certain as NASA only had limited control over *Skylab* by that point. It fell almost entirely into the water, but some of the debris missed the ocean, and instead tumbled down across the Nullarbor and Esperance. Some 24 pieces fell in the garden of 17-year-old Esperance local, Stan Thornton – he had heard about the *Examiner*'s prize, grabbed a few bits of debris, and hopped a plane to San Francisco. The newspaper paid out the reward. Nobody was injured; the larger pieces mostly burned-up on re-entering the atmosphere.

For its part, the Shire of Esperance issued NASA with a light-hearted A$400 fine for 'littering'. Years later, in 2009, a California DJ, Scott Barley, collected donations from his listeners to pay off NASA's fine and received a key to the city of Esperance in response. Others decided to use the event to promote the state; the National Archives of Australia note that a piece of *Skylab* was sent to the 1979 Miss Universe pageant in Perth, posed over by Miss Australia and Miss America, while the Kalgoorlie Tourist Bureau decreed the Goldfields as 'Skylab Country' and invited US President Jimmy Carter to visit and offered to name a Skylab museum after him.

The Americans declared that the fragments of *Skylab* were 'finders keepers' and you can see original bits of the station in Esperance and Balladonia – and quite possibly find some of your own if you are prospecting or fossicking in the Nullarbor.

wide-open skies and dusty Outback scenery that forms such an important part of the Australian national identity. It also serves as a metaphorical bridge linking WA with the rest of the country to the east.

Heading east from Norseman, your first stop comes after 220km: the **Balladonia Hotel Motel** (Eyre Hwy; ✎ 9039 3453; w balladoniahotelmotel.com.au; **$$**), an excellent place to overnight with well-kept rooms, a good restaurant and caravan facilities. The roadhouse also has a museum, with an emphasis on the *Skylab* (see box, opposite), with replica pieces of the station and documents from NASA.

East of Balladonia is the '**90 Mile Straight**' – the name surviving Australia's conversion to the metric system – 146.6km of highway without a turn or bend in sight. The end of the straight is marked by the roadhouses of **Caiguna**, with **Cocklebiddy** a further 65km on.

Those with an interest in birds should consider the 50km detour off the highway to the **Eyre Bird Observatory** (✎ 9039 3450; w birdlife.org.au/visit-us/observatories/eyre). Established in 1977 by Birds Australia and located in an old telegraph station (built in 1897), they offer numerous multi-day programmes on bird identification and surveying – highlights include the gorgeous pink, red and white Major Mitchell's cockatoo. Overnight bookings are available – the road here is 4x4-only, but if you book two nights or more, the caretakers will meet you at a 2WD-accessible point on the track where you can leave your car, and ferry you the rest of the way.

Continuing east from Cocklebiddy, **Madura** and **Mundrabilla** are the next stopping points (you can drive 20km south from Mundrabilla to the Great Australian Bight; ask the roadhouse for information and road conditions), before arriving in **Eucla** (population: 37), from where it's 12km to the South Australian border. The **Eucla Motel** ✴ (Eyre Hwy; ✎ 9039 3468; w euclastay.com.au; **$$$**) has bright, sunny rooms and a good restaurant. In 1877, **Eucla Telegraph Station** opened and became an important relay point for communications between WA and the rest of the world – though it closed only 50 years later. Today, the abandoned structure is slowly being eaten by sand dunes – a spooky and eerie sight. A short drive south of the highway, Eucla's derelict jetty juts out from the beautifully isolated beach, where you can enjoy good swimming and snorkelling in the Great Australian Bight. You can't get to the jetty in a 2WD, but you can walk there (20 mins) from the telegraph station through the dunes (if you've got a high-clearance 4x4, you can drive the same path).

THE BRADT STORY

In the beginning

It all began in 1974 on an Amazon river barge. During an 18-month trip through South America, two adventurous young backpackers – Hilary Bradt and her then husband, George – decided to write about the hiking trails they had discovered through the Andes. *Backpacking Along Ancient Ways in Peru and Bolivia* included the very first descriptions of the Inca Trail. It was the start of a colourful journey to becoming one of the best-loved travel publishers in the world; you can read the full story on our website (bradtguides. com/ourstory).

Getting there first

Hilary quickly gained a reputation for being a true travel pioneer, and in the 1980s she started to focus on guides to places overlooked by other publishers. The Bradt Guides list became a roll call of guidebook 'firsts'. We published the first guide to Madagascar, followed by Mauritius, Czechoslovakia and Vietnam. The 1990s saw the beginning of our extensive coverage of Africa: Tanzania, Uganda, South Africa, and Eritrea. Later, post-conflict guides became a feature: Rwanda, Mozambique, Angola, and Sierra Leone, as well as the first standalone guides to the Baltic States following the fall of the Iron Curtain, and the first post-war guides to Bosnia, Kosovo and Albania.

Comprehensive – and with a conscience

Today, we are the world's largest independently owned travel publisher, with more than 200 titles. However, our ethos remains unchanged. Hilary is still keenly involved, and **we still get there first**: two-thirds of Bradt guides have no direct competition.

But we don't just get there first. Our guides are also known for being **more comprehensive** than any other series. We avoid templates and tick-lists. Each guide is a one-of-a-kind expression of an expert author's interests, knowledge and enthusiasm for telling it how it really is.

And a commitment to wildlife, conservation and respect for local communities has always been at the heart of our books. Bradt Guides was **championing sustainable travel** before any other guidebook publisher. We even have a series dedicated to Slow Travel in the UK, award-winning books that explore the country with a passion and depth you'll find nowhere else.

Thank you!

We can only do what we do because of the support of readers like you – people who value less-obvious experiences, less-visited places and a more thoughtful approach to travel. Those who, like us, take travel seriously.

Bradt GUIDES
TRAVEL TAKEN SERIOUSLY

Part Three

EAST OF PERTH

KALGOORLIE-BOULDER Page 228. Historically one of the state's – and the nation's – most important cities, Kal has spent most of its existence serving as WA's wallet. The character and period architecture here still stands, you can tour the Super Pit, mine and pan for your own gold, and eat at some of country WA's best restaurants and Outback pubs. This is one of the state's most underrated tourism destinations – and without the pivotal role its population played in pulling a reluctant WA into the federation, there might not have been a united Australia without it.

LAKE BALLARD Page 238. On this dry lake, Antony Gormley's 51 simple metal figurines – representing locals and visitors – is one of Australia's most mind-blowing outdoor art exhibits. Going at sunrise or sunset adds a bit of extra magic to a visit – which already inspires deep contemplation on the connection between humans, nature and isolation.

YORK Page 248. WA's oldest inland town makes for a fine afternoon amble as you walk past Heritage building after Heritage building, including the Town Hall – one of our favourite structures in the state. Stay overnight at some of rural WA's best boutique accommodation and throw in a hot-air balloon ride over the bucolic surrounding farmland.

ROCK HOPPING Page 250. The massive granite outcrops that dot the Wheatbelt's bucolic farmland can mostly be climbed and provide fantastic vistas over the landscape. The best-known is Wave Rock, whose distinctive vertical black stripes makes it look like, well, a wave that's about to crash. Other well-known rocks include Elachbutting Rock in Mukinbudin, Kokerbin Rock near Quairading and Gorge Rock in Corrigin. Hop in your car and tackle half a dozen of them over a few days, while stopping off for some fantastic hearty food at the local country pubs en route.

DRYANDRA WOODLAND Page 256. This 28,000ha national park is a good example of what the Wheatbelt looked like before European settlement and is also home to woylies, bilbies, possums, malas, quendas and boodies, among others. The Barna Mia sanctuary here provides night-time viewing opportunities and you're sure to see something.

8

The Goldfields

Elegant architecture, Outback wilderness, ghost towns and (of course) gold – the Goldfields is where the Australian icons of your imagination come to life. The lifeblood of the region is the yellow metal, and the spectacular Super Pit and Golden Mile in Kalgoorlie – on top of some of the world's wealthiest real estate – have been WA's wallet for over a century. Towns here came and went as fast as the prospectors, and the resulting abandoned settlements provide an eerily silent meander through history – although some, like Broad Arrow and Kookynie, still have operational pubs, making for an unforgettable evening of enjoying a pint in a ghost town. Driving on through endless Outback scrub and woodland to the deeply moving *Inside Australia* figures on Lake Ballard – a world-renowned masterpiece – and the Menzies clock tower, which finally got its clock a century after being built, before hauling the metal detector out of the boot to look for a nugget in your own patch of Outback dust, is every Perth office worker's escapist fantasy. You are not going to forget this place.

COOLGARDIE

Once WA's third-largest city, the gold-rush town of Coolgardie is known as 'The Mother of the Goldfields'. Although the crush of prospectors are long gone, the town's grand buildings stand proudly and have turned Coolgardie into an 1890s living museum. Standing on its massively wide – and mostly empty – main street, where grandiose buildings remain almost the same as they were in their heyday, you can imagine the ghosts of yesteryear shuffling along the footpaths, into and out of the buildings and waiting on the side of the road for their carriages to pick them up.

The town got its start in 1892, with the discovery of nearly 500oz of gold by two prospectors, Arthur Bayley and William Ford, at Fly Flat (today's Coolgardie). Heeding warnings that, due to water shortages, prospecting in the Eastern Goldfields area was only possible after rains, they set off together – and while one of their horses was taking a drink from a native well, Ford spotted gold and the two began successfully prospecting the area. Their find coincided with the exhaustion of many of the goldfields in east Australia, and consequently led to one of the biggest gold rushes in the country's history, as prospectors flocked west. Within a few years the railway also arrived, and Coolgardie became the most important centre in WA outside Perth. It peaked in the late 1890s with a population of about 25,000, but the good times didn't last long – Coolgardie was no exception to the boom-bust cycle of other gold-rush towns in the state. It took less than 20 years for the party to end, after which the town went into terminal decline. Today, Coolgardie is often incorrectly thought of as a ghost town – there are about 800 residents, though its empty streets will have you looking around for any tumbleweeds blowing through.

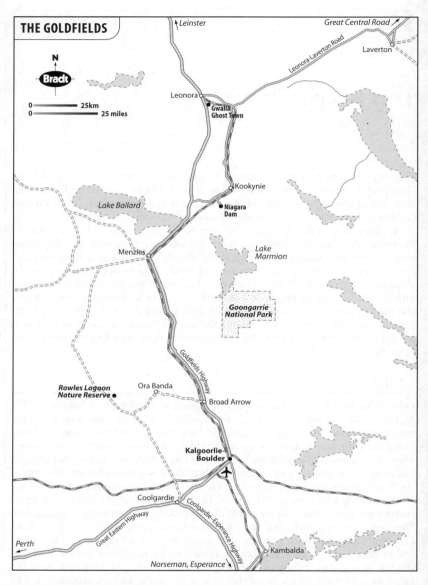

GETTING THERE AND AWAY Coolgardie is on the Great Eastern Highway, 550km/ 6 hours from Perth and 40km/30 minutes from Kalgoorlie. Esperance is 370km/ 4 hours south on the Coolgardie–Esperance Highway.

Getting to Coolgardie is difficult without your own transport. Transwa's thrice-weekly coach service linking Kalgoorlie and Esperance stops in Coolgardie (from Esperance 4hrs 45mins; from A$60), but only once a week. The Perth–Kalgoorlie *Prospector* train stops at Bonnie Vale, an abandoned mine site 14km north of town, but there are no buses or taxis from there to Coolgardie. If you don't have your own transport, you should take the train to Kalgoorlie and then get a bus or taxi to town.

WHERE TO STAY AND EAT Options are limited in Coolgardie. Unless you are a historian or a prospector, it is better to stay and eat in Kalgoorlie (page 231), 40km away.

🏠 **Denver City Hotel & Diner** (26 rooms) 73 Bayley St; 📞 9026 6031; w denvercityhotel. com.au. This atmospheric & Heritage-listed inn has seen its share of controversy in recent years. The on-site pub was the focus – for better or for worse – of the 2016 film *Hotel Coolgardie*, which showcased the negative experience of 2 Finnish backpackers in the Outback, who were subject to boozy, lewd & misogynistic behaviour from pub regulars. Thankfully, it has been under different management for some time now. Rooms inside the main building have shared facilities, while donga-style rooms outside have en suites. The pub offers sizable portions of the usual no-frills meals. **$$**

WHAT TO SEE AND DO Most of Coolgardie's sights are clustered along the parallel streets of Bayley and Sylvester. Head to the visitor centre (see below) to pick up a copy of the **Glory Days Boom or Bust Heritage Trail** (also available as an app), a self-guided drive/walking tour (complete with audio narration) that takes in 65 points of interest in Coolgardie as well as the nearly two-dozen Heritage-listed buildings – though the buildings themselves are easy enough to help you imagine the Coolgardie of yesteryear, the audio guide enhances the experience.

The best place to start your tour of Coolgardie is undoubtedly the Heritage-listed **Warden's Court Building** ✸ (62 Bayley St), built in 1898 from local sandstone. With its balconies and columns, its façade is one of the most photographed in the state. It once settled disputes between landowners and miners over boundaries, but today it hosts the **Coolgardie Visitor Centre and Goldfields Exhibition Museum** (📞 9026 6090; ⏱ 08.30–16.00 Mon–Fri, 10.00–15.00 Sat–Sun; A$4/$2 adult/senior & child) showcasing dramatic photographs of the gold-rush days and the **Waghorn Bottle Collection**. Valued at A$500,000, it belongs to local residents Frank and May Waghorn, who collected specimens from all over the world – some bottles date from as far back as 300BC.

Next door to the visitor centre is the Heritage-listed **Post Office Complex** (56 Bayley St; ⏱ 09.00–17.00 Mon–Fri), originally built in 1894 but subject to a recent A$3 million restoration. Still a functioning outlet of Australia Post, the building's elaborate and intricate verandas, colannades and chimneys have made it a richly representative surviving structure of the period. A few doors down is the **RSL Building** (33 Bayley St), formerly the Marvel Bar Hotel and another Bayley Street masterpiece. Constructed as a symbol of the town's wealth at the turn of the 20th century, it operated as a hotel until 1927, when it lost its liquor licence. Its arches,

ROAD TRIP: GOLDEN QUEST DISCOVERY TRAIL

At nearly 1,000km in length, the award-winning Golden Quest Discovery Trail (w goldenquesttrail.com) is an authoritative dive into the history, culture and social fabric of the Goldfields. The highly accessible self-drive trail is described in a 162-page guidebook by Barry Strickland, which can be purchased in hard-copy form (recommended, to take with you in areas of poor reception) or downloaded from the website. Starting in Coolgardie, the route takes in 25 sites replete with local legends and history – highlights include the Lake Ballard reserve (page 238) and the townsites of Menzies, Leonora and Laverton before finishing in Kalgoorlie-Boulder. The trail's accessibility, coverage of key sites and depth make this an excellent first road trip in the Goldfields.

pilasters and highly elaborate parapet now look somewhat oversized and ambitious for its setting, but that only adds to its appeal.

Built in 1895 for Coolgardie's first magistrate and mining warden, **Warden Finnerty's Residence** (19 Morgan St; ☎9080 2111; ◷ 11.00–16.00 Sat–Wed; A\$4/2 adult/child) was built by the Bunning brothers (of hardware store fame) and is an excellent example of period architecture, its green-and-gold striking verandas, shutters and windows designed for the uncooperative local climate. But the interior is what makes it stand out; it has been furnished to the standards of 1800s high society in the Goldfields and gives a taste of what life was like then for the 'top-end-of-town' folk.

KALGOORLIE-BOULDER

Kalgoorlie has a reputation among West Australians as an anachronism, a time-capsule frontier town where mining is king, lady luck is queen, the law is somewhat hazy and anything goes. But beneath the rough-and-tumble veneer of WA's largest Outback town lies an understated cosmopolitan vibe, apparent through its dynamic embrace of flamboyant architecture, fine galleries and some excellent restaurants – all that mining money has to be spent somewhere!

Aboriginal peoples have been here for thousands of years, and the Wangkatha (also called Wongi) are the major group. Kalgoorlie was founded in 1893 on the site of a major gold find by Irish prospectors Paddy Hannan, Thomas Flanagan and Daniel Shea, which immediately ignited a rush of prospectors to the area, including from nearby Coolgardie. However, it was some of the world's richest gold reefs, found shortly after at Boulder by Will Brookman and Sam Pearce, that proved durable over time and prevented Kalgoorlie from entering the same boom-bust pattern that befell other gold-rush towns like Coolgardie and Cue.

The concentration of several dozen gold mines around town is known as the Golden Mile, sometimes referred to as the richest area in the world. The Great Boulder Mine was the first to be established in 1893 and was considered the largest and wealthiest, churning out stratospheric profits. The 1903 completion of the Goldfields Water Supply Scheme, engineered by Irish engineer C Y O'Connor (see box, page 95), allowed potable water to arrive from Perth and further solidified Kalgoorlie's viability. Trams, railways and the other trappings of urban life began popping up to support the growing population, and the town grew.

In the 1970s, a collapse in gold prices nearly shut down the entire Golden Mile, but by the end of the decade prices rebounded and so did the town. In the 1980s, controversial and high-profile businessman Alan Bond attempted to combine the various leases and mining operations in the Golden Mile to create one enormous open-cut mine; although Bond himself could not pull the deal off, the project did eventually go ahead and, in 1989, what is now known universally as the 'Super Pit' opened. Gold mining still drives the Kalgoorlie economy today, accounting for about half of the region's economic output and employing about one-quarter of the workforce.

The City of Kalgoorlie-Boulder formed from the merging of the twin cities of Kalgoorlie and Boulder into one unified local government area in 1989 (locally referred to as just Kalgoorlie). The two towns are one seamless area and it is indistinguishable where Kalgoorlie ends and Boulder begins. Together, they form the fifth-biggest centre in WA with a population of about 30,000.

Despite its rich fortunes, Kalgoorlie is undeniably a town with social tensions. In 2016, the Aboriginal Legal Service of Western Australia declared it to be in a 'state of social emergency' after the death of 14-year-old Aboriginal boy Elijah Doughty at the hands of a white man sparked riots and civil unrest (see box, opposite). Street

THE CASE OF ELIJAH DOUGHTY

In late August 2016, racial tensions in Kalgoorlie exploded into the open following the death of 14-year-old Aboriginal Elijah Doughty, who was killed on a motorbike following a collision with a ute driven by a 56-year-old white man, whose identity remains suppressed by the courts.

On 28 August, the man arrived home to find that two of his motorbikes had been stolen. The following day, he went to an area of town popular with dirtbike riders and saw Doughty riding one of his motorbikes. The man gave chase to Doughty in his Nissan Navara ute along a dirt track, but when Doughty turned suddenly on his motorbike the two vehicles collided. Doughty's injuries were catastrophic and he died instantly. There is no evidence that Doughty knew he was on a stolen motorbike; his friends claimed it was given to him by someone else.

The next day, a crowd gathered to protest at the Kalgoorlie Courthouse, and tensions escalated; a dozen police officers were injured in the unrest as protestors broke down the gates of the court. The ute driver was charged with manslaughter, instead of the higher charge of murder, which precipitated a riot in the Kalgoorlie CBD.

The trial was held a year later in the Supreme Court of Western Australia and the lead-up was marked by heated and, at times, racist social media posts in Kalgoorlie towards Aboriginal people. The ute driver was found not guilty of manslaughter, and was instead convicted of the lesser charge of dangerous driving causing death, with a three-year jail sentence. This prompted outrage in some quarters and among social justice advocates, who noted that the driver had been travelling at unsafe speeds in difficult terrain and at a distance too close to Doughty for safety.

Following the verdict, vigils were held for Doughty across Australia. An emergency race relations summit followed, where then-state premier Colin Barnett conceded racism was a problem that concerned the state government and an attempt was made to better coordinate agencies to deliver better outcomes for Aboriginal peoples. However, progress has remained very slow, and the town is still considered to be simmering.

drinking and anti-social behaviour are common occurrences, which resulted in the introduction of point-of-sale alcohol restrictions in 2020. The crime rate is high and there is a visible police presence in town so it pays to keep your wits about you, especially at night.

GETTING THERE AND AWAY Kalgoorlie is the terminus of the Great Eastern Highway, 600km/7 hours from Perth. It forms a T-junction with the Goldfields Highway, which travels south to Norseman (190km/2 hours) and Esperance (400km/4 hours) and north to Leonora (235km/2½ hours) and Wiluna (530km/5½ hours).

Transwa's *Prospector* train connects Kalgoorlie and Perth (7hrs; from $93), while Transwa coaches run to Esperance three times per week (5hrs; from A$63).

Qantas and Virgin Australia offer flights to Perth from Kalgoorlie-Boulder Airport (1hr), about 5km southwest of the Kalgoorlie CBD directly to the west of Burt Street in Boulder. You will need to take a taxi into town as there's no public bus, but it's a short enough trip.

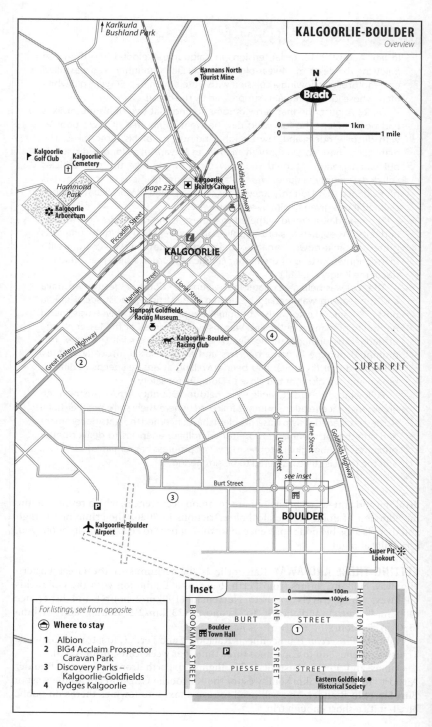

KALGOORLIE-BOULDER
Overview

Karlkurla
Bushland Park

Hannans North
Tourist Mine

N

Bradt

0   1km
0   1 mile

Kalgoorlie
Golf Club

Kalgoorlie
Cemetery

Goldfields Highway

*Hammond
Park*

Kalgoorlie
Health Campus

page 232

Kalgoorlie
Arboretum

Piccadilly Street

KALGOORLIE

Hannan Street

Lionel Street

Great Eastern Highway

Signpost Goldfields
Racing Museum

Kalgoorlie-Boulder
Racing Club

(4)

(2)

SUPER PIT

Lane Street

Goldfields Highway

Burt Street

see inset

(3)

P

Kalgoorlie-Boulder
Airport

Lionel Street

BOULDER

Super Pit
Lookout

For listings, see from opposite

Where to stay

1 Albion
2 BIG4 Acclaim Prospector
   Caravan Park
3 Discovery Parks –
   Kalgoorlie-Goldfields
4 Rydges Kalgoorlie

Inset

0   100m
0   100yds

BROOKMAN STREET

BURT

Boulder
Town Hall

LANE STREET

STREET

HAMILTON STREET

(1)

P

PIESSE

STREET

STREET

Eastern Goldfields
Historical Society

GETTING AROUND Kalgoorlie's TransGoldfields bus network offers three circular routes: the 861 leaves from the Palace Terminal on Hannan Street and heads north through the suburbs of Piccadilly and Hannans, while the 862 and 863 both go to Boulder (the 862 from the Palace Terminal, the 863 across the street from the Exchange Hotel).

Taxi services include Twin City Cabs (☎9021 2177) and Go Gold Taxi (☎9093 0333).

TOURIST INFORMATION

☑ Kalgoorlie-Boulder Visitor Centre Kalgoorlie Town Hall, 316 Hannan St; ☎9021 1966; w kalgoorlietourism.com; ⏱ 09.00–15.00 Mon–Fri, 09.00–noon Sat

---

WHERE TO STAY *Map, page 232, unless otherwise stated*

🏠 Quest Yelverton (48 apartments) 210 Egan St, Kalgoorlie; ☎9022 8181; w questapartments. com.au. Stylish serviced apartments with kitchenettes, & some with multiple bedrooms; larger units have laundry facilities & a spa bath. On-site swimming pool & BBQ facilities. A great choice for longer stays. **$$$$**

✳ 🏠 Rydges Kalgoorlie [map, opposite] (91 rooms) 21 Davidson St, Kalgoorlie; ☎9080 0800; w rydges.com. A good upscale choice; units are contemporary & spacious with spas in all rooms. The pool is heated. Continental b/fast is included in some rates; full b/fast available for an extra charge. **$$$$**

🏠 Discovery Parks – Kalgoorlie Goldfields [map, opposite] 286 Burt St, Boulder; ☎9039 4800; w discoveryholidayparks. com.au. Close to the airport, features cabins, powered & unpowered sites; some powered sites are en suite. The grounds feature a restaurant/dining hall as well as BBQ, swimming pool & playground. Dogs allowed. *Cabins* **$$$$**, *sites* **$**

🏠 The View on Hannans (128 rooms) 430 Hannan St, Kalgoorlie; ☎9091 3333; w theviewonhannans.com.au. 4-star motel featuring large bathrooms & tea-/coffee-making facilities, but a bit plain for the price. Laundry & BBQ facilities. **$$$$**

✳ 🏠 Palace Hotel (70 rooms) 137 Hannan St, Kalgoorlie; ☎9021 2788; w palacehotelkalgoorlie. com. A local icon, the memorable Palace, built in 1897, oozes charm & old Goldfields' ambience at every turn. The decorative mirror in the foyer was a gift to the hotel from future US President Herbert Hoover, who supposedly fell in love with one of the barmaids here while serving in the Goldfields as a mining engineer before entering US politics (see box,

page 242). Rooms range from suites to backpacker offerings; some of the standard rooms are simply decorated, but the overall ambience makes up for it. The hotel's central location can make it a bit loud at night. The Balcony Bar & Restaurant, Hoover Café & Gold Bar are attached (page 232). **$$$**

🏠 The Plaza (100 rooms) 45 Egan St, Kalgoorlie; ☎9080 5900; w plazakalgoorlie.com. au. Tasteful, contemporary rooms offering all the modern conveniences & balconies, some with views of town, one block south of Hannan St. Rooms are a bit larger than standard & b/fast is available for an extra charge at the attached Plaza Restaurant. **$$$**

🏠 Quality Inn Railway Motel (95 rooms) 51 Forrest St, Kalgoorlie; ☎9088 0000; w railwaymotel.com.au. A very good option directly opposite the train station. Comfortable & bright rooms feature leather recliners & double-glazed windows, some with kitchenette; accessible rooms & 2-bedroom apartment available. The attached Carriages Restaurant offers b/fast & dinner. **$$$**

🏠 BIG4 Acclaim Prospector Caravan Park [map, opposite] 9 Ochiltree St, Kalgoorlie; ☎9021 2524; w big4.com.au/caravan-parks/wa/ golden-outback/acclaim-prospector-holiday-park. A reliable option from this national chain, with powered & unpowered sites & studio & family cabins with kitchens. Camping & caravan sites feature a camp kitchen & BBQ facilities, while the grounds have a swimming pool & playground & can offer gas bottle swap/ refills & short-term caravan storage. *Cabins* **$$$**, *sites* **$**

🏠 Albion Hotel [map, opposite] (37 units) 60 Burt St, Boulder; ☎9093 1399. Built in Federation Filigree-style in 1897, the historic Albion was

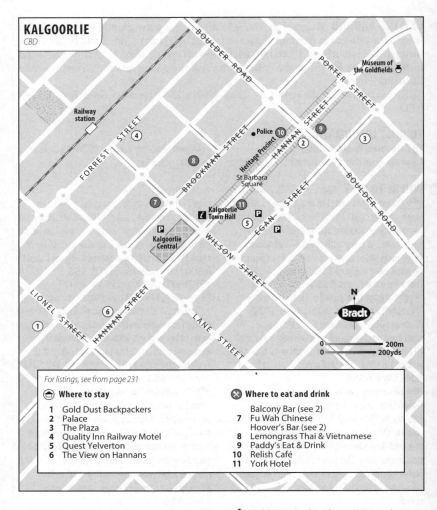

Railway station

Museum of the Goldfields

FORREST STREET

BOULDER ROAD

PORTER STREET

BROOKMAN STREET

HANNAN STREET

• Police

Heritage Precinct

St Barbara Square

Kalgoorlie Town Hall

Kalgoorlie Central

STREET

EGAN

BOULDER ROAD

WILSON STREET

LIONEL STREET

HANNAN STREET

LANE STREET

N

Bradt

0 ————— 200m
0 ————— 200yds

For listings, see from page 231

Where to stay

1 Gold Dust Backpackers
2 Palace
3 The Plaza
4 Quality Inn Railway Motel
5 Quest Yelverton
6 The View on Hannans

Where to eat and drink

   Balcony Bar (see 2)
7 Fu Wah Chinese
   Hoover's Bar (see 2)
8 Lemongrass Thai & Vietnamese
9 Paddy's Eat & Drink
10 Relish Café
11 York Hotel

renovated in the late 1990s to come as true to its original form as possible. The comfortable if standard rooms are all en suite & have a kitchenette. The attached bistro (⏱ 11.30–14.30, 17.30–20.30 daily) is known for its steak. **$$**

Gold Dust Backpackers (27 rooms) 192 Hay St, Kalgoorlie; ☎ 9091 3737; e golddust@ westnet.com.au. A good place for information on backpacker work options; AC dbl, trpl & dorm rooms, plus 2 large lounge rooms. Kitchen; also offers a pick-up/drop-off service from the bus & train stations. **$**

✗ WHERE TO EAT AND DRINK *Map, above*

Most restaurants are clustered on Hannan Street in Kalgoorlie or Burt Street in Boulder.

✳ ✗ **Balcony Bar & Restaurant** 137 Hannan St, Kalgoorlie; ☎ 9021 2788; w palacehotel kalgoorlie.com; ⏱ 16.00–22.00 Mon–Sat. Inside

the Palace Hotel (page 231); grab a table on the balcony overlooking Hannan St & the clock tower. The menu features an ample selection of meat &

seafood, & pavlova stars in the dessert section. Last time I was here, I had a sensational steak. They also offer a vintage wine list. $$$

✷ ✗ **Paddy's Eat & Drink** 135 Hannan St, Kalgoorlie; ☎6002 2207; w exchangekalgoorlie. com.au; ⏰ 11.00–midnight daily. In the Exchange Hotel, Paddy's hearty, filling burgers & warm atmosphere have a way of recharging the soul after a hard day in the Outback scrub. The beef & Guinness pie isn't bad either. This place is a personal favourite & I always call in at least once whenever I'm in town. $$$

✗ **York Hotel** 259 Hannan St, Kalgoorlie; ☎9021 2337 w yorkhotel.com.au; ⏰ 11.00–midnight Mon–Sat. Dating to 1901, this rustic hotel restaurant serves decent steaks & burgers, but the 'flagship sandwich' – steak on Turkish bread – is the star item. A range of starters & salads also features. Good balcony views out over Hannan St. $$$

✗ **Fu Wah Chinese Restaurant & Takeaway** 6/6 Wilson St, Woolworth's Plaza; ☎9021 6242; ⏰ 11.00–14.00, 17.00–21.30 daily. The pick of Kal's Chinese eateries & a local favourite, Fu Wah has an extensive menu & is recommended for its soup & fried rice dishes. $$

✗ **Hoover's Bar & Bistro** 137 Hannan St, Kalgoorlie; ☎9021 2788; w palacehotelkalgoorlie. com; ⏰ 07.00–16.00 daily. Named after its famous guest, & in an exquisite setting in the Palace Hotel (page 231) with stained glass, decorative ceiling, chandelier & old-world mirrors, the Hoover offers morning & afternoon teas in addition to its b/fast & lunch offerings. While the menu could be a bit more creative, this is a solid bet & the atmosphere makes it a winner. B/fasts here are particularly hearty. $$

✗ **Lemongrass Thai & Vietnamese** 5/4-90 Brookman St, Kalgoorlie; ☎9021 8009; ⓕ LemongrassKalgoorlie; ⏰ 11.30–14.30 & 16.30–21.30 Mon–Sat, 16.30–21.30 Sun. This local favourite for southeast Asian specialties adjusts its menu to the season. Expect winter soup & noodle dishes, tasty spring rolls & stir-fries & more exotic specials like sugar cane prawn. $$

✗ **Relish Café** 162 Hannan St, Kalgoorlie; ☎9091 9992; ⓕ relishkalgoorlie; ⏰ 06.00–15.00 Mon–Sat, 08.00–14.00 Sun. Quirky café with a hipster menu featuring take-away sandwiches & healthier options like banana & coconut chia pudding, as well as more decadent, sugar-filled snacks like cheesecake & pretzel fudge. $

OTHER PRACTICALITIES

Kalgoorlie Health Campus 15 Piccadilly St, Kalgoorlie; ☎9080 5888

West Australian Police Lot 4911 Brookman St, Kalgoorlie; ☎9021 9777

WHAT TO SEE AND DO

Gold sights The **Kalgoorlie Heart of Gold Discovery Tour** (w goldindustrygroup. com.au/kalgoorlie-heartofgold-discovery-trail) is a great starting point to the 'Golden Mile' and understanding Kalgoorlie's history. Available as an app, this self-guided walking tour (2km; about 1hr) takes you around 11 sites in the Kalgoorlie CBD (all but three are on Hannan Street), starting with the gold bar replica at the Market Arcade and finishing at the Museum of the Goldfields (page 235).

Super Pit & Lookout ✷ (Outram St, Boulder; w superpit.com.au; ⏰ 07.00–19.00 daily; free) Kalgoorlie's signature attraction is recognised country-wide. This is one of the biggest mines in Australia – almost 28,350kg of gold are mined out of the 500m-deep pit annually. The viewing platform is on Outram Street, just off the Goldfields Highway, and staring down into this neatly terraced abyss and seeing its haulage vehicles – gargantuan up close, but which look like insects in the Super Pit's massive expanse – is an unforgettable experience. You can also check mine operator KCGM's website for when blast times are and view a blast (a detonation to break apart rock, making it easier to remove) from the lookout.

The Super Pit is one attraction where it pays to invest a bit more and book a guided tour to see the workings inside the pit itself. **Kalgoorlie Tours & Charters** (250 Hannan St, Kalgoorlie; ☎ 9021 2211; e info@kalgoorlietours.com.au; w kalgoorlietours.com.au) is recommended and authorised by KCGM; they

THE STORY OF MODESTO VARISCHETTI

Mine accidents don't usually have a happy ending, but the story of Italian miner Modesto Varischetti in the Goldfields bucked the trend.

On 19 March 1907, Varischetti was one of 160 miners underground at the mine at Bonnie Vale, 12km from Coolgardie, when a thunderstorm arrived. Although the mine was evacuated, Varischetti was somehow left behind – 220m under the surface – as it began to flood. Unable to get out, he became trapped, incredibly and miraculously, in an air pocket underneath 15m of water.

Though the evacuated miners presumed that Varischetti had drowned, the mine manager, Josiah Crabb, thought there was a slim chance he may have survived and an alert was put out. The next day they were astounded when they heard Varischetti's tapping from below. The West Australian government snapped into action, sending an air hose and specialist divers on a train to Coolgardie – setting a speed record in the process of 12 hours. On Varischetti's sixth day in the air pocket, divers reached him and were able to give him some sustenance, but they were still unable to get him out. They continued to visit him daily, but it was not until day nine that enough water had been pumped out to allow a rescue. Varischetti finally emerged from his ordeal on 28 March, but with barely a scratch on him.

Varischetti returned to the mines soon after and continued to work there until he died of fibrosis in 1920. Tom Austen's book *The Entombed Miner* documents the story. Varischetti is buried in the Kalgoorlie Cemetery, and you can visit his grave.

offer 1½- and 2½-hour tours that travel on the same access roads as the dump trucks, show you the old mine shafts and offer excellent vantage points of modern mining machinery and operations. As this is a working gold mine, there are safety requirements in place to be able to take the tour, including wearing appropriate clothing. KCGM also runs a free community tour on Boulder Market Day (the third Sunday of every month) – book at the **Eastern Goldfields Historical Society** (Old Boulder Power Station, Hamilton St, Boulder; w kalgoorliehistory.org.au; ⊕ 09.00–14.00 Mon–Fri) from 08.30 on the day; first come, first served. This long-standing organisation is dedicated to preserving and educating about the Goldfields and holds a series of objects, documents and over 60,000 photographs in its collection showing the development of the region. A good place for novice gold prospectors in their site research.

Hannans North Tourist Mine ✳ (130 Goldfields Hwy, Kalgoorlie; ✆ 9022 1664; w hannansnorth.com.au; ⊕ 09.00–16.00 Sun–Fri; adult/concession/child/family A$15/12.50/8/45) Originally one of the first mines in the Goldfields in 1893, this is no longer a working mine like the Super Pit but instead a must-see interactive tourist experience, enjoyable for both adults and kids. Visitors can mine their own gold, clamber aboard a haul truck and even visit the underground refuge chamber, designed to keep miners alive in the event of disaster (one of my favourite parts of the grounds). Period buildings have also been relocated here and there is a set-up where you can experience life at an 1890s prospector's campsite. Gold-pour demonstrations usually occur during school holidays – call to verify times.

Museum of the Goldfields (17 Hannan St, Kalgoorlie; ☎9021 8533; w museum. wa.gov.au/museums/museum-of-the-goldfields; ⏱ 10.00–15.00 daily; free, donations welcome) The Kalgoorlie branch of the Western Australia Museum, this is a good place to learn about the region's mining history. Home to the state's largest collection of gold bars and nuggets, it also chronicles how Kalgoorlie's Outback geography – often the first stop for travellers coming west – has impacted the state's development. Permanent exhibitions include a relocated miner's cottage, opulent period-era mining office boardrooms and a Heritage-listed hotel that has been remodeled to contain exhibits and galleries. The main gallery traces the Gold Rush's

HOW TO PROSPECT FOR GOLD

So, like thousands that have entered these lands before you, you have come down with Gold Fever. What's the cure? Prospecting is an accessible and enjoyable activity, even if you don't find the motherlode.

The first question many novice prospectors have is: where should I look? It's the legwork here that pays – research, research, research. Look for old goldfields, old mining sites and ghost towns (which, in this region, would have been built near gold finds). Historical societies and local libraries (such as the Local History Archives at Boulder Town Hall) can be great sources of information – look for old town plans and maps, mining registers and grants etc that may indicate areas where there have been gold finds.

When you have located where you would like to prospect, investigate what permissions you need to go ahead. The most commonly issued permit to tourists is the Miner's Right, and can be issued at any mining registrar's office – such as the one in Kalgoorlie (cnr Hunter & Broadwood St; ☎9021 9499). This will allow you to prospect on Crown land. The Department of Mines, Industry Regulation and Safety publishes the 'Seven Golden Rules for Prospecting' which will point you in the direction of what permit you need, and this can be downloaded from their website (w dmp.wa.gov.au/Documents/Minerals/ Minerals_-_Seven_golden_rules_for_prospecting.pdf). Stiff penalties apply if you don't have the right permit.

Next, make sure you have the right equipment. Most commonly this will involve hiring a metal detector, a large and small spade, a pan, a pick and plenty of water. There is a technique to using a metal detector – try to keep it as low to the ground as you can, and move it in a slow, steady motion. Some people also bring a smaller detector called a 'pinpointer', which can help direct you to a metal more quickly once your larger detector has found a signal. Often nuggets can be close to the surface – the Welcome Stranger, the biggest found in Australia by two Cornish miners in 1869, was only 3cm under the surface. It weighed 72kg and was 61cm long.

If you are a true novice – it's a great day's fun to go on an organised prospecting tour to learn the ropes. **Gold Nugget Tours** in Kalgoorlie (w tours88.com.au; ⏱ by appointment) offers all-day tours with equipment hire and instruction, taking you to a lease just north of town. **The Prospector's Patch** (260 Hannan St; w prospectorspatch.com.au; ⏱ 09.00–17.00 Mon–Fri, 09.00–noon Sat) is perhaps the premier resource in the area – they provide equipment sales and hire, can assist with planning and their general wealth of knowledge, passion and enthusiasm make their shop a must-stop if planning a prospecting run.

influence on the area. The Gold Vault has a display of nuggets and holds half of the state's gold collection.

Kalgoorlie A great walk to do in conjunction with Heart of Gold Discovery Tour (page 233), the **Heartwalk** (w heartwalkcbd.com) is a collection of over 60 public art murals by local artists. Jason Dimer's *Kgungka Thurtu* (*Sister Girl*) dot painting, in honour of his deceased younger sister, is a personal favourite, as is Brenton See's *Freedom in Red*, an ode to the spectacular flora and fauna of the Goldfields bush. A map (and kids' activity sheets) can be downloaded from the website, and many of the murals are along Hannan Street.

Elsewhere on Hannan Street is the **Government Precinct,** a Heritage-listed complex of buildings all designed by the same architect, J H Grainger, and consisting of the Old Post Office, Warden's Court, Mines Department and Courthouse. In 2013, they were amalgamated and restored into a contemporary new courthouse, at a cost of nearly A$42 million. One of the notable features of this precinct is the stately and still-functioning clock tower, built from soft pink stone and topped with a gold dome. Unfortunately, views are only from the outside looking up – it is not open to the public.

Next to the precinct is **St Barbara Square**, dedicated to the patron saint of miners. The placement of a statue and fountain on this square in 1999 was a highly appropriate dedication to the mining industry, its workers and, as the plaque notes, those who have died in the industry. Kalgoorlie Market Days are held here on the first Sunday of each month. Barbara's Feast Day, when the dedication took place, is on 4 December and marked with a festival.

Continuing south along Hannan Street, you'll reach **Kalgoorlie Town Hall** (316 Hannan St; ⟍9021 9600; ⊕ guided tours only, 10.30 Mon & Wed, A$5). Though a notch below that in Boulder, it is still a very impressive sight – the powder-pink edifice of this Heritage-listed building is one of Hannan Street's most beloved local landmarks. Built as a catch-all in 1908 with theatre, council chambers and municipal offices, the upstairs foyer now hosts a local Sporting Hall of Fame. The inside foyer also has a commemorative statue of prospector Paddy Hannan. The statue of Hannan outside the Town Hall is a replica, and has a drinking fountain inside Hannan's handbag. The **Kalgoorlie-Boulder Visitor Centre** (page 231) is located here and can assist you with booking a guided tour – the only way to see the inside.

Signpost Goldfields Racing Museum (14 Meldrum Av, Kalgoorlie; ⟍9021 2303; w kbrc.com.au; ⊕ 09.00–15.30 Mon–Fri, 09.00–noon Sat; free) On the grounds of the Kalgoorlie-Boulder Racing Club, this museum showcases many exhibits from horse racing including a restored hansom cab, old 'photo finish' equipment used by judges, and Melbourne Cup memorabilia. The club's website includes information about the track and a calendar of upcoming races.

Hammond Park (Memorial Dr, Kalgoorlie; ⟍9021 9600; ⊕ 09.00–17.00 daily) Just 2km north of the CBD, this park offers a peaceful retreat from the city nestled in the middle of the Outback. The ponds attract a number of local birds and you'll also spot peacocks roaming around. The grounds feature a miniature Bavarian Castle, and also a children's playground. Adjacent to the park is the dog-friendly Kalgoorlie Arboretum (free), set on 26ha of native bush representative of the Great Western Woodlands (page 218) and featuring bushwalks through the eucalyptus; there's also a picnic area and small dam that attracts birds like red wattlebirds and mistletoe birds. The Katunga Lookout in the adjacent Karlkurla Bushland Park is a local favourite to watch sunrises and sunsets.

Boulder The main reason to visit this part of town is to admire the magnificent, Heritage-listed **Boulder Town Hall** ✳ (116 Burt St; ☎ 9021 9817; ◷ 10.00–13.00 Mon–Fri; free). Built in 1908, this Federation Free Classical-style building captures the spirit of the turn-of-the-century Goldfields and is truly eye-catching, with its white clock tower and verandas contrasting against the red bricks. Inside, cast-iron pillars support an elevated horseshoe-shaped seating veranda with ornate balustrade. Over the decades the hall has hosted numerous musical performances, including Victorian opera singer Dame Nellie Melba. Inside the theatre is the **Goatcher Curtain**, considered a priceless work of art – one of the last working stage curtains in the country, it was painted by Philip Goatcher with a depiction of the Bay of Naples and Mount Vesuvius. It gets lowered on Tuesdays, Wednesdays, Thursdays and Boulder Market Days. The Town Hall also contains the **Local History Archive** and the **Goldfields War Museum** (◷ 10.00–16.00 Mon–Fri; entry by donation) which covers the involvement of local residents in wars from the Boer War to the 21st century, though artefacts, documents and images.

DAY TRIPS AROUND KALGOORLIE-BOULDER

Heading north from Kalgoorlie on the Goldfields Highway, your first stop, 38km away, is the one-pub town – quite literally – of **Broad Arrow**. What differentiates this ghost town from the others that litter the highway is that its pub – the only thing left in town, which has been abandoned for a century – is still functioning. The **Broad Arrow Tavern** (492 Railway St; ☎ 9024 2058; 🇫 broadarrowtavern; ◷ 11.00–19.00 daily) is enormously popular with Kal folk looking for an afternoon out – the burgers here ('Broady Burgers') are worth the drive up and are very reasonably priced. The 1971 comedy film *Nickel Queen* was set at the tavern.

In Broad Arrow is a turning to **Rowles Lagoon Nature Reserve**, the only freshwater wetland in the Goldfields, 55km west along the Ora Banda–Davyhurst Road and the Ora Banda–Carbine Road. It hosts dozens of species of waterbird like spoonbills and herons. The amount of water in the wetlands varies dramatically, from dry to flooded; swimming is possible when there is enough water. This is a popular campground (managed by DPaW– there are no fees, but advance bookings are not accepted); however, last time I ventured out here, the road was in such poor condition that I had to stop and turn around.

Back on the highway, continuing north from Broad Arrow to Menzies you'll come to the turning for **Goongarrie National Park**. Gold was discovered in this area just after it was in Coolgardie; in 1890, Goongarrie was actually a town known as Ninety Mile – though it was abandoned quickly and essentially became a ghost town by 1910. Today only three old railway cottages remain (part of the Golden Quest Discovery Trail; see box, page 227). Camping is available at the homestead complex (bookings through DPaW Goldfields Office; ☎ 9080 555; e kalgoorlie@ dpaw.wa.gov.au; fees apply) and is surprisingly comfortable, and its distance from the highway means it is often quiet.

THE NORTHERN GOLDFIELDS

The sparsely populated Northern Goldfields host Lake Ballard, a postcard-perfect clock tower on the main street in Menzies, and the Gwalia Ghost Town mining exhibit – and the whole area can be explored as a rewarding though long day trip from Kalgoorlie. If you are going to be in Kal, don't pass up a chance to come out here.

MENZIES Most Australians would assume a town named Menzies is named after Robert Menzies, the country's longest-serving prime minister, who held office from 1939 to 1941 and then again from 1949 to 1966. The town *is* named after a Robert Menzies, but a completely different one (and, incidentally, an American): Leslie Robert Menzies, from Baltimore, Maryland, was the first person to take up a mining lease here.

Situated 130km north of Kalgoorlie, Menzies's current claim to fame is the eccentric history behind its **clock tower**. When the Town Hall and Shire Office (124 Shenton St) was built in 1896, it included provisions for a clock tower – the tower was constructed, but legend has it that the clock was purchased from England and it went down with the Royal Mail Steamer *Orizaba* when it sank off Rottnest Island in 1905. The clockface on the tower was not replaced, and so it sat bare for the next 95 years – until an actual clock was finally installed on the tower in 2000.

It's a great story, but one the Shire of Menzies says may not be true. There is no record of a clock ever being bought from England, no record of one being transported on the *Orizaba*, nor any purchase or cost estimates for a clock in government records. Former Shire CEO Greg Carter told the *West Australian* in 2000 that '[T]he story would certainly have suited politicians rather than their unwillingness to provide for a clock'.

Inside the historic former Lady Shenton Hotel, **Menzies Visitors' Centre** (35 Shenton St; ✎ 9024 2702; ⊕ 08.30–noon Mon–Fri, 13.00–16.30 Mon–Fri) has maps and a short walking tour brochure of the town. There are limited options for accommodation and meals in Menzies, so you are better off staying in Kalgoorlie, which is a little over an hour away.

Lake Ballard ✳ (w lakeballard.com) Menzies is the closest town to Lake Ballard, home to Turner Prize winner Antony Gormley's spectacular *Inside Australia* outdoor gallery – one of the defining art pieces of WA, and perhaps the entire country. Unveiled in 2003, these 51 metal figures (the 'insiders') reside on the 4,900ha salt lake, a collection of locals and out-of-towners visiting Menzies. Gormley used a laser scanner to record their images at the Menzies Hotel, and their names are posted on the website.

The multi-award-winning film *Inside Australia*, available for purchase from Artemis Media's website (w artemisfilms.com), takes a look inside the making of the gallery – from the initial reaction of the shire police, who thought Gormley was crazy (the shire president thought someone was playing a prank on her when she first heard about it), to Gormley recounting how he managed to convince reluctant townspeople and those from the Aboriginal community to pose nude for the body scanners. The photos were used to create moulds cast in steel alloy – though the figures have significantly less mass than their real-life models. It is entertaining and fundamental pre-requisite viewing for a visit here.

The lake is a perfect setting for the sculptures. There is a small hill a few hundred metres out (which you can climb for a bird's-eye view) that elegantly frames the scene. The sculptures themselves are simple and scattered about – you can't see all of them from any one vantage point, and some require a bit of a hike to reach (there's no signposting or signage). I find it a place that inspires deep contemplation about the relationship between humans and nature, isolation and remoteness.

Lake Ballard is 51km from Menzies on an unsealed road; it is suitable for 2WD vehicles but check conditions first – although I have never had a problem in my 2WD. Free camping is permitted at the lake but only at designated sites. There is no water available, and fire restrictions apply. One word of warning: bring a fly net to put over your hat.

KOOKYNIE Continuing north from Menzies, after 40km you'll reach the Kookynie Road, which leads east to this living ghost town home to about a dozen people and a thriving hotel-pub, the Grand Hotel Kookynie (☏ 9031 3010; 🅕 grandhotelkookynie). Still in its original building, it attracts about ten times the town's population most nights – often mining and rail contractors, though also plenty of tourists. One of the most prominent regulars is Willie the Horse, who drops in every now and again. The restaurant is highly regarded, and the hotel has an extensive collection of photographs and artefacts of the town's history. Unlike many West Australian ghost towns, which can feature rubble, interpretive signage and little else, Kookynie still has some buildings standing. The ruins of the old Cosmopolitan and National pubs are worth a look as are the restored Cumberland Street shops.

An unusual availability of fresh water is why the town has been able to cling on. **Niagara Dam**, 12km south from Kookynie on the road from the highway, is a swimming and camping spot.

LEONORA The biggest town in the northern Goldfields, around 103km north of Menzies on the Goldfields Highway, Leonora is best known for the award-winning Gwalia Ghost Town and the Leonora Loops (see box, below). There isn't a whole lot in town itself, and Tower Street, the main high street, can seem shabby and at times derelict. The town does have a **Heritage Trail** that you can download from the shire's

---

ROAD TRIP: LEONORA LOOPS

Built to be complementary to the Golden Quest Discovery Trail (see box, page 227), the Leonora Loops are actually two different drives, each with 15 interpretive sights – the 350km Darlot Trail, which loops east and north of Leonora, and the 300km Agnew Trail, which loops west and north of town. Each loop can be done in a day and has a different theme. Storytelling is the emphasis and at each stop there is a steel cutout figure with a tale. Be sure to set your odometer to zero at the start of the trail so you can easily monitor your progress; the sites are denoted in kilometre distance markers from Leonora.

The theme of the **Agnew Loop** is 'Survival in a Strange Land', with the figures telling a social history of the Outback. Some of the sites are a fairly lukewarm and redundant mix of wells, creek pools, cemeteries and ghost town homages that can seem to only marginally differ from those elsewhere in the Goldfields. The real attraction is being out in some of the most remote open land in the world, and pondering, as you look at the sites, how people were able to make a go of it in some of the most harsh and inhospitable conditions on earth.

The **Darlot Loop** is more nature-focused and its theme is 'Much More than Mulga', showcasing different landscapes of the area. It makes for a nice, if not spectacular, day out – the desert eucalyptus and the terraces, a breakaway formation, are the highlights. If you only have time to do one of the loops, the Darlot is probably the more varied and offers something different if you are heritage-trailed out.

Both loops are mostly unsealed, though suitable for 2WD vehicles driven with care. Check conditions with the Shire of Leonora. The visitor centre (page 240) has a 90-page guidebook for the loops, and a brochure is available to download at ⓦ goldenquesttrail.com/wp-content/uploads/2015/07/Leonora-Loop-Trails-Brochure.pdf.

From Laverton, the Great Central Road runs for nearly 1,200km to the town of Yulara, in Northern Territory, near Uluru. The route is part of the larger Outback Way that bills itself as 'Australia's Longest Shortcut', starting in Laverton and ending in Winton, Queensland. The road is mostly used as a shortcut to get to Uluru, Alice Springs or Queensland, and being able to avoid the 'right angle drive' of crossing the Nullarbor east to Port Augusta and then heading north to Alice Springs. But it is a truly epic drive, trundling through the vast Outback – and passing some of the world's most remote real estate. Over the distance you'll pass breakaways, caves and waterholes, but expect a lot of scrub and dirt. You may see kangaroos, emus, dingoes and perhaps even camels.

The desert road is mostly unsealed and a 4x4 is recommended. Occasionally it is in good enough condition to be accessed by 2WD – *some* have made it – but the fleet of abandoned cars dotting the roadside all the way to the NT is testament to the risk of this. Check conditions with the Shire of Laverton (w laverton.wa.gov. au); it is also worth calling the three roadhouses on the WA side of the border, since they will have up-to-date information on conditions in their areas. In the highly expensive event of a breakdown, Paul Ashboth in Warburton (0428 838 476) is your contact person for vehicle recovery. This is remote country, so have enough food, water and activities to be able to wait for hours. There is no unleaded fuel on the Great Central Road – BP has developed 'opal fuel', which is an equivalent, but was developed to combat petrol-sniffing. If you are unsure whether your vehicle can use opal fuel, contact the manufacturer.

A permit to drive through Aboriginal lands is required to travel on the Great Central Road. For tourists, this can often be obtained instantaneously (and for free) at w dplh.wa.gov.au/entrypermits. The permit gives you three days to travel from Laverton to the WA/NT border, but only gives you permission to travel the road and enter the roadhouses and their attached accommodations. Department permits are only valid in WA.

Your first stop, 300km east of Laverton, is the **Tjukayirla Roadhouse** (7 rooms; 9037 1108; w tjukayirlaroadhouse.com.au; ⊕ 08.00–17.00 Mon–Fri, 09.00–15.00 Sat–Sun), which has a restaurant and a shop, plus extensive

website or purchase from the visitors' centre (cnr Tower & Trump St; 9037 7016; ⊕ 09.00–16.30 Mon–Fri).

GWALIA ✳ If you only have time to visit one ghost town in the Goldfields, it should be this one. A A$3.3 million upgrade from the Shire of Leonora helped make it a 2019 Western Australian Heritage Award winner, and today it is one of the country's best interactive ghost town experiences. It also hosts the northern Goldfields' best accommodation (which is the primary reason to base yourself in Leonora for a stay in the area).

The Sons of Gwalia mine operated from 1897 to 1963 and is notable because US president Herbert Hoover was its first manager (see box, page 242). The old mine office houses the **Gwalia Museum** (15 Manning St; w gwalia.org.au; ⊕ 09.00–16.00 daily; free), which features an electric tram, restored postal truck and numerous other vehicles. Outside the museum in the grounds, the Fraser and Chalmers steam winder, which used to lower men down into the shafts for their shifts, is one of only three left in the world. Wander among the deserted cottages and you'll see hops, the camping facilities including showers. There are a few Aboriginal art caves in the vicinity, with art estimated to be around 5,000 years old. Ask the roadhouse about access.

The main townsite of the Western Deserts and the Shire of Ngaanyatjarraku, **Warburton** comes next, 250km east of Tjukayirla. The **Warburton Roadhouse** (45 rooms; 8956 7656; w warburtonroadhouse.com.au; 08.00–17.00 Mon–Fri; 09.00–15.00 Sat–Sun) has en-suite motel rooms, cabins, caravan and camping sites, as well as a restaurant. Next door is the **Cultural and Civic Centre**, housing the indigenous **Tjulyuru Regional Arts Gallery** (09.00–16.00 Mon–Fri, other times by appointment; by donation) with work from local artists and one of the world's largest collections of community-controlled indigenous art. Apart from the roadhouse and gallery, a separate permit is required to enter the town itself (contact DPLH for more information).

The last stop before the NT border is the **Warakurna Roadhouse** (14 rooms; 8956 7344; w warakurnaroadhouse.com.au; 08.30–17.00 Mon–Fri, 9.00–15.00 Sat–Sun) in the Rawlinson Ranges, which has a restaurant and powered and unpowered camping sites. The **Yurliya Art Gallery** is nearby (8955 8399; w warakurnaartists.com.au) showcasing hand-woven baskets, sculptures and paintings. Behind the roadhouse is the **Giles Weather Station** where you can witness the daily launch of the weather observation balloon for the Australian Bureau of Meteorology. Warakurna is 235km east of Warburton, and 118km west of the border at Docker River.

You might think that these roadhouses are the remotest in Australia, but you'd be wrong. The 1,325km-long **Anne Beadell Highway** links Laverton to Coober Pedy, South Australia, and the **Ilkurlka Roadhouse** (9037 1147) is the only facility on this 4x4-only remote desert track, 600km from Laverton. There is only one self-contained unit available, but there are campgrounds. The shop will operate outside normal hours if you knock and/or ask around. This road is not to be taken lightly – you need to be completely self-sufficient with your own comms systems, and you need to be able to make your own vehicle repairs. Plan on a minimum of five days to drive the whole route.

state school and other vestiges of old Goldfields' life. There are also good views into the open-cut mining pit.

Where to stay and eat

Hoover House B&B (3 rooms) 15 Manning St; 9037 7122; e museum@gwalia.org.au; w gwalia.org.au/hoover-house/accommodation. The best place to stay in the northern Goldfields. Dating from 1897, the building was designed by Herbert Hoover as the residence for the mine managers. Rooms are tastefully decorated in period style with ample views; there is an on-site café during the day. There is a free RV site;

however, all vehicles must have a sealed grey-water container & meet criteria (available on the website). Camping is not permitted. **$$$**

Leonora Motor Inn (60 rooms) 48 Tower St; 9037 6444; e reception@leonoramotorinn. com.au. A solid choice, the motel rooms here have all the standard amenities & there are serviced apartments as well. The motel has a laundry & does room service. **$$**

LAVERTON The town of Laverton, 123km east of Leonora, is best known as the gateway to the Great Central Road – a 1,200km route through the depths of the

A FUTURE PRESIDENT IN THE GOLDFIELDS

Before becoming the 31st President of the United States, Herbert Hoover trained as a geologist at Stanford University in California, and upon graduation took a job Bewick, Moreing & Co, a London-based mining company that operated in WA. They sent him to Coolgardie, where he proved to be a highly competent inspection engineer – his initial role in the Goldfields. When asked to evaluate Gwalia as a potential site, he liked what he saw, recommended the purchase and wrote a development plan, and so was the natural choice to become the first manager of the mine – at age 23 – when it opened in 1898.

As manager, Hoover had something of a slash-and-burn style. He implemented longer working hours, brought in immigrant labour at lower wages, ended numerous salary bonuses and even implemented some new policies like making shift changes no longer occur at ground level to save productivity time. Not surprisingly, he had an antagonistic relationship with the unions. However, under Hoover's watch, the Gwalia mine become one of the most profitable in the Goldfields. He was also rumoured to be something of a night owl – the Palace Hotel in Kalgoorlie (page 231) displays a poem that may have been written by him to a barmaid mistress. Despite Hoover's aptitude as a mine manager and his efforts to ingratiate himself in some parts of Kalgoorlie society, his bosses found him difficult to work with, and the company solved that conflict by promoting him – and sending him to China.

Outback into Northern Territory (see box, page 240). Other sights in the town include the **Explorers Hall of Fame** at the **Great Beyond Visitor Centre** (5 Augusta St; ☏ 9031 1361; e greatbeyond@laverton.wa.gov.au; ⊕ 09.00–16.30 Mon–Fri, 09.00–13.00 Sat–Sun), where past explorers 'speak' to you about the motivations for their expeditions and the hardships they endured in the process. Elsewhere, the **Laverton Outback Gallery** (Augusta St; ☏ 9031 1395; ⊕ 08.00–16.00 Mon–Fri) displays pieces from the local Wongatha artists, including things like scarves and painted emu eggs. The gallery is a co-operative and most of the purchase price goes to the artists. If you have to stay the night here – try the **Desert Inn Hotel** (26 rooms; ☏ 0931 1188; **$$**), which has a pub.

9

The Wheatbelt

The Wheatbelt is Western Australia's answer to Big Sky Country, a place where the temptation to roll the windows down, crank up the radio and just drive is irresistible. This massive grain-growing area stretches from the Indian Ocean just north of Perth to the edge of the Outback between Southern Cross and Coolgardie. Driving down from the Perth Hills, the landscape opens up into a palette of colour: two-lane roads rolling through green fields dotted with eucalyptus, golden hay bales spread out like squares on a chequerboard, studs of light brown granite outcrops and snow-white salt lakes glittering in the sun, all beneath an oh-so-blue sky. Grain and farming are king here – particularly wheat and sheep. However, this was not naturally open land prior to European settlement – much of it was cleared to make way for farming, and the resulting environmental change (combined with the effects of introduced and invasive species) had catastrophic impacts on native animals like numbats and the burrowing bettong, who lost their habitats.

For visitors, however, the Wheatbelt's most famous drawcard is the big, distinctively streaked rocks. Wave Rock in Hyden is the best known, but there are many others that are just as intriguing – including the third-biggest monolith in the country. But there is plenty more to discover besides – York is the earliest inland settlement in the state, home to some wonderfully preserved Heritage buildings, and the area has started to embrace its Aboriginal heritage too, with local operators springing up to introduce it to visitors. Further south, close to the Peel Region, the salt lakes and eucalypt bush provide a unique landscape with unique fauna, and you can take a night tour to look for small marsupials.

The Wheatbelt is home to several Aboriginal groups, who have been here for at least 45,000 years: the Njaki Njaki Nyoongar traditional lands are in the southern part of the region, the Ballardong Nyoongar traditional lands in the central and eastern parts, the Yued Nyoongar traditional lands are north of Perth, and the traditional lands of the Gubrun peoples are in the northwestern part.

THE AVON VALLEY

The Avon Valley makes for a great long weekend; base yourself in any of the three towns and enjoy the glorious old buildings and fine dining each provides, capped with a hot-air balloon ride over the rolling farmland. This is the Wheatbelt's largest population centre, with about 19,000 people residing in the Northam, York and Toodyay shires collectively, and it has the best services to match – it's a destination in its own right, but the hotels and restaurants make it a good base if you're looking to explore the rocks a bit closer to Perth and not as far out as Hyden.

NORTHAM With a population of around 6,500, Northam is the Wheatbelt's largest town, bisected by the Avon River. Gazetted in 1836, it has one of the largest collections of Heritage-listed buildings in the state, which is a primary reason to visit. Nonetheless, despite its (by Australian standards) age, Northam developed slowly – it wasn't until the state government decided to send the railway to the Eastern Goldfields through here in the early 1890s that Northam really began to grow, eclipse York and become the region's main town. A town reaction against over-alcoholism in the later stages of the 1800s saw temperance become a key movement here – Northam became known as 'Temperance Town' – and you will find homages to that on the heritage walks (though that reputation for temperance largely ended when the railway to the Goldfields opened). You'll also find nods to white swans – this is the only place in the state where they have thrived, and seeing them on the picturesque Avon River from the suspension bridge in the early morning mist is a memorable experience.

Northam is Ballardong Noongar country, and a visit to Bilya Koort Boodja – one of the state's premier Noongar culture centres – is a must while you are here. Artefacts have been found indicating Aboriginal presence here going back at least 40,000 years.

Getting there and around Northam is only 96km/90 minutes east of Perth, just off the Great Eastern Highway. Transwa's *AvonLink* train runs from Perth's Midland Station (1hr 20mins; from A$21 one-way), while *MerredinLink* and the *Prospector* cover the same route on their way to the Eastern Wheatbelt and Goldfields, but depart from East Perth Station (both 1hr 40mins). A Transwa coach also operates from East Perth (1hr 35mins; from A$21 one-way).

Avon Valley Taxis (◥9622 2936) and **Northam Taxis** (◥0428 807 048) will get you around town, but if you're planning on exploring the wider area – and you should – you realistically need your own car.

Tourist information and tour operators

🛈 **Northam Visitor Centre** 2 Grey St; ◥9622 2100; ☉ 09.00–16.00 daily. Operates the **Historical Buildings Bus Tour** ✳ (A$15pp) showcasing the stories behind Northam's history, & can assist with **self-guided heritage walks** ✳ (about 90mins). Also has an art gallery as well as local crafts for sale.

Windward Balloon Adventures Withers St; ◥9621 2000; w ballooning.net.au. The Wheatbelt's gentle yet colourful landscape make ideal territory for hot-air ballooning. This award-winning outfit runs sunrise flights of about an hour, finishing with a champagne breakfast afterwards (from A$300pp).

 Where to stay Northam (and the entire Avon Valley, for that matter) has some wonderful Heritage accommodation.

🏠 **Farmer's Home Hotel** (16 rooms) 112 Fitzgerald St E; ◥6500 3920; w farmershomehotel.com. This elegant hotel was founded in 1866 by George Throssell – who would go on to become Premier of Western Australia. Under later owners in the 1800s, it gained a reputation as a site for illegal gambling, but today offers beautifully decorated country-style rooms with touches of modern luxury (Bluetooth speakers, USB charging points, Aesop toiletries) – the 'Farmhouse' rooms feature elements from the original hotel, such

as stained-glass windows. The Temperance Bar serves a good selection of local wines & there is a Dome Café here too. **$$$$**

🏠 **Duke's Inn** (31 rooms) 197 Duke St; ◥9670 3450; w dukesinn.com.au. The Heritage-listed Duke has a huge range of recently renovated rooms, from tiny converted 'stables' to self-contained chalets & older rooms with shared facilities. The restaurant has a varied menu with twists on favourites like Mexican parmigiana, & there is a sports bar with free pool table. **$$**

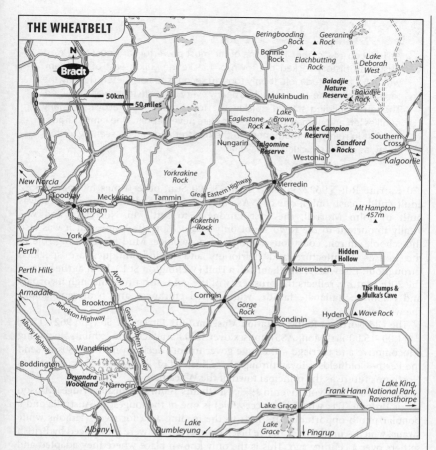

Bradt

50km

50 miles

🏠 **Northam Caravan Park** (12 cabins, 23 pitches) 150 Yilgarn Av; ☎ 9622 1620; w northamcaravanpark.com. Just northeast of town, these recently renovated cabins are a great deal starting at under A$100 per night. Powered & camp sites available; pets accepted if you are in a caravan. Facilities include an atrium with birds, laundry, dump point & camp kitchen. *Cabins* **$$**, *sites* **$**

✗ Where to eat and drink

✗ **Lume Bar & Bistro** 187 Fitzgerald St E; ☎ 9636 5250; w lumenortham.com.au; ⏰ 11.00–14.30, 17.00–21.00 Mon–Sat. Distinctive Italian- & Indian-inspired menu featuring gnocci, arancini, butter chicken & tandooris. Finish off with affogato & tiramisu. **$$**

✗ **Café Yasou** 175 Fitzgerald St E; ☎ 9622 3128; w cafeyasou.com.au; ⏰ 08.00–16.00 Mon–Fri, 08.00–noon Sat. Award-winning café that knows its coffee. Innovative b/fasts like Turkish eggs & Aussie benedict, plus a big selection of pastries. **$**

✗ **Lucy's Tearooms** 122 Fitzgerald St E; ☎ 9622 8628; w lucys-tearooms.business.site; ⏰ 08.00–15.00 Mon–Fri, 08.00–noon Sat. The oldest café in Northam, dating from the 1940s, this homely cafe does a variety of coffees, cakes & b/fasts – try the homemade quiches. **$**

What to see and do Northam's historic buildings make for a pleasant stroll (see opposite for details of guided tours). The best known is **Morby Cottage**

245

(70 Katrine Rd; 9622 3881; 11.00–15.00 Sun, other times by appt; A$5/2 adult/child – cash only), one of WA's oldest residences, dating from 1836. It was built by John Morrell, the first European to settle in Northam, and was vitally important to the town – not only was it Morrell's home, but it was also the school, church, courthouse, shop and post office. Mud played a big role in the house's architecture and heirlooms and period antiques are speckled throughout. Elsewhere, **Northam Town Hall** (Wellington St E), built at the turn of the 20th century, reflects the prosperity of the gold rush times through its ornate and elaborate Italianate façade, with arched entrances and pediments above the windows.

The **Old Northam Railway Station Museum** (401 Fitzgerald St W; 9621 1739; 11.00–15.00 Fri–Mon; A$5) houses over 1,000 artefacts and exhibits, including a locomotive and carriage – the state government's decision in the 1880s to send the Perth–Goldfields railway through here, instead of Toodyay or York, cemented Northam's future as the principal town of the Wheatbelt.

Built across the Avon River in 1975, Northam's 100m **suspension bridge** (Minson Av or Broome Tce; wheelchair accessible) is one of the longest in Australia and a popular photo opportunity. It's next to the feeding area for river's famous white swans, which – unlike their native black counterparts – were introduced by British settlers over a century ago. This is the only known place where they adapted and thrived and the swans have consequently become protected. The bridge is also the starting point for the **Avon Descent** (w avondescent.com.au) – an annual two-day, 124km whitewater race from Northam to Bayswater held in August. If you want to canoe or kayak on the river, you will need to bring your own as there are no hire facilities in town.

Bilya Koort Boodja – Centre for Nyoongar Culture and Environmental Knowledge

(w bilyakoortboodja.com; 09.00–16.00 daily; adult/child A$10/5) Aiming to protect and educate about the Noongar and the Ballardong peoples, and their traditional land practices, this engaging interactive centre runs a variety of workshops, including programs in bushfood tasting and boomerang painting, and also sells local Noongar art.

TOODYAY Originally known as Newcastle (but renamed in 1910 to avoid confusion with Newcastle, NSW), the small town of Toodyay began to thrive when a convict depot was established with the arrival of the Europeans in the 1830s. When it closed in 1872, Toodyay shifted gears to farming and has followed the ebbs and flows of agriculture since, with growing support from tourism – this is true bed-and-breakfast country.

Getting there and away Toodyay is 28km/20 minutes north of Northam. By train, Transwa's *AvonLink*, *MerredinLink* and *Prospector* services all stop at Toodyay en route between Perth and Northam (page 72).

↑ **Where to stay and eat**

🏠 **Pecan Hill B&B** (4 rooms) 99 Beaufort St; ☏9574 2636; w pecanhill.com.au. Overlooking the surrounding pecan orchards of the Avon Valley (hence the name), this is a truly tranquil, comfortable & homely property. Rooms have access to a veranda & outdoor pool, & a good cooked b/fast is served in the morning. Owners Helen & Graham are warm & welcoming. **$$$**

✳ 🏠 **Ipswich View Homestead** (5 rooms) 195 Folewood Rd; ☏9574 4038; 🖿 ipswichview. Built in the 1860s, the bright, elegantly appointed rooms are the epitome of country charm, with views across the valley. Good b/fast; tea/coffee available all day. Owners Alan & Bonnie are great hosts. **$$**

✕ **Alicia's Estate Winery & Restaurant** 525 Nerramine Dr; ☏9574 5458; w aliciaestaterestaurant.com.au; ⏱ 10.00–16.00 Fri–Sun. The owners here have roots in France & Poland, & the winery has Zinfandel, Shiraz & honey mead. The German & Central European-style menu is really worth trying, with schnitzel, goulash & *zwiebelrostbraten* – sliced beef fillet in onion sauce – alongside plenty of potato dishes. Have the strudel for dessert. **$$**

✕ **Cola Café** 128 Stirling Tce; ☏9574 4407; w colacafe.com.au; ⏱ 08.00–16.00 daily. This nostalgic, 1950s café & museum – featuring a vast memorabilia collection curated over the last 45 years – specialises in what it calls 'retro tucker' (ie, food from the period). **$**

Shopping Toodyay has gained a reputation for being an artisan's haven and there are plenty of interesting independent shops lining Stirling Terrace.

Blue Moon Crystals 121D Stirling Tce; ☏0427 554 456; ⏱ 09.30–16.00 Mon & Wed–Sat, 09.30–15.00 Sun. All your gemstone needs; also sell crystals, bracelets & charms. Psychic readings can be booked here – ring in advance for availability.

The Book Shed 112B Stirling Tce; ☏0497 912 672; w thebookshed.com.au; ⏱ 10.00–14.00 Mon–Fri, 10.00–13.00 Sat. Used & vintage books

at this indie retailer stocking everything from Star Trek comics to classic novels.

Christmas 360 113 Stirling Tce; ☏9574 5884; w christmas360.com.au; ⏱ Apr–Dec 09.00–17.00 daily, though check website for exact dates. Billed as one of the biggest Christmas stores in the state. Dolls, figurines, nutcrackers, ornaments & anything even remotely Christmas related is seemingly on offer here.

What to see and do There are nearly 100 Heritage-listed places in the Shire of Toodyay, and the **Living History Walking Trails** ✳ – get a copy from the visitor centre (7 Piesse St; ☏9574 9380; w toodyay.wa.gov.au/visit-toodyay; ⏱ 09.00–16.00 Mon–Fri, 09.00–15.30 Sat–Sun) – offer an excellent overview to many of them. All are very manageable and do not last more than an hour. The focal point of the Yellow Trail is the gloriously interactive **Newcastle Gaol Museum Precinct** ✳ (13 Clinton St; ☏9574 2435; ⏱ 10.00–15.00 daily; A$6), a historical complex focused on Toodyay's convict past – you can wander around the old lock-up cells, police stables, exercise yard and even an old period courtroom – and you can learn more about famous convict, Moondyne Joe (see box, page 248).

Elsewhere, the Green Trail follows the banks of the Avon to take in two sights of interest. Housed inside a 150-year-old mill, **Connor's Mill Museum** (Piesse St; ☏9574 2431; ⏱ 10.00–15.30 daily; admission A$2.50) is an interactive ode to wheat farming in the district, using historic machinery to demonstrate how wheat was turned into flour. Nearby, Gothic **St Stephens Anglican Church** (132 Stirling Tce; ☏9574 2203) was one of the first buildings constructed in the area, dating from

TOODYAY'S FAVOURITE CONVICT

One of the state's most famous renegades, Joseph Johns – aka 'Moondyne Joe' – was transported as a convict to WA in 1853 and, given a new lease of life with a pardon shortly after arriving, moved to Toodyay. But he could not stay out of trouble. In 1861, he was convicted of stealing a horse, and then escaped from the Toodyay Gaol on the same horse he stole, using the judge's own saddle in the process. He was quickly caught, but prison security in Toodyay wasn't so great; he apparently just took a saddle and left. Caught again, this time he was sent to Fremantle Prison, where he was pardoned in 1864. Still unable to stay out of trouble, he found himself on the wrong side of the law and returned to Fremantle Prison in 1865 – escaping three times in four months. In 1866 he even escaped from an 'escape proof' cell at Fremantle Prison. Moondyne Joe's evasiveness became legendary and gained him a following even among law-abiding West Australians. His nickname of 'Moondyne' refers to Moondyne Hill in what is now Avon Valley National Park, which was one of his reputed hiding spots.

Indeed, Moondyne Joe is behind what was considered to be the most cunning escape from Fremantle Prison – he dug out a crawlspace from a wall, using stones to hide the gap, and when it was time he left his clothes behind to trick the guards into thinking he was still inside the prison – thus escaping in his underwear. On another occasion, when he was planning to leave WA and cross to the Eastern States, he broke into one of Toodyay's general stores for supplies and ended up with several dozen ladies' handkerchiefs – how that was supposed to help his journey across the Nullarbor is anyone's guess.

Wherever he went, Moondyne Joe always seemed to wind up back in Toodyay; he gained a sympathetic following among the local population, who seemed to regard him as an entertaining annoyance rather than any sort of hardened criminal. His reputation outlives what seems to be his relatively minor yet repetitive exploits, as is often the case with bush legends. But a word of warning: it is hard to separate fact from fiction with Moondyne Joe. Several songs and poems were written about him and on every first Sunday in May, Toodyay holds an annual Moondyne Festival in honour of its favourite outlaw.

Moondyne Joe died in 1900 at the age of 74 at the Fremantle Asylum, after several years of declining mental health. He is buried in Fremantle Cemetery (page 96).

1862, and its brick façade and deeply steeped roof give the building a handsome stature. Services are still held here.

The shortest of the routes, the Orange Trail (which can be tagged on to the end of the Yellow Trail) leads through the Heritage-listed **Catholic Precinct**, anchored by **St John the Baptist Church** (36 Stirling Tce; ✆9622 5411); this was occupied by monks until 2018, and services are still held here.

YORK Founded in 1831, WA's oldest inland settlement has an absolute ripper of a town hall and a main street that is just bursting with heritage, culture and elegance. York's undeniable charm, coupled with some excellent restaurants, make it very popular with Perth weekenders. When the Covid-19 lockdown was lifted in WA, this was the first place we returned to.

Wheat and grain production to feed the nascent Swan River settlement – now Perth – was the reason for the district's and town's founding. It was named York because the European surveyors here felt the landscape resembled Yorkshire in England. Sheep farming arrived soon after the district's foundation; agriculture and farming, specifically wheat, grains and wool, have been the mainstays of the town ever since.

Getting there and away York is 35km/20 minutes south of Northam and 96km/80 minutes from Perth – take the Great Eastern Highway past Mundaring, and then turn on to the Great Southern Highway. Transwa coaches between East Perth and Albany (via Northam) stop here; fares from East Perth (2hrs) start at A$18 and from Northam (30mins) A$8.70.

Tourist information
York Visitor Centre 81 Avon Tce; \9641 1301; w visit.york.wa.gov.au; ⊕ 09.30–16.00 daily

Where to stay and eat
York has some excellent accommodation and restaurants and is probably the best place to stay in the Avon Valley. However, it can be relatively pricey – consider staying in Northam (page 244) if your budget is tight.

The GrandHouse York (10 rooms) 48 Panmure Rd; \9641 2880; w thegrandhouse. com.au. One of our go-tos in the area. The elegant, tastefully furnished rooms have very comfortable beds & are well heated for chilly Wheatbelt nights. Continental b/fast inc & can be served in your room; cooked b/fast extra. **$$$**

York Palace Hotel (20 rooms) 145 Avon Tce; \9641 2454; w theyork.com.au. Built in 1909 & decorated in the style of the early 20th century, heritage rooms here are gorgeous & feature high ceilings with all the mod-cons, while terrace accommodation is bright, clean & comfortable. The Lord Forrest Suite is worth splurging for, with its veranda & views to Mount Brown. **$$$**

Imperial Homestead (5 rooms) 83 Avon Tce; \9689 4239; w imperialhomestead. com.au. Opened in 1886, this beautiful building is where the working class stayed & where gold miners transited during the latter years of the 19th century – rooms have been well restored with en suites far above the expectations of the original client base. The on-site restaurant is excellent & is worth visiting even if you are not staying here – the kangaroo loin with sweet potato is some of the best we've had, & the seafood paella is good too. **$$**

York Travellers Rest Caravan Park 2 Eighth Rd; \0414 510 503; w yorktravellersrest. com.au. Powered & unpowered sites, featuring a camp kitchen, coin laundry & BBQ area. Pets welcome. **$**

What to see and do
Like Coolgardie, York is a town where every building seems to have a story and its main street, Avon Terrace, is its centrepiece. The visitor centre publishes three highly recommended walking routes (w visit.york.wa.gov.au/ Profiles/visitors/Assets/ClientData/York_Walk_Trails-webversion.pdf), of which the 3km 'Pubs and Parapets' tour is my favourite, but it is equally rewarding to just leave your car and go for a wander. You can also download the 'Avon Terrace' app, which provides a guided audio tour of the street.

The best starting point for any exploration is **York Town Hall** ✳, one of our favourite buildings in WA, and as you approach its grand exterior you will instantly see why. Built in 1911, the Edwardian building is a true architectural showpiece and a highlight of Federation Free style – its red-brick exterior complemented by pastel yellow columns and an ornate clock at the top. It looks stylishly out-of-place among the much more modest, though still decorative, buildings elsewhere along the main street. Its prominence masks a rather checkered history, though – it was condemned less than 20 years after it was built, requiring substantial reinvestment to bring it up to standard; the council struggled to pay off the building's construction, and it was underutilised for most of its early existence. Today, however, it is used as an exhibition space and – far from its rough start – serves as a living postcard for the town.

Across the road from the Town Hall is the gruesome **Rabbit Shed**, built for people to turn in rabbit hides from when the animal was an out-of-control pest in this area in the 1930s.

Heading north along Avon Terrace, you'll reach the **York Motor Museum** (116 Avon Tce; ☏9641 1288; w yorkmotormuseum.com; ⊕ 09.00–16.00 daily; A\$12/9/3 adult/senior & student/child), one of the state's finest car museums, which showcases 100-year-old vehicles, race cars and other period vehicles through the decades. Next door is the National Trust-listed **Courthouse Complex** (132 Avon Tce; ☏9641 2072; ⊕ 10.00–16.00 Thu–Mon), originally built in the 1850s although the cells and court room were, astonishingly, still used as late as the 1980s. Other buildings of note include the **Old Council Chambers** (151 Avon Tce), which housed the fire brigade for nearly 70 years, and the **Sandalwood Yard** (cnr Avon Tce & Ford St; ☏9641 1765; ⊕ 10.00–16.00 daily), which was a big industry in York – the building is now home to the York Society, who aim to ensure historical preservation in the shire.

MERREDIN, HYDEN AND THE BIG ROCKS

The service centre for the Eastern Wheatbelt, with a population of about 2,800, Merredin is best known as the jumping-off point for exploring the region's 'big rocks'. Rising unexpectedly and dramatically out of cleared farmland or eucalypt scrub, these granite outcrops – scattered in isolation across the region – are millions of years old and form part of one of the world's most ancient landscapes. Created from magma solidifying under the earth, before becoming exposed through eons of soil erosion, these golden-brown domes look jarringly and intriguingly out of place against the surrounding flat agricultural land. The outcrops differ wildly in size – some tower above the surface, while others are barely discernable.

The exposed rocks are also good for collecting water, and therefore create microhabitats that are very different from the surrounding area. A number of small native marsupials like bandicoots and possums can be spotted here, and the rocks are popular spots for wildflower enthusiasts to search for orchids. Water pools on the rocks are called gnammas. Aboriginal people relied on these gnammas for their water sources and guarded, marked and cared for them as they sustained life.

The best-known outcrop is Wave Rock in the town of Hyden, famous for its distinctive 'surf wave' shape and vertical streaks, but many Wheatbelt locals do not consider it the best in the area. There are hundreds, perhaps thousands, of rocks scattered across the whole region, and in recent years a two- or three-day self-drive circuit around the Eastern Wheatbelt has become a popular road trip. The vast majority of rocks are 2WD-accessible on good roads, and almost all of them have walking trails leading to the top that can be done in under an hour. When you see a small tower or stack of pancaked rocks, you have reached the peak.

GETTING THERE AND AWAY Merredin is about halfway between Perth (260km west) and Kalgoorlie (333km east) on the Great Eastern Highway; it's about 3 hours to both. The *Prospector* train stops here for 27 minutes during its East Perth–Kalgoorlie runs – services to Kalgoorlie take 3½ hours and it's a little less to East Perth. The *MerredinLink* train runs Monday, Wednesday and Friday from East Perth and back the same day (3hrs 20mins). Tickets start at A$49 one-way to/from Perth and A$60 one-way to/from Kalgoorlie.

Hyden is 330km/4 hours from Perth along the Brookton Highway and 360km/4 hours 15 minutes from Kalgoorlie, through Southern Cross. Transwa coaches operate from East Perth to Hyden on Tuesday, Thursday and Sunday, stopping at the roadhouse in town (4½hrs; from A$58). The coach continues to Esperance, arriving 5 hours later (from A$60 return). The return route to East Perth runs only on Tuesday and Thursday.

TOURIST INFORMATION AND TOUR OPERATORS

⚡ Central Wheatbelt Visitors Centre
85 Barrack St, Merredin; `9041 1666;
w wheatbelttourism.com; ⏱ 08.30–16.30 Mon–Fri. Pick up a brochure mapping out Merredin's Heritage Walk or the self-drive routes in the area.

☀ Njaki Njaki Aboriginal Cultural Tour `0407 984 470; e mick@njakinjaki.com.au; w njakinjaki.com.au. Traditional Owner

Mick's walking tours are famous throughout the Wheatbelt. Learn about connections between the Njaki Njaki & the land, Aboriginal bush tucker & the Dreamtime stories. Mick offers 2 tours; a 2hr 'Peak Merredin' tour highlighting the Aboriginal history of the area & an all-day tour to traditional & historical sites of the local Aboriginal people.

WHERE TO STAY AND EAT

Merredin is not bursting with amenities but still provides the most range in the region. If you are planning excursions to the outcrops in the northern or central Wheatbelt, or are heading further afield to Coolgardie or Kalgoorlie, it makes sense to use Merredin as a base.

Merredin

🏠 Merredin B&B (5 rooms) 30 Bates St; `9041 4358; w atozvisual.com/biz/merredinbedandbreakfast/index.html. Housed in a 1930s bank building, this B&B offers period furniture, country style & a good b/fast. Probably your best bet for staying in town, which is a 5–10min walk away. **$$$**

🏠 Merredin Motel & Gumtree Restaurant (11 rooms) 30–34 Gamenya Av; `9041 1886; w merredinmotel.com. Standard motel rooms with kitchenette items such as toasters, fridge & a microwave. The Gumtree Restaurant (open to guests only) provides frozen but homecooked meals for guests to heat in their rooms. Continental & box lunches available. **$$**

✖ Northside Tavern 58 Bates St; `9041 1635; f northsidetav; ⏱ 11.00–midnight daily. Massive portions offset the standard pub-fare nature of the menu; we did not even finish half of ours. Try the Neptune parmi. **$$**

✖ Café 56 56A Barrack St; `9041 5000; f cafe56merredin; ⏱ 06.30–14.30 Mon–Fri, 07.30–14.00 Sat–Sun. Fantastic full b/fasts & a teeming pastry case make this establishment an excellent spot to fuel up before heading out to the rocks. A real highlight in an otherwise thin dining scene. **$**

✖ Wild Poppy Café 88 Barrack St; `0435 013 780; w wildpoppycafe.com.au; ⏱ 08.00–16.00 Tue–Fri. This bright & trendy café has an innovative lunch menu with dumplings, Thai chicken salad & pulled pork tacos. Also does a good classic b/fast plus milkshakes, smoothies & a wide variety of coffees/teas & pastries. **$**

Hyden

🏠 Wave Rock Hotel/Motel (55 rooms) 2 Lynch St; `9880 5052; e waverockmotel@westnet.com.au. Standard en-suite motel units get the job done. There are 3 on-site restaurants – the Bush Bistro (⏱ 06.00–21.00 daily), specialises in steaks & has ample children's meals;

while the Sandalwood & the Gimlet cater for groups (bookings essential). The Sandalwood also serves b/fast for private diners (⏲ 07.00–09.00 daily). **$$$**

🏠 **Wave Rock Resort** (14 villas) Wave Rock Rd; ☎ 9880 5022; e waverock@wn.com.au. On the banks of Lake Magic, 1.5km from Wave Rock, these villas have fully equipped kitchens, dining areas, AC & partially screened verandas. A cottage equipped for disabled guests is also available. A great choice for families who want some space & privacy. **$$$**

🏠 **Wave Rock Caravan Park** 1 Wave Rock Rd; ☎ 9880 5022; e waverock@wn.com.au. Well-established, pet-friendly facility with en-suite powered sites, backpacker accommodation, self-contained cabins & camping. **$**

✘ **Wave Rock Café** Wave Rock Rd; ☎ 9880 5182; ⏲ 09.00–17.00 daily. At the visitor centre, 500m from Wave Rock, this café has decent lasagne & pastries. A good pick-me-up after a long drive. **$**

WHAT TO SEE AND DO

Merredin While the town doesn't boast a huge number of attractions, there are a few sights of note worth visiting if you have time between the rocks. A real treat for vehicle enthusiasts, **Merredin Military Museum** (Great Eastern Hwy; ☎ 9041 1505; ⏲ 10.00–15.00 daily; A$10/free adult/child) houses numerous examples of conflict vehicles from World War I that have been restored to their original condition – with the museum's prize exhibit being an Iroquois helicopter, of which only one other is on display in the state, at the Bull Creek Aviation Heritage Museum in Perth. The neighbouring **Merredin Railway Museum** (Great Eastern Hwy; ☎ 0438 814 339; ⏲ 09.00–15.00 Mon–Sat, 11.00–14.00 Sun; A$10/free adult/child) is also worth a look and features an original 1897 locomotive.

Merredin boasts a couple of Heritage-listed buildings, such as the **Town Hall** (18 Mitchell St; no entry to the public), which has a memorial clock tower said to be a replica of Big Ben, and **Cummins Theatre** (31 Bates St; ☎ 9041 3295; w cumminstheatre.com.au; ⏲ 09.00–15.00 Mon–Fri), built in 1928 from the demolished Tivoli Theatre in Coolgardie (owned by James Cummins, former mayor of Kalgoorlie), supposedly with bits of gold in its bricks. Performances are still held here (check the theatre's website) and office staff are happy to let you have a quick look at the main theatre.

A short walk from the centre, **Merredin Peak** is the highest point (361m) in town, accessed by two 2.4km loop trails: the Rock Walk (30mins) and the Bush Walk (about an hour, as it goes through bush before joining the Rock Walk). Go at dusk; some of the most glorious sunsets I've ever seen in Australia have been from the top of Merredin Peak.

Merredin is a grain powerhouse and the Co-Operative Bulk Handling (CBH) receival silo on the edge of town – one of the biggest in the southern hemisphere – can hold over half a million tons of it. Part of the Public Silo Trail, **Merredin Silo Art** ✳ is the work of Kyle Hughes-Odgers, who used 200 litres of paint to create bright artworks on the sides of these enormous structures, each depicting a story about Merredin, its community and agricultural history. As this is an operational agriculture site, you have to view the work from the ample parking bay (suitable for caravans) on the Great Eastern Highway.

Hyden The **Visitors' Information Complex** (Wave Rock Rd) hosts a restaurant (see above) and a wildlife complex (⏲ 09.00–17.00 daily; A$12/5 adult/child) where you can spot albino kangaroos, wombats and a plethora of friendly native birds. There is also an eclectic **Miniature Soldiers' Museum** (⏲ 09.00–17.00; A$5) with over 10,000 handmade pieces owned by the same man, Alex Smith, who collected them over 60 years; the soldiers represent hundreds of years' worth of battles. There is also a

Lace Museum (w waverocklaceplace.com.au; ⏰ 09.00–17.00; A$5/2.50 adult/child) on site, with pieces dating back to the 1600s, alongside antique wedding dresses and an off-cut from the wedding veil of Princess Diana.

The Big Rocks The following itinerary takes in some favourite rocks in the Eastern Wheatbelt. Come prepared; distances can be long and the towns you pass through are *small*. While most will have a tiny or automated petrol station, there is no guarantee it will be open or working when you visit. Accommodation and restaurants are very thin in this area, so it pays to pack your own meals and snacks or ring ahead to scope out what will be on offer. Be sure take a very good paper-based road map (page 56).

Day 1 (Merredin–Beringbooding or Elachbutting Rock) Heading north from Merredin, your first stop is **Talgomine Reserve** after 45km. The reserve is known for its gumtree woodlands and, in wildflower season, for its carpets of everlastings; walking up Mt Moore (383m) offers views over the gums to **Lake Campion Reserve**, a salt lake, a further 15-minute drive northeast and a good birdwatching spot. From there head 25km north on Jolly Road (which turns into Cornish Road) to **Eaglestone Rock** which, as the name suggests, is a popular place to spy eagles. The easy-to-moderate climb to the top of the rock provides nice views over another salt lake, Lake Brown; the contrast between the white of the salt and the golden brown of the rock makes for particularly good photos.

Travelling northwards again, reverse back and head for **Mukinbudin**, 35km away, known as 'Mukka' to the locals and the only town of any note on today's itinerary. The welcome sign to the shire – reading 'Classic Dry Red' – has seen hundreds of humorous snapshots. Fill up here and stop for a coffee or snack at the roadhouse; these are the last facilities for a while. The unmanned visitors' information hut, next to the public toilets on Shadbolt Street, has a very good road map of the shire – it's not a bad idea to take a photo of it for when 4G signal fades.

Heading north from town, after 50km you will arrive at the ghost town of **Bonnie Rock**. A series of droughts and the Great Depression killed off the townsite – the Town Hall is still standing, but that's about it. If ghost towns interest you, you're better off heading to the Goldfields (page 225). Continue for 15km west from Bonnie Rock to **Beringbooding Rock** ☀, a spectacular outcrop which holds the biggest rockwater catchment in Australia – almost eight million litres! The highlights here are an enormous gnamma hole, framed by a granite wall behind it with classic 'wave' streaks, a balancing boulder and hand paintings from Kalamaia Aboriginal peoples. A further 15km along Masefield Road is **Geeraning Rock**, which has an old hand-dug well, and then 7km beyond that is **Elachbutting Rock** ☀ – my favourite rock in the region, and one which many Wheatbelt locals consider to be more impressive than the more famous Wave Rock. Similar in shape, Elachbutting also boasts a 'wave' pattern, though not as pronounced as at Wave. There is a 5km self-drive loop plus a walk through a spooky cavern (called Monty's Pass), a natural amphitheatre, indigenous drawings and paintings and tons of birdlife – Major Mitchell's cockatoos are often seen here. If you have a 4x4 you can drive to the top of the rock.

The 20km area between Beringbooding and Elachbutting has free camping facilities and it makes sense to take advantage of those; otherwise, head back to Merredin for the night.

Day 2 (Beringbooding or Elachbutting Rock–Hyden) Around 90 minutes south from Elachbutting Rock are the **Sandford Rocks**, part of an 800ha reserve.

There is a wonderful trail here looking down on a natural amphitheatre, plus native peaches, sandalwoods and myrtles; look out for rock wallabies and purple peacock beetles too. A further 12km southwest is the townsite of **Westonia**, often described as where the Goldfields meets the Wheatbelt. The town has maintained the distinctive look of its mining boom days a century ago – it is well worth having an amble up Wolfram Street and back to admire the preserved building façades. There is fuel and a few facilities in town.

A 45-minute detour northeast of Westonia on an unsealed track off the Koorda– Bullfinch Road, **Baladjie Rock** is a popular picnic spot, surrounded by woodland and with a phenomenal view over a salt lake. The sunset colours here are nothing short of breathtaking and there are caves, curious rock formations and ponds, and interesting streak wave formations.

Head back to Merredin on the Great Eastern Highway and then take the turning south to **Narembeen** (71km), stopping at the **Grain Discovery Centre** (1 Currall St; ☎9064 7055; ☉ 09.00–17.00 daily; gold coin donation), joined with the Narembeen Roadhouse. Showcasing the history and future of farming in the Wheatbelt, the centre has a number of interactive grain and CBH exhibits, including tracing what supermarket products come from Wheatbelt grain. One of the highlights is a fully restored 1950s farmhouse kitchen – it is like a time capsule. Your next stop is **Mt Walker**, 30km east of Narembeen. There is a glorious hidden amphitheatre in the rock called **Hidden Hollow**, tucked away behind vegetation. A walking trail goes up to the top of the amphitheatre and provides excellent views of the surrounding farmland.

From Mt Walker, it is 46km south to the region's signature attraction: **Wave Rock** ✳ (A$12 per vehicle). Formed 2.7 billion years ago, it's not particularly high at 15m (though it is 110m long) – but the reason to come here is because the streaky rock looks like a giant tidal wave about to crash over a surf break. The processes of weathering and erosion have given the rock formation a concave shape, and chemical deposits running down the surface have left dark streak marks – creating the iconic tidal wave look. It's something of a rite of passage for visitors to stand at the base and have their photo taken while making a surf pose.

In addition to the base and summit walks, the 1.7km return **Hippo's Yawn Loop** follows an easy, flat path from the base of Wave Rock to a remarkable 13m-high granite formation shaped like the mouth of a yawning hippo. The walk then loops back through native bush and sandalwood trees (with lots of ring-neck parrots) to the car park. It's easy to combine with a hike up the rock; the **Wave Rock Walk Circuit** is the longest of the lot at 3.6km return, taking in Wave Rock, Hippo's Yawn, and heaps of native bush before returning you to the car park.

About 19km north is **Mulka's Cave**, home to many Aboriginal hand stencils and paintings. According to an Aboriginal story, Mulka was the son of a couple who were forbidden to marry. As a result, Mulka, though huge and tall in size, was born with crossed eyes and could not hunt as he couldn't throw a spear effectively. He therefore resorted to eating children, and lived in the cave – the handprints high up the cave wall show his enormous size.

It's a good idea to use Hyden's built and/or camping facilities as a base for the night (page 251).

Day 3 (Hyden–Merredin) Start your morning with another stroll around Wave Rock, and then head west along the Kondinin–Hyden Road. After 85km, you will reach **Gorge Rock**, atop which is a big, deep rockpool that was for many years the de facto swimming pool for locals and many older Wheatbelt families have fond memories of spending lazy summer days here. Although swimming is no longer allowed, the rock is still a great place to relax, look for orchids and enjoy spectacular views of the countryside. It's another 23km to the town of **Corrigin**, where the **Corrigin Hotel** (17 Walton St; ☎ 9063 2002; w corriginhotel. net; ⊕ noon–14.00 & 18.00–20.30 daily; $$) is the best place in the area for lunch – they do a good steak sandwich. Corrigin is also famous in the Wheatbelt for its **dog cemetery**, where pet owners have been laying their faithful to rest since 1974. There are inscriptions on the gravestones; a dog statue marks the entrance on the Brookton Highway.

Heading north from Corrigin, your next stop is **Kokerbin Rock**, the third-largest monolith in Australia at 122m high. Three Devil's Marbles – giant, round boulders – are here and there's an excellent walkway to the top. From here, proceed north to Tammin on the Great Eastern Highway, from where it is 25km north to the 341m-high **Yorkrakine Rock**, your final stop on this tour. Aboriginal women used this site as a place to give birth.

To get back to Merredin (88km away), head north on Kwolyin West Road (which turns into the Kellerberrin–Shackleton Road), until you reach the Great Eastern Highway at Kellerberrin. From there, Merredin is 58km east.

THE LAKES AND THE SOUTHERN WHEATBELT

A lot of rain that falls in the southern Wheatbelt does so in shallow depressions that take a long time to drain away – which has lead to the formation of large pans of salt spread irregularly over hundreds of kilometres. Collectively known as The Lakes, most of these salt pans spend the year completely dry, but they can fill in seasons of very heavy rain – and when that happens it can leave a lake full for years. Indeed, the flooding that resulted from torrential rains early in 2017 could still be seen in the area's lakes three years later.

While most visitors just whizz by here on their way to Esperance, it's worth slowing down a bit and spending a day leisurely exploring the small towns and salt lakes.

LAKE KING The best place to spend the night if you are breaking up a long trip from Perth to Esperance, this tiny community, 124km south of Hyden, is known for the 10km-long **Lake King Causeway**. The longest road built across a salt lake in the state, it is a mesmerising and highly photogenic place to stop the car and take in the views. Afterwards, enjoy a filling dinner at the **Lake King Tavern Motel** (Lot 165 Varley Rd; ☎ 9874 4048; w lakekingtavernmotel.com.au) – the town's awesome rammed-earth pub and probably the best place to stay in this part of the Wheatbelt. Also in town, the open-air **Bush Engineers Tractor Museum** (Newdegate Rd; ⊕ 24hrs) is a monument to country ingenuity, displaying tractors built and modified by local farmers. Lake King is also the jumping-off point for **Frank Hann National Park**, 78km east on an inland sandplain accessed via the Lake King–Norseman Road (4x4 only). At 60,000ha, this remote national park has no facilities; visitors mainly come for the variety of banksias found here.

LAKE GRACE This is the best-known of the lake communities, although the lake itself – 50km long and 7km wide – is actually 8km west of the townsite. A lookout offers beautiful views of the lake's colours and you can walk on the lakebed when it is dry. In town, the **Australian Inland Mission Hospital Museum** (Stubbs St; ☎ 9881 2064; ⊕ 13.00–16.00 Wed–Thu, other times by appt) allows you to walk through and envision what an old rural bush hospital was like – you can see period wards and duty rooms. The mission hospital was established in 1926 by the Presbyterian Church to serve isolated communities, serving an area of 16,000km². It closed in 1952 and, by the 1980s, the building was derelict and scheduled for demolition; until a group of volunteers fundraised to restore it, and the museum opened in 1992.

A photogenic 50km drive leads south from Lake Grace to **Pingrup**, passing alongside the pink waters of the Chinocup lake system. Every March the **Pingrup Races** (w pingrupraces.com.au) are held in town, featuring six horse races throughout the day and 'two-up' in the evening, an Australian gambling game (usually played on ANZAC Day) where coins (usually two) are thrown up in the air at the same time and players bet on the combination of heads-or-tails resulting from the toss.

LAKE DUMBLEYUNG This vast lake, 80km west of Lake Grace, was made famous in 1964 when Donald Campbell set the world water speed record on its waters, hitting 444.7kph in his craft, the *Bluebird*. A replica of the *Bluebird* can be seen in Dumbleyung town on Absolon Street. The lake has considerably variable water levels; when full, you can jet ski or sail, but at other times it can be completely dry.

DRYANDRA WOODLAND Located 30km north of Narrogin – itself about 90km northwest from Dumbleyung (first go 40km west to Wagin, then 50km north to Narrogin) – lies this ecologically significant woodland, a surviving example of what the Wheatbelt was like before European settlement and the clearing. Dryandra survived in its natural state because it was considered too hilly and rocky for clearing and grazing. As such, it is a vitally important habitat for native fauna and is WA's newest national park, gazetted in January 2022.

Several walking trails, ranging from 1km to 12.5km, explore the bushland and there are high chances of animal sightings – I have never failed to see kangaroos here and on multiple occasions have also sighted echidnas. The most famous resident of Dryandra, however, is the endangered numbat (*Myrmecobius fasciatus*), a marsupial that looks like a cross between a chipmunk and a squirrel. About 30cm long and weighing up to 500g, numbats are diurnal and love termites, which they lap up with their long, sticky tongues. There are fewer than 1,000 left as introduced species such as foxes and feral cats have gotten the better of them across the years. WildfilmAustralia produces an excellent half-hour documentary on the numbats of Dryandra, available on YouTube (w youtube. com/watch?v=xUy_JOQFg9o).

While your chances of seeing a numbat in the wild are fairly low, the **Barna Mia Nocturnal Animal Sanctuary** ✳ 🕿 9881 2064; w parks.dpaw.wa.gov.au/site/barna-mia-nocturnal-wildlife-experience; A$22/16 adult/child, bookings essential) provides guaranteed opportunities for small marsupial sightings. The nocturnal guided tour explores the sanctuary, fenced off to protect their grounds from predators; as the guide puts down their fruit bowls down at various stations, the little animals come out into the open – expect to see the likes of the rabbit-eared bilby, fat-tailed boodie and rufous hare-wallaby.

Getting there and away Dryandra is about 170km/2 hours south of Perth and about 15 minutes north of Narrogin. It can easily be visited as a day trip from Perth, a stop-over on your way to Albany, or in conjunction with some sites in the Peel Region. It can also be added on to a trip to the Lakes or Kokerbin Rock. The reserve's main access road is a signposted turn-off on the Narrogin–Wandering

Road. Roads inside the woodland are unsealed but well-maintained and easily suitable for 2WD.

Where to stay and eat Accommodation is available in the park. **Lions Dryandra Village** (8 huts; 9884 5231; w dryandravillage.org.au; **$$**) has comfortable en-suite facilities, or you can camp at either the **Congelin Campground** (8 caravan bays, with toilet facilities and gas BBQs; **$**) or the **Gnaala Mia Campground** (27 caravan bays & 8 tent sites; toilet facilities, BBQ shelters & open fire pits; **$**).

Part Four

THE MID WEST TO GASCOYNE

THE PINNACLES Page 268. These mysterious limestone outcrops, part of a gold-and-yellow sand and dune desert 2 hours north of Perth, were likely caused by erosion over eons – but they provide an eerie moonscape in the here and now; there isn't an experience like it anywhere else in the state. The surrounding towns are famous for their rock lobster and also have good beaches and wildlife experiences.

KALBARRI Page 285. Gorge hikes with great beaches are an impactful one-two punch at this holiday town north of Geraldton. Kalbarri National Park recently received a multi-million-dollar facelift with the installation of a new skywalk offering breathtaking views out over the red bluffs and gorges, and the 7km hike across the gorge floors of the Murchison is one of the best day walks in the state. The coast features great snorkelling and sheltered waters too, and there's some good restaurant options for such a small town.

MID WEST WILDFLOWERS Page 288. The Mid West explodes in a kaleidoscope of colour during the late winter and early spring, and the breathtaking carpets of wildflowers – particularly pink, white and gold everlastings, stretching as far out as the horizon – are an unforgettable site. Take in a hearty dinner at one of the regions many country pubs after a day of exploring.

NINGALOO REEF Page 304. Friendly whale sharks – the world's biggest fish – ply the waters off these spectacular reefs, which rival those in Queensland. One of the best spots in the state – maybe the world – for snorkelling, and just a few steps into the water from the beach you'll see rainbow-coloured coral gardens, spectacular tropical fish, turtles and rays. You'll be amazed how close to the shore they come.

FRANCOIS PERON NATIONAL PARK Page 298. With its red-orange dunes and cliffs abutting azure and turquoise waters, this peninsula where desert meets sea gives the impression that this is the spot where Mother Nature fell over and spilled her paint palette. The many viewpoints and swimming spots here are also some of the best places in the state to view dolphins, stingrays and dugongs – I have even seen a thorny devil here.

Geraldton, the Mid West & Indian Ocean Drive

Balmy days, golden-sand beaches, dazzling wildflowers and breathtaking Outback expanses – the imagery of the Mid West is where the West Australian stereotype come to life. As you head north from Perth, you'll pass a string of sleepy seaside villages hugging the coastline, where the rock lobster and fishing industries still drive major portions of the economy. Geraldton, the state's biggest city north of Perth, is increasingly hip, has a growing trendy restaurant and cultural scene, and its residents have taken the term 'beach lifestyle' and turned it from tired cliché into a proud civic identity. Inland, one of the world's most spectacular wildflower displays blooms every spring – you will see several endemic species, like the wreath flower – and paddocks and parks turn into widespread carpets of pinks, whites, golds and lavenders. As you keep heading east, the vast Outback landscape and million-acre station country starts to gently unfold as the dirt changes into oranges and reds, cattle roam freely and it seems like you can gaze forever off into the horizon.

CHITTERING VALLEY AND NEW NORCIA

Around 45km north of Guildford in Perth's Swan Valley, the Chittering Valley is also known for its wine and produce but stands out from its urban neighbour thanks to its more noticeably rural landscape, embracing the hills of the Darling Range. The towns of Muchea (pronounced moo-shay) and Bindoon, both on the Great Northern Highway, and Gingin, just off the Brand Highway to the west, anchor the region. New Norcia, Australia's only monastic town, sits on the valley's northern fringe.

GETTING THERE AND AWAY The Great Northern Highway is how the majority of visitors access the area. Transwa coaches do service Bindoon (1hr 20mins; A$37 return) and Gingin (1hr 15mins; A$37 return) from Perth, but you are not going to get much out of a visit here unless you have your own transport.

TOURIST INFORMATION

Chittering Visitor Centre 6180 Great Northern Hwy, Bindoon; 9576 4664; w visitchittering.com.au; ⏲ 10.00–13.00

Mon–Tue & 09.00–16.00 Wed–Fri, plus Mar–Dec 10.00–14.00 Sat–Sun

WHERE TO STAY

Orchard Glory Farm Resort (20 chalets) 41 Mooliabeenee Rd; 9576 2888;

e orchardglory@westnet.com.au; w orchardglory. com.au. Large chalets with televisions, kitchens

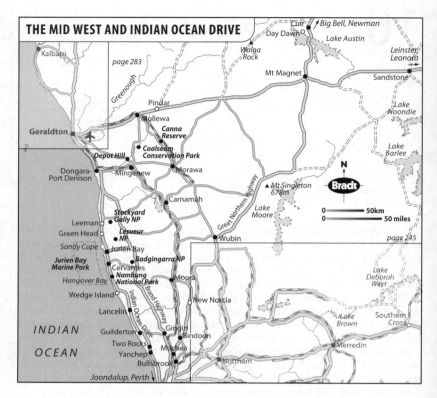

page 283

THE MID WEST AND INDIAN OCEAN DRIVE

page 245

& separate living/dining areas make this a good option for longer stays. You can pick fruit from the orchards & feed the farms animals. **$$$$**

🏠 **Bindoon's Windmill Farm** (2 chalets) 132 Kay Rd, Bindoon; 🗞9576 1136; e miltonandjoan@ windmillfarmstay.com; w windmillfarmstay.com. Just 2km north of Bindoon, this is a good option for groups thanks to its large en-suite chalets (1 can hold 12 people, the other 17) surrounded by hills & orchards. **$$$**

🏠 **Enderslie House B&B** (6 rooms) 15 Peters Rd, Muchea; 🗞9571 0595; w enersliehouse.com. au. Sprawling farmstead-style accommodation with large lounge/dining room common area; en-suite rooms have a homey, comfortable feel but no televisions. There are animals on the property (alpacas, kangaroos, emus), & the owners will invite you to help feed them if you are so inclined. Cooked & continental b/fast. **$$$**

🏠 **Treetops Guesthouse** (2 rooms) 289 Powderbark Rd; 🗞0411 018 565; e treetopsguesthouse@westnet.com.au; w treetopsguesthousewa.com.au. On 2.5ha of pastoral land, the rooms have access to a veranda, & there is a DVD & book library plus gardens with native plants. B/fasts, lunches & dinners can be provided; the owners also run a native herb & spice business, which they use in their meals. Pets can stay with prior arrangement for A$20. Good value. **$$**

✕ WHERE TO EAT AND DRINK

✳ ✕ **Stringybark Winery** 2060 Chittering Rd; 🗞9571 8069; w stringybarkwinery.com.au; 🕘 noon–20.30 Wed–Thu, noon–21.30 Fri–Sat, 09.00–20.30 Sun. A visit to this rustic winery is a must if you are in the region – the chilli mussels are sensational, & the steaks & Turkish breads are good too. Have the crème brûlée for dessert. Their house wines complement the menu wonderfully. **$$$**

✳ ✕ **Scottallian Hotel** 6626 Great Northern Hwy; 🗞9576 1400; w hotelscottallian.com. au; 🕘 noon–21.00 Mon–Thu, noon–23.00 Fri,

11.00–23.00 Sat, 11.00–21.00 Sun. Great little pub off the highway, 10km north of Bindoon, offering hearty burgers, steaks & onion rings. A local legend. $$

✗ **Bindoon Bakehaus** 27 Binda Pl, Bindoon; 🖀 9576 0069; w bindoonbakehaus.com.au; ⏰ 07.00–15.30 Mon–Sat, 08.00–15.30 Sun. At the end of Bindoon's main shopping strip, right off the Great Northern Highway, this popular bakery & its vast assortment of pies, rolls, breads, pastries & hot drinks is the perfect morning tea stop or rest break if you're driving through the area. You can also pick up wraps for a picnic. The chilli con carne pie is a hit; they also have kangaroo pies. $

WHAT TO SEE AND DO

Local produce Like its neighbour to the south, the Chittering Valley is an area of table produce and many fruits, vegetables and wines are grown and produced here. The 110km, self-guided **Chittering Farm Flavour Trail** explores a dozen or so farm gates around Bindoon and Gingin; pick up the brochure at the Chittering Visitor Centre or download it from their website (page 261).

On the fourth Sunday of each month, the **Bindoon Farmers Market** (⏰ 08.30–12.30), held at the corner of the Great Northern Highway and Gray Road, showcases the best of the region's produce – eggs, preserves and wine alongside handicrafts and local skin products. Other recommended farm gates include:

Little Eeden Farm 429 Cook Rd; 🖀 0429 149 354; w littleeedenfarm.com; ⏰ by appointment. Bush honey specialists – try the chilli & smoked varieties.

✳ **Local Goat** 867 Coonabidgee Rd; 🖀 0418 714 107. This phenomenal cheese shop is open by appointment only, but it's well worth making one & stopping by. A sustainably managed small goat herd – numbering about 50 – are raised & live on the owners' 60ha farm; the goats' milk produces award-winning cheeses – we just love their camembert & feta. They do gelatos from goats' milk too.

Nesci Estate Cnr Great Northern Hwy/Wandena Rd, Lower Chittering; 🖀 9571 4102; ⏰ noon–17.00 Sat–Sun. One of the area's first vineyards, the estate has a beautiful stone-&-timber cellar door with excellent whites. The owners cleared the bush off the land by hand in the 1940s.

✳ **The Orchard** 1378 Chittering Rd; 🖀 9571 8074; w theorchardperth.com.au; ⏰ 09.30–16.00 Thu–Sun. A 15-min drive from Muchea, the 10,000 citrus trees here provide rich bounty for the orchard's fruit-picking tours (adult/child A$20/12). If you don't feel like wandering the groves, take a fresh juice in their café – the perfect antidote to a hot afternoon.

Oversby's Citrus 6422 Great Northern Hwy, Bindoon; 🖀 0400 440 227; ⏰ 08.00–17.00 daily. Has a variety of oranges & mandarins – look for the green combi that marks their farm gate.

Wootra Farm 164 Wells Glover Rd; 🖀 9576 0986; w wootrafarmbedandbreakfast.com; ⏰ Aug–Oct 10.00–15.00 Wed–Sun. Since being established in 2013, this asparagus farm has grown from 500 crowns to a whopping 120,000. Also a B&B.

Gingin Gravity Discovery Centre (1098 Military Rd; 🖀 9575 7577; w gravitycentre.com.au; ⏰ 10.00–16.00 Tue–Thu & Sun, 10.00–19.30 Fri–Sat; A$22/14 adult/child, A$48/30 adult/child for observatory too) This hands-on interactive exhibition focuses on gravity, cosmology and physics, and features a retractable-roof observatory and powerful telescopes for their Friday and Saturday night observatory sessions. The 45m 'Leaning Tower of Gingin' leans at a 15-degree angle, designed to re-create some of Galileo's experiments, while the Solar System Walk follows a 1km model of our solar system. There's also a café on site, which is open for dinner for those doing night-time observatory visits (bookings essential).

Scenic drives The undulating hills, vineyards and orchards of the Chittering Valley make it especially suitable for driving. The best-known route is the roughly 40km drive on **Chittering Road** from Bullsbrook to just south of Bindoon; there aren't

Almost 57km north of Bindoon, the monastic town of New Norcia (**w** newnorcia. wa.edu.au) was founded in 1847 by Spanish Benedictine Monks, and it is still used by them today – though just nine remain. The settlement evolved into a full town and the buildings and architecture took on the Spanish heritage of the founders. Flour mills, olive groves, schools and a church sprang up – and today the entire town is registered on the National Estate. Visitors are welcome to join mass, which occurs at 07.30 Monday to Saturday (in the monastery oratory) and 09.00 on Sunday (in the Abbey Church).

The **New Norcia Museum and Art Gallery** (New Norcia Rd; **** 9654 8056; **⊕** 09.30–16.30 daily; A$12.50/free adult/child) provides a great overview of the town's history, with artefacts and artwork tracing the transformation from bush mission into monastic settlement, including plenty of European exhibits brought from Spain and Italy by the monks. There is also an impressive art gallery of religious works. Guided town tours (2hrs) are at 11.00 and 13.30 – book at the museum.

Strolling through the one-street town is a delight, with a mix of architectural styles in the various buildings set in rolling farmland. The mission-style **Abbey Church**, with its wonderful yellow-and-white clock tower, handsome brown-stone building and red roof has an old German pipe organ from the 1930s and is where Rosendo Salvado, New Norcia's first abbot, is interred. The Gothic-revival **St Gertrude's College** was established for girls in 1908 as a boarding school and **St Ildephonsus** was built for boys in 1913; there was also an orphanage for indigenous children. Both are now closed and used as group accommodation facilities.

If you'd like to stay, a variety of accommodation is available in the old buildings, including at the convent and colleges; contact the main office (**** 9654 8018) for more information. New Norcia has also gained a reputation as a foodie town; you can find locally produced olive oils, wines and other treats for sale in the gift shop inside the museum.

many stopping-off points, but the point is to take in the scenery – the valley views towards the gentle hills, speckled with cattle pastures, dams and bushland scrub have a cathartic effect. Some easy loops include taking Teatree Road from just south of Bindoon, to its T-junction at Mooliabeenee Road, and then either on to Gingin or turning right and then almost right again immediately on to Cresthill Road, which will put you back at the highway just a bit north of Bindoon. Another route is up towards New Norcia (see box, above); take Calingiri Road off the highway, and then do a semi-circle past town back to the highway just north of New Norcia. Wildflower season in spring is also vibrant in the Chittering Valley – expect to see fringe lilies, kangaroo paws, wattles, red and yellow banksias, leschenaultias and cowslip orchids.

NORTH TO GERALDTON: INDIAN OCEAN DRIVE AND AROUND

If the name 'Indian Ocean Drive' conjures up ideas of a dreamy ride alongside glittering oceans, with winding hairpins beneath dramatic cliffs and photograph-worthy lookouts every few kilometres… Well, forget it, but know that many West Australians make that mistake too. Indian Ocean Drive isn't like that, and it doesn't turn a drive up north into a glamorous riviera adventure.

What the road *did* do when it opened in 2010, however, was provide a quicker alternative for Perth residents to reach the time-capsule beachside communities of Cervantes, Jurien Bay and Leeman/Green Head – an area collectively known as the Turquoise Coast – than the traditional inland Brand Highway. At 269km long, the road goes from Yanchep in Perth's far northern fringes (page 113) to a T-junction just south of Dongara-Port Denison in the Mid West region, though most of the seaside towns are technically in the Wheatbelt.

The drive itself is pleasant enough, starting within the densely packed eucalypt woodlands just north of Yanchep, which then slowly fade out in place of the rolling green hills of the Wheatbelt, before a seemingly endless array of scrub- and bush-covered sand dunes. There *are* occasional glimpses of the Indian Ocean, but you have to crane your neck to see them, which isn't advised – Indian Ocean Drive has become notorious as a place of horror crashes, with nearly 50 since 2017 alone despite none of the hairpin turns and distracting scenery one expects from coastal roads. Keep your focus, even though the road seems deceptively gentle.

The bulk of WA's tourist traffic out of Perth heads south, not north, and the result is that many communities along Indian Ocean Drive – including as close as Lancelin – have not been overrun with development and still retain the old beach shack vibe of yesteryear. That culture has become as much a part of the experience here as the dramatic Pinnacles, snorkelling and lobster lunches.

GETTING THERE AND AWAY The following towns are all on the coastal side of Indian Ocean Drive, between Perth and Geraldton. Transwa coaches ply the route between the two major cities, stopping at Lancelin, Cervantes, Jurien Bay and Leeman/Green Head.

GUILDERTON Taking its name from Dutch coins found here from a 1600s shipwreck, Guilderton is best known for its acclaimed town beach, which won recognition as the cleanest in Australia in 2015. The town sits on the Moore River Estuary, the mouth of which provides sheltered swimming when the sandbar separating it from the sea is exposed. This yin and yang of the ocean's chop and the river's gentleness is one of Guilderton's selling points – many visitors like to have a surf or do a bit of ocean snorkelling before swapping over to a kayak or a canoe to paddle up the gentle river. Canoes and kayaks can be hired from the foreshore to use in either the ocean or the river. The Moore River is also very popular for fishing, especially for bream. For river cruises, try Phil Cook at **Moore River Tours** (✆9577 1600 or 0439 039 766; e moorerivertours@westnet.com.au; w mooreriverholidays.com.au) while **Explorer Boat Hire** (Guilderton Foreshore; ✆0488 984 942; e explorerboathire@ westnet.com.au; ⊕ weekends & school holidays, call ahead at other times) rents out all sorts of canoes, kayaks and pedal craft.

LANCELIN Framed by giant cake-icing white sand dunes and turquoise waters, pretty Lancelin is famous among West Australians for its surfing, sandboarding and windsurfing. Once a quaint fishing hamlet, it has transformed itself into the adventure sports capital of the Turquoise Coast while retaining its ramshackle beach-chic look.

Where to stay and eat In addition to the following, **Lancelin Beach Breaks** (w lancelinbeachbreaks.com.au) is an aggregation site for the area's holiday homes, with properties to suit most mid-range budgets.

10

Midway between Lancelin and Cervantes, unique Wedge Island is an isolated community home to some 350 shack inhabitants – and they really are shacks, made from scrap metals and corrugated materials, and without electricity or running water. There is no accommodation, dining or services of any kind here, other than an unattended shack that sells ice and bait on an honour system. The shacks were first built in the 1950s by holidaymakers from the Mid West and Wheatbelt, though in later years Perth residents, attracted to the off-grid lifestyle and ample fishing opportunities, also built them. Construction continued into the 1980s, before the WA government's 1989 Squatter Policy saw shacks start to be dismantled and removed, and Wedge was transferred to the jurisdiction of the then-Department of Conservation and Land Management (CALM) in the mid-1990s and new shack construction banned. The 'Wedge' in 'Wedge Island' is named not after its shape but rather after Bob Wedge, a pioneer in the area, or Charles Wedge, a surveyor – the account is disputed.

However, no-one in Wedge actually owns their shack – they sit on unvested public land, which the government gives leases to the shackholders. The state government, however, feels the community is environmentally unsustainable, due to the impact on continued unplanned growth and wants to remove the shacks to allow for formal development – this has been an ongoing battle between shack users, local government and state government since the Shire of Dandaragan removed its first shacks in 1968 at Kangaroo Point and Hangover Bay.

The environment, however, has started to weigh in more forcefully on the side of the state bureaucrats, and coastal erosion is becoming a major threat to the shacks – one was lost to the waves in 2018, and others are in danger. The site has thus become one of the first examples in Australia of a 'managed retreat' strategy

🏠 **Lancelin Beach Hotel** (26 rooms) 1 North St; 📞 9655 1005; w lancelinbeachhotel.com.au. Metres from the beach, the en-suite rooms have AC but otherwise seem a bit pricey for what you get. The on-site Dunes Restaurant (🕒 11.00–21.00 daily) has a varied & tasty range of mains including Indonesian beef curry & crab linguini. **$$$**

🏠 **Experience Lancelin Holiday Park** Hopkins St; 📞 9655 1056; e info@lancelincaravanpark.com.au; w lancelincaravanpark.com.au. Pet-friendly & with a new spa, this accommodation offers a range of powered sites & unpowered sites, plus camp kitchen, indoor pool & rec centre. Pet friendly. Cabins **$$$**, sites **$**

🏠 **Lancelin Lodge YHA** 10 Hopkins St; 📞 9655 2020; e lancelin@yha.com.au; w yha.com.au/ hostels/wa/midwest/lancelin. Private, multi-bed dorm & family rooms inc Wi-Fi & linen. Guests can use the bikes free of charge & there is also a communal kitchen. **$**

🍴 **Endeavour Tavern** 58 Gingin Rd; 📞 9655 1052; w endeavourtavern.com.au; 🕒 11.30– 14.00 & 18.00–20.00 Mon–Fri, 11.30–14.00 & 17.30–20.00 Sat–Sun. This hearty dinner spot offers a variety of seafood dishes, from chilli mussels & panko calamari to a fisherman's basket, complemented by ribs & steaks. **$$**

🍴 **Lobbster Trap Café** 91 Gingin Rd; 📞 9655 1127; 🕒 08.00–15.00 Fri–Mon. The focus of this popular café is, unsurprisingly, lobster, but it also serves a host of filling b/fasts alongside gourmet burgers, curries & toasties at lunch. **$$**

What to see and do Stretching for 2km, the height, steepness and variety of Lancelin's **sand dunes** ✳ have led some to claim that the town is Australia's premier **sandboarding** destination. The dunes are often teeming with an array of 4x4 and off-road vehicles, so it's better to book a sandboard in advance than risk driving up

– where the government is gradually moving people out of the danger zone, rather than implementing immediate measures like seawalls and sandbags. As the residents are licensees and not landowners, the government has prevented residents from taking their own actions and no new shacks are permitted to be built to replace threatened ones.

The shackholders have fought back. In 2012, the National Trust issued an assessment recommending that the shacks here (and just north at Grey) be put on the Western Australia Register of Heritage Places due to their historical and social value. The shacks are seen as representative of historic Australian beach culture; however, the Heritage Council of Western Australia has yet to make a final decision.

The current licence for the shackholders expires in 2022 and the future of the perpetually under-threat community is very much under a cloud.

In the meantime, day trips to this iconic and one-of-a-kind West Australian community are still possible. Until 2010, the community was accessible only by 4x4 – until Indian Ocean Drive opened, which made 2WD travel possible and, some say, changed the face of the community by removing access barriers. Even still, the sealed turn-off road (Wedge Rd) from Indian Ocean Drive goes only the outskirts of town, where there is a parking bay – the remaining 1km or so into the community is still either by 4x4 or on foot.

Leave your car behind and wander through town to the glorious beach on the other side of the dunes. There is also ample fishing – the main reason the original licensees came here in the first place. If you have a 4x4, take care when driving, even if you are experienced – the sand is particularly soft, and vehicles have been lost after getting bogged and swept away by the tide.

from Perth and find they are all out. You can reserve one at the **Have A Chat General Store** (13 Whitfield St; ☎ 9655 1054; ⏲ 05.00–17.00 Sun–Fri, 07.00–17.00 Sat) or on the town's website (w lancelin.com.au/product/sandboard-rental-bookings), which also provides a map of where 2WD vehicles can park. Tour operator **Perth Quad** (☎ 0404 491 921; e perthquad@gmail.com; w perthquad.com.au) offers ATV, UTV, Motocross and sandboarding experiences that are supervised and have safety demonstrations, starting at A$129 per person depending on the type of vehicle chosen. It also has a sandboard hire facility.

Lancelin also has a reputation as one of the world's great spots for **windsurfing**. A reef protects the bay's inner waters, offering a variety of surf conditions to suit all abilities – beginners can stay in the more tranquil waters closer to shore, while pros can catch larger waves beyond the reef. For equipment and lessons, try **Werner's Hotspot** (☎ 0407 426 469; e windslanc@hotmail.com; w wernershotspot. blogspot.com).

Lancelin Beach and **Back Beach** are the main beaches, to the north and south of town respectively, and both are great for swimmers.

CERVANTES Cervantes is an instantly likeable place, with an air of relaxation wafting over it along with the sea breeze. The town is named after a US (not Spanish!) whaler ship – the *Cervantes*, which in turn was named after *Don Quixote* author, Miguel de Cervantes – which sunk off the coast here in 1844, although the crew all made it out safely. The town has made hay of this 'Spanish' connection and many of the streets have names celebrating the flavour of Iberia, such as Aragon, Seville and Cadiz. The three main reasons to Cervantes – and they are whoppers – are the Pinnacles, lobster and stromatolites.

Where to stay and eat

RAC Cervantes Holiday Park (11 accommodations) 35 Aragon St; 9652 7060; e reservations@raccervantesholidaypark.com.au; w parksandresorts.rac.com.au/cervantes. Recently redesigned, this park is right on the beach & features 3 multi-bedroom, poolside villas (though pricey) & powered & unpowered sites for caravans & tents. There is an on-site café that does b/fasts & other meals, plus heated outdoor pool, BBQ area & rec centre. *Villas* $$$, *sites* $

Cervantes Pinnacles Motel (40 rooms) 7 Aragon St; 9652 7145; e reservations.pinnacles@bigpond.com; w cervantespinnaclesmotel.com.au. Rooms in the motel are clean & comfortable if unspectacular; a reasonable if not flash buffet b/fast is available at a steep charge. Behind it is the **Pinnacles Edge Resort** (same address & phone number – they share reception & facilities – w pinnaclesedgeresort.com.au) whose 26 spa suites are bright, clean & comfortable & a better choice if your budget allows. $$

Cervantes Bar & Bistro 1 Cadiz St; 9652 7009; w cervantesbarandbistro.com.au; ⏱ 11.00–late daily. Our must-stop for dinner when we are in town, this laidback tavern serves a rich & diverse menu including local specialities like full lobster & marinated octopus, plus healthier options like halloumi & quinoa salad. $$$

Lobster Shack 37 Catalonia St; 9652 7010; w lobstershack.com.au; ⏱ 11.00–15.00 daily. The restaurant at this West Australian institution (see below) features its title in a whole host of forms – lobster chowder, lobster fritters, lobster roll, etc – but also offers traditional fish & chips, oysters, mussels & seafood platters. Pricey, but you should stop here at least once. $$$

What to see and do

Lobster Shack ✳ (37 Catalonia St; 9652 7010; w lobstershack.com.au; ⏱ shop 09.00–17.00 Mon–Thu, 09.00–21.00 Fri–Sun; lunch 11.00–15.00 daily) A Turquoise Coast legend, this western rock lobster (see box, opposite) factory and restaurant (see above) is the creation of the Thompson family – the 'shack' is a reference to the shack settlement that the family lived in near here when David Thompson Sr and his three sons started the business in the 1960s. Since then, their single-boat business has blossomed to become a full fleet and tourism cornerstone of the region; the processing facility opened in 2008. Self-guided tours take you into the live processing plant via overhead walkways, where you can see facilities that can hold up to 20 tonnes of lobster, and you can learn about how the lobsters are packaged and shipped live all over the world. They also run a 90-minute sea lion trip to the islands around Cervantes (Sep–Apr only).

Thirsty Point Skip the main town beach on the foreshore and come here instead, at the end of Seville Street. The beach (good for swimming) wraps around the 'point', which juts out into the sea – you can see the waves colliding at an angle from both ends. There is a boardwalk leading through the dunes to a viewpoint, where you can look out over the kite- and windsurfers who congregate to make the most of the windy conditions. The *Cervantes* shipwreck is about 1km southwest from Thirsty Point, in only about 2m of water.

Nambung National Park and the Pinnacles ✳ (Off Indian Ocean Rd; 9652 7913; A$15 per vehicle) The darlings of a million tourist pamphlets, the Pinnacles are the centrepiece of this desert national park – thousands of thin limestone towers (up to and over 4m) that have spawned up out of the orange sand. The landscape here has been compared to the moon or the set of a science-fiction film, but I don't

THE WESTERN ROCK LOBSTER

Sometimes called 'crayfish' in WA, the extremely valuable western rock lobster (*Panulirus cygnus*) is found only off the west coast of Australia, mostly between Perth and Geraldton. Aside from its succulent meat, it is known for its tiny spines – important for defence, since they don't have claws – and two large antennae. Lobsters can weigh up to 5kg and live for over 20 years. They tend to reproduce in the southern winter – the eggs attach to the underside of the female's tail and, when they hatch, the tiny larvae (only millimetres in length) spend nearly a year drifting in the ocean, ending up hundreds of kilometres away from the coastline. Though most do not make it, the ones that do survive grow large enough to be swept back near to the shore by a series of winds and currents. They eventually become transparent, after which they swim dozens of kilometres to reefs closer to shore, where they spend their childhood and gain their red pigmentation.

Western rock lobsters eat a varied diet of algae, dead animal matter and crustaceans – and they are themselves eaten by large fish and octopuses. The latter have especially become a bane to fisherman as they have learned how to squeeze into and out of traps to eat rock lobsters that have been caught but not yet hauled in.

The annual catch in WA is managed by a quota system to ensure sustainability after breeding stocks became low – an annual commercial quota (6,615 tonnes in 2020–21) is then divided up and allocated to licencees. There is also a recreational sector, with about 25,000 recreational fishermen taking rock lobsters each year. The West Australian government estimates the sustainable limit is 8,000 tonnes per year. The industry is worth A$5 billion to the state economy; 95% of the commercial catch gets exported to China.

think those descriptions do it justice. Surrounded by Outback scrub and huge white sand dunes on one side and the Indian Ocean on the other, they do look remarkably out of place. Perhaps *Mad Max* meets *The Beach* is a better fit.

Scientists believe that the Pinnacles were formed from quartz sand dunes that stood atop limestone and lay inland from the coast, some 25,000 to 30,000 years ago. As cracks formed in the limestone, this was gradually filled by plant roots, water and sand, all of which eroded the limestone – when the wind eventually carried away the detritus, the Pinnacles were revealed. A walking trail and a sealed, 2WD- and wheelchair-suitable road lead through the park. Both start from behind the **Pinnacles Desert Discovery Centre** (9652 7913; 09.30–16.30 daily), which has displays and exhibits chronicling the geology of the national park.

After exploring the Pinnacles, head to the other side of Indian Ocean Drive (still within Nambung National Park) to the unfortunately named **Hangover Bay**. This acclaimed beach is partially reef protected, and good for swimming and snorkelling; being outside town, it is often relatively secluded. There are picnic and barbecue facilities here, making it a great place for lunch.

Lake Thetis ❋ Just 2km out of town – turn on to Hansen Bay Road, not Indian Ocean Drive – the muddy grey humps on the shores of Lake Thetis are stromatolites – descendants of some of the oldest living things on earth. These stromatolites have been growing for over 3,000 years. The cyanobacteria that built

10

these are very similar to earth's earliest lifeforms and are believed to be responsible for significantly increasing the amount of oxygen in the atmosphere when they first appeared. Today, however, there are few places in the world where they, and their thrombolite cousins (page 140), can be found. An easy 1.5km trail goes around the lake; the first 300m are wheelchair accessible and lead to a viewing platform. Regrettably, many of the stromatolites here have been damaged and crushed by humans, and a management plan is being developed to combat this.

A few kilometres from the lake is a steep staircase leading to the top of a dune, which provides a good panorama of Hansen Bay and Cervantes.

JURIEN BAY Only 22km away from Cervantes – but about three times the size – Jurien Bay has become a popular long-weekend spot for Perth residents, with the most accommodation and services of all the towns on Indian Ocean Drive. It's best known for its sea lions, pretty beaches and biodiversity, but has recently been building an increasing portfolio of adventure activities too.

Tourist information
Turquoise Coast Visitor Centre 67 Bashford St; 9652 0870; w visitturquoisecoast.com.au; ⏱ 09.00–17.00 Mon–Fri, 09.00–13.00 Sat

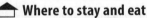

Where to stay and eat

The Heights B&B (3 rooms) 495 Jurien Bay Vista; 9652 1100; e theheightsbandb@wn.com.au; w jurienbayheightsbandb.com.au. A 10min drive west of town, this family-run B&B is set in very peaceful surroundings on the inland side of Indian Ocean Drive. En-suite rooms feature Netflix, while the property has a well-equipped common area & kitchen. **$$$**

Jurien Bay Hotel (32 rooms) 5 White St; 9652 1022; e office@jurienhotel.com.au; w jurienhotel.com.au. These budget en-suite rooms are the best value in the region. This hotel is also a major entertainment hub, with an on-site sports bar & regular live music. **$$**

Jurien Bay Tourist Park Roberts St; 9652 1595; e stay@jurienbaytouristpark.com.au; w summerstar.com.au/caravan-parks/jurien-bay. Overlooking the coast, this pet- & family-friendly complex offers relatively new holiday units sleeping up to 6, plus powered & unpowered sites.

Also has laundry facilities, ablution blocks & a sewer dump point. **$$**

Murray St Grill 12 Murray St; 9652 2114; w murraystgrilljurienbay.com; ⏱ 11.00–21.00 Wed–Sun. With a focus on sustainable produce & reducing food waste, this is a great place for burgers & steaks – though their pear, walnut & halloumi salad (among others) will leave vegetarians happy – with a sizeable tapas menu too. **$$**

Sandpiper Tavern & Pizzeria 12 Roberts St; 9652 1229; w sandpipertavern.com.au; ⏱ kitchen 11.00–14.00 & 17.00–20.00 daily, bar from 11.00 daily. Nearly 40 different types of pizza headline here – everything from your classics like margherita & quattro formaggi to others topped with chia seeds & Thai chilli prawns. There's also a range of interesting dessert pizzas, as well as fish & chips & chicken parmis. **$$**

What to see and do The Jurien Bay shoreline simply sparkles, with clear turquoise water lapping against sugar-white sands, and a large reef system providing outstanding sheltered swimming and snorkelling. The seagrass meadows in the reef system provide vital nursing grounds and you can see butterflyfish and lionfish, as well as octopuses and corals. There are myriad grottos and small rocky islands offshore, where tropical and temperate species are found as the two biogeographic regions converge, creating a rich mix of marine life.

Extending about 100km from Green Head to Wedge Island, and 5.5km out to sea, a limestone reef system known as the **Jurien Bay Marine Park** ✳ creates numerous lagoons here and is home to the rare Australian sea lion (*Neophoca cinerea*), of which there are only a few thousand remaining in the wild. These islands serve as resting points for the sea lions after their open-ocean feeding expeditions, and they also breed here. With their beady eyes and curious and playful nature, they often draw comparisons to puppies and are known to approach swimmers and divers on their own. Various operators run trips to the islands: **Turquoise Safaris** (☏ 0458 905 432; e info@turquoisesafaris.com.au; w turquoisesafaris.com.au) is probably your best bet, with 2½-hour tours to watch or swim with the sea lions, but **Jurien Bay Oceanic Experience** (☏ 9652 2436; e info@jurienbayoceanic.com. au; w jurienbayoceanic.com.au) and **Sea Lion Charters Jurien Bay** (☏ 0427 931 012; e info@sealioncharters.com.au; w sealioncharters.com.au) offer similar excursions.

If you'd rather head to the skies than underwater, you might want to contact **Jurien Bay Skydive** (65 Bashford St; ☏ 9652 1320; w skydivejurienbay.com), which offers solo and tandem jumps from multiple altitudes. **Jurien Bay Adventure Tours** (Bashford St; ☏ 1300 462 383; e info@jurienbayadventuretours.com; w jurienbayadventuretours.com.au) offers a 3,000m jump as well as snorkel and sandboarding experiences and tours to the surrounding national parks.

Lesueur National Park

A 20-minute drive north of Jurien Bay, this significant biodiversity site is home to almost 1,000 plant species – about 10% of WA's total – and is protected because of its conservation importance. Covering some 27,000ha, Lesueur is notable for its mesas – Mt Lesueur (313m) and Mt Michaud (310m) – named after Charles-Alexander Lesueur, an artist, and Andre Michaud, a botanist, both of whom were on the *Naturaliste*. Most of the park is covered in low shrub, wandoo and mallee woodland as well as grass trees, with some sandstone outcrops, and a 4km return trail leads to the top of Mt Lesueur.

The time to come here is the spring wildflower season – headlined by banskias, grevilleas, bottlebrush and heaps of orchids. I particularly enjoy looking for different colours of kangaroo paw here – pinks, oranges, whites and purples. The national park rivals the Fitzgerald Biosphere and the Stirling Range for its intense concentration of wildflower and flora species; while it lacks a drawcard like Bluff Knoll or Barrens Beach, if you are at all into wildflowers, this is a must-stop. Expect to see beautiful splendid fairywrens, western rosellas and Carnaby's cockatoos too.

To reach the park, take Jurien Road from Indian Ocean Drive, and then a left on to Cockleshell Gully Road. All roads are 2WD suitable.

Sandy Cape

This sheltered beach, 12km north of Jurien Bay, is a local favourite, accessed by an unsealed but 2WD-suitable road. You can swim, snorkel and fish here, as well as head into the dunes to sandboard. If you have a 4x4, you can also visit the remains of a World War II radar installation south of the cape – operating between 1943 and 1945, all that is left are two concrete bunkers and some remains of the radar's base. There are rumours that the radar station was attacked by a Japanese plane, which would make this the furthest south the Japanese came during the war – but nothing has been proven.

GREEN HEAD AND LEEMAN

With only about 500 residents between them, these two communities – 18km apart – are your first stops in the Mid West region after you cross the boundary from the Wheatbelt. The Shire of Coorow, in which the two towns lie, is traditionally heavy-duty farming country – settlers arrived in and around Coorow townsite, 110km inland, almost a century before Green

Head and Leeman were established. The area's spectacular three bays, and the 2.5km walkway linking them, are the main visitor draw. The centrepiece is circular **Dynamite Bay**, sheltered by white- and golden-rock cliffs and an excellent choice for family swimming and snorkelling. **South Bay** and **Anchorage Bay**, south and north, respectively, are also good for swimming. Lookouts abound along the walkway, which also includes plenty of interpretive signage with information about bush tucker and regional history and benches to rest along the way.

Around 25km from Green Head (4x4 only), **Stockyard Gully National Park** is home to a series of caves created by an ancient underground river system. The main cave is nearly 300m long, with a sandy floor; there is a 1.3km return walk trail that takes you into a limestone tunnel, big enough though that you can stand in. There are bat colonies here, so steer clear if that bothers you. If you don't have a 4x4, some Jurien-based outfits run tours to the caves (page 271). The park got its name as early drovers used to rest their cattle here.

DONGARA-PORT DENISON Separated by the Irwin River, the twin towns of Dongara and Port Denison have delightfully contrasting personalities – Dongara is all about stately and graceful colonial architecture, while Port Denison has a lazy, ambling beachcomber attitude that complements its postcard-worthy coastline. Put them together and it's a great place to idle away a few days, exploring the beach, estuary and walking trails – there's even a rum distillery. It's also much quieter than Geraldton, and so makes a good alternative base for those seeking a slower pace.

Getting there and away Dongara-Port Denison is 65km/30 minutes south of Geraldton and 350km/3½ hours north of Perth on the Brand Highway. Transwa coaches serve Dongara – starting at A$30 return to Geraldton (1hr) and A$121 return from East Perth (6hrs). There is also a stop in Port Denison.

Tourist information
Dongara-Port Denison Visitor Centre 9 Waldeck St; 9927 1404; w dongaraportdenison.com.au; 09.00–15.00 Mon–Fri, 10.00–13.00 Sat

Where to stay and eat
Dongara Hotel Motel (28 rooms) 12 Moreton Tce; 9927 1023; w dongarahotel. com.au. On one of Dongara's main arteries, these contemporary rooms come with LED TVs, AC & plush beds. There's an outdoor pool & children's area, & the on-site restaurant offers filling b/fasts (extra charge) & burgers, steaks & Asian-inspired mains for lunch & dinner. **$$**

Seaspray Beach Holiday Park 79–81 Church St; 9927 1165; e stay@ seaspraybeachholidaypark.com.au; w seaspraybeachholidaypark.com.au. A real favourite with families, right on the beach 2.5km from Dongara, with a wide range of accommodation including multi-bedroom chalets, motel units & powered sites. Pets welcome in some – check before booking. The on-site café does great

coffee & has a variety of b/fast & lunch options – the place is often full with non-guests. **$$**

Southerly's Harbour View & Restaurant 60 Point Leander Dr; 9927 2207; w southerlystav.com; 10.00–23.00 daily. Easygoing tavern offering hearty burgers & an award-winning steak sandwich. Their 'Taste of Irwin' tapas plates focus on local ingredients like Abrolhos scallops & ribs infused with local Illegal Tender Rum sauce (page 274). **$$**

Starfish Café White Tops Rd; 0474 382 672; w starfishcafedenisonwa.wordpress.com; 08.00–14.00 Thu–Sun. Charming & quaint café right on South Beach. Eggs, cooked b/fasts, burgers & salads are all served here, but the real sensation is the fruit smoothies – a perfect way to cool down after a morning on the beach. **$$**

What to see and do The area was first settled by Europeans in 1850 – Dongara means 'place of seals' in the Wattandee language, though the seals are now mostly long gone due to overhunting in the 1800s. The area's raison d'être is farming and agriculture, but it grew slowly due to transport issues and distance; when the Irwin Roads Board was created in 1871, it extended all the way to the South Australian border.

Dongara is renowned for its colonial architecture, and a short heritage walk takes in over a dozen charming sights. The best known is the beautifully restored, four-storey **Royal Steam Flour Mill**, visible from the Brand Highway and an icon of the town, which makes a great photo opportunity but is unfortunately not open to the public. Built in 1894, it is made from local limestone and red brick, with an iron gable corrugated roof. Capable of producing six tonnes of flour per day, the mill closed in 1935 and was used as an army camp in World War II. Other highlights include the town's police station, courthouse and gaol – collectively known as the **Irwin District Museum** (3 Waldeck St), built in 1871 and used for its intended purpose until 1983. The buildings are Heritage listed and made of local limestone – a fascinating look at an early Australian government complex, and you can see the gaol cells and living quarters of the staff. Pick up a trail map at the visitor centre (see opposite) or purchase a more in-depth version with additional sites (A$5) from the **Irwin District Historical Society** (inside the Irwin District Museum; 5 Waldeck St; \ 9927 1323; w irwinhistory.org.au; ⊕ 10.00–noon Mon–Sat).

A network of six walking routes, collectively known as the **Thungara Trails**, stretch across the town taking in coastal views, lookouts, historical buildings and the Irwin Estuary. Perhaps the highlight of these is the 4.6km **Calico Trail**, a good introduction to Port Denison that can be walked or cycled. The start point is **Granny's Beach** (5 McIntyre Cove), a calm beach protected by a rock wall that provides great swimming for families; the **Green Beanie** coffee van (cnr McIntyre Cove & Point Leander Dr, \ 0417 935 411; ⊕ 07.00–noon daily) is just across the street, with a variety of coffees and teas to power you up before your walk. The trail then travels north up the shore along Ocean Drive to the **Ocean Drive Lookout** (which you will climb Sandy's Ladder, a series of steps, to get to), with its dazzling views of the estuary and ocean. Along the way you will pass **Nun's Pool**, a fabulous snorkelling spot that is protected by reefs. Next to Nun's Pool are the **ANZAC Memorial Soldiers** – a metal installation of 15 silhouette soldiers in different poses, commissioned for the centenary of ANZAC.

From there you continue inland on Ocean Drive, passing along the boardwalk of the **Irwin River Estuary**, where you can spot waterbirds such as cormorants, pelicans and egrets. Make a left at Point Leander Drive to reach historic **Russ Cottage** (Parker St; ⊕ 09.30–noon Wed & Fri). Built in 1868, it is a period example of a workers' home – the furniture in it today is symbolic of a yeoman's cottage from that era. Titus Russ, family patriarch, was a squatter; the cottage was finished in 1868, reportedly with Russ carrying the limestone from quarry to site in a wheelbarrow himself. It was lived in until the early 1960s and retained by the Russ family until later that decade when it was bought by the Shire of Irwin, and then restored by the Irwin District Historical Society. A short extension to the route (about 1km) can be added by continuing on Point Leander Drive, past the marina to the white-and-red **Fisherman's Memorial Lookout and Obelisk**, commemorating those who have died in the many shipwrecks along this stretch of coast.

From the lookout, you can follow another Thungara Trail – the 2.7km Fisherman's Trail – past jetty ruins and fig trees down to **South Beach** ✳, the wide-sweeping,

10

sparkling jewel of the region popular with surfers, kiteboarders and all sorts of water activities.

A must-visit if you enjoy spirits is **Illegal Tender Rum Co** ✳ (35 Illyarrie Rd; ☎ 9927 2555; w illegaltenderrumco.com; ⏲ 11.00–17.00 Sat–Sun), a multi-award-winning rum distillery that offers tours of the rum-making process (A$30) – everything from distilling to bottling. The cellar door has a range of rums – tastings are available (A$5), and come with a talk from the producers about how the varying rums are made. Owner and distiller Codie Palmer believes the award-winning difference here is his use of dark brown sugar in the product instead of cheaper molasses.

CENTRAL GREENOUGH HISTORIC SETTLEMENT (91 Gregory Rd; ☎ 9926 1084; w centralgreenough.com; ⏲ 09.00–15.00 daily; adult/child A$10/5) About halfway between Dongara-Port Denison and Geraldton, and well-signposted from the Brand Highway, lies one of the best-preserved towns in WA – a window into the 1800s and the lives of the original European pioneers in the area who arrived as farmers. Many of the limestone buildings are managed by the National Trust and have been filled with period artefacts – the visitor's guide on entry provides a self-guided (4km) walk through the settlement. One of the appeals of a visit here is the easy access of the bulk of the sites – just off the Brand Highway, it makes a convenient afternoon stopping point if heading to/from Geraldton, or an easy day trip from the city.

Heritage listed, the three-storey limestone and brick **Clinch's Mill** – resembling a quaint old gingerbread farmhouse – was built to supply settlers and prospectors in the Murchison with flour. The grace and character of the building, and neighbouring **Cliff Grange**, a house for the mill manager, are highlights of a planning and construction method of the time showcasing unanimity of style and materials. The mill closed in 1922 and neither of the buildings are open to the public.

Also in the settlement, but a few kilometres out from the central precinct, is the interactive **Greenough Museum and Gardens** (Phillips Rd; ☎ 9926 1890; w greenoughmuseum.org.au; ⏲ 08.30–15.00 Tue–Sun; A$9/7/free adult/concession/child), set in the 1862 Maley Homestead, showcasing the history of the area through collections of artworks, documents and period costumes. John Maley began his apprenticeship at the age of ten as an engineer. Overseeing construction of Greenough's mill, at 21 he had the homestead built next to the mill to prepare for marriage and family life. Maley stayed on in Greenough and became one of the local power-brokers, opening several businesses before economic setbacks in the 1890s (when he was in his 50s) shuttered his local financial empire – he died in the house in 1910. The lovely garden is brimming with fruits like mulberries.

WALKAWAY RAILWAY STATION MUSEUM (Railway Station, Padbury Rd; ☎ 9926 1976; w walkawaymuseum.org.au; ⏲ 10.00–16.00 Tue–Fri, 13.00–16.00 Sat–Sun, closed summer months; adult A$5) Built in 1886, this station served the community for 80 years before it stopped being attended in 1966, and in its heyday played a vital role in linking Geraldton and Perth. Its centrepiece is its locomotive and restored carriage, but you can see the old station master's quarters as well. There are loads of railway exhibits plus local history about the town and its families.

ELLENDALE POOL Set against a hilly backdrop among the gum trees, this is a local, if overrated, favourite beauty spot, some 30km inland from the Brand Highway. Traditionally it's been a popular place to swim, but today warning signs urge you

to avoid contact with the water – even so, families still flock here for picnics and a kick around. On your way there, stop at the photogenic **Alinta Wind Farm** lookout on Walkaway–Nangetty Road; the car park features a turbine for you to inspect, and has information boards detailing the capacity of these 80m-tall turbines.

LEANING TREES A Mid West icon, these remarkable red river gum trees (*Eucalyptus camaldulensis*) on the Brand Highway grow horizontally along the ground rather than vertically due to an adaptation against strong salt-bearing winds. There is a car park where you can stop to take photographs.

GERALDTON

Lots of places claim to have the tired cliché of 'beach culture' in their fabric, but Geraldton – WA's third-most populous area after the Perth Metro and Bunbury – is one place where it is actually true. It isn't a surfer vibe like at Margaret River, nor a yachtie atmosphere like at Cottesloe. Geraldton enjoys a laidback, relaxed feeling – think chucking a sickie on a Thursday afternoon, putting on your sandals and sunglasses and heading down to the foreshore with your book to enjoy a drink at one of the many cafés lining the shore, or taking the sailboat out for a cruise. Owning a boat, kayak or some other form of watercraft is almost a legal requirement here, as Geraldton's bursting marina attests.

Sitting on the shores of Champion Bay, the town's gentle atmosphere and low-key sights mean that it's overlooked on the tourist circuit, but it is a great place to unwind for a few days, with a wealth of good restaurants, hotels and cafés. Its location near the likes of Kalbarri, the Abrolhos Islands and the Wildflower Circuit (page 288) also makes it a great base for exploring the wider region.

HISTORY The Geraldton area has abundant natural resources, which led Aboriginal peoples here some 40,000 years ago – the Yamatji are the Traditional Owners of this land and speak a language called Wajarri. These same resources also drew Europeans here – there is evidence that European explorers were in the region during the 1600s – particularly the Abrolhos Islands, 80km off the coast of Geraldton, where the *Batavia* wrecked (sometimes the Geraldton region is also called the Batavia Coast) – but there's no evidence they landed or explored the area where Geraldton townsite sits today. The first recorded formal European interest came from British explorer George Grey in 1839, on his expedition back to Swan River from Shark Bay – Grey felt the pastoral potential of the Geraldton area was great. However, subsequent reports by other parties disagreed with Grey, and settlement of the area was delayed. Over the next few years more of a consensus was reached, and the combination of coal deposits along the Irwin River – along with lead discoveries in the nearby Murchison – resulted in the first lots of land going up for auction in late 1849. Surveyor Augustus Gregory mapped out the town plan, and the town was named after Charles Fitzgerald, who was Governor of Western Australia from 1855 to 1862. The town got its official proclamation in 1871.

Convict labour was involved in the establishment of Geraldton right from the start – convicts built the original jetty at the port at Gregory Street. The development of agriculture and mining led to the laying of railway track and the expansion of the Port of Geraldton, which would become one of the state's most economically important – lead ore was one of the port's original main money-spinners. The Point Moore Lighthouse opened in 1878 to assist ships going into and out of the port and

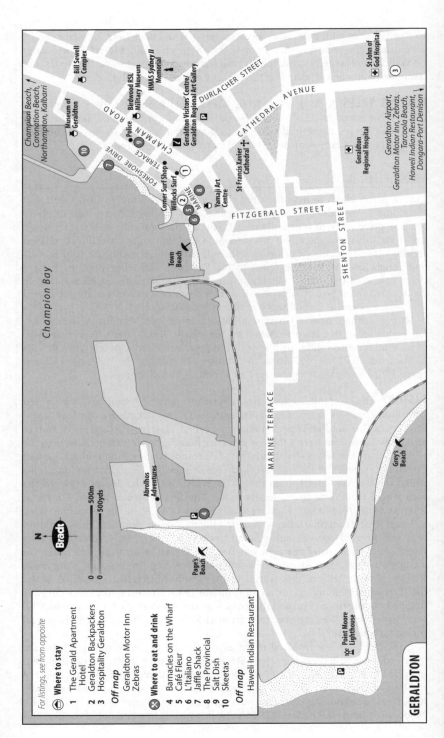

For listings, see from opposite

Where to stay
1 The Gerald Apartment Hotel
2 Geraldton Backpackers
3 Hospitality Geraldton
Off map
Geraldton Motor Inn
Zebras

Where to eat and drink
4 Barnacles on the Wharf
5 Café Fleur
6 L'Italiano
7 Jaffle Shack
8 The Provincial
9 Salt Dish
10 Skeetas
Off map
Haweli Indian Restaurant

GERALDTON

Champion Beach,
Coronation Beach,
Northampton, Kalbarri

Champion Bay

Page's Beach

Abrolhos
Adventures

Town Beach

Corner Surf Shop
Willocks Surf

N
Bradt
0   500m
0   500yds

Museum of
Geraldton

Bill Sewell
Complex

Police
Birdwood RSL
Military Museum
HMAS Sydney II
Memorial

FORESHORE DRIVE
TERRACE
CHAPMAN ROAD
DURLACHER STREET
CATHEDRAL AVENUE

Geraldton Visitors' Centre/
Geraldton Regional Art Gallery

Yamaji Art
Centre

MARINE TERRACE
MARINE

FITZGERALD STREET

St Francis Xavier
Cathedral

SHENTON STREET

Geraldton
Regional Hospital

St John of
God Hospital

Geraldton Airport;
Geraldton Motor Inn, Zebras;
Tarcoola Beach,
Haweli Indian Restaurant;
Dongara-Port Denison

Grey's Beach

Point Moore
Lighthouse

in the 1890s a railway opened linking Perth and Geraldton. The port later became a hub of wheat and livestock trade – still an economic mainstay of the area inland of town.

The post-war period saw diversity in the local economy; organisations such as the Geraldton Fishermen's Cooperative (founded in 1950) helped take the local lobster industry global, and the lifting of the Australian government's ban on iron-ore exports caused the town to become a hub – indeed, iron ore is Geraldton's top export today, well ahead of grains. The A$30 million redevelopment of the foreshore in 2007 revitalised the city centre, and today the town and region are considered to be growth centres for the state.

GETTING THERE AND AWAY As the biggest city north of Perth, Geraldton is a transit junction. With your own vehicle, the drive from Perth is 415km/4 hours. You have two options – taking Indian Ocean Drive, which is usually a bit slower but has more facilities en route, or the quicker Brand Highway which travels inland. Both join up again just south of Dongara-Port Denison.

Qantas and Virgin Australia both fly to Perth from Geraldton Airport (1hr), about 10km east of town on Geraldton–Mt Magnet Road. Transwa coaches run to/from East Perth (around 7hrs; from A$70 one-way).

GETTING AROUND TransGeraldton is the city's public bus network and it operates three routes, all originating at Anzac Terrace. Route 850 goes north along Chapman Drive to St George's Beach, Sunset Beach and Drummond Cove, while Route 851 takes a more inland route but also goes to St George's and Sunset Beaches, but then heads east towards the Chapman Valley. Route 852 is probably of limited use to tourists, heading along the North West Coastal Highway to some of the inland suburbs.

Private car is the most convenient option for travelling in town; parking is usually ample and convenient. Otherwise, try Geraldton Associated Taxis (131 008) and Geraldton Greenough Taxis (9964 7070).

TOURIST INFORMATION

Geraldton Visitor Centre Chapman St; 9956 6670; w visitgeraldton.com.au; 09.30–13.30 Mon, 09.00–16.00 Tue–Fri, 09.30–13.30 Sat–Sun. Located in the Geraldton Regional Art Gallery.

WHERE TO STAY *Map, opposite, unless otherwise stated*

The Gerald Apartment Hotel (40 rooms) 25 Cathedral Av; 9918 0100; e hello@thegerald.com.au; w thegerald.com.au. The premier option in town (with a price tag to match), the 7th-floor apartments have lounge, well-equipped kitchenette & dining area, with great views over town. More modest 'classic rooms' have blackout curtains & waterfall showers; some rooms interconnect for families. The rooftop bar has views out to the port, while the newly added boutique bar has over 50 gins. **$$$**

Hospitality Geraldton (47 rooms) 169 Cathedral Av; 9921 1422; e geraldton@hospitalityinns.com.au; w geraldton.wa.hospitalityinns.com.au. Tastefully appointed rooms, free laundry facilities & the quality licensed restaurant make this the pick of the motels in the CBD. **$$$**

Nesuto Geraldton [map, page 283] (80 studios) 298 Chapman Rd; 1800 834 314; e geraldton@nesuto.com; w nesuto.com/geraldton. Overlooking Champion Bay, these bright, spacious studios & multi-bedroom apartments come with kitchenette & courtyard; premier studios have separate living area & a washing/drying machine. Outdoor pool & hot tub & BBQ facilities. Great value for prices that come in at just above that of a motel. **$$$**

Nightcap at Wintersun Hotel [map, page 283] (38 rooms) 441 Chapman Rd; 9923 1211;

e info@nightcaphotels.com.au; w nightcaphotels. com.au. Part of a countrywide chain, these reasonably priced rooms & apartments are clean & stylish. On-site restaurant, 2 bars & outdoor pool make this a great social choice. **$$$**

🏠 **Geraldton Motor Inn** (60 rooms) 113 Brand Hwy; ☎ 9964 4777; e reception@gminn. com.au; w geraldtonmotorinn.com.au. You can't miss this distinctive green-&-white motel from the highway as you drive into town. Spacious but basic rooms are comfortable enough & there is an on-site bar, beer garden & bottle shop. The location is handy if you are overnighting on your way up north or down south. **$$**

🏠 **Zebras** (6 rooms) 2 Glendinning Rd; ☎ 0427 089 385; e info@zebrasgeraldton.com; w zebrasgeraldton.com. This unique, comfortable guesthouse in Tarcoola Beach brings a touch of Africa to the west coast – each room is themed around an animal (lion, leopard, elephant, buffalo,

rhino & zebra). All come with tea/coffee facilities, flatscreen televisions & rainfall showers. A mainstay choice for many travelling through town; it's our go-to when we pass through. There's also a shared kitchen & lounge. **$$**

🏠 **BIG4 Sunset Beach Holiday Park** [map, page 283] 4 Bosley St; 9938 1655; w sunsetbeachpark.com.au. With beachfront access, this quiet & dependable option offers chalets (inc 1 wheelchair-accessible), motel units & powered sites. A good option if you want to stay outside the CBD. *Chalets* **$$**, *sites* **$**

🏠 **Geraldton Backpackers** 172 Marine Tce; ☎ 9904 7342; w geraldtonbackpackers.com. au. Right on the foreshore, dorms are divided by gender though private rooms also available. Located in a Heritage building that was originally a large residence & supposedly the site of the first Freemasons meeting in the area. Excellent value. **$**

✖ WHERE TO EAT AND DRINK *Map, page 276*

✖ **Barnacles on the Wharf** 70 Connell Rd; ☎ 9964 4820; w barnaclesgeraldton.com.au; ⏰ 08.00–14.00 Mon–Fri, 17.00–19.30 Fri, 10.00–14.00 Sat. Award-winning fish & chips, plus locally caught seafood – including very reasonably priced western rock lobster. **$$$**

✳ ✖ **L'Italiano** 204 Marine Tce; ☎ 9964 9291; w litalianorestaurant.com; ⏰ 17.00–late Wed–Sun. Our first port of call when we are in town, this little but popular family-run restaurant serves a Sicilian-inspired menu plus terrific gelato for dessert. Try the cannelloni, though you can't go wrong with the pizzas. Be sure to book ahead. **$$$**

✳ ✖ **Skeetas** 3/219 Foreshore Dr; ☎ 9964 1619; w skeetas.com.au; ⏰ 06.30–23.00 daily. Bright & airy restaurant down by the marina that serves stylish & trendy plates (if a bit pricey) across the day. Last time I was here, I had a terrific crab linguini. Strong local wine list, plus a range of craft beers. **$$$**

✖ **Haweli Indian Restaurant** 8/75 Barrett Dr; ☎ 9921 1930; w haweli.com.au; ⏰ 11.00–14.30 & 16.30–21.30 daily. In the Woolworth's strip mall at the top of the hill eatery in Wandina, this serves dependable Indian classics. Signature dishes include leg of lamb marinated overnight & chicken breast filled with cheese & covered in an onion & tomato gravy. Limited seating – a take-out option for most. **$$**

✖ **The Provincial** 167 Marine Tce; ☎ 9964 1887; w theprovincial.com.au; ⏰ 16.30–midnight Tue–Sat. Classics like scotch fillets are done well here, but there is a creative starter menu of items like prawn & chorizo skewers, & Chinese dumplings of chicken & mushroom. There is a varied pizza menu – try the fig & prosciutto – plus an extensive cocktail list. Live music in the outdoor courtyard on Fri & Sat nights. **$$**

✖ **Salt Dish** 35 Marine Tce; ☎ 9964 6030; 🄵 saltdishcafe; ⏰ 07.00–15.00 Mon–Sat, plus 17.30–22.00 Fri–Sat. Down near the Esplanade, this café is known for its creative take on traditional dishes, such as spring pea bubble & squeak, beetroot risotto, buttermilk fried calamari & strawberry Dutch babies. **$$**

✖ **Café Fleur** 186 Marine Tce; ☎ 9949 9750; 🄵 cafefleurgeraldton; ⏰ 07.30–15.00 Mon–Fri, 07.30–14.00 Sat–Sun. With the slight air of a Parisian bistro, this colourful café serves a mixed menu featuring the likes of croquettes, nasi goreng & fish wings. Gets busy at lunchtime. **$**

✖ **Jaffle Shack** 188 Marine Tce; w jaffleshack. com.au; ⏰ 07.00–15.00 & 07.00–14.00 Mon–Fri. This small chain serving hearty jaffles (toasted sandwiches) & delicious waffles has 2 branches in Geraldton – this one, directly next to Café Fleur, & another on the foreshore. Good for a quick snack or a chatty lunch. **$**

OTHER PRACTICALITIES

Geraldton Regional Hospital 51–85 Shenton St; ☏ 9956 2222; ⊕ 24hrs
St John of God Hospital 12 Hermitage St; ☏ 9965 8888; ⊕ 24hrs

Western Australian Police Force 21 Marine Terrace; ☏ 9923 4555; ⊕ 24hrs

WHAT TO SEE AND DO Most sights are clustered in Geraldton's compact CBD, making it possible to visit them as part of a self-guided walking tour using the city map on page 276.

HMAS *Sydney II* Memorial ✳ (Gummer Av; ⊕ 24hrs; free) Geraldton's signature landmark, dedicated to the loss of the HMAS *Sydney II*, Australia's greatest naval tragedy, this monument atop Mt Scott was declared a national memorial on 21 May 2009. On 19 November 1941, the HMAS *Sydney II* did battle with a German warship, the HSK *Kormoran*, resulting in the loss of both ships – however, the survivors came exclusively from the *Kormoran*, while all 645 hands on the *Sydney* were lost (see

THE *BATAVIA* MUTINY

The Mid West coast is notoriously treacherous, a fact attested by its numerous shipwrecks. Perhaps the most famous is that of the *Batavia*; indeed, this part of the state is sometimes called the Batavia Coast after the vessel. Belonging to the Dutch East India Company, it left the Netherlands in 1628 with 270 souls and was on its way to the Dutch East Indies to take on spices when it hit a reef at the Houtman Abrolhos Islands and was marooned. The voyage's commander, Francisco Pelsaert, along with the ship's captain, Adrian Jacobsz (who reported to Pelsaert), left with a few others to try and find help in what is today Indonesia. That left Jeronimus Cornelisz, the third-ranking member of the crew, in charge.

Cornelisz then began a campaign to take control, with the overall goal of seizing a rescue ship and using the enormous riches in the *Batavia*'s cargo to start a new life. He began a campaign of terror – sending men on hopeless missions for food and water, where his confidants would murder them. But Cornelisz was a hapless captain, who chose poor henchmen, and that ended up being his undoing. Cornelisz send an unarmed group to West Wallabi Island to find water, certain they would fail and die, but when they found it, they remained on the island. Cornelisz then sent an armed crew to murder them, but they failed, with the West Wallabi survivors making makeshift weapons and being able to fend off the attack. Pelsaert returned on a rescue ship 3½ months later and, with the combined forces of the survivors on West Wallabi, comprehensively defeated the mutineers, but the damage was done. Only about one-third of the *Batavia*'s crew and passengers survived the ordeal; Cornelisz and his men were responsible for 115 murders and as punishment he had his hands chopped off and was hung.

The shipwreck was discovered nearly 300 years later on Morning Reef, near Beacon Island in the Abrolhos (page 282), along with evidence of human activity and artefacts. The remains of the *Batavia*'s hull were reconstructed and are now on display in the Batavia Gallery at the Shipwrecks Museum in Fremantle (page 95). Artefacts from the *Batavia* are on display at the Museum of Geraldton.

page 301 for more details on the battle). The entrance to the area is marked by two bollards that were used by the *Sydney* on her last stay in Geraldton.

The centrepiece of the exhibit is the Dome of Souls, the latticework of which is made up of 645 seagulls, representing the crew of the Sydney and inspired by a real-life flock of seagulls that appeared over a crowd at the dedication of the memorial during the playing of *The Last Post*. The dome is held up by seven pillars, representing both the states and territories of Australia and the seven seas, while the circular podium is made up of materials from the seven states and territories to represent the national nature of the crew and the tragedy. The altar is designed to resemble a ship's propeller, the black granite Wall of Remembrance lists the crew, their rank and home base while the stele was modelled after a ship concept and can be seen towering above Geraldton for kilometres. In bronze, towards the sea, is the statue of the waiting woman – who she is waiting for, we don't know – that has become symbolic of all the families and friends of loved ones who died in the tragedy.

Museums and historical sights

At the marina, the **Museum of Geraldton** (2 Museum Pl; ✆ 9431 8393; w museum.wa.gov.au/museums/museum-of-geraldton; ⊕ 09.30–15.00 daily; free, donations welcomed) – the Mid West branch of the West Australian Museum – is a good introduction to the town's maritime past, Aboriginal history and local fauna and flora. The Shipwrecks Gallery showcases discoveries from four Dutch wrecks – the *Batavia* (see box, page 279), *Gilt Dragon, Zuytdorp and Zeewijk* – and additionally, in 3D film, the *Sydney* and the *Kormoran*. A longboat that is a replica of the *Batavia* sails from in front of the museum every last Sunday of the month.

Military and war buffs will love the **Birdwood RSL Military Museum** (cnr Chapman Rd & Forrest St; ✆ 9964 1520; ⊕ 09.00–noon Mon & Thu, 17.00–19.30 Fri, noon–15.00 Sun; donations requested), cataloguing hundreds of artefacts and displays of Geraldton's and Australia's military history, including metals, used weapons and even handmade flags that were carried into battle. Exhibits rotate frequently.

Listed on the National Trust, the graceful and elegant **Bill Sewell Complex** (cnr Champan Rd & Bayly St) was originally a depot for convicts, before being repurposed as a hospital in 1868. A 650m trail leads around the complex and free guided tours are available on Tuesdays and Thursdays. The old gaol onsite was not closed until 1984 and served the Mid West for over a century; today it is a craft centre (⊕ 10.00–15.30 Mon–Fri & 09.00–noon Sat).

Galleries

The town has a thriving arts scene, and one of the best places to witness this is the **Geraldton Regional Art Gallery** (24 Chapman Rd; ✆ 9956 6750; w artgallery. cgg.wa.gov.au; ⊕ 09.00–16.00 Tue–Fri, 09.30–13.30 Sat–Sun; donations requested). Opened in 1984 in the Heritage-listed Town Hall, it hosts significant exhibitions year-round alongside the permanent City Collection, started in the late 1950s, showcasing works by local and national artists. The gallery also runs the prestigious Mid West Art Prize, held every two years – a major influence on the arts scene in WA. Showcasing a wide range of Aboriginal art including paintings, weavings, textiles and prints, **Yamaji Art Centre** (189 Marine Tce; ✆ 9965 3440; w yamajiart. com; ⊕ 09.00–16.00 Mon–Fri) supports indigenous artists in the region and offers numerous workshops, tours and talks for visitors.

St Francis Xavier Cathedral

(Cathedral Av; ⊕ daily – tours 14.30 Sun, Mon, Wed & 16.00 Fri; tour costs A$5) Built between 1916 and 1918, the large, imposing

Above   One of Australia's biggest mines, Kalgoorlie's 500m-deep Super Pit is the Goldfields' signature attraction (TV/S) page 233

Right   Broome has been the centre of WA's pearling industry since the late 19th century (TA) page 342

Below   The state's first permanent European settlement, Albany has a long history of whaling — today documented in the world's only whaling station tourist attraction (TA) page 199

Above   A replica of the Brig *Amity*, which arrived on WA's shores in 1826, on show at the Museum of the Great Southern (BP/WAM) page 197

Left   ANZAC history is part of Albany's DNA, and is best explored at the National **ANZAC Centre** (TA) page 197

Below   Coolgardie is one of the state's best examples of a gold-rush town (DW/S) page 225

Top left   Geraldton's HMAS *Sydney II* Memorial commemorates Australia's greatest naval tragedy (t/S) page 279

Above left   Today a museum and hostel, Fremantle Prison is one of 11 sites on UNESCO's Australian Convict Sites grouping (JT/S) page 94

Above right   Carnarvon was home to a NASA tracking station in the 1960s and 1970s, supporting the *Skylab* mission — which crashed off the coast of WA in 1973 (t/S) pages 220 & 300

Below   Built by German monks in 1918, Beagle Bay's Sacred Heart Church is known for its remarkable pearl-adorned interior, showcasing both Aboriginal and European motifs (MC/S) page 346

Above At Lucky Bay, kangaroos come down to the sand from the surrounding bush to eat the seaweed that washes ashore (LTO/S) page 216

Left Almost every morning since the 1960s, a pod of bottlenose dolphins has visited the shores of Monkey Mia in Shark Bay (EH/S) page 297

Below The Ningaloo Coast is famed for its whale sharks, best seen between March and August (LB/S) page 304

Top left   Active day and night, short-beaked echidnas are seen across the state (KG/S) page 9

Above left   Once widespread, the numbat is today only found in small patches of jarrah forest such as Dryandra Woodland (KG/S) page 256

Above right   Koalas are not endemic to WA, and Yanchep National Park is one of only two places in the state where you can see them (BM/S) page 113

Below   Estuarine (or saltwater) crocodiles are prevalent across the waters of the Kimberley, but the safest place to see them is Malcolm Douglas Crocodile Park (TA) page 345

Above left   Carnaby's black-cockatoo are endangered (i/S) page 10

Above right   Flocks of galahs are common in drier areas (i/S) page 10

Left   The black swan is WA's state emblem (i/S) page 9

Below left   Endemic to southern Australia, the malleefowl is classed as vulnerable (WOT/S) page 186

Below right   Lake Argyle is home to about one-third of the world's population of hooded plovers (JJ/S) page 10

Above left The world's smallest penguin, the little penguin is the face of Penguin Island, just off the coast of Rockingham (EQR/S) page 101

Above right The brilliantly coloured red-winged fairywren is endemic to the South West (FM/S) page 11

Below left The endemic Christmas Island hawk-owl is a favourite among visitors to the island (SS) page 365

Below right The Cocos (Keeling) Islands are good for birdwatching, with notable species including the red-footed booby (CITA) page 371

Above Christmas Island is renowned for its annual crab migration — one of the greatest natural displays in the world (CN/S) page 365

and eye-catching domes and towers of this Catholic cathedral are unmissable as you enter the CBD. Designed by Priest John Hawes, whose architectural influence across the Mid West is profound, there are echoes of Italian (the striping) and Californian churches (the mission-style towers), though Hawes's intention was to use simplicity to make a grand building. While the cathedral certainly catches the eye, notice the lack of ornamentation and fine detail as you tour. The grounds also host the **Monsignor Hawes Heritage Centre and Museum** (✆ 9937 9504; ⊕ 10.00–16.00 daily; donations requested), which explores the monsignor and his work further.

Point Moore Lighthouse (Marine Tce) At 34m high, this red-and-white striped lighthouse can project light some 26km out to sea and is still in operation today. Made from prefabricated iron, it entered operation in 1878 and is the oldest surviving Commonwealth lighthouse in the state. The lighthouse is not open to the public but there is information around the base.

Foreshores A popular pastime in Geraldton is to walk along the manicured grass lawns of the **Geraldton Foreshore**, busy with playing children, cyclists and swimmers preparing for a dip in Champion Bay. The Esplanade has a 360-degree lookout and provides good views of town and the ocean – sometimes sea lions hop on to the rocks here. North of the CBD along Chapman Road is the **Beresford Foreshore**, home to Lucy Humprey's *Horizon* sculpture – a 1.5m acrylic sphere with water inside, whose reflection of the sunset is one of the most photographed objects in town.

Beaches and watersports Geraldton is firmly enmeshed in the West Australian psyche as one of the state's beach capitals, and the locals fiercely embrace this tag. There are two beaches in the CBD itself – **Champion Beach** and **Town Beach** – if you don't mind the gritty port backdrop for scenery. Champion Beach is the bigger of the two, right against the grassed foreshore area, while Town Beach lies adjacent to the Esplanade. Both are great for family swimming, but there isn't much snorkelling potential. On the western 'thumb' peninsula, around a 20-minute walk from the CBD, **Page's Beach**, **Point Moore** and **Grey's Beach** are also suitable for swimming; Page's and Point Moore have some snorkelling sites as well, and Point Moore and Grey's are popular with fishermen. A similar walking distance north and south, respectively, **St George's Beach** and **Tarcoola Beach** round off the portfolio of highlight beaches in town. St George's has more facilities (such as a playground, barbecue and ablutions) but both are swimmer-friendly.

Further north, 30km from town and signposted off the Brand Highway, dazzling **Coronation Beach** could well be the prettiest beach in Geraldton. Its extensive reef makes for excellent sheltered swimming and snorkelling while the winds coming in off the ocean also make it a good surfing and kitesurfing location. Based on the beach, **Kitewest** (Coronation Beach Camp; ✆ 0449 021 784; e info@kitewest.com.au; w kitewest.com.au) offer surfing, kite- and windsurfing lessons, SUP yoga, equipment rentals and watersports tours. On Geraldton's northern fringe, 6km from the CBD, **Sunset Beach** is one of the best for wind- and kitesurfing, while another 7km north, **Drummond Cove** is also popular among locals. The waves are more intense at Sunset Beach which makes it a good one for surfers. In the CBD, **Corner Surf Shop** (103 Marine Tce; ✆ 9921 3127; w cornersurf.com.au; ⊕ 09.00–17.00 Mon–Fri, 09.00–16.00 Sat, 10.00–15.00 Sun) and **Willocks Surf** (127 Marine Tce; ✆ 9921 8623; w willockssurf.com; ⊕ 09.00–17.00 Mon–Fri, 09.00–16.00 Sat, 10.00–15.00 Sun) stock surfboards and bodyboards, as well as associated clothing.

Fishing can be had at all the beaches listed, within regulations – herring and sand whiting are caught routinely but also tailor and tarwhine. The deep sea off Grey's Beach and Point Moore serves up pink snapper and dhufish, among others. For day and multi-day fishing trips, contact **Abrolhos Adventures** (154 Connell Rd; ✆ 9942 4515; e admin@abrolhosadventures.com.au; w abrolhosadventures.com. au) and **Offshore Charters WA** (✆ 0428 531 231; e kim@offshorecharterswa.com. au; w offshorecharterswa.com.au). Both also organise whale watching, trips to the Abrolhos (see below) and crayfish pot pulling.

Houtman Abrolhos Islands Often referred to as Australia's Galápagos, the 122 coral-fringed islands that make up this pristine, reef-laden archipelago are home to an astounding array of marine life and are a breeding ground for an estimated two million birds. BirdLife International has classified the islands as an Important Bird Area, and the endemic Abrolhos painted buttonquail (*Turnix varius scintillans*) is found nowhere else on earth. The islands are also home to 26 species of land reptile, marine turtles, sea lions and countless species of fish, as well as the tammar wallaby – the first marsupial seen by Europeans in Australia in the 1600s. There are also 140 species of native flora on the island, and all are protected.

Situated 60km west of Geraldton, the islands are divided into three groups: the Wallabi (north), the Easter (centre) and the Pelsaert (south). Aside from their natural importance, the islands are also a key historical site in the early European exploration of Australia, among the first parts of Australia seen by Dutch explorers in the early 1600s; 'discovery' was credited to Dutch captain Frederick de Houtman, after whom the islands are partially named. 'Abrolhos' is a Portuguese term that was interpreted to mean 'open your eyes' – a warning about the many reefs that have claimed numerous ships along this stretch of coast (including the *Batavia*; see box, page 279).

Guano mining – the harvesting of bird excrement, which was an excellent agricultural fertiliser – was a major industry in the early Federation period and ruins of guano jetties and even a railway can still be seen on Rat and Pelsaert Islands. Guano mining relied on manual labour – the terrain made machines impractical, and they also scared the birds – and hand-tools were used to loosen and collect the guano. Fishing has also always been a major economic activity here, and even today small settlements of about 100 western rock lobster fishermen live seasonally on the islands. Black pearls are cultivated here, and there are commercial fisheries.

For the visitor, the islands offer a wealth of fantastic diving, fishing and snorkelling opportunities. You can also dive to the *Batavia* – cannons still visible – which sits in about 5m of water. A number of Mid West operators run trips to the islands, including Abrolhos Adventures and Offshore Charters WA (see above). There is no accommodation on the islands and you need to be completely self-sufficient, including having your own fresh water, but multi-day excursions are possible including boat stays.

NORTH OF GERALDTON TO KALBARRI

Driving north from Geraldton, the Brand Highway becomes the North West Coastal Highway and continues to pass through farmland, pasture and paddocks framed by low-rising hills, dotted with haybales and the occasional windmill – it's all very photogenic. When you get to Northampton, most visitors to Kalbarri will leave the highway and turn on to Horrocks Road – which changes its name several times – all the way to Kalbarri, with similar pastoral scenery. You can, instead,

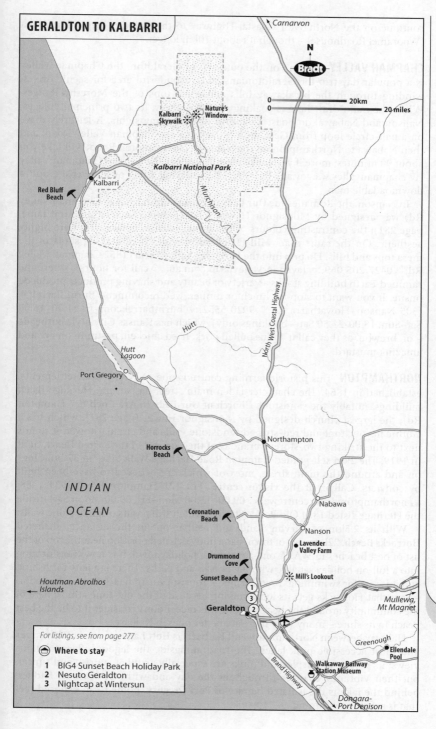

GERALDTON TO KALBARRI

↑ Carnarvon

N

Bradt

0   20km
0   20 miles

Nature's Window

Kalbarri
Skywalk ☀

Kalbarri National Park

Kalbarri

Murchison

**Red Bluff
Beach** ↖

Hutt

North West Coastal Highway

Hutt
**Hutt
Lagoon**

Port Gregory ○

Northampton

**Horrocks
Beach** ↖

Nabawa ○

INDIAN

OCEAN

Nanson ○

● **Lavender
Valley Farm**

**Coronation
Beach** ↖

**Drummond
Cove** ↖

Sunset Beach ↖

☀ **Mill's Lookout**

①
③
②

Geraldton

*Houtman Abrolhos
Islands*
←

*Mullewa,
Mt Magnet*

Greenough

● **Ellendale
Pool**

**Walkaway Railway
Station Museum**

Brand Highway

*↓ Dongara-
Port Denison*

For listings, see from page 277

⌂ **Where to stay**

1   BIG4 Sunset Beach Holiday Park
2   Nesuto Geraldton
3   Nightcap at Wintersun

continue on the North West Coastal Highway to the Kalbarri turn-off at Ajana (Wooramel Roadhouse) – though it's about 10km longer.

CHAPMAN VALLEY Starting on the outskirts of Geraldton, the Chapman Valley is a popular day trip for Geraldtonians and a wonderful area for scenic drives, winding through the breakaway hills and mesa tops of the Moresby Ranges. While the main draw here is soaking up the scenery, its two principal villages, Nanson and Nabawa, do boast a handful of interesting sights. A leisurely drive on a half-circle loop from Geraldton to Nabawa on Chapman Valley Road, and then Nabawa to Northampton on the Nabawa–Northampton Road, will take you about 90 minutes; more if you make plentiful stops. The Shire of Chapman Valley (w chapmanvalley.wa.gov.au) has suggested driving trails on its website and a downloadable map.

In Nanson, the Romanesque **Our Lady of Fatima Church** (2445 Chapman Valley Rd) was designed by Monsignor Hawes (of St Francis Xavier Cathedral fame, page 281); the contrasting colours of the stones used in construction are highly aesthetic. On the same road, **Mill's Lookout** provides breathtaking shots of the mesa tops and hills. Do pop into the **Lavender Valley Farm** (1852 Chapman Valley Rd; \0427 205 069; w lavendervalleyfarm.com.au; ⏱ call for hours), where the rammed-earth building stocks a variety of beauty and shaving products produced onsite. If you want to stop for lunch or dinner, we'd recommend **Burnt Barrel** ✳ (305 Nanson–Howatharra Rd; \9920 5552; w burntbarrel.com; ⏱ 11.00–16.00 Sat–Sun, 18.00-21.30 Sat – bookings only), which has Kansas City-style barbecue – or 'brewbq', as they call it – plus pulled pork, fried chicken, pastrami on rye and amazing mustard.

NORTHAMPTON This historic farming centre is one of WA's oldest settlements, established in 1864. The character-laden main street has several Heritage-listed buildings, notably the sandstone **Church of Our Lady in Ara Coeli** (27 Hampton Rd), the largest church designed by Monsignor Hawes (page 281), which has a Gothic flavour to it and red-striped sandstone walls and circular tower. It stands next to the striking two-storey verandas of the **Convent of the Sacred Heart**, built in 1919. The 2km self-guided **Hampton Road Heritage Walk** takes in 37 buildings on and around the main street, most of which are believed to have been built by convicts. Call in at the **visitor centre** (Lot 121 Hampton Rd; \9934 1488; ⓕ northamptonvisitorcentrewa; ⏱ 09.00–15.00 Mon–Fri, 09.00–noon Sat) inside the Heritage-listed 1884 Old Police Station, which still has its original stone walls.

With its 2.5km of curving sand and reefbar out in the distance, sheltered **Horrocks Beach**, 22km west of town, has a hotly debated position near the top of the list of best beaches in WA. A one-time shack holiday town, it is now transforming into a full-on holiday satellite with big houses and parks. There is a jetty for fishing and it is safe for swimming. Brad Farmer – Tourism Australia's 'beach ambassador' – says that Horrocks gets its lofty ranking because of the old-time atmosphere of the community around the beach. While it is nice, I don't consider it to be the best beach in its shire – in my view there are better ones in Kalbarri.

Halfway between Northampton and Kalbarri is **Hutt Lagoon**, one of WA's larger and most accessible pink lakes. The road alongside the lagoon offers fabulous views; its palette of purples and pinks are especially artful at sunrise and sunset, but their vibrancy changes throughout the day and with the seasons. Hidden behind the lake is the isolated hamlet of **Port Gregory**, home to an exposed reef that is safe for swimming.

KALBARRI

The gem in the Mid West's jewel box, Kalbarri's spectacular contrasting scenery – dramatic gorges and cliffs in the famed national park alongside magnificent coastal landscapes – have made this little town a West Australian synonym for 'holiday' for decades. A growing and increasing surfing presence has added to this reputation; there has even been talk that the town may supplant Margaret River as a stop on the pro-surfing circuit.

Be warned: Kalbarri's reputation as a sublime tourist spot often exceeds its capacities, as this is still a small town of only about 1,500 people. It is not uncommon or unheard of for accommodation here to get booked out weeks and sometimes months in advance, so you'd do well to book ahead.

GETTING THERE AND AWAY Kalbarri is 570km/6 hours north of Perth and 150km/90 minutes north of Geraldton. Note that Kalbarri is not on the North West Coastal Highway; if heading north from Perth or Geraldton, the most common access point is the Stephen Street turn-off – the road changes its name several times but takes you past Port Gregory and Hutt Lagoon (page 284). Alternatively, a longer (10km more) route is the Ajana–Kalbarri Road, the turn-off for which is 49km north of Northampton.

Transwa coaches go to/from East Perth (8½hrs; from A$87 one-way) and Geraldton (2½hrs; from A$30 one-way). Integrity Coach Lines will drop you at the Binnu General Store, 78km away, from Perth or up north. From there you will need to contact Kalbarri Shuttle, which is run by the Kalbarri Backpackers YHA (pre-book at ℡9937 1430), to take you into town.

TOURIST INFORMATION AND TOUR OPERATORS

Kalbarri Visitor Centre 70 Grey St; ℡9937 1104; w kalbarri.org.au; ⏱ 09.00–17.00 Mon–Fri, 10.00–14.00 Sat–Sun

Kalbarri Abseil ℡9937 1618; e kabseil@ bigpond.net.au; w kalbarriabseil.com. Runs abseiling tours into the Z-Bend Gorge in Kalbarri National Park, suitable for all experience levels.

Kalbarri Adventure Tours ℡0419 943 795; e kalcanoe@wn.com.au; w kalbarritours.com.au.

Half- & full-day canoe & hiking excursions inside the gorges of Kalbarri National Park.

Kalbarri Boat Hire & Canoe Safaris Grey St; ℡9937 1245; w kalbarriboathire.com. Self-guided half-day canoe treks along the Murchison, suitable for all abilities with meals en route, as well as kayaks. They also hire out seemingly all manner of watercraft – kayaks, canoes, SUPs, canoes & pedal boats.

WHERE TO STAY

Gecko Lodge Kalbarri 9 Glass T; ℡9937 1900; e stay@geckolodgekalbarri.com.au; w geckolodgekalbarri.com.au. Luxury B&B with spa suites that come with comfortable robes – there's also a penthouse suite with a 65-inch TV. **$$$**

Kalbarri Edge Resort (76 rooms) 22 Porter St; ℡9937 0000; e reservations@kalbarriedge. com.au; w kalbarriedge.com.au. Self-contained studios & apartments make this a good upmarket option for families or those seeking a bit more privacy & facilities. Studios have microwaves, mini-fridges & freezers, while suites have hotplates,

washer/dryer & private balcony with BBQ. On-site restaurant. **$$$**

Kalbarri Palm Resort (78 rooms) 8 Porter St; ℡9937 2333; e stay@palmresort.com. au; w palmresort.com.au. Central option with standard but comfortable & clean motel units. Suites & a villa available for larger groups or families. A solid choice. **$$**

Murchison River Caravan Park 92 Grey St; ℡9937 1005; e mcp@wn.com.au; w murcp. com. Right on the waterfront, with shaded powered & non-powered sites as well as cabins. Facilities include camp kitchen, playground, fish-cleaning station & a dump point. *Cabins* **$$$**, *sites* **$**

🏠 **Kalbarri Backpackers YHA** 51 Mortimer & Woods St; ☎9937 1430; w kalbarribackpackers.

com. 6–12-bed dorm rooms available, plus 2 dbls. Swimming pool on site as well as an undercover BBQ area & community kitchen. Fishing, snorkelling & other activity gear available for hire. **$**

✖ WHERE TO EAT AND DRINK

✖ **Finlay's Kalbarri** 13 Magee Cres; ☎9937 1253; w finlayskalbarri.com.au; ⊕ 17.00–22.00 Wed–Sat, noon–22.00 Sun. A brewery & outdoor seafood restaurant showcasing regional specialties like Shark Bay cockles & Exmouth coconut & panko prawns. The seafood linguini packs a punch & the brewery is very popular – so much so that they were able to expand after just a few years of operation. Their Murchison Hazy Pale & Jakes Point India Pale Ale were both medal winners at the Perth Royal Show. They are also dog-friendly & there's a campfire that adds spirit to the experience. **$$$**

✖ **Upstairs Restaurant** 3/10 Porter St; ☎0408 001 084; w upstairsrestaurant.com.au; ⊕ 17.00– 22.00 Thu–Mon. Trendy dinner & tapas restaurant with local seafood such as pink snapper & shellfish. Desserts are done in-house. A bit pricey but worth it; reservations essential. **$$$**

* ✖ **Buddha's Bites** 8 Porter St; ☎0488 054 693; 🇫 buddhasbiteskalbarri; ⊕ 17.30–20.30 Wed–Sat. Thai restaurant that does a great beef rendang, plus curries, burgers & wraps. **$$**

✖ **Red Bluff Bakery & Café** 10 Porter St; ☎9937 1045; ⊕ 06.00–18.00 Mon–Sat, 06.00– 17.00 Sun. Great pies, b/fast wraps & coffees plus good-value lunch options. **$$**

✖ **Black Rock Café** 80 Grey St; ☎9937 1062; ⊕ 07.00–14.00 Tue–Sun, 17.00–19.30 Wed–Sat. Wonderful b/fast spot on the main street; our favourite place for a good morning start, with coffees & a varied cake selection. **$**

✖ **Jetty Seafood Shack** 1/365 Grey St; ☎9937 1067; ⊕ 16.30–20.30 daily. The ocean line-caught fish & chips here are high quality & the service is good. Burgers available also if you prefer something land-based. **$**

WHAT TO SEE AND DO

Kalbarri National Park * Spectacular enough to make the cover of this guidebook – no easy feat in a state full of jaw-dropping scenery – huge (186,000ha) Kalbarri National Park captivates visitors with its brightly coloured gorges, sensational wildflowers, dramatic sea cliffs and scenic panoramas. For visitors, the park appears disjointed, though it actually isn't; the larger, northern section – most famous for its gorges – is 40km northeast of Kalbarri, while 6km south of town, the southern section offers coastal bluffs, cliffs and a bird's-eye view of the dramatic pounding they take from the Indian Ocean. The access points for these two main areas are not near each other – Kalbarri townsite and about 45km separates them.

Carved over millions of years as the Murchison made its way to the Indian Ocean, the **Murchison River Gorges** (⊕ 06.00–18.00 daily; A$15/vehicle for the inland gorges; free if you are going to the coastal section of the park) provide some of the best views and hiking in WA. The array of colours – red, orange, brown, white – of the gorge walls, often in stripes or layers and contrasting with the blue-greens of the Murchison on the gorge floor, presents a palette that is especially powerful in wildflower season when it is complemented by pink pokers, white spider orchids, purple starflowers and yellow sennas (among others). Kalbarri Adventure Tours (page 285) organise guided activities here.

Accessed by an 800m walk from the car park, **Nature's Window** is one the most photographed views in the state, an opening through a natural rock arch at the top of a gorge cliff that captures the Murchison as it makes a horseshoe-shaped curve thorough the formations. From here, you can return to the car park or continue to enjoy one of the best hikes in the state – the 8km, Class 4 **Loop Trail**. Proceeding across the tops of the gorges, before descending into them and along the banks of the Murchison, this steep trek crosses varied terrain – including sandy banks and rock edges. You can swim in the Murchison if it is deep enough. Be warned, though: the steep ascent back up to Nature's Window at the end of the loop – after you have already done 7km, and often in hot weather – is very demanding. There are numerous other gorge walks in the park; call in to the Kalbarri Visitor Centre (page 285) for more information.

Another park showpiece is the recently opened **Kalbarri Skywalk**, which is actually two separate 100m-high lookouts, each protruding 25m over the edge of the gorge to hover over the Murchison – with sensational views over the surrounding landscape. The path up to the viewpoints is wheelchair-accessible.

The southern end of the national park features stunning coastal cliff scenery – brilliant reds and chalk whites against the sparkling blues of the Indian Ocean. There are wildflowers here too – among them pink-purple parakeelyas, red Murchison roses and orange-white acorn banksias. Some cliffs – such as that at Red Bluff and

THE MONACO OF WESTERN AUSTRALIA

In 1969, the West Australian government put in place quotas on wheat production, substantially cutting the amount of wheat that farmers could sell on the market. One such farmer, Leonard Casley, had around 9,900 acres of wheat ready to sell from his 18,500-acre farm in the Shire of Northampton, but the quota meant he was only permitted to sell 99 acres of that. After a series of court fights with the government, Casley decided to get around the quotas by seceding and forming his own nation – and thus the Principality of Hutt River was born on 21 April 1970, with Casley as monarch, declaring himself 'Prince Leonard'.

The secession was not recognised by any country in the world, including Australia – though amusing bureaucratic stuff-ups could happen from time to time, such as when the Australian Tax Office (ATO) sent Casley a letter saying that he had been declared a non-resident for income purposes, which Casley gleefully embraced and used in his many court fights against the government. Casley gained enormous publicity both inside WA and nationwide, and began to implement the full trappings of independence – postage stamps, banknotes and passport stamps when you entered the principality. Casley even commissioned composer Keith Kerwin to write a national anthem.

Casley's battles with the Australian government continued off and on over the decades, and the principality became a tourist sight in its own right – with Casley's wife Shirley operating a tearoom on site. At one point nearly 1,000 tourists a week were flocking to Hutt River Principality, with the passport stamps gaining enduring popularity.

Prince Leonard handed over the principality to his son Prince Graeme in 2017, and Leonard Casley died in February 2019 at the age of 95. But Prince Graeme's reign would be short-lived: Covid-19 and the ATO teamed up to take down Hutt River, with the former resulting in the principality closing its borders to tourists in January 2020, and the latter winning a A$3 million back-tax judgment against the Casleys. Prince Graeme confirmed to the media in August 2020 that the principality would be dissolved and the farm sold to pay off the tax debts – a buyer was found in late 2021, but the 'principality' will not reopen for tourists.

Pot Alley – have steep walking trails that lead down to beaches. **Red Bluff Beach** is suitable for swimming – the bluff provides a breathtaking backdrop – though when I have swum here, there has been an undercurrent a bit too strong for my liking, so proceed with caution.

Swimming, snorkelling and surfing There are two ideal swimming spots in the region. Right on the foreshore in Kalbarri, **Chinaman's Beach** is a sheltered rivermouth connecting the Indian Ocean to the Murchison River, while **Blue Holes Beach** ✳, just 2km south of town, is a protected marine environment with both submerged and exposed reefs – lots of marine life is visible very close to the shore such as butterfly fish and rock lobsters. A further 1km from Blue Holes is **Jacques (Jake's) Point**, famed for its left-hand surf break, which challenges experienced surfers. The interior bay is known as Little Jake's and is more suited for beginners and intermediates.

WILDFLOWER COUNTRY: MOORA TO MINGENEW

There are roughly 12,000 species of wildflower in WA, and over half are found nowhere else – the state is truly one of the world's great wildflower hotspots, and its epicentre is the inland Mid West. Each spring, the region erupts into one of the world's most dazzling shows of colour, with carpets of wildflowers appearing in almost every nook and cranny. The two headliners are the much-loved pink, white and gold everlastings and the endemic wreath flower (*Lechenaultia macrantha*), an amazing natural circular bouquet of pink, red and white flowers that form a ring around a centre of green growth that resembles a Christmas tree branch. Every West Australian strives to come here at least once for one of nature's greatest floral shows – seeing the wreath flowers, particularly, is on every West Australian bucket list (see box, page 290) – and many of those who visit, including ourselves, end up turning it into an annual pilgrimage.

Most of the regions in the state stake a claim to being 'Wildflower Country' but your central focus should probably be the area which, when looked at on a map, forms an upside-down triangle – with the northern Wheatbelt town of Moora being the apex, the town of Yalgoo in the Mid West being the northeast point and Geraldton being the northwest point. This is a vast area, so you're best to focus on one or two spots – all the shires in the area will be able to give you advice and suggestions of what to see in their areas and it is worthwhile to call ahead, as they will know what is blooming where and can also provide advice on what kind of season they are having. It often pays to just drive and explore, however – we found one particular route from Carnamah to Morawa that isn't denoted as a wildflower hotspot, but whose numerous carpets of everlastings made it a personal favourite of ours and a must-do on all of our trips.

GETTING THERE AND AROUND Moora is 167km/2 hours north of Perth. From Moora, it's 195km/2 hours 45 minutes north to Mingenew, and then another 84km/1 hour 10 minutes north to Mullewa. Geraldton is 100km/1 hours 10 minutes west of Mullewa and Dongara-Port Denison is 54km/1 hour west of Mingenew. Your own vehicle is a necessity in this region; public transport will get you to the staging towns but not to the reserves where the action happens.

WHERE TO STAY AND EAT Some pre-planning is essential; you will pass many small towns through here, but they were built to support the surrounding pastoral and agriculture industries, not tourism. Services, accommodation and dining can be extremely limited especially on weekends; on Saturdays in this part of the state many things shut at noon. Give heavy consideration to basing yourself in Geraldton (page 277), Dongara-Port Denison (page 272) or Moora and making day trips from there. Pack a lunch to take with you.

🏠 **Drovers Inn** 1 Dandaragan St, Moora; 📞9651 1108. The pick of the offerings in the area, the recently renovated motel units behind the main building are clean, spacious & bright. The restaurant inside the 1909 building does quality fish & chips among other offerings, but it does get very busy so reserve ahead. **$$$**

🏕 **Canna Camping** Self-serve sites with no bookings required – however, there are no rubbish or dump points, but there is an ablution block with hot showers & a BBQ (gas is BYO). No petrol available. Turn on to Offszanka Rd from the Wubin–Mullewa Rd; the campsites are at the tiny, tiny townsite 3km down the road. **$**

🏕 **Coalseam Camping** (16 sites) Unpowered sites but toilets are provided. There is a max 3-night stay during wildflower season. Generators are only permitted for 2hrs in the morning & 2hrs in the late afternoon. **$**

✕ **Mingenew Hotel** Midlands Rd; 📞9928 1002; ⏰ call for hours. First opened in 1899, this place does good pizzas & steaks alongside satisfactory motel rooms. **$$**

✕ **Jeanne d'Moore** 103 Gardiner St; 📞0497 857 975; w jeannedmoore.com.au; ⏰ 08.00–15.00 Mon-Fri, 08.00–13.00 Sat. French-inspired café & homeware/gift shop showcasing a wide variety of teas, baguettes, croissants & pastries. Great spot for a snack & an unusual find in the area. **$**

WHAT TO SEE AND DO The following sights follow a rough south–north route from Moora.

Badgingarra National Park
Roughly 45km from both Cervantes and Moora on the Brand Highway, this 13,000ha national park is brimming with wildflowers, even in poor seasons. The best way to explore is on the 3.5km Iain Wilson Nature Trail through the low scrub, where banksias and kangaroo paws are common. Note, though, that the trail can be strenuous and steep in sections.

Mingenew
This small town, 84km south of Mullewa and 54km west of Dongara, often falls off the usual tourist wildflower track but is a favourite among locals. **Depot Hill**, 12km from town, is a haven for orchids, including donkey, spider, sun, cowslip and snail orchids, while **Mingenew Hill**, in town itself, has everlastings and lilies. You can also find fairy orchids in the region.

Coalseam Conservation Park ✳
Widely seen as one of the go-to places for wildflowers by West Australians, and one of the centrepieces of Wildflower Country, this park is especially known for its yellow and white pom-pom flower carpets. There are many viewpoints and plateaus that provide stunning vistas into the riverbed: the 3.2km **Plateau Loop Trail** offers a good vantage point of the wildflowers in the valley, as does the 600m **Irwin Loop Lookout**. You can easily walk down to the valley floor along the (dry) riverbed, where there are lots of exposed old (though tiny) fossils – we have seen plenty. You can also see exposed coalseams there too; coal was discovered here in 1846 and WA's first coal mine was here; however, the coal was not high enough in quality for significant, profitable commercial mining (the major finds were later in Collie, in the South West). There are shafts so take care with children. The **Miners Walk Trail** (700m return) takes you to a viewing platform to a coal shaft (no longer used). The park

10

There are two highly dependable (and signposted) spots to find these sought-after flowers, so don't fret that you don't know where to look or worry that you won't find any. The first is about 10km north of the town of **Pindar**, which is 30km east of Mullewa. An unsealed road takes you just inside West Australian Station Country (which begins behind the small town) where, depending on how good the season has been, you can see hundreds or just a few dozen of the wreath flower. The spot is signposted – you'll pass the entrance to Tallering Station on the way. Pindar itself is a highly photogenic one-road town, with a sprinkling of old veranda houses that ooze classic Australiana. It also has a gorgeous tearoom inside a Heritage-listed old hotel – **The Old Pindar Hotel** (17 Sharpe St; ☏0478 398 162; e admin@pindarhotel. com; ⏰ call) opens seasonally for wildflower tourists.

The other equally dependable spot for wreath flowers, is along the **Morawa–Yalgoo Road**, about 30km from Morawa. Again, the location is simply signposted on the side of the road; however, you don't have to look for the sign – the wreath flowers love roadside shoulders and enormous rows of them bloom there, making them readily obvious when you drive by. Failing that, though, look for campervans and drivers pulled over on the side of the road. That's a sure sign there is something interesting.

has unsealed roads but they are well-formed and 2WD suitable; it's about 30km north of Mingenew.

Canna Reserve ✱ In wildflower season, this is one of our favourite places in Australia – the carpets of white and gold everlastings seem to expand unrestricted in every direction, and every turn you take provides a different but equally spectacular photo opportunity. The caravan/camping area is the best place for everlastings; the nearby dam has a short walk and is a good place to look for orchids. It's rarely crowded and often flies below the radar as a wildflower site in the state. Roughly 40km north of Morawa, head north on the Wubin–Mullewa Road; the reserve is signposted from there.

Mullewa Its proximity to major wildflower reserves and wreath flower sites arguably makes Mullewa the capital of Wildflower Country, but the town has seen better days – Mullewa's decline is evident almost immediately as you drive in. You are better off staying and eating in Geraldton, 100km away. Nevertheless, it's the starting point for two drive trails; the 115km, 13-stop **Northern Loop** and the 145km, 14-stop **Southern Circuit**, the latter of which takes in Coalseam and Pindar (see box, above). The highlight of the Northern Loop is a section around the Greenough River where you will find **Bindoo Hill Nature Reserve**, an area that was an old glacier moraine. However, you would probably be wiser to just cherry-pick a few highlights to concentrate your time at, like Coalseam and Canna, and then travel up to Pindar, otherwise you risk having the lasting memory of your wildflower trip be the inside of your car.

Back in town, the 2.8km **Mullewa Wildflower Walk**, opposite the caravan park, showcases the variety of flora here with lots of spider orchids and everlastings. Aside from wildflowers, the beautiful **Our Lady of Mt Carmel Church and Priest House Museum** (18 Doney St; ☏9961 1165; ⏰ 10.00–noon daily; A\$2) is arguably the greatest work of Monsignor Hawes (page 281) and evokes a Spanish mission. The stones came from a local quarry.

THE MURCHISON AND WESTERN GOLDFIELDS

Heading east from Geraldton on the Geraldton–Mt Magnet Road, the bluffs and wheat farms give way to the classic Outback scenery – red dirt and scrub. Gold mining put this area on the map in the 1890s – the original Europeans were prospectors and some of the finds here rivalled those in the Goldfields – and later stations popped up. Most visitors head this way en route to the Pilbara or Kimberley, but there are a few interesting detours worth exploring – even if you aren't a prospector.

MT MAGNET   With a population of about 800, this is the biggest town in the region and a transit crossroads; if you are going north from Perth to Port Hedland or the Kimberley, or from Geraldton to the Goldfields, you will pass through here. The town's turn-of-the-century Goldfields architecture is well preserved; download the Shire's **walking tour** from w mtmagnet.wa.gov.au. It's also worth popping into the **Wirnda Barna Arts Centre** (76 Hepburn St; ℡ 0438 757 274; w wirndabarna. com.au), showcasing Aboriginal artists from the surrounding Badimaya and Wajarri Country and exquisite paintings inspired by the Murchison landscape. If you are here in September, the **Astro Rocks Fest** celebrates astronomy and the connections to Aboriginal culture – meaning is often assigned to the stars and other astronomical matters, which then informs law and custom. The **Swagman Roadhouse** (599 Hepburn St; ℡ 9920 8000; w swagmanrh.com.au) is the best place for a meal and to fill up the car.

ROAD TRIP: WOOL WAGON PATHWAY

This 1,248km, three-day, deep inland drive leads from Geraldton to Exmouth through deep historical pastoral country. The first section (350km) leads from Geraldton to the Shire of Murchison – the only shire in Australia that does not have a town. The shire is instead a collection of a few dozen pastoral stations. You have two solid accommodation options: the homestead of **Wooleen Station** (℡ 9963 7973; w wooleen.com.au; all meals included; **$$$$**), 38km south of Murchison; or the **Murchison Oasis Roadhouse & Caravan Park** (6 motel rooms; ℡ 9961 3875; e murchisonoasis@westnet. com.au; **$$$**), in Murchison itself and home to a small shop. The second day takes you 300km to Gascoyne Junction, from where it's a long 610km, 7-hour trip to Exmouth. Plan that last day carefully as there is no petrol en route. Check road conditions with the shires beforehand to verify suitability for your vehicle.

There are a few natural sites of interest in the Shire of Murchison, such as the saddle-like **Errabiddy Bluff** (turn-off 1km from Murchison), **Wooramel Gorges** (145km north of Murchison) and **Bilung Pool** (150km north of Murchison) – but the real attraction is the Outback experience of true isolation, wide-open spaces, iconic scenery and the contemplation of just how it would have been to make it in such a harsh environment.

See *Gascoyne Murchison Outback Pathways* by Samille Mitchell, available from w outbackpathways.com, for more information.

10

SANDSTONE If heading to the Goldfields, the next town you will reach is Sandstone, 154km east on the Mt Magnet–Sandstone Road. The reason to come out this way is to see **London Bridge**, a flat-arch rock formation looking out over the Outback scrub; it's only a few well-signposted kilometres out of town. Sandstone's picturesque main street hosts the **Sandstone National Hotel** (17 Payne St; ☏ 9963 5801; � SandstoneNationalHotel), which does a good pub meal, but you're better off staying in the **Alice Atkinson Caravan Park** (☏ 9963 5859) if you don't need a motel room.

CUE Eighty kilometres north of Mt Magnet is Cue, a National Trust-listed living museum of gold-rush architecture (see box, below) that is some of the best in the state. Austin Street, Cue's wide main thoroughfare has changed precious little in the past century. Wandering up and down past its charming, locally quarried stone buildings and corrugated ironworks is a real trip back in time. Pick up a free **Heritage Walking Trail** pamphlet from the Visitor Centre (72 Austin St; ☏ 08 9963 1198; w cue255.wixsite.com/cuecrc; 🕑 08.30–15.30 Mon–Fri) and follow the

QUEEN OF THE MURCHISON

Gold was first found in Cue in the early 1890s by an Aboriginal prospector known as Governor. Another prospector, Michael Fitzgerald, found gold on what is today Austin Street – apparently by using sticks to turn over rocks, after a drought had killed the grass there. His partner, Tom Cue, was the one who actually registered the find – the first registration for the area – and that is likely why the town took Cue's name when it was gazetted in 1893.

Within days of Fitzgerald's find, several hundred miners flooded into the area, with numbers eventually reaching such a crescendo that poems were written capturing the spirit of the migration, such as *Along the Road to Cue* by Andree Hayward. The region became covered in goldfields, and the optimism of those early prospectors is reflected in the upbeat names they gave their mines and leases: Golden Stream, Light of Asia, Cue Victory and Hidden Treasure.

As one newspaper later put it, however, it was 'deep gold' rather than 'surface gold' that made up Cue – and things didn't really take off until a major gold reef was found just outside town in 1892. The Great Fingall Mining Company's mine at Day Dawn Reef – 8km south and so named because of the shimmer the sun's light made off the reef at sunrise and sunset – became one of the most important in WA and Cue became a boom town.

At its height, Cue had 10,000 residents and another 3,000 lived at Day Dawn. The area had three newspapers, a hospital, numerous stamp mills, and the streets were lined with hotels with names like the Excelsior, the Great Britain and the Miners Arms.

It wasn't to last, however. World War I drew young men into the army and away from the goldfields, meaning the Great Fingall Mining Company was gone by 1918 and many of the area's other mines did not reopen when the war ended. Later, the Great Depression and fall in gold prices signaled the end of Cue as a major centre. By the 1930s, Cue's population had fallen to a few hundred and the surrounding mining towns like Day Dawn had been abandoned. Today, Cue has fewer than 200 residents and serves to support the surrounding mining and pastoral industries.

route past the police station, post office and courthouse, all of which are still in use today. The trail also takes in the remains of the old goal, which you can freely access and wander through to imagine what life as a turn-of-the-century prisoner in the Outback must have been like. Stay at the stately **Queen of the Murchison** ✻ (24 rooms; 53 Austin St; ☎(08) 9963 1625; w queenofthemurchisonguesthouseandcafe. com.au; **$$**), built in the 1930s and still retaining its high ceilings and a wide staircase. The owner, Joyce, is a wealth of information and frequently dines with guests at the on-site café-restaurant.

There are a few ghost towns around Cue. **Day Dawn**, 8km south, is home to the Great Fingall Mine Office – the mine's old administration building (see box, opposite), a Federation Italianate-style structure that is on the state's register of historic places. Also nearby, **Big Bell** (30km southwest of Cue) was abandoned a few decades later than Day Dawn – the Fingall Mine closed in 1918 and Day Dawn was abandoned by the 1930s. Its showpiece ruin among the slabs is the Big Bell Hotel, an old Art Deco building that purportedly had the longest bar in WA when the premises were still active. For safety reasons, visitors are not allowed inside the buildings at either town.

One final attraction in the vicinity lies 48km east of Cue on the Cue–Dalgaranga Road: **Walga Rock**. At 5km in diameter and 1.5km in length, it's the second-biggest monolith in Australia after Uluru. It houses one of the state's largest collections of Aboriginal rock art, with nearly 1,000 pictures, including what are purported to be images of ships that sailed along the West Australian coast, possibly as early as the 1600s. Some of the art at Walga is 10,000 years old. Visitors are allowed to climb to the top, but the rock is of substantial cultural significance to the local Wadjari custodians and respectful behaviour is required.

The Gascoyne & Ningaloo

Welcome to the most spectacular corner of the world... that you've never heard of. The least-populous of WA's regions, the Gascoyne is true Outback country – its main town, Carnarvon, has landed squarely on the contemporary foodie circuit for its luscious tropical fruits (especially bananas) and delectable seafood. But the main draws here are on the coast: UNESCO-listed Shark Bay, known for its friendly dolphins that come right up to the shoreline; and the dazzling Ningaloo reef system, which is more accessible than – and in many people's eyes, superior to – the Great Barrier Reef. Inland are the Kennedy Ranges, which burst with nature's geological colour palette, and Mt Augustus – often called 'the world's biggest rock', which is about double the size of Uluru and a lot older.

SHARK BAY

A UNESCO World Heritage Site since 1991, Shark Bay is internationally recognised for its outstanding natural beauty, ecosystems and geological history. At Australia's most westerly point, sticking out the side of the state like a right-handed thumb and finger, Shark Bay covers an area of 2.2 million hectares and is made up of two bays separated by the Peron Peninsula (where Denham and Monkey Mia are), and bounded to the west by Edel Land Peninsula and Dirk Hartog Island. Famous for its dramatic cliffs, red and orange-hued sand dunes, and frequent sightings of the 'Big Five' in the bays – dolphins, dugongs, rays, sharks and turtles – the area is perhaps most famous for its stromatolites (the oldest 'living fossils' on earth, page 5) at Hamelin Pool.

This is the traditional land of the Malgana, Nhanda and Yingkarta – in Malgana, this area is called Gutharraguda, meaning 'two waters'. This was the site of the first European landing in Australia; on 25 October 1616, Dirk Hartog arrived here accidentally when his ship, the *Eendracht*, was blown off-course by a storm while on its way to Indonesia. The Dutch, however, were not particularly impressed by the land and made no attempts to start a colony; the land was largely turned over after British settlement in the 1850s to pearling and pastoralism, the latter of which remains important today.

Despite its fame, Shark Bay is a love-it-or-leave-it kind of place. If you're interested in fishing, boating and wildlife – and are quite happy to strike out on your own – you will think this place a paradise and want to stay for decades, as many here have. If, however, you are looking for a more traditional classic beach holiday, you will find it a bit of a letdown and are better off heading to Exmouth or Geraldton. And if you don't have your own 4x4 or boat, you will need a bucket of money to hire one or join a tour – a holiday here can get pretty expensive if you don't want to end up marooned in and around Denham, the area's main (albeit tiny) settlement of about 600 people.

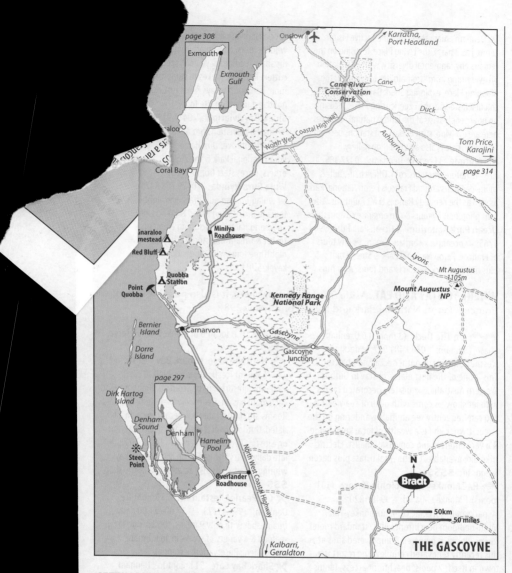

Onslow

Karratha,
Port Headland

page 308

Exmouth

Exmouth
Gulf

Cane River
Conservation
Park

Cane

Duck

North West Coastal Highway

Ashburton

Tom Price,
Karajini

page 314

...aloo

Coral Bay

Gnaraloo
Homestead

Red Bluff

Quobba
Station

Point
Quobba

Minilya
Roadhouse

Lyons

Mt Augustus
1105m

Mount Augustus
NP

Kennedy Range
National Park

Bernier
Island

Dorre
Island

Carnarvon

Gascoyne

Gascoyne
Junction

page 297

Dirk Hartog
Island

Denham
Sound

Denham

Hamelin
Pool

North West Coastal Highway

Steep
Point

Overlander
Roadhouse

N

Bradt

0   50km
0   50 miles

THE GASCOYNE

Kalbarri,
Geraldton

The Gascoyne & Ningaloo   SHARK BAY

GETTING THERE AND AWAY Denham lies 128km/1 hour 20 minutes from the main North West Coastal Highway; turn off at the Overlander Roadhouse. Integrity Coach Lines run services to the Overlander from Perth, and from there you can transfer to Shark Bay Coaches to reach Denham or Monkey Mia. By air, Rex flies from Perth Airport to Monkey Mia (3hrs 15mins; from A$250 one-way).

TOURIST INFORMATION AND TOUR OPERATORS Multiple operators run tours to Francois Peron National Park, Edel Land/Steep Point and Dirk Hartog Island.

Shark Bay World Heritage Discovery & Visitor Centre 53 Knight Tce, Denham; 9948 1590; w sharkbayvisit.com.au; ⏰ 09.00–16.30 Mon–Fri, 09.00–13.00 Sat-Sun; adult/child A$11/6.

11

On Denham's main street, this interactive visitor centre has 3 parts: the Living Place, focusing on the region's environmental diversity, with information on everything from stromatolites to seagrass; the Mapping Place, exploring Shark Bay's indigenous & colonial history; & the Experiencing Place, focusing on how people's use of the land & natural resources here are evolving, such as pastoral stations becoming reserves. There is also an exhibition gallery.
Naturetime 3 Leeds Ct, Denham; ✆0427 385 178; w naturetimetours.com. Offers half-, full- & multi-day tours around Francois Peron National Park, as well as the Kennedy Ranges & Mt Augustus. Also runs photography tours & can organise custom tours.
Ocean Park Aquarium 1 Ocean Park Rd; ✆9948 1765; w oceanpark.com.au. Organises day tours of Francois Peron National Park & Steep Point, plus half-day Dirk Hartog Island tours. Also runs

specialist diving & marine sa[...] wildlife tours. The aquarium its[...] inc shark feedings & you can see [...] critters from sea snakes to stonefish[...] more benign stingrays & sea turtles. [...] good restaurant on site too.
Shark Bay Aviation ✆0417 919 0[...] w sharkbayaviation.com.au. Offe[...] scenic flights over Dirk Hartog Island, [...] Peron National Park & the Zuytdorp Cliffs, amo[...] others; prices start from A$125.
Wula Gura Nyinda ✆0429 708 847; w wulagura.com.au. Offers overnight & single-day tours to Dirk Hartog Island & Francis Peron, with an Aboriginal focus including elements of bush tucker & Dreamtime stories. They also run cultural nighttime tours with didgeridoo meditation plus kayak/SUP tours.

WHERE TO STAY AND EAT Aside from the listings here, it is also possible to camp at Francois Peron National Park and Steep Point (page 298).

✳ 🏠 **On The Deck** (3 rooms) 6 Oxenham Chase, Denham; ✆0409 481 957; e deckie@ westnet.com.au; w onthedecksharkbay.com. This is one of the best places to stay in Outback Western Australia. Exquisitely decorated rooms with jet showers come with bush or sea views & you can frequently see animals wandering up the street. Owner Phil is a wealth of local knowledge & a very entertaining conversationalist. Electric trike hire available. Continental b/fast plus bacon & eggs inc. **$$$$**
🏠 **RAC Monkey Mia Dolphin Resort** (101 rooms) 1 Monkey Mia Rd; ✆9948 1320; w parksandresorts.rac.com.au/monkey-mia. Multi-bedroom beachfront villas, standard motel rooms, dorms & powered & unpowered sites at this recently renovated complex. The resort is a town in itself: 2 pools, beachfront access, tennis court, 2 restaurants & camp kitchen. Great for families — but not cheap. Note there is also a surcharge of A$15pp/day (or A$35 per family)

as the resort is located in Monkey Mia Reserve. **$$$$**
🏠 **Heritage Resort Shark Bay** (27 rooms) 73–75 Knight Tce, Denham; ✆9948 1133; w heritageresortsharkbay.com.au. Right in town, each room has an ocean view & en-suite facilities. Rooms are comfortable but décor can seem a bit dated. Outdoor pool & well-regarded restaurant on-site (🕐 07.30–09.30, noon–14.30 & 17.30–late daily) — try the garlic cob & the Shark Bay whiting — & there is also an attached bottle shop. **$$$**
✗ **Old Pearler Restaurant** 71 Knight Tce, Denham; ✆9948 1373; 🕐 17.00–21.00 daily. Quaint spot with only 9 tables, showcasing local seafood & a variety of steaks in an intimate atmosphere. Reservations essential. **$$**
✗ **Shark Bay Café** 51 Knight Tce, Denham; ✆9948 3222; 🕐 07.30–14.00 daily. The best b/fast spot in town, although they also do some mean sushi at lunch. **$**

WHAT TO SEE AND DO The following sights can be visited independently or as part of the 160km, 2WD-suitable **Shark Bay World Heritage Drive** ✳; you can download a map at w cdn-sharkbaywa.pressidium.com/wp-content/uploads/2017/04/SBWHA_A2_Brochure.pdf or get a hard copy at the visitor centre.

Hamelin Pool stromatolites ✳
At 3.5 billion years old, these stromatolites are the oldest 'living fossils' (they are still growing slowly) in the world and provide

a glimpse of what the planet may have been like way back then. Hamelin Pool is one of only two places in the world that have living stromatolites, along with Lake Thetis (page 269), and the Hamelin colony is the larger of the two. The fluctuating salinity of the water here has helped to preserve them by keeping away predators that might eat the algae growing on the stromatolites. A raised triangular wooden boardwalk with detailed information boards allows visitors to see the stromatolites up close without damaging them – the boardwalk was damaged by Cyclone Seroja in 2021 but is due to reopen in early 2023. The area itself has profound natural beauty; the jet-black colour of the stromatolites contrasting against the many azures of the water is remarkable. No matter how tempted you may be, however, swimming is strictly prohibited. Hamelin Pool is only 35km down Shark Bay Road from the North West Coastal Highway turn-off, so it is possible as a detour if not exploring the rest of Shark Bay.

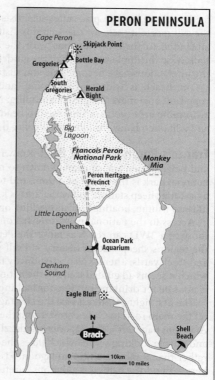

Beaches and swimming Just north of Shark Bay Road, midway between Denham and the highway, is the unique **Shell Beach** made up of millions of *Fragum* cockle shells, which have thrived because the hypersalinity of the water has made the habitat unsuitable for many predators. At some points, the depth of the shells is more than 10m – you are free to go into the water here. A further 30km from Shell Beach is **Eagle Bluff**, where a beige sandy cliff descends sharply down to the blue-green sea, which is good for snorkelling. A 400m boardwalk next to the lookout car park provides a great vantage point for spotting marine animals. Just 5km north of Denham, **Little Lagoon** is a sheltered swimming spot (and can be fairly shallow a long way out) connected to the sea by a small creek (which you can also explore) – turtles, stingrays and even stonefish have been known to pass through the creek and into the lagoon.

Monkey Mia (Entry: A$15/5 adult/child) A 20-minute drive northeast of Denham, this conservation park offers one of the best dolphin-watching experiences in the state. Almost every morning since the 1960s, a pod of bottlenose dolphins has visited the shores here. Their visits were initially spurred by local fishermen giving them some of their morning catch; not the type of animal to pass up a good deal, the dolphins quickly put two and two together and today it has grown into a supervised feeding experience, where a small group of dolphins are offered fish by park visitors – chosen and supervised by the park ranger – up to three times daily while the rest of the crowd watches on. Feeding times vary on when the dolphins are around, but generally start at 07.45 and conclude by noon. The guidelines to regulate dolphin feedings have been in place after scientists discovered in the 1980s and 1990s that the calf mortality rate for the dolphins visiting the beach was extraordinarily high, attributed to their interactions with the humans harming their survival skills. Following the implementation of the guidelines, the calf mortality rate plunged and the interactions have become safe and sustainable for the dolphins.

The beach is wide and sweeping, and the waters outside the dolphin-only roped-off area make for great swimming. Note the dolphins often venture into the swimming area (you are supposed to head for the shore if they come within 50m) and will often hang around after feeding times.

Francois Peron National Park
Known for its spectacular red, orange, white and beige dunes, which tumble down to meet a turquoise-blue sea, this 52,500ha national park is the image of a thousand tourist brochures and book covers. Once a pastoral sheep station, today the area is known for its sensational scenery, marine life and fishing, boating and snorkelling opportunities.

Access to the national park is by 4x4 only (see page 295 for tour operators), but those in a 2WD can reach as far as the **Peron Heritage Precinct**, which documents the region's sheep station history – a self-guided walk explores the shearing shed and stock yards. There is also a regionally famous hot tub with artesian waters here, which it seems all guided tours to the national park stop for a dip in. Note the water is not safe for drinking but fine for bathing.

The first sight of interest past the Heritage Precinct is **Big Lagoon** – a 10km detour off the main road to Cape Peron. From the air on a scenic flight (contact Shark Bay Aviation, page 296), this lagoon is a dazzling array of turquoise water, white sand and purple-looking scrub, which takes the shape of an inlet with circular side pools rather than a more traditional lagoon. Fishing, canoeing and kayaking are terrific here – mind the fishing regulations carefully as the northern waters of the lagoon are a protected nursery. Dolphins and dugongs also sometimes visit.

Otherwise, the park's main attractions are on the northwest tip of the Peron Peninsula: **Cape Peron** and **Skipjack Point**. Perched at the confluence of two different water bodies, the cape attracts a diverse range of marine life and you are likely to see some of the 'Big Five' (dolphins, dugongs, turtles, rays and sharks) here. There is beach fishing here, but the currents can be fierce – don't swim. The 1.5km **Wanamalu Trail** connects Cape Peron with the two viewing platforms at Skipjack Point, precariously hovering over the cliff edge but offering wonderful coastal views.

DPaW manages the campsites in the national park (A\$11/7 adult/child); booking ahead is not possible. **South Gregories**, **Gregories** and **Bottle Bay** all have camping facilities and are within about 10km of each other. Gregories has a reef system that is good for snorkelling, while South Gregories and Bottle Bay have launches for small boats. Fishing is very popular at all three sites, particularly for bream and whiting. Returning back towards Denham, **Herald Bight** – along a side track, which goes for 5km off the main track towards the eastern end of the peninsula – is another camping, fishing and boat-launching spot that has the remains of an old cannery.

Steep Point
The westernmost part of the Australian mainland, Steep Point is on the Edel Land Peninsula. Taking the wonderfully named Useless Loop Road – high-clearance 4x4 only – it is about 150km from the North West Coastal Highway turn-off. The 200m-high **Zuytdorp Cliffs** – stretching from Steep Point all the way 200km down to the Mid West – are WA's answer to the Bunda Cliffs on the Nullarbor, dropping straight down into the Indian Ocean. DPaW manages the **Shelter Bay**

campsite here and, unlike in Francois Peron National Park, advance bookings are required. This is isolated, rugged terrain with no facilities, and you need to be fully prepared for all circumstances.

Dirk Hartog Island (w dirkhartogisland.com) Jutting north from Steep Point, this 620km² island – the largest in WA – is believed to be the place where the first European to reach Australia landed in 1616 (page 18). Today, having been converted from pastoral leaseland into a national park in 2009, the island's main draws are beaches, dramatic scenery and wildlife watching. The west side of the island is very rugged with cliffs, while the sheltered eastern side has beaches. At Cape Inscription, Hartog left a plate with details of his 1616 voyage; a lighthouse overlooks the site. Mystery Beach is known for its varied flotsam, while on the eastern side, Turtle Bay, Sandy Point and Louisa Bay are fantastic snorkelling spots.

The Return to 1616 ecological project, an attempt to return the island to the state it was in when Hartog arrived, was launched in 2012 and had eradicated feral introduced animals as of 2018, while relocations of native animals like dibblers, Shark Bay bandicoots, banded hare-wallabies and rufous hare-wallabies are ongoing; chuditches, desert mice, boodies and other natives will also be re-introduced until 2030. This is also the only place in Australia where this subspecies of black-and-white fairywrens are found, and there are plenty of eagles and ospreys too. Thousands of loggerhead turtles lay eggs here in the summer, and humpback whales pass by in September.

Day trips are possible with the operators listed on page 296, but for independent travellers with a 4x4 the island operates the *Hartog Explorer* barge from Steep Point, which carries one vehicle across at a time – there is, however, a maximum of 20 4x4s allowed on the island at any one time (and the *Hartog Explorer* is not cheap: A$340 each way in the high season, and bookings must be minimum 48 hours in advance). Accommodation comes in the form of the Eco Lodge (6 rooms & 1 villa; \9948 1211; e escape@dirkhartogisland.com), a rustic oceanfront retreat with shared kitchen, bar and pool table; five-day all-inclusive packages are available. The three-bedroom ocean villa has a kitchenette and can sleep seven (minimum five-night stay). You can also camp at multiple spots around the island – see DPaW's site for locations.

CARNARVON

Tell a West Australian that you are going on holiday to Carnarvon and the reaction is likely to range from bemusement to shock. The Carnarvon of today, however, is not the 'Boganville by the Sea' of 20 years ago – with an attractive natural setting, an evolving foodie culture and some excellent museums, the town makes a worthwhile place to spend a few days and explore the Kennedy Ranges and the southern Ningaloo Coast. Plus, as the biggest town between Geraldton and Karratha (a distance of 1,100km), it's also the best place to break up a trip to the north.

European settlement began here in 1876 and the pastoral industry dominated; the town was gazetted in 1883, and the jetty's opening in 1899 cemented the town's place as a regional centre. However, after World War I agriculture began to take hold, and produce – particularly bananas – came to define the town. Carnarvon remains closely linked to the yellow fruit in the West Australian psyche.

GETTING THERE AND AWAY Carnarvon is just west of the North West Coastal Highway; Geraldton is 480km/5 hours to the south, and Karratha is 638km/

6 hours 40 minutes north. Integrity Coach Lines run overnight services from Perth to Carnarvon (12hrs; from A$174 one-way), while Rex flies non-stop from Perth (2hrs; from A199 one-way).

TOURIST INFORMATION

 Carnarvon Visitor Centre 21 Robinson St; 9941 1146; **w** carnarvon.org.au; ⏲ 09.00– 17.00 Mon–Fri

---

🏠 WHERE TO STAY AND EAT

🏠 **Best Western Hospitality Carnarvon** (45 rooms) 6 West St; 0041 1600; **w** carnarvon. wa.hospitalityinns.com.au. A clean, comfortable option; motel rooms are bright & airy though standard. The Sails Restaurant has cooked b/fasts & interesting dinner options like whisky-infused oysters & coconut curry prawns. **$$$**

🏠 **Carnarvon Motel** (61 rooms) 34 David Brand Dr; 9941 0600; **w** carnarvonmotel.com. au. Though the décor is a bit dated, this is a clean & reliable place to stay & very good value. There's an outdoor pool, & the on-site restaurant is known for its 'hot rocks' cooking style – using volcanic rocks heated to over 400°C – but it can get busy, so make a booking. **$$**

🏠 **Coral Coast Tourist Park** 108 Robinson St; 9941 1438; **w** coralcoasttouristpark.com.au. Centrally located, this complex offers everything from deluxe spa suites to en-suite powered & unpowered sites. On-site facilities include swimming pool, laundry, boat parking & car-wash bay. Suites **$$$**, sites **$**

✱ ✖ **A Taste of Thai by Fon** 17 Hubble St; 0409 911 198; 🔳 ATasteOfThaiByFon; ⏲ 11.00–20.00 daily. Authentic Thai street food in a residential neighbourhood. Doug & Fon will explain to you the variants of pad Thai across the country as well as the local ingredients they use, both seafood & greens. Seating is limited so book ahead if you want to dine in. **$$**

WHAT TO SEE AND DO

Heritage Precinct (1 Annear Pl, Babbage Island; 9941 3423; ⏲ 09.00–15.00 daily) The Carnarvon Heritage Precinct is based around the old port and jetty built to service the pastoral industry in the late 1890s, and today is a nod to the town's original European settlement links, with a number of period buildings and features. Once the longest jetty in the northern WA at 1,493m, the **One Mile Jetty** was closed down a few years ago due to safety concerns and then wiped away entirely in 2021 by Cyclone Seroja. While you can't walk it for now (the Carnarvon Heritage Committee is currently in the process of a multi-million-dollar fundraising drive to restore it), you can visit the **One Mile Jetty Centre**, home to a museum that documents both the history of the jetty and the battle between the HMAS *Sydney* and the HSK *Kormoran* (see box, opposite) – the lifeboat used by the *Kormoran*'s survivors is on display here. The precinct also houses a few other museums: the **Railway Station Museum**, which displays the Kimberley Steam Train – the last steam train used in northwest WA; the **Shearer's Hall of Fame**, which focuses on the area's pastoral history; and the old **Lighthouse Keeper's Cottage**, a restored cottage that was the home of the lighthouse keeper until the 1970s. There is also a 400m boardwalk that goes through the surrounding mangroves.

Carnarvon Space and Technology Museum (Mahony Av; 9941 9901; **w** carnarvonmuseum.org.au; ⏲ Oct–Mar 10.00–14.00 & Apr–Sep 09.00–16.00 daily; adult/child A$18/10) Carnarvon has an unsung role in space exploration – NASA had a tracking station here in the 1960s and 1970s, with a staff of over 200 before it closed in 1974. It supported the *Gemini*, *Apollo* and *Skylab* programs,

On 19 November 1941 off the Gascoyne coast, the HMAS *Sydney* encountered the German ship, HSK *Kormoran*, which was masquerading as a Dutch merchant ship to hide its real mission – to lay mines in order to disrupt allied shipping. Though the *Sydney* was the superior ship, all 645 of its hands were lost; while 318 of the 380 hands on the *Kormoran* survived and came ashore near Carnarvon. Many survivors were kept in Carnarvon gaol for a few days before being transported to POW camps.

The loss of life was the largest in Australian naval history and questions abounded as to how the ship was lost. The German crew claimed, and were believed by the Australians, that the *Sydney* got too close to the *Kormoran* in the battle, negating its advantages in armour and weapons and allowing the *Kormoran*'s armaments to penetrate the *Sydney*'s hull. Conspiracies emerged, however; a popular (unfounded) one was that a Japanese submarine was also involved in the attack on the Sydney and assisted the *Kormoran*.

Though the approximate location of the battle was known, the wrecks of both ships were not found until 2008, off Shark Bay. Monuments and remembrances line the Coral Coast; aside from the memorial in Geraldton (page 279), there is a Remembrance Walk along the Fascine, Carnarvon's main waterway, which has the names of the Australian crew etched on a wall and points to the direction of the sinking, and a memorial near Red Bluff (page 287).

including Neil Armstrong's mission to the moon in 1969, and data was relayed through Carnarvon to Houston. The museum's highlight is undoubtedly the 'Apollo Experience' – a capsule simulating a blast-off in which you shake, rattle and roll.

Gwoonwardu Mia (146 Robinson St; ☎ 9941 1989; w gahcc.com.au; ⊕ 09.30–15.30 Mon–Fri) Celebrating the indigenous peoples of the Gascoyne's five language groups – the Yinggarda, Bayungu, Malgana, Thadgari and Thalanyji – this interactive cultural centre houses exhibitions focused on indigenous use of astronomy, history (including Aboriginal history during European settlement of pastoral stations) and also showcases numerous artefacts like grindstones and shields; there are also burrowing bees – one of the world's largest bee species – which live in the Gascoyne. There is also a shop selling art, and tours can be arranged.

Farm gates The banana is king in Carnarvon, with the variety grown here being particularly sweet. Plantations line the roads into town; the rectangular area bounded by North River Road, South River Road, Bibbawarra Road and the North West Coastal Highway is known as the 'Fruit Loop' as it passes several plantations, some with open farm gates and stalls. **Morel's Orchard** (486 Robinson St; ☎ 9941 8368; ⊕ call for hours) is the place for tropical fruit ice creams – the black sapote is especially tasty – while **Bumbak's** (449 North River Rd; ☎ 9941 8006; ⊕ 09.00–16.00 daily) has a range of banana products, including a nice banana jam. **Westut Plantation** (605 Robinson St; ☎ 9941 4979; ⊕ 09.00–17.00 daily), next to the Caltex Station, sells a range of tropical and exotic fruits – look hard for the path from Caltex, as it can be a bit tricky to spot.

The Gascoyne & Ningaloo CARNARVON

11

Some 50km off the coast of Carnarvon, Bernier and Dorre islands represent one of the darkest periods of European colonisation in WA. In an effort to prevent Aboriginal peoples from 'spreading diseases' to Europeans, around 800 Aboriginal people were rounded up and sent to 'lock hospitals' – men to Bernier, women to Dorre – from 1908 to 1919. It is estimated that 200 of them died. Children were also forced to the lock hospitals. The patients were vaguely diagnosed with 'venereal disease', but it is likely that many Aboriginal people sent there were never sick to begin with. European settlers with venereal disease were not subjected to the same measures.

The lock hospitals closed in 1919, and in 1986 the sites were protected under the Aboriginal Heritage Act. The Lock Hospital Workgroup has launched a remembrance project; learn more about their work and this dreadful period in history at w lockhospital.com.au. There is a memorial to the atrocity at the Carnarvon Heritage Precinct – *Don't Look at the Islands* features a bronze sculpture of a girl facing the islands and covering her eyes.

EXCURSIONS FROM CARNARVON

Point Quobba Known locally as the 'Aquarium' for its spectacularly clear sheltered waters, coral reefs and marine life, Point Quobba is immensely popular with Carnarvon locals and is something of the 'town beach' – despite it being 75km north of town and there also being a beach in Carnarvon. Just 1km from Point Quobba are the **Blowholes**, where water shoots up out of sea caves, sometimes as high as 20m. The high, rugged cliff faces here are steep and beautiful, with natural waterfalls tumbling down to the rough surf. The 'King Waves Kill' sign at the entrance to the Blowholes is a local landmark – and a warning to heed, so be careful when venturing near the edge.

If you want to overnight in the area, there are three options: **Quobba Homestead** (❧ 9948 5098; w quobba.com.au; **$**), 10km north of the Blowholes; **Red Bluff** (❧9948 5001; w quobba.com.au; **$$$$–$$**), a further 41km north; and a further 39km beyond that, the remote **Gnaraloo Homestead** (❧ 9315 4809; w gnaraloo. com; **$$$**), which marks the southern end of Ningaloo Reef. Note that you cannot travel along Gnaraloo Road all the way to Coral Bay or Exmouth; the road ends just past Gnaraloo.

Kennedy Range National Park

Kennedy Range National Park Roughly 200km east and then north from Carnarvon, this remote national park – home to a series of sandstone and shale cliffs, rising 100m – makes an outstanding day trip. Erosion, wind and water have chiseled away at the rock and caused the shapes we see today; the desert climate means you may see euros here, as well as dozens of reptile species including goannas. Numerous walking trails weave through the park – they are all Class 3 or 4, requiring moderate fitness. The **Honeycomb Trail** (600m return) leads to a remarkable spot where honeycomb-like holes have eroded into the high rockface – the changing colours of the rocks from soft oranges to browns, reds, pinks and purples, depending on where you are standing and the light conditions, are incredible. The **Temple Gorge Trail** (2km return) takes you past a pyramid-like formation into some narrow gorges which, similar to the Honeycomb Trail, have striking colour combinations of reds and oranges.

To get to the park from Carnarvon, take the Carnarvon–Mullewa road to the tiny settlement of Gascoyne Junction, 175km to the east. The Kennedy Ranges run north–south and access is from the east side. The turn-off from Gascoyne Junction north to the ranges is about 1km east of the townsite; the road is unsealed, but it is 2WD suitable. The entrance to the national park is about 50km north of here.

Camping is available at **Temple Gorge Campground** (A$11/3 adult/child) or you can stay at the **Junction Pub and Tourist Park** in Gascoyne Junction (4 Viveash Way; \9943 0868; w junctiontouristpark.com; **$$$**).

Mt Augustus

This is often called the largest rock in Australia, but that is not technically accurate – Mt Augustus is actually an anticline in geological terms. But rising 715m above the surrounding land and 1,106m above sea level – compared with Uluru's 348m and 863m respectively – Mt Augustus is a whopping 8km across, 1.6 billion years old (almost a billion years older an Uluru), and certainly something you will never forget as long as you live. Also unlike Uluru, the tourism industry is yet to really discover Mt Augustus, so you will have the place (more or less) in splendid isolation.

The Traditional Owners of the area are the Wajarri – their name for Mt Augustus is 'Burringurrah', the name of a boy in Wajarri tradition who ran away from an initiation ceremony and was then killed by a spear; you can supposedly see him laying down in the rock formations.

Surrounding Mt Augustus is the eponymous national park, criss-crossed by a dozen or so walking and driving routes. The 49km **Loop Drive** takes you around the entire base, while the **Summit Trail** (12km return; Class 4) walk offers amazing views over the surrounding bush. Aboriginal engravings can be found along the **Ooramboo Trail** (500m return; Class 3) and at Mundee's **Petroglyph Trail** (Class 3, 300m return).

You can get to the park in a 2WD, but it is a long, remote drive (300km from Gascoyne Junction) on an unsealed road. Be prepared with spare tyres and other equipment for emergencies, and contact the relevant shires for road conditions before setting off. Just 6km before the entrance to the park on the west side is **Emu**

ROAD TRIP: KINGSFORD SMITH MAIL RUN

Known as Smithy, Charles Kingsford Smith (1897–1935) was one of Australia's most accomplished aviators, whom Sydney Airport is named after. Early on in his career, Smith worked in transport in the Gascoyne, founding the Gascoyne Transport Company in 1924 which carried mail from Carnarvon to Meekatharra in the Mid West. The route still exists today: the Kingsford Smith Mail Run (4x4 required) follows his path for 834km over a leisurely four days. Day one (177km) follows the sealed road from Carnarvon to Gascoyne Junction, followed by a trip on day two to the Kennedy Ranges, overnighting again in Gascoyne Junction (see above). Day three (320km) takes you to Mt Augustus National Park and day four (345km) to Meekatharra, your end point. To get the most out of this trip, however, rejig your timetable a bit; if you have only four days, do the Kennedy Ranges on the first day, overnighting in Gascoyne Junction; then go to Mt Augustus on the second day, thus allowing for an extra day there.

An excellent companion for this trip is *Gascoyne Murchison Outback Pathways* by Samille Mitchell, available from w outbackpathways.com.

Hill, which offers well-worth-it views of Mt Augustus. The only accommodation option in the park is the well-run **Mt Augustus Tourist Park** (☏ 9943 0527; e mtaugustustouristpark@skymesh.com.au; w mtaugustustouristpark.com; **$$$**) with self-contained units, motel rooms, powered and unpowered sites plus a petrol station and small shop.

THE NINGALOO COAST

Although its big brother, 70km off North Queensland, gets all the attention, the Ningaloo Reef is in many people's eyes even better than the Great Barrier. It is certainly one of Australia's most underrated gems – its isolation, located in one of the country's least-populated areas, has protected it from overdevelopment and crushing tourist hoards. While the Great Barrier *is* bigger, Ningaloo is a lot more accessible – as a fringing reef, rather than a barrier reef, it extends much closer to the shoreline and in many places you just walk into the water off the beach and you're there.

The largest reef in the world near a land mass, at 300km long, it became UNESCO-listed in 2011 because of its incredible biodiversity – it is home to over 200 species of coral and 500 animal species; it is on the migratory routes of dolphins, whales, dugongs and rays; and is an important nesting site for turtles. The area is most famed, however, for its gentle whale sharks – the biggest fish in the ocean (it can reach over 20m in length and over 40 tonnes in weight) with a mouth over 1m long. Best seen between March and August, their distinctive polka-dot pattern – white spots on grey skin – is unique to the individual, in the same way no two snowflakes are alike. Ningaloo is also just one of two places in Australia where you can swim with humpback whales; numerous operators take divers and snorkellers out and swimming with these giants can be the experience of a lifetime.

Beach fishing, reef fishing and deep-sea fishing are also very popular at Ningaloo. Emperor and cod can often be found here and species such as Spanish mackerel, marlin, mahi mahi and wahoo further afield – but there are many more besides. Make sure you are up to date about regulations before casting a line. Boat launches are at Exmouth Marina, Bundegi and Tantabiddi, just past Jurabi on the western side of the cape.

Ningaloo is on the North West Cape, which is shaped like a shark fin. Bundegi Beach, 15km north of Exmouth at the top of North West Cape, is where the reef starts and it extends down the western side of the peninsula. The many canyons and vistas of Cape Range National Park run down the middle of the cape.

GETTING THERE AND AWAY Access to the Ningaloo Coast is along the Minilya–Exmouth Road, off the North West Coastal Highway; the turn-off is just past Minilya Roadhouse. Coral Bay is 237km/2 hours 30 minutes north of Carnarvon, and Exmouth is a further 140km/90 minutes north from there. Fuel up each time you leave Exmouth – opportunities to fill up are limited on the cape's western side.

Integrity Coach Lines run to both Coral Bay and Exmouth from Carnarvon, Geraldton and Perth (see w integritycoachlines.com.au for times and fares). The region's airport is at Learmonth, served by QantasLink flights from Perth (1hr 150mins; from A$318 one-way). Learmonth is 37km south of Exmouth; if you don't have your own vehicle or aren't hiring a car at the airport, you need to book an airport transfer in advance (ring the visitor centre) as there's no public transport and taxis don't necessarily await flights; try Coral Coast Tours (☏ 0427 180 568; e coralcoasttours@yahoo.com.au; w coralcoasttours.com.au; from A$95pp).

CORAL BAY ✳ To West Australians, the tiny hamlet of Coral Bay (population about 200) is synonymous with holidaying at Ningaloo. Founded as a tourism spot by pastoralist Charlie French 100 years ago – 'Billie' was his wife's name, which somehow got turned into the 'Bill' in 'Bill's Bay' – the area began growing in popularity due to the spectacular coral gardens and the marine life they attract in the calm and sheltered water.

Tour operators

Boat tours

Coral Bay EcoTours Shop 4, Peoples Park; 📞 9942 5885; w coralbayecotours.com.au. Run a variety of full-day whale & manta ray safaris, as well as shorter coral-viewing & turtle tours.

Ningaloo Marine Interactions Shop 12, Coral Bay Arcade; 📞 9948 5190; w mantaraycoralbay. com.au. Offers a variety of snorkel & quad biking tours, as well as a trip to swim with manta rays.

Fishing

Mahi Mahi Fishing Charters Shop 13, Coral Bay Arcade; 📞 9942 5874; w mahimahifishingcharters. com.au. Offers half-, full-day & private charters.

Seaforce Coral Bay 1 Robinson St; 📞 0429 034 540; w seaforcecharters.com.au. Deep sea & game fishing charters, with half-, full- & multi-day options available.

🏠 Where to stay and eat

🏠 **RAC Ningaloo Reef Resort** (34 rooms) 1 Robinson St; 📞 9942 5934; e reservations@ ningalooreefresort.com.au; w parksandresorts. rac.com.au/ningaloo. Just a stone's throw from the ocean, this complex boasts studio rooms all the way up to 2-bedroom apartments with spa baths. All rooms have cooking facilities & there is a guest laundry & outdoor pool. The on-site Shades Café (🕐 07.30–10.30, 11.30–14.30 & 17.30–20.30 daily) has a wide-ranging menu of pizzas, burgers & meat dishes. **$$$$**

🏠 **Ningaloo Coral Bay Bayview** Robinson St; 📞 9385 6655; e reservations@ningaloocoralbay. com; w ningaloocoralbay.com. A family-run venture founded by Bill & Alison Brogan in 1973, this holiday village offers bright & comfortable en-suite lodge rooms complete with kitchenettes, plus detached houses, budget cabins with stoves, backpacker dorms & a handful of powered & unpowered sites. Nearby **Bill's Bar** (46 Robinson St; 📞 9948 5156; 🕐 11.00–late; **$$**) has local seafood as well as a range of pub options. **$$$**

What to see and do Coral Bay is immensely popular for all kinds of water activities, from fishing and snorkelling to swimming with manta rays, which do not have barbs on their tails. See above for recommended operators. Try to book a tour that includes snorkelling at the **Blue Maze** – about 2km from shore, so you need a boat to get there – home to an enormous number of fish, marine life and coral, forming a maze-like pattern.

Bill's Bay is Coral Bay's star attraction, right at the end of Robinson Street, the settlement's main thoroughfare. The impossibly varied shades of sparkling blue, overlaying calm, sheltered waters and the proximity of wildlife like dugongs, turtles and manta rays, make this one of the state's favourites. The reef is just offshore (about 100m or so) and heaving with marine life – this is a great spot for young snorkellers. Five hundred metres south of Bill's Bay is **Purdy Point**, with its almost unbelievable array of colours – red and beige hills and rocks disappearing into ever-changing blue shades of water as it deepens in stages off the coast. Some of my favourite photographs I've taken of beaches anywhere in the world have been at Purdy Point. The snorkelling and coral here are top-notch too – boats do come by though, so watch out. A little south of Purdy Point is **Paradise Beach**, with its awesome drift snorkel and gloriously massive coral gardens.

Skeleton Bay Reef Shark Nursery is just north of Bill's Bay, where in summer gentle (and mostly harmless) young reef sharks arrive and come right up to the shoreline –

the water is clear, and the sharks are black, making sightings easy. **Maud's Landing**, just north of Skeleton Bay around the tip of Point Maud, is the best beach fishing spot in town; take the road past the airstrip to get there.

EXMOUTH AND THE NORTH CAPE Exmouth, the base town on the cape's northeastern tip, has a population of about 2,500. Today it is best known for Ningaloo Reef, but Exmouth wasn't born that way – the town began in 1967 to support the Harold Holt Naval Communications Centre and navy base, which the Americans used to communicate with submarines. American cars were driven, Greenbacks were used as currency and even a baseball diamond was built here. In 1992, with the end of the Cold War, the Americans withdrew from Exmouth and handed over control of the facility to Australia. Today, though, the area has completely turned over to tourism and the reason to come is obvious – WA's answer to the Great Barrier Reef, the dazzling and spectacular Ningaloo Reef, and array of beaches where you just step into the water and you're among corals and marine life.

Tourist information and tour operators

Ningaloo Visitor Centre 2 Truscot Cres; 9949 3070; w ningaloocentre.com.au; ⊕ 08.30–16.00 daily

Diving, snorkelling & boat tours
Dive Ningaloo 0456 702 437; w diveningaloo. com.au. Offers diving tours of Exmouth Navy Pier, as well as dive & snorkel tours out to the Murion Islands & whale shark swims.
Ningaloo Blue 2/1 Kennedy St; 9949 1119; w ningalooblue.com.au. Highly experienced operator specialising in whale shark & humpback whale tours.
Ningaloo Ecology Cruises 9949 2255; w glassbottomboat.com.au. Numerous coral-viewing, snorkelling & whale-watching glass-bottom-boat tours.
Ningaloo Whale Sharks Cnr Learmonth & Kennedy Sts; 9949 4777; w ningaloowhalesharks.com. Winner of the Gold Medal for Best Adventure Tour in Western Australia, these guys offer both humpback whale

& whale shark tours & reef-diving trips. They use spotter planes find the animals.
Ocean Eco Adventures 3/2 Ross St; 9949 1208; w oceanecoadventures.com.au. Runs whale shark & humpback whale tours, reef kayaking & turtle-swimming trips; they also offer microlight flights.

Fishing
Evolution Fishing Charters 0477 901 445; w evolutionfishingcharters.com.au. Private charters under championship angler Craig White (aka 'Whitey') – maximum 6 persons, this can be economical if you have a group. They also have a multi-night live-aboard tour.
Ningaloo Sportfishing Charters 0437 917 427; w ningaloosportfishing.com. Day tours & week-long live-aboard options.
On Strike Charters 0458 136 848; w onstrike. com.au. Highly regarded operator with heaps of tournament accolades, offering veteran experience in game, sport, reef & fly-fishing among others.

Where to stay and eat
Mantarays Ningaloo Beach Resort (68 rooms) Madaffari Dr; 9949 0000; w mantaraysningalooresort.com.au. With direct access to Sunrise Beach, this simple yet luxurious resort houses spacious bungalows & apartments (some with spa) plus bright, airy en-suite rooms with sofas. There's a large outdoor pool, & the award-winning restaurant (⊕ 06.30–10.00, noon–17.00, 17.30–21.00 daily) has excellent

seafood alongside light snacks such as prawns & spring rolls that can be ordered 14.00–17.00. Recommended for both staying & eating. **$$$**
Ningaloo Lodge (36 rooms) 1/3 Lefroy St; 9949 4949; w ningaloolodge.com.au. Family-owned, motel-style lodge with big communal kitchen, large alfresco area, games room, laundry & outdoor pool. Rooms do feel cramped, but

all have en suites. A good mid-range option, especially for longer stays. **$$$**

🏠 **RAC Exmouth Cape Holiday Park** (25 cabins) 3 Truscott Crescent; 📞 9949 1101; w parksandresorts.rac.com.au/exmouth. Recently renovated, family-friendly complex featuring cabins, motel rooms & powered & unpowered sites. There's a brand-new outdoor pool, children's wading pool, bike hire, camp kitchen & games room, & the dorm rooms have been converted into en-suite studios. *Motel units* **$$$**, *sites* **$**

✕ **Whaler's Restaurant** 2 Murat Rd; 📞 9949 2416; w whalersrestaurant.com.au; ⏲ 07.30–10.30, 11.30–14.00, 17.00–21.00 daily. Popular, relaxed seafood restaurant with stylish indoor & outdoor areas; the latter overlooks a beautiful swimming pool. Favourites include Exmouth tiger prawn gnocchi, New Orleans seafood gumbo & a gluten-free seafood medley, but the steaks are good too. Have the key lime pie for dessert. Regular live music; bookings recommended for dinner. **$$$**

✕ **Adrift Café** 8 Huston St; 📞 9949 2058; w adriftcafe.com.au; ⏲ 08.30–14.00 & 18.00–20.30 Mon–Fri, 18.00–20.30 Sat–Sun. Laidback but creative café serving good home-cooked meat dishes like Mexican chilli chicken salad alongside decent vegetarian options like red lentil & bean dhal. **$$**

✕ **BbqFather** 112 Murat Rd; 📞 9949 4905; w thebbqfather.com.au; ⏲ 17.30–21.00 Mon–Sat. Italian restaurant with some native Italian-speaking staff, serving up tasty wood-fired pizzas & variety of smoked meats & pastas. The homemade gelato is a great way to end a meal. **$$**

✕ **Whalebone Brewing Company** 27 Patterson Way; 📞 0457 447 117; w whalebonebrewing.com.au; ⏲ noon–22.00 daily. Operated by 2 local families, this trendy craft brewery produces several types of beers including pale ales, IPAs, stouts & lagers, washed down with pizza. Their beers are now stocked in a growing number of shops around WA. Dog friendly; regular live music from travelling musicians. Walk-ins only, take-away available. **$$**

What to see and do Home of the visitor centre (see opposite), the **Ningaloo Aquarium and Discovery Centre** (2 Truscott Crescent; 📞 9949 3070; w ningaloocentre. com.au; ⏲ Apr–Oct 08.30–16.30 Mon–Fri, 09.00–16.30 Sat–Sun, Nov–Mar 08.30–16.30 Mon–Fri, 09.00–13.00 Sat–Sun; adult/child A$19/14) is a good place to orient yourself before exploring the area. There are three galleries: En Route to Exmouth featuring local history, Reef to Range introducing the region's plants and animals here, and the Cape Range highlighting local geology and landscapes. The aquarium is one of the country's largest live reef showcases and has over 100 species of fish, including angel fish and clown fish, as well as reptiles.

Aside from those within Cape Range National Park (page 308), there are dozens of other world-class **beaches** and swimming spots within easy reach of Exmouth, and one of the pleasures is just finding a patch of sand you can enjoy on your own. The 300m-long **Exmouth Navy Pier**, 14km from Exmouth, is still in active naval use but may be dived through a tour operator (see opposite) – it is one of the best dive sites in the state, covered in corals and sponges with heaps of marine life swirling around and underneath.

At **Lighthouse Bay**, 17km from Exmouth, you can see the remains of the SS *Mildura*, a cattle ship that ran aground in a cyclone in 1907 and is now a marine sanctuary. South of Lighthouse Bay is the nudist-friendly **Mauritius Beach**, where you'll also find the **Jurabi Turtle Centre** – an open-air educational display about the area's marine turtles. The beach area is a sensitive nesting site for three species of marine turtle: green, loggerhead and hawksbill. From December to March, DpaW conducts turtle-interaction tours leaving from Jurabi – book at the Ningaloo Visitor Centre (see opposite) or at w ningaloocentre.com.au. If you are looking to watch nesting turtles, it is highly recommended you visit the website of the Ningaloo Turtle Program (w ningalooturtles.org.au) and read their 'Turtle Watching Code of Conduct'.

CAPE RANGE NATIONAL PARK

Fringing the turquoise waters of the Ningaloo Coast, this 47,655ha national park is the turquoise jewel in WA's crown. The state's best beaches and most colourful and diverse marine life are a few steps off the beaches, while the inland canyons and gorges along the limestone range of the cape's spine provide a magnificent backdrop. The marine life – turtles, rays, and fish – is the main draw; swimming with the whale sharks here is an iconic West Australian experience.

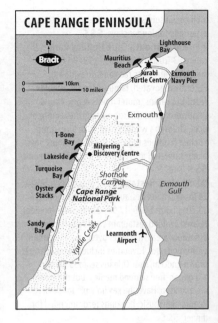

CAPE RANGE PENINSULA

Getting there and around Most, though not all, of the park is 2WD accessible – certainly you will not have much trouble accessing the park's spectacular beaches and some of the canyons and gorges in a 2WD, though have a map to verify that the route you are taking is suitable for your vehicle. It can be a long drive from Exmouth – the road around the cape is sealed up to Yardie Creek (91km from Exmouth) and make sure your petrol tank is full before you set out. Be warned: there's also no drinking water available and not much shade either, so come prepared.

Where to stay and eat There are a handful of campsites inside the national park; bookings (up to six months in advance) are essential; visit w parks.dpaw.wa.gov.au/park-stay for camp-specific information.

Sal Salis Ningaloo Reef (14 tents) ☎9949 1776; w salsalis.com.au. Right on the beach, a few minutes' drive from Turquoise Bay, these luxurious eco-tents have hand-made beds & are en suite. There is a main lodge where guests gather for drinks in the evening; it also has board games & a library. Rates are pricey, but include all meals (from a gourmet chef), drinks from the bar & equipment hire such as kayaks. **$$$$**

What to see and do The **Milyering Discovery Centre** (☎9949 2808; ⊕ 09.00–15.45 daily) near Lakeside provides a huge range of information about both Ningaloo and Cape Range, and is a good place to visit before exploring.

Beaches and water activities Lakeside, Turquoise Bay and Oyster Stacks are the premier **snorkelling** sites within the national park. **Lakeside** is the most northerly of the three, a sheltered sanctuary zone that provides opportunities to see lots of bigger fish as well as rays and turtles. The entry point is 400m south of the car park and is well marked; a circular snorkel trail goes about 150m out to some coral gardens here. Just north of Lakeside, **T-Bone Bay** (which has north and south beaches) also offers good swimming, and occasionally huge green, loggerhead and hawksbill turtles.

The most famous of Ningaloo's snorkelling areas and considered one of the best beaches in WA, **Turquoise Bay** ✳ is 12km south of Lakeside. There are two distinct snorkelling areas here: the drift snorkel, which you enter from the southern end and allow the current to carry you over the corals and then exit at the sandbar; and the bay snorkel, usually calm, on the other side of the sandy point. Currents can be very strong at the sandy point separating the two – do not swim between them.

Just 6km south of the bay is the compact snorkelling area, **Oyster Stacks** – the outer edge of the reef is only about 300m from shore, so there are a lot of corals and fish packed inside a small area. The shore here is rocky, not sandy, so be careful entering, and only snorkel at high tide when water is covering the reef, otherwise you may damage the corals. You can check tide times at Milyering Discovery Centre (page 308). Continue south from Oyster Stacks for 14km to reach **Sandy Bay** ✳, home to spectacular white beaches, some coral formations, shallow waters and good kitesurfing, and often few people.

Walking and driving trails There are numerous walks through the park, most taking less than an hour – though graded Class 4, they are well worth the effort for the stunning visuals, and you are likely to see rock wallabies (I often do). The **Yardie Nature Walk** (Class 1; 1.2km return), coupled with the **Yardie Gorge Trail** (Class 4; 750m return), is a particular highlight – the Gorge Trail offers fantastic views over the creek and en route you can spy numerous birds nesting in holes inside the gorge walls – look out in particular for osprey nests. The **Shothole Canyon Walk** (Class 4; 100m return) is perhaps the most spectacular, but unfortunately access is 4x4 only – the views from here into the gorges and to the other cliffs are breathtaking. The cape was once an ancient seabed, and the range was formed by the earth's crust throwing it up – these magnificent folds can be enjoyed on a scenic drive (suitable for 2WD) along **Charles Knife Road**, which provides views down into the gorges. Lookout points are scattered along the way.

Part Five

THE NORTH & INDIAN
OCEAN TERRITORIES

KARIJINI NATIONAL PARK Page 316. Swim inside plunge pools tucked inside deep-red gorges or hike along the spinifex-framed ridges in pure Outback country. The colours in WA's headline national park will sear into your memory and you will never forget your time here.

MURUJUGA NATIONAL PARK Page 328. This open-air natural gallery of Aboriginal rock art is tens of thousands of years old. Among the etchings and drawings you'll see on the hill-like stacks of red-coloured rocks are those of extinct animals that once co-existed with humans here.

BROOME Page 337. WA's winter gem is the perfect antidote for the grey, cold and rain down south. The water of picture-perfect Cable Beach is a shade of blue that has to be seen to be believed, framed with white and pink frangipani and swaying palm trees. While here, also pay a visit to the World War II flying boat wrecks, dinosaur footprints and crocodile park.

GIBB RIVER ROAD Page 348. One of Australia's iconic road journeys, this winter-only 4x4 track through the Kimberley takes you past magnificent waterfalls, huge gorges and one of the country's most iconic stations in El Questro. The Gibb is so connected with the Kimberley in the state's psyche that it will often be assumed by locals that if you are coming up here, this is the reason why.

PURNULULU NATIONAL PARK Page 353. These massive, orange-and-brown beehive striped sandstone domes are one of the world's most curious spectacles in one of its most remote locations. Walking here makes you reflect on nature, isolation and the human spirit in a way that few other places can.

ABORIGINAL ART GALLERIES In one of the world's best places to buy and browse Aboriginal art, the many galleries around Halls Creek (see box, page 352) have all manner of paintings, carvings and crafts produced by highly talented artists from the area. Visitors are welcome and the galleries can often provide opportunities to meet artists.

CHRISTMAS ISLAND CRAB MIGRATION Page 365. Each October and November, millions of red crabs make their way from the island's forests to the sea as part of their annual breeding regimen – a truly spectacular sight, unparalleled in the natural world.

12

The Pilbara

What green is to Ireland, red is to Australia – something that becomes crystal clear in the geological mosaics of Western Australia's top mining region. Mining makes the Pilbara (pronounced *PIL-burra*, not *pil-BARRA*) – and WA – run, and you'll be reminded of that at almost every turn here. The mining industry metaphorically settles, often uneasily, among some of the classic landscapes that form the backbone of the state's psychological identity. To really understand WA, you need to spend at least some time in this region.

The star attraction is the world-class Karijini National Park, where deep gorges, natural plunge pools and the state's tallest peaks make for a red experience of a lifetime. It's so famous that it often dwarfs the region's other attractions, but there's plenty else not to be missed. Millstream-Chichester National Park, with the Fortescue River flowing through it, has gorgeous plateau scenery and rock formations, some permanent pools and is of major significance to Aboriginal culture – there are over 30 Aboriginal language groups represented in the region. Murujuga National Park is home to a natural rock art gallery with some of the world's most ancient works, some 50,000 years old, and the Burrup Peninsula is a place that tries to find a balance between the economic importance of modern oil and gas exploration, with the cultural importance of historical preservation and environmental conservation. Meanwhile, the state's biggest national park – remote, 1.3-million-hectare Karlamilyi – will delight the adventurous with its pure Outback landscapes and isolation.

There are plenty of chances for beach and marine endeavours as well. The 42-island Dampier Archipelago is a haven of reefs, shoals and islands teeming with wildlife, while the Mackerel Islands off Onslow are home to plenty of turtles, dugongs and dolphins. East of Port Hedland, Eighty Mile Beach is one of Australia's most important sites for migratory waders.

The region's two principal towns – Karratha and Port Hedland – are studies in contrast, with one embracing its natural surrounds and the other embracing its economic fortunes and fate as a FIFO centre. Both have ample mining cash floating around, as well as some complex societal undercurrents.

ONSLOW AND THE MACKEREL ISLANDS

Often called 'Cyclone City' due to the frequency of cyclones, Onslow is otherwise known for its enormous salt-mining operations – the salt flats here are 9,000ha – and for being the most southerly site in Australia to be bombed by the Japanese in World War II. In tourist terms, it's the jumping-off point for the **Mackerel Islands** (w mackerelislands.com.au), ten islands scattered up to 22km off the coast, which have developed as an eco-tourism destination – snorkelling at the fringing reef, beach fishing, kayaking and turtle-watching are a few of the activities to be had, as well as guided 4x4 sunset tours.

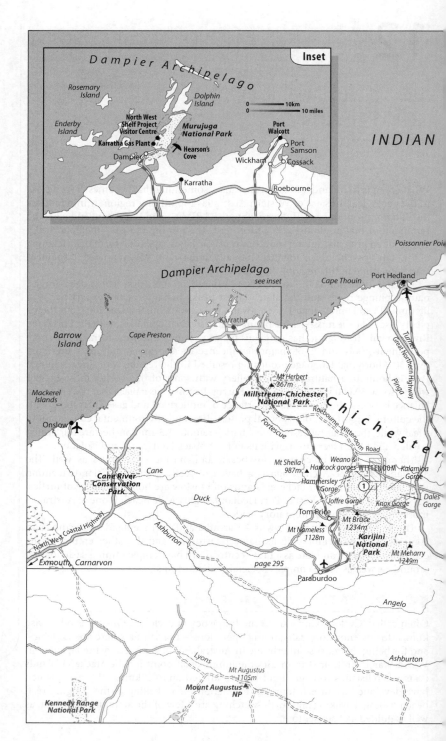

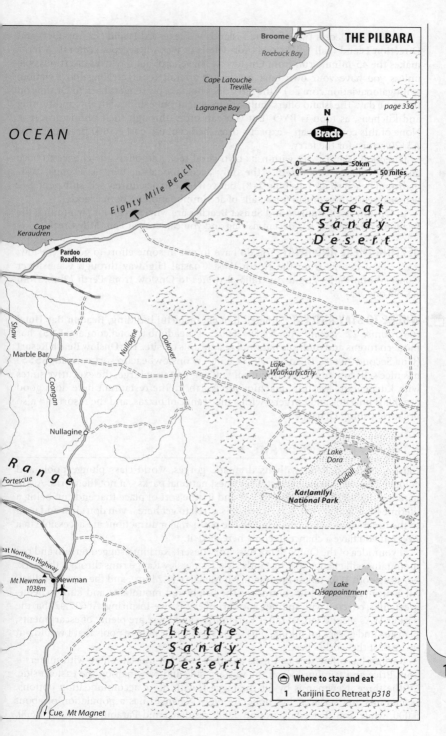

THE PILBARA

Broome

Roebuck Bay

Cape Latouche
Treville

Lagrange Bay

page 336

N

Bradt

0 ———————— 50km
0 ———————— 50 miles

OCEAN

Eighty Mile Beach

*Great
Sandy
Desert*

Cape
Keraudren

Pardoo
Roadhouse

Shaw

Marble Bar

Nullagine

Oakover

Lake
Waukarlycarly

Coongan

Nullagine

Lake
Dora

Rudall

**Karlamilyi
National Park**

R a n g e

Fortescue

eat Northern Highway

Mt Newman
1038m

Newman

Lake
Disappointment

*Little
Sandy
Desert*

Cue, Mt Magnet

⌂ **Where to stay and eat**
1 Karijini Eco Retreat *p318*

The Pilbara ONSLOW AND THE MACKEREL ISLANDS

12

315

Visitors can access two of the ten islands – Thevenard Island (⊕ Apr–Oct) and Direction Island (call ☏9184 6444 for details of when it accepts visitors). A ferry makes the 45-minute run from Onslow to Thevenard, but day trips aren't possible unless you have your own boat or charter aircraft (contact Ningaloo Aviation; w ningalooaviation.com.au) – the ferry does not take passengers back to Onslow on the same day. The island offers multi-room beachfront cabins with air conditioning and kitchens, as food is BYO (but you can order through their online grocery). None of this comes cheap – expect a three-bed cabin to cost A$660 per night, plus A$120 return for the ferry.

Direction Island is set within its own coral reef, and offers the chance to have an entire island to yourself – the only accommodation here is a single two-bedroom beach shack (sleeping 2–8), but you have to be entirely self-sufficient. See w mackerelislands.com.au for details of accommodation on both islands.

In Onslow itself, **Sunrise** and **Sunset Beaches** are where to go for swimming; the **Beadon Creek** groyne has decent fishing and you can crab at **Four Mile Creek**.

GETTING THERE AND AWAY You do have to put in some effort to get to Onslow; it's a 90km detour from the North West Coastal Highway through Cane River Conservation Park. Virgin Australia also flies to Onslow from Perth (2hrs; from A$299 one-way).

 WHERE TO STAY AND EAT Situated in a characterful building, **Beadon Bay Hotel** (66 rooms; 22 Second Av; ☏9184 6002; w beadonbayhotel.com.au; **$$$**) has modern rooms and multiple bars and restaurants on site. The **Onslow Beach Resort** (Cnr Second Ave & Third St; ☏9184 6586; w onslowbeachresort.com.au; **$$$$**) has nice self-contained apartments; if you're going to splurge, the executive suites with kitchen and washing machine are worth it. The restaurant here does good breakfast burritos and burgers, with a nice range of pizzas, and the resort can also organise fishing charters.

KARIJINI NATIONAL PARK ✳

Karijini National Park, with its dramatic gorges, world-class plunge pools and colourful terrain, is one of Australia's finest national parks – if not the world. A trip here is a highlight of any visit to WA and it's the sort of place that ends up being a lifetime highlight as well. Be warned, it is a trek to get here – you don't just add it on to the itinerary as a side trip – but all the park's major attractions are accessible in a 2WD. If you have a chance to come here, take it.

If your idea of the Outback is a dusty, dry desert, Karijini's rugged terrain and red mountains will change that instantly. The Hamersley Range runs through the park, boasting both WA's tallest mountain, Mt Meharry (1,249m), and the second-tallest, Mt Bruce (1,234m). The contrast of the bright-red mountains and almost neon-green hills, covered with spinifex and shrubbery, is awe-inspiring. At 627,422ha, the park is WA's second largest (after Karlamilyi), and there are plenty of escarpments, plateaux and gorges for hiking, plus some spectacular plunge pools that I would put up against the world's best.

Karijini has a few service towns at either end that tourists share with miners – Tom Price and Paraburdoo on the western side and Newman on the eastern side. Of the three, Newman is by far the biggest, with more accommodation options, restaurants and services, but none are *big* – Newman has a population of about 5,000, while Tom Price has around 3,000 residents and Paraburdoo about 1,600.

None are particularly near the park, either – Tom Price is an hour away and Newman almost two. There is camping available in the park itself, plus luxury eco-tents (which are often booked out months in advance); and while lots of visitors do choose this option, we usually try to stay in Tom Price and drive in.

You'll want to come between May and October – summer is scorching. Whenever you come and wherever you choose to say, book well in advance.

The Traditional Owners of the land Karijini sits on are the Banyjima, Kurrama and Innawonga peoples. 'Karijini' is the Banyjima name for the Hamersley Range – there is evidence Aboriginal peoples have lived here for at least 30,000 years.

GETTING THERE AND AWAY From Perth you have two options, both about 1,500km; the Great Northern Highway inland through Cue and Newman, then across Karijini Road to the park's entrance; or take the coastal road (Brand Hwy/NW Coastal Hwy) past Carnarvon, turning off at the famous Nanutarra Roadhouse. The coastal route is slightly longer; both options have fantastic scenery once you get to the Pilbara and if Karijini is your main destination you may want to take one road up and the other back. Regardless, if coming from Perth direct to Karijini/Tom Price you will need to make this a two-day drive – do not think about driving this route at night – and, as such, it may make sense to take the coastal route since there are far more accommodation options as you pass through Geraldton and Carnarvon.

Integrity Coach Lines does the job in 27 hours going up from Perth, and 32 coming back to Perth, starting at A$596 return to/from Tom Price. Qantas flies from Perth to Paraburdoo Airport (1hr 45mins; from A$378), 9km from Paraburdoo and 71km from Tom Price.

GETTING AROUND Entrance to the park is A$15 per vehicle, per day. There are two main entrances (Station West and Station East), both accessed from Karijini Drive – from Tom Price, take the Tom Price–Paraburdoo Road and the turn-off is a few kilometres after. From there, the road connects to the Great Northern Highway, which is somewhat the park's de facto eastern boundary and is the road to Newman.

The western side of the park is home to the Eco Retreat plus the Four Gorges lookout, while the eastern side of the park is where you will find Dales Gorge and some of the more famous plunge pools, as well as the visitor centre. For both sides, turn on to Banjima Drive, which effectively forms a rough semi-circle connecting the two ends, but the middle part is 4x4 only. This means you can enter either end of the park with a 2WD, but to go between them you have to come back out on to Karijini Drive. It is very possible to 'do' Karijini in a 2WD and not have to rough it – just be prepared to drive a bit. A full petrol tank in a standard 2WD should get you from either gateway town to the park's main areas, but make sure you carry extra petrol as there is no fuel in the park or on the way. Paraburdoo, 80km south of Tom Price, can also be used as a gateway – the commercial airport is also there.

Hamersley Gorge, in the northwest of the park, is accessed differently – take Munjina Road north along the western boundary of the park.

TOURIST INFORMATION AND TOUR OPERATORS

Karijini Visitor Centre Banjima Dr; 9189 8121; w parks.dpaw.wa.gov.au/site/karijini-visitor-centre; ⊕ 09.00–15.30 Wed–Mon, 09.00–15.00 Tue. In a building designed to represent a goanna, this should be your first stop in the park. Numerous displays & exhibits are centred around local Aboriginal culture & the physical geography & geology of the area.

Tom Price Visitor Centre 1 Central Rd; 9188 5488; w tomprice.org.au; ⊕ 08.30–17.00 Mon–Fri, 08.30–12.30 Sat–Sun

Flying Sandgroper ☎0419 637 300; w flyingsandgroper.com.au. With bases in Exmouth & Tom Price, this adventure operator offers full- & half-day tours taking in Hamersley Gorge, plus multi-day options combining Karijini with Ningaloo, Broome & Perth. They also offer 4x4 hire from Tom Price with, importantly, 300km per day.

Lestok Tours ☎9189 2032; w lestoktours.com. au. Half- & full-day tours of the gorges including

swimming at Handrail Pool. They also organise mine tours at Rio Tinto. Tours originate/end in Tom Price.

Remtrek Tours ☎9189 8121; w remtrek.com. au. Stargazing astro-tours from the Dales Gorge Campground, with several large telescopes. They also offer 4x4 driving, remote travel preparation & safety courses – great if you're planning a trip to remote national parks like Karlamilyi.

 WHERE TO STAY AND EAT Accommodation is limited and can fill up very quickly in Tom Price and well in advance; look towards Newman (page 322) if you are having difficulty. For those who want to stay in the national park, try Karijini Eco Retreat or **Dales Gorge Campground** (140 sites), managed by DPaW (w parks.dpaw. wa.gov.au/park-stay); maximum two-night stay applies during peak season.

✳ 🏠 **Karijini Eco Retreat** [map, page 314] (40 units) Karijini, off Weano Rd; ☎9286 1731; e reservations@karijiniecoretreat.com.au; w karijiniecoretreat.com.au. Aboriginal-owned, with an emphasis on sustainability, this glamping site has become famous in WA for its deluxe en-suite eco-tents, complete with solar-powered lights & composite timber floors. Unpowered sites & eco-cabins are also available. Their Outback-style restaurant (reservations required) uses traditional bush tucker ingredients & take-away lunches can be arranged; there's also a camp kitchen with BBQ. It is very popular so book well in advance. **$$$$**

🏠 **Tom Price Hotel Motel** Central Rd, Tom Price; ☎9189 1101; w tompricehotel.com.au. Standard motel rooms – it benefits from the lack of options in & around town. Attached restaurant & bottle shop. **$$$$**

🏠 **Tom Price Tourist Park** (32 rooms) Nameless Valley Dr, Tom Price; ☎9189 1515; e info@ tompricetouristpark.com.au; w summerstar.com. au/caravan-parks/tom-price. In the shadow of Mt Nameless, this offers powered & unpowered sites, backpacker rooms, en-suite cabins & A-frame chalets with kitchens. The best option if you want to stay in or around Tom Price. *Cabins* **$$$**, *sites* **$**

✕ **The Pickled Bean** Stadium Rd, Tom Price; ☎0437 289 052; ⊕ 07.00–12.30 Mon–Sat, 08.00–11.00 Sun. Homely café with good b/fasts, coffee & pressed juices – a great stop to fuel up before you head out to the gorges. **$**

✕ **Red Breeze** 21 Stadium Rd, Tom Price; ☎9189 3461; 🄵 redbreeze; ⊕ 10.00–15.00 & 17.00–21.00 daily. Asian restaurant with classics like satay chicken, sushi platters, spring rolls & wonton soup. **$**

WHAT TO SEE AND DO It may help to think of Karijini in terms of gorges.

Eastern side
Dales Gorge West to east, the major sites here are Fern Pool, Fortescue Falls, Three Ways Lookout and Circular Pool. There are car parks at Fortescue Falls and Circular Pool, and Dales Gorge has a campground. Hiking trails link or pass all four sites; a combination Class 2 and Class 3 hike on the edge of the gorge, or a Class 4 hike into the gorge itself.

From Fortescue Falls car park, it is about a 1.2km (Class 3/4) hike down into the gorge to the spectacular freshwater **Fern Pool**. It's a fantastic place for swimming – there's a waterfall pouring down from a long shelving ledge, and greenery around the other three sides. You can also go up under and behind the waterfall for a unique viewpoint. If you enter the water, please do so quietly and respect the land's Traditional Owners. The Creation Serpent is said to live here – having arrived after travelling through the Pilbara landscape, its movements creating the waterways. En route to Fern Pool you'll pass **Fortescue Falls** – another glorious swimming spot, highlighted by a long waterfall that slides its way down red rockface; the stepped appearance of the rock to the right of the falls adds drama to the scene. From here, there's an optional 800m (Class 3) detour to **Fortescue Falls Viewpoint**, where a viewing platform gives a beautiful aerial vantage point of the falls.

From the viewpoint, you have three options: go back to the car park, continue on the **Gorge Rim Trail** (2km; Class 3) to the Three Ways Lookout and Circular Pool, or stay in the gorge, bypass the viewpoint and continue on to Circular Pool by doing the **Dales Gorge Hike** (2km; Class 4). Many people mix both trails: follow one of the hikes on the way out and the other on return. If you choose the Gorge Rim Hike, you will get to Circular Pool by descending at the **Three Ways Lookout** (and, conversely, if you do the Dales Gorge Hike, you will come up and out at Three Ways). **Circular Pool** itself is, unsurprisingly, a circular-shaped natural swimming pool, but its main USP is its sheer colours – an incredible mix of reds, oranges, whites, pinks, greys, some dark, some light, some bright and some soft – making a beautiful, steep natural backdrop to the blue waters of the pool. There is also a **lookout** at the top of the gorge near the Circular Pool car park. Once you've finished swimming, looking or just relaxing, retrace your steps and exit via the climb back at Three Ways.

Kalamina Gorge Given its location, on a 4x4-only track off Banjima Road, Kalamina is not one of Karijini's 'headline' gorges – but the crowds are often thinner, making it a good option if you are looking to break away from the pack. Though not as deep as others, the gorge is still accessed by a Class 4, 3km return trail which leads down to the permanent pool, with a seasonal waterfall – **Kalamina Falls**. Walking along the gorge floor is not as demanding as the other hikes; you will pass rockpools and some colourful rock walls, until you reach the end point at Rock Arch Pool.

Western side

Weano Gorge Weano Gorge is often downplayed, but for our money **Handrail Pool** ✳ – your reward at the end of the **Lower Weano Gorge hike** – is one of the most spectacular plunge pools in the country, if not the world. If you are able to negotiate the Class 5, 1km walk – do so. It starts off easy, but don't be fooled – there are steep, slick descents, narrow passageways and, at times, you have to walk through water – an elderly man slipped and died here in April 2021. As grumpy as you may feel on the difficult and slow trek down, all is forgotten once you get your first glimpse of Handrail Pool – so named because of the handrail you grip as you descend. The deep, steep, red, orange and pink rockface walls contrast with the brilliantly coloured water, occasionally making a green-tinted border where the two meet. The water's small waves reflect off the walls of the gorge, and there is an echo when you speak.

The gorge's other walk is also difficult: the Class 4, 1km **Upper Weano Gorge hike**. There are steep sections and it can be difficult going, but the views are worth it – rockpools, beautiful gorge wall scenery and Karijini's trademark colours.

If the two hikes feel too challenging, there are two shorter walks to a pair of lookouts – the **Junction Pool Lookout** (overlooking Junction Pool) and the **Oxer Lookout** (with views over the Four Gorges – Weano, Red, Junction and Joffre).

To get here, take Banjima Road from Park Entrance Station West, then turn on to Weano Road. Weano Gorge has a day-use area and a car park at the very end of the road, 38km from the park entrance.

Hancock Gorge Accessed from the same car park as Weano Gorge, Hancock Gorge is home to the immensely challenging **Spider Walk** – so named because to

On the northern edge of Karijini, at the base of the gorge of the same name, the town of Wittenoom is the site of one of the biggest industrial disasters in Australian history. In the first half of the 20th century, abundant quantities of blue asbestos were discovered in the Wittenoom and Yampire gorges, both in the national park. Mining operations commenced, and in 1946 the town of Wittenoom was established to cater to the workers and their families.

The health problems associated with asbestos mining are well-known today. If an asbestos fibre enters your body – through breathing or swallowing – it can lead to serious conditions, including cancer, as the body is unable to process the fibres. One of the most common forms of asbestos-exposure cancer is mesothelioma, which affects the lining of the lungs. Onset of the cancer, however, does not happen quickly – it can take decades, even as long as 40 years, for the cancer to develop. For those who develop mesothelioma, the long-term prognosis is very poor, and many patients die within 18 months of diagnosis. Hundreds of miners fell ill, as did members of their families, as asbestos tailings stuck from everything including the laundry and could linger in the air as airborne particles. In 2018, news site Perth Now published a heartbreaking, early 1950s photograph of two young toddler boys in Wittenoom innocently playing in asbestos dust, with the caption and story noting that they both died of mesothelioma in their 30s.

These catastrophic health risks, however, were not well documented at the time of Wittenoom's foundation, though there are questions about how much the government and medical community did know. The mine closed in 1966 because of falling profits as well as health concerns, and although the town's population shrunk quickly many residents remained. Wittenoom stayed in business thanks to tourism – its proximity to the gorges remained a draw – and there were still a few hundred people living in (and moving to) the town as late as the 1980s; the Fortescue Hotel did not close until 1992.

The townsite is still extremely dangerous today – airborne asbestos tailings and particles remain a problem, and there are three million tons of them sitting in Wittenoom Gorge. The government de-gazetted Wittenoom in 2007, disconnected its electricity supply and had it removed from maps to discourage tourists from visiting, and attempted to buy out existing landowners. However, under existing laws, the West Australian government could only compulsorily acquire land if it was related to public works. Some Wittenoom residents refused to leave, and as of 2022 there were still two remaining residents. The same year the McGowan government introduced the Wittenoom Closure Bill amending the law to allow compulsory acquisition of land in Wittenoom, and Lands Minister Ben Wyatt put the figure of Wittenoom workers and residents who have died of asbestos-related sickness at over 2,000. The Australian Asbestos Network details the history of the town at w australianasbestosnetwork.org.au/asbestos-history/asbestos-wittenoom, and former residents have started the Facebook page Lost Wittenoom.

Do not visit Wittenoom under any circumstances. There is no safe level of exposure, no safe way to navigate through the town (even in a closed vehicle) and even one particle can bring death.

get through the passageway, you have to stick your legs and arms out to the sides of the narrow chasm like a spider. There are rock steps, uneven ground and you will have to negotiate through water. **Kermit's Pool**, the end point, is beautiful but can feel narrow, and the colours darker than the other pools, surrounded by steep walls. This is a Class 5, 1.5km trek – while it can seem fun when you read about it, this is the only one in Karijini I have had to turn back on before finishing.

Joffre Gorge The Class 5, 3km walk through Joffre Gorge leads to the incredible **Joffre Falls** – almost perfectly centred at the end of a narrow gorge, as if it knows it's the showpiece. The falls seem to curve towards the bottom like someone slouching into their chair. When you're at the bottom of the gorge, your vantage point can make it seem like you're standing at the bottom of a giant tin can. If you don't want to do the hike, there is a lookout just 100m from the car park.

To get here, follow Banjima Road from Park Entrance Station West, pass Weano Road, then take the access road.

Knox Gorge Knox Gorge has a lookout and a hike (Class 5, 2km) along the gorge floor. If you are short on time, this is one you can skip; while it is beautiful and has the standard array of colours, rockpools and so on, it lacks a singular 'wow' feature like Joffre Falls, the Spider Walk or Handrail Pool.

To get here, take the road to Joffre Falls. The very end of this road – 6km from the turn-off – has a car park where you can access the gorge.

Northern side
Hamersley Gorge Disconnected from the other popular gorges in the park, Hamersley Gorge – in the northwest, and accessed on a different road – is a somewhat gentler gorge than its cousins. The rock here has some distinctive geology behind it and looks almost diagonally patterned in parts down the long face to the water. There are some waterfalls here, plus a fabulous swimming plunge pool, and the gorge is significantly wider – which gives broader views and permits a less claustrophobic feeling. The walk down is also a bit more relaxed – a Class 3, 400m hike that almost feels like a stroll compared to some of the other gorges. Access is via Munjina Road, at the western end of the park – take Karijini Road to the Hamersley–Mt Bruce Road, and from there it's 30km to the Munjina Road turn-off (and another 24km to the gorge).

The 'Four Mountains' Though the Stirling Range in the Great Southern gets all the attention, WA's tallest mountains are actually in the Pilbara, close to Karijini's gorges. The state's second-highest peak at 1,234m, **Mt Bruce** is very accessible from Karijini Road, near the western entrance to the park. There are three walks here, the shortest of which is the **Marandoo View Walk** (Class 2; 500m), with views out over the mine site. The **Honey Hakea Walk** (Class 3; 4.6km) has good vistas of the surrounding mountains and scrub, while the **Summit Walk** (Class 5; 9km) takes you to the top with even grander panoramas of the craggy Pilbara mosaic. The views into Karijini and out to the Marandoo mine site make this a great spot for contemplation and reflection about the yin and yang of the economic use of the land that powers the state's economy and the livelihood of its residents, in stark contrast against the geographic beauty and cultural value of this landscape. If you can't get to Millstream-Chichester, it is worth doing this one for the views.

Mt Meharry (1,249m) pips Mt Bruce as tallest mountain by only 15m, but it is considerably more challenging to reach this peak. You can drive to the summit along a difficult 4x4 track – accessed from Juna Downs and the Great Northern Highway – but call the visitor centre ahead of time for conditions and information.

There are two other peaks that are good for climbing – Mt Nameless and Mt Sheila, both outside Karijini near Tom Price. **Mt Nameless** (1,128m), also known as Jarndunmunha, looks over the town like a sentinel, its shape somewhat similar to a right triangle; you can drive to the summit in a 4x4, or hike up (Class 4; 4.5km) starting from the speedway. The summit affords views of the town and mine site. Smaller **Mt Sheila** (987m) is north of Tom Price – again 4x4 only – and about 40km west of Hamersley Gorge – access is via the private Tom Price Railway Road, so you will need to get a permit first from the Tom Price Visitor Centre (page 317).

NEWMAN

Karijini's eastern gateway is primarily a mining town, purpose-built in the 1960s by the Mount Newman Mining Company. Many people think of Newman as a dusty service centre and nothing else, but it does offer some interesting attractions in its own right, making it a good stopover point if you aren't tackling Karijini and instead are taking the Great Northern Highway up to Port Hedland or the Kimberley. You'll quickly notice the famous Pilbara red dust all over town, which gives the footpaths here a unique crimson tint.

A 4x4 will maximise your visit as it gives you access to the Waterhole Circuit and places like Mt Newman – it may make it worth spending two or even three days here. With a 2WD, your options are more limited and it may make more sense to take the mine tour, use the facilities and services to recharge and relax for a day and then head on to wherever you're going next.

GETTING THERE AND AROUND Newman is on the Great Northern Highway, 1,200km/14 hours from Perth. You will need to stop somewhere along the way – Cue (page 292) is your best bet. In the north, Port Hedland is 450km/5 hours away. Karijini is 200km/2 hours from town.

Integrity Coach Lines can get you to Newman from Perth in about 15 hours (from A$259 one-way), but only if you get the direct coach – if you have to transfer in Port Hedland you are looking at around a 30–40-hour trip.

TOURIST INFORMATION

Newman Visitor Centre Cnr Fortescue Av & Newman Dr; 9175 2888; w newman.org.au; 09.00–17.00 daily. Organises mine tours & chalet accommodation, plus information about the waterholes around town.

WHERE TO STAY AND EAT Many of the hotels in town have well-regarded restaurants and bistros.

Mia Mia (91 rooms) 32 Kalgan Dr; 0499 800 100; e reservations@miamianewman.com. au; w miamianewman.com.au. This 'house in the desert' has bright rooms in an attractive setting; splurge on the executive suite & enjoy a spa bath, kitchenette, outdoor terrace with BBQ & 70" smart TV. The popular on-site Acacia Restaurant has a mix of steaks & other mains like mushroom pappardelle. **$$$$**

Seasons Hotel (89 rooms) 77 Newman Dr; 9177 8666; e reservations@seasonshotel. com.au; w seasonshotel.com.au. Rooms here have a pleasant – if a bit standard – décor but are spacious enough. The on-site steakhouse is excellent & incorporates regional ingredients. **$$$$**

🏠 **Capricorn Village** (239 rooms) Lot 10 Great Northern Hwy; 📞 0429 940 612; e reservations@ outbacknetwork.com.au; w capricornvillage.com. au. Comfortable motel-style complex with free laundry, a golf range, sport courts, fitness centre & pool. The on-site Capricorn Bar & Grill does hearty steaks; they also have a buffet. **$$$**

🏠 **Newman Hotel** (190 rooms) 1401 Newman Dr; 📞 9175 9300; e reception@newmanhotel. com.au; w newmanhotel.com.au. Bright, airy & comfortable rooms with large bathrooms; sgl rooms feel a bit tight but do have desks. The restaurant has a large selection of pizzas & burgers. **$$$**

🏠 **Newman Visitor Centre Chalets** (6 Chalets) Cnr Newman Dr & Fortescue Av; 📞 9175 2888; e nvcmanager@bigpond.com; w newman. org.au. A unique option, surrounded by old mining equipment from Mt Whaleback. The modern chalets come with good en suites, microwaves, fridges & private BBQ area. A good option if you are looking for a bit more privacy than the big hotels elsewhere in town. **$$$**

🏠 **Oasis @ Newman** (394 rooms) 44 Great Northern Hwy; 📞 9328 1100; e admin@ oasisnewman.com.au; w www.oasisnewman. com.au. While rooms here are comfortable & well equipped with built-in wardrobes, it can feel hard to escape the FIFO camp feeling. It is worth booking an Oasis Queen room, which has an outdoor veranda & more homely vibe than some of the smaller standard rooms. Facilities include a gym, recreation room with pool table & large alfresco area. The restaurant buffets at b/fast & dinner are very good value – ask about special offers, as the A$50 meal option where you get both buffets plus a take-away lunch is a great deal. **$$$**

✗ **Whole Foods Café** 79 Giles Av; 📞 0400 210 836; ⏰ call for hours. At the Fortescue Golf Club, this café has become almost legendary among travellers for its high-quality b/fasts & lunches – an essential & very pleasing pit stop if passing through. **$$$**

WHAT TO SEE AND DO Opened in 1968, the **Mt Whaleback Mine** is today the largest open-cut iron-ore mine in the world at 5km long by 1.5km wide – the trains that take the ore from the mine average 2.5km in length. Guided tours (90mins) depart from the visitor centre daily at 09.15 (A$35/20 adult/child). The site was originally called Mt Whaleback because of its shape, though those features are no longer recognisable today. Note that this is a working mine site and so appropriate clothing (closed-in shoes etc) must be worn.

Those with their own 4x4 and an access permit (available from the visitor centre) can explore the **Newman Waterhole Circuit** – the unofficial moniker of a string of waterholes and pools outside town; the visitor centre has a comprehensive list of them all. The track is quite rugged and, generally, the circuit refers to six waterholes – **Kalgan's Pool**, **Eagle Rock Falls**, **Three Pools**, **Silent Gorge**, **Weeli Wolli** and **Wunna Munna**. Kalgan's Pool is probably the most famous, and was used as a filming location in the 2003 film *The Japanese Story*, which was screened at the Cannes Film Festival. Three Pools is another permanent pool in a gorge that is good for swimming; the colour of the gorge walls turns an awesome shade of red-pink at sunrise and sunset, which makes it a popular camping spot. Eagle Rock Falls is actually two falls – one 12m high, the other 60m – and the water tumbles and snakes down a spectacular red cliff. The pool here is permanent, even though the falls only flow after heavy rains.

The most accessible pool in the area is **Gingianna Pool**, which you can get to in a 2WD. Popular among locals, it is a tranquil spot with lots of trees, good for camping and whiling away an afternoon, though the size of the pool depends on recent rainfall.

The summit of **Mt Newman** (1,038m) offers great views out over the area; a 4x4 can get you about halfway up (you'll need a permit from the visitor centre), but you'll have a challenging hike to reach the summit. Also nearby, 35km north of Newman, is the **Hickman Crater**, formed by a meteorite, which despite being 30m deep and about 260m wide was not discovered until 2007, by geologist Arthur Hickman, remarkably, when he was using Google Earth. It's believed the crater is between 10,000 and 100,000 years old – so there is a high probability it occurred while humans were living in Australia.

KARRATHA, DAMPIER AND POINT SAMSON

Long thought of as a dull mining town, Karratha is actually surprisingly upbeat and pleasant once you lift the bonnet, with a whirlwind of natural activities in the vicinity and some rich history at its core. The first major town you reach once WA's coastline makes its major turn eastwards, Karratha and its surrounding attractions stretch west to east along the coast, with the North West Coastal Highway forming a southern boundary. West of town is the magical Dampier Archipelago and the Burrup Peninsula – now Murujuga National Park – which is home to one of the world's greatest open-air Aboriginal rock art galleries, where you can wander among images tens of thousands of years old. Also nearby is one of the north's most spectacular swimming beaches at Hearson's Cove.

East of Karratha is the heritage ghost town of Cossack, the old gaol at Roebourne and the relaxed seaside village of Point Samson, a favourite Pilbara weekend haunt. Anchoring it all in the middle is Karratha itself – which, while short on attractions, has excellent services and shops, making it a very pleasant base.

HISTORY Aboriginal peoples have been in this area for tens of thousands of years – the name 'Karratha' means 'good country' or 'soft earth' – though the word's use to apply to the area reputedly came from it being applied to a station. The Traditional Owners of this land are the Ngarluma and the Yindjibarndi. Traditional life here revolved around the availability of food, water and other resources; the Yindjibarndi language has survived and there are still a few hundred speakers of it in the area – a dictionary was published in 2003 by Wangka Maya, the Pilbara Aboriginal Language Centre. The Ngarluma language has not fared as well and Wangka Maya estimates there are fewer than 20 speakers left.

The first European settlements were founded in the mid 1800s, and the township of Nickol Bay was established in 1866, with Roebourne and Cossack following. But the arrival of Europeans severely disrupted Aboriginal societies – many Aboriginals were exploited on pastoral stations for slave labour or paid pittance wages until a three-year strike in 1946, when a group of close to a thousand Aboriginal workers from multiple stations walked off to protest horrible working conditions. The strike lasted for three years and resulted in some concessions, but many never returned to the stations.

Despite this, the area remained pastoral-oriented until the 1960s, when Dampier was developed into a port to support mining operations, primarily iron ore. Karratha itself was built in the late 1960s; mining continued to expand and Karratha became the region's principal town from around the mid 1970s. Iron ore remains the main driver of the economy today, alongside natural gas, ammonia and sea salt operations; the city has low unemployment, high wages and a young population. Today the City of Karratha has a population of about 21,000, making it one of the biggest regional towns in WA.

GETTING THERE AND AWAY Karratha is 7.5km north of the North West Coastal Highway; turn off at Madigan or De Witt roads. The town is 1,530km/15 hours 30 minutes from Perth, 638km/6 hours 30 minutes from Carnarvon and 236km/

2 hours 30 minutes from Port Hedland. Integrity Coach Lines serves Karratha from Perth (24hrs; from A$298 one-way) and Port Hedland (3hrs 30mins; from A$96 one-way). Karratha Airport, just northwest of town on the road towards Dampier, is served by Qantas and Virgin Australia from Perth (2hrs; from A$373 return).

GETTING AROUND The TransKarratha public bus service connects Karratha with Dampier, Roebourne, Wickham and Point Samson. The 880 goes from Dampier to Point Samson (2hrs) and the 881 is the reverse; note the bus does not stop at Cossack or Murujuga National Park.

Taxis
Karratha Silver Taxis ☎ 13 50 60
Premier Taxis ☎ 0439 747 800

TOURIST INFORMATION AND TOUR OPERATORS

ℹ Karratha Visitor Centre Lot 4548 De Witt Rd; ☎ 9186 8056; w karrathaiscalling.com.au; ⏱ 10.00–14.00 Tue–Sat

HeliSpirit Karratha ☎ 9144 2444; w helispirit. com.au. Runs a range of aerial sightseeing flights, including a 3hr heli-dive in the Dampier Archipelago & an 18min flight over Hearson's Cove & the resource industry plants.

Experience Murujuga ☎ 9144 4112; w experiencemurujuga.com. 90min guided walking tours of Murujuga National Park, led by traditional custodians of the land who share their knowledge on not only the rock art but local plants, bush tucker & bush medicine. Tours leave at 08.00 from Nganjarli — you'll need your own transport to reach the national park.

Ngurrangga Tours ☎ 6373 1440; w ngurrangga. com.au. Offers a range of day trips to Murujuga, specialising in rock art & bush tucker, plus tours to Millstream-Chichester & to witness the Staircase to the Moon at Hearson's Cove.

Pilbara Dive and Tours ☎ 0410 890 077; w pilbaradiveandtours.com.au. Offers a variety of dive trips & PADI courses in & around Karratha, as well as a seasonal 'Island & Snorkel Tour' in the Dampier Archipelago.

WHERE TO STAY

🏠 Best Western Plus the Ranges (73 apartments) Lot 1090 De Witt Rd, Karratha; ☎ 1300 639 320; e reservations@ therangeskarratha.com.au; w therangeskarratha. com.au. Probably the best place to stay in town: stylish & spacious serviced apartments in a tranquil garden with pool, designed to give an 'oasis' feel. Apartments have separate bedrooms with 4-poster bed & large wardrobe, full bathrooms, kitchens & laundry & private balcony. Indicating that the clientele is here for business, not pleasure, the on-site restaurant, My Second Home, is closed on weekends. **$$$$**

🏠 Karratha International Hotel (80 rooms) Cnr Hillview Rd & Millstream Rd, Karratha; ☎ 9187 3333; e reservations@kih.com. au; w karrathainternational.com.au. Modern amenities like smart TVs & workspaces set these rooms apart from other motel-style options. There's also an on-site pool, gym & restaurant. **$$$$**

🏠 Point Samson Resort (12 rooms) 56 Point Samson–Roebourne Rd, Karratha; ☎ 9187 1052; e reservations@pointsamson.net; w pointsamson.net. Rooms here are motel-style but come with king-sized beds. There's also a 3-bed lodge with outdoor kitchen & individual en suites. The location on Point Samson has a relaxed vibe & it's a place to go to get away from it all. **$$$$**

🏠 Comfort Inn & Suites (20 rooms) 2–4 Matebore St, Nickol; ☎ 9144 0777; w choicehotels. com/western-australia/karratha/comfort-inn-hotels. A solid choice: well-equipped suites feature washing machines, fully equipped kitchens & spacious bathrooms, all set among the attractive grounds. **$$$**

🏠 Karratha Central Apartments (84 units) 27 Warambie Rd, Karratha; ☎ 9143 9888; e reservations@karrathacentralapartments. com.au; w karrathacentralapartments.com.au. Popular & well-appointed choice, with a great location in the centre of Karratha. The well-kept grounds feature a swimming pool; apartments have full kitchens, studios are large & have kitchenettes. **$$$**

🏠 **Samson Beach Chalets & Caravan Park** (14 chalets & 20 bays) 44 Bartley Ct, Karratha; 📞 9187 0202; e chalets@samsonbeach. com.au; w samsonbeach.com.au. Spacious, resort-style chalets, set in attractive gardens with a pool. There is also a 20-bay caravan park, fish & chips shop & a tavern. *Chalets* **$$$**, *sites* **$**

🏠 **Discovery Parks – Pilbara Karratha** 70 Rosemary Rd, Karratha; 📞 9185 1855; e karratha@ discoveryparks.com.au; w discoveryholidayparks. com.au/caravan-parks/western-australia/pilbara-pilbara-karratha. Bungalows, cabins, motel rooms & powered sites headline at this reliable chain.

The grounds feature an activity room, dump point, swimming pool & general store. Pet friendly – ring ahead first. *Cabins* **$$$**, *sites* **$**

🏠 **Dampier Mermaid Hotel** (68 rooms) 5 Nielsen Pl, Dampier; 📞 9183 1222; e info@ dampiermermaid.com.au. Although the rooms are fairly standard, this is ideally located in Dampier for those wanting to be closer to the Burrup Peninsula. The on-site restaurant does OK burgers & steaks. **$$**

🏠 **Econo Lodge** (42 rooms) 1 Dwyer Pl, Millars Well; 📞 9185 2411; e book@karrathamotel.com. au; w karrathamotel.com.au. A comfortable mid-range choice, with standard (though well-decorated) motel rooms, communal kitchen, on-site parking for a variety of vehicle types & a café. **$$**

✖ WHERE TO EAT AND DRINK

✖ **Onyx on Sharpe** 1 Sharpe Av, Karratha; 📞 9185 6666; w www.onyxkarratha.com.au; ⏰ 16.00–22.00 Tue & Wed, 16.00–midnight Thu, 11.00–midnight Fri–Sat, 11.00–22.00 Sun. Steak heavy – most of the beef comes from the Great Southern – though there is also some locally caught seafood on the menu. Don't overlook the entrees, such as bao buns & French onion soup. **$$$**

✖ **Soak in Dampier** 6 The Esplanade, Dampier; 📞 0438 522 558; w soakhospitality.com.au; ⏰ 05.00–15.00 Tue–Thu & 05.00–22.00 Fri–Sun. Though pricey, this has nice views to the archipelago & serves locally caught fish & chips & an all-day b/fast featuring 'loaded scrambled eggs' with kransky. **$$$**

✖ **Bollywood Lounge** 23 Sharpe Av, Karratha; 📞 9144 1804; w bollywoodlounge.net; ⏰ 17.00–21.30 Mon–Sat, 17.00–21.00 Sun. Slightly kitschy but atmospheric Indian restaurant with a wide selection of starters & interesting mains, including some Indian-Chinese fusion. Nut dishes are particularly well done. **$$**

✖ **North West Brewing Co** 100 Mooligunn Rd, Karratha; 📞 0107 2214; f NorthWestBrew; ⏰ 11.00–22.00 daily. Karratha's first & only craft brewery has a variety of lagers, pale ales & IPAs, alongside some local vodkas, gins & whiskeys. The

burgers are quality – try the Argentinian lamb burger. Located in the industrial area just south of town, but they offer a courtesy bus to the centre; ring for details. **$$**

✖ **Burger Bus** Central Av, Dampier; 📞 0455 514 287; ⏰ 09.00–14.00 Mon & Wed, 09.00–14.00 & 17.00–20.00 Tue, Thu & Fri. The place to stop for lunch in Dampier, with ham, steak, chicken & fish burgers & desserts like ice-cream sandwiches. **$**

✳ ✖ **Bushlolly Café** 5–15 Sharpe Av, Karratha; 📞 9185 1953; w bushlolly.com; ⏰ 07.30–14.00 Mon–Fri. Award-winning Aboriginal café specialising in bush tucker – both fresh & frozen. Dishes are infused with native ingredients like myrtle & bush tomato. **$**

✖ **Empire 6714** 180/26 Sharpe Av, Karratha; 📞 9143 0068; w empire6714.com.au; ⏰ 05.30–14.00 Mon–Fri, 06.30–14.00 Sat–Sun. Good b/ fasts headline here, with interesting twists like waffles benedict & Japanese vegetable pancakes. They also have decent bagels. **$**

✖ **Lo's** 24 Sharpe Av, Karratha; 📞 0438 186 688; f losbistro; ⏰ 06.00–16.00 daily. Another place with interesting b/fasts, this Asian fusion restaurant serves bubble waffles, miso kimchi beef benedict & Taiwanese radish cake, alongside rice burgers & egg rolls for lunch. **$**

WHAT TO SEE AND DO

Karratha One of the best ways to explore Karratha's Aboriginal history is on the **Yaburara Heritage Trail**, a interconnecting network of trails that start from the water tanks behind the visitor centre (page 325). Highlights include the Aboriginal

Artefact Scatter, an old tool-making spot where you can still see remains of original materials; the Shell Midden, where Aboriginal women extracted shellfish caught offshore; grinding stones, used on seeds and spinifex; and multiple rock art and engraving sites, though they tend to be more recent – in the last 5,000 to 10,000 years. The trail was named by the Ngarluma in honour of the Yabunaka people – traditional inhabitants whose society no longer exists as a result of the catastrophic impact of colonialisation.

Dampier ✳ With a population of around 1,500, Dampier townsite, 20km west of Karratha, is one of the Pilbara's three main centres for exporting iron ore. Despite its raison d'être, however, it boasts a relaxed beach vibe thanks to its pretty palm-lined esplanade curving around the water; there is good swimming at **Shark Cage Beach** and **Hampton Harbour Beach.** The Dampier Foreshore underwent a A$13.6 million upgrade in 2019 and also has shaded adventure playgrounds for kids and good beach fishing. On arrival into Dampier, note the statue of the **Red Dog** – a kelpie who wandered around the Pilbara in the 1970s and became an unofficial mascot of the region (see box, below).

The town is the jumping-off point for the **Dampier Archipelago**, comprising 42 islands within a 50km radius of Dampier that offer terrific opportunities for fishing, swimming, diving and snorkelling. The area is an important nesting site for hawksbill, loggerhead and green turtles, while migrating humpback whales frequent the waters between July and September; you're also likely to spot bottlenose dolphins and manta rays. Dolphin Island and Easterby Island probably have the best beaches and are open for camping. Not all islands are open, however, as some are closed to the public for environmental reasons – check with the visitor centre (page 325). If you don't have your own boat, a number of local operators organise boat charters and diving trips (page 325).

The archipelago is also of massive importance to Aboriginal peoples. There are over a million examples of rock art and petroglyphs here, which hold enormous cultural significance as a reminder of law, custom and tradition. Many of the

THE PILBARA MASCOT

On arrival into Dampier, on the left-hand side of Central Avenue, you will find a curious statue alongside the 'Welcome to Dampier' sign – that of the Red Dog. This friendly kelpie roamed across the Pilbara in the 1970s, winning friends wherever he went. He had multiple owners, but the region as a whole adopted him. Although originally named Tally Ho, his wanderings left him with a coat of characteristic Pilbara red dust and so he took on the moniker of 'Red Dog'. According to one story, Red Dog was unaware that one of his owners, John Stazzonelli, had died in a motorcycle accident and so he set off through the Pilbara looking for him. Red Dog also met a tragic end, believed to have been poisoned in 1979.

The dog, and the Pilbara's love for him, have captured the imagination of many people passing through – enough that it has inspired three books and two films. Nancy Gillespie's 1983 book called *Red Dog* compiled people's recollections of him in the Pilbara, while Louis de Bernieres's 2002 book was the basis for the 2011 movie, *Red Dog*, and a 2016 prequel, *Red Dog: True Blue* ('True Blue' is slang meaning, loosely, something that is very Australian). For more information, see w reddogwa.com.

12

petroglyphs represent animals and people; they serve as an overview of the natural history of the area, as the animals in the drawings changed (such as thylacines) as they became extinct and new animals arrived. Some estimates peg the oldest etchings at 20,000 years old.

Hearson's Cove Northeast of Dampier is the very popular and scenic Hearson's Cove, one of the best-known swimming spots in the Pilbara. Looking out to Nickol Bay, it is penned in by hills, the rich reds and browns of which contrast with the turquoise of the water and the gold of the sand. Note that the tide here is extreme: when it is in, there is good swimming in the clear water (look out for sea snakes) and when it is out, you can walk across the mudflats and look for turtles. Come during full moon from March to November to witness the natural phenomenon known as the **Staircase to the Moon** – a magical optical illusion where the light of the moon reflects on the mudflats at low tide.

There is also a bit of European settler's history at Hearson's Cove – F T Gregory's expedition on the *Dolphin* landed here in 1861. Gregory was a surveyor who arrived in Swan River as a boy in one of the first European arrivals in 1829, and his arrival marked the first sustained contact between European settlers and Aboriginals in the Pilbara, as well as setting the stage for the eventual pastoral settlement.

Murujuga National Park ✳ Covering the northern end of Burrup Peninsula, Murujuga National Park is one of the most spectacular and important Aboriginal rock art galleries in the world. There are over a million drawings here, many dating back almost 50,000 years if not more, and the national park is in the process of being inscribed on the UNESCO World Heritage List.

If you have been to other rock art sites, Murujuga may seem a bit different. The drawings here are not in caves or on cliff tops – instead, the etchings are found on small red rocks that have been stacked in gigantic piles. Spotting the art is a bit like looking for orchids – it can be very difficult at first, but once you find your first one it gets easier and easier. My favourite drawing is one of a jellyfish with extra-long tentacles, though you will see plenty of creatures here including humans and unrecognisable animals that have probably been extinct for tens of thousands of years. Note that the open-air site lacks signage and railings, but this just adds to the mystique (though there is now a 700m boardwalk at Nganjarli). If you don't fancy striking out on your own, various local operators run guided tours (page 325).

'Murujuga' means 'hip bone sticking out' in Yaburara. Almost all of the art here is in petroglyph form; Aboriginal peoples believe that the images were made by the Marga – creation spirits. While some of it is believed to be 50,000 or even 60,000 years old, varying sea levels around Australia and the presence of marine animals in many drawings, indicate that much of it would be much more recent – around the 6,000- to 8,000-year mark – as in different periods of Aboriginal habitation of Australia, this area would have been far inland.

Just south of the national park is the **North West Shelf Project Visitor Centre** (Burrup Rd; ☏ 9158 8292; ☉ 09.00–noon Wed, also 09.00–noon Tue–Thu during school holidays; free), located within the Karratha Gas Plant. The Burrup Peninsula is home to massive natural gas exploration, and this centre has interactive displays and exhibits on the process of discovery, extraction and refinement. One-third of Australia's oil and gas is produced here; it has generated A$35 billion in investment over its 35 years of operation and is Australia's largest natural resource development project. Despite this, it is estimated that only about one-third of the shelf's reserves have been exploited. The plant provides for much of the state's domestic consumption; the pipeline from here to Bunbury is the longest in Australia (roughly 1,600km) and accounts for nearly all of the South West's consumption.

Roebourne A 30-minute/40km drive from Karratha along the North West Coastal Highway brings you to Roebourne, which got its start in 1866 as a mining and pearling centre. Many of its stone buildings have been restored, most notably the **Old Roebourne Gaol** (5 Queen St; ☏ 9182 1060; ⊕ 09.00–15.00 Mon–Sat; A$5), which opened in 1896 with cells segregated by race. It was shut down in 1924 due to the closure of the Cossack port and subsequent declining population, though it reopened as a prison facility again in the 1970s for about a decade, before finally closing its doors permanently in 1984. Today it houses a museum with displays and artefacts showcasing both the colonial and indigenous history of the Roebourne area as well as the gaol.

Roebourne is also known as a creative hub, particularly for Aboriginal artists, and the **Ganalili Centre** (38 Roe St; ☏ 6118 5286; w ganalili.com.au; ⊕ 09.00–17.00 Mon–Sat, 09.00–14.00 Sun), housed in the refurbished Victoria Hotel, is a good place to learn about and buy art and textiles produced by Yindjibarndi artists.

Cossack ✳ Cossack was established in the 1870s, originally named Port Walcott but dutifully renamed in 1871 after the HMS *Cossack* visited the town with the Governor of Western Australia, Frederick Weld. It served as the first port in this part of the Pilbara, though was quickly made obsolete and redundant – much of the pearling industry packed off to Broome, the Gold Rush fizzled and the waters here were not adequate for the larger boats coming online at the time. The settlement sputtered, town administration dissolved and Cossack was a ghost town by the 1950s. Since then, however, the town's buildings have been immaculately restored, giving visitors a taste of what life was like in an 1800s Outback pearling town.

Consider exploring the buildings on the main street on foot and driving out to the others – download a copy of the Class 2, 3km **Cossack Heritage Trail Brochure** from the City of Karratha's website (w karratha.wa.gov.au/sites/default/files/uploads/2016Cossack-brochure-web.pdf). The courthouse is a highlight; designed by famed West Australian architect George Temple-Poole, the stone used in the building is from the ballast of ships and the veranda is noted for the decorative pillars. Also noteworthy is the old brown-and-black stone customs house – again designed by Temple-Poole – once the centre of activity, as food and alcohol were imported here and wool and pearl materials were exported from here. Today a small café (☏ 9182 1060; ⊕ 08.30–14.30 Wed–Sun; $) operates there and is a good place to have a pie and a coffee. If you want to spend the night in a ghost town, the old police barracks have been converted into a simple yet comfortable B&B with shared facilities (5 rooms; ☏ 0488 364 587; w cossack.org.au/accommodation-camping; $).

A good time to come is during the **Cossack Art Awards** (w cossackartawards.com.au), held over three weeks in July and August, where works from all over Australia are displayed inside several of the Heritage buildings – over A$80,000 of prize money is distributed, making it one of the richest competitions in the country.

Cossack is 14km north of the North West Coastal Highway at Roebourne; take the Point Samson–Roebourne Road and then turn on to Cossack Road.

Point Samson A very popular weekend spot for Karratha residents, this seaside village is known for its excellent beaches and relaxing lookouts over the water. It became a major port in 1902 with the construction of a lengthy (1,900m) jetty that could handle the newer, bigger ships that the Cossack jetty couldn't – thus kick-starting Cossack's decline. In the mid 20th century, it was a major export hub for Wittenoom's asbestos (see box, page 320); when the asbestos mine closed and iron producers began building their own facilities, Port Samson's importance began to rapidly decline – the jetty was no longer used commercially by the mid 1970s and, over time, it succumbed to cyclones and dereliction, before being completely removed in the early 1990s. It is almost impossible to imagine it now, strolling through the sleepy seaside atmosphere, but this was once the Pilbara's main arrival point.

Honeymoon Cove and **Point Samson Beach** are your best bets for swimming, snorkelling and fishing (the former is good for beach fishing), and there is a boat launch at **Johns Creek Boat Harbour**. Point Samson Adventure Rentals (Lot 259 Macleod St; w pointsamsonadventure.com.au/equipment-hire) hires out half- and full-day snorkel gear (A$15/A$25) and also half- and full-day bike hire (A$20/A$30). Overlooking the water, the **Samson Beach Tavern** (Miller Cl; ↘9187 1414; ⊕ from 11.30 Wed–Mon, meals served noon–14.00 & 17.30–20.30; $$) is a good spot for a beer and fish and chips.

To get to Point Samson, take the Roebourne–Point Samson Road to its end – it's 23km from Roebourne. En route you'll pass the purpose-built mining town of **Wickham**, constructed in the 1970s and named after the captain of the HMS *Beagle* who surveyed the area here in 1840. You can take a detour through town to reach **Port Walcott**, the major iron-ore port known for its massive 2.7km wharf. Nearby is **Boat Beach**, home to **Port Walcott Yacht Club**, which offers good swimming.

MILLSTREAM-CHICHESTER NATIONAL PARK

Deeply significant in Aboriginal culture and a 'holy land' for the Yindjibarni people, the 200,000ha Millstream-Chichester National Park is an area of diverse beauty, with permanent pools taking their water supply from underground aquifers, palm trees and spinifex of varying shades of green, which contrast with the red hills and rock formations. It has a very diverse ecosystem of fauna due to the presence of permanent water, and it has been estimated that over 300 species of animal can be found here, including flying fox and euro (a type of kangaroo) – though it's not common to see much as the animals are not very active in the hot weather. The park is, however, a good spot (after rains) to see Sturt's desert pea (*Swainsona formosa*) – the small, circular black 'pea' inside the long, red flower petals is an emblem of the Pilbara – and the conical, feathery, purple-pink mulla mulla (*Ptilotus exaltatus*).

The drive from Karratha to Python Pool is only a little over an hour, along mostly good, quick sealed roads (and what isn't sealed is 2WD suitable). You will be surprised how quickly you arrive from town. For visitors, the main points of interest can be grouped into two areas – the northern Chichester area around Python Pool, which many consider the park's signature attraction, and the southern Millstream area.

GETTING THERE AND AROUND Arriving at Millstream-Chichester National Park from Karratha is straightforward. From the North West Coastal Highway, take Warlu Road into the park. When you arrive at Roebourne–Wittenoom Road inside the park, turn left to access the Chichester Range section or right to head further south to Millstream Road and access that part of the park.

Many people combine a trip to Millstream with one to Karijini. You can access the unsealed Rio Tinto Rail Access Road from Tom Price – although you do need a permit (enquire at the Tom Price Visitor Centre; page 317). It's 176km to Millstream from there. A longer route (235km) runs from the Hamersley Gorge area at Karijini; take Nanutarra Road north to Fortescue Crossing Road, for 10km to the junction with the Roebourne–Wittenoom Road, where you'll go north – this does not take you to Wittenoom. These are unsealed roads, so ring the visitor centres to check conditions before setting out.

The Chichester and Millstream sections of the park are connected by the unsealed Roebourne–Wittenoom Road. As you head south from Chichester to Millstream, you'll turn on to the unsealed Millstream–Pannawonica Road, and then the unsealed Millstream Road. Python Pool to the Millstream Homestead is 61km.

The entrance fee is A\$15 with a private vehicle.

WHERE TO STAY AND EAT Visiting the park is easily done as a day trip from Karratha, but if you do want to overnight DPaW bush camps with pit toilets are available in the Millstream end at **Stargazers Campground** (15 sites; no power) and the **Miliyanha Campground** (27 sites; generator can be used at set times). In the Chichester section, bush camping is available at **Snake Creek** – again, generators can only be used at set times.

WHAT TO SEE AND DO
Northern section: Chichester Range
Arriving from Karratha, this is the first part of the park you will reach. **Mt Herbert** (367m) is your first stop with a 600m return walk trail to the summit, giving views out over the plain. You'll then proceed to **Python Pool** ✳ along a beautiful road with a gorgeous panorama lookout over the red hills, escarpments and valleys, and their bright green vegetation cover. Python is a plunge pool with a spectacular backdrop – a large cliff wall of red, white and orange folded rock, which gives the impression that the pool is being screened off from what's behind it.

You can also walk to Python Pool from Mt Herbert along the beautiful if challenging **Camel Trail** (Class 4; 16km return) – the terrain is basalt and sandstone, which used to be covered by camel teams. WA isn't often associated with camels, but the state is actually home to the largest herd of feral camels in the world – there are about 150,000 of the humped mammals in the state, though you are exceedingly unlikely to see one here anymore, as they live mostly in the deserts today (such as Karlamilyi). Introduced in the 1840s as work animals, they caused enormous damage to the state's agricultural and pastoral industries (usually by damaging fencing) – so much so that the state declared them pests in the 2007 Biosecurity and Agriculture Management Act, and jurisdictions across Australia began culls in 2009. En route you will pass **McKenzie Spring**, which used to be a watering hole for the camels passing through. If you can manage it, it is better to start at Mt Herbert, so you can relax in Python Pool at the end and get picked up from there.

The road to the Chichester Range section of the park from Karratha is sealed most of the way, then there is a roughly 15km section of unsealed road (2WD suitable but rough in places) and then it gets sealed again before Mt Herbert, all the way to the Snake Creek camping area. Karratha to the Mt Herbert Lookout is only 117km, taking about 90 minutes to drive; it's only about 4km further to Python Pool. Visiting the Chichester Range section of the park is very viable as a day or even half-day trip from Karratha.

Southern section: Millstream The Millstream section of the park is centred around the Fortescue River. Owing to the abundance of freshwater here, much of which has overflowed into pools, there is a variety of flora and fauna such as geckos and lizards and you may even see a dingo; abundant yellow sennas add colour to the setting.

The **Millstream Homestead Visitors Centre**, housed in an attractive period building with deeply steeped roof and wide veranda, is a good orientation point; it doesn't have any staff, but does contain a lot of information about the park's history, significance to Aboriginal peoples and the local environment. The Class 1, 750m return **Homestead Trail** offers a glimpse of what pastoral life was like here in the 1930s, told through the perspective of a young teenager. The trail also leads to **Jirndawurrunha Pool**, though swimming is not allowed here or in the neighbouring streams and pools due to their cultural significance to Aboriginal peoples.

There are, however, two places where you can swim. **Nhanggangunha Deep Reach Pool**, often just called Deep Reach Pool, is permanent, ringed by trees and shrubbery, and fed by the aquifer. The Yinjibamdi believe the Wagyl serpent (page 131) lives here. Canoeing is also permitted. This pool is on Millstream Road, a few hundred metres before the homestead. On Snappy Gum Drive, which Millstream Road loops into, is **Murlamunyjunha Crossing Pool**, which has a similar tree/shrubbery backdrop though there is some hill scenery behind it. A Class 3, 6.1km walk leads to the Crossing Pool from the homestead, with interpretive signage along the way about bush plants and how they can be used. Snappy Gum Drive is often accessible for 2WD, but not always – there will be signs up about its status.

PORT HEDLAND AND SURROUNDS

On paper, Port Hedland and Karratha appear to be similar places – both are mining towns of roughly the same size, on or near the water. But in reality they have developed very different personalities. Whereas Karratha has shaken off its gritty port town image to incorporate a community feel, Port Hedland very much embraces FIFO culture. Mining and shipping operations are front-and-centre and the port – one of the busiest in the world – is right in the middle of town, along with its assorted railway lines and facilities. That being the case, most visitors stay here for just one night on their way to Broome, Karratha or Newman – though if you are interested in industry and port operations, you have come to the right place.

Port Hedland essentially has two parts; a northern section on the coast, where the port is; and South Hedland, a community 13km south on the highway that was purpose-built in the 1960s and 1970s, home to its schools, health campus and other businesses. South Hedland, however, has a notorious reputation in WA for its high crime rate, particularly car break-ins, so you are better off staying in the northern part of town.

The Kariyarra are the Traditional Owners of this land – their name for the area is 'Marapikurrinya', which means 'hand pointing straight', with 'nya' being a location marker – the name refers to the shape of the land, creeks and coastline here.

GETTING THERE AND AWAY Port Hedland is just north of the Great Northern Highway, which merges with the North West Coastal Highway a few kilometres east. Exit the highway on Powell or Wallwork Road to access South Hedland, or Wilson Street for the port area. It's 236km/2 hours 30 minutes to Karratha, 450km/5 hours to Newman and 600km/6 hours to Broome. Perth is 1,620km away and the drive takes two days, the quickest route being inland along the Great Northern Highway through Cue and Newman.

Integrity Coach Lines runs services from Perth (about 30hrs; from A$298 one-way), Newman (6hrs; from A$128), Broome (6hrs 40mins; from A$136) and Karratha (3hrs; from A$96). Port Hedland's airport is south of town on the Great Northern Highway; both Qantas and Virgin Australia fly from Perth (2hrs; from A$500 return).

GETTING AROUND The TransHedland provides a public bus service. Route 870 connects South Hedland and Port Hedland in about 40 minutes (and there is an express 23-minute service); routes 871 and 872 are 20-minute circulars around South Hedland that go clockwise and anticlockwise, respectively.

Hedland Taxis (◄ 9173 1010; w hedlandtaxis.com.au) has wheelchair-accessible cabs.

TOURIST INFORMATION
▉ **Port Hedland Visitor Centre** 13 Wedge St; ◄ 9173 1711; e info@visitporthedland.com.au; w visitporthedland.com.au

WHERE TO STAY AND EAT
🏠 **Hospitality Port Hedland** (40 rooms) Webster St; ◄ 9173 1044; e porthedland@ hospitalityinns.com.au; w porthedland. wa.hospitalityinns.com.au. The Port Hedland branch of this WA chain offers modern motel rooms (it is worth getting one with an ocean view), swimming pool & BBQ facilities. The on-site Pilbara Room Restaurant has a cocktail bar & serves some good Asian-inspired dishes like Japanese scallops. **$$$**

🏠 **Discovery Parks Port Hedland** 2 Taylor St; ◄ 9173 1271; e porthedland@discoveryparks.com. au; w discoveryholidayparks.com.au/caravan-parks/western-australia/pilbara-port-hedland.

Cabins, economy rooms & powered & unpowered sites; good facilities including camp kitchen, activity room, laundry & dump point. Pet-friendly. *Cabins* **$$$**, *sites* **$**

✗ **Hedland Harbour Café** 5 Wedge St; ◄ 9173 2630; ⏰ 04.00–14.30 Mon–Fri, 04.30–14.00 Sat–Sun. Catering to early rising shift workers, this café offers good salads featuring the likes of lamb & Thai beef. Burgers use local beef. **$**

✗ **Silver Star Café** 12A Edgar St; ◄ 9140 2207; ⏰ 06.00–15.00 daily. With an atmospheric location in a preserved railway carriage, this is a good place to stop for a coffee & filling b/fast. **$**

WHAT TO SEE AND DO The **Port Hedland Peace Memorial Seafarer's Centre** (Cnr Wilson & Wedge St; ◄ 9173 1315; w phseafarers.org) is a mission agency of the Anglican church, whose role is to provide wellbeing and spiritual care for seafarers. For visitors, they offer a 90-minute **Harbour Tour** (A$55/30 adult/child), which combines a presentation about the organisation and the port, with a run around the harbour in one of their boats, picking up seafarers who want to come ashore.

Iron isn't the only major industry in town. **Pilbara Tours** (13 Wedge St; ◄ 0408 933 108; e enquiries@pilbaratours.com.au; w pilbaratours.com.au) run a 3-hour **Salt Eco Tour** (A$65/40 adult/child) to the wetlands east of town, around the Ridley River, to see how Rio Tinto makes salt. They also operate a 90-minute **Twilight Industry Tour** (A$50/25 adult/child), offering a glimpse of port operations as night falls, as well as fishing charters in the wetlands (from A$300).

The visitor centre can also arrange guided **bus tours** of the town led by a local historian, taking in sites like the old World War II rifle range, and the lookout honouring the victims of the sinking of the SS *Koombana*, a steamer with 80 passengers and 74 crew that went missing off the coast here in 1912 but was never found – believed to be the victim of a cyclone.

EAST OF PORT HEDLAND: MARBLE BAR, CAPE KERAUDREN AND EIGHTY MILE BEACH As you head east on the Great Northern Highway towards Broome and the Kimberley, there are a couple of worthwhile detours off the highway. The first of these, around 150km south of the highway along the sealed Marble Bar Road through the rolling red Coongan Hills, is **Marble Bar** – where the town sign reads 'Warmest Welcome from Australia's Hottest Town'. The record temperature here was 49.2°C in 1905, though they nearly topped that in 2018 at 49.1°C; it also holds the record for most consecutive days over 100°F (37.8°C) – 160 days from 31 October 1923 to 7 April 1924. The town was named after the nearby mineral deposits that were first thought to be marble but later discovered to be jasper, a colourful variety of quartz. The bar and deposits cross and line the Coongan River and Chinaman's Pool – the colourful stripes on the white deposit make it look like something out of a geological candy store. While you can't take any of the jasper, fossicking for colourful Pilbara stones is a popular activity in the area.

From Marble Bar, if you continue south for 112km you will reach the old Gold Rush town of **Nullagine**, where it is said the first Australian diamonds were discovered in 1895. Contact the Shire of East Pilbara to discuss road conditions; accommodation comes in the form of the **Nullagine Hotel** (☏ 9176 2000; w nullaginehotel.com.au; **$$$**), which also runs a pub and a general store, and the shire also operates a caravan park.

Back on the Great Northern Highway, 150km from Port Hedland is the Pardoo Roadhouse, opposite which is the unsealed road to **Cape Keraudren** (A$12/ vehicle), a 4,800ha coastal reserve that is a popular haunt for fishers and crabbers. Camping is permitted, though the reserve is electricity-free; ATVs and quad bikes are prohibited. The cape also marks the start of the splendid-but-misnamed **Eighty Mile Beach** – the longest uninterrupted beach in WA, it's actually 220km (137 miles) long.

The Eighty Mile Beach Marine Park is a Ramsar Wetland of International Importance and attracts thousands of birds each year – sand plovers, red knots and curlews among them. Dolphins, dugongs and turtles also visit. Behind the dunes is **Eighty Mile Beach Caravan Park** (5 cabins, 150 powered sites, 50 unpowered sites; ☏ 9176 5941; e stay@eightymilebeach.com.au; w eightymilebeach.com.au; cabins **$$$**, sites **$**; walk-ins only), with fresh water, a mini-general store and well-kept ablution blocks. You can walk to the beach from the caravan park; Eighty Mile Beach is remote country though, so come with supplies.

KARLAMILYI NATIONAL PARK

At over 1.3 million hectares, Karlamilyi is WA's biggest national park, but also its most remote – it's suitable only for experienced and completely self-sufficient visitors who have high-clearance 4x4s, ample supplies of fuel, water and food, a satellite phone, a highly detailed map (Hema does a good one) and excellent bush and remote navigational skills. The Martu people are the Traditional Owners of this area and hold native title of over 13 million hectares of the western deserts, but that does not include the national park. They were among the last Aboriginal groups to make contact with Europeans – 'Karlamilyi' is their word for the Rudall River, which flows through the park. The main communities here are at Punmu (☏ 9176 9110) and Parnngurr (☏ 9176 9009), both of which have very limited fuel and shop facilities – ring ahead for access and permit requirements. Do not rely on fuel or water facilities anywhere in the park.

Karlamilyi is sandwiched between two deserts – the Little Sandy Desert to the southwest and the Great Sandy Desert to the northeast, both of which are home to numerous sand dunes and salt lakes. The park's main landmark is the **Desert Queen Baths**, a waterhole encased in red, rocky hills which, in parts, have a gorge-like feel, with rockfaces reaching down to the water. Feral camels are known to wander through Karlamilyi – do not approach them. There are also plenty of kangaroos, wallabies and reptiles around, as well as acacias and hakeas.

There are two access tracks: one from Marble Bar, 420km away, and another from Newman, 260km away.

The Pilbara KARLAMILYI NATIONAL PARK

12

335

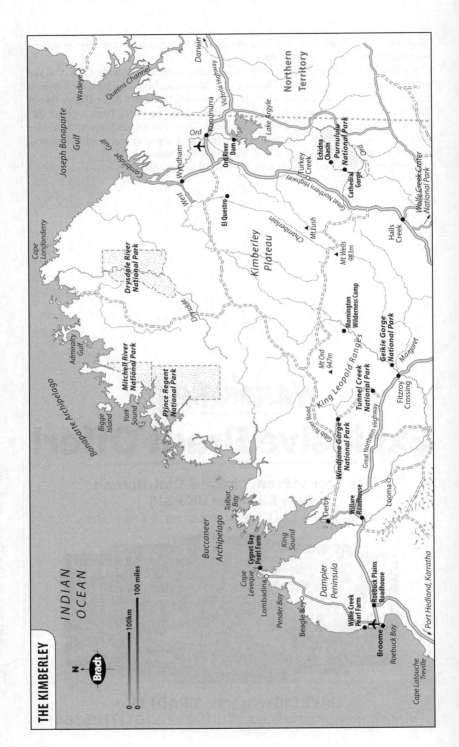

13

The Kimberley

As you head north from the Pilbara, the landscape transforms dramatically from red dust and spinifex to a lush, green tropical setting and then, as you head east, opens up more into pockets of savannah. This is the legendary Kimberley, home to pearls, crocs, million-acre cattle stations and violent rainstorms that make Niagara Falls blush.

The jewel in the crown is arguably Broome, WA's winter playground, with world-class Cable Beach, exquisite pearl shops and laidback locals among the brightly coloured frangipani. I say 'arguably' because Kununurra, on the other side of the region and less well-known, has its own fervent band of supporters who champion its striped sandstone rock formations, incredible Lake Argyle, and the town's rare pink diamonds and frontier spirit. I know people who have worked for a few years in Kununurra and then returned to other parts of WA, and they tell me that 10, 20 or even 30 years later the spirit of Kununurra still hasn't left them and they return regularly.

Whichever town wins the debate, both Broome and Kununurra are places that will stay with you long after you leave. In between the Kimberley's two bookends, there are dramatic gorges, cascading waterfalls, one of Australia's most iconic 4x4 tracks in the Gibb River Road and the spectacular and unique Purnululu National Park, with its orange-and-brown striped domes.

The Kimberley is thought and spoken of in two sections: the West Kimberley, which comprises Broome and Derby, and the East Kimberley, which is Kununurra and Halls Creek. Tell many West Australians that you are planning a trip to the Kimberley, and they will imagine you chaining cannisters of petrol to the back of your 4x4 as you set off for six weeks. That may have been true at one time, but not today – many (but not all) of the key sights are accessible along 2WD-suitable sealed roads, with a petrol station within reach. And while it *is* a long way from Perth – driving to Broome from the state capital is likely to take you three days, and Kununurra four – there are creative options, like hopping on a flight from Perth to Darwin in Northern Territory, hiring a car there and making the 9-hour drive to Kununurra. The whole of the Kimberley, from Kununurra to Broome, can be driven across in about 11 hours. There are also commercial flights from Perth to both Broome and Kununurra.

BROOME

The focal point of tourism in the Kimberley and the region's biggest town, schizophrenic Broome is a tale of two cities. In winter, the warm weather, clear waters, buzzing restaurants, exquisite pearl shops and lush tropical setting make it one of WA's greatest tourist destinations with a vibrancy and energy that is often missing in other West Australian country towns. In summer, however, temperatures soar, the rains come, the humidity becomes so thick you can cut it with a knife and

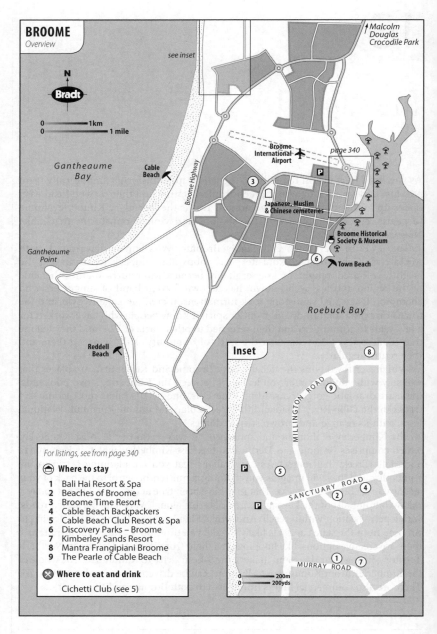

BROOME
Overview

↑ Malcolm
Douglas
Crocodile Park

see inset

N

Bradt

0 ————— 1km
0 ————— 1 mile

*Gantheaume
Bay*

Cable
Beach ↖

Broome Highway

Broome
International
Airport ✈

page 340

3

Japanese, Muslim
& Chinese cemeteries

Broome Historical
Society & Museum

6 ↖ Town Beach

*Gantheaume
Point*

Roebuck Bay

Reddell
Beach ↖

Inset

8

MILLINGTON ROAD

9

5

2 SANCTUARY ROAD **4**

MURRAY ROAD **1** **7**

0 ———— 200m
0 ———— 200yds

For listings, see from page 340

⊖ **Where to stay**

1 Bali Hai Resort & Spa
2 Beaches of Broome
3 Broome Time Resort
4 Cable Beach Backpackers
5 Cable Beach Club Resort & Spa
6 Discovery Parks – Broome
7 Kimberley Sands Resort
8 Mantra Frangipiani Broome
9 The Pearle of Cable Beach

⊗ **Where to eat and drink**

Cichetti Club (see 5)

super-venomous jellyfish flood those clear waters, putting Cable Beach – one of
the state's most famous beaches – off-limits and making Broome a highly alcoholic
misery cocktail. So if you're planning a visit, go in winter.

Sitting on a small peninsula – the term 'Broome' is used for both the city and
the area – the town was founded in 1883 by John Forrest, who went on to become
WA's first premier, as a port for the pearling industry. Forrest named the town after

Frederick Broome, who was Governor of Western Australia at the time. There are 84 Aboriginal communities in the Shire of Broome; the Yawuru, who are the Traditional Owners of the land here and the waters of Roebuck Bay, hold native title for Broome townsite, which they call Rubibi. The early pearling industry was not kind to Aboriginal peoples – many were forced to dive for pearls in terrible conditions or work on board the luggers. Pearling workers were also heavily recruited from Asia, giving the town a multi-cultural character from its inception that it retains and celebrates today. Pearling continued to be Broome's mainstay, with the demand for pearl buttons fueling the industry; in 1910, it was the biggest pearling centre in the world. But during World War II it became an important allied base in the Pacific Theatre. On 3 March 1942, the town suffered an air raid by Japanese fighters, killing almost 100 people (page 344). The event remains an important part of the town's psyche and history.

In the 1950s, plastics and polyesters began to replace pearls as a textile and pearls started being emphasised as jewellery – and so the first pearl cultivation farms began to crop up, transforming the industry to its foundation. Tourism also slowly emerged in the 1980s, capitalising on the town's beautiful setting and warm winter climate, and is today vital to its economy.

GETTING THERE AND AWAY Broome sits 40km west of the Great Northern Highway (exit at Roebuck Plains Roadhouse), 598km/6 hours from Port Hedland, 203km/2 hours from Derby and 396km/4 hours from Fitzroy Crossing. It will take you about three days to drive up from Perth, overnighting likely around Cue and then Port Hedland.

Integrity Coach Lines run services from Port Hedland (6hrs 40mins; from A$136 one-way), while Greyhound runs intra-Kimberley routes to Derby (2½hrs; from A$59 one-way), Fitzroy Crossing (5½hrs; from A$108 one-way), Halls Creek (9hrs; from A$138 one-way) and Kununurra (14hrs; from A$191 one-way), with onward services to Darwin (26hrs; from A$342 one-way).

Broome International Airport is only 2km from the city centre; lounging at one of the cafés in the CBD and watching the planes descend on final approach is a popular local pastime. Qantas and Virgin Australia both offer flights from Perth (2½hrs; from A$460 return, but that price can rise significantly). Skippers Aviation offers intra-Kimberley flights from Broome to Fitzroy Crossing (1hr 10mins) and onwards to Halls Creek (55mins) but they are not cheap – from A$990 return. Airnorth flies to Kununurra (1hr 30mins) but it is again expensive – fares can be around the A$550 return mark. They also offer onward flights to Darwin.

GETTING AROUND The Broome Explorer Bus (w bebus.com.au) is geared to tourists and connects the CBD, Chinatown and Cable Beach (24hr passes start from A$15). Otherwise, there are plenty of taxi companies: Broome Transit (☎131 008; w broometaxis.com.au), Chinatown Taxis (☎9192 3316; w chinatowntaxis. com.au) and Pearl Town Taxis (☎131 330) are reliable.

TOURIST INFORMATION AND TOUR OPERATORS

ℹ Broome Visitor Centre 1 Hamersley St; ☎9195 2200; w visitbroome.com.au; ⊕ 09.00–16.00 Mon–Fri, summer 09.00–noon Sat
Broome Hovercraft Eco Adventure Tours ☎9193 5025; e info@broomehovercraft.com.au; w broomehovercraft.com.au. Offers a

variety of boat tours around Broome including a 3hr 'Dinosaur Adventure Tour' exploring the footprints at Gantheaume Point (page 344) & a 90min tour of Roebuck Bay's WWII shipwrecks (page 344).

13

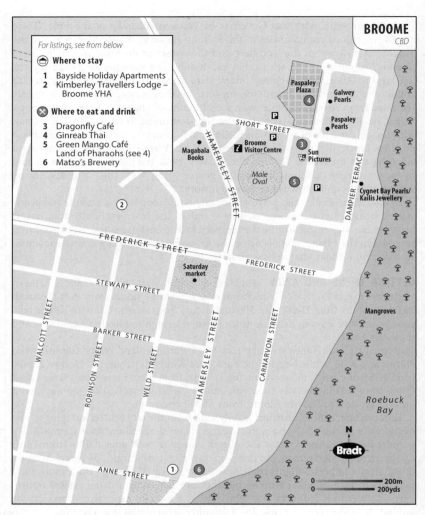

BROOME
CBD

For listings, see from below

🛏 **Where to stay**

1 Bayside Holiday Apartments
2 Kimberley Travellers Lodge –
   Broome YHA

❌ **Where to eat and drink**

3 Dragonfly Café
4 Ginreab Thai
5 Green Mango Café
   Land of Pharaohs (see 4)
6 Matso's Brewery

Paspaley
Plaza

Galwey
Pearls

Paspaley
Pearls

SHORT STREET

Magabala
Books

Broome
Visitor Centre

Sun
Pictures

Cygnet Bay Pearls/
Kailis Jewellery

Male
Oval

DAMPIER TERRACE

HAMERSLEY STREET

FREDERICK STREET

FREDERICK STREET

Saturday
market

STEWART STREET

Mangroves

WALCOTT STREET

BARKER STREET

ROBINSON STREET

WELD STREET

HAMERSLEY STREET

CARNARVON STREET

Roebuck
Bay

N

Bradt

ANNE STREET

0   200m
0   200yds

🏠 **WHERE TO STAY**   *Map, page 338, unless otherwise stated*

Broome is very popular and often gets booked out at peak times, so reserve well
in advance.

☀ 🏠 **Bali Hai Resort & Spa** (31 villas) 6
Murray Rd; 📞9191 3100; w balihairesort.com.
Tranquil, Asian-inspired resort comprised of self-
contained villas with private courtyards & BBQ, some
of which have multiple bedrooms. On-site massage
spa & Asian-Australian restaurant are both high
quality, & walking distance to Cable Beach. **$$$$**
☀ 🏠 **Cable Beach Club Resort & Spa** (225
rooms) 1 Cable Beach Rd W; 📞9192 0400; e info@
cablebeachclub.com; w cablebeachclub.com.

Mixing colonial & Asian motifs, this upmarket
choice features spacious & stylish studios, some
with ocean views & timber floors. There are also
multi-bedroom bungalow & apartment options,
& villas that have their own pool. Multiple
restaurants on site, with Italian (see opposite) &
Thai among others, & there is also a salon & spa.
A great place to splurge. **$$$$**
🏠 **Kimberley Sands Resort** (72 rooms) 10
Murray Rd; 📞9193 8300; e info@kimberleysands.

com.au; w kimberleysands.com.au. Stylish, tranquil & family-friendly resort; elegant rooms have a touch of the tropics to them, with marble-tiled bathrooms. Stunning outdoor pool area, & the award-winning on-site restaurant features delicious fare with local ingredients. **$$$$**

🏠 **Mantra Frangipani Broome** (60 units) 15 Millington Rd; 🖂 9195 5000; e frangipani.gm@ mantra.com.au. Near Cable Beach, the 1-, 2- & 3-bedroom apartments here are well-appointed, with private outdoor shower, terrace & BBQ, & the grounds have 2 swimming pools – 1 with a waterfall. A solid choice. **$$$$**

🏠 **The Pearle of Cable Beach** (70 rooms) 14 Millington Rd; 🖂 9194 0900; e info@thepearle. com.au; w thepearle.com.au. Luxurious resort with a range of homely, tastefully decorated rooms & upscale villas featuring their own private pool. The gorgeous gardens surround the infinity-edge pool & BBQ area, overlooked by the Pearle Café (which serves complimentary b/fast). A great option if you're looking for privacy & seclusion. **$$$$**

🏠 **Bayside Holiday Apartments** [map, opposite] (12 apts) Cnr Hamersley & Anne St; 🖂 9195 5200; e stay@baysideholidayapartments. com.au; w baysideholidayapartments.com.au. This small, well-contained resort offers spacious, good-value 1- & 2-bedroom apartments (the latter with full kitchens). Outdoor pool & shared BBQ facilities. **$$$**

🏠 **Broome Time Resort** (58 rooms) 1 Cable Beach Rd E; 🖂 9194 1700; e stay@ broometimeaccommodation.com.au; w broometimeaccommodation.com.au. Popular & reliable motel-style option in town & near the beach; all rooms have a kitchen & fridge. Outdoor pool & on-site gallery showcasing local indigenous art; continental b/fast inc. **$$$**

🏠 **Beaches of Broome** (42 rooms) 4 Sanctuary Rd; 🖂 9192 6662; e bookings@ beachesofbroome.com.au; w beachesofbroome. com.au. A short walk from Cable Beach, this budget option is more upmarket than your traditional backpackers'. Dbl en-suite rooms have a stylish flourish to them with contemporary colour schemes & bathrooms behind double sliding doors; though private rooms & dorms are basic. Standard continental b/fast inc; there's also a bar, guest laundry, pool table & communal kitchen. A good option for large groups. **$**

🏠 **Cable Beach Backpackers** (25 rooms) 12 Sanctuary Rd; 🖂 1800 655 011; e mail@cablebeachbackpackers.com; w cablebeachbackpackers.com. Lively backpackers' catering to 18–30s, offering well-priced dorms & private rooms – AC rooms are worth the extra money. Prices go up in the dry season. Communal kitchen, outdoor pool, licensed bar (with happy hour) & volleyball court. Jobs are sometimes advertised for those with the legal right to work in Australia. **$**

🏠 **Discovery Parks – Broome** 91 Walcott St; 🖂 9192 1366; e broome@discoveryparks.com.au; w discoveryholidayparks.com.au/caravan-parks/ western-australia/kimberley-broome. Powered & unpowered sites are on offer at this reliable chain. The grounds feature a boat launch, restaurant, playground & laundry. Pet-friendly. **$**

🏠 **Kimberley Travellers Lodge – Broome YHA** [map, opposite] (22 rooms) 9a Bagot St; 🖂 9193 7778; e lodge@kimberleywild.com.au; w kimberleytravellerslodge.com.au. Right by the airport but not that close to the beach, this offers basic but well-priced dorm facilities, alongside tour desk & bar. B/fast inc. **$**

✗ WHERE TO EAT AND DRINK *Map, opposite, unless otherwise stated*

✗ **Cichetti Club** [map, page 338] 1 Cable Beach Club W; 🖂 9192 0411; w cablebeachclub. com/dine; ⏱ 07.00–09.30, 11.00–15.00 & from 18.00 Tue–Sat. At the Cable Beach Club, this Italian restaurant with twinkly outdoor terrace serves pastries & toasties for b/fast, paninis for lunch & 2- & 3-course set meals for dinner. The focaccia is good. Reservations essential. **$$$**

✗ **Dragonfly Café** 3/6 Carnarvon St; 🖂 9192 3222; ⏱ 06.30–14.00 Mon–Fri, 07.00–14.00

Sat–Sun. Great b/fast & lunch spot with dishes done really well. Try the Spanish beans for b/fast; they also do a good eggs benedict. **$$**

✳ ✗ **Ginreab Thai** Paspaley Plaza, Carnarvon St; 🖂 9192 2533; w ginreabthai.com.au; ⏱ lunch 11.00–14.00 Mon–Fri, dinner 17.00–21.00 daily. Authentic Thai with terrific pad Thais, spring rolls & prawn crackers. **$$**

✳ ✗ **Matso's Brewery** 60 Hamersley St; 🖂 9193 5811; w matsos.com.au; ⏱ 11.30–21.00 Mon–Fri, 08.00–21.00 Sat–Sun. Calling itself

Australia's most remote brewery, Matso's produces a variety of exotic beers with flavours like lemon, mango, chilli, 'chango' (mango & chilli) & ginger. They also do b/fasts – eggs benny & smashed avo – plus burgers, salads & seafood for lunch & dinner – try the ribs & the lobster bisque, or the 'green bowl' if you're a vegetarian. $$

✗ **Green Mango Café** 2/12 Carnarvon St; ☎ 9192 5512; ⏰ 07.00–14.00 daily. Popular b/fast & coffee spot – try the chilli scrambled eggs. Good juices too. $

✗ **Land of Pharaohs** 20 Carnarvon St; ☎ 9192 6469; ⏰ 10.30–20.00 Mon–Sat. Good kebab, rice & falafel dishes on one of Broome's busiest streets. A great place to sit & relax over lunch. $

SHOPPING

✳ **Magabala Books** 1 Bagot St; ☎ 9192 1991; w magabala.com; ⏰ 09.00–16.30 Mon–Fri. One of Australia's leading indigenous book publishers, this not-for-profit also plays a leading role in promoting Aboriginal writers & in facilitating the contributions of Aboriginal writers to Australian literature. This shop is a landmark & features a whole range of Aboriginal literature & authors – a must-visit if you have an interest in the field.

Markets w broomemarkets.com.au. On the grounds of Broome's courthouse gardens, there are over 100 stalls at the long-standing **Saturday market** (8 Hammersley St; ⏰ Apr–Oct 08.00–13.00, Nov–Mar 08.00–noon), from fashion to pottery to street food. From Jun to Sep there is also a **night market** at Town Beach on Thu (16.00–20.00), plus a **Staircase to the Moon night market**, also at Town Beach, on the night of the full moon between Apr & Oct. At both markets, heaps of food stalls with varied cuisine from burgers to Chinese & satays to pizza can be had, making them a good place for a cheap, filling comfort food dinner. You'll also be able to find jewellery, clothing, homeware & craft stalls with things like candles & soap.

Pearls Broome is the pearl capital of Australia (& maybe the world) &, despite the town's small size, many pearl companies maintain showrooms here. The price of pearls varies significantly based

TYPES OF PEARL

You are likely to come across several types of pearl as you shop through Broome. From the *Pinctada maxima* oyster off the Kimberley coast, **Australian South Sea** pearls are considered one of the most highly sought-after in the world, and typically produce the largest pearls. They have excellent lustre and come in whites, silvers and pinks, and in a variety of shapes. They are not to be confused with **South Sea pearls**, which come from the coasts of southeast Asian nations like Indonesia, the Philippines and Vietnam; though they also come from *Pinctada maxima* oysters and have excellent lustre, these pearls are smaller than Australian South Sea pearls and come in whites, golds and creams.

Tahitian pearls are often black, though come in other colours like green, and are roughly the same size as South Sea pearls. They come from the coastlines of South Pacific islands like French Polynesia, and come from the *Pinctada margaritifera* oyster.

From the *Pinctada fucata* oyster, **Akoya pearls** have historically been produced in Japan. Significantly smaller than the other three aforementioned pearls listed– as much as half the size – akoyas come in a variety of shapes and are often white, pink or grey.

Finally, **Freshwater pearls** are associated with Chinese production, and come from mussels. Size can range from smaller than Akoyas to as big as Tahitians, but the colour is often enhanced. Freshwater pearls account for the vast majority of pearl production in the world.

on a whole range of factors such as size, colour & type of pearl (see box, opposite), which makes it impossible to give a blanket price estimate for, say, a necklace – you could pay anywhere from a few hundred to a few thousand to tens of thousands of dollars. However, you can find authentic pieces of pearl at much lower prices.

Cygnet Bay Pearls 2/23 Dampier Tce; ✆9192 5402; w cygnetbaypearls.com.au; ⏱ 09.00–16.00 Mon–Fri. A pearl titan, with the oldest continuously operating farm, which you can visit north of Broome (page 347). Founder Dave Brown was instrumental in the early success of Australian cultivation & in building an overall larger industry.

Galwey Pearls 24 Dampier Tce; ✆9192 2414; w galweypearls.com.au; ⏱ 10.00–14.00 Mon–Fri, 10.00–13.00 Sat. Another longstanding &

respected firm, this family business specialises in South Sea & Tahitian pearls.

Kailis Jewellery 3/23 Dampier Tce; ✆9192 2061; w kailisjewellery.com.au; ⏱ 09.00–15.00 Mon–Fri, 09.30–13.00 Sat. Hailing from the same Greek island as the Paspaleys, Kailis opened the first pearl jewellery store in Broome in the 1970s & helped foster the domestic Australian market for the jewels.

Paspaley Pearls 2 Short St; ✆9195 1600; w paspaley.com; ⏱ 09.30–15.00 Mon–Thu, 09.30–14.30 Fri–Sat. Nicholas Paspaley arrived in Australia as a migrant from the Greek island of Kastellorizo & started his pearling business as a young adult in the 1930s. The family went on to become significant pioneers of the cultivation industry & this remains one of the best-known shops in town.

WHAT TO SEE AND DO

Cable Beach ✳ One of WA's most famous beaches, this iconic 22km stretch of chalk-white sand and azure blue water is a true sight to behold. The colour of the water here – known as 'Cable Beach Blue' – is magnificent and, somehow, one the crayon companies missed. The beach got its name from the underwater telegraph cable that connected Australia to the rest of the world, which came ashore here in the late 1800s.

The sea may look enticing, but be warned of what lies beneath. Though generally croc-free, the waters are occasional frequented by the odd juvenile – normally quick to be noticed and shutting the beach. That being said, don't swim anywhere here unless you have been advised comprehensively and conclusively that it is safe. More worrisome are the box jellyfish and Irukandji (see box, page 344) – stinger season here is between November and May, and I personally would steer completely clear of the water in the Kimberley, not just Broome, during this time. The Western Australia Department of Health and the Shire of Broome report that nobody in Broome has died of a box jellyfish sting since records began – so don't be the first. I have swum here many times outside stinger season and had only great experiences – it really does live up to its reputation as one of the best beaches in Australia.

Cable Beach's tide patterns are big, and the sunsets over the Indian Ocean are colourful spectacles drawing crowds of tourists and locals every night. A camel ride along the beach is a popular way to enjoy the sunset: **Red Sun Camels** (✆ 9193 7423; w redsuncamels.com.au), **Broome Camel Safaris** (✆ 0419 916 101; w broomecamelsafaris.com.au) and **Sundowner Camel Tours** (✆ 0477 774 297; w sundownercameltours.com) offer similar tours, starting from A\$70.

Also on the beach, **Ultimate Watersports** (✆ 9999 1839; w ultimatewatersports. com.au; ⏱ May–Sep) has a huge range of equipment and instruction on offer – jetpacks, tubing, SUPing, kayaking and wakeboarding, just to name a few. They also offer a brilliant 2½-hour jet-ski tour of the Cable Beach and Broome coastline, taking in mangroves and marine park sanctuaries, starting from A\$180 (shared jet-ski) or A\$280 (your own jet-ski).

Some people say that the Irukandji – a tiny but highly venomous box jellyfish – are present in Broome's waters during only the wet season, but that is a myth. Though more prevalent during that time, these jellyfish exist in the coastal waters of northern Australia year-round – and can be very difficult to see owing to their small size (often just a few centimeters wide) and translucence.

Irukandji stings can be insanely painful. Victims are said to suffer from 'Irukanji syndrome', which includes vomiting, sweating, headaches, anxiety, severe limb and back pain and high blood pressure. Irukandji syndrome can last for days and many sting victims require hospitalisation – some have died, but not in Broome. The best way to protect yourself is by wearing stinger suits in the water, to heed warnings and avoid the water completely during stinger season. The good news is that Broome Hospital is very well-versed in what to do if someone has an encounter with a stinger. But that's also the bad news...

Town Beach Bookending the town centre at the southern end, the mudflats here make this a great place to witness the **Staircase to the Moon** phenomenon also seen in Karratha (page 328). Its location – a 1km walk south down Robinson Street from the CBD – provides easy access and a beautiful outlook into the waters of Roebuck Bay. The area is also known for its Heritage-protected **Dutch shipwrecks**; on 3 March 1942, 15 flying boats – most of them carrying Dutch refugees fleeing the Japanese invasion of Indonesia – were destroyed here by Japanese raiders. About 80 people were killed in the attacks; when the tide is low enough (ask at the visitor centre for times), you can see the wrecks and walk out to them.

Cemeteries On Port Drive, Broome's Japanese Cemetery (thought to be the largest outside Japan), Chinese Cemetery (for the local Chinese community) and Muslim Cemetery (for largely Malay pearl divers) are testaments to both Broome's multi-ethnic makeup and the dangers of pearl diving in which the 'bends', cyclones, shipwrecks and numerous other hazards killed thousands over the years. There is also an Aboriginal cemetery just south of the Japanese one; though there are not direct 'pearl diver' graves here, many Aboriginal people were 'blackbirded' – essentially forced into slavery – to work in the industry. Many did so as 'skin divers' – pearling without the use of equipment – and died doing so.

Reddell Beach With its red cliffs and 1.7km stretch of sand, red, gold and brown rocks and blue water, this colourful, lesser-known beach a short drive southwest of town is a far-less-crowded alternative to Cable Beach and is good for swimming. At nearby **Gantheaume Point**, just to the north of the beach, the waters are home to some 120-million-year-old dinosaur footprints, preserved in the reef rock a few dozen metres out at sea. They can be seen via a walking trail, but only at low tide; Broome Hovercraft Eco Adventure Tours (page 339) also offer a 3-hour tour.

Broome Historical Society and Museum (67 Robinson St; ☎ 9192 2075; w broomemuseum.org.au; ⊕ 10.00–16.00 Mon–Fri, 10.00–13.00 Sat–Sun; A$12/ free adult/child) Formed in 1975 due to citizens' concerns about the removal and destruction of Broome's historical objects and artefacts, this volunteer-staffed historical society now has a collection spanning three buildings – the town museum is inside an 1890s old general store, while more memorabilia is in the former mess hall for the Public Works Department. However, the highlight is the restored Sailmaker's Shed, which won UNESCO's Award of Honourable Mention in 2013. Originally owned by Charles Bagge, a Swede who worked in the pearl industry before entering into sail-making, this single-story metal shed displays some of the tools and exhibits from the craft, which produced the sails for the pearling luggers in the town's early days. There is an extensive virtual museum on the website that makes for good background reading and viewing prior to a trip to town.

Malcolm Douglas Crocodile Park ✳ (Broome Rd; ☎ 9193 6580; w malcolmdouglas.com.au; ⏰ 14.00–17.00 daily) If you want to get up close with salties, the daily feeding tour (15.00; A$35/20 adult/child) at this family-run park is a safe – behind huge fences – but fascinating experience, as staff lob hunks of meat over the top of the see-through barriers. The deep, loud thunderclap made by the salties' jaws when they slam shut is truly terrifying. Look closely as you explore the park; you'll see how hard it is to tell the difference between a stalking croc in the water and a rotting log or piece of detritus. In the Kimberley wilds, you won't know a croc is there until it has already got you.

Sun Pictures (8 Carnarvon St; ☎ 9192 1077; w broomemovies.com.au) Built in 1903, this facility has been showing movies to Broome locals and visitors for over a century – before 'talkies' (films with spoken words) had come about. Today it is on the State Register of Historic Places, its tired tin frame and simple veranda still luring customers in. The facility is half-open and half-covered; back in the day, seasonal flooding did not close the facility or stop films showing – it just meant moviegoers had to lift up their feet. There is a grassed area in front of the screen and you're welcome to sit there, though be warned that mozzies can visit, and you can hear the planes overhead landing at the airport (pretty loudly). Unique for sure – but a large piece of this town's social history. It continues to show new films as the world's oldest operating 'picture gardens'. Check the website for films and times.

THE DAMPIER PENINSULA AND CAPE LEVEQUE

Sitting 200km north of Broome and shaped like a pyramid of whipped cream is the Dampier Peninsula and its apex, Cape Leveque. Home to red pindan cliffs and hills fronting white sands and aqua waters, the area is not only rich in nature but culture too, as four major Aboriginal communities – One Arm Point (Ardyloon), Lombadina, Beagle Bay and Djarindjin – still dot the peninsula; check with the visitor centre in Broome to confirm current permit requirements or access fees before you set off. The Traditional Owners are the Bardi Jawi and Nyul Nyul peoples.

Historically, Broome residents loved to hop in their 4x4s and tackle the notoriously difficult Cape Leveque Road to find a secluded beach for the weekend. However, the great news for visitors is that, after much consultation and debate, the road became fully sealed as of November 2020, making it much more accessible and 2WD suitable (and providing much better access to services in Broome for remote communities). The first time we came up here in 2017, the road was still a difficult 4x4-only track, and we didn't have a 4x4. Thankfully, the postie was offering tours from Broome in his mail truck, so we booked and hopped on board. It was a working post run and so we had to hold parcels in our laps – but this just added to the enjoyment! Sadly the mail run tour no longer operates, and though Cape Leveque Road is now 2WD suitable, you will still need a 4x4 to access many of the peninsula's sites and find a spot of paradise to camp at. A (long) day trip from Broome is possible, and a very small number of specialist operators offer built accommodation – but this is not motel or B&B country and you will need to plan your overnight stay in advance. Check with the Broome visitor centre for advice on where you can and can't go; at the time of writing, plans were being drafted to post signage along the road with notices to tourists on which grounds and communities are accessible and which are prohibited or require permits.

WILLIE CREEK PEARL FARM (Willie Creek Rd; w williecreekpearls.com.au) Owned by the Banfield family and just 40km north of Broome, this is one of the state's biggest pearl producers. Family patriarch Don Banfield used to drive limousines for Lord McAlpine, whose investment spurred Broome's tourism industry in the 1980s – it was this relationship that led the Banfields to move to Broome in 1989 and start a bus service. It is home to two of the world's last fully restored pearl luggers and historic pearling equipment, including diving gear and hand-pumps, which paint a vivid picture of how hard life was for those in the industry. A suite of trips is offered, including farm tours (A$75) where you visit the hatchery and see how the pearls are cultivated, harvested and then turned into jewellery. You can also pre-book a hearty lunch (A$35) and a scenic helicopter flight around the farm, plus a helicopter transfer to/from Broome.

BEAGLE BAY ✳ Around 130km north of Broome, this Nyul Nyul community is notable for its gorgeous, Heritage-listed **Sacred Heart Church**, built by German Pallottine monks in 1918. Its chalk-white exterior belies a vibrant, tropical interior of aqua walls decorated with local pearl shells and both European and Aboriginal motifs, and there's also a spectacular altar made entirely from mother of pearl shells. The church is usually open for visitors to wander in – if not, mass is at 17.00 on Saturday and 08.00 on Sunday.

Beagle Bay also has a dark side to it – a number of Aboriginal children who were part of the Stolen Generations were relocated here after being separated from their families. Enquire at the Broome visitor centre about entry requirements to the community.

LOMBADINA ✳ (w lombadina.com) This Bardi community takes cultural tourism to a new level, with numerous high-quality fishing, crabbing and kayaking tours – their excellent 2-hour 'Ancient Footprints' tour (A$50) takes in the community, swimming beach and – the highlight – ancient human footprints that have been fossilised in rock. Accommodation is available – fully equipped en-suite cabins with their own kitchens plus ten single rooms that share facilities (bathroom and kitchen) – book well in advance. Day passes to enter the community and visit the beach (A$10) are required and can be bought on arrival at the community office – but do double check the entry requirements at Broome visitor centre before setting off. The town's 1934 Christ the King mangrove-and-paperbark church – the materials were cut by hand – is well worth a visit for its almost idyllic simplicity, with the roof's wooden beams clearly visible as you stand inside – close your eyes and you can imagine yourself in the South Pacific. Lombadina was an outpost of the Beagle Bay Mission.

Lombadina and the community of Djarindjin sit side-by-side but are under separate governance. Djarindjin was once part of the Lombadina mission but became its own community in 1985. The **Djarindjin Roadhouse** (📞0447 513 123; **w** djarindjin.org.au) has 24 en-suite air-conditioned rooms, 24-hour fuel and a café (🕐 09.30–19.00 Fri–Wed and 09.30–17.00 Thu); full board available. Ring the community (📞9192 4940) or ask at the Broome visitor centre for current entry requirements.

CYGNET BAY PEARL FARM (Broome–Cape Leveque Rd; **w** cygnetbaypearlfarm. com.au) In 1946 family patriarch Dean Brown came up to the Kimberley with a tent and began cultivating pearls, first for buttons and then later for jewellery. Since then, what is now Cygnet Bay Pearl Farm has grown to be one of the Kimberley's scions of pearl production. A range of experiences are on offer (all A$37) including 1-hour farm tours, where pearl cultivation is demonstrated, to traditional Aboriginal pearl shell carving – ochre is carved into the shells, and used as cultural and ceremonial objects – and a class on pearl grading where you can learn how to assess pearls. There are also boat tours (from A$220) out to explore the Kimberley's giant tides – to Waterfall Reef and the fast currents of Escape Passage.

The farm also offers a variety of accommodation – safari tents, pearlers shacks (purpose-built in the 1960s to house pearling crew), powered caravan and camping sites, and a private master pearlers' retreat, originally the family home of the farm's owner, and today sleeping eight. There is also a restaurant overlooking the farm's pool serving an interesting menu of Asian-inspired dishes, including local Cygnet Bay pearl meat. Reservations for eating and sleeping are essential.

PENDER BAY This 4x4-only accessible bay (Pender Bay Road is accessed from Cape Leveque Road) is where, each August, one of the world's largest migrations of humpback whales cruise by – you can observe them from lookouts here. Tidal variations allow for mollusk-spotting at low tide and eagles are about too. The water is safe for swimming; it's about a 5-hour drive from Broome. If you want to overnight, **Pender Bay Escape** (📞0429 845 707; **f** penderbayescape) is a bush campground owned by the Goojarr Goonyool Aboriginal Corporation; their emphasis is on being low-key and sustainable, and they can book out months in advance.

DERBY AND THE BUCCANEER ARCHIPELAGO

Known for being the western gateway to the Gibb River Road (see box, page 348), Derby is a sizeable Outback town (population: 4,500) on the edge of the King Sound with a good range of accommodation and services. While it is comfortable enough as a base for a day or two, there isn't a whole lot here to engage visitors for longer than that. The town's claim to fame is that the King Sound has the biggest tidal variations in Australia, which can reach nearly 12m. Though the water is not suitable for swimming due to croc risk, the **Derby Jetty** at King Sound is a popular place to enjoy the mudflats, both with locals fishing and those who come to watch the sunset.

Derby's main street is an impressive sight thank to the **boab trees** that line it. This stumpy tree has become something of an emblem for the town, and it hosts an annual **Boab Festival** (**w** derbyboabfestival.org.au) in July, with several nights of live music. Around 5km south of town is the notorious **Derby Prison Boab**, which is reputed to be over 1,000 years old and has a huge 14m base. It was used as a holding area for Aboriginal prisoners being transported to and from Derby in the 1890s.

Arguably the most iconic road trip in WA, this 660km, 4x4-only drive infused with Outback and frontier spirit leads from Derby to Kununurra through the untamed wilds of the far north. It can take a week or more to do the drive – the road itself is not that challenging, and many 4x4 drivers do it with no problems, but there are a number of sights along the way that invite explorers to linger.

The road dates to the 1960s, when the national government sought infrastructure projects and provided funding to allow the state government to begin planning and construction on a road through north Kimberley to assist the beef and cattle industry. Before then, very rough, slow unsealed tracks linked cattle stations to the ports at Derby and Wyndham – the poor quality of the tracks was a major logistical and economic problem for the industry. What is today the Gibb River Road partially follows these tracks, and was completed in 1967.

The road is chock full of some of Australia's most rugged and beautiful gorge, waterfall and Outback scenery, with plenty of swimming holes and camping opportunities. Windjana Gorge and Tunnel Creek are highlights (page 350), as is El Questro (page 360). In between are landmarks like **Bell Gorge**, with a waterfall cascading 150m into a plunge pool ringed by orange rockwalls – one of the Kimberley's most magnificent swimming spots. Elsewhere, **Mornington Wilderness Camp**, run by the Australian Wildlife Conservancy, is a birding paradise covering 3,000km^2 of land encompassing gorges and savannah, with over 200 species recorded, including purple-crowned fairywrens. The conservancy offers guided birdwatching tours, and there is on-site accommodation and a licensed restaurant. The area also encompasses **Dimond Gorge**, with its 30m-high walls and waterfall. Proceeding northeast brings you to another string of gorges close to the road – **Adcock**, **Galvans** and **Manning**, the latter of which is home to waterfalls (of varying magnitudes) and swimming opportunities. **Barnett River Gorge**, nearby, also has good swimming.

There are various options to fuel up en route – the Mt Barnett Roadhouse has diesel and petrol available, as do Drysdale Station and El Questro. For accommodation, there are a few camping points, but there are some station stays and wilderness lodges (such as Mornington) en route. There's even a tyre and repair mechanic – **Over the Range Tyre and Mechanical Repairs** (☎ 9191 7887 & 9191 7857) – that services the Gibb. Regardless, careful planning is needed to sketch out your route, sleeping points, food and fuel. If you have the time and the vehicle, this is a must-do in the Kimberley.

Many tourists in Derby come to visit the **Buccaneer Archipelago**, an unspoilt group of roughly 1,000 small rocky islands home to mangroves, rainforest and beautiful sandy beaches, that start about 50km from town. Some of the fauna here includes taipans, native quolls and dragon lizards, and though the rocky islands don't have a whole lot of vegetation, there are pockets of rainforest and mangroves. There is no public transport or ferries to the archipelago, but a number of operators run tours. The archipelago's signature attraction is **Horizontal Falls** in Talbot Bay – the huge tidal flows cause a vast amount of water to pass so rapidly through the gaps in the cliff bases here that the water levels on either side don't have time to equalise, creating a 'horizontal' waterfall effect that looks like giant rapids.

Broome-based **Horizontal Falls Seaplane Adventures** (14 Gus Winckel Rd; w horizontalfallsadventures.com.au) runs seasonal seaplane trips to the falls from Derby, Broome and Cape Leveque, in which you fly out and then cruise through the gorges, with lunch and swimming opportunities in Talbot Bay. It's the trip of a lifetime but not cheap – prices start from A$800 per person. They also do extended day tours of the Buccaneer Archipelago (from Broome and Cape Leveque only), overnight tours (from Derby) with accommodation on their houseboat and meals included, and a 24-hour tour of the falls and the archipelago, which includes a fishing charter and an overnight houseboat stay at Talbot Bay.

Another popular attraction is **Cockatoo Island**, which was an iron-ore mining site off and on until 2015. Today, the CockatooI s (w cockatoois.com) resort is made up of the old workers' accommodation and is the reincarnation of a previous resort attempt in the 1990s by Alan Bond. The attraction here is the complete and total isolation in one of the world's last frontier paradises – a place of tropical fish, archipelago views and utter seclusion.

GETTING THERE AND AWAY Derby is 220km/2 hours 30 minutes from Broome; take the Great Northern Highway to just past the Willare Roadhouse, then turn north on to the Derby Highway. Greyhound services Derby from Broome (2½hrs; from A$59 one-way) and Kununurra (11hrs; from A$162 one-way).

WHERE TO STAY AND EAT

🏠 **Derby Lodge** (35 units) 15 Clarendon St; ☏ 9193 2924; e stay@derbylodge.com.au; w derbylodge.com.au. Probably the pick of the town, with motel-style rooms in the lodge (some with shared bathrooms) alongside self-contained studio apartments & 1- & 2-bedroom cottages, all of which have, importantly for this part of the world, great AC. **$$$**

🏠 **Spinifex Hotel** (48 apartments) 6 Clarendon St; ☏ 9191 1233; e info@spinifexhotel.com.au; w spinifexhotel.com.au. Decent option with sgl rooms & motel suites. There's also an on-site coin laundry, restaurant & bottle shop. **$$$**

🏠 **Kimberley Entrance Caravan Park** (200+ sites) 2/12 Rowan St; ☏ 9193 1055; e kecp@westnet.com.au; w kimberleyentrancecaravanpark.com.au. Plenty of powered & unpowered sites available, & they are pet friendly. On-site camp kitchen is fully equipped. **$**

✗ **Jila Gallery Café** 18 Clarendon St; ☏ 9193 2560; w jilacafe.com.au; ⏰ call for hours. Good pizzas & pastas on offer here, with a few deviations from Italian like Thai beef curry & Spanish steak. They do full b/fasts on weekends. **$$**

✗ **Lwoy's Chinese Restaurant** 2 Loch St; ☏ 9191 1554; w lwoyschinese.com.au; ⏰ 09.00–17.00 Sun–Fri. A long-standing favourite in Derby – they opened in 1981 – the classic Chinese fare here is well priced & good value. A decent place to wind up at in the evening – you will not leave hungry. **$**

CENTRAL KIMBERLEY

As you continue east on the Great Northern Highway, you enter the central Kimberley and arrive at **Fitzroy Crossing.** While the town doesn't offer much to visitors, it is a convenient jumping-off point for three national parks: **Geikie Gorge National Park**, **Windjana Gorge National Park** and **Tunnel Creek National Park**; the former is accessible in a 2WD, but the latter two are not (though there are worthwhile organised tours). Windjana Gorge and Tunnel Creek are only 37km apart and can be accessed from the Gibb River Road (turn on to the Fairfield–Leopold Downs Road); the proximity of the two means that many operators will combine them both into the same (long) day trip. Award-winning **Kimberley Wild**

(9 Bagot St, Broome; w kimberleywild.com.au) runs a highly regarded Windjana/ Tunnel Creek one-day tour, departing from and returning to Broome.

WINDJANA GORGE NATIONAL PARK (Entry: A$15/vehicle) Tucked between vertical limestone cliff faces reaching up to 100m, this spectacular 3.5km-long gorge has a striking orange-and-black appearance and is dissected by the Lennard River. The land here is integral to the legend of Jandamarra (see box, opposite). There are three walking trails, the highlight of which is the **Gorge Trail** (Class 4; 7km) that runs down into gorge and along the river. Windjana Gorge was part of the Devonian Reef system 375 million years ago and today you can see numerous fossils in the rocks, including that of a nautiloid (a cephalopod with a shell resembling a spiral) on the Class 3, 2km return **Time Walk**. There are freshwater crocs in the water, which are very different from salties and much, much less aggressive and dangerous (see box, below) – I know people who have swum here but it's not something I'd be willing to try.

TUNNEL CREEK NATIONAL PARK ✳ (Entry: A$15/vehicle) Home to WA's oldest cave system, at about 20 million years old, this national park is lots of fun. The **Subterranean Trail** (Class 4; 2km) takes you inside the 750m cave tunnel, which has a very dramatic and foreboding entrance, and once inside you wade through water to get to the other side – make sure you bring a torch, preferably one for your head. There are freshies in the water with you – if you are an organised tour, your guide will probably point them out! Look up to spy branches and other debris near the roof of the tunnel, lifted there and lodged by the floodwaters.

GEIKIE GORGE NATIONAL PARK A 22km drive northeast of Fitzroy Crossing, this national park is much more accessible than the other two in the area – the road is sealed and 2WD suitable. The Fitzroy River flows through the park, overlooked by orange-and-black limestone cliffs on either side, with a wide and dramatic chalky-white base. From April to October, DPaW rangers run 1-hour boat tours through the gorge, highlighting geology and the environment (from A$50/14 adult/child), while **Darngku Heritage Cruises** (Forrest Rd, Fitzroy Crossing; ☏9191 5552) also operates cruises with an emphasis on Aboriginal connections

---

BE CROCWISE

In 2017, the West Australian Government introduced its 'Be Crocwise' safety campaign to prevent attacks and, while you are in the Kimberley, you need to ensure that you are indeed crocwise as these huge beasts are skilled predators – and you are unlikely to know one is around until it's already got you.

A few safety points:

- Always assume a waterway has crocs in it, unless definitively stated otherwise by reliable entities;
- Don't get too close to the water's edge, and camp at least 50m away from it;
- Don't think that freshwater can't have saltwater crocodiles – salties will happily be in both.

See page 11 for more on WA's crocodiles.

A man of the Bunuba people from the area around Fitzroy Crossing, Jandamarra is an Aboriginal legend. He was a skilled herdsman and tracker, and began working for the police in order to have charges against him dropped for killing sheep; he also helped capture Aboriginal (Bunuba) warriors near Derby. One night in 1894, he suddenly turned on the police – he shot the constable he was working for, Bill Richardson, as he slept, and freed a series of Aboriginal prisoners, who told him of their concerns about the police back in Fitzroy Crossing, and of their fears that Europeans were going to conquer Bunuba Country.

Jandamarra began to lead the Bunuba in something of a guerilla campaign against the Europeans over the course of three years. He had hopes of a pan-Aboriginal uprising, but this did not materialise; despite this, Jandamarra took on mythical status for his ability to attack the police and European settlers and then quickly disappear into the hills and mountains around Windjana Gorge and Tunnel Creek. The latter was where he met his end in 1897, killed by another Aboriginal tracker from a different tribe.

Numerous books have been written about Jandamarra, as well as a film from the ABC and indigenous film company Wawili Pitjas in 2011 called *Jandamarra's War*. Banjo Woorunmurra and Howard Pedersen's book *Jandamarra and the Bunuba Resistance* won the WA Premier's Book of the Year Award and can be bought at Magabala Books in Broome (page 342).

to the land, culture and history. There are also four walking trails in the park (all Class 3, three of which are under 2km), exploring the riverbank and gorge. You are likely to see native figs and passion fruit, as well as heaps of bats and corellas, alongside freshwater crocodiles.

WHERE TO STAY AND EAT In Fitzroy Crossing – which the Gibb River Road does not pass through, but the Great Northern Highway does – you have two options. The **Fitzroy River Lodge** (277 Great Northern Hwy; \ 9191 5141; e reservations@ fitzroyriverlodge.com.au; w fitzroyriverlodge.com.au; $$$$) is an attractively verandaed accommodation with motel units, safari tents and studios, as well as powered and unpowered sites and a bar and restaurant serving three meals a day. Opened in 1897, the **Crossing Inn** (35 Skuthorp Rd; \ 9191 5080; e crossinginn@ bigpond.com; w crossing-inn.com.au; $$$) has motel rooms, powered and unpowered sites, plus the on-site Homestead Restaurant serving breakfast and dinner.

HALLS CREEK, PURNULULU NATIONAL PARK AND SURROUNDS

HALLS CREEK The main (and perhaps only) reason to stay in Halls Creek – which the ABC quoted Magistrate Colin Roberts calling in 1994 'the most lawless town in the state' – is as a base for exploring the two nearby national parks or to break up longer drives. Crime, especially youth crime, is prevalent; the ABC reported in 2021 that the crime rate had doubled in the past ten years, with government funding and attempts at youth-engagement programmes proving largely ineffective. Choose your accommodation carefully – I've recommended what I feel is the most reliable option in town – and you are likely to find warning signs in car parks around town about valuables in your vehicles.

13

The East Kimberley is an excellent place to see and learn about magnificent Aboriginal art. Numerous Aboriginal groups live in the Shire of Halls Creek, including the Jaru and the Kija peoples. There is a very strong tradition of ochre paintings here, with the Kimberley's rich earth producing a number of bold ochre pigments that help set Kimberley's Aboriginal art apart from that found elsewhere. The volume of galleries in remote Aboriginal communities that welcome visitors, with on-site artists who you can meet, make the area in and around Halls Creek a particularly good place to explore and educate yourself about Aboriginal art.

Yarliyil Art Centre 300 Great Northern Hwy; ☏ 9168 6723; ⏰ call for current hours. Has over 100 member artists, some working daily. Paintings, prints, & carvings among others are on offer.

Laarri Gallery Yiyili Community; ☏ 9191 7195; ⏰ Mon–Fri 09.00–14.00, weekends by appointment. 120km west of Halls Creek (signposted from the Great Northern Highway), this gallery run by Gooniyandi artists features traditional & contemporary Aboriginal art as well as handbags, scarves, canvases & crafts.

Warlayilti Art Centre Balgo Community; ☏ 0407 123 478; w balgoart.org.au; ⏰ 09.00–17.00 Mon–Fri, weekends by appointment. Some 250km south of Halls Creek, off the Tamani Rd, this centre specialises in prints & silk-scarf dying, working with over 200 artists from 3 local indigenous communities – Kururrungka, Mulan & Wirramanu. It is requested you call in advance of a visit.

Warmun Art Centre Warmun Community; ☏ 9168 7496; w warmunart.com.au. Owned by the Gija people, this centre offers an array of beautiful paintings & other items like boomerangs, with over 60 local artists producing works. Warmun is 161km north of Halls Creek, just off & signposted from the Great Northern Highway.

Getting there and away Halls Creek is on the Great Northern Highway, 686km/7 hours from Broome and 380km/4 hours from Kununurra. Greyhound buses also serve the town from Broome (9hrs; from A$138 one-way) and Kununurra (4hrs; from A$121 one-way).

Where to stay and eat

The Kimberley Hotel (80 rooms) Roberta Av; ☏ 9168 6101; e stay@kimberleyhotel.com.au; w kimberleyhotel.com.au. Secure compound featuring a welcoming outdoor pool & comfortable, homey rooms & apartments with kitchen & private decking area. On-site Gabi's Restaurant serves hearty b/fasts (inc a 'breaky burger') while the sports bar serves classic pub fare for lunch & dinner. **$$$**

WOLFE CREEK CRATER NATIONAL PARK The second-largest crater in the world – 880m across, and roughly 60m deep – Wolfe Creek is the site of a meteorite impact, around 300,000 years ago. Europeans first sighted the crater during an aerial survey in 1947, but Aboriginal people have known about it for much longer; they believe a giant snake emerged from the ground to help create the Wolfe Creek and Sturt Creek. It is an impressive yet eerie sight to come across this gaping circular hole in the middle of a flat Outback landscape. While you are not allowed to climb down the crater, you can walk up to the rim (a difficult 400m climb) or take a 70-minute scenic flight over it with Northwest Regional

Airlines (☏9168 5211; w northwestregionalair.com.au; from A$325pp), departing from Halls Creek. You can camp at Wolfe Creek Crater – though you need to be completely self-sufficient. Access (4x4 only) to the national park is along Tamani Road, about 150km/2 hours south of Halls Creek. From the turn-off it's another 25km into the park.

PURNULULU NATIONAL PARK ✳ (Entry: A$15/vehicle) On the UNESCO World Heritage List since 2003, the magnificent beehive-resembling orange-and-black sandstone domes of the Bungle Bungle Range (not to be confused with Kununurra's Bungle Bungles; page 359) are the highlight of this national park. Some reaching 250m in height, the domes themselves are made of sandstone, and were carved out of erosion from waterways. The distinctive striping is due to cyanobacteria, which require moisture. The darker stripes have their presence, while the orange bands indicate areas of dryness that can't support the cyanobacteria. Europeans did not first sight them until 1983 – when a helicopter pilot spotted them and took a documentary crew there. They had been known, however, to the Aboriginal peoples who had lived here for at least 20,000 years.

Sometimes Bungle Bungle is used synonymously with Purnululu, but that is a mistake – Bungle Bungle is a range *within* Purnululu, and the park itself is several times larger. The park is split into two sections – northern and southern – and try to plan your itinerary so that you have ample time to explore both. However, if you have time to do only one side, then make it the southern section – where you can explore the dramatic Cathedral Gorge as well as the beehive domes. Like most things in the Kimberley, the park is subject to seasonal closures. Organised tours will often stop by the end of September because, even by that early on, the temperature in the gorges can be upwards of 50°C.

Getting there and around
The park's access road is a turn-off from the Great Northern Highway, 108km north of Halls Creek and 272km south of Kununurra. While distances within the park might seem quite manageable when looking on a map, this is misleading – the road is a *terrible*, rough, high-clearance 4x4-only track, causing a blowout in drive times. Though it's only 53km from the turn-off to the visitor centre, you should allow a couple of hours of drive time. Don't even think about trying this with a 2WD; you might even be refused entry to the park altogether. The closest petrol stations are both on the Great Northern Highway: one at Warmun, 53km north, and the other back in Halls Creek.

From the visitor centre, the road T-junctions at Gorge Road from where you can head either into the northern section, anchored by Echidna Chasm, or the southern section, with Piccaninny and Cathedral gorges.

Tourist information and tour operators
There are multiple operators offering guided tours in and scenic flights over Purnululu, departing from Halls Creek or Kununurra.

ℹ Visitor Centre ☏9168 7300; ☺ dry-season only 08.00–noon & 13.00–16.00. At the entrance to the national park, the centre offers some information, souvenirs & basic provisions (but do not rely on this).

Aviair Lot 319 Laine Jones Dr, Kununurra; ☏1800 095 500; w aviair.com.au. 2hr scenic flights departing from Kununurra (from A$435pp), as well as a full-day tour (from A$810pp) where you land at the park & take guided walks into Cathedral Gorge.

Bungle Bungle Guided Tours Lot 319 Laine Jones Dr, Kununurra; ☏1800 899 029; w bunglebungleguidedtours.com.au. Guided

13

walks & day trips with flights from Kununurra, plus overnight stays at Bungle Bungle Savannah Lodge (see below).
Bungle Bungle Caravan Park See below. 4x4 guided day tours (from A$339pp), taking in Echidna Chasm, Cathedral Gorge & the Livistona palms.
Kingfisher Tours Shop 2/20 Messmate Way, Kununurra; ✆9168 2718; w kingfishertours.com.

au. 2hr scenic flights departing from Kununurra (from A$420pp), plus 6hr options with a guided tour of the southern gorge (from A$790pp), & an extended north & south day tour (from A$1,200pp).
Savannah Lodge See below. Guided tours of the domes & gorges (from A$319pp, A$419 if you add Echidna Chasm). Tours begin from the Bellburn airstrip inside the park.

Where to stay and eat
Aside from the options listed here, DPaW operates the **Kurrajong Campground**, 5km along Gorge Road from the visitor centre in the park's northern section, and the **Walardi Campground**, which is about 12km from the visitor centre in the southern section – book for both in advance.

Bungle Bungle Caravan Park ✆9168 7220; e bookings@bunglebunglecaravanpark. com.au; w bunglebunglecaravanpark.com.au; ◷ 1 Apr–30 Sep. 1km off the Great Northern Highway on the park access road but with 2WD access, this caravan park offers en-suite cabins, safari tents & powered & unpowered sites plus laundry & BBQ area; their 'baravan' has beer, wine & pre-mixed spirits. Their bush-style restaurant also does a dinner buffet. A good option for those without their own 4x4, as they also offer bus tours into the park & scenic flights. *Cabins* $$$$, *sites* $
Bungle Bungle Savannah Lodge (27 cabins) ✆9168 2213; w bunglebunglesavannahlodge.com.au; ◷ mid-Apr–mid-Sep. In the southern section of the park,

this eco-camp offers en-suite cabins, each with hot-water shower, timber flooring & fan, plus the only swimming pool in Purnululu. Rates include b/ fast & dinner, served either in your cabin or alfresco under the stars. You do pay for the experience, but a significant advantage is that you get to explore the park without having to do the extensive drive in & out each day. $$$$
Bungle Bungle Wilderness Lodge (40 units) ✆1300 336 932; e info@aptouring.com. au; w aptouring.com.au/experiences/wilderness-lodges/bungle-bungle. In the southern section of the park, this eco camp owned by venerable operator APT offers en-suite safari tents with hot water. Rates include buffet b/fast & a 3-course dinner; packed lunches also available. $$$$

What to see and do
Northern section (Bungle Bungle Range) This is home to one of the real highlights of the park: the **Echidna Chasm**, accessed via a Class 4, 2km return walk from the car park. The chasm is very narrow, often just a few metres wide, but also very tall (up to roughly 180m in some places) – and the light that reflects off the walls makes for a variety of hues – noon is the best time to come for the best colour effect.

The **Mini Palms Trail** is another glorious walk (Class 5; 4.4km return), leading to the centre of the Bungle Bungle Range, where Livistona palms grow from the cliffs and down in the gorge. You can access this walk from the Bloodwoods car park or combine it with the **Escarpment Trail** (Class 3; 7.2km return) from Echidna Chasm, through spinifex, woodland and across dry creek beds. There are lookouts near both the Echidna Chasm and the Bloodwoods car parks.

Southern section (Bungle Bungle Range) The best place from which to explore the southern section is Piccaninny car park, 27km from the visitor centre. From here, the short **Domes Walk** (Class 3; 1km return) is a great introduction to the beehive domes, with close-up views of the differing layers of sediment. A longer, scenic walk (Class 4; 2km return) along the beehives leads to the spectacular **Cathedral Gorge**, a large natural amphitheatre known for its majestic beauty and fantastic acoustics. At the centre is a water pool, surrounded by white sand – the colours reflecting off the rock walls here are simply beautiful, and is one of the park's highlights. For a real challenge, the **Piccaninny Gorge Trek** (Class 5; 20km return) explores the park's largest gorge, delving into the heart of the Bungle Bungle Range with beehive domes, cliffs, seasonal waterholes and wildlife en route, like spinifex pigeons, rock wallabies and skinks. The trail is unmarked and takes at least two days to complete; you must register at the visitor centre before undertaking this hike, and you also need to have a personal locator beacon or a satellite phone.

The southern side of the park also has a pair of good lookouts – **Piccaninny Creek** (Class 3; 3km return), just past the Cathedral Gorge track, gives a panoramic outlook towards the domes; and **The Window** (Class 4; 6km return), a striking circular hole in a sandstone dome.

KUNUNURRA AND SURROUNDS

With its rustic, tropical feel, Kununurra (population: 7,500) will be your first stop in Western Australia if driving across from Northern Territory. But as the state's most-distant outpost – a four-day drive from Perth – it is often an afterthought on a WA travel itinerary, when it should be a highlight. There are a plethora of worthwhile sights here that lodge their way into your imagination long after you've left, from Lake Argyle and its breathtaking Infinity Pool to the mini-Bungle Bungles at Mirima National Park, not to mention some of Australia's best gorges and swimming pools at El Questro and the rarest gems on the planet – pink diamonds.

Kununurra is a new town – it was gazetted only in 1961. The fast-flowing Ord River and good soils had long made the Kimberley ripe with agricultural potential and then, in the early 1960s, the Kununurra Diversion Dam was erected on the Ord to irrigate this land, and Kununurra was built as its service centre and the focal point of the surrounding new irrigated agricultural land that could hold water year-round (as the Ord withered significantly in the 'dry', making year-long agriculture a problem). One of the appeals of Kununurra townsite was that it was situated close enough to farms to allow farming families to live in town instead of on isolated properties. The dam was completed and opened in 1963; the Ord River Dam that created Lake Argyle, and holds 20 times more water than Sydney Harbour, was opened in 1971. Today, however, Kununurra is a townsite of extremes – where rich agricultural bounty and diamond shops co-exist uneasily with poverty and inequality. You're unlikely to run into trouble here, but you do need to keep your wits about you and your car door locked.

The Shire of Wyndham-East Kimberley is home to about 40 Aboriginal communities. The Miriwoong Gajerrong are the Traditional Owners of the land; it is believed that the name 'Kununurra' comes from 'Goonoonoorrang', which is the Miriwoong word for the river. Miriwoong Country includes what is now Kununurra, Lake Argyle, the Ord River and also crosses over into the adjacent Northern Territory lands. Displacement owing to agricultural development severely disrupted traditional life, and art and painting have become a key way for the Miriwoong to retain their connection to place and country, and tell the stories and share knowledge associated with their culture and their land; the East Kimberley has become a focal point for West Australian Aboriginal Art.

GETTING THERE AND AROUND Kununurra is on the Victoria Highway, which is what the Great Northern Highway becomes as it heads east from the Cockburn

Rest Area. Broome is 1,065km/11 hours away, while Darwin is 850km/9 hours across the border in Northern Territory. Note that you have to pass through an agricultural checkpoint when you enter WA from NT, which will involve a few quick questions from the friendly officers at the manned checkpoint – be sure to declare and disclose anything if you aren't sure whether you are allowed to take it into WA. Depending on the time of year, you may be better off breaking up the trip to Broome into two days, if the rains are heavy enough that driving is slow-going or, in winter, if the drive can't be completed during daylight hours. Greyhound also services Kununurra from Broome (14hrs; from A$191 one-way) and Darwin (10hrs from Kununurra, 12hrs from Darwin; from A$169 one-way).

Virgin Australia and Airnorth fly to Kununurra from Perth (3hrs 20mins; from A$498 return); the latter also flies to Broome (1hrs 30mins; from A$620 return) and Darwin (1hr; from A$320 return).

Bert's Taxi Service (📞0408 938 343) and Taxi Services Kununurra (📞9168 1521) will get you around town, though if the weather is good you should be able to explore on foot.

TOURIST INFORMATION AND TOUR OPERATORS The waters of Lake Argyle, Lake Kununurra and the Ord River provide ample opportunities for boat cruises.

 Kununurra Visitor Centre 75 Coolibah Dr; 📞9168 1177; w visitkununurra.com; ⏰ 09.00–16.00 Mon–Fri, 09.00–13.00 Sat. You can buy passes to El Questro here, & the helpful staff can assist with booking all manner of tours.
Department of Parks and Wildlife (DPaW) Lot 248 Ivanhoe Rd, Kununurra; 📞9168 4200; ⏰ 08.00–16.30 Mon–Fri. Organises permits for visiting the more remote national parks in this area (page 361).
Kununurra Cruises 4A Coolibah Dr; 📞9168 2882; w kununurracruises.com.au. Offers a Lake Kununurra sunset dinner cruise, with a menu featuring locally caught barramundi.

Lake Argyle Cruises 530B Lake Argyle Rd; 📞9168 7687; w lakeargylecruises.com. Runs a number of morning & sunset options on Lake Argyle, as well as kayak, SUP & BBQ pontoon hire & fishing charters. Their 'Best of Lake Argyle' tour is a real winner, combining lake swimming with birdwatching & fossicking for zebra stone.
Triple J Tours Lot 2253 Coolibah Dr; 📞9168 2682; w triplejtours.com.au. A well-respected & award-winning operator that specialises in the Ord River. Day cruises exploring the river's scenery up to the Ord Top Dam are very popular, as are sunset cruises.

WHERE TO STAY *Map, opposite*

* 🏠 **Freshwater East Kimberley Apartments** (60 apartments) 19 Victoria Hwy; 📞1300 729 267; e stay@freshwaterapartments.net.au; w freshwaterapartments.net.au. 2.5km out of town, this complex features stylishly decorated apartments, all with kitchen & some with multiple bedrooms; bathtubs have a relaxing outdoor setting. Complimentary airport transfers & an inviting pool. An excellent option. **$$$$**
🏠 **Kununurra Country Club Resort** (88 rooms) 47 Coolibah Dr; 📞9168 1024; e stay@kccr.com.au; w kununurracountryclub.com.au. Reliable option with clean, homely rooms, which have all the mod cons but the décor is a bit ordinary. On-

site restaurant (page 358), plus swimming pool, valet & 24hr laundry. **$$$$**
🏠 **Kimberley Croc Motel** (29 rooms) 20 River Fig Av; 📞9168 1411; e stay@kimberleycrocmotel.com.au; w kimberleycrocmotel.com.au. Catchy name, & you can throw the dice by asking for a 'mystery room', which could be any on the property – from standard motel rooms to a garden room overlooking the tropical grounds. All are clean & comfortable, if standard, & some are pet friendly. Complimentary airport transfers, pool, shared kitchen, BBQ area & on-site fish & chip shack round off the facilities. **$$$**
🏠 **Lake Argyle Resort & Caravan Park** 525 Lake Argyle Rd; 📞9168 7777; e resort@lakeargyle.

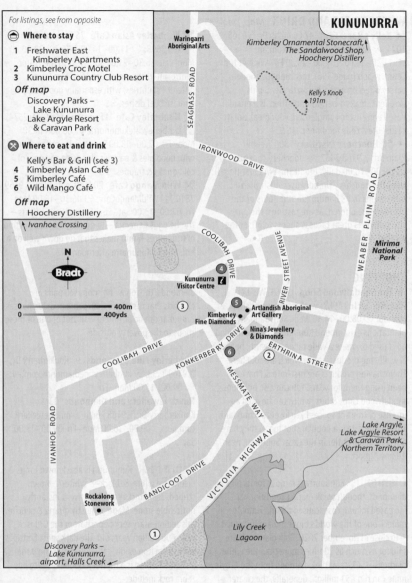

For listings, see from opposite

🏠 **Where to stay**
1 Freshwater East
   Kimberley Apartments
2 Kimberley Croc Motel
3 Kununurra Country Club Resort
Off map
   Discovery Parks –
   Lake Kununurra
   Lake Argyle Resort
   & Caravan Park

✕ **Where to eat and drink**
   Kelly's Bar & Grill (see 3)
4 Kimberley Asian Café
5 Kimberley Café
6 Wild Mango Café
Off map
   Hoochery Distillery

Waringarri
Aboriginal Arts

Kimberley Ornamental Stonecraft,
The Sandalwood Shop,
Hoochery Distillery

Kelly's Knob
191m

SEAGRASS ROAD

IRONWOOD DRIVE

WEABER PLAIN ROAD

*Mirima
National
Park*

Ivanhoe Crossing

COOLIBAH DRIVE

RIVER STREET AVENUE

Kununurra
Visitor Centre

Artlandish Aboriginal
Art Gallery

Kimberley
Fine Diamonds

Nina's Jewellery
& Diamonds

ERTHRINA STREET

KONKERBERRY DRIVE

COOLIBAH DRIVE

MESSMATE WAY

IVANHOE ROAD

VICTORIA HIGHWAY

BANDICOOT DRIVE

Lake Argyle,
Lake Argyle Resort
& Caravan Park,
Northern Territory

Rockalong
Stonework

*Lily Creek
Lagoon*

*Discovery Parks –
Lake Kununurra,
airport, Halls Creek*

N

0 ——— 400m
0 ——— 400yds

Bradt

13

com; **w** lakeargyle.com. On Lake Argyle, this resort
offers a variety of luxury villas, cabins & powered
& unpowered sites. It's 35m Infinity Pool is the
centrepiece (also open to non-guests, page 360);
restaurant open for 3 meals a day. *Cabins* **$$$$**,
sites **$**

🏠 **Discovery Parks – Lake
Kununurra** Lakeview Dr; ☎ 9168 1031;
e kununurra@discoveryparks.com.au;

w discoveryholidayparks.com.au/caravan-parks/
western-australia/east-kimberley-lake-kununurra.
A moderately priced option overlooking the
lake, with spacious & comfortable en-suite
cabins featuring kitchens, outdoor terraces &
some with spa bath. Powered & unpowered sites
also available; the grounds include a laundry,
swimming pool & boat launch. Pets welcome –
ring for details. *Cabins* **$$$**, *sites* **$**

✕ WHERE TO EAT AND DRINK   *Map, page 357*

✕ **Kelly's Bar & Grill**   47 Coolibah Dr; ✆9168 1024; w kununurracountryclub.com.au; ◷ 11.30–14.00 & 17.00–20.30 Fri–Wed. At the Country Club (page 356), this laidback, modern eatery offers an extensive pizza menu plus excellent steaks & barramundi. There is a broad-based wine list to complement your meal. Smart casual dress code for dinner. $$$

✳ ✕ **Hoochery Distillery**   300 Weaber Plain Rd; ✆9168 2467; w hoochery.com.au; ◷ 09.00–16.00 daily. Producing WA's first (legal) rum, the Hoochery proudly uses Australian ingredients in its handmade still. Tours of the distillery are offered, as are tastings; the on-site café does great tacos & sliders to offset the alcohol. $$

✕ **Kimberley Asian Café**   75 Coolibah Dr; ✆9169 3698; ◷ 11.00–14.00 & 16.30–21.00 Mon–Sat, 16.30–21.00 Sun. Next to the visitor centre, interesting menu of Asian fare from different countries, with especially good satay & Chinese beef dishes. $$

✕ **Kimberley Café**   4 Papuana St; ✆9169 2574; ▯ kimberleycafekununurra; ◷ 06.00–14.30 Mon–Fri, 07.00–13.00 Sat. Popular coffee shop with good pies & pastries alongside a variety of cold drinks & frappes. $$

✕ **Wild Mango Café**   20 Messmate Way; ✆9169 2810; ▯ WildMangoCafe; ◷ 06.30–15.00 Mon–Fri, 07.00–13.00 Sat–Sun. Scrumptious b/fasts – try the eggs benedict – to go with a wide selection of fruit juices & milkshakes that go down well on a hot, humid Kununurra afternoon. $$

SHOPPING

✳ **The Sandalwood Shop**   Lot 51, Weaber Plain Rd; ✆9169 1987; w thesandalwoodshop. com.au; ◷ 08.00–14.30 Wed–Sun. Sandalwood plantations exist around Kununurra, & sandalwood oil is used to create a wide range of health, beauty & wellbeing products, all of which are sold here. Their shaving products are first-rate & I have been using them for years. You can also buy pure sandalwood chips & bits, which can be used as incense or to scent spaces like closets or cupboards. The on-site café is a popular spot too, & they have a second retail outlet in the Great Southern, near Albany Airport.

Diamonds   Kununurra is famous for its pink diamonds, though weak market conditions & increased mining costs caused the Rio Tinto Argyle mine – one of the world's biggest diamond mines – to close in November 2020. Pink diamonds are sold for as much as 20 times more than the white diamond – a 1-carat pink diamond from the Argyle mine can run A$1 million. Generally, the clearer the diamond, the more valuable it is, but this does not apply to rare naturally coloured diamonds like those from the Argyle mine. Instead, the more colour that these diamonds show, the more they are worth.

Though best known for its pink diamonds, the mine actually produced 9 colours of diamond, including blue, red & purple. If you are interested in purchasing – or just window-shopping – pink diamonds, the following shops sell pairs of earrings that cost more than some people's houses, though it can be jarring to walk out of one of these shops to the poverty outside.

Kimberley Fine Diamonds   93 Konkerberry Dr; ✆9169 1133; w kimberleyfinediamonds.com.au; ◷ 09.00–13.00 Mon–Fri

Nina's Jewellery and Diamonds   13 Konkerberry Dr; ✆9168 2646; w ninasjewellery. com.au; ◷ 09.00–16.00 Mon–Fri, 09.00–13.00 Sat

Zebra rock   Kununurra is also known for its distinctive white-&-black- & white-&-brown-striped, zebra rock – an attractive & instantly noticeable stone. Made of mostly quartz & sericite, this sedimentary rock deposit from the Ord is at least 600 million years old. The dark spots & stripes come from iron oxide – though exactly how the patterns formed is a mystery. Good places to buy zebra rock include:

Kimberley Ornamental Stonecraft   269 Farm River Rd; ✆9168 3642; w kimberleystonecraft. com.au; ◷ 09.00–17.00 Mon–Fri. A recommended family-owned & operated gallery that makes a variety of products from the zebra rock, including things like bowls & ornaments. They also sell pieces of pure zebra rock.

Rockalong Stonework 15 Bandicoot Dr; ☎9168 3038; w rockalong.com.au; ⊕ call for hours. Another family-run operation producing a variety of items like spice racks, candle holders & more.

WHAT TO SEE AND DO

Lake Kununurra Like Lake Argyle (see below), this is a manmade lake, a consequence of the Diversion Dam (part of the Ord River Irrigation Scheme), 5km west of town on the Victoria Highway, which is an interesting feat of engineering in itself. The lake is surrounded by extensive Ramsar-protected wetlands – good for birdwatching, and you can see long-tailed finches, black kites and bowerbirds – though you may get mixed opinions on the viability of swimming here – locals tell me they don't do it (and I listen to locals in Croc Country!). Your best bet is to enjoy a boat cruise with one of the operators listed on page 356. Elephant Rock (also called the Sleeping Buddha) is also on the eastern side of the lake; depending on the angle, part can resemble an elephant's head, but in its entirety it can look like a sleeping buddha laying on his back. Celebrity Tree Park, on the Victoria Highway towards the western end of town, is a good vantage point to see the formation.

Aboriginal art ✳ Kununurra has some excellent Aboriginal art galleries. One of the oldest galleries in the Kimberley, and the first to be completely Aboriginal-owned, **Waringarri Aboriginal Arts** (16 Speargrass Rd; ☎9168 2212; w waringarriarts. com.au; ⊕ 08.30–16.30 Mon–Fri, 10.00–14.00 Sat) showcases Miriwoong culture, supporting over 100 artists. **Artlandish Aboriginal Art Gallery** (10 Papuana St; ☎9168 1881; w aboriginal-art-australia.com; ⊕ 09.00–16.00 Mon–Fri, 09.00–13.00 Sat) is a great place to learn about local Aboriginal art and has works to suit all budgets.

Kelly's Knob The tallest point in Kununurra (191m), this is a great vantage point from which to take in the town. Take Speargrass Road to Kelly Road, which leads to the car park – from where the lookout is accessed by a 1.2km return hike.

Mirima National Park ✳ (Entry: A$15/vehicle) If you can't make it to Purnululu (page 353), then this 2,067ha national park – just 2km from Kununurra on the outskirts of town – is a good substitute, with similar (although far smaller) orange-and-black-striped beehive domes, the striped bands formed by black algae and lichens overlaying the sandstone. Signposted walking trails – the longest is 2.2km, the rest under 1km – offer good views of the sandstone formations and lookouts over Kununurra. This is a majestic place to come and watch the sunset; you'll often have it to yourself. It instantly became one of our favourite places in Kununurra. Wallabies, kites and finches are common here.

Ivanhoe Crossing Once part of the Kununurra–Wyndham Road, this concrete causeway over the Ord River is now a mini-waterfall, with water all year round cascading off the causeway. It's a very scenic and unique river crossing, still used by vehicles today when the water levels are low enough. It's not safe for swimming as saltwater crocs are present, but it is a popular spot for fishing. To get there, take Ivanhoe Road north from Kununurra (it's in the western end of town).

AROUND KUNUNURRA

Lake Argyle and the Ord River Dam Bigger than Sydney Harbour, and part of the Ord River Irrigation Scheme, Lake Argyle is a huge, manmade freshwater lake, filled in 1974. Its storage capacity is almost 11 billion cubic metres, and the lake has a maximum depth of 63m. A Ramsar-protected wetland, it's also wonderfully scenic, with a backdrop of red and orange hills and escarpments dotting the landscape. You can swim in the lake, and the cruises that ply through here stop to do so (see page 356 for details). There is even an annual Lake Argyle Swim (w lakeargyleswim. com) on the first Saturday of each May, with race distances of 10km and 20km.

However, if sharing the lake with an estimated 35,000 crocodiles (freshwater!) isn't to your liking, then Lake Argyle Resort's **Infinity Pool** ✳, one of the most spectacular swimming pools in Australia, is for you. It overlooks the lake and its hills, with terrific views from the pool as though on some high aquatic balcony. Day passes are available from the resort (page 356), and they can also arrange lake cruises and even scuba diving.

Lake Argyle is 90km south of Kununurra; to get there from town, head east on the Victoria Highway, almost to the Northern Territory border, and then turn off on to Lake Argyle Road.

El Questro ✳ (☏ 1800 837 168; w elquestro.com.au; ⊕ Apr–Oct) This vast,

2,832km² station had been running cattle since 1903, though the original claim was not pegged until 1958 – the lease application by Charles Torrence McMicking named this area 'El Questro', though nobody is sure why. In 1991, then-leaseowners Will and Celia Burrell recognised the natural beauty of the area and turned El Questro into one of the Kimberley's signature tourism destinations. Today it is owned by American corporate Delaware North and boasts hot springs, gorges, plunge pools, waterfalls and pockets of rainforest. Set between the sandstone cliffs of the Cockburn Range, **Emma Gorge** is probably its most famous attraction, accessed by a challenging 1.6km hike – but with a plunge pool as your end reward, at the base of 65m cliffs. The palm-fringed thermal hot pool at **Zebedee Springs** is also very popular, as are the waterfalls and pools of **Amalia Gorge**.

Roughly 100km west of Kununurra, the area is a destination itself and El Questro operates multiple luxury accommodation options in the homestead, the station or in en-suite safari tents; camping is also available. Access is 4x4 only; however, you can visit for the day and hire a 4x4 in Kununurra. Drop into their Kununurra office (75 Coolibah Dr, same as the visitor centre) to buy a visitor's pass (from A$22), pick up a park map and discuss itinerary options. Guided tours and airport transfers are possible.

Wyndham This small town, 106km from Kununurra along the Great Northern

Highway, is best known for the **Five Rivers Lookout**, where five rivers – the Ord, Pentecost, Durack, Forest and King – join together and flow out into the ocean. The lookout is signposted from town; also note the giant (20m-long) **crocodile statue** near the entrance to town. However, there is not much else to Wyndham, and driving through here you might think it is a town left behind – for decades, this was the main settlement of the East Kimberley before it was surpassed by Kununurra in the 1980s.

THE REMOTE NORTH KIMBERLEY

The Kimberley's remote northwest coast features rugged and isolated national parks where getting there is an experience itself, and half the fun. This is, however, one of the most remote, isolated and inaccessible areas in Australia (and perhaps the world). It is for experienced 4x4 drivers only, and you need to be fully self-sufficient and equipped to handle emergencies. Bring a full medical kit, personal locator beacon and satellite phone, as well as vehicle repair equipment.

This area is not day-trippable from Kununurra unless you have an airplane or a helicopter or are willing to fork out for a scenic flight. **HeliSpirit** (↘ 9161 4512; w helispirit.com.au) offers flights over Mitchell Falls, starting with 6-minute orbits around the falls to longer flights (48mins) around the park, while **Kingfisher Tours** (↘ 9168 2718; w kingfishertours.com.au) offers a full-day scenic flight and guided tour of the falls and **Aviair** (↘ 1800 095 500; w aviair.com.au) does a combined scenic flight/helicopter/guided tour. **Kimberley Air Tours** (↘ 9168 2653; w kimberleyairtours.com.au) will fly you out from Broome or Kununurra to Mitchell River to do the falls hike, and then fly you back the same day.

DRYSDALE RIVER NATIONAL PARK

At almost 4,500km², this park is a true wilderness experience – there are no roads, airstrips, visitor facilities or marked trails, and you have to be completely self-sufficient as you explore the river, gorges and waterfalls. The park is so big, so unspoiled and so undeveloped, it's hard to have two similar trips here, but it is not for beginners. Some of the few visitors who come here use helicopters; others play it safe and enjoy a scenic flight over the park.

One of the park's star attractions is the cascading **Morgan Falls**, which tumbles down a tiered rock face into the Drysdale River (not safe for swimming due to saltwater crocs). From there you can reach **Euro Gorge**, which has a nice permanent pool, waterfall and excellent scenery. **Solea Falls** is another major waterfall – a roughly 15m torrent pouring down a large, semi-circular rockwall.

To reach the park, take the track from Carson River Station off Kalumburu Road. Entry requires a permit from the Kalumburu Aboriginal Corporation and you will also need to register with DPaW's office in Kununurra (page 356).

MITCHELL RIVER NATIONAL PARK

This 1,153km² park is a staggering highlight of any trip to the Kimberley – if you can get there, that is. Home to some of the best waterfalls in the country, its showpiece is the four-tiered **Mitchell Falls** – an iconic Kimberley landmark. The falls are accessed by the well-marked **Mitchell Falls Walk** (8.6km return), which leads from the DPaW campsite. On the way (800m from the campsite) you will pass **Mertens Falls** – which is actually a single waterfall, underneath which there is indigenous Bradshaw rock art. Continuing from Mertens Falls, you will arrive at **Mertens Gorge** – another dramatic waterfall, dropping into a deep, narrow gorge, before ending at Mitchell Falls. Allow an entire day for this walk – this gives you ample time to explore the many sites and take in the beauty of the area.

Getting there and away

Access to the national park is via the Mitchell Plateau Track. Take Kalumburu Road from the T-junction at Gibb River Road to Warrender Road (159km), from where you can access the track. It's about 85km from the turn-off to the campground via the King Edward River crossing, which has varying degrees of difficulty depending on the water level. The Mitchell Plateau Track's bark is bigger than its bite, but it is rough going and you do need to plan thoroughly and keep your attention focused.

Where to stay

The **DPaW campground** has generator-powered and unpowered camping areas (ask DPaW for availability before setting out). There is also the **Mitchell Falls Wilderness Lodge** (↘ 1300 336 932; e info@aptouring.com.au; w aptouring.com.au/experiences/wilderness-lodges/mitchell-falls; **$$$$**), run by APT, which has en-suite tented cabins with hot showers, and serves meals in its impressive pavilion.

GINGER MEADOWS

In 1987, 24-year-old American beauty queen Ginger Meadows was on a yacht cruise around the Kimberley coast following the America's Cup (which was held in Perth that year), when she and a friend decided to go for a dip at the King Cascades. A huge, 4m saltwater crocodile sighted them almost immediately, and trapped them up against the huge rockface in waist-deep water. The two women began splashing and yelling at the crocodile, who apparently paused; but then Ginger, possibly panicked, decided to try and make a break for it and swim for the banks. She did not get far and was taken by the croc; her friend made it out alive. The attack gained worldwide attention. A few days later, the police found Ginger's body; but when they retrieved it, this irritated another crocodile who then lunged at the body bag – luckily the police were able to successfully defend it.

PRINCE REGENT NATIONAL PARK With no roads into the park, access here is by scenic flight or boat – **Kimberley Quest** (✆ 9193 6131; w kimberleyquest.com.au) stop here on their multi-day cruises of the Kimberley. The park's jewel is **King Cascades**, a beautiful, terraced waterfall that drops down into a pool, though it does have a sad history – this is where American model Ginger Meadows was killed in 1987 by a saltwater crocodile after going for a swim (see box, above), so don't be tempted to get in the water. Another signature attraction is **Mount Trafalgar**, a lonely block in an otherwise flat landscape – it looks a bit like someone plopped down a huge footstool in the middle of the bush. A pass from the Dambimangari Aboriginal Corporation (w dambimangari.com.au) is required to enter the park (A$35pp). Visits to some sites may require you to engage a local guide – the Aboriginal Corporation will have information.

14

The Indian Ocean Territories

Federally governed from Canberra, subject to West Australian law and yet far closer to Indonesia than Australia, Christmas Island and the Cocos (Keeling) Islands are remote, external Australian territories.

The main reason to visit these two territories are the sublime beaches and, in the case of Christmas Island, the enormous red crab migration – one of the world's most remarkable wildlife spectacles. However, they are not easy 'tag-ons' to a trip to WA; their isolation and limited transport options mean they usually require dedicated visits in their own right. The vast majority of visitors fly in from Perth; three days in each is enough time to explore.

Note that there is a time difference – Christmas Island is an hour behind Perth (GMT+7), while the Cocos (Keeling) Islands are 90 minutes behind (GMT+6.30). Both territories use the same West Australian dialling prefixes, and both use Australian dollars.

CHRISTMAS ISLAND

Known primarily for its huge annual red crab migration, Christmas Island is the closest thing West Australians have to Hawaii with its warm, clear waters, tropical forests, cultural diversity and splendid geographic isolation.

Far closer to Indonesia than Australia – it is about 350km south of Java, but nearly 1,000km away from the West Australian mainland – it got its name because European captain William Mynors, of the British East India Company, sighted it on Christmas Day 1643, though it had originally been sighted by Europeans a few decades earlier. However, humans did not settle here until almost 250 years later in 1887, when Britain annexed it to mine the phosphates that were discovered there. The island was administered from Singapore, and the Christmas Island Phosphate Company was set up, bringing in Chinese, Malay, Singaporean and Sikh labourers – forming the foundation of a multi-cultural society that remains in place today.

Japan conquered the island during World War II but made little use of it and it was returned to the British at the end of the war. However, the island's days as part of the British Empire were numbered – Australia was keen to secure its phosphate supply and saw southeast Asia as vital to its national defence; at the same time, Britain was looking to decolonise and exit the area. Australia negotiated to purchase the island for $20 million Malaya and British Borneo dollars and it became part of the nation on 1 October 1958 – a date that is today celebrated as 'Territory Day' on Christmas Island.

The island is part of Australia and Christmas Islanders are Australian citizens. They are represented in parliament in the Division of Lingiari, an electoral division of the Northern Territory; despite this, West Australian law applies here, West Australian courts have jurisdiction and West Australian government departments provide essential services, such as schooling.

Owing to its proximity to Indonesia, Christmas Island has become associated with migration in the 21st century (see box, opposite), and the island jolted unexpectedly into the national consciousness in 2001 due to the MV *Tampa* affair, when the Norwegian freighter rescued hundreds of Afghan asylum seekers at sea just north of the island; the Australian government refused access and had Australian special forces board the ship. The refugees were taken to Nauru instead, and the incident became an issue in that year's federal election – one that is considered to have helped John Howard's coalition government be re-elected.

In recent years, tourism has emerged as a key driver of the island's economy, as well as infrastructure development. Just under 2,000 people live on the island today, with about 700 of them living in Flying Fish Cove, the capital (often just called 'The Settlement'). A plurality of the island's residents are Chinese, though Malay, Indian and European Australians have strong communities. English, Malay and Chinese are spoken on the island. This diversity is also seen in the Islamic, Buddhist, Taoist and Christian communities.

GEOLOGY AND NATURAL HISTORY Think of 135km² Christmas Island as an anvil tipped on its side, with the long top part forming the eastern end, a narrow rectangular middle section, and two base spurs sticking up and down at the western end, much smaller and thinner than those at the eastern end. Essentially, the island should be considered as a long plateau with cliffs and rainforest.

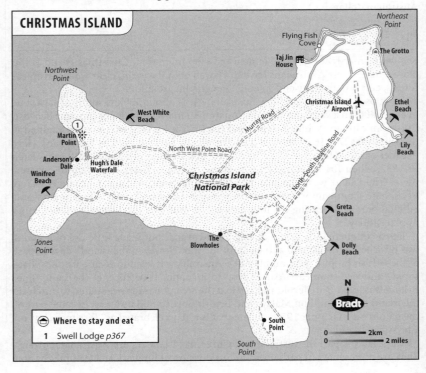

CHRISTMAS ISLAND

Northeast Point
Flying Fish Cove
Taj Jin House
The Grotto
Northwest Point
West White Beach
Christmas Island Airport
Ethel Beach
Murray Road
Martin Point
North West Point Road
Lily Beach
Anderson's Dale
Hugh's Dale Waterfall
Christmas Island National Park
North–South Baseline Road
Winifred Beach
Greta Beach
Jones Point
The Blowholes
Dolly Beach
N
Bradt
South Point
South Point
0   2km
0   2 miles

Where to stay and eat
1 Swell Lodge *p367*

The island is actually the peak of a vast basalt volcanic seamount, which first came about 60 million years ago. The coastline is predominantly sea-cliff, with some narrow beaches and bays, and there is an extensive underground cave system. A reef surrounds the island producing very steep drop-offs – with water depth plunging to about 500m. Much of the interior of the island is tropical rainforest.

Recognising how centuries of isolation and lack of settlement had preserved the island's unique plants and animals, the Government of Australia gazetted Christmas Island National Park in the 1980s, which today covers about two-thirds of the island in the central and western ends.

Fauna There are tens of millions of crabs on Christmas Island, with nearly two-dozen species found here (see box, page 366). The most famous of these is the **Christmas Island red crab** (*Gecarcoidea natalis*), whose annual migration from the forest to the ocean to lay eggs is one of the island's main draws – and one of the greatest natural displays in the world. The island's crab population has spiked from a fairly stable 40–50 million to almost 200 million today, attributed in part to successful control of the yellow crazy ant population, who had previous been killing the crabs. During the migration, males go first, and then females join along the way. The males dig burrows and then do their return migration; the females stay behind with the eggs, a process that can take some weeks. The females then drop their eggs into the sea and commence their return migration. The larvae from the eggs remains at sea for a few weeks before the baby crabs return to the shore, becoming adults and participating in the migration themselves after three to five years. The red crab is about 12cm wide and has a lifespan of about 20 to 30 years.

The migration usually begins after the first major rainfall of the season, most often in October or November (but that's not guaranteed). The phase of the moon heavily influences how fast the migration proceeds, and so the it can be longer some years, shorter in others, and sometimes also comes in waves. The migration normally occurs all over the island – the beach in Flying Fish Cove (page 368) can be a good place to watch, but information is normally posted around the island. Just be aware that sometimes roads can close during this time to protect the crabs.

The huge variety of native species, relative proximity to Asia and rainforest ecology make Christmas Island one of Australia's premier destinations for **birdwatching**. There are hundreds of species here; with its fire-red chest, the striking red-and-black Christmas Island frigatebird (*Fregata andrewsi*) is a favourite, as is the Christmas Island hawk-owl (*Ninox natalis*). You'll also find kingfishers, hawks and owls among tens of thousands of seabirds, who nest here. Parks Australia offers a free app that you

THE CRABS OF CHRISTMAS ISLAND

In addition to the famous red crabs, Christmas Island has a truly rainbow assortment of crab species, from white stripe and purple to yellow and yellow-eyed. You will see them everywhere, just be careful – every year crabs are run over and killed by drivers, and it's considered a harbinger of bad luck if you do so.

The world's largest land crustaceans, giant robber crabs (also known as coconut crabs; *Birgus latro*) are seen all over the island, weighing up to 4kg and measuring up to 1m. They can live for as long as 70 years and have excellent climbing abilities. They got their name from their proclivity to make off with anything they find that is not bolted down – whether they think it's food or not. They will even take pots and pans.

Endemic to the island, Christmas Island blue crabs (*Discoplax hirtipes*) are a brilliant turquoise shade and about 12cm; they live in freshwater, particularly on the western side of the island. They were not recognised as a distinct species until 2012.

can download from the Christmas Island National Park website (w parksaustralia. gov.au/christmas) that will help you match location to species and identify calls.

This is also a great place to **turtle**-watch, with endangered green turtles and critically endangered hawksbill turtles prevalent; the former nest on the beach year-round and hatchlings are often visible. Whale sharks also gather here from November to March, who come to feed.

GETTING THERE AND AWAY Most visitors to Christmas Island arrive by air. Virgin Australia is the only airline in town and flies to Christmas Island from Perth twice a week (3½hrs). They also fly from the Cocos (Keeling) Islands to Christmas Island (from A$588 return, 90mins). The airport is 8km from Flying Fish Cove, and it is highly recommended that you book your airport transfer in advance. Indian Ocean Experiences (see opposite) offer transfers from A$25 one-way, or ring Island Crabbie Transport (see below).

There are no scheduled ferries or boats, though occasional yachts call in. Requirements for entry are the same as for the rest of Australia.

GETTING AROUND To hire a 2WD or 4x4, try Sea Eye (58 Gaze Rd; w contact@sea-eye.net; w sea-eye.net) – but book well in advance as stock is limited. The Christmas Island website (w christmas.net.au) also has a useful car-hire booking engine that allows you to compare models and prices. The only sealed roads are in and around the island's northeast point, where Flying Fish Cove is; all other roads are either unsealed or are tracks. The North–South Baseline Road connects the airport to South Point, at the southeastern end of the island; going east to west, Murray Road connects to the North West Point Road.

There is a taxi service, Island Crabbie Transport (☏0439 215 644), but it operates only limited hours – evenings during the week and afternoons on weekends. They can also be booked for tours.

TOURIST INFORMATION AND TOUR OPERATORS

Christmas Island Visitor Centre 1 Gaze Rd, Flying Fish Cove; ☏9164 8382; w christmas.net.au; ⊕ 08.00–16.00 Mon–Fri, 09.00–noon Sat. Can help with bookings & organised tours.

Christmas Island Wet'n'Dry Adventures
📞 0439 215 290; w divingchristmas.com. Has several dozen dive sites to choose from – the WWII shipwrecks & cave dives are particular highlights. **Extra Divers** 📞 0475 247 789; w extradivers. com.au. Offers scuba & freediving along with snorkelling & boat charters, & a choice of 37 dive sites. They cater to all experience levels & can also offer accommodation.

Indian Ocean Experiences 📞 0439 215 667; w indianoceanexperiences.com.au; see ad, 3rd colour section. These are your best option for tours – they run day trips taking in beach walks, crab migrations & birdwatching, as well as 1- & 2-week package tours taking in both Christmas Island & the Cocos (Keeling) Islands.

WHERE TO STAY
The island's remoteness and small population make for high prices, at times similar to the WA Outback. Cancellation policies can be very restrictive – make sure you read the fine print before booking. The bulk of the island's accommodation is located on Gaze Road in Flying Fish Cove. Though small, the range is varied – everything from eco-lodges to motel units.

Flying Fish Cove
🏠 **Hibiscus House** (2 rooms) Gaze Rd; 📞 0438 811 953; e contact@hibiscushousechristmasisland. com; w hibiscushousechristmasisland.com. With a beautiful veranda & garden, this homey accommodation has a stately feel to it thanks to the wooden floorboards & French doors & is a relaxing place to spend a few days. Laundry & kitchen facilities. **$$$$**

🏠 **Cocos Padang Lodge** (4 units) Murray Rd; 📞 9164 7500; e info@cocospadanglodge.cx; w cocospadanglodge.cx. Heritage accommodation that housed mine workers until the 1960s, within walking distance of shops. Very, very comfortable & stylish, with each unit having flatscreen TV, full kitchen & a laundry. Surcharge applies if you're staying fewer than 3 nights. **$$$**

🏠 **Mango Tree Lodge** (4 rooms) 123 Gaze Rd; 📞 9164 7189; w mangotreelodge.cx. Stylish place with a great garden; rooms here have private balcony or patio, & outside there is a jacuzzi. Laundry services & airport transport can be arranged. **$$$**

🏠 **The Sunset** (12 rooms) Unit 4/55–63 Gaze Rd; 📞 9164 7500; e info@thesunset.cx; w thesunset.cx. One of the island's more budget

options, this motel-style facility has an outdoor pool overlooking the ocean, as well as communal kitchen; some rooms have ocean views. **$$$**

🏠 **VQ3 Lodge** 60 Gaze Rd; 📞 9164 7500; e info@ vq3lodge.cx; w vq3lodge.cx. A budget option, or what passes for one on Christmas Island; standard & superior (ocean views) rooms are clean, comfortable & have all modern conveniences including en suite & TV. There is access to kitchen & laundry facilities. Surcharges apply for shorter bookings. **$$$**

Elsewhere on the island *Map, page 364*
🏠 **Swell Lodge** (2 chalets) 📞 1300 790 207; e contact@swelllodge.com; w swelllodge.com. Billing itself as one of the world's most exclusive eco-lodges, & the only accommodation inside the national park, this fully inclusive luxury facility offers visitors pristine coast & jungle alongside a private chef & blissful solitude. Daily guided tours are included, & each chalet has its own private walking path through jungle with heaps of forest birds. Access is 4x4 only, though airport transfers are available. Be under no illusions about cost, however – you pay for the experience. From A$1,656/night for 2 guests. **$$$$**

WHERE TO EAT AND DRINK
All of the following are in Flying Fish Cove. The dining scene is fairly limited and, owing to the island's location, there is a heavy Asian influence. For self-caterers, **Christmas Island Supermarket** (9 Gaze Rd; 📞 9164 8370; ⏰ 09.00–17.00 Mon–Fri, 09.00–13.00 Sat) and **Kedai al-Barakah** (1 Masjid Rd; 📞 9164 7330; ⏰ 07.30–21.00 daily) are your go-tos.

✖ **Golden Bosun Tavern** 51 Gaze Rd; 📞 9164 7486; ⏰ 16.00–midnight Tue–Sat, 16.00–22.00

Sun. Steak sandwiches & chicken dishes here, as well as fish like wahoo & standard sides like garlic bread & chips. Specials are reasonable, with dishes like Moroccan chicken. A good choice if you're missing Australian pub food & ambience. **$$$**

✗ Chinese Literary Association 13 Gaze Rd; ☏9164 8299; ⏱ 10.00–14.00 & 18.00–21.00 Tue, Wed, Fri, Sun, 18.00–21.00 Thu, 10.00–14.00 Sat.

Often called 'Le Cla', this place has an array of fried rice & noodle dishes &, at dinner, stir-fries. Some alcoholic drinks available. A good place to fill up. **$**

✗ Smash Espresso Bar 63 Poon Saan Rd; ☏9164 8884; ⏱ 06.00–13.00 Mon–Fri, 07.00–11.00 Sat. Upbeat place with good coffee, burgers & quality b/fasts like eggs benedict. **$**

WHAT TO SEE AND DO

Diving The waters around the island make for some fantastic diving, with grottos, caves, coral and marine life. It is a particularly good place to see a wide range of shark species, including whale sharks from November to March, as well as dolphins and manta rays, coral gardens and huge walls, and visibility is amazing in the calm, clear and seemingly perpetually warm waters. See page 367 for operators who organise dive excursions.

Flying Fish Cove (The Settlement) Looking from above like a fistful of beach has been shoehorned in between the cliffs, the island's main settlement is not named after piranhas or some other aquatic animal – the HMS *Flying Fish* was a British survey ship that collected specimens here in the late 1800s. Today, Flying Fish Cove is a relaxed cultural melting pot, with Chinese, Malay, Muslim, Buddhist, Australian and Christian influences, and many colourful festivals highlighting the diversity such as Vesak Day (a Buddhist holy day), Territory Day and Chinese New Year celebrations. The settlement's different areas reflect its cultural mix: the residential Malay Kampong Precinct, next to the port, is the heart of the island's Muslim community; the original houses were made from timber. Elsewhere, Poon Saan – meaning 'halfway up the hill' – has traditionally been the home of the Chinese community, and is noted for its Singapore-style houses. The outdoor cinema is also here (films every Saturday at 19.30 and every other Wednesday – tickets cost A$5); films play rain or shine, so bring an umbrella.

Buddhist temples are dotted in Poon Saan, like Si Mian Fo Temple, while Taoist temples, such as Tai Pak Kong Temple, can be found in the main town. The two-storey Administrator's Residence, **Tai Jin House** (21 Jln Pantai; ☏ 0427 569 459; ⏱ 09.00–noon Mon–Fri) is representative and symbolic of European rule of the island – both in the grand colonial architecture of the residence and in its cliff-top location with sweeping views out over the water and the town. Community functions are often held in the gardens here, and there is also a gun emplacement which recalls the defence of the island and its takeover by the Japanese during World War II. The house is today the site of a local history museum.

Flying Fish Cove Beach is very popular with locals, despite the port at the northern end. It is considered one of the Indian Ocean's best shore-diving sites, with brightly coloured corals and fish just metres off the shore. It's also a good place to witness the red crab migration (page 365).

Also nearby, just a few minutes' drive from the centre of town and by the golf course, is **The Grotto** – a cave boasting a fresh seawater pool that looks like a natural jacuzzi (though, the water is much less warm). It's especially scenic when the sunlight beams down, giving the appearance that someone is shining a spotlight on to it. It is a bit of a trek down the rocks to get there, but there is a rope to help you get back out again. It's accessed by a sealed road, making it one of the island's most accessible outings.

Christmas Island National Park At 85km², Christmas Island National Park comprises the majority of the island's land mass and there are some outstanding short walks exploring much of the island's most dramatic scenery. The main way in from Flying Fish Cove is on Murray Road; the East-West Baseline Road also cuts alongside the spine of the park.

In the wild and woolly west, the 1.4km trail from the car park (4x4) to **Winifred Beach** passes through rainforest before descending to the rugged beach – its rocky shore and rough surf provide a good backdrop while watching the seabirds. **The Dales**, at the centre of the island's west coast, is a wetland with waterfalls, streams, forests and gorges. Its ample water supply allows it to be a haven for blue crabs (though red crabs also pass through here) and birds, including Abbott's booby. Here you'll find **Martin Point** (4x4), home to a lookout over the breaking surf that is the place to come for glorious sunsets – a 400m walk from the car park leads to the viewing platform to see the coral reef as well as several species of booby.

From the Dales car park, a 1km boardwalk track leads to **Hugh's Dale Waterfall** (4x4) – you can go under the water here – and then another trail continues for 800m to the small gorge and stream at **Anderson's Dale** (4x4). One of the island's longest walking trails, the 10km (but relatively flat) **Perpendicular Wall Trail** (4x4) starts at Martin Point and passes through forests, with great cliff views and plenty of crab- and birdwatching opportunities – it's about 2 hours each way on the track (which is not a loop). Just north of the Dales is **West White Beach** (4x4), where there is a spectacular coral reef hugging the shore; the 1.4km access track weaves through rainforest.

On the eastern side of the park, **Greta Beach** is an excellent place to see turtles (year-round) and red crabs (in migration season). The beach is accessibly by 4x4 only, about halfway between North East Point and South Point. Unfortunately, there is a pollution problem here – especially plastic. Just south of Greta is the **Dolly Beach Walk**, where a 1km (mostly boardwalk) trail leads through forest to Dolly Beach with a coral reef. Turtles nest here and there are red crabs during the migration.

On the central part of a long stretch of southern coast, a track leads through rainforest to get to the **Blowholes**, where there is an elevated walkway and viewing platforms to see the water spray up when there are swells.

CHRISTMAS ISLAND CASINO

During the 1990s, Christmas Island was home to one of the world's most profitable casinos. Seeking to take advantage of the island's proximity to Indonesia, the casino was the brainchild of Perth developer Frank Woodmore as a way to attract gamblers from Asia, who suffered from lack of choice due to Indonesian gambling regulation – and the Christmas Island Casino did so with abundance and abandon.

The good times always end, though, and what was a profitable idea and a smash hit in 1993 quickly fell victim to the Asian financial crisis of the late 1990s. As the crisis bit, the amount of money available for gambling dried up, and the casino's doors shut almost as quickly as they opened. The casino was gone by 1998. However, the decline of the phosphate mining industry and the winding back of the Australian government's detention centre on the island have renewed the focus on its teetering economy. The idea of reopening the casino has been mooted as a way to supercharge the island's tourism industry but, although it has gained some support, the issue has yet to fully come to a head and the casino remains closed.

Lily Beach and Ethel Beach Just north of the midpoint on the island's eastern coast, **Lily Beach** has a rockpool that, when the tide is right, is good for swimming – the cliffs here are grand, making for quite a sight when the waves crash into them, and it is a tranquil spot to relax. From the beach, a boardwalk leads past blowholes to **Ethel Beach**, which has good swimming and snorkelling and is a good spot to see crabs.

South Point Near the southern tip of the island, 16km south of Flying Fish Cove, South Point was a major settlement during the island's phosphate mining days, though that has been long gone since the 1970s. The Heritage-listed remains here include a historic railway station (not in use), with good views over the coastline, and three Chinese temples that you can visit. Though the overgrown ruins are fun to look at, do be careful – the structural conditions of some aren't great.

THE COCOS (KEELING) ISLANDS

Part of two atolls, these 27 coral islands – 900km west of Christmas Island and 2,750km northwest of Perth – are your classic tropical paradise, brimming with coconut trees, colourful reefs and sandy beaches. The latter are the main reason people come; unspoiled, uncrowded beaches with terrific snorkelling and diving. Three to seven days is enough time for most people – keep in mind that the flight schedule here is twice weekly, so you will have a minimum stay requirement due to lack of transport.

Although sighted by Captain William Keeling in 1609, the islands did not become inhabited until English merchant Alexander Hare put down here in 1826 The islands' history, though, has been dominated by the Scottish Clunies-Ross family who arrived the year after and established copra plantations (see box, page 372) – an industry that became the islands' economic mainstay.

The islands were formally annexed by the United Kingdom in 1857, and transferred to Australia as a territory in 1955; a 686m airstrip that was built by the Royal Air Force in World War II was the attraction for Australia (though the islands did not have a major role in the war, in World War I the *Sydney* won a battle against the German cruiser *Emden* here, which then beached on a reef). Singapore – which the islands were a part of in 1955 – had little interest in keeping them and continuing to pay for their upkeep. The government bought out the Clunies-Ross lands in 1978 and, in 1984, the islands' residents voted to integrate with Australia in a referendum; Clunies-Ross was declared bankrupt in 1986 and moved to Perth in 1991.

As with Christmas Island, the Cocos (Keeling) Islands are not part of WA; however, the islands do apply West Australian law, where applicable, and WA provides state-level services. They do have a shire council – the Shire of the Cocos (Keeling) Islands, which has seven seats – and at the federal level, Cocos (Keeling) Islands residents vote in the Division of Lingiari in the Northern Territory.

Today the islands have a population of 600, most of whom are Cocos Malays, descendants of those brought here in the 19th century to work on the plantations. Their identity is unique, incorporating elements from southeast Asia and Great Britain, and they speak a Malay dialect as their first language; however, English is also spoken and understood. Islam (Sunni) is the island religion and the Cocos Malay are a conservative people. Visitors should dress modestly and cover their shoulders and knees; don't photograph people without their permission, and don't enter a mosque without a Cocos Malay escort.

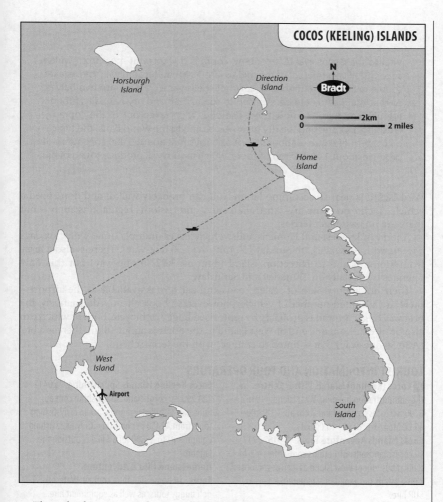

N

0   2km
0   2 miles

Horsburgh
Island

Direction
Island

Home
Island

West
Island

Airport

South
Island

The 14km² territory is low, small coral atolls; the highest point is only 6m. It is warm and humid, and cyclones can strike. While there are no endemic mammals, there are heaps of crabs – look out for purple land crabs (*Gecarcinus ruricola*)– and the waters host nearly 500 different types of fish as well as rays, turtles and dolphins. The islands are an important stopping point for migratory birds; expect to see green junglefowl, red-footed boobies and sooty terns.

Your main foci will be the two inhabited islands – West Island and Home Island, connected by a ferry, but very distinct from one another – and the uninhabited Direction Island, which has what is considered one of Australia's greatest beaches in Cossies Beach. West Island is the largest island in the group, with a length of 10km; it hosts the airport and a range of accommodation and dining, and is where most visitors base themselves.

GETTING THERE AND AROUND Virgin Australia flies to the Cocos (Keeling) Islands on Tuesday and Friday, from Perth (6hrs) and Christmas Island (90mins); flights can be expensive, from A$1,500 return, and can involve a fuel stop. The airport on

14

West Island is near to accommodation; you can probably walk it and don't need a vehicle. Yachts do come in – Australian entry and customs regulations apply – but there are no passenger ferries.

A ferry links West and Home islands, which leaves multiple times a day, six days a week, with no service on Sunday (30mins; A$2.50 one-way). There is also a ferry from Home Island to Direction Island (30mins; A$2.50 one-way) but this only operates twice daily on Thursday and Saturday.

There are about 15km of sealed roads and car hire is available at the airport – there are a limited number of vehicles, however, so book ahead. Alternatively, the best way to get around is probably by motorised buggy or bicycle, both of which can also be hired. From one end of West Island to the other is about 10km; there is a bus (A$0.50 one-way) that is timed to connect with the ferry schedule.

TOURIST INFORMATION AND TOUR OPERATORS

Cocos (Keeling) Islands Visitor Centre In the administration building, West Island; 9162 6790; w cocoskeelingislands.com.au; 08.00–15.00 Mon–Fri, 10.00–15.00 Sat
Cocos Islands Adventure Tours 9162 7717; w cocosislandsadventuretours.com. Offers a 2-hr guided bus tour of West Island as well as motorised canoe safaris (no experience required) & kayak/SUP hire.

Cocos Keeling Islands Sportfishing 0412 124 290; w cocosislandssportfishing.com.au. Runs half- & full-day lagoon, ocean & fly-fishing tours from A$450 per half-day (they have fishing equipment) to A$800 for a full day outside the lagoon.
Home Island Hire & Adventure Tours w homeislandhire.com.au. Waterbike & golf buggy tours, as well as equipment hire.

WHERE TO STAY AND EAT The Cocos are expensive – budget a minimum of A$250 per night for accommodation. There are often minimum stay restrictions, too – keep in mind that, unless you have your own yacht, the limited number of flights mean you will have to stay for a certain number of nights anyway. That being said, you generally do get what you pay for, and there is some brilliant accommodation here. You can book through the visitor centre website, which also has a selection of holiday houses.

You are allowed to **camp** at Scout Park (West Island) and Direction Island; facilities are basic and include eco-toilets, wood-fired barbecues and picnic tables – no drinking water is available. You need a permit – the Shire of the Cocos Islands' website (w shire.cc) has information.

Cocos Beach Resort (28 suites) West Island; 9162 6640; w cocosbeachresort.com. Though the lime-green paint is a bit jarring, these rooms have all modern conveniences & the executive suite has 4 bedrooms. The aptly named ocean suites have lovely views. **$$$**

Cocos Cottages (3 cottages) West Island; ☏ 9201 9391; w cocoscottages.com. With views to the lagoon & other islands, these 2-bedroom, somewhat stately cottages have great outdoor verandas, outdoor showers & fully equipped kitchens. A popular choice & deservedly so. $$$$

Cocos Seaview (3 apartments) West Island; ☏ 9162 6620; w cocosseaview.com. In the West Island settlement, these tranquil, well-appointment apartments have kitchenettes, & guests have access to free laundry. $$$

Oceania House (4 rooms) Home Island; ☏ 0403 070 501; w oceaniahousecocosisland.com. Heritage-listed & with lagoon views, the former residence of the Clunies-Ross family sits on 4.8ha & has been beautifully kept & restored. Guests have use of a full kitchen. $$$

Saltmakers by the Sea West Island; ☏ 9162 7716; ☐ saltmakersbythesea; ⏰ 08.00–11.00 &

17.00–20.00 Mon, Wed, Thu, Sat, Fri, 17.00–20.00 Fri & Sun. Café with theme-night dinners such as steak, pizza, tapas & where coconut stars across the menu. Book ahead. $$$

Cocos Club West Island; ☏ 9162 6688; ☐ CocosClubInc; ⏰ 17.00–20.00 daily. Pub & social gathering spot with pool, sport, films & hearty dinners. Their 'Parmi Nights' are popular. $$

Tropika Restaurant & Pulu Lounge West Island; ☏ 9162 6702; w cocosbeachresort.com. At the Cocos Beach Resort, this Malay restaurant with fresh seafood is open for b/fast, lunch & dinner 7 days a week; b/fast options include nasi lemak or more western options. They can also do packed lunches & BBQ for guests who are going to spend a day at Direction Island. Overall – a really good choice. $$

WHAT TO SEE AND DO Water activities are the main reasons to come here. The best snorkelling is at Direction Island – about a 10-minute walk down the beach from the ferry point is 'The Rip', a fantastic snorkelling spot, perhaps unfortunately named (it's safe), where you can see huge arrays of coral, fish, reef sharks, starfish and sea urchins. Direction Island is also known for **Cossies Beach** – named after Sir Peter Cosgrove ('Cossie'), the former Australian Governor-General – which is seen as one of the country's best beaches. At 300m long on the lagoon, it is the perfect location for a stereotypical, lazy tropical afternoon thanks to its palms, marine life and shallow, calm waters. Starting from the jetty, the 3.5km **Heritage Trail** does a loop of Direction Island with 25 interpretive panels about its history along the way documenting everything from its life as a station to its military use.

Beach and jetty fishing are popular in the lagoon and out in the ocean, and there is a huge variety of fish from trout to yellowfin tuna to wahoos. **Pulu Maraya**, a small uninhabited island just off West Island, can be accessed via a reef walk (dependent on tides) from Scout Park at the southern end of West Island. There is lagoon snorkelling; gear can be hired at the visitor centre.

There are a pair of **surfing** spots on the islands, known as 'The Spot' and 'The Shack'. You have to be careful because the breaks are on top of a reef and so monitoring the tides is important; the Spot is by far the gentler of the two. You need to bring your own board – there are no hire facilities on the islands. The Yacht Club (also on West Island) is where kitesurfers like to hang out – the calm, flat conditions make it ideal for beginners.

For a bit of culture, try the free **Home Island Visitor Centre & Museum** – sometimes just called the Cocos Museum (ring ahead to the Shire Office (☏ 9162 6649) as the museum is only open during Shire Office hours (07.00–16.00 Mon–Thu, 07.00–noon Fri), and you have to go to the office to get the key) – which has a number of displays on local culture, history and plant/animal life. It is also known for its collection of shadow puppets – a traditional storytelling method which the islands' early Javanese labourers brought here with them. Unfortunately, shadow puppetry skills were not passed down on the Cocos and so the craft is no longer in practice.

Appendix 1

GLOSSARY

Australian English is, generally, very similar to English in other parts of the world. If you speak North American English or British English, you will have no problems at all understanding, or being understood by, Australians. Australian English also does not have the same huge variations in spoken accent or dialect as, say, England or the United States. Though there are some subtle differences, you're unlikely to pick up what part of Australia a person is from by their accent.

There are, however, some vocabulary differences that you may come across. The following is a list of the most common terms.

ambo	A paramedic (or a trained volunteer) who responds to a medical emergency in an ambulance
ankle biter	A child
ANZAC	Australia and New Zealand Army Corps. Revered by both countries, ANZAC played an important role in World War I; their role there, and at Gallipoli, is often seen as a turning point in establishing an Australian identity separate from that of the United Kingdom.
argy-bargy	An argument, though something of a dated term
arvo	Afternoon
bail up	To surprise someone and trap them in an unexpected, or unwanted, conversation
barrack for	To support a sports team. Do not use the American term 'root', which is (offensive) slang for having sex.
bash	Fight
bathers	Swimming suit
battler	Commonly used as a political term, meaning hard-working middle-class Australians. Can also mean someone fighting the odds.
billy	Something used to boil water, often for tea at campsites
biscuit/bikkie	A cookie (not a fluffy piece of bread as in the US)
bludger	Someone who is lazy and takes hand-outs from others
bogan	A loud, somewhat obnoxious, and definitely unclassy individual
bush	Anywhere that is not a town or city. Can also mean a small town.
bush lawyer	Someone unqualified who takes on the case of someone else, as in an argument
bush telegraph	Gossip

chockers	Very busy
chook	A chicken (as in the bird, not someone who is afraid of something)
chuck a wobbly	Kick up a fuss
cop	Can be a police officer, but can also be to suffer something unexpected or negative (ie: 'Tom copped it from the neighbour after he parked on his lawn').
crook	Sick, unwell
damper	A type of savoury roll or scone, common in colonial times
dill/drop kick	Moron, idiot
dobber	A tattler or snitch, someone who 'tells on' someone
Dreamtime, Dreaming	Aboriginal stories and beliefs relating to how the land, plants and animals were created
Esky	An ice chest/portable cool box to store food in
fizzer	Something not living up to expectations
footy	Australian Rules Football (AFL)
go bush	Leave the city
gold coin	Small donations at museums. A\$1 and A\$2 coins are gold in colour – hence when a museum asks for 'gold coin donation' it means to drop a coin into the donation box.
grog	Liquor or alcohol
hoon	A youth who is a careless or reckless driver, usually deliberately
icy pole	Popsicle/ice lolly
Jackaroo/Jillaroo	A young stockman or stockwoman (rancher) in the bush
lolly	Candy/sweets
Outback	Very remote area; not the same as 'bush'. In the West Australian context, it's used for anything north of Kalbarri or east of the Wheatbelt/Great Southern, but not the Indian Ocean Territories.
pick	Choose, but it also means to guess (ie: 'I'm trying to pick your accent')
Pom or Pommie	A British person
regions	Rural Australia, generally referring to a place outside the state/territory capital cities (ie: 'house prices are lower in the regions')
rego	The annual registration document of a car
ripper	Amazing/awesome
roo bar	A tough metal bar on the front of a car, intended to absorb the blow in the event of hitting an animal
rort	A scam
Sandgroper	A West Australian
servo	Petrol station
shonky	Poor quality
shout	To offer to pay for something for someone, ie: a drink or meal
sly grog	Bootleg liquor
snag	Sausage
squiz	To take a look
station	Large ranch
stoush	Fight, argument
stubby	Small bottle of beer
swag	Sleeping bag

tall poppy	Braggart, show off
true blue	Something very Australian
tucker	Food
ute	Pick-up truck
yakka	Difficult or challenging work – use an adjective like 'tough' or 'hard' in front of it

Appendix 2

FURTHER READING

BOOKS
Aboriginal history and culture

Broome, Richard *Aboriginal Australians* Allen & Unwin, 2019.

Greenwood, Mark & Denton, Terry *Jandamarra* Allen & Unwin Children's, 2013. An illustrated, award-winning children's story that is considered a classic.

Haebich, Anna *The Stolen Generations: Separation of Aboriginal Children from their Families in Western Australia* Western Australian Museum, 1999.

Morgan, Sally *My Place* Fremantle Press, 2021. Sally Morgan's story about a false sense of identity and exploration to learn about her Aboriginal roots. Considered to be a landmark in Aboriginal literature.

Palmer, Kingsley *Noongar People Noongar Land* Aboriginal Studies Press, 2016.

Pascoe, Bruce *The Little Red Yellow Black Book: An Introduction to Indigenous Australia* Aboriginal Studies Press, 2018.

Scrimgeour, Anne *On Red Earth Walking: The Pilbara Aboriginal Strike, 1946–1949* Monash University Publishing, 2020.

Autobiographies and memoirs

Barry, Bernice *Georgiana Molloy: The Mind that Shines* Pan Macmillan Australia, 2016.

Barry, Paul *The Rise and Fall of Alan Bond* Random House Australia, 1991.

Day, David *John Curtin: A Life* HarperCollins, 2000.

Facey, A B *A Fortunate Life* Penguin Books, 1981.

History, politics and culture

Aldrian-Moyle, Sue-Lyn *Surfing Down South – Discovering Margaret River and Yallingup* Margaret River Press, 2014.

Bunbury, Bill & Bunbury, Jill *Many Maps: Charting Two Cultures: First Nations Australians and European Settlers in Western Australia* University of Western Australia Press, 2020.

Davis, Russell Earls *A Concise History of Western Australia* Woodslane, 2018.

Dia, Melody *FIFO – Fit In or F**k Off* Magabala Books, 2022. FitzSimons, Peter *Batavia* Random House, 2011.

Forrestal, Peter & Jordan, Ray *The Way It Was: A History of the Early Years of the Margaret River Wine Industry* Margaret River Press, 2017.

Frame, Tom *HMAS Sydney: Australia's Greatest Naval Tragedy* Hachette Australia, 2018.

Gilleland, Ray *The Nullarbor Kid* Allen & Unwin, 2014

Kells, Stuart *Argyle: The Impossible Story of Australian Diamonds* Melbourne University Press, 2021.

Kelly, Lorraine & King, Norma *Goldfields Stories: Early Days in Western Australia Lozs Loot & Luxuries*, 2018.

Kennedy, Peter *Tales from Boomtown: West Australian Premiers from Brand to Barnett* University of Western Australia Press, 2014.

Layman, Lenore & Fitzgerald, Criena (editors) *110 Degrees in the Waterbag: A History of Life, Work and Leisure in Leonora, Gwalia and the Northern Goldfields* Western Australian Museum, 2014.

Lewis, Tom & Ingman, Peter *Zero Hour in Broome: The Untold Story of the Attacks on Northwest Australia in 1942* Avonmore Books, 2012.

Marsh, Bill *The Complete Book of Australian Flying Doctor Stories* HarperCollins, 2013.

Statham-Drew, Pamela *James Stirling: Admiral and Founding Governor of Western Australia* University of Western Australia Press, 2005.

Language

Cox, Felicity & Fletcher, Janet *Australian English Pronunciation and Transcription* Cambridge University Press, 2017.

Dixon, R M W *The Languages of Australia* Cambridge University Press, 2011. Considered a masterpiece of linguistic study.

Mackman, Doreen *Wajarri Dictionary: The Language of the Murchison Region of Western Australia* Irra Wangga Language Centre, 2011.

Peters, Pam *The Cambridge Guide to Australian English Usage* Cambridge University Press, 2007.

Richards, Kel *The Story of Australian English* NewSouth Publishing, 2015.

Rooney, Bernard *Nyoongar Legacy: The Naming of the Land and the Language of its People* Batchelor Press, 2011.

Natural history and wildlife

Barrett, Russell & Tay, Eng Pin *Perth Plants: A Field Guide to the Bushland and Coastal Flora of Kings Park and Bold Park* CSIRO, 2016.

Calderwood, Mark, Grguric, Benjamin & Jacobson, Mark *Guidebook to the Pegmatites of Western Australia* Hesperian Press, 2007.

Fetherston, JM, Stocklmayer, Susan, & Stocklmayer, Vernon *Gemstones of Western Australia* Geological Survey of Western Australia, 2017.

Hansen, Vivienne & Horsfall, John *Noongar Bush Tucker: Bush Food Plants & Fungi of the South-West of Western Australia* University of Western Australia Publishing, 2019.

Hoffman, Noel *Orchids of South-West Australia* Orchids WA, 2019.

Laurie, Victoria *The Southwest: Australia's Biodiversity Hotspot* University of Western Australia Publishing, 2015.

Marsh, Loisette *Field Guide to Sea Stingers and Other Venomous and Poisonous Marine Invertebrates of Western Australia* Western Australian Museum, 2010.

Martin, Stella *Australian Wildlife* Bradt Guides, 2020.

Neville, Simon *Birds of Western Australia: The Field Guide* Woodslane, 2018.

Shine, Richard *Australian Snakes: A Natural History* New Holland, 1998.

Stone, Doug *Gold Atlas of Western Australia* Outdoor Press, 2013.

Tyler, M J & Doughty, P *Field Guide to Frogs of Western Australia* Western Australian Museum, 2009.

Wajon, Eddy *Colour Guide to Spring Wildflowers* Wajon Publishing, 1999.

Perth

Stories of Perth Brio Books, 2016. An anthology of stories about the West Australian capital from a deliberately diverse collection of writers.

White, Terri-Ann *Perth: A Guide for the Curious* University of Western Australia Publishing, 2016. Drawing a wide range of views, this work explores what gives Perth its sense of identity.

Whish-Wilson, David *Perth* New South Books, 2020. Wonderfully written book exploring the elements and characters that give the city its life and pulse.

Sport

Everett, Les *Fremantle Dockers: An Illustrated History* Slattery Media Group, 2014.

Nicholson, Matthew, Stewart, Bob & de Moore, Greg *Australia's Game: The Complete History of the Australian Game of Football* Slattery Media Group, 2021.

Slattery Media Group *Time to Fly: The Pictorial Story of the Eagles' 2018 AFL Premiership* Slattery Media Group, 2018.

USEFUL WEBSITES

w **dmp.wa.gov.au/Minerals/Prospectors-fossickers-1525.aspx** WA Department of Mines and Petroleum – information for prospectors and fossickers

w **emergency.wa.gov.au** Real-time information on bushfires and natural disasters

w **sharksmart.com.au** Shark Smart (shark activity website)

w **timeout.com/perth** Up-to-date listings for events and goings on in the capital

w **transport.wa.gov.au/mediaFiles/licensing/DVS_DL_B_DriveSafeFull_0.pdf** *Drive Safe: A Handbook for Western Australian Road Users*

w **travelmap.mainroads.wa.gov.au** Updates on road closures, traffic alerts and other information

w **thewest.com.au** *The West Australian* (the state's major daily newspaper)

w **winecompanion.com.au/wineries/western-australia** Information about the state's wines and wineries

Appendix 2 FURTHER READING

A2

NOTES

Index

Page numbers in **bold** indicate major entries; those in *italics* indicate maps.

INDEX OF ADVERTISERS